Linguistics: The Cambridge Survey

Volume I
Linguistic Theory: Foundations

# Linguistics: The Cambridge Survey

# Linguistics: The Cambridge Survey

*Edited by Frederick J. Newmeyer*

University of Washington

# Volume I
# Linguistic Theory: Foundations

CAMBRIDGE
UNIVERSITY PRESS

Published by the Press Syndicate of the University of Cambridge
The Pitt Building, Trumpington Street, Cambridge CB2 1RP
40 West 20th Street, New York, NY 10011–4211, USA
10 Stamford Road, Oakleigh, Melbourne 3166, Australia

First published 1988
First paperback edition 1989
Reprinted 1990, 1993

Printed in Great Britain at the Athenaeum Press Ltd, Newcastle upon Tyne

*British Library cataloguing in publication data*

Linguistics: the Cambridge survey.
Vol. 1: Linguistic theory: foundations
1. Linguistics
I. Newmeyer, Frederick J.
410   P121

*Library of Congress cataloguing in publication data*

Linguistics theory.
(Linguistics, the Cambridge survey; v. 1)
Includes indexes.
1. Linguistics. I. Newmeyer, Frederick J.
II. Series.
P121.L567 vol. 1   410 s [410]   87-24915

ISBN 0 521 30832 1 hardback
ISBN 0 521 37580 0 paperback

# Contents

# Contributors to Volume I

*Stephen R. Anderson* Program in linguistics, The Johns Hopkins University
*Avery D. Andrews* Department of Linguistics, Faculty of Arts, Australian National University
*Mary E. Beckman* Department of Linguistics, The Ohio State University
*Hans Basbøll* Nordisk Institut, Odense University
*Bernard Comrie* Department of Linguistics, University of Southern California
*Mürvet Enç* Department of Linguistics, University of Wisconsin
*Steve Harlow* Department of Language, University of York
*Laurence R. Horn* Department of Linguistics, Yale University
*Patricia Keating* Department of Linguistics, University of California, Los Angeles
*Paul Kiparsky* Department of Linguistics, Stanford University
*William A. Ladusaw* Board of Studies in Linguistics, University of California, Santa Cruz
*David Lightfoot* Department of Linguistics, University of Maryland
*James McCloskey* Board of Studies in Linguistics, University of California, Santa Cruz
*Alice ter Meulen* Department of Linguistics, University of Washington
*Geoffrey K. Pullum* Board of Studies in Linguistics, University of California, Santa Cruz
*R. H. Robins* Department of Phonetics and Linguistics, School of Oriental and African Studies, University of London
*Nigel Vincent* Department of Linguistics, University of Manchester
*Amy S. Weinberg* Department of Linguistics, University of Maryland
*Arnold M. Zwicky* Department of Linguistics, The Ohio State University and Department of Linguistics, Stanford University

# Preface

This is the first of four volumes that comprise the series, *Linguistics: the Cambridge survey*, a comprehensive introduction to research results and current work in all branches of the field of linguistics, from syntactic theory to ethnography of speaking, from signed language to the mental lexicon. Our goal has been to balance depth of coverage with ease of reference and affordability, and we have therefore settled on sixty relatively short chapters in four volumes as best being able to provide thorough overviews of the various subdivisions of the field.[1]

This first volume, *Linguistic theory: foundations*, covers the internal structure of the language faculty itself, that is, it deals with the grammatical properties of language, both synchronic and diachronic. In addition to chapters covering the particular grammatical components such as the syntactic and the phonological, the volume contains several chapters which, as far as we know, are quite unique, on the *interfaces* between those components. It also delves into topics that arise in conjunction with research on the foundations of linguistic theory, such as the mathematical properties of grammars, the relationship between the fields of linguistics and the philosophy of language, and linguistic typology. A special feature is the appendix by R. H. Robins on the history of linguistics.

Volume II, *Linguistic theory: extensions and implications*, considers the evidence for, and the implications of, the core conceptions of linguistic theory. Most of its chapters take some aspect of linguistic study, such as the real-time processing of language, the representation of language in the brain, speech errors, first and second language acquisition, and so on, and examine the extent to which they provide support for the generativist approach to language. Other chapters explore the boundaries between linguistic theory and theories based in cognition and communication, and the volume closes

---

[1] Unfortunately, circumstances have prevented coverage of four topics that were originally slated to be represented by *Survey* chapters: linguistics and artificial intelligence; linguistics in literary analysis; language and education; and linguistics and semiotics.

with a debate between Derek Bickerton and Pieter Muysken on the theoretical implications of the properties of creole languages.

The fields of psycholinguistics and neurolinguistics are covered in Volume III, *Language: psychological and biological aspects*, which contains such chapters as 'Language perception,' 'Language production,' 'Second language acquisition,' and 'The biological basis for language.' Additionally, two interesting topics are covered that do not often find their way into surveys of the field: 'The evolution of human communicative behavior' and 'Linguistics and animal communication.'

Volume IV, *Language: the socio-cultural context*, covers sociolinguistics and fields allied to it such as anthropological linguistics, ethnography of speaking, the organization of discourse, and conversation analysis. Microsociolinguistics, macrosociolinguistics, and applied sociolinguistics are given equal representation, as well as the 'variationist' approach pioneered by Labov and Hymes's more 'ethnographic' orientation.

Needless to say, the field does not compartmentalize neatly into sixty discrete subdivisions; as a result, there is a certain amount of overlap between chapters, both within and across volumes. To the greatest extent possible, we have striven to ensure that where overlap of subject matter occurs, the overlapping chapters present different aspects of the phenomenon covered or present different viewpoints about the same aspect. The following paragraphs should help the reader choose in advance which of two (or more) overlapping chapters will contain material most directly meeting his or her immediate interest.

Two chapters deal with creole languages. In Volume II Chapter 14 comprises contributions by Derek Bickerton and by Pieter Muysken, as well as a debate between them. Derek Bickerton's contribution, 'Creole languages and the bioprogram,' defends the idea that creoles are in some sense 'closer' to universal grammar than other languages are. Pieter Muysken's contribution, 'Are creoles a special type of language?,' argues the contrary position, namely that creoles have no priveleged theoretical status. William A. Foley's 'Language birth: the process of pidginization and creolization' in Volume IV, approaches these languages from a sociolinguistic standpoint.

The lexicon is the subject of Avery D. Andrews' 'Lexical structure' in Volume I and Karen D. Emmorey and Victoria A. Fromkin's 'The mental lexicon' in Volume III. The former studies its properties with respect to the other components of the grammar, the latter from the point of view of psycholinguistics.

Four chapters deal with language acquisition, two with first and two with second. The two chapters in Volume II, 'Grammatical principles of first language acquisition: theory and evidence,' by Thomas Roeper, and 'Second language acquisition and grammatical theory,' by Suzanne Flynn, are focussed almost entirely on the question of whether current central conceptions of linguistic theory are borne out in acquisition; the Volume III chapters, 'Where learning begins: initial representations for language learning' by Lila R. Gleitman *et al.* and 'Second language acquisition' by Ellen Broselow, are considerably broader in their scope. Also, Gleitman *et al.* focus on earlier stages of acquisition than does Roeper; the Flynn chapter is weighted primarily to the acquisition of syntax, the Broselow chapter to phonology.

Other chapters that treat similar phenomena in Volumes II and III are weighted to their grammatical dimension in the former volume, and much more broadly in the latter. Thus, the chapters 'Brain structures and linguistic capacity' by Mary-Louise Kean and 'Grammar and language processing' by Lyn Frazier in Volume II are more oriented to questions of linguistic theory than the Volume III chapters, 'Language production' by Merrill F. Garrett, 'Language perception' by Giovanni B. Flores d'Arcais, and 'Neurolinguistics: an overview of language–brain relations in aphasia' by Sheila E. Blumstein.

Finally, two chapters treat the field of discourse analysis. Ellen F. Prince's 'Discourse analysis: a part of the study of linguistic competence,' in Volume II, examines the boundary between grammatical principles and those grounded in communication, while the Volume IV chapter, 'The organization of discourse,' by Diane Blakemore, spells out the pragmatic principles that contribute to appropriate discourses.

We hope that whether you are a beginning student of linguistics or an established specialist in one of its subdisciplines, you will find in *Linguistics: the Cambridge survey* a wealth of information, insight, and challenging ideas.

# Acknowledgments

Assembling a work of this scope and size requires the close collaboration of many. To those who offered their talents, their time, and their attention we owe our deep gratitude. Just as in a chorus, for the sound to have its effect, no single voice should stand out. So it is in this work. Contributors performed their parts admirably, providing thoughtful appraisals of their areas of research. Readers of these volumes will be indebted to the authors for their skill in guiding them through the paths of modern linguistics.

To those listed as members of the Board, we also owe our appreciation for their support and thoughtful counsel. We would like to express our gratitude to Ellen Eggers for preparing the subject indexes, and a special thanks goes to Mark Meade for shepherding the manuscripts, for holding contributors close to schedule, and for maintaining his equilibrium during smooth and rocky times.

*Frederick J. Newmeyer*
*and Robert N. Ubell*

# 1 Generative linguistics: an overview

*Steve Harlow and Nigel Vincent*

## 1.0. Background

In this introduction we review briefly the general pattern of development in generative linguistics during recent years and identify what seem to us to be major current themes and prospects for the future. Comparing the mid 1980s with the 1960s reveals an interesting pattern of similarities and differences. In general, the goal of the generative linguistic enterprise remains substantially the same – the search for explanatorily adequate characterizations of the properties of natural languages – although there is, as in the 1960s, considerable disagreement over the precise interpretation of this goal and the methods to be employed in pursuit of it.[1] At the same time, the growing maturity of the subject has led to a considerable shift in emphasis away from particularistic solutions to problems of linguistic analysis and towards a search for general theoretical principles from which the facts of particular constructions follow as consequences. See Chapter 2 of this volume for further discussion and examples from the domain of syntax.

Other territory familiar to a time-traveler from the 1960s is the material which forms the actual topic of linguistic theories and analyses. In syntax, for example, many of the constructions which formed a major focus of

---

[1] Although it is a hallmark of generative linguistics that particular descriptions should capture linguistically significant regularities in the data and that linguistic theories should be couched in such a form as to admit only grammars which permit such characterizations, there are, at the very least, significant differences in emphasis on the factors which are relevant to theory evaluation. Much theoretical linguistics, particularly but not exclusively under the influence of Chomsky, has come to see its central task as the formal modeling of the knowledge that native speakers may be hypothesized to have of their languages and the, possibly innate, faculty or faculties by which they are enabled to acquire those languages. More succinctly, on this view linguistics involves the study of grammars rather than of languages, and the investigation of the general form that grammars may take rather than of the contents of particular grammars (see Chomsky 1986: chs. 1 and 2 for recent discussion of one view of the implications of such an approach). Chomsky repeatedly stresses as a fundamental goal the task of explaining the problem of (first) language acquisition. (See Lightfoot in Chapter 12 of this volume for an articulation of this view and its consequences.) Linguistics in that view is thus considered to be a part of the study of human mental capacities. Lexical functional grammar stresses the importance of human linguistic processing for the form of linguistic theories and the representations they admit, while generalized phrase structure grammar, at least in Gazdar *et al.* (1985:5f), takes a position of studied agnosticism with respect to the connection between linguistics and psychology.

investigation in the 1960s are largely the same. Phenomena such as *wh-*movement, raising constructions, anaphora, passives, equi constructions, reflexives, etc. are as much a matter of current concern as they ever have been. Indeed, as Sag (1982:427) remarks:

> Few linguists would take seriously a theory of grammar which did not
> address the fundamental problems of English grammar that were
> dealt with in the framework of 'standard' transformational grammar
> by such rules as There-insertion, It-extraposition, Passive, Subject–
> Subject raising and Subject–Object raising.

Yet there have been new constructions which have been the focus of much attention in recent years, e.g. 'parasitic gaps' (Engdahl 1983) and 'switch-reference' (Haiman & Munro 1983; Finer 1985). The former is a good example of the way the enormous growth in the range of languages investigated has had a considerable impact (cf. also Huang 1982 on Chinese, and Hale 1982 on indigenous languages of Australia, as well as several contributions to Bresnan 1982).

In another respect too the situation is remarkably similar to that of the 1960s: generative linguistics reveals a number of schismatic tendencies, just as it did twenty years ago.

At the same time, the scene is entirely different: the content of theoretical frameworks is radically different from the earlier period. In syntax, the early 1980s saw the development of serious nontransformational contenders in the field (prefigured by work by Michael Brame in the 1970s (Brame 1976, 1978): lexical functional grammar (LFG), generalized phrase structure grammar (GPSG) and, more recently, head-driven phrase structure grammar (HPSG). Even government–binding theory (GB), the contemporary direct descendant of the 'standard theory' (Chomsky 1965), bears little superficial resemblance to its progenitor.

## 1.1. Phonology

In phonology, *The sound pattern of English* (Chomsky & Halle 1968, henceforth *SPE*) sparked off a generation of research which focussed around three sorts of issue:

(a) the nature of phonological alternations and the kinds of rules, conventions, and orderings that are necessary adequately to model morphophonemic systems;

(b) the inventory of distinctive features and associated questions such as binarity;

(c) a concern for suprasegmental phenomena following on from the ground-breaking *SPE* work on English stress.

As research progressed, it became clear that a number of fundamental assumptions of that program would have to be revised or even scrapped. In particular, the kind of derivational, rule-based format that worked well for classic types of morphophonemic alternation proved unnecessarily cumbersome and unilluminating when stress and kindred phenomena were investigated more thoroughly. Hence, the development of metrical trees and grids (Liberman & Prince 1977) with subsequent controversies as to whether both are necessary or only grids (e.g. Prince 1983; Selkirk 1984b) or only trees (Giegerich 1985). For a general introduction, see now Hogg & McCully (1987). At roughly the same time, it was becoming clear that linear representations were not adequate for certain types of morphophonemic process, notably those involving tone, perseverative nasalization, segmental length, vowel harmony, etc. A single linear, vertically segmented phonological representation came to be replaced therefore by multi-tiered autosegmental representations (Goldsmith 1976), and more generally, the geometry of phonological representations came to be more central than the form of phonological rules. In all of this, a notable returner to the theoretical fold was the syllable, which was seen to fill a number of crucial roles: natural domain for the statement of phonotactic restrictions (Hooper 1976), possible domain for the scope of phonological processes (Kahn 1976), natural environment for the assignment of stress, and definer of certain types of phonological class (Selkirk 1984a). A concern with the form of representations (for which see now also Clements 1985 and Archangeli 1985, among others) has not however completely replaced an interest in derivational history, which has now been developed within the context of a structured, level-ordered lexicon in lexical phonology (see Mohanan 1986 for a survey and references and also the useful collection of papers in *Phonology Yearbook*, 2 (1985)).

## 1.2. Morphology

Perhaps inevitably, the interest in nonlinear aspects of phonology led to a concern with similar issues in morphology, usually identified as 'non-concatenative,' following McCarthy (1979, 1981). Serious attention to morphological phenomena such as reduplication, infixing, and the peculiar properties of Semitic-type 'interdigitation' of consonantal roots and vocalic affixes has produced a number of theories, again concerned as much with the form of the representation as with the rules required to generate the relevant output. The immediate future therefore seems to hold a period of taking stock and reconciliation in which the many new dimensions of phonological and morphological structure currently permitted are explored and tested one against the other. In other words, it remains for the disciplines of phonology and morphology to sort out where autosegmental, metrical, and lexical approaches overlap and where they complement each other; where there are different analyses and where there are simply variant ways of stating the same new insights. This conclusion resembles quite closely the situation in syntax.

A common way of conceptualizing the form of a grammar has been a series of components. In particular, under the so-called 'standard theory' of transformational generative grammar – roughly that model which can be characterized by adding the view of syntax and semantics to be found in *Aspects of the theory of syntax* (Chomsky 1965) to the view of phonology expounded in *SPE* – it was assumed that a grammar consisted of a syntactic component, in turn divisible into phrase structure, transformational and lexical components, a semantic component, and a phonological component. In addition, Chomsky and Halle (*SPE*: 11) argued for the need for a 'readjustment component' to mediate between the output of the syntax and the input to the phonology. Within such a framework, theoretical debates might arise, as it were, 'component-internally,' about the directionality of phonological rules, the nature of phonological primitives, rule interaction (e.g. rule ordering, the cyclicity of transformations), the form of semantic rules, etc. Equally, however, disputes might center on the boundaries between components. Thus, it might be argued that certain boundaries were unnecessary, as when generative semantics challenged the need to recognize a 'division of labour' between syntax and semantics (see Newmeyer 1986 for a historical account). Alternatively, where a boundary was generally agreed to be necessary, the question might arise as to the right place to draw it. The conflict between 'abstract' and 'concrete' phonology (see Lass 1984: ch. 9, for a convenient summary and also Basbøll, in Chapter 7 of this volume) is essentially of the latter kind, dealing as it does with the proper assignment of material to the phonological and lexical parts of a linguistic description.

Whatever the subsequent importance of the component view in theoretical terms, it has left its mark in the way in which the discipline came to be institutionally subdivided. Whatever stance one takes on the abstract vs. concrete debate, one is a phonologist if one is professionally involved in questions of that kind and a syntactician if one's working life is spent, say, on questions relating to the form and functioning of transformations. Naturally, it is not precluded that some polymathic scholars should contribute to more than one subdiscipline thus defined. These divisions of the discipline not only affect matters of theory, but also more tangible things like the classification of books in libraries, the growth of specialized journals, the topics of conferences and workshops, and the hiring of academic staff in order to achieve balance and coverage of the discipline within a department. They also, therefore, determine the kinds of courses that are taught and the kinds of training and skills required of future generations of researchers. Terms such as 'phonology' or 'syntax' may therefore be taken to refer as much to subdisciplines of theoretical linguistics as to subcomponents of the models of natural language such theoretical work proposes.

Naturally, the match between components and subdisciplines may change, and this has happened dramatically during the evolution of generative linguistics in the case of morphology. As long as this was a separately defined level, as it had been within a post-Bloomfieldian conception of language, it was reasonable to think of a particular publication as being about morphology or of a particular scholar as working on morphological issues. Within the standard theory of generative grammar, by contrast, it was difficult even to raise questions of morphology in a unified way, since the model tended to assign them either to phonology or syntax (see Anderson, in Chapter 6 of this volume, for further elaboration of this point). One of the more significant shifts of the last decade or so, dating from such papers as Halle (1973), Jackendoff (1975), and from Aronoff's (1976) seminal dissertation, has been the return of morphology as a separate domain of inquiry. Significantly, since the component view has at the same time been being eroded, this return is not necessarily, and not always, linked to the setting-up of a separate morphological component but rather to the (re-)recognition of a clear set of morphological problems and issues with their own terms of reference. For an exchange that highlights both a class of morphological problems and the nature of their integration into a formal model of language, see Anderson (1982) and Jensen & Stong-Jensen (1984).

## 1.3. **The lexicon**

The converse case of a component without an attendant sub-discipline is the lexicon. Under the standard theory view, the reason is not hard to find, since classical transformational grammar shares the Bloomfieldian view that the lexicon is the repository of idiosyncrasies and irregularities – as it were, the waste products of syntax and phonology rather than material fit for investigation in its own right. Yet the case of the lexicon is rather special, since it is the one component within the standard view that interacts with all others, and therefore may be involved in a range of what we characterized above as 'boundary' disputes. For example, within phonology any move to reduce the range of data regarded as predictable by rule entails a compensatory increase in lexical statements, so that a pair such as *verbose/verbosity*, if not related by the *SPE* rule of trisyllabic laxing, could be connected by a lexical redundancy rule (Jackendoff 1975) or a via-rule (Hooper 1976). Or again, the giving up of transformations as a means of establishing relations between *arrive* and *arrival* or between *send* when it subcategorizes for [ __ NP PP] and [ __ NP NP] ('dative movement') involves finding alternative means for connecting the related pairs in the lexical lists. Thirdly, it has been argued that one can dispense with transformations such as affix-hopping if one treats inflected forms as whole items accessible via separate lexical entries. The logical cumulation of all these lines of argument would be to treat a grammar as one vast lexical store, with respect to which a variety of competing generalizations might be made. The generalizations would be statable in terms of the form of the representations in the store and of the connections that can be established between those entries.

## 1.4. **Diachronic change**

If we think of a grammar as involving at minimum a structured lexicon and at maximum separate syntactic, morphological, and phonological components, we might seem to be omitting two major areas of professional concern, namely phonetics and semantics. In one sense this omission is right, since the study of phonetics seems just as much the province of physics, engineering, and biology as it does of linguistics, and likewise semantics might be argued to be the proper responsibility of philosophers and logicians. On this view, the pure study of sound and meaning lies outside linguistics, which is concerned with the study of the nature of the relation between sound and meaning. An argument that such a state of affairs is more than an accident of the organization of academic institutions is to be found in the facts of language change. Phoneticians and semanticists study aspects of language that do not change over time, or at least only on the kind of time-scale that counts as evolution rather than as history. A reflection of this is the fact that this book does not contain chapters on phonetic or semantic change. Phonologists, morphologists, and syntacticians, by contrast, have to deal with the consequences of diachrony, as is evidenced in the fact that the present volume has parallel chapters on theory and change in each of these three sub-areas. Indeed, it is one of the more welcome of recent developments that data from linguistic change have been seen as pertinent to the development of proper models of language structure and not as areas simply of curiosity and anecdote.

The diachronic criterion can also be used to identify a theoretical issue whose importance is reflected in the chapter divisions of this volume, namely that of the syntax–phonology interface. Other interfaces are certainly conceivable; indeed in one sense, as we have already argued, the lexicon interfaces with all three of phonology, syntax, and morphology. Examples of problems at the morphology–syntax interface would be the status of clitics or the nature of periphrases. At the phonology–morphology interface we find issues relating to the productivity of certain types of alternations. The point is that in diachronic terms it makes sense to see an aspect of phonology being morphologized or a syntactic pattern such as compounding becoming lexicalized – indeed the terminology in *-ized* has precisely this dynamic implication. By the same token, however, phonology cannot become syntax or *vice versa*: we have here the projection to a different level of the Saussurean argument for the arbitrariness and, more important in the present context, the logical independence of the linguistic sign. It is not surprising therefore to see Pullum and Zwicky (in Chapter 10 of this volume) defending the inviolability of the syntax–phonology border, whereas in other areas the evidence of linguistic change always, and linguistic structure sometimes, leads to the abandonment of certain component boundaries within the model.

The past decade has thus seen the re-emergence of morphology as a topic for study in its own right, the concern being not so much – as was traditionally the case – with the linear structure of morphologically complex forms, as with the ways in which morphology is nonlinear. This latter issue has been taken up either at the level of representation, as in McCarthy's work already alluded to and as in Marantz's (1982) classic study of reduplication, or at the level of morphological rules, as in Anderson's attempt (1982 and this volume) to revive the classical word-and-paradigm model. This concern with nonlinearity in various guises represents a convergence with developments in phonology, where the rise of metrical and autosegmental models has promoted the treatment of a wide variety of phenomena as either entirely nonlinear (e.g. tone and perseverative nasalization; see Goldsmith 1985; Pulleyblank 1986), or as only accidentally linear, as in the suggestion that what makes a consonant a consonant is not any intrinsic property of consonantality but its occurrence in one of the non-nuclear positions in the syllable (onset or coda). Once things are approached in this fashion, it is possible in phonology, as already in syntax, to adopt a declarative style of formulation, giving conditions on possible syllable constituencies or on admissible metrical trees or grid configurations. Classic principles such as cyclicity, already a dead-letter in syntax, now become subsumed as part of the notation, while other kinds of rule ordering are eliminated at the expense of component ordering, e.g. syntax before morphology, or level ordering, as in the lexical phonology approach (Mohanan 1986). This multi-tier approach, which has come in recent years to seem so appropriate in the domains of morphology and phonology, has even begun to raise its head in syntax, most notably in Sadock's (1985) intriguing proposals for what he calls 'autolexical syntax,' in which the morphological and syntactic aspects of particular constructions may be represented on different tiers. The recent development of so-called double analyses in GB (e.g. Zubizarreta 1985) indicates another area where form of representation is taking over some of the descriptive and analytic burden from sequential, rule-based approaches.

## 1.5. **Syntax**

In syntax there are still substantial differences of opinion about the classification of a range of linguistic phenomena and, hence, concomitant disagreement about the mechanisms or principles responsible for them. Government–binding theory, for example, views pronominal anaphora, reflexives, control, raising, *wh*-movement, and quantifier scope as different manifestations of a common set of principles, and research in that paradigm has been largely concerned with the investigation of the general principles governing the distribution of different subtypes of NP involved in these constructions (anaphors, pronominals, traces, R-expressions) with the goal of providing a unified theory. Other paradigms dispute the interpretations of the data which drive the search for these generalizations (cf. Pullum & Borsley 1980), with consequent differences of opinion about the generalizations to be captured.

Nonetheless, despite these often profound disagreements, there has at a global level been a considerable degree of convergence in several domains over the past decade or so. Among the areas that one can point to is a general agreement that linguistic systems are modular. That is to say, the complex of linguistic behavior that we observe is the consequence of the interaction of a number of (semi-)independent systems (e.g. phonology, morphology, syntax, semantics, pragmatics (cf. Chapter 10), each of which is characterized by its own primitives and operations. This is in striking contrast to, and is arguably a reaction against, the position taken by generative semantics in the 1960s (cf. Newmeyer 1986).

McCloskey, in Chapter 2 of this volume, draws attention to the often covert agreement in metatheoretical assumptions. He points, for example, to a general shift from procedural to declarative styles of description and the abstraction away from particularized analyses towards more general formalizations, from which the particular facts fall out as consequences, as noted above. Declarativeness is particularly striking in LFG and GPSG, but it is just as much a feature of GB in terms of well-formedness conditions on levels of representation. Another more specific aspect of convergence is the emphasis on the local nature of syntactic phenomena. Even syntactic constructions such as 'unbounded dependencies' are now viewed by most theories as a manifestation of the sum of a set of local conditions. Theories differ considerably at the implementation level over how this locality is to be represented and, indeed, over the domains over which it holds (see Chapter 2 for details), but it is difficult to conceive that future developments will lead to this view being abandoned.

The role of the lexicon is something which has grown in importance in syntax as well as in phonology/morphology. One can identify two main aspects: the first is the role played by lexical categories (centrally N, V, A, and P) in constraining the output of grammars. In GB the role of lexical categories as governors/Case assigners together with the requirement of the empty category principle (ECP) constrains the distribution of empty categories. In GPSG the restriction of the domain of metarules to rules introducing lexical categories serves both to constrain the set of rules which a grammar can contain and also results in a similar effect to the ECP as far as *wh*-movement is concerned. The second is the contribution made by lexical entries themselves (see Andrews, in Chapter 3 of this volume). In GB, for example, lexical entries contain information about the Case and θ-role assigning properties of lexical items, which interact with other principles of the theory to determine significant aspects of syntactic structure. In GPSG and LFG the content of lexical entries plays an equally, if not more, significant role. This, again, stands in sharp contrast to the generative linguistics of the 1960s. Needless to say, there are considerable differences between theories over the actual content of lexical entries and the way in which they interact with the syntax (see Chapter 3 for further discussion). Given the emergence of the significance of the lexicon in current work, it is to be expected that this tendency will persist. Indeed, in a more recent development, head-driven phrase structure grammar (HPSG) (Pollard 1984, 1985; Sag forthcoming) the role of syntactic rules is reduced to a bare minimum, all significant syntactic and semantic processess being driven by information contained in lexical entries.

If the re-emergence of the syllable and of morphology is something surprising from the perspective of the 1960s, a topic of a fundamental nature which rather surprisingly re-emerged during the past decade in syntax is that of the formal status of natural languages. Chomsky's (1957) contention that context-free (CF) phrase structure grammars are inadequate for the characterization of natural languages came under challenge from Gerald Gazdar (1982). Pullum & Gazdar (1982) discussed at length a range of constructions which had been claimed to demonstrate that human languages are not context-free. They argued that these constructions had been incorrectly characterized (e.g. Postal's 1964 argument for the non-context-freeness of Mohawk), or that the standard interpretation of the construction confused strong generative capacity with weak generative capacity (e.g. the argument from English *respectively* constructions). The program of research which led to the development of GPSG was predicated on the assumption that it was preferable to start from the weakest hypothesis compatible with the data, and it succeeded in showing that interesting analyses of a wide range of natural language phenomena could be given in terms of a system which is extensionally equivalent to a CF grammar. Recent work (Culy 1985; Shieber 1985) has demonstrated to the satisfaction of the major protagonists of the GPSG position (Gazdar & Pullum 1985) that at least some natural languages (Swiss German and Bambara) are not context-free. The logic of the GPSG approach dictates a progressive relaxation of the restrictive hypothesis embodied in the CF claim.

The recent resurgence of interest in this issue is perhaps related to the fact that natural language processing by computer is a field which has grown in importance in recent years. The mathematical status of natural languages in terms of their position on the Chomsky hierarchy (Chomsky 1963) is in itself an interesting issue which has been used to motivate claims and counter-claims in the literature for the superiority of one theory over another (e.g. Gazdar 1982:130ff; Kaplan & Bresnan 1982:263). There has been a widespread assumption that it would be desirable for the class of grammars for natural languages to be the weakest possible, commensurate with the empirical evidence. (Recall that one of Chomsky's (1957) arguments in favor of transformational grammars was founded on a demonstration that grammars with weaker string-defining properties are inadequate for the definition of some string sets which are attested in natural languages.) More recently, this question has been linked to the issue of natural language parsability. Gazdar remarks:

> The sentences of a natural language can be parsed. We do it all the time. Furthermore, we do it very fast (see Marslen-Wilson 1973 for relevant psycholinguistic evidence). But 'for transformational grammars, it is not known that processing time can be any less than the a doubly exponential function of sentence length' (Peters 1979). Transformational grammars thus fail to provide even the beginnings of an explanation for one of the most important, and most neglected, facts about natural languages: parsing is easy and quick. Sentences of a context-free language are provably parsable in a time which is, at worst, proportional to less than the cube of the sentence length (Valiant 1975, Graham 1976). Many context-free languages, even ambiguous ones, are provably parsable in linear time (Earley 1970:99). These parsability results, and the avenues of research that they open up, provide a significant conceptual motivation for constraining natural language grammars to CF generative capacity. (Gazdar 1982:133f)

The relevance of language type (on the Chomsky hierarchy) to parsability is, however, not as clear-cut as Gazdar's remarks would suggest.[2] In a number of

---

[2] The status in terms of weak generative capacity of the languages defined by the theories discussed above is, in order of increasing power: GPSG – context-free (but see also Uszkoreit & Peters 1986); LFG – probably context-sensitive (Bresnan & Kaplan 1982; Gazdar & Pullum 1985:20); GB – probably recursive. As for the status of natural languages, Gazdar & Pullum (1985:11) state: '. . . we do not believe that any currently known facts lead one to believe that the N[atural] L[anguage]s fall outside

publications Berwick and Weinberg (Berwick 1984; Berwick & Weinberg 1982, 1984) have argued that the connection between the two is considerably more complex. Essentially, what is at issue is that the standard results from parsing theory give 'worst case' results – i.e. they state what the worst possible parsing times are for a whole class of grammars. As is apparent from Gazdar's comments, particular grammars within a given class may well have much better parsing results than the class as a whole. (See Perrault 1984, and Weinberg in Chapter 15 of this volume, for a discussion of the issues involved.) An alternative view, therefore, would be that the greatest efficiency is to be achieved by matching the parser much more closely to the grammar (cf. Marcus 1980).[3]

It would thus appear unlikely, in our current state of knowledge, that the issue of parsability will provide a clinching argument for or against any of the currently competing theories. Barton (1986:80) states: '. . . GPSG and other modern theories seem to be (very roughly) in the same boat with respect to complexity. In such a situation, the linguistic merits of various theories are more important than complexity results.' Nonetheless, these questions seem to be becoming one of the standard issues to be addressed and they may well play an even more significant role in future (see also Barton, Berwick & Ristad 1987). Although Gazdar's remarks were directed at the human capacity for language processing, the issue has achieved a greater degree of poignancy as a result of the massive increase in computing power (at considerably lower cost) which is available on modern computers. This development has contributed to an upsurge of interest in computer natural language processing, in which the practicality of a product depends significantly on the parsing efficency of the system. It is as yet too early to predict the outcome of these efforts, but it is conceivable that those linguistic theories which lend themselves to computational applications may enjoy an advantage in terms of research funding which may influence their status in the wider linguistic community – cf. Newmeyer's comments (1986:35–51) on the nonlinguistic factors which led to the predominance of transformational grammar in the 1960s.

the I[ndexed] L[anguage]s . . .' (Indexed languages are a proper subset of the context-sensitive languages and a proper superset of the context-free languages.)

[3] The worst case parsability result for CFPSGs which Gazdar cites in the quotation given in the text ('Sentences of a context-free language are provably parsable in a time which is, at worst, proportional to less than the cube of the sentence length') assumes that the length of the input string is the predominating factor. As Weinberg (Chapter 15 in this volume) points out, if the number of rules in the grammar is very large, the size of the grammar may come to play a crucial role in parsing times. The rules of a GPSG, when expressed in 'Immediate dominance/linear precedence' (IDLP) format, form a compact set, but if, for parsing purposes, they are expanded out by a preprocessor, the number of rules involved may be very large indeed – 'trillions' according to Shieber (1984:4). It would be possible in principle to avoid this situation by not expanding the grammar into a set of fully instantiated phrase structure rules, but by doing the required matching 'on the fly' as the parse proceeds. Such IDLP parsing has been argued by Barton (1985) to give exponential parsing times.

Contacts with the computing world are also reinforcing one of the consequences of the contacts with philosophical logic which developed during the late 1960s and 1970s and which are outlined in ter Meulen's chapter in this volume. On the one hand, a much higher standard of formal precision has been introduced into both discussions and theories and, on the other, the linguist's tool bag is now considerably larger. For example, feature systems have now been given a formal definition in terms of function theory by both GPSG and LFG and the operation of unification (which forms the basis of the interpreter for the PROLOG programming language) is used by GPSG, LFG, HPSG, Kay's functional unification grammar (Kay 1984), and unification categorial grammar (Zeevat, Klein & Calder 1987). It is difficult to imagine that nontransformational theories would have made any significant impact on the linguistic scene without the fertilization of ideas that has arisen out of these contacts. They have made it possible to demonstrate that mathematically more constrained theories can provide the basis for realistic theories of natural language syntax. We expect that this is a trend which will continue to develop.[4]

## 1.6. Semantics

Semantics can no longer be parodied as 'grammar minus syntax.' Semantics has become a growth area in linguistics. As Enç's and Ladusaw's contributions to this volume reveal, the dominant paradigm of the past decade has been the truth-conditional approach deriving from the foundational work of Richard Montague (Montague 1974). As noted above, this tradition has had the effect of introducing higher standards of mathematical rigor in areas other than semantics and it has, of necessity, played a crucial role in nontransformational theories by allowing entailment relations between sentences (such as actives and passives) to be captured at the semantic level (e.g. Gazdar *et al*. 1985 for GPSG, and Halvorsen 1983 for LFG). It has not played any significant role in GB (but see, for example, Heim 1982 and Chierchia 1984, 1985 for work in formal semantics sympathetic to the GB framework).

As Ladusaw points out in Chapter 4 of this volume, model-theoretic semantics has received most attention and consequently has been worked out to a greater extent than alternatives. As work in this area has matured, there

---

[4] It is worth commenting in this context that categorial grammar, while it has never achieved the status of a paradigm in linguistics, has seen many of its ideas being adopted by other theories and has contributed solutions to outstanding problems in linguistics which may yet prove to be influential. Steedman (1985) shows how a categorial grammar, augmented with rules of 'partial combination' can be used to give an insightful analysis of coordination and of intersecting dependencies in Dutch (and presumably Swiss German). Dowty's (1982a, b) categorial reconstruction of grammatical relations has been adopted by GPSG and HPSG. HPSG also shows strongly the influence of categorial grammar in its treatment of subcategorization. Unification categorial grammar, categorial grammar to which unification has been added, gives an example of influence proceeding in the opposite direction.

have been two major interconnected patterns of development: the extension of the theory to account for a wider range of semantic phenomena and an increasing concern for a more principled relationship between the syntactic entities of natural languages and their interpretations. One of the consequences of these trends has been extensions of the ontology of the semantic theory to incorporate a richer universe of individuals (e.g. Carlson's 1978 distinction between 'kinds,' 'objects,' and 'stages,' and Chierchia's 1984, 1985 analysis of gerunds), or the assignment of a richer structure to the model (Keenan & Faltz 1985). (See Ladusaw's chapter for further discussion of these issues.)

More recently, the field has seen the emergence of alternatives to the standard Montague version of truth-conditional semantics, notably discourse representation theory (Kamp 1981; Heim 1982) and situation semantics (Barwise & Perry 1983). Discourse representation theory (DRT) offers an alternative, but still model-theoretic, approach to the treatment of anaphora and quantification which provides new solutions to traditional problems – notably a unified treatment of bound anaphora and coreference and the apparent failure of phrases such as *a donkey* in *Every farmer who owns a donkey beats it* to have its usual existential force. It is too early to make a serious estimate of the impact which DRT will have on generative linguistics, but already interesting modifications of Kamp's original formulation are beginning to appear (e.g. Klein & Johnson 1986; Klein to appear) which render the theory more compatible with the general program of research in compositional semantics which Bach (1976) has termed the 'rule-to-rule' approach.

Situation semantics offers a more radical alternative to the possible worlds semantics adopted by Montague. Sentences are not true or false in possible worlds, but describe situations, where these are part of the world. Situations, in their turn, are sets of 'facts' which consist of a location, a relation and a truth value. A sentence describes a situation when the fact corresponding to the sentence is a member of the situation. This approach, among other things, allows sentences to represent partial information. The evaluation of the truth of a sentence does not require access to global information about the state of the universe. It thus offers the basis for a reconciliation between model-theoretic semantics and a psychological theory of semantics (cf. Ladusaw's chapter). Cooper (1984) gives a reconstruction of Carlson's (1978) ontology, using the tools of situation semantics, and shows how the theory can provide an account, in terms of partial information, of the progressive/non-progressive distinction in English. (See also Gavron 1986a, b, for further development of the theoretical framework and an analysis of the semantics of prepositional phrases.) To date, work in situation semantics has not been greatly concerned with the mapping from syntax to semantics, but this is an area which is now starting to receive attention (Cooper 1986; Cooper & Engdahl in preparation) and may well lead to new possibilities.

In conclusion, we share the view of most contributors to this volume that considerable progress has been achieved since the birth of generative linguistics thirty years ago. Although we may still be far from realizing the goals of the subject, however these are defined, there is a much better understanding of a wide range of linguistic phenomena and a much greater degree of sophistication in analyses. Although there is still the same lack of consensus as there has been for much of the subject's history, the debate is now rather less vituperative and the contemporary heterodoxy and the broader horizons of workers in the field look more likely to result in profitable cross-fertilization of ideas.

*REFERENCES*

Anderson, S. 1982. Where's morphology? *Linguistic Inquiry* 13: 571–612.
Archangeli, D. 1984. Underspecification in Yawelmani phonology and morphology. Doctoral dissertation, MIT.
Archangeli, D. 1985. Yokuts harmony: evidence for co-planar representations in non-linear phonology. *Linguistic Inquiry* 16: 335–72.
Aronoff, M. 1976. *Word-information in generative grammar*. Cambridge, MA: MIT Press.
Bach, E. 1976. An extension of classical transformational grammar. In *Problems in linguistic metatheory: proceedings of the 1976 conference at Michigan State University*, pp. 183–224.
Barton, G. E. 1985. The complexity of ID/LP parsing. *Computational Linguistics* 11: 205–18.
Barton, G. E., Berwick, R. C. & Ristad, E. S. 1987. *Computational complexity and natural language*. Cambridge, MA: MIT Press.
Barwise, J. & Perry, J. 1983. *Situations and attitudes*. Cambridge, MA: MIT Press.
Berwick, R. 1984. Strong generative capacity, weak generative capacity and modern linguistic theories. *Computational Linguistics* 10: 189–202.
Berwick, R. & Weinberg, A. 1982. Parsing efficiency, computational complexity and the evaluation of grammatical theories. *Linguistic Inquiry* 13: 165–91.
Berwick, R. & Weinberg, A. 1984. *The grammatical basis of linguistic performance*. Cambridge, MA: MIT Press.
Brame, M. 1976. *Conjectures and refutations in syntax and semantics*. New York: Elsevier.
Brame, M. 1978. *Base generated syntax*. Seattle: Noit Amrofer.
Bresnan, J. (ed.) 1982. *Mental representation and grammatical relations*. Cambridge, MA: MIT Press.
Carlson, G. 1978. Reference to kinds in English. Circulated by Indiana University Linguistics Club, Bloomington.
Chierchia, G. 1984. *Topics in the syntax and semantics of gerunds*. Doctoral dissertation, University of Massachusetts at Amherst. Published by the University of Massachusetts Graduate Linguistics Association.
Chierchia, G. 1985. Formal semantics and the grammar of predication. *Linguistic Inquiry* 16: 417–43.
Chomsky, N. 1957. *Syntactic structures*. The Hague: Mouton.
Chomsky, N. 1963. Formal properties of grammars. In R. D. Luce, R. R. Bush & E. Galanter (eds.) *Handbook of mathematical psychology*, vol. II. New York: Wiley.
Chomsky, N. 1965. *Aspects of the theory of syntax*. Cambridge, MA: MIT Press.
Chomsky, N. 1986. *Knowledge of language*. New York: Praeger.
Chomsky, N. and Halle, M. 1968. *The sound pattern of English*. New York: Harper & Row.
Clements, G. N. 1985. The geometry of phonological features. *Phonology Yearbook* 2: 223–52.

Cooper, R. 1984. *Aspectual classes in semantics*. Report no. CSLI-84-14-C, Center for the Study of Language and Information, Stanford University.
Cooper, R. 1986. Verb-second – predication or unification. *Working Papers in Scandinavian Syntax*. Trondheim: Linguistics Department, University of Trondheim.
Cooper, R. & Engdahl, E. In preparation. Situation semantics for long-distance dependencies.
Culy, C. 1985. The complexity of the vocabulary of Bambara. *Linguistics and Philosophy* 8: 345–51.
Dowty, D. 1982a. Grammatical relations and Montague grammar. In Jacobson & Pullum (1982).
Dowty D. 1982b. More on the categorial analysis of grammatical relations. In Zaenen (1982).
Earley, J. 1970. An efficient context-free parsing algorithm. *Communications of the ACM* 13: 94–102.
Engdahl, E. 1983. Parasitic gaps. *Linguistics and Philosophy* 6: 5–34.
Finer, D. 1985. The syntax of switch reference. *Linguistic Inquiry* 16: 35–56.
Fodor, J. & Katz, J. 1964. *The structure of language*. Englewood Cliffs: Prentice-Hall.
Gavron, J. M. 1986a. Situations and prepositions. *Linguistics and Philosophy* 9: 327–82.
Gavron, J. M. 1986b. Types contents and semantic objects. *Linguistics and Philosophy* 9: 427–76.
Gazdar, G. 1982. Phrase structure grammar. In Jacobson & Pullum (1982).
Gazdar, G. & Pullum, G. 1985. *Computationally relevant properties of natural languages and their grammars*. Report no. CSLI-85-24, Center for the Study of Language and Information, Stanford University.
Gazdar, G., Klein, E., Pullum, G. & Sag, I. 1985. *Generalised phrase structure grammar*. Oxford: Basil Blackwell.
Giegerich, H. 1985. *Metrical phonology and phonological structure*. Cambridge: Cambridge University Press.
Goldsmith, J. 1976. Autosegmental phonology. Doctoral dissertation, MIT.
Goldsmith, J. 1985. Vowel harmony in Khalka Mongolian, Yaka, Finnish, and Hungarian. *Phonology Yearbook* 2: 253–75.
Graham, S. L. 1976. On-line context-free language recognition in less than cubic time. In *Proceedings of the Eighth Annual ACM Symposium on the Theory of Computing* pp. 112–20.
Groenendijk, J. & Stockhoff, M. (eds.) To appear. *Proceedings of the Fifth Amsterdam Colloquium*. Amsterdam: Mathematisch Centrum.
Groenendijk, J., Janssen, T. & Stockhoff, M. (eds.) 1981. *Formal methods in the study of language. Part 1*. Mathematical Centre Tracts 135, Mathematisch Centrum, Amsterdam.
Haddock, N. Klein, E. & Morrill, G. (eds.) 1987. *Working papers in cognitive science*. Vol. 1: *Categorial grammar, unification grammar and parsing*, Centre for Cognitive Science, University of Edinburgh, Edinburgh.
Haiman, J. & Munro, P. 1983. *Switch-reference and universal grammar*. Amsterdam: Benjamins.
Hale, K. 1982. On the position of Warlpiri in a theory of typology. Circulated by Indiana University Linguistics Club, Bloomington.
Halle, M. 1973. Prolegomena to a theory of word formation. *Linguistic Inquiry* 4: 3–16.
Halvorsen, P. K. 1983. Semantics for lexical-functional grammar. *Linguistic Inquiry* 14: 567–615.
Heim, I. 1982. *The semantics of definite and indefinite noun phrases*. Doctoral dissertation, University of Massachusetts at Amherst. Published by the University of Massachusetts Graduate Linguistics Association.
Hogg, R. M. & McCully, C. 1985. *Metrical phonology: a coursebook*. Cambridge: Cambridge University Press.
Hooper, J. B. 1976. *Introduction to natural generative phonology*. New York: Academic Press.
Huang, J. C. T. 1982. Logical relations and the theory of grammar. Doctoral dissertation, MIT.
Huck, G. J. & Ojeda, A. E. (eds.) Forthcoming. *Syntax and semantics*, vol. 20. Orlando, FA: Academic Press.
Jacobson, P. & Pullum, G. (eds.) 1982. *The nature of syntactic representation*. Dordrecht: Reidel.
Jackendoff, R. 1975. Morphological and semantic relations in the lexicon. *Language* 51: 639–71.
Jensen, J. & Stong-Jensen, M. 1984. Morphology IS in the lexicon. *Linguistic Inquiry* 15: 474–98.

Kahn, D. 1976. Syllable-based generalizations in English phonology. Doctoral dissertation, MIT.

Kamp, H. 1981. A theory of truth and semantic representation. In Groenendijk *et al*. (1981).

Kaplan, R. & Bresnan, J. 1982. Lexical functional grammar: a formal system for grammatical representation. In Bresnan (1982).

Kay, M. 1984. Functional unification grammar: a formalism for machine translation. In *Proceedings of Coling 84*. Menlo Park: Association for Computational Linguistics.

Keenan, E. & Faltz, L. 1985. *Boolean semantics for natural language*. Dordrecht: Reidel.

Klein, E. To appear. VP ellipsis in DR theory. In Groenendijk & Stockhoff (to appear).

Klein, E. & Johnson, M. 1986. Discourse, anaphora and parsing. In *Proceedings of the 11th International Conference on Computational Linguistics and the 24th Annual Meeting of the Association for Computational Linguistics*. Institut fuer Kommunicationsforschung und Phonetik, Bonn University.

Lass, R. 1984. *Phonology*. Cambridge: Cambridge University Press.

Liberman, M. & Prince, A. 1977. On stress and linguistic rhythm. *Linguistic Inquiry* 8: 249–336.

Marantz, A. 1982. Re reduplication. *Linguistic Inquiry* 13: 435–82.

Marcus, M. 1980. *A theory of syntactic recognition for natural language*. Cambridge, MA: MIT Press.

Marslen-Wilson, W. D. 1973. Speech shadowing and speech perception. Doctoral dissertation, MIT.

McCarthy, J. 1979. Formal problems in Semitic phonology and morphology. Doctoral dissertation, MIT.

McCarthy, J. 1981. A prosodic theory of nonconcatenative morphology. *Linguistic Inquiry* 12: 373–418.

Mohanan, K. P. 1986. *The theory of lexical phonology*. Dordrecht: Reidel.

Montague, R. 1974. *Formal philosophy: selected papers of Richard Montague* ed. by R. Thomason. New Haven: Yale University Press.

Newmeyer, F. 1986. *Linguistic theory in America*. 2nd edn. New York: Academic Press.

Perrault, C. R. 1984. On the mathematical properties of linguistic theories. *Computational Linguistics* 10: 165–76.

Peters, S. 1979. How semantics keeps syntax psychologically computable. Paper presented to the Cognitive Studies Seminar, University of Sussex.

Pollard, C. 1984. Generalized context-free grammars, head grammars and natural language. Doctoral dissertation, Stanford University.

Pollard, C. 1985. Phrase structure grammar without metarules. In *Proceedings of the 4th West Coast Conference on Formal Linguistics*. Stanford: Department of Linguistics, Stanford University.

Postal, P. 1964. Limitation of phrase structure grammars. In Fodor & Katz (1964).

Prince, A. 1983. Relating to the grid. *Linguistic Inquiry* 14: 19–100.

Pulleyblank, D. 1986. *Tone in lexical phonology*. Dordrecht: Reidel.

Pullum, G. & Borsley, R. 1980. Comments on two central claims of 'trace theory'. *Linguistics* 18: 73–104.

Pullum, G. & Gazdar, G. 1982. Natural languages and context-free languages. *Linguistics and Philosophy* 4: 471–504.

Sadock, J. 1985. Autolexical syntax *Natural Language and Linguistic Theory* 3: 379–440.

Sag, I. 1982. A semantic theory of 'NP movement' dependencies. In Jacobson & Pullum (1982).

Sag, I. Forthcoming. Grammatical hierarchy and linear precedence. In Huck & Ojeda (forthcoming).

Selkirk, E. 1984a. On the major class features and syllable theory. In M. Aronoff & R. Oehrle (eds.) *Language sound structure*. Cambridge, MA: MIT Press.

Selkirk, E. 1984b. *Phonology and syntax*. Cambridge, MA: MIT Press.

Shieber, S. 1984. Direct parsing of ID/LP grammars. *Linguistics and Philosophy* 7: 135–54.

Shieber, S. 1985. Evidence against the non-context freeness of natural language. *Linguistics and Philosophy* 8: 333–43.

Steedman, M. 1985. Dependency and coordination in the grammar of Dutch and English. *Language* 61: 523–68.

Uszkoreit, H. & Peters, S. 1986. On some formal properties of metarules. *Linguistics and Philosophy* 9: 477–94.

Valiant, L. G. 1975. General context-free recognition in less than cubic time. *Journal of Computer and System Sciences* 10: 308–15.

Zaenen, A. (ed.) 1982. *Subjects and other subjects*. Bloomington: Indiana University Linguistics Club.

Zeevat, H. Klein, E. &. Calder, J. 1987. Unification categorial grammar. In Haddock, Klein & Morrill (1987).

Zubizarreta, N. L. 1985. The relation between morpho-phonology and morphosyntax: the case of Romance causatives. *Linguistic Inquiry* 16: 247–90.

# 2 Syntactic theory*

*James McCloskey*

## 2.0. Introduction

The study of syntax, for reasons that have never been clear (to me, at least) has always been a more acrimonious business than the pursuit of sister-disciplines in formal linguistics. Phonologists, morphologists, semanticists and phoneticians can all survive and cooperate in courteous disagreement, but syntacticians seem to thrive on a more robust diet of anger, polemic and personal abuse. It may well be that this robust atmosphere leads to progress and to good work in the long term, but there can be little doubt but that in the shorter term it tends to obscure certain points of basic agreement and to obfuscate, rather than clarify, the points of real disagreement.

My aim in this short review will be to survey some current approaches to the study of syntax, and to attempt to distinguish between areas in which there is broad agreement about principles and analyses, and areas in which there is real disagreement. Certain limitations will be imposed and these should be mentioned explicitly from the outset. I will be concerned only with 'generative' theories of syntax – by which I mean roughly those theories which see themselves as continuing in one way or another the research tradition established by Noam Chomsky in *Syntactic structures* (1957) and in *Aspects of the theory of syntax* (1965). One exclusion that this will impose is that I will not consider work in categorial grammar, although this theory represents a rich and active tradition and one that interacts a great deal with some of the theories that will be considered explicitly here.[1] Nor will it be possible to consider every theory of syntax which would merit

* I am grateful to Fritz Newmeyer, Sandra Chung and in particular to David Perlmutter for help and advice in the preparation of this chapter. I would also like to acknowledge the support and hospitality of the Syntax Research Center of the University of California, Santa Cruz during its preparation. The work was supported in part by NSF Grant BNS84-05596.
[1] For work in categorial grammar, see Dowty (1978, 1979, 1982a, 1982b, 1985), Bach (1979, 1981, 1982, 1983), Schmerling (1979, 1983), Ades & Steedman (1982), Steedman (1985a, b), Flynn (1983). *Head-driven phrase structure grammar* (HPSG), as developed recently by Carl Pollard and others (see Pollard 1984, 1985; Goldberg 1985; Sag 1985) might be seen as an amalgam of categorial grammar and GPSG (for which, see below).

the name 'generative' by the criterion of tracing its ancestry to *Syntactic structures* and *Aspects of the theory of syntax*. I will consider explicitly only the frameworks known as *government and binding* (GB), *generalized phrase structure grammar* (GPSG), *lexical functional grammar* (LFG) and *relational grammar* (RG) respectively. It is fair to say, I think, that these are the theories that currently attract most interest and which represent the most active paradigms of research.[2]

One way to approach the task of defining the current theoretical scene, and of determining what progress, if any, has been made in recent years, is to ask what the most controversial issues in syntax were ten years ago. What is the status of those controversies now and to what extent has consensus been achieved concerning those issues in the intervening period?

Before addressing these particular issues, it seems right to broach a topic of a rather broader character – broader in that it has to do with the general strategy of research rather than with particular empirical proposals.

There is a characteristic which distinguishes all the theories being considered here from almost all earlier work in generative grammar, a characteristic having to do with the overall organization of grammatical description. In work of the 60s and 70s, the task of analyzing a particular domain of facts consisted largely in specifying a set of rules (phrase structure rules and/or transformations) and a way in which the rules interacted (how, for instance, they were ordered with respect to one another in application) to define derivations. Grammatical sentences were those for which legal derivations were defined: ungrammatical sentences were those for which no legal derivation was defined. The rules proposed tended in general to be quite specific, in that they were particular to individual constructions in individual languages. Work of this period is therefore full of references to the 'French passive rule' or the 'English relativization rule,' and so on. The task of the general theory of grammar was seen largely as being that of defining a notational system within which such rule systems could be formulated, a system which would allow for the statement of all possible rules and disallow the impossible.

More recent work has a very different orientation. The view of what a syntactic representation in essence consists of is not different in a fundamental way from the views commonly held in the 60s and 70s. Then as now, most theories view the syntactic analysis of a sentence as having at its core a phrase structure tree, annotated in various ways to account for the anaphoric and other links holding between various positions within the

---

[2] See Sells (1985) for surveys of GB, LFG and GPSG. For GB, the basic references are Chomsky (1981, 1982, 1986a, b); for LFG, the basic reference is Bresnan (1982a). For GPSG see Gazdar *et al.* (1985), and for RG see Perlmutter (1983), Perlmutter & Rosen (1984). *Arc-pair grammar* (Johnson & Postal 1980) is a close relative of relational grammar.

sentence, and associated with a representation of the sentence's interpretation.[3] However, what is very different in recent work is the view of how these structures arise and are recognized as being either well-formed or ill-formed. Syntactic representations are seen now as being constructed by very general mechanisms (such as the principles of *X-bar theory*, hereafter *X̄-theory*, which define what it is to be a well-formed phrase structure) which are 'then' subjected to a battery of conditions on well-formedness which filter out unwanted structures (those corresponding to ungrammatical sentences).[4] Such conditions may apply to syntactic structures at a number of different levels of representation, depending on the number of such levels recognized by the theory in question. Furthermore, the filtering conditions proposed tend not to be specific to a particular construction (such as the passive construction); rather they are formulated in as general and as streamlined a way as the data will allow, and will typically have consequences for many different constructions. There is also a strong tendency to explain particular facts as far as is possible in terms of general principles of grammar rather than in terms of principles unique to the language being investigated. Among the filtering conditions that have been proposed, for example, are general principles having to do with the relation between the argument-structure of a predicate and the syntactic structures in which the predicate may appear (the 'completeness and uniqueness conditions' of LFG, for instance, or the 'θ-criterion' of GB), or general principles governing the distribution of syntactic features in phrase structure trees (the 'head feature convention' and 'foot feature principle' of GPSG, for example), or principles which govern the relation between anaphoric elements and their antecedents (the three principles of binding theory in GB). In all these cases, such general principles perform analytic tasks previously performed by numerous particular conditions attached to particular rules in particular languages. In modern work, it is not the existence of a list of rules which recognizes and legitimizes a set of structures as well-formed; rather it is this conspiracy of very general filtering and licensing conditions.

One of the most dramatic illustrations of this tendency to factor out general principles, rather than simply supply a list of rules, is the way in which the phrase structure rules familiar from generative work in the 50s,

---

[3] Positions differ as to whether or not the interpretation can be represented in terms of the same vocabulary and constructs as the phrase structural representation. The level of logical form (LF) in GB is defined in terms of phrase structure trees; the level of functional structure in LFG is defined in terms of structures quite different from phrase structure trees; GPSG makes no appeal at all to a *representation* of the sentence's interpretation, but rather defines a model-theoretic interpretation directly on the phrase structural representation of the sentence's syntax. It should also be stressed that relational grammar and arc-pair grammar are two important current theories that make no appeal to phrase structures of the traditional type in syntactic analysis.

[4] Or assign to the sentence some intermediate status between full well-formedness and complete ungrammaticality (see Chomsky 1986b).

60s and 70s have been dismembered and, in a sense, eliminated. One of the few uncontroversial assumptions that emerged from the 60s was the position that the grammar of a given language had as its base a list of phrase structure rules of the general form in (1):

(1) $A \rightarrow X\ Y\ Z$

Such rules define as well-formed a substructure like that illustrated in (2):

(2)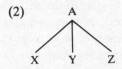

A rule like (1) specifies precedence relations (e.g. that X precedes Y and Z) and hierarchical relations (e.g. that A immediately dominates X, Y and Z) simultaneously and totally. Much recent work separates out these two functions, hierarchical structure and linear order being specified by different subsystems.

Hierarchical relations are defined by the general principles of phrase structure, known collectively as $\bar{X}$-theory. Here too an effort has been made to extract the general pattern from the lists of rules common in earlier work. The essential ideas do not differ substantially from one theory to another, although there is, of course, much disagreement at the level of specifics. The basic unit of syntax is the *maximal projection*; these are the phrases which are 'large enough' in some sense to move (in those theories which permit movement), to bind pronouns and empty positions and to fill argument positions. Each maximal projection is constructed around a 0-level category, of which there are two kinds: *lexical categories* (nouns, verbs, adjectives and, arguably, prepositions) and *nonlexical categories* (Comp(lementizer) and, more controversially, Infl(ection)).[5] One widely accepted view is that the basic cross-categorical schema is as in (3):

(3)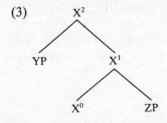

where the relative order of elements is understood to be unspecified. YP in (3) is known as the *specifier* of the construction. ZP is known as the *complement* of $X^0$. And both $X^0$ and $X^1$ are known as the *head* of the maximal

---

[5] Infl corresponds essentially to the category Aux(iliary) of earlier work.

projection. When it is necessary to distinguish the two notions of *head*, $X^0$ can be called the *lexical head*. Finally, both $X^1$ and $X^2$ are known as *projections* of $X^0$. Particular phrase structure configurations are made available for a given language by instantiating X in (3) as a particular category, and by allowing the lexical requirements of $X^0$ to determine the number and type of complements it will have as sisters.[6]

Linear order of constituents is defined by separate conditions – linear precedence rules in GPSG, and in GB principles having to do with the direction in which case or semantic roles are assigned. In both cases, the domain of application of these conditions is considerably broader than the very particular structures defined by a traditional phrase structure rule like (1).

We will see a number of other instances of this general strategy as we proceed to look at more specific domains of analysis.

There are, of course, certain elements in the grammatical system of any language which are irreducibly stipulative and particular. Lexical specifications, for instance, which contain all the idiosyncratic and unpredictable information peculiar to individual words or morphemes, must simply be listed. It is a question explicit or implicit in much current work to what extent the grammatical systems of given languages can be viewed as being defined completely by the interaction between this layer of unavoidably stipulative and particular information, and a system of otherwise rather general principles, some belonging to the general theory of grammar, some peculiar to the given language. Work in GB pursues this possibility in a particularly explicit and energetic way (Chomsky 1986a, for instance, suggests that syntactic rules, in the sense traditionally understood, may be completely eliminable), but the investigation of this option is clearly a very general theme in current work in a number of different frameworks.

Turning to more particular issues, let us address the question of what has become of the controversies that aroused the passions of syntacticians ten years ago. This can probably best be done by considering the taxonomy of grammatical domains traditional in generative grammar. We will consider first '*wh*-movements,' then the 'cyclic NP-movements.' The general conclusion will be that a surprising degree of consensus has in fact emerged over the past ten years with respect to all these phenomena.

---

[6] For more detail on X̄-theory, see Chomsky (1970, 1986a: 80–4, 1986b: 2–4), Jackendoff (1977), Bresnan (1982b), Pullum (1985). Controversy remains about the question of whether or not a phrase can have a phrase at the same bar-level as its head, or if there must always be a descent in bar-level from mother to head. The analysis of the clausal categories S and S′ also remains controversial.

## 2.1. *Wh*-movements

*Wh*-movement constructions[7] are those whose crucial identifying property is. that an anaphoric link is established between an empty position within S and a position external to S and peripheral in the larger clausal structure of which S is a part. This kind of link is characteristic of relative clauses, constituent questions, clefts, comparative clauses and certain kinds of adverbial clauses in many languages. Examples from English are given in (4), in which the S-external binder is indicated by italicization, and the bound empty position within S is indicated by ' ___ .'

(4) a. This is the one *which* I really like ___
 b. I wonder *what* he wants to do ___
 c. He came back just *when* I said he would ___

Two properties of this binding relation have been the focus of theoretical concern. The first is that in English and many other languages the link between binder and empty position can apparently be made across an unlimited number of syntactic boundaries, in the sense that the empty position may be contained within a subordinate clause which is itself contained within an arbitrarily large number of higher clauses which exclude the binding position:

(5) a. That's the guy *who* I think he said you ought to make sure that you talk to ___
 b. *Who* do you think we should say we were thinking of inviting ___ ?

This observation notwithstanding, the relation of *wh*-binding is subject to a number of structural conditions, known as 'island constraints' since they were first investigated by Ross (1967). 'Islands' are syntactic configurations of a particular degree or type of complexity into which the relation of *wh*-binding may not reach. The examples in (6) are typical, exemplifying the 'complex NP constraint,' the 'subject condition,' the '*wh*-island constraint' and the 'adjunct island condition' respectively:

(6) a. *$*How tall$ did you know [$_{NP}$ a man [$_{S'}$ that [$_S$ was ___ ?]]]
 b. *$*Who$ [$_S$ did [$_{NP}$ your obsession with ___ ] annoy your father?]
 c. *That's the car [$_{S'}$ *which* [$_S$ I wanted to know [$_{S'}$ what [$_S$ you did with ___ ]]]]
 d. *That's the kind of job *which* my husband sleeps [while I take care of ___ ]

---

[7] Also known as 'A′ binding' constructions in recent GB work, as 'unbounded dependency' constructions in a lot of work (particularly GPSG), or as 'constituent control' constructions in LFG.

*Wh*-binding into a clause contained within a noun phrase is ungrammatical (the complex noun phrase constraint); *wh*-binding into a noun phrase that is itself in subject position is ungrammatical (the subject condition); *wh*-binding into a clause already built around another instance of *wh*-binding is also ungrammatical (the *wh*-island constraint). And finally, *wh*-binding into a clause which is an adjunct (i.e. serves an adverbial function) is ungrammatical.

The controversy surrounding such constructions in the mid-70s centered on the question of whether or not their apparently unbounded character should be taken at face value, and on the related question of how the island constraints were best analyzed. Chomsky (1973) argued that *wh*-binding is always accomplished by means of syntactic movement of a phrase from the empty position within S to the binding position outside S. He argued further that this movement was subject to a locality requirement known as the 'subjacency principle,' which demanded that no more than one NP or S node be crossed in the course of any one application of the rule. Subjacency (in combination with certain other assumptions) yielded an account of many of the island conditions first discussed by Ross. Of the constraints exemplified in (6), for instance, three at least have an immediate explanation in terms of subjacency, in that they involve movement across two or more boundaries of the crucial type (NP or S). The complex noun phrase constraint (see 6a) involves movement in a single step at least across the S-boundary of the clause within NP and across the NP-boundary itself. Similarly, the subject condition (6b) involves movement across both the boundary of the NP subject and across the highest S-boundary. Finally, the *wh*-island constraint (6c) involves movement across both the first and the second S-boundaries. Subjacency also requires that in grammatical instances of 'long' movement, as in the examples of (5), a moved phrase makes the journey from the empty position to the binding position not in a single step (this would involve the crossing of two S-boundaries, in violation of subjacency), but rather in a series of smaller steps from one clause-initial position to the next highest:

(7) the man [*who* [ₛ you thought [that [ₛ you should say [that [ₛ you would hire___]]]]]]

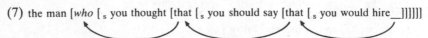

No one of these moves crosses more than one S-node, and subjacency is therefore not violated.

The position that the relation of *wh*-binding always reflects the application of a movement rule, and furthermore one that always applies in a series of locally bounded hops, as in (7), was extremely controversial, and gave rise to a dispute surprising in retrospect in its intensity. An alternative view, propounded notably by Joan Bresnan, in an important series of papers (1975, 1976a, 1977) maintained that *wh*-movement applied in an unbounded way, that there were also deletion rules which obeyed the island constraints and which acted over unbounded domains, and was thus led to reject the subjacency interpretation of the island facts.

The overwhelming consensus in modern work tends clearly toward some version of the view originally proposed in Chomsky (1973). Virtually every modern theory[8] analyzes the apparently unbounded relationships exhibited in (5) as being in fact made up of a series of smaller, quite local, links.

There are a number of factors to which the emergence of this consensus might be attributed. Firstly, no equally attractive account of the island phenomena emerged to compete with the subjacency interpretation. Secondly, the very elegant account of island effects in Italian proposed by Luigi Rizzi (1982a, first published in 1980) was extremely influential. This analysis provided very clear support for what was the central idea of the subjacency proposal – namely, that it is the crossing of *two* boundaries of the relevant type (NP and S' for Italian, according to Rizzi) that is crucial for determining ungrammaticality.[9]

Finally, investigation of a variety of languages turned up evidence that the clause-initial stopping-off points postulated by the theory of subjacency in the derivation of examples like (5) did indeed play a crucial role in establishing the link between binder and bound position in *wh*-constructions. The evidence accumulated was of two kinds. It can be argued for a number of languages that the stopping-off points postulated by subjacency are formally and visibly marked in one way or another. For another group of cases, it can be argued that the hypothesis that a phrase passed through these intermediate positions on its way to its ultimate destination, plays some crucial role in explaining other grammatical phenomena.[10]

For these reasons and others, it is now widely accepted that apparently long movements, as in (5), are in fact best analyzed as being compositions of smaller, more local links.[11] One can discern two variants of this basic idea – variants which, in large part, cut across theoretical divides. Consider a simple example like (8), with the approximate structure illustrated in (9):

[8] Arc-pair grammar (Johnson & Postal 1980) being an exception.
[9] Rizzi's work is also important in being the first proposal to exploit the notion of a 'parameter'. The basic idea is that a principle defined by the general theory of grammar may allow a small range of options in its formulation among which individual languages may choose. A small difference in parameter setting (e.g. the choice of S as a bounding-node for subjacency in English, but S' in Italian) will account, it is hoped, for a whole network of subtle and connected differences between the two languages in question. The exploitation of this general idea has been crucial in the subsequent development of GB. See Chomsky (1981, 1986a), Rizzi (1982b), Huang (1982), Koopman (1984), Travis (1984).
[10] Kayne & Pollock (1978), McCloskey (1979), Harlow (1981), Torrego (1984), Chung (1982), Wheeler (1978), du Plessis (1977).
[11] One of the larger reasons why this conclusion has been of importance is that from it developed a general concern for the discovery of locality conditions on a wide variety of grammatical processes and principles. This too is a feature of much current work. For general discussion, see Koster (1978), Bouchard (1984), Culicover & Wilkins (1984).

(8) (Let me ask you) *who* you thought that you saw _____

(9)

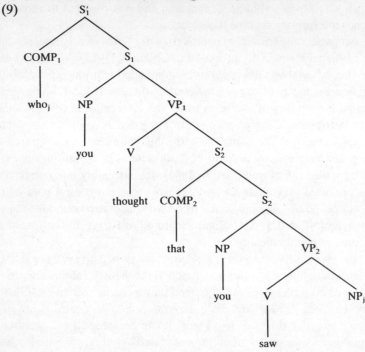

In Chomsky's original conception the COMP-nodes played a distinguished and crucial role in establishing the link between the binder *who* and the empty NP-position it binds in $S_2$. Stated in movement terms, what happens is that *who* originates in the NP-position in $S_2$, moves first to $COMP_2$ and then to $COMP_1$. Avoiding the movement metaphor, one might say that the anaphoric link between *who* and the empty NP-position in $S_2$ is in fact a composition of two more local links – one link between *who* and $COMP_2$ and another link between $COMP_2$ and the empty NP-position. Neither of these links violates subjacency, in the sense that neither is made across more than one S-boundary. This view, which involves assigning a distinctive and important role to the COMP-node in obviating subjacency violations, was, until very recently at least, the view taken by and large in orthodox GB work. It is also the view taken in much LFG work (see Kaplan & Bresnan 1982; Zaenen 1983).[12]

Opposed to these 'COMP theories' of *wh*-phenomena, one can set what might be called 'path theories' of the same phenomena. If one looks at the structure in (9), it is apparent that one can trace a path through the tree beginning with the empty NP-node, going up to $VP_2$, from there to $S_2$, to $S_2'$;

[12] More recent LFG work, however, departs somewhat from these assumptions. See Kaplan & Zaenen (1985), Sells (1985: 179–86).

from there to $VP_1$ and to $S_1$ and finally to $S_1'$, which immediately dominates *who*. The two positions (the bound NP-position and the binder *who*) can, then, be seen as being connected by a path consisting only of very local (i.e. mother-to-daughter) phrase structure connections. One can then begin to account for certain properties of these constructions by requiring that each local link on this path meet certain conditions, or, alternatively, that the path itself, viewed globally, meet certain conditions.

This general strategy is characteristic of GPSG, and also of certain traditions within GB stemming from the work of R. S. Kayne (Kayne 1981a, 1983; Pesetsky 1982; Longobardi 1983, 1985).

The principal difference between work in GPSG and GB in this domain, is that in GPSG the path through the tree is marked explicitly by means of the syntactic feature SLASH, which takes as its value a syntactic category (ultimately the category of the gap). This feature must appear on each node in the tree which forms part of the path between binder and bound position. In the case of (8), we will have the tree structure in (10):

(10)

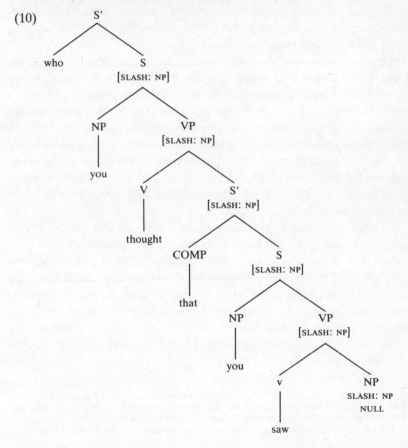

In the work of Kayne, Longobardi, and Pesetsky, however, the nodes along a path are not marked explicitly in any way.

The difference is not merely notational. GPSG owes its existence, in a sense, to the idea that context-free phrase structure grammars should be taken seriously as models of syntactic description for natural language. For this reason, work in GPSG is committed to a particularly radical version of the idea that all grammatical processes are subject to locality conditions. In particular because it restricts itself to using only the expressive power made available by context-free grammars, the only grammatical domains that can be inspected and acted upon by the devices of GPSG are the local trees consisting of a mother and its immediate daughters. Applied to the particular problem under consideration here, what this means is that in a structure like (9) or (10) no grammatical principle or rule can refer simultaneously to the binder *who* and the NP-position that *who* binds. Nor can any rule or principle refer, for instance, to the binder *who* and the intermediate COMP-position COMP$_2$, since they are neither in the sister nor the mother–daughter relation. GPSG, therefore, is not in a position to define properties of *wh*-constructions by referring to global properties of the paths that link the binding and the bound positions.

The central strategy of the GPSG enterprise is to account for grammatical phenomena by stating conditions which govern the appearance and distribution of syntactic features in the local subtrees consisting only of a mother and its daughters. Since the path between a *wh*-binder and the position it binds is marked by the appearance of the feature [SLASH], and since the empty positions which are bound in *wh*-constructions are assumed to be marked with the feature [NULL], properties of these constructions can be accounted for in terms of the general or particular principles which govern the distribution of these features. But all such principles must refer only to local subtrees.[13]

Consider an example. It follows from a very general condition (the lexical head constraint) that the feature [NULL] can appear only on a category which is a sister to a lexical category. From this it follows that the examples in (11) will be ungrammatical, since they all involve the appearance of the feature [NULL] on a category (i.e. the empty position) which is not a sister to a verb, preposition, noun or adjective. (11a) illustrates the famous and familiar 'COMP-trace effect' – that is, the impossibility of having an empty category in subject position adjacent to an overt complementizer.

---

[13] This is not totally accurate as it stands. In early unpublished work, Gerald Gazdar discusses the possibility of using rules of the form A→[B[$_C$ D E]] while remaining within the context-free languages as far as weak generative capacity is concerned. Such rules analyze two 'layers' of phrase structure at once, as it were. Such rules, though, have played no role in analytic practice as GPSG developed.

(11) a. *Who did you say [that [$_S$ ___ [$_{VP}$ had arrived]]]
     b. *How many did Sandy borrow [$_{NP}$ ___ [$_{N'}$ books]]

Consider another example. Two of the most general principles governing feature distribution in GPSG are the head feature convention (HFC) and the foot feature principle (FFP). Consider the tree in (12) (where H is the head of the category X).

(12)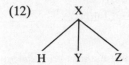

'Head' features are those which, if they appear[14] on a mother-node, must also appear on its head. So in (12), for instance, any head features which appear on the category X must also appear in identical form on the category H. 'Foot' features behave differently. The FFP holds that any foot feature which appears on a daughter must be matched by an identical feature on the mother. So in the case of (12) again, foot features appearing on any or all of H, Y or Z must also appear on X. More generally, the foot features appearing on a mother-node must represent the union of all the foot features which appear on the nodes which it immediately dominates.

Now the feature [SLASH] which defines the path between a binder and the position it binds in a *wh*-construction, belongs both among the foot features and the head features. Its distribution, therefore, is governed by both the HFC and by the FFP. Consider what this means in the context of a schematic tree like the one in (13).

(13)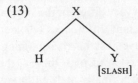

In a structure like (13), [SLASH] appears on Y. Since it is a foot feature, it must also appear on the mother of Y, namely X. But since it is also a head feature, if it appears on X it must also appear on the head of X, namely H. The effect of this conspiracy of general principles is that [SLASH] may appear on a non-head category, *only* if it also appears on the head. In turn this means that a *wh*-binder may bind a position within a non-head constituent, only if it also binds a position within the head constituent.[15] From this result, the following array of data (illustrating the 'parasitic gap' phenomenon discussed in detail by Engdahl 1983) is predicted.

---

[14] The term 'appears' here represents a radical oversimplification of the actual proposal. For more precision and detail, see Gazdar *et al*. (1985: ch. 7).

[15] The caveat of the previous footnote is important in establishing the full range of this prediction.

(14) a.   the kind of proposal *which* people reject ___ [without considering the consequences]

b.   *the kind of proposal *which* people reject the main idea [without considering ___ ]

c.   the kind of proposal *which* people reject ___ [without considering ___ ]

(15) a.   *Who* did [your obsession with cars] most annoy ___ ?

b.   **Who* did [your obsession with ___ ] annoy your father?

c.   *Who* did [your obsession with ___ ] annoy ___ ?

In the examples in (14), Y of (13) is the adjunct phrase *without considering* . . . and H is the VP headed by *reject*. The *wh*-binding can reach into the non-head adjunct clause only if it also reaches into the head of the construction (the VP which the adjunct clause modifies). In the examples of (15), Y is the subject NP, H is the VP headed by *annoy* and X is S. Once again, *wh*-binding can reach into the non-head constituent (the subject NP) only if it also reaches into the head (the VP).

Notice that we have in this an account of two of the island constraints discussed earlier – see (6) above – namely the subject condition, as exemplified in (15b) and the adjunct island condition, as exemplified in (14b).[16] Notice too that the account provided illustrates the general strategy that we argued earlier was characteristic of most current work in syntax – whereby principles that are in themselves simple and general interact to provide an account of what seem to be complex and unrelated arrays of facts.

The work of Kayne (1981a, 1983), Longobardi (1983, 1985) and Pesetsky (1982) also makes crucial use of the notion of a path through the tree, linking binder and bound position, but the ideas are set in a very different theoretical context, that of GB. There are at least two important differences between these proposals and the GPSG proposals we have just been examining. Firstly, and as already pointed out, in the GB version of path theory, the nodes which in sequence constitute a path are not formally marked in any way, and the formalities of feature distribution can therefore play no role in determining whether or not a path is well-formed. Secondly, in the GB version, one inspects the geometry of the entire path between an empty position and its binder, to determine whether or not a given structure is well-formed. The exact sense in which this is so will become clearer as the discussion proceeds.[17]

---

[16] GPSG has been largely agnostic about the analysis of the complex NP constraint and of the *wh*-island constraint. See Maling & Zaenen (1982) for some proposals, however.

[17] Another important difference is that Kayne's well-formedness condition on paths (the 'connectedness condition') is taken to apply at the level of logical form (LF). LF is a level of representation, defined in terms of the same constructs and primitives as more obviously syntactic levels of representation, which is derived from s(urface) structure by movement operations, and which is the input to the procedures of

In Kayne's conception, the kind of path we have been considering is known as a *g-projection* (mnemonic for 'government-projection'). Strictly speaking, a g-projection links not an empty position and its binder, but rather the *governor* of an empty position and a node which immediately dominates an antecedent for the empty position. The condition imposed on paths (known as the 'connectedness condition') is that an empty position must have a g-projection such that one of its nodes immediately dominates an appropriate antecedent for the empty position. Speaking more loosely, we can say that the connectedness condition demands that an empty position have an antecedent in its g-projection. Consider an example like (16) with the structure in (17):

(16) (I wonder) *what* he said he wanted ___

(17)

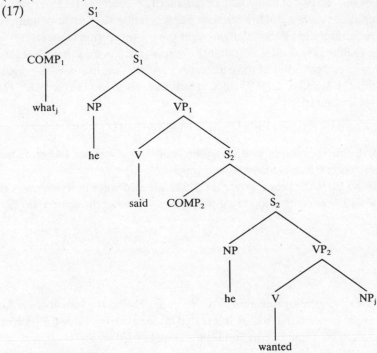

semantic interpretation. It is at this level that such things as scope of quantifiers are indicated explicitly. Kayne (1981a) has argued that certain scope phenomena are subject to a restriction exactly like the 'COMP-trace effect' (illustrated in (11a) above). Since this effect is one of the things accounted for by the connectedness condition, the connectedness condition itself must apply to a representation in which scope is marked explicitly and in which empty categories occupy the positions occupied by quantified NP at S-structure. This is the level of LF. The general idea that 'visible' syntactic movement almost always has an 'invisible' counterpart in LF and that both types of movement are subject to some of the same constraints is a guiding principle of much recent work in GB. GPSG is a radically monostratal theory, and makes no appeal to a level of representation like LF. It is therefore in principle impossible for this analysis to be translated directly into GPSG. I know of no attempt to account for the relevant data within GPSG.

In (17) $NP_j$ has a g-projection which originates with its governor, the verb *wanted*, goes up by way of $VP_2$, $S_2$, and $S'_2$ to $VP_1$, $S_1$, and $S'_1$. This last node immediately dominates an antecedent for $NP_j$, and the structure is thus well-formed with respect to the connectedness condition.

This is the sense in which, on this view of matters, a global, or non-local, requirement is imposed on the path structure: *somewhere or other* along the path there has to be a node which immediately dominates an appropriate antecedent for the empty category whose governor is at the bottom of the g-projection.

The sense, however, in which this proposal still deserves to be known as a local analysis of *wh*-phenomena is that the conditions which determine what counts or does not count as a well-formed g-projection inspect only nodes linked by the relation of immediate dominance (i.e. mother–daughter pairs). The empirical substance of the connectedness condition lies in the conditions that it requires these mother–daughter links in a g-projection to meet.

The preliminary condition is that the empty position must have a lexical governor (i.e. a governor of the category $V^0$, $A^0$, $N^0$, or, in some languages, $P^0$). Thus the familiar 'COMP-trace effect' illustrated in (18) (see also 11a above) is accounted for:

(18) *\*Who* did you think [s that [s ── [vp would come ] ] ]

In (18), the empty subject position has no lexical governor and therefore has no g-projection which contains its antecedent.

Starting from the lexical governor, there are two ways in which one can proceed with the construction of a g-projection. Consider the subtree in (19):

(19)

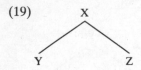

If Z is already in the g-projection (say by virtue of being the lexical governor of the empty position that we are interested in), one can continue the path up to its mother X if one of two conditions is met.[18] Either:

---

[18] The following account takes great liberties in the sense that it conflates the proposals of Kayne and Longobardi and considerably simplifies both. It is true to the spirit of both in a general way, however, and also anticipates subsequent developments in a way that will be useful in later discussion. The principal difference between the informal account presented here and the formal proposals actually made by Kayne (1983), is that for the second condition below Kayne requires not that Y govern Z, but rather that Y and Z be 'in a canonical government configuration.' For VO languages, this means, in essence, that Y must be to the left of Z. The construction of g-projections, therefore, proceeds smoothly up right branches, but blocks when attempting to move from a left branch (in an English-like language) to its mother. Longobardi (1983, 1985) suggested adding the requirement that Y govern Z, essentially to derive the adjunct island condition.

(i) X is a projection of Z (in the sense of $\overline{X}$-theory)

or:

(ii) Y governs Z in a head–complement relation.

Consider how this will account for the data we have been examining.

**The complex NP constraint.** See (6a) above. The configuration for this constraint is (20):

(20)

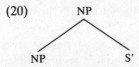

where S' contains an empty category whose potential antecedent is outside the dominating NP. For this structure to be legal, there has to be a g-projection rising from the lexical governor of the empty category, through NP in (20) and on up to a node which immediately dominates the potential antecedent. This path must have the mother–daughter pair ⟨NP–S'⟩ as one of its links. But this cannot be. NP is not a projection of S', nor is S' in a head–complement relation with its sister NP.

**The subject condition.** See (6b) above. This is illustrated again in (21).

(21) a. *What do [NP books about __ ][VP interest you]?
    b. *What is [talking about __ ] dangerous?

In each case, we have the structure in (22):

(22)

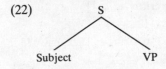

Where Subject contains an empty category linked to an antecedent outside S. The path in this case must go from Subject up to S. But this again is impossible, since S is not a projection of Subject (whether this is NP or S') and Subject is not in a head–complement relation with its sister.

**The adjunct island condition.** See (6b) above. This is illustrated again in (23).

(23) a. *Who were you embarassed [because you talked to __ ]?
    b. *It was Susan who I got bored [while I talked to __ ]

Here we are dealing with structures like (24):

(24)

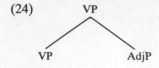

Since the adjunct phrase has an empty position whose antecedent is outside VP, the g-projection must be able to include the pair ⟨VP – adjunct phrase⟩ as a link. But this too is impossible, since again neither of the crucial conditions is met.[19]

Finally, one might ask how the 'parasitic gap' phenomenon, discussed earlier with respect to GPSG, can be accommodated in this general view of matters. Recall that this is the situation in which two empty positions share a single *wh*-binder as antecedent. The most important observation here is that certain types of violations notably violations of the subject condition or of the adjunct island condition, either disappear completely or are greatly improved, when a second empty position appears in the larger structure and, in some sense, 'supports' the otherwise illegal gap inside the island-structure. This is the sense in which the gap inside the island is 'parasitic' on another gap. The relevant examples are given again in (25) (for the subject condition) and in (26) (for the adjunct island condition).

(25) a. *Which official* will [NP friends of __ ][VP run for office]?
  b.  *Which official* will [NP friends of Kennedy] [VP vote for __ ]?
  c.  *Which official* will [NP friends of __ ] [VP vote for __ ]?
(26) a. *the kind of book [*which* [S people [VP criticize the author] [AdjP without having read __ ]]]
  b.  the kind of book [*which* [S people [VP criticize __ ] [AdjP without understanding the author's philosophy]]]
  c.  the kind of book [*which* [S people [VP criticize __ ] [AdjP without understanding __ ]]]

In Kayne's analysis, the (a) examples in the above are ungrammatical because the g-projection from the empty position can rise no further than a certain point in the tree – the Subject NP in the case of (25), the Adjunct Phrase (whatever category that is) in the case of (26). In neither case is there an antecedent for the empty category within this g-projection. Call this the 'failed' g-projection. In the (b) examples, a g-projection rises from the empty position within VP. Call this the 'successful' g-projection, since it is the existence of this path through the tree that makes these examples grammati-

---

[19] The connectedness condition will not yield an account of the *wh*-island condition unless supplemented in some way.

cal with respect to the connectedness condition. In the relatively good examples of (25c) and (26c), what is interesting is that we have *both* the failed projection of the (a) example, *and* the successful projection of the (b) example in a single tree structure. And the way in which these two g-projections interact somehow lessens the degree of unacceptability evident in (25a) and (26a). In these relatively well-formed structures, the topmost node of the failed g-projection forms a subtree with two of the nodes on the successful g-projection. This is illustrated in (27), in which nodes on g-projection are circled.

(27) a.    *Subject condition*

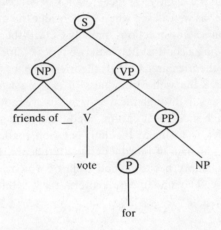

   b.    *Adjunct island condition*

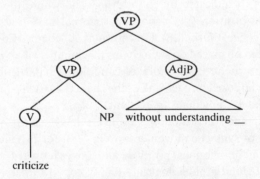

It is this contiguity of g-projections which, on Kayne's analysis, renders grammatical the parasitic gaps in (25b) and (26b). For a detailed explication of the proposal, see Kayne (1983).

Before getting lost in the finer details, we should pause and consider some general points. Notice first that we have here another instance of the general strategy we have already discussed several times. A single condition (the connectedness condition) accounts for a broad and complex array of facts that in earlier days (in work of the 60s, for instance) would have required a list of particular conditions on particular rules.

Notice too that we have another instance of the strategy of analyzing apparently unbounded cases of *wh*-binding as sequences of local connections (mother–daughter links, as in GPSG).

Finally, and at a slightly more particular level, notice that both the theories that we have considered so far share the intuition that a crucial factor in the licencing of an empty category in a *wh*-construction, is that it should stand in a close relationship with a lexical category. This close relation is *sisterhood* in GPSG, but the slightly less local relation of *government* in GB.[20] This is a general theme, as we will see when we consider the more orthodox strain of GB thought on *wh*-constructions, namely COMP-theories.

We have been drawing a contrast between two types of 'local' theories of *wh*-phenomena: path theories and COMP-theories. The basic strategy in path theories is to have the well-formedness of a given *wh*-construction depend on there being a path through the tree of successive mother–daughter pairs, each pair of which must meet certain conditions. The strategy in the case of COMP-theories is to make the link between binder and empty position by postulating a chain of intermediate antecedents, each of which (ultimately) binds the empty position, and each of which is (ultimately) bound by the *wh*-phrase. The fundamental pattern, then, is the one in (28):

(28) $[XP[+WH]_j \ldots XP_j \ldots XP_j \ldots XP_j \ldots]$

where all but the initial *wh*-phrase are phonologically empty, where the relation of binding is indicated by co-indexing, and where the initial *wh*-phrase is in an A'-position (i.e. a position external to S but within S'). Structures of the general form (28) are known as A'-chains. Conditions of well-formedness can be placed on such chains in a number of ways: they can be imposed on the structure as a whole; or conditions (in particular, locality conditions) can be imposed on each link of the chain (i.e. each pair consisting of an empty XP and its immediate antecedent).

The traditional, and still orthodox, view in GB has been that such chains arise only by way of syntactic movement. So in (28), for instance, the *wh*-phrase originates in the rightmost position, and moves leftwards to the third position, leaving behind a phonologically empty copy (*a trace*). From this position it then moves leftwards again, leaving a trace, and so on to its

[20] *Government* is a less local relation than *sisterhood* in the following sense. Although when node *a* governs node *b*, *a* and *b* are typically sisters, this need not always be the case. In particular, a governed element, under the right conditions, may be immediately dominated by a node which is a sister to its governor. See Chomsky (1986b) for detailed discussion.

ultimate destination. Given this view, (28) can be represented in the abbreviated form (29):

(29) [WH . . . $t_1$ . . . $t_2$ . . . $t_3$ . . .]
    (where *t* is mnemonic for 'trace')

To illustrate: an example like (30) will now be analyzed as in (31):

(30) I wonder *which house* he said we should buy ___ ?
(31) I wonder [$_{S'}$ *which house* [$_S$ he said [$_{S'}$ *t* [$_S$ we should buy *t* ] ] ] ]

A'-chains could also be viewed as being created directly by phrase structure mechanisms, rather than by movement. The empirical issues separating these two views of chain formation are very subtle and complex, and we will have nothing to say about the issue here. The informal account to be presented here of the constraints on *wh*-binding, is intended to be neutral between the two conceptions.

The traditional view was also that every element but the lowest in an A'-chain (i.e. all but the fourth in (28) and (29)) must be in COMP-position (i.e. a position which is sister to S and which is dominated by S'). The role of COMP-position as a distinguished position with respect to *wh*-movement has, however, been considerably diminished in the most recent work on the question as we will see shortly.

The most comprehensive recent treatment of *wh*-phenomena within GB is Chomsky's monograph *Barriers* (Chomsky 1986b). The framework developed there represents a significant departure from earlier work in a number of respects. One view of what the theory does is that it attempts to incorporate the insights of Kayne and Longobardi (as described above), along with similar insights due to Huang (1982) and, at a slightly more distant remove, Cattell (1976), into a COMP-theory of *wh*-phenomena. The essential insight to be found in all these works (in one form or another) is that phrases which are complements to lexical categories are transparent in a way that other phrases are not. They are transparent in the sense that the relation of *wh*-binding can reach into them to bind an empty position more easily than it can reach into other kinds of phrases. This insight is built in a very fundamental way into the *Barriers* framework.

In the original development of the idea of subjacency (Chomsky 1973, 1977; Rizzi 1982a), the crucial nodes (called *bounding nodes*) for subjacency in a given language, were simply listed once and for all. NP and S were taken to be the bounding nodes in English, and any movement which crossed two or more bounding nodes gave rise to a violation of subjacency. In the *Barriers* framework, the crucial nodes (known as *barriers*) are not listed, but defined. The definition of *barrier* incorporates in a fundamental way the intuition of

Cattell, Huang, Kayne, and Longobardi that categories which function as the complement to a lexical category (cf. (3) above) permit movement across their boundaries more freely than do other maximal projections.

A *blocking category* for a node *a* on this view, is a node which contains *a*, and is a maximal projection which is not the complement to a lexical category. A *barrier*, in turn, for a node *a* is a category which is a *blocking category* for *a* (other than S), or which is a maximal projection which immediately dominates a *blocking category* for *a*.

Movement, then, yields a degree of unacceptability proportional to the number of barriers crossed. Movement across one barrier yields a minor violation; movement across two barriers yields a sharply worse violation; and movement across more than two barriers yields a more severe violation still.[21]

The ultimate effect of these definitions is to incorporate the idea that lexically governed categories are transparent to movement, in a way that categories not so governed are not. Before considering how this is so, however, we should consider a problem that arises immediately.

Notice that given these definitions, and the traditional idea that *wh*-movement is movement to COMP, simple structures like (32) pose problems:

(32) $[_{S'}$ COMP $[_S$ John $[_{VP}$ saw *who*$]]]$

Structure (32) is the source for the embedded interrogative clause in *I wonder who John saw*, which would be derived, on the traditional view, by direct movement of *who* to the clause-initial COMP-position. Such an analysis is not possible in the revised framework of assumptions. VP in (32) is a barrier for *who* since it is not lexically governed. S is then also a barrier for *who* since it immediately dominates VP. Movement of *who* to COMP would therefore violate subjacency, in that two barriers would be crossed.

In response to this problem, Chomsky proposes that adjunction to VP is also an option. *Who* in (32) first adjoins to VP and then moves to COMP. The final structure for the embedded clause is, then, (33):

(33) $[_{S'}$ *Who* $[_S$ John $[_{VP} t [_{VP}$ saw *t*$]]]]$

In (33) no barrier intervenes between any trace and its immediate antecedent in the A'-chain. Adjunction to a category is not considered to involve crossing the boundary of that category, nor is movement from an adjoined position. Therefore neither the first nor the second movement crosses any barrier.[22]

---

[21] The informal account presented here simplifies away many subtleties and complexities – having to do, in particular, with the precise definition of what we call vaguely here the 'head-complement relation,' and with the analysis of adjunction-structures.

[22] Allowing moved phrases to adjoin promiscuously to higher categories would, of course, undo this set of

This is one sense in which COMP has, in this scheme, lost its distinguished role in the analysis of *wh*-movement. It is not the only target position to which *wh*-phrases move. There is another.

One of the new proposals to emerge from *Barriers* is the idea that the two clausal categories S and S' are in fact regular and rational with respect to X̄-theory. That is, they are projected from 0-level categories like any other maximal projection, and they have the same specifier and complement structure as any category. S' is taken to be a (maximal) projection of Complementizer (COMP), while S is taken to be a (maximal) projection of Inflection (INFL). The picture that then emerges of clausal structure is the one in (34).

(34)

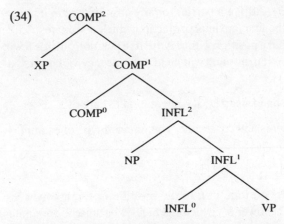

COMP$^0$ is the locus of elements such as *that*, *whether* and *for* in English. The target position for *wh*-movement is the XP specifier position within the projection of COMP. *Wh*-movement is therefore just another instance of movement to specifier position, just as passive and raising involves movement to the specifier position (that is, the subject position) of S (analyzed as INFL$^2$). In this sense too, then, COMP-position has no special status with respect to *wh*-movement.

Now consider how this system of definitions yields an account of the island constraints we have already discussed a number of times.

For the subject condition, the relevant structure is (22), and the relevant examples are (6b) and the like. In (22) Subject is a barrier because it is a maximal projection (either NP or S') which is not lexically governed. S is also a barrier because it immediately dominates Subject which is a blocking category for anything inside it. Therefore, movement from a position within Subject of (22) to a position beyond S (as in 6b) will yield a violation.

proposals completely. To meet this problem, Chomsky proposes that adjunction is possible only to non-argument maximal projections, and furthermore that adjunction to S is impossible.

For the complex NP constraint the relevant example is (6a), and the relevant structure is the schematic one in (20). In (20), S′, not being a complement to any lexical category, is a barrier for any element within its boundaries. NP is also, therefore, a barrier for material within S′, since it is maximal and immediately dominates S′. Movement from a position within S′ to a position beyond NP will therefore involve the crossing of two barriers and a severe violation results.

For the adjunct island condition the structure that must be assumed is (35), with the adjunct phrase attached either to INFL[1] or directly under S.

(35) $[_S$ Her husband sleeps $[_{AdjP}$ while she takes care of the laundry]]

Given the structure in (35), AdjP is a barrier for any position within it, and S is a barrier because it is the first maximal projection which dominates AdjP. Therefore, movement from a position within AdjP to a position outside S will involve the crossing of two barriers and will yield a subjacency violation,[23] as illustrated in (36):

(36) *What* does her husband sleep $[_{AdjP}$ while she takes care of ___ ]?

Consider finally the *wh*-island constraint. The relevant type of example is (6c). The relevant structure is (37).

(37) $[_{S'} wh_j [_S \ldots [_{S'} wh [_S \ldots t_j \ldots ]]]]$

Here, movement from the position of $t_j$ to the position of $wh_j$ involves the crossing of one barrier (the lower S′, which is a barrier because it dominates S, which, not being the complement to a lexical category, is, in its turn, a blocking category for $t_j$). It is a difficult and subtle question whether this result is sufficient. *Wh*-island violations are typically quite weak, but it is arguable that they are properly regarded as being, in general, of a lower degree of acceptability than this analysis would suggest. This is the conclusion drawn by Chomsky (1986b: 36–9), who adds additional mechanisms to make these structures involve more robust violations.

This framework, then, accommodates all the island constraints we have been examining in this review.[24]

But there is a little more than this to be said about the analysis of *wh*-phenomena in the *Barriers* framework. We have just seen how the frame-

---

[23] Note that we must not assume the structure in (24). If this structure were available, then an element moving from AdjP could first adjoin to VP, crossing just one barrier, then n.ove on to the specifier position of COMP, crossing no barriers. Perhaps, though, one could attribute the very weak character of many violations of the adjunct island conditions (compare *Who did you leave after seeing?* or *That's the paper that you were going to kill yourself if you didn't finish, isn't it?*) to the availability of a structure like (24), at least as an option.

[24] The discussion of the parasitic gap phenomenon in *Barriers* is rather inconclusive, see Chomsky 1986b: 54–68.

work essentially incorporates the insights of Kayne and Longobardi in the analysis of the island constraints. But notice now the contrasts in (38)–(40):

(38) a. ?*Who* did you lie [$_{AdjP}$ while praising ___ ]
    b. **How copiously* did you lie [$_{AdjP}$ while praising them ___ ]
(39) a. ?*Which book* do scholars know [$_{S'}$ how [$_S$ Joyce wrote ___ ]]
    b. **How* do scholars know [$_{S'}$ which book [$_S$ Joyce wrote ___ ]]
(40) a. ?*Which jobs* do you not like [$_{NP}$ people [$_{S'}$ who get ___ ]]
    b. **How* do you not like [$_{NP}$ people [$_{S'}$ who get jobs ___ ]]

In the (a) example of each of (38)–(40), we have a standard island violation – of the adjunct island condition in (38), the *wh*-island constraint in (39), and the complex NP constraint in (40). In all the (a) examples it is an *argument* that has been moved out of the island to yield a violation. Notice now the contrast with the (b) examples. These are sharply less acceptable than the (a) examples. The difference between the (a) examples and the (b) examples is that the latter all involve movement of an *adjunct* (a phrase that is not an argument but rather serves an adverbial function) from within an island. The question now arises: why does movement of an adjunct from within an island give rise to a more severe violation than movement of an argument from within an island? One of the basic aims of the *Barriers* framework is to provide an answer to this question.[25]

Subjacency is not the only principle that checks *wh*-constructions for well-formedness. The traces left by *wh*-movement must also satisfy the empty category principle (ECP). The ECP, as originally conceived of in Chomsky (1981), involved a disjunction of two clauses. The first clause incorporated the insight that we have already had occasion to comment on a number of times – namely, that traces can be legitimized (in part) by being in a close relation (government) with a lexical category. The second clause offers an alternative. This clause says that a trace can also be legitimized by being governed by its antecedent. So we have the rough formulation in (41).

(41) *The empty category principle*
    A trace left by syntactic movement must be governed *either* by a
    lexical category, *or* by its antecedent.

This principle is the basis of the account of the 'COMP-trace effect,' discussed a number of times already. Example (42) is ungrammatical because the trace in the embedded subject position is governed neither by a lexical category (there is none close enough) nor by its antecedent. Its antecedent is the trace $t_j$. This element cannot govern the trace in subject position because of the intervening complementizer *that*.

---

[25] The line of research to be reported on here grows out of work by James Huang (1982) and by Lasnik & Saito (1984).

(42) *[$_{NP}$ the guy [$_{S'}$ *who*$_j$ [I said [$_S$ $t_j$ that [$_S$ $t_j$ [$_{VP}$ would come]]]]]]

Consider now the status of adjuncts with respect to the ECP. Adjuncts, by their nature, cannot be lexically governed. Since they are, by definition, not arguments, they cannot be in the complement of a lexical category in the X̄-bar schema (3). Therefore, if an adjunct moves, its trace can be legitimized with respect to the ECP only by being governed by its antecedent.

Now one of the most interesting innovations of the *Barriers* framework is the way in which the theory of government and the theory of subjacency are related. We have already seen how the notion of 'barrier' is defined and put to use in the definition of subjacency. But the important point that we have not so far considered is the role that the notion of 'barrier' also plays in the definition of government. It has, in fact, a crucial role. Put succinctly, *two* barriers block movement; *one* barrier blocks government. Stated a little more precisely: for any two positions *a* and *b*, if there are two barriers which include *b* but which do not include *a*, then movement from position *b* to position *a* is impossible. If there is one barrier that includes position *b*, but does not include position *a*, then an element in position *a* cannot govern an element in position *b*.

This linking of subjacency and government (anticipated in the work of Kayne 1981a, 1983) is quite a daring move. The relation of government is implicated in almost every subdomain of the grammatical system. Case assignment depends on government; the theory of agreement depends on government; the theory of anaphora (in the broad sense) depends on government. The move that links all these subsystems, and connects them all to the theory of movement by way of the concept of a barrier, will generate a complex web of related empirical predictions – a set of expectations about how arrays of facts in very different grammatical domains will correlate, once a decision has been made about how government works in a particular phrase structural configuration. The working out of these correlations and expectations constitutes the main focus of the program of research initiated with the publication of *Barriers*.

Returning to more immediate concerns, however, what does this theoretical move have to say about the problem of the contrasts between movement of arguments and movement of adjuncts illustrated in (38)–(40)? The trace of an adjunct depends on government by its antecedent to be licensed. Government is blocked by a single intervening barrier. In all the (b) cases in (38)–(40), there is at least one barrier that includes the adjunct trace but excludes its antecedent. This is why the (a) examples all involve a subjacency violation, however weak. The presence of this barrier means that the adjunct traces in the (b) examples of (38)–(40) cannot be governed by their antecedents. Therefore all these examples involve *both* a subjacency violation (like the (a) examples) *and* an ECP violation. The (a) examples involve *only* a subjacency violation. Hence the contrast in acceptability.

Many further ramifications follow from this general line of analysis. If it is assumed that the ECP holds at the level of logical form (as seems to be necessary; see footnote 17), and if it is further assumed that *wh*-phrases must move to an A'-position at that level, even when they do not move visibly in the syntax, then a range of predictions follow for constructions in which *wh*-phrases do not move syntactically (in, for instance, multiple *wh*-questions) and for languages in which *wh*-movement seems to play no role in the visible syntactic system at all (such languages as Chinese and Japanese, for instance). The investigation of these matters forms one of the major topics of research that has grown out of the *Barriers* proposals and their immediate ancestors (Huang 1982; Lasnik & Saito 1984, in particular).

The major research topics opened up by *Barriers* include, firstly, the question of whether or not government phenomena in general, and subjacency phenomena will actually correlate in the way in which that framework suggests that they should. The question of differences in behavior as between arguments and adjuncts crosslinguistically, and of the implications that those differences have for subjacency and for the ECP, is also central. Finally, the nature of the ECP itself is a core topic. Is the disjunctive formulation in (41) correct, or must traces meet both the requirement of lexical government and of antecedent government simultaneously? Or can lexical government be reduced to a species of antecedent government, as argued ultimately by Chomsky (1986b)? The investigation of these topics has barely begun at the time of writing.

Before leaving the topic of *wh*-constructions, let us briefly note again the common threads running through all the analyses we have been considering. Firstly, it is almost universally agreed that the apparently unbounded character of *wh*-movement is illusory. All the theories we have considered construct the long *wh*-movement link from a sequence of local connections. Secondly, all the theories share the intuition that the lexical categories play a crucial role in the licensing of *wh*-constructions – either by making an empty category legal in the source position of *wh*-movement, or by making larger categories transparent for the binding of that empty position by an antecedent. Finally, and on a more general level, it is important to say that all the theories we have considered here achieve considerable success in the general aim of explaining a complex array of apparently unrelated facts by appealing to a few very general principles and their manner of interaction. In this, all these theories have achieved significant advances over the kinds of proposals commonly available in the 60s and 70s.

## 2.2. **NP-movements**

If one looks at 'classical' transformational grammar of the middle and late 60s, the transformations which were known as the cyclic NP-movements were those which dealt with such relationships as are exemplified in the passive construction, dative movement, raising to object and raising to subject. These are illustrated in (43a–d).

(43) a. Kennedy was assassinated by Oswald
b. I showed my brother the picture
c. I have always considered him to be a genius
d. Prices seem to be higher here

Classical treatments of these phenomena were transformational. Passive, as in (43a), involved the movement of an NP from postverbal to preverbal position within a single clause. Dative movement as in (43b), involved the movement of a prepositional object to the object position of a clause and the subsequent deletion of the preposition (this to relate (43b) to *I showed the picture to my brother*). These movements operated within the bounds of a single clause. The raising cases were biclausal, in that they involved the movement of an NP across exactly one clause boundary. Raising to object, illustrated in (43c), involved the movement of an NP (the pronoun *him* in the case of (43c) from the subject position of a nonfinite complement clause to the object position in the immediately higher clause (this in part to account for the relationship between, for instance, (43c) and *I have always considered that he was a genius*). Finally, raising to subject involved movement of an NP from the subject position of a nonfinite complement clause to the subject position of the immediately higher clause (this in part to account for the relationship between (43d) and *It seems that prices are higher here*).

The controversy surrounding such structures in the mid 70s centered on two questions:

(A) Are these relations properly seen as transformational?
(B) Do they involve direct reference to grammatical relations such as subject, direct object, indirect object and so on?

Classical transformational grammar answered 'Yes' to (A) (as we have just seen) and 'No' to (B). This second answer was part of a larger pattern of scepticism about the utility of appeal to relational notions in syntactic analysis.

Both of these aspects of the traditional wisdom came under severe attack in work of the mid 70s. The development of relational grammar from 1974 on grew from the conviction of Perlmutter, Postal, and others that the correct answer to (B) is a firm 'Yes.' There were two sources for this conviction. The first was that these operations *could* be thought of in relational terms. Passive, for instance, is the promotion of the object in a clause to be the clause's subject; dative movement is the promotion of an indirect object to the status of a direct object in the same clause; raising can be seen as the ascension of a complement subject to the status of subject or direct object of an immediately higher clause.

The second, and more important, source for the conviction was the realization that if one thought of NP-movement phenomena in these terms, crosslinguistic formulations of the relevant rules were easily to hand. Syntactic operations like those illustrated in (43) are to be found in many or all languages. But the ways in which grammatical relations are formally marked (in terms of case marking or constituent order, for instance) vary widely from one language to another. There seemed, therefore, to be no way to adapt the traditional formulation of passive (which, put loosely, was simply: 'Move an NP from postverbal position to preverbal position') in such a way as to be applicable in languages with syntactic profiles very different from that of English. Yet such languages clearly had passive constructions and dative movement and raising to subject and so on. Perlmutter and Postal argued that the way to factor out the common core of all these processes in different languages was to state the rules in terms of grammatical relations, and then to have language-particular rules to determine how various grammatical relations were realized in given languages. This was a challenge that at the time was ignored rather than met by mainstream generative thinking. Since that debate was opened, though, the question of the proper analysis of NP-movement phenomena has been inextricably linked with the question of what status should be afforded to relational notions in syntactic theory.

Relational grammar, and its descendant, arc-pair grammar, developed from this beginning into a rich and elaborate theory of grammar whose primitives were grammatical relations, and whose basic operations were promotions or demotions on the hierarchy in (44):

(44) Subject   Direct object   Indirect object   Obliques

Clause structure is seen not in traditional phrase structural terms but rather in terms of networks of grammatical relations. The basic strategy in relational grammar is to define general, crosslinguistic constraints on such networks, and thus indirectly on the operations of promotion, demotion and ascension. One of the hallmarks of this work is that it has exposed its constructs to the test of dealing with a very broad range of languages and language types to a much greater extent than any other theory of syntax.

Relational grammar has had very little to say about the lexicon, or about the relation between the lexicon and syntax; but the observation that the kinds of relationships and processes illustrated in (43) are typically lexically governed, led also in the mid 70s to an attack from a different perspective, on the answers traditionally given to questions (A) and (B). To say that an operation is lexically governed is to say that its application or manner of application depends on the presence in a clause of a particular predicate. Raising to subject, as in (43d), for instance, works with the adjective *likely*, but not with the adjective *probable*.

(45) a.  John is likely to arrive late
    b. *John is probable to arrive late

Dative movement works with *show* or with *give*, but not with *donate*:

(46) *My mother donated the hospital a new scanner

Furthermore, although for most verbs dative movement is 'optional,' for at least some it is 'obligatory.' Compare (47) and (48):

(47) a.  John showed his mother the picture
    b.  John showed the picture to his mother
(48) a.  I envy you your new life-style
    b. *I envy your new life-style to you

Raising to object is, in general, optional (for the small number of verbs that allow the possibility at all), but for at least one verb, namely *take*, it is 'obligatory.' Compare (49) and (50):

(49) a.  I believed Paul to be a genius
    b.  I believed that Paul was a genius
(50) a.  I took Paul to be a genius
    b. *I took that Paul was a genius

Even passive fails with certain verbs and classes of verbs:

(51) a. *A week was lasted by the festival
    b. *A ton is weighed by my young brother
    c. *My father is resembled by his dog

These kinds of idiosyncrasies were seen as the hallmarks of lexical structure and of lexical operations. Therefore a line of thought developed in the mid and late 70s which saw all the operations we have been discussing, as well as related ones, as being lexical operations on the argument-structure of particular predicates.

Passive, for instance, could be seen as a rule relating the lexical entries for two forms of the same verb – its active form and its passive participle. That argument which was linked with the object argument in the active member of the pair, is linked with the subject argument in the passive member of the pair.

Raising verbs could be seen as verbs which take subjectless, nonfinite complements, whose lexical entries were annotated in one way or another to show that the subject of the verb also functioned as subject of its complement.

Dative movement could also be analyzed as a rule linking related lexical entries – an entry in which the verb took a direct object and a PP-complement, with an entry in which the verb took a direct object and a second object.

Since all these operations were in the lexicon, it was natural and easy to restrict their application to particular predicates.

Such proposals were developed in various different ways by a number of authors in the mid and late 70s (Brame 1976, 1978; Bresnan 1978; Dowty 1978, 1979; Gazdar 1982). These developments were frequently associated with a desire to eliminate completely any appeal to transformational operations and to eliminate also the consequent appeal to multiple levels of syntactic representation.

Since these proposals were first developed, the question of the proper analysis of NP-movement constructions has also been inextricably linked with questions having to do with the proper division of labor between syntactic and lexical processes.

If we now consider the current theories that we have been examining in this review, GPSG and LFG are the two which directly continue this tradition of lexical analysis of NP-movement phenomena. Both eschew transformations completely, and therefore, *a fortiori*, make no appeal to movement rules in analyzing NP-movement dependencies. Both generate the structures in (43) directly by means of phrase structure mechanisms, and establish the relation between, say, a passive sentence and its active counterpart, by appealing to lexical or semantic rules.[26]

As to the question of the theoretical status of grammatical relations, GPSG and LFG take very different views. GPSG follows classical transformational grammar in not recognizing grammatical relations as primitive concepts of the theory. To the extent that any appeal at all is made to relational notions, this is done indirectly. David Dowty (1982a, b) working within categorial grammar, has developed a conception of grammatical relations in

---

[26] This is something of an oversimplification for GPSG, in the sense that, for the analysis of passive, GPSG appeals to the notion of a *metarule*. A metarule is a rule which relates the existence of one phrase structure rule in a syntactic system to the existence of another in the same system. Put loosely, metarules make statements of the form: 'If there exists a rule of type *A*, then there also exists a rule of type *f(A)*,' where the 'output' rule has a form which is some function of the form of the 'input' rule. In the case of passive, *A* would be any VP-rule headed by a transitive verb, *f(A)* would be the corresponding 'passivized' form of the same VP. Metarules were one of the hallmarks of GPSG work in its earliest days, but their use has decreased steadily as other aspects of the theory (in particular, feature-passing mechanisms) have been developed. Furthermore, given the lexical head constraint (due to Flickinger 1983) which restricts metarules to taking as input only those rules which introduce a lexical head, metarules can probably be regarded as a species of lexical rule (see Pollard 1985 for discussion).

which they are not primitives but are rather defined in terms of the compositional structure of a clause – in terms, in other words, of the order and manner in which the component parts of the meaning of a sentence are composed to provide the interpretation of the sentence as a whole. Consider an example like (52):

(52) $[_{NP_1}$ Julia] gave $[_{NP_2}$ the dog]$[_{NP_3}$ a bone]

In defining the interpretation of such an example, the argument-structure of the verb *give* is the core around which everything else is built. To this, one adds first the interpretation of $NP_3$, then the interpretation of $NP_2$, and finally, the interpretation of $NP_1$. Thus one can define the grammatical relation borne by an NP in terms of the order in which its interpretation is combined with the interpretation of the verb of the clause. The subject is that NP whose interpretation is added in last; the direct object is that NP whose interpretation is added in second last; and the indirect object is that NP whose interpretation is added in third last. Notice that this ordering mirrors exactly the hierarchy of (44). One can thus refer to grammatical relations, and produce relational analyses, without taking the step of admitting the relations themselves as theoretical primitives. To the extent that GPSG makes any use at all of relational concepts in syntactic analysis, it does so by borrowing and adapting Dowty's categorial analysis.

LFG, on the other hand, has relational analyses at its core, and furthermore, follows RG in taking grammatical relations to be primitives of syntactic theory. In a sense, one can see LFG as drawing together the two traditions we have been discussing – the lexical tradition and the relational tradition in the analysis of NP-movement dependencies. The principle differences between LFG and RG are firstly that LFG makes use of standard phrase structural notions (annotated with relational information) in the analysis of clausal structure, and secondly that operations which RG takes to be syntactic, LFG takes to be lexical. Consider passive as an example. The argument-structure of verbs in LFG is given in terms of grammatical relations. So a simplified version of the lexical entry for *give* might look like (53):

(53) **give**: GIVE⟨SUBJ⟩⟨OBJ⟩⟨*to*-OBJ⟩

This says, in essence, that *give* takes three arguments – one realized syntactically as a subject, another realized syntactically as a direct object, and a third realized syntactically as object of the preposition *to*. These representations would be further annotated to indicate, perhaps, that the subject argument is an *agent*, the object argument a *theme* and the indirect object argument a *goal*. Passive can then be conceived of as a lexical operation with the rough formulation in (54):

(54) OBJ → SUBJ
    SUBJ → *by*-OBJ

Applied to (53), this will yield an entry for the passive participle *given* like that in (55):

(55) **given**: GIVE⟨SUBJ⟩⟨*to*-OBJ⟩⟨*by*-OBJ⟩

Since the annotations for argument type are constant across such manipulations, the new subject argument will now be the *theme*; the new *by*-object argument will be the *agent* and the *to*-object will still be the *goal*. Inserted in the appropriate syntactic frame, this entry will yield (56), which is now related to (52) in the appropriate way and interpreted in the appropriate way:

(56) A bone was given to the dog by Julia

Raising (both raising to subject, as in (43d) and raising to object, as in (43c) will also be analyzed in the lexicon. A raising trigger like *seem* will have as part of its lexical entry an equation which identifies its subject with the subject of its complement. So given (57):

(57) Many students seem to have passed

we account for the fact that the NP *many students* functions, for many purposes, as subject to both the matrix predicate *seem* and to the complement VP *to have passed*.

In accepting the position that grammatical relations are primitive concepts of syntactic theory, LFG is able to incorporate many of the insights and analyses of RG. As long as the analyses, concepts, and laws of RG can be reinterpreted as lexical operations or as constraints on lexical operations, this incorporation can proceed smoothly.

If we consider now GB, it is apparent that there is a sense in which, with respect to the treatment of NP-movement relationships, it is the most conservative of the theories we are mainly considering here. We have isolated two main themes in the controversy concerning NP-movement: the proper role of grammatical relations in syntactic theory, and the appropriate division of labor as between lexical and syntactic processes. We began the review by considering the positions taken with respect to these two controversial issues in classical transformational grammar of the 60s. In that theory, grammatical relations had no place (as primitives at least), and the NP-movement relationships were seen as transformational relationships. GB is conservative in this domain in the sense that it continues to deny any role to grammatical relations (as traditionally understood) in syntactic analysis, and also in that it continues to assume that syntactic movement is an important part of the analysis of these constructions. As we will see, though, there is, in this domain also, more of a consensus than this brief sketch might suggest.

The earliest work in relational grammar stressed the difficulty of arriving at appropriately general, crosslinguistic formulations of operations like passive, if one relied on something like the classical conception of the rule. This was, in essence, (58):

(58)   i. Move the initial NP to a postverbal position and mark it with the preposition *by*.

   ii. Move the NP which immediately follows the verb to initial position.

   iii. Turn the verb into its passive participle form.

   iv. Insert the auxiliary *be*.

Built into this formulation in a fundamental way are many of the particulars of English syntax and it thus provides no way of factoring out those elements of the passive construction which are common to, say, Hebrew, French, Japanese, and Swahili.

A closely related difficulty is that this traditional formulation is full of the kind of construction-specific and language-specific conditions which GB works so hard to avoid, since they increase the descriptive potential of the theory so far beyond the range of phenomena actually found in the syntactic systems of natural languages. Such a theory, for instance, could describe a language just like English except that it had a rule moving an adjective phrase from clause-final position to a position just to the left of the verb, simultaneously inserting the auxiliary *would* and adding the marker *whether* in clause-final position. Such a rule is neither less natural nor less expected than the traditional passive rule as sketched in (58). But this is clearly wrong.

The current GB analysis of NP-movement phenomena attempts to avoid both of these difficulties by factoring the operation known informally as 'passive' into a set of interacting lexical and syntactic mechanisms and principles. The hope is that by having this conspiracy of mechanisms replace the elaborate specifications in (58), those kinds of descriptive options, and the unwanted power they bring with them, can be eliminated completely. Furthermore, the principles and operations that take the place of (58) will be, it is hoped, sufficiently general as not to be applicable only to a single language or language type. We can thus hope to have a theory of what it is that the constructions known as 'passives' in various languages have in common. Similar remarks apply to all the NP-movement phenomena. This 'modular' approach to the problem is, of course, part of the more general 'modular' strategy we have already commented on extensively.

One of the principles at the core of the GB analysis of NP-movement phenomena is the case filter.[27] This principle demands, in its commonest formulation, that every phonologically specified NP have an abstract Case. Abstract Case is a feature assigned to an NP by a governing element – by a verb or preposition, or, in the case of nominative, by the element AGR. AGR is a subcomponent of the element $INFL^0$ in the clausal schema (34). It governs the NP in subject (i.e. specifier) position of (34) and is responsible, ultimately, for the appearance of agreement morphology on V.

A further set of interacting principles determines that an NP may move *only* to a semantically empty subject position. By semantically empty positions (or *nonthematic* positions as they are called) I mean NP-positions which are not assigned a semantic role by any predicate. One of the distinguishing characteristics of such positions is that they may be occupied by *pleonastic* elements – pronouns with no semantic content, whose only function is to fill a syntactic position which has been assigned no role in the semantic interpretation of a sentence. Some English examples are given in (59):

(59) a. *It* appears that they are not coming
  b. *There* exists no solution to this problem

GB argues that it is a fact that such elements may appear only in subject position, and concludes that there is a general principle demanding that all complement positions (the ZP-positions of the schema (3) above) be semantically contentful, that is, that every complement position must be assigned a semantic role by the predicate $X^0$. Positions which are assigned semantic roles are known as θ-*positions*. Now if an NP were to move from one θ-position to another, it would end up having to meet double semantic requirements. It would have to carry the semantic role assigned to the position from which it moved and also carry that assigned to the position to which it moved, and it would have to meet whatever kinds of semantic restrictions (animacy or abstractness or whatever) might be associated with both roles. This, it is argued, is a state of affairs that is impossible in principle.[28] If it were in fact possible for an NP to bear double semantic roles in this way, then one might expect examples such as (60) to be grammatical:

(60) *A woman is greeting

and interpretable in such a way that the NP *a woman* signified simultaneously the greeter and the greeted. From this it is concluded that NP may move only to semantically empty (nonthematic) positions.

Now, since only non-complement positions may be nonthematic, accord-

---

[27] This grew out of work by Rouveret & Vergnaud (1980), and was further developed in Chomsky (1980, 1981). For recent proposals as to its status and functioning, see Chomsky (1986a).

[28] This is one of the consequences of the θ-*criterion* introduced and discussed in Chomsky (1981).

ing to the discussion above, NP may never move to a complement position. NP may only move to specifier position in the clausal schema (34).[29] If we have movement to the specifier position (called informally the subject position) of S, analyzed as $INFL^2$, we are dealing with NP-movement; if we have movement to the specifier position within S' (or $COMP^2$ as it should properly be known), we are dealing with *wh*-movement. For present purposes, we can draw from this brief discussion two important conclusions:

(i) From this set of positions, it follows that NP-movement may operate only to a semantically empty subject position.

(ii) Semantically empty, or nonthematic, positions may, in general, suffer two fates. Either they will be filled with a pleonastic element (a dummy pronoun, as in (59)), or they will be filled by an NP moving from some other position.

Notice how conclusion (i) eliminates many descriptive options previously available in transformational grammar. Notice too that NP-movement is not now a listed rule in the syntactic system of any given language. It is, rather, a completely general syntactic operation (or relation between positions), which cannot be adorned with specific conditions, as in classical transformational grammar, but whose application is constrained by the kinds of general considerations we have been examining.

Consider now how this set of assumptions deals with the facts of NP-movement. Recall that one of the controversial questions that arose in discussion of the mid 70s was whether or not passive and related NP-movement constructions were properly seen as transformational or as lexical processes. In the context of the GB analysis of such phenomena, this question, in a way, makes no sense. The construction known as passive, on this view of matters, arises from a complex interaction between lexical properties, syntactic operations, and general principles of grammar constraining both. But one of the ways in which GB departs from traditional thinking is that at the root of the passive construction lies a lexical operation. The application of the morphological operations which create passive participles has two effects on a verb:

(i) It makes the verb's subject position nonthematic.

(ii) It deprives the verb of its ability to assign Case.

These two effects are in fact linked in a systematic way. Luigi Burzio (1986) has observed that it is a general fact that verbs which take nonthematic subjects fail to assign Case to the position they govern (i.e. they are intransi-

---

[29] This is true of movement by substitution. Two kinds of movement are recognized in GB – substitution and adjunction. Adjunction is constrained by a different set of principles, for which see Chomsky (1986b).

tive). This is one part of what has become known as *Burzio's generalization*. If this is true, then only (i) need actually be stated as the morphological effect of forming a passive verb; (ii) will follow by default.

When inserted in a phrase structure tree, this passive participle will yield structures like (61):

(61) $[_S[_{NP}\ ][_{INFL}1$ was $[_{VP}$ murdered $[_{NP}$ Julia$][_{PP}$ by the butler$]]]]$

Here the initial NP position is empty because it is assigned no semantic role (this, in turn, as a result of the morphological operation which derived *murdered* from *murder*). Since the initial NP is empty and nonthematic, movement is *possible* to this position. Consider now the NP *Julia*. The passive participle *murdered* has been deprived of its ability to assign Case. Therefore, if the NP *Julia* remains in this position, it will not be assigned Case, and a violation of the Case filter will result. This NP, therefore, *must* move, if a grammatical structure is to be derived. In this way, the grammatical (62) is derived:

(62) Julia was murdered by the butler

This analysis has a number of interesting properties which should be pointed out. Note first that it is still, in an important sense, a *transformational* analysis of passive, in the sense that a movement operation continues to be a crucial part of the derivation of a passive sentence. It is also, however, a *lexical* analysis, in the sense that movement is triggered by lexical properties of the passive participle. Thirdly, this is a fundamentally *non-promotional* analysis of passive. Many of the relational theories that we have been examining see passive fundamentally as the *promotion* of an object to the status of a subject. In the GB analysis we have just sketched, the promotion (i.e. movement of an NP to a subject position) is, so to speak, an accidental by-product of what happens to a verb when it is turned into a passive participle, and of how those lexically assigned properties interact with the Case filter. In particular, if a passive verb has a complement which does not require Case (recall that the Case filter applies specifically to NP), then movement will not be forced and there will be no 'promotion.' This is how such examples as (63) are analyzed:

(63) It has been said $[_{S'}$ that the recession is over$]$

Note that in (63) the nonthematic position created when the passive participle *said* is created has been filled with the pleonastic *it*. The non-promotional character of this analysis has a variety of other empirical consequences, which have been explored for instance in Marantz (1982, 1985).[30] Note finally, that

---

[30] Note that this is not to claim that non-promotional analyses of passive can be formulated only in GB and not in relational theories like LFG or RG. They can. Historically, though, both these theories, in

this account of passive is not as closely tied to the structure of a particular language as was the classical transformational analysis. It depends on the notions of Case, of Case-assigning ability, of nonthematic position and of generalized syntactic movement, none of which are supposed to be particular to any one syntactic system rather than another. There remains an important issue in this domain, however. The logic of the argument which derives the restriction that an NP may move only to a nonthematic subject position, implies that the schema for the analysis of clausal structure in (34), in which a rigid structural distinction is drawn between subjects (outside VP) and complements (inside VP), *is* universal. This is, of course, controversial in the extreme.

The analysis of raising to subject is very similar to the analysis of passive. It is an inherent lexical property of a raising verb like *seem* that it has a nonthematic subject position. It follows, then, from Burzio's generalization that such a verb will not be able to assign Case. It is also a lexical property of a verb like *seem* that it takes a clausal complement. These properties can be seen in (64):

(64) *It* seems [$_{S'}$ that prices are higher than here]

In (64) we see that *seem* has a clausal complement and its subject position is occupied by the pleonastic element *it*. Now if *seem* takes a finite clause as complement (as in (64)) we might expect that it would also take a nonfinite clause as complement. If this circumstance arose, we would have the structure in (65):

(65) [$_S$[$_{NP}$ ][INFL$^0$[$_{VP}$ seem [prices to be higher]]]]

Now nonfinite clauses have a special status with respect to Case theory. In particular, there is no general mechanism which will assign Case to the subject of a nonfinite clause (since they lack agreement effects, and therefore the element AGR which assigns nominative Case to the subjects of finite clauses). Therefore, if the NP *prices* remains *in situ* in (65) a violation of the Case filter will result. So this NP can and must move to the higher subject position, where it can be assigned nominative Case, and a grammatical outcome results, namely (66):

(66) Prices seem [*t* to be higher]

This, in essence, is raising to subject. Notice that it results from the same combination of lexical and syntactic considerations as does passive, except that in this case, the relevant lexical properties are inherent rather than morphologically derived.

their mainstream variants at least, have been committed to promotional analyses. It is less clear that a non-promotional analysis can be formulated in GPSG.

Consider finally raising to object. The traditional analysis of raising to object is unavailable to GB. The traditional analysis involves moving an NP from complement subject position to the object position of an immediately higher clause. Lexical and relational analyses, as well as the traditional analysis, all agree that in the final structure for a raising to object construction, the postverbal NP and the nonfinite complement do not form a constituent. That is, in a case like (67), the NP *him* and the phrase *to be a genius* do not form a constituent. GB rejects this position, and instead supposes that the NP *him* and the phrase *to be a genius* (an instance of INFL$^1$ in (34)) do form a constituent (in fact a clause):

(67) I believed [ [$_{NP}$ him][to be a genius] ]

This position is forced, essentially, since *believe* clearly takes a clausal complement, as in (68):

(68) I believed [that he was a genius]

But by the logic we discussed earlier, GB has been led to a conclusion that movement is possible only to a nonthematic subject position. This conclusion is incompatible with any analysis which moves a subject NP out of a complement clause into an object (i.e. VP-internal) position. Therefore, GB assumes that no movement is involved in 'raising to object' structures. Rather the structure, at every level, is (69):

(69) I believed [$_S$ him to be a genius]

But how can this structure be legal? We have just seen that there is, in general, no mechanism for assigning Case to the subject of a nonfinite clause. How is it then, that (69) does not give rise to a violation of the Case filter? The answer that GB provides is that it is a property of this class of verbs (the defining property of raising to object verbs) that they can govern an NP across the S-boundary of their complement. Now since *believe* does assign a semantic role to its subject, it does, by Burzio's generalization, assign Case to an NP that it governs. Since *believe* governs the initial NP of its complement clause, it assigns it Case, and the structure (69) surfaces as legitimate. If *believe* is then passivized, it will lose its ability to assign Case, the complement subject will have to move, and we will have the pattern in (70):

(70) a.   He is believed [*t* to be a genius]
     b.  *It is believed [him to be a genius]

Thus GB, on the one hand, and all other current theories on the other, assign quite different constituency relationships to examples such as (43c). It is one of the enduring embarrassments of the field that this apparently routine question of constituency has proven so difficult to resolve one way or the other (see Postal 1974; Bresnan 1976b; Bach 1977).

In summary, GB has moved away from the classical position and towards theories such as GPSG and LFG in recognizing that lexical properties, some intrinsic, some morphologically derived, are seen to be at the heart of NP-movement relationships. It admits no role to grammatical relations at all, whether as primitives or as defined concepts of the theory of grammar. It substitutes instead a complex web of interacting concepts and principles, centering on government, Case-assignment and semantic role assignment.

The role of movement transformations has been correspondingly reduced and marginalized, in the sense that movement is now simply a consequence of other properties of the relevant constructions. This is not to say that it is an unimportant property of the GB analysis of NP-movement phenomena that it involves movement, nor to say that the GB analysis is now a notational variant (in the famous phrase) of lexical analyses. On the contrary, the fact that movement still figures at all in the analysis generates an interesting set of empirical predictions. Since movement plays a role in the analysis, NP-movement constructions should show the typical properties of movement; principles that constrain movement operations in general, should also constrain NP-movement structures. In particular, NP-movement should exhibit ECP effects. The ECP (discussed above in connection with *wh*-movement constructions) is a principle that imposes certain restrictions on the traces left by movement rules. It requires (in its classical formulation) that such traces be governed either by a lexical category, or by their antecedent. This being the case, NP-movement structures should show the effects of the operation of this principle. In particular, there should be certain systematic similarities between the way in which *wh*-movement operates in a language and the way in which NP-movement operates in a language. Kayne (1981b) argues that such correlations hold in French; Chung & McCloskey (1987) argue that they hold in Irish.

As a conclusion, it is worth pointing out, perhaps, that in the decomposition of passive and the other NP-movements, we have another dramatic instance of the general strategy of factoring processes and constrictions in particular languages into an interacting web of general principles. This is clearly the distinguishing mark of syntax in the 80s.

*REFERENCES*

Ades, A. & Steedman, M. 1982. On the order of words. *Linguistics and Philosophy* 4: 517–58.
Bach, E. 1977. Review of *On Raising: one rule of English grammar and its theoretical implications*, P. Postal, MIT Press. *Language* 53: 621–54.
Bach, E. 1979. Control in Montague grammar. *Linguistic Inquiry* 9: 393–426.

Bach, E. 1981. Discontinuous constituents in generalized categorial grammar. In V. A. Burke & J. Pustejovsky (eds.) *NELS* 11: 1–12.

Bach, E. 1982. Purpose clauses and control. In P. Jacobson & G. K. Pullum (eds.) *The nature of syntactic representation.* Dordrecht: Reidel.

Bach, E. 1983. On the relation between word-grammar and phrase-grammar. *Natural Language and Linguistic Theory* 1: 65–89.

Bouchard, D. 1984. On the content of empty categories. Doctoral dissertation, MIT.

Brame, M. 1976. *Conjectures and refutations in syntax.* New York: Elsevier North-Holland.

Brame, M. 1978. *Base generated syntax.* Seattle: Noit Amrofer.

Bresnan, J. 1975. Comparative deletion and constraints on transformations. *Linguistic Analysis* 1: 25–74.

Bresnan, J. 1976a. Evidence for a theory of unbounded transformations. *Linguistic Analysis* 2: 353–99.

Bresnan, J. 1976b. Nonarguments for Raising. *Linguistic Inquiry* 7: 485–501.

Bresnan, J. 1977. Variables in the theory of transformations. In P. Culicover, T. Wasow & A. Akmajian (eds.) *Formal syntax.* New York: Academic Press.

Bresnan, J. 1978. A realistic transformational grammar. In M. Halle, J. Bresnan & G. Miller (eds.) *Linguistic theory and psychological reality.* Cambridge, MA: MIT Press.

Bresnan, J. (ed.) 1982a. *The mental representation of grammatical relations.* Cambridge, MA: MIT Press.

Bresnan, J. 1982b. Control and complementation. *Linguistic Inquiry* 13: 343–434. Also in Bresnan (1982a).

Burzio, L. 1986. *Italian syntax: a government–binding approach.* Dordrecht: Reidel.

Cattell, R. 1976. Constraints on movement rules. *Language* 52: 18–50.

Chomsky, N. 1957. *Syntactic structures.* The Hague: Mouton.

Chomsky, N. 1965. *Aspects of the theory of syntax.* Cambridge, MA: MIT Press.

Chomsky, N. 1970. Remarks on nominalization. In R. Jacobs & P. Rosenbaum (eds) *Readings on English transformational grammar.* Waltham. Ginn & Co.

Chomsky, N. 1973. Conditions on transformations. In S. R. Anderson & P. Kiparsky (eds.) *A festschrift for Morris Halle.* New York: Holt, Rinehart & Winston.

Chomsky, N. 1977. On WH-Movement. In P. Culicover, T. Wasow & A. Akmajian (eds.) *Formal syntax.* New York: Academic Press.

Chomsky, N. 1980. On binding. *Lingustic Inquiry* 11: 1–46.

Chomsky, N. 1981. *Lectures on government and binding.* Dordrecht: Foris.

Chomsky, N. 1982. *Some concepts and consequences of the theory of government and binding.* Cambridge, MA: MIT Press.

Chomsky, N. 1986a. *Knowledge of language: its nature, origin and use.* New York: Praeger.

Chomsky, N. 1986b. *Barriers.* Cambridge, MA: MIT Press.

Chung, S. 1982. Unbounded dependencies in Chamorro grammar. *Linguistic Inquiry* 13: 39–77.

Chung, S. & McCloskey, J. 1987. Government, barriers and small clauses in Modern Irish. *Linguistic Inquiry* 18.2: 173–237.

Culicover, P. & Wilkins, W. (1984). *Locality in linguistic theory.* New York: Academic Press.

Dowty, D. 1978. Governed transformations as lexical rules in a Montague grammar. *Linguistic Inquiry* 9: 393–426.

Dowty, D. 1979. Dative 'movement' and Thomason's extensions of Montague grammar. In S. Davis & M. Mithun (eds.) *Linguistics, philosophy and Montague grammar.* Austin: University of Texas Press.

Dowty, D. 1982a. Grammatical relations and Montague grammar. In G. K. Pullum & P. Jacobson (eds.) *The nature of syntactic representation.* Dordrecht: Reidel.

Dowty, D. 1982b. More on the categorial analysis of grammatical relations. In A. Zaenen (ed.) *Subjects and other subjects. Proceedings of the Harvard Conference on Grammatical Relations.* Bloomington: Indiana University Linguistics Club.

Dowty, D. 1985. Type raising, functional composition, and non-constituent coordination. Paper presented to the Tuscon Conference on Categorial Grammar, May 31–June 2, 1985. To appear in the *Proceedings.*

du Plessis, H. 1977. WH-movement in Afrikaans. *Linguistic Inquiry* 8: 723–6.

Engdahl, E. 1983. Parasitic gaps. *Linguistics and Philosophy* 6: 5–34.

Flickinger, D. 1983. Lexical heads and phrasal gaps. In M. Barlow, D. Flickinger & M. Wescoat (eds.) *Proceedings of the Second West Coast Conference on Formal Linguistics*. Stanford: Stanford University Linguistics Dept.

Flynn, M. 1983. A categorial theory of structure-building. In G. Gazdar, E. Klein & G. K. Pullum (eds.) *Order, concord and constituency*. Dordrecht: Foris.

Gazdar, G. 1982. Phrase structure grammar. In P. Jacobson & G. K. Pullum (eds.) *The nature of syntactic representation*. Dordrecht: Reidel.

Gazdar, G., Klein, E., Pullum G. K. and Sag, I. 1985. *Generalized phrase structure grammar*. Cambridge, MA: Harvard University Press; London: Blackwell.

Goldberg, J. 1985. Lexical operations and unbounded dependencies. In W. Eilfort, P. Kroeber & K. Peterson (eds.) *CLS* 21: Part I.

Harlow, S. 1981. Government and relativization in Celtic. In F. Heny (ed.) *Binding and filtering*. Cambridge, MA: MIT Press; London: Croom Helm.

Huang, J. 1982. Logical relations in Chinese and the theory of grammar. Doctoral dissertation, MIT.

Jackendoff, R. 1977. *X-bar syntax: a study of phrase structure*. Cambridge, MA: MIT Press.

Johnson, D. & Postal, P. 1980. *Arc pair grammar*. Princeton: Princeton University Press.

Kaplan, R. & Bresnan, J. 1982. Lexical functional grammar: a formal system for grammatical representation. In Bresnan (1982a).

Kaplan, R. & Zaenen, A. 1985. Unbounded dependencies in LFG. XEROX PARC, Palo Alto. ms.

Kayne, R. 1981a. ECP extensions. *Linguistic Inquiry* 12: 93–133. Also in Kayne (1984).

Kayne, R. 1981b. On certain differences between French and English. *Linguistic Inquiry* 12: 349–71.

Kayne, R. 1983. Connectedness. *Linguistic Inquiry* 14: 223–49. Also in Kayne (1984).

Kayne, R. 1984. *Connectedness and binary branching*. Dordrecht: Foris.

Kayne, R. & Pollock, J.-Y. 1978. Stylistic inversion, successive-cyclicity and move NP in French. *Linguistic Inquiry* 9: 595–621.

Koopman, H. 1984. *The syntax of verbs*. Dordrecht: Foris.

Koster, J. 1978. *Locality in syntax*. Dordrecht: Foris.

Lasnik, H. & Saito, M. 1984. On the nature of proper government. *Linguistic Inquiry* 15: 235–89.

Longobardi, G. 1983. Connectedness and island constraints. In J. Gueron, H. G. Obenauer & J.-Y. Pollock (eds.) *Levels of linguistic representation 2*. Dordrecht: Foris.

Longobardi, G. 1985. Connectedness, scope and c-command. *Linguistic Inquiry* 16: 163–92.

Maling, J. & Zaenen, A. 1982. A phrase structure account of Scandinavian extraction phenomena. In P. Jacobson & G. K. Pullum (eds.) *The nature of syntactic representation*. Dordrecht: Reidel.

Marantz, A. 1982. Whither move NP? In A. Marantz & T. Stowell (eds.) *MIT Working Papers in Linguistics*, vol. 4. Cambridge, MA: MIT Dept. of Linguistics and Philosophy.

Marantz, A. 1985. *On the nature of grammatical relations*. Cambridge, MA: MIT Press.

McCloskey, J. 1979. *Transformational syntax and model theoretic semantics: a case study in Modern Irish*. Dordrecht: Reidel.

Perlmutter, D. (ed.) 1983. *Studies in relational grammar 1*. Chicago: University of Chicago Press.

Perlmutter, D. & Rosen, C. (eds.) 1984. *Studies in relational grammar 2*. Chicago: University of Chicago Press.

Pesetsky, D. 1982. Paths and categories. Doctoral dissertation, MIT.

Pollard, C. 1984. Generalized phrase structure grammars, head grammars and natural language. Doctoral dissertation, Stanford University.

Pollard, C. 1985. Phrase structure grammar without metarules. In M. Cobler, J. Goldberg & S. Mackaye (eds.) *Proceedings of the Fourth West Coast Conference on Formal Linguistics*. Stanford: Dept. of Linguistics, Stanford University.

Postal, P. 1974. *On raising*. Cambridge, MA: MIT Press.

Pullum, G. 1985. Assuming some version of X-bar theory. In W. Eilfort, P. Kroeber & K. Peterson (eds.) *CLS* 21: Part 1.

Rizzi, L. 1982a. Violations of the *wh*-island constraint in Italian and the subjacency condition. In Rizzi (1982c). First published (1980) in *Journal of Italian Linguistics* 5: 157–95.

Rizzi, L. 1982b. Negation, *wh*-movement and the null subject parameter. In Rizzi (1982c).

Rizzi, L. 1982c. *Issues in Italian syntax*. Dordrecht: Foris.

Ross, J. 1967. Constraints on variables in syntax. Doctoral dissertation, MIT.

Rouveret, A. & Vergnaud, J.-R. 1980. Specifying reference to the subject: French causatives and conditions on representations. *Linguistic Inquiry* 11: 97–202.

Sag, I. 1985. Grammatical hierarchy and linear precedence. Center for the Study of Language and Information, Stanford University. ms.

Schmerling, S. 1979. A categorial analysis of Dyirbal ergativity. *Texas Linguistic Forum* 13: 96–112.

Schmerling, S. 1983. Two theories of syntactic categories. *Linguistics and Philosophy* 6: 393–421.

Sells, P. 1985. *Lectures on contemporary syntactic theory*. Stanford: Center for the Study of Language and Information, Stanford University.

Steedman, M. 1985a. Dependency and coordination in the grammar of Dutch and English. *Language* 61: 523–68.

Steedman, M. 1985b. Combinators, categorial grammars and parasitic gaps. Paper presented at the Tucson Conference on Categorial Grammar, Tucson, Arizona, May 31–June 2, 1985. To appear in the *Proceedings*.

Torrego, E. 1984. On inversion in Spanish and some of its effects. *Linguistic Inquiry* 15: 103–29.

Travis, L. 1984. Parameters and effects of word order variation. Doctoral dissertation, MIT.

Wheeler, E. 1978. The '*Se 'Sann* construction in Scottish Gaelic. In J. Kegl, D. Nash and A. Zaenen (eds.) *NELS* VII. *Proceedings of the Seventh Annual Meeting of the North Eastern Linguistic Society*.

Zaenen, A. 1983. Syntactic binding. *Linguistic Inquiry* 14: 469–504.

# 3 Lexical structure

*Avery D. Andrews*

In this chapter I examine lexical structure: the form of the specifications on lexical items that determine how they fit into and function in syntactic structure. I will begin by examining 'classical' transformational grammar, in which the concept of lexical structure gradually emerged as a distinctive component of grammar, closely related to semantics. Then I will examine the way in which the classical ideas are taken up and modified in a number of current theoretical approaches, including generalized phrase structure grammar (GPSG), the government–binding theory (GB), relationally-based theories such as lexical-functional grammar (LFG), relational grammar and arc-pair grammar, and, finally, theories derived from Richard Montague's approach to syntax. Although these constitute a fairly representative collection of approaches, they are not exhaustive. Furthermore, we will not be able to examine all aspects of lexical structure within these theories.

## 3.1. **Classical transformational grammar**

In this section I will examine three phases in the development of classical TG, those represented by Chomsky's *Syntactic structures* (1957) and *Aspects of the theory of syntax* (1965), and also the post-*Aspects* phase, represented by generative semantics and lexicalism/interpretive semantics as developed in Jackendoff's *Semantic interpretation in generative grammar* (1972). These frameworks illustrate the gradual emergence of the concepts that are now taken to be central for lexical structure.

### 3.1.1. *Syntactic structures*

In *Syntactic structures* there was no distinct component of the grammar concerned with lexical structure. A set of ordered and nonrecursive context-sensitive rewriting rules generated a large but finite set of phrase markers, from which grammatical transformations produced the set of surface structures. In this theory there was no principled distinction between rules introducing lexical items and other sorts of phrase structure rules. Just as we might have a phrase structure rule expanding S to NP VP, so we might have phrase structure rules such as these:

(1) a.
$$V \rightarrow \left\{ \begin{array}{l} V_1/N_{anim} \text{—} (Det) \ N_{anim} \\ V_2/N_{inan} \text{—} \\ \dots \end{array} \right\}$$

    b. $V_1 \rightarrow$ {murder, assassinate, impersonate, . . .}

    c. $V_2 \rightarrow$ {elapse, jam (meaning 'get stuck'), break (intransitive), . . .}

Rules of this kind conflate two kinds of information which we now consider to be distinct (McCawley 1968): information about the kind of grammatical structure a word can appear in, such as whether a 'direct object' (here represented as Det followed by $N_{anim}$ or $N_{inan}$ after the verb) can appear, and information about the semantic categories of the surrounding NP. Thus rule (1a) says that a verb (category V) can be rewritten as a $V_1$ if it is preceded by an animate noun ($N_{anim}$) and followed by another one (with an optional intervening Det), or as a $V_2$ if it is preceded by an inanimate noun ($N_{inan}$). Then rules (1b) and (1c) say what verbs belong to these categories.

Although the lexicon does not appear as a distinct component in this theory, we can say that the way in which a lexical item fits into the syntax is indicated by a single symbol, its 'grammatical category symbol,' which is the symbol that appears to the left of the arrow in the rule that introduces the item.

The unsatisfactory nature of this treatment soon became apparent. One problem is that there are no fundamental principles governing the contextual restrictions that a language might place on lexical insertion – there is just a maze of context specifications in phrase structures rules, which might easily differ in almost any respect from what they actually happen to be. Therefore, in *Aspects of the theory of syntax*, Chomsky proposed a far more structured and restrictive account of these contextual dependencies.

### 3.1.2. *Aspects of the theory of syntax*

*Aspects* proposed several fundamental revisions in the theory of phrase structure. Two major motivations for these revisions were (a) the overwhelming majority of instances of context-sensitive rule application involved the insertion of lexical items; (b) the contextual restrictions on the insertion of a lexical item could almost always be stated in terms of its close neighbors, usually its sisters. Chomsky therefore proposed that the functions previously fulfilled by the phrase structure rules be divided into two: context-free categorial rules would account for the distribution of phrase types, while a lexicon with context-sensitive lexical insertion would account for the distribution of lexical items in the resulting phrase structures.

This proposal was implemented by means of another innovation in the nature of phrase structures themselves which was imported from phonology. In *Syntactic structures*, the categories of constituents were represented by atomic symbols with no internal structure or natural classification: in the rules given in (1), $N_{anim}$ has no more intrinsic connection with $N_{inan}$ than it has with V or any other symbol, and neither do $V_1$ and $V_2$ have any special relationship to each other or to V. In the *Aspects* theory, categories were viewed as complex structures composed of more elementary units called *features*. A verbal position would then be seen as having the major category feature $[+V]$, as well as contextual features distinguishing between, for example, transitive and intransitive verbal positions.

The phrase structure rules, together with other principles controlling the distribution of features, generated a 'deep structure', in which 'preterminal' nodes such as N and V represented positions into which a lexical item could be inserted if its own feature did not conflict with those of the position. Thus the lexical structure of an item becomes a complex of features, rather than just an atomic category symbol.

Apart from the major categories (V, N, etc.), three other types of features were proposed in *Aspects*, two of which remain significant today. In the first place, there were grammatical features such as tense, gender/noun class, number, and case. Lexical items are typically compatible with a wide range of values for these features, which are often expressed inflectionally. But lexical items are sometimes inherently specified for them, the commonest instance being nouns specified for gender/noun class. They have retained importance in syntactic theory, and have been developed with especial thoroughness in GPSG.

The other type of feature which is still current are the strict subcategorization features. The basic observation behind strict subcategorization was that it is necessary in English to classify verbs and other major parts of speech in terms of the kinds of sequences of sisters that they occur with. We have verbs such as *elapse*, which absolutely reject any kind of following NP, verbs like *discern*, which require one, verbs like *put*, which demand to be followed by an NP and a PP in that order, and so on. On the other hand, there are many other sorts of constituents, such as locative PPs, sentence adverbs like *evidently*, and so on, whose occurrence is neither required nor excluded by the choice of particular verbs (except by general semantic restrictions: *One plus eleven equals twelve in Russia* is strange because the facts of arithmetic do not vary with geographical location). Chomsky argued that the items whose presence verbs were sensitive to occurred under the VP as sisters to the verb, while those that were ignored were further away.

To implement the restrictions, a lexical item is equipped with a subcategorization feature which represents the sequence of sisters that it may have: *elapse*, which allows no sisters, has the feature [+ — ]; *murder*, which calls for one NP sister, has [+ — NP]; *put*, which demands an NP and a PP, has [+ — NP PP], and so forth. A universal principle of syntax then deposits on subcategorizable nodes a subcategorization feature determined by the context of the node. Lexical insertion requires that the features of the item and the node match.

Although current linguistic theories no longer use this technical theory of subcategorization, they all employ some sort of device to specify the structural environments of verbs and other kinds of lexical items, and many of the issues raised in the *Aspects* theory retain importance. An especially prominent one is the status of subjects. In the *Aspects* theory itself, verbs did not subcategorize for their subjects, since the subject is not a sister to the verb. This, furthermore, seemed well-motivated: since all verbs have subjects, no information would be conveyed by including the subject in subcategorization.

Some subsequent theories have followed *Aspects* in this regard, including GPSG and the version of GB presented in Chomsky (1981). Others, such as relational grammar, LFG, and other variants of the GB,[1] have found cause to include the subject in subcategorization.

The third kind of features were selectional features. These classified nouns into types such as *physical*, *abstract*, and *animate*, and also verbs and other predicators as being preceded or followed by nouns of various selectional types. A verb such as *kill*, for example, would carry a feature specifying that it be followed by a noun with the feature [+animate]. Then a sentence such as *John killed the doorknob* would be ruled out as ill-formed because this requirement is not satisfied. Selectional features were abandoned by most linguists when McCawley (1968) argued that the phenomena they accounted for should be explained in terms of principles of semantics rather than syntax.

### 3.1.3. Early successors to the *Aspects* theory

Generative syntax after *Aspects* was dominated by the attempt to integrate semantics into syntactic theory.[2] The principal burden that the new concern for semantics imposed on the theory of lexical structure was that of explaining how verbs and other predicates impose semantic roles on the surrounding noun phrases – how it is, for example, that in (2a) John receives a car from Mary, while in (2b) these relationships are reversed:

---

[1] Such as that proposed in Keyser & Roeper (1984).
[2] An attempt which was initiated by Katz, Fodor and others, in work such as Katz & Fodor (1964), Katz & Postal (1964).

(2) a. Mary gave a car to John
b. Mary received a car from John

Two major approaches quickly emerged: 'generative semantics' and 'lexicalism/interpretive semantics,'[3] which differed radically in many respects, especially in their treatment of lexical structure. In addition to the major schools, a body of ideas about semantic roles was founded in different forms by Gruber (1965) and Fillmore (1968). Although these never produced theoretical schools with wide allegiance, they have been extremely influential in the subsequent development of the subject.

## Generative semantics

Generative semantics restructured syntactic theory in such a way that the issue of lexical structure disappeared, or at any rate was thought to disappear. *Aspects*-style deep structures were abandoned in favor of underlying structures in which universal semantic primitives were arranged in complex patterns built out of an extremely restricted set of node types (NP, V and S, equivalent to the logical concepts of term, (*n*-place) predicate, and proposition), arranged in a small number of configurations. A superficially simple sentence such as:

(3) Mary killed John

would have as its underlying representation a multi-clausal structure along the lines of (4). In the proposal of McCawley (1968b), which became accepted as standard, transformational rules would combine together the underlying semantically primitive verbs of (4) under a single V-node, yielding a structure like (5). Another transformation would then replace this structure with the overt lexical item *kill*. In this system, lexical structures are the environments for these replacement rules. The nature of these environments (in technical terms, the structural descriptions of the lexical replacement rules) seems to have been regarded as quite uninteresting.

Since the basic predicates in the underlying structures of generative semantics were linguistic universals, no special notation was needed to indicate how they assigned semantic roles to their arguments. Rather, a universal convention would assure that the first argument of CAUSE was the causer, the second the thing caused, etc. Thus the semantic roles of the participants in a situation were to be read off the underlying representation in terms of universal (although somewhat arbitrary) conventions.

---

[3] See Newmeyer (1986) for a general discussion of these approaches and the differences between them.

(4)

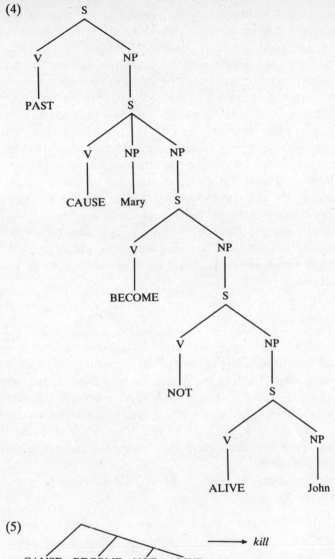

(5)

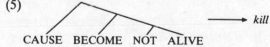

$$\text{CAUSE BECOME NOT ALIVE} \longrightarrow \textit{kill}$$

## Semantic roles

It is an intriguing fact about language that there is a strong correlation between the semantic role of an NP (the nature of the role its referent plays in the action designated by the predicator) and its syntactic position. For example, if an English verb has a meaning similar to *give*, with participant A transferring possession of participant B to participant C, and if the verb is

65

ditransitive, participant A will always be the subject, C the first object, and B the second object. Generative semantics provided one form of answer to this problem: since the semantic roles are presumably imposed by the semantic structure of the verb, the transformational principles applying to similar underlying structure might be expected to produce similar results.

But the most empirically important work on semantic roles was conducted outside of standard generative semantics by Gruber (1965) and Fillmore (1968). Working in quite different frameworks,[4] these authors proposed classifications of the semantic roles taken by the arguments of many common types of verbs, and principles relating the semantic role of an NP to its syntactic realization. Gruber, for example, identified 'agents' (who cause things to happen), 'themes,' (whose nature, position or status changes), 'sources' (places from which things originate, or conditions they cease to be in), and 'goals' (places where things go, conditions they attain). Although the technical proposals they advanced have not been generally adopted, their classifications and terminology have been taken up by linguists of many theoretical persuasions.

## Lexicalism/interpretive semantics

Lexicalism/interpretive semantics, advocated by Chomsky (1970a, b and elsewhere) and most thoroughly developed and exposited by Jackendoff (1972), held much more closely to the *Aspects* theory. Conventional lexical items were retained, and the task of assigning semantic roles to NPs was taken on by the subcategorization frame. Therefore some notation was needed to express the fact that the subject of *kill* is its agent (the causer of death), the object the theme (one who dies), etc. Subcategorization features were the device most widely assumed.

In Jackendoff's account, for example, the lexical structure of the verb *buy* was to be represented as:

(6) *buy*
$$
\begin{bmatrix}
+V \\
+[\text{NP}\underline{\quad}\text{NP} & (\text{from NP}) & (\text{for NP})] \\
\text{agent} \quad \text{theme} & \text{source} & \text{secondary} \\
\text{goal} & & \text{theme}
\end{bmatrix}
$$
(excerpted from Jackendoff 1972, example (2.56))

Jackendoff adopted Gruber's terminology for semantic roles, and intended

---

[4] Gruber proposed what was essentially a precursor of generative semantics, with lexical items replacing complexes of semantically more primitive items. Fillmore attempted to use semantic roles (or more precisely, their labels), as structural primitives of syntax, functioning analogously to prepositions or case markers. Associated with these theoretical differences was a terminological one: Gruber called semantic roles 'thematic relations,' while Fillmore called them 'deep cases.'

them to be understood as names for variable positions in the semantic structure representing the meaning of the verb (Jackendoff 1972:38–43).

Example (6) departs in two ways from the *Aspects* theory of strict subcategorization. First, it mentions the subject (following in this respect the *Aspects* notation for selection restrictions). Second, it specifies the preposition used with some of the arguments, thereby imposing restrictions on the internal structure of a sister PP rather than merely mandating its presence.

Although Jackendoff did not address this problem, the treatment of prepositions can be squared with the *Aspects* theory by making the identity of the preposition of these phrases available as a feature of the PP, so that a subcategorization such as '. . . to NP . . .' is formalized as '. . . [+*to*] . . .' (A [+P] specification would presumably be redundant.) This is essentially the treatment of prepositional subcategorization proposed in GPSG, and depends on the proposal of Chomsky (1970a) that phrasal categories as well as lexical and preterminal ones are complexes of features.

Subjects, on the other hand, require a real change to the theory. We must suppose that a predicate has some number of 'internal' arguments, which appear in the subcategorization feature, and at most one 'external' argument, which is not subcategorized for, and is interpreted to be the subject by a rule which Williams (1980) calls 'predication.'[5] Although rejected in the relationally based approaches and those based on Montague's syntax, the distinction between internal and external arguments is central in GB.

Alongside of subcategorized NP, which seemed to function logically as arguments, receiving their semantic roles from the verb or other predicator, Jackendoff recognized the existence of what have since become known as 'adjuncts,' which seem to provide their own semantic roles, or to function as operators or predicates applying to the remainder of the clause.[6] In a sentence such as *Mary killed John in the kitchen*, the phrase *in the kitchen* is an adjunct: it serves to locate the action referred to by *Mary killed John*. Adjuncts were not generated as sisters to the verb, and so were not subcategorized. This fits in nicely with their failure to receive a semantic role from the verb. The argument/adjunct distinction and its structural correlates continue to play a strong role in most syntactic theories, even though it is often difficult to tell how to distinguish them in practice.

### 3.1.4. Problems with subcategorization features

There are a number of difficulties with the classical conception of subcategorization features, two of which I will discuss here. Both derive from the fact that the theory makes incorrect predictions about linguistic typology.

---

[5] See Williams (1980), Chomsky (1981) and Zubizarreta (1985) for various expositions of this idea.
[6] In generative grammar, the properties of adjuncts were first noted by generative semanticists (Lakoff 1970), who treated them as remnants of clauses superordinate to the main verb.

The first problem was pointed out by Heny (1979:340) and Chomsky (1981:31), and derives from the fact that subcategorization features explicitly specify the linear order of the items subcategorized for, redundantly providing information that is already specified in the PS rules. This problem is not merely esthetic, but leads to empirically false results. For according to the theory there could be a language whose PS rules impose little or no ordering on the sisters of the verb, this being provided idiosyncratically by the lexical entries of individual items. We might have a PS rule such as (7), and lexical entries such as (8):

(7)
$$VP \rightarrow \left( \left\{ \begin{array}{c} NP \\ AP \\ PP \\ V \end{array} \right\} \right) *$$

(8) [glark, V, +[AP—NP]]
[blig, V, +[NP—AP]]
[gnil, V, +[PP PP—]]
[shlom, V, +[NP—PP NP]]

.
.
.

The VP rule (7) generates random sequences of V, NP, PP and AP, with each verb selecting the kind of sequences that it appears with.

Under the classical theory, this kind of grammar is formally no more complex or bizarre than that of English, and is therefore characterized as something we should expect to find in many human languages. But this is clearly wrong. If word order in a language is highly variable, it varies uniformly for large classes of verbs, rather than each verb calling for its own peculiar order variant. The *Aspects* theory allows this kind of non-occurring linguistic system because of the redundant specification of ordering information in PS rules and subcategorization frames: avoiding such redundancy is an important goal of current theories of subcategorization.

The second problem concerns another aspect of word order typology. Classical subcategorization nicely fits the word order patterns of typical SVO languages such as English, Swahili or Bahasa Indonesia, in that the verb and its object show a clear tendency to group together as a unit with adjuncts (and other arguments) coming afterwards in what is called 'SVOX' order. SVXO order does not, on the other hand, seem to occur as the unmarked option.

Classical subcategorization implies that we should find a similar phenomenon with verb-final languages: the verb and object should cluster together with the other nonsubject arguments as a verbal-final constituent, excluding the adjuncts, which might then appear either before or after the subject, yielding SVOX or XSOV order. But there does not seem to be any noticeable tendency for this to happen. In fact, most often the relative order of the object and other arguments and adjuncts is more or less free, and there is no reasonably direct evidence for a VP.[7] Standard subcategorization theory thus implies that verb-final languages accidentally happen to contain principles which obscure the presence of the underlying VPs that the theory requires. This is not a very plausible claim.

## 3.2. **Generalized phrase structure grammar**

Generalized phrase structure grammar (GPSG) presents what is probably the least radical revision of the theory of lexical structure provided in *Aspects*, although it originated in the late 70s. The treatment I will discuss is based on the theory as formulated in Gazdar, Klein, Pullum & Sag (1985; henceforth GKPS). In this theory, each rule introducing a lexical category introduces an integer-valued feature 'SUBCAT'. Thus the following rules might introduce transitive and intransitive verbs:

(9) a. VP→ V[SUBCAT 1]
    b. VP→ V[SUBCAT 2] NP

Transitive and intransitive verbs are then specified as [SUBCAT 2] or [SUBCAT 1], respectively. Although this is somewhat reminiscent of the *Syntactic structures* framework, [SUBCAT 1] and [SUBCAT 2] are taken as features of the V, so that the two types of V are recognized as related by the theory.

The essential difference between this and the *Aspects* theory is that the SUBCAT features are objects introduced by the PS rules themselves, rather than by an independent convention that scans the environment of a prelexical node. From this, a number of important consequences follow.

One is an explanation of the restriction of subcategorization to sisters. In the *Aspects* framework, subcategorization is an exception to the general context-freeness of the base, and there is no explanation for the fact that it is limited to the sisters of the preterminal node receiving the subcategorization features. But if the subcategorization feature is introduced by the rule producing the preterminal node, as in GPSG, there is no exception to context-freeness, and furthermore, the sisterhood restriction follows from context-freeness.

[7] Of course, it sometimes does happen that verb and object group together. In Turkish, for example, the verb and a non-case-marked direct object seem to form a constituent, but not a verb and a case-marked one. There appears to be no reason to believe that other subcategorized complements (which are all case-marked) belong to this constituent (Erguvanli 1984:20–8).

A more straightforwardly empirical consequence is the possibility of a measure of indirectness between subcategorization specifications and the form of the environments in which lexical items actually appear. GPSG does not specify the grammatical structures of a language directly with conventional PS rules, but employs various kinds of principles which can be regarded as determining a *set* of conventional PS rules. In early GPSG, the 'metarule' was the principal such device. A metarule is a rule which accepts a set of PS rules as input, and produces an expanded set of PS rules as output.

An important metarule is the passive, an early form of which might be represented informally as:

(10) If *S* (a set of rules) contains a rule of the form:
    VP→ V NP . . .
  then add to *S* a rule of the form:
    VP→ V[+PASS] . . . PP[+BY]

This is supposed to say that if your set of rules contains one expanding a VP to V followed by an NP, followed possibly by other things, then the set of rules is to be expanded to contain a rule expanding the VP to a V marked with the feature [+PASS], followed by the other material, if any, and finally followed by a PP whose preposition is *by*.

In an appropriate formalization, a node specification that is inherited from the rule being operated upon, such as the V above, will retain all of its features except those that are explicitly changed by the metarule, including the SUBCAT feature. Thus the effect of the metarule (10) on the set of rules (9) will be to add to it the rule:

(11) VP→ V[SUBCAT 2, +PASS] PP[+BY]

This new rule has the same SUBCAT features as rule (9b), so the same class of verbs will be introduced into the structures produced by it, but with passive morphology. This treatment of subcategorization thus allows one class of verbs to be inserted into two systematically related classes of environments without deriving one of the environments from the other with a transformation.[8]

The indirect connection between subcategorization features and actual environments is even more important in current GPSG, where the basic work of defining the permissible phrase structures is done by two distinct types of principles, immediate domination (ID) rules, and linear precedence (LP) rules. These may be thought of as principles that admit a set of ordinary PS rules. A well-formed phrase structure is then one that can be generated by the set of admissible PS rules.[9] ID rules specify what kinds of nodes may appear

---

[8] Although metarules like (9) resemble transformations in certain respects, there are important differences in their technical operation and empirical consequences.

[9] They can also be thought of as directly constraining phrase structure (Shieber 1984).

as daughters to a given kind of mother, without saying anything about linear order. An ID rule corresponding to (9b) would be:

(12) VP→ V[SUBCAT 2], NP

The comma symbolizes the fact that the order in which the elements to the right of the arrow are listed is not significant. Example (12) admits both (9b) and its mirror-image, where the NP precedes the V.

Order is specified by the LP principles, which hold for the output of all the ID rules. English has an LP principle to the effect that lexical heads precede their complements, which leaves (9b) as the sole rule admissible from (12), and also that NP precede AP and PP.

This ID/LP format captures the empirical generalization that the order of sister categories tends to be independent of the category of the mother, and furthermore solves the redundancy problem of the *Aspects* framework. For a verb such as *kill* would be specified as being a V[SUBCAT 2], which requires it to be introduced in a VP expanded by rule (12). But this rule says nothing about the order of the V and the NP constituents.

Since lexical items are specified only for the types and numbers of subcategorized items, and not for their linear order, a grammar such as (8) has no simple counterpart in GPSG. Note, for example, that the LP principle placing AP before the verb and NP after it, needed for the lexical item *glark*, would rule out the NP V AP order needed for *blig*.[10]

In so far as lexical structure is concerned, GPSG represents a restriction of the *Aspects* theory: subcategorization features are not implanted by a special context-sensitive mechanism, but by the PS rules themselves, in the same way as other features. Furthermore, as in *Aspects*, the lexical structures relevant to syntax are not directly involved in semantics: subcategorization features do not assign semantic roles.

## 3.3. Government–binding theory

In GB, lexical structure is elaborated along different, and somewhat more complex, lines. In the first place, although it is a transformational theory, its general organization is quite different from that proposed in *Aspects*.

A prominent feature of the theory is that the expressive power of the transformational component is virtually eliminated. There is one transformation, 'move α,' which re-orders constituents in a universally prescribed way. The effects of what used to be language-specific transformations such as passivization are achieved by various components that impose constraints on

---

[10] A grammar weakly equivalent to (8) could be produced by subdividing AP, NP, etc. into categories identical in internal structure, but distinguished by the ID and LP rules. But this would be highly marked in any event, and presumably ruled out by independent constraints on the form of phrase structure.

the operations of move α and other rules (such as the co-indexing rules involved in anaphora).

The central level of representation in the theory is a level called 'S-structure.' From this two additional levels are derived. Overt surface structure, or 'phonological form,' is produced by 'stylistic' rules and perhaps certain universal principles, and 'logical form' (the input to semantic interpretation) is produced by move α. S-structure corresponds roughly to the output of the 'structure preserving' transformations (Edmonds 1976), such as passive, raising and *wh*-movement. It is derived by move α from a level 'D-structure,' which is like *Aspects* deep structure in that D-structure configurations reflect semantic role assignment in a relatively direct way.

The structural organization that results is:

(13)

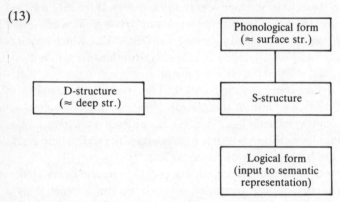

Lexical items impose restrictions on their environments at the level of D-structure and S-structure.

There is a basic distinction between 'internal' (nonsubject) arguments, which are subject to something like classical subcategorization at D-structure, and 'external' arguments (subjects), which lexical items are also specified for at D-structure. Then there is a theory of 'Case marking,' which amounts in effect to a kind of subcategorization at D-structure. Below, I will discuss in turn internal arguments, external arguments, and Case marking. Although all of these devices satisfy the original concept of 'subcategorization' (subdividing major categories such as 'noun' and 'verb'), the term 'subcategorization' is normally reserved for specifications of internal arguments.

### 3.3.1. Internal arguments

GB avoids the redundancy problem by invoking some form of the theory of grammatical functions presented in *Aspects*. There 'subject' was defined as

'NP under S' ([S, NP]), 'object' as 'NP under VP' ([VP, NP], etc.).[11] The basic idea is that predicates don't have classical subcategorization frames, but are specified as taking 'subjects,' 'objects,' etc. (by various means, which may be rather indirect). Since the definitions of the grammatical functions don't specify linear order, the redundancy problem does not arise.

This idea is implemented in a number of ways in the GB literature. One is that of Zubizarreta (1985:249), where we find lexical entries with subcategorization features such as these:

(14) cry:     arg
    hit:     arg, arg
               ⟨ __ NP⟩
    believe: arg, arg
               ⟨ __ S⟩
               ⟨ __ NP⟩
    hand:   arg,   arg,     arg
               ⟨ __ NP⟩ ⟨to __ ⟩

The first 'arg' symbol in each entry represents the subject, which is the external argument and therefore not subcategorized. The second 'arg' of *hit* is subtended with ⟨ __ NP⟩, which is supposed to indicate that this argument is expressed as an NP sister to the verb (strictly speaking, the ' __ ' should be omitted, since it does not convey information). In the entry for *believe*, the second 'arg' is specified as being expressed by either an NP or an S. The entry for *hand* expresses the crucial feature of this proposal, that subcategorization restrictions do not specify the order of sisters with respect to each other. One argument of *hand* is specified as being an NP, the other as associated with *to*, with no indication of their relative order. Since the subcategorization specification does not convey information about order, this can be determined by other components of the grammar without redundancy.

Although Zubizarreta does not provide an explicit theory of just what can appear in a subcategorization specification, her formulations are consistent with her idea that it specifies only the category of the subcategorized item. Idiosyncratic prepositions can be treated in this manner if we suppose that they impose a feature on their containing PP, as suggested above.

One problem with Zubizarreta's approach arises with 'double object' constructions in sentences such as:

(15) a. Mary gave John a snake
    b. John showed Mary a picture
    c. John handed Mary a letter

[11] Although these grammatical functions were defined in the terminology, they didn't do any actual work in the theory.

It seems hard to escape the conclusion that the two postverbal NPs in such examples are both subcategorized complements of some kind. In the case of *hand*, for example, both must be present in order for a grammatical sentence to result. Therefore one would expect these constructions to have a constituent structure like:

(16)

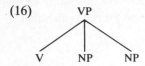

But then the notation ⟨ ___ ⟩ fails to pick out a unique NP. Thus these subcategorization features cannot assign the 'recipient' role to the first postverbal NP and the 'theme' (thing received) role to the second.

Under the assumptions of *Aspects*, these examples do not pose a serious problem, not only because subcategorization features specify the linear order of sisters, but also because transformations can be used to derive double object structures from underlying structures in which there is only a single object, with one of the NPs represented as a PP.[12]

But such an analysis is not consistent with GB, because there is a central principle, the 'projection principle' (Chomsky 1981:29, 38), which asserts that the subcategorization properties of lexical items must be met at all levels: dative movement would clearly produce violations of this principle.

One attempt to solve this problem was made by Stowell (1981), who proposed that the verb+first object in a double object construction formed a 'complex word,' which subcategorized the second object. But this proposal extends the concept of 'word' so far beyond its conventional boundaries that it is quite unclear that empirical content remains. A 'complex word' can, for example, contain a relative clause, or a quantifier that participates in scope ambiguities with things outside of it:

(17) a. Mary showed the agent who interviewed her all of the letters
     b. Some teacher assigned every student a 20,000 word essay

Cattell (1984) takes another approach, distinguishing subcategorization for first and second objects by superscripting the former with 1. He also, for reasons that needn't concern us here, represents the dominating category (the mother of the subcategorizer and subcategorizee). Thus *hand* would get a subcategorization feature like (18) (adapted considerably to suit the present context):

---

[12] In the analyses which seem ultimately to have found the widest acceptance (Emonds 1972; Jackendoff 1973), the recipient was expressed as object of the preposition *to* in underlying structure, with a rule of 'dative movement' transforming structures of the form [V NP [to/for NP]] into double object structures, reversing the order of the NPs.

(18) hand:   Agent   Theme     Goal
            [NP, VP]   [NP$^1$, VP]
                       [PP, VP]

But this notation is clearly *ad hoc* and non-explanatory. For example, it does not rule out the possibility of a verb being subcategorized for two [NP, VP]s, which would presumably yield a double object construction in which the order to the two NPs was free. While some languages are more liberal than English in the ordering possibilities for double objects, this seems to be a general property of the construction in these languages rather than an idiosyncratic property of lexical items.

In addition to the double object problem, these accounts of subcategorization share with the classical theory the false prediction that verb-final languages should show a noticeable tendency for verb and object (and other nonsubject arguments) to be adjacent and inseparable by adjuncts. But, as discussed above, no such tendency seems to exist. Although GB workers have proposed various devices to account for specific instances,[13] the fact that object–verb adjacency does not appear to be the unmarked case remains problematic.

### 3.3.2. The external argument

Following work in relational grammar,[14] Burzio (1981) argued that predicates could be specified as taking or not taking an external argument, and this proposal has been generally adopted in GB. External arguments are typically 'agentive' subjects, and predicates without external arguments are typically 'non-agentive' verbs such as intransitive *boil*, *spin*, etc., although the situation is more complicated than this (Rosen 1981). Verbs without an external argument are called 'unaccusative' verbs, following Perlmutter.

In Zubizarreta's format, an unaccusative verb would receive a lexical entry like:

(19) boil:   arg
        ⟨ __ NP⟩

This entry differs from that for *cry* in (14) in lacking an unsubcategorized (external) argument, instead having one subcategorized as __ NP. In underlying structure, this verb will take an object, but no subject.

In many languages, such as English, a requirement that all clauses have a syntactic subject applies, so that a transformation (move α) must shift the arguments of these verbs from object to subject position. In other languages,

---

[13] Such as rules of movement and 'scrambling,' or 'virtual structures' (Zubizarreta & Vergnaud 1982).
[14] Perlmutter (1978, 1983a), Perlmutter & Postal (1984).

such as Italian (Perlmutter 1983a) this requirement does not apply to overt form, so that these verbs can appear in clauses which appear at least superficially to have an unfilled subject position.[15]

Although verbs are marked to determine whether or not their subject position is filled in D-structure, they cannot determine the category of the filler, since they do not subcategorize this position. The *Aspects* theory's asymmetry between subject and object is thus preserved, although in a modified form.

### 3.3.3. Case marking

The basic principle governing case is:

(20) *The Case filter:*
A lexicalized NP must bear a Case feature in S-structure.

'Case' with a capital C is here understood not as morphologically marked case, but as an abstract feature which will be present even in languages such as Swahili or Chinese which lack case marking on NPs (it is usually assumed however, that Case will be congruent with morphological case where the latter is present).

Case is assigned in various ways. English tense markers (assumed to occur under node INFL immediately dominated by S) assign nominative Case to the subject of a finite sentence, while the complementizer *for* assigns accusative Case to the subjects of infinitives. Infinitival clauses themselves have no ability to assign Case to their subjects, so we get paradigms like:

(21) a.   It would be odd for John to leave
     b.   It is odd that John left
     c.   *It would be/is odd John to leave/to have left

Since the Case filter applies at S-structure, it constrains the output of the rules producing passives:

(22) a.   It would be odd for John to be rejected
     b.   It is odd that John was rejected
     c.   *It would be/is odd John to be/to have been rejected

While tense and certain complementizers assign Case to subjects, transitive verbs and prepositions assign Case to their objects. If a verb is passivized, it loses this ability, so the verb's object must be shifted to subject position or

[15] Acehnese (Durie 1985) appears to be an even more radical exception to the requirement that clauses have a subject, since Italian requires verb agreement with the unaccusative NP, which may be regarded as a kind of substitute for the subject, or an indication that the unaccusative argument is at some stage or in some sense a subject (Perlmutter 1983a). But in Acehnese, the single argument of an unaccusative predicate behaves in all respects like an object, with no indications of subject status at all.

beyond in order for the Case filter to be satisfied. The Case filter thus amounts to a device whereby words may subcategorize for derived structure environments.

Although similar to ordinary subcategorizations, Case marking is less restricted in certain respects. Subcategorization applies only to sisters, and obeys a principle (the projection principle – Chomsky 1981:37–8) requiring that any argument that is subcategorized by a predicate receive a semantic role from that predicate. But the standard GB analysis of the classical 'subject-to-object raising' verbs such as *believe* has them assigning Case to the subject of their infinitival complement clause, a position to which they are not sister, and to which they do not assign a semantic role:

(23)

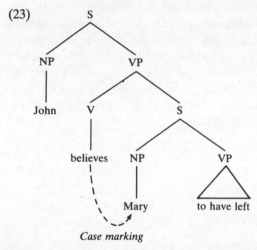

*Case marking*

In effect the Case-marking properties of *believe* allow it to subcategorize at surface structure for a following overt complement subject, a possibility which is absent for predicates such as *odd*. Case marking and subcategorization are also distinct in that passive verbs subcategorize (and assign a semantic role to) an object NP, but don't assign Case to it.[16] Unfortunately, there is as yet no general theory of what Case-marking principles look like. There are only verbal statements of what they are supposed to do in various languages.

It is also not entirely clear how to integrate the theory of abstract Case marking with the behavior of morphologically marked case. In fact, in a study of case marking patterns in languages with complex systems of morphological case,[17] Rothstein (1985) concluded that Case theory was not in fact able to control NP-movement as desired, and proposed an alternative based on a principle that predicates require S-structure subjects.

[16] Oddly, Chomsky (1981:164) asserts that subcategorization features are Case-assigners, evidently forgetting about passives.

[17] The languages considered were Icelandic (Andrews 1982), Russian (Pesetsky 1982) and Basque (Levin 1982, 1983).

### 3.4. **Relationally based theories**

'Relationally based' theories, such as relational grammar (Perlmutter 1983b), its formalized derivative arc-pair grammar (Johnson & Postal 1980), and lexical-functional grammar (Bresnan 1982a), make a more fundamental break with the *Aspects* theory. In these theories, the basic phrase structure relations of domination and linear order are not the sole constituents of syntactic structure. Rather there are also 'grammatical relations,' such as 'subject' and 'object,' which directly relate noun phrases to the clauses that contain them. These relations are viewed as structural primitives, in the sense that there is no language-universal scheme for reading off the grammatical relations of noun phrases from their phrase structure constituency relations.

A clause, then, minimally takes the form of a predicator and a collection of arguments, each with a different relational label. In relational grammar, this is customarily diagrammed as a tree-like network with labels on the arcs, while in LFG it is notated as a set of 'attribute–value' pairs, the attributes being the names of grammatical relations, the values representing the bearers of those relations. Thus a sentence such as *John handed a snake to Mary* would receive representations such as these:

(24) a. *Relational grammar representation:*

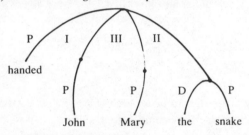

b. *LFG representation:*

$$
\begin{bmatrix}
\text{SUBJ [PRED 'John']} \\
\text{PRED 'Hand}\langle\text{SUBJ, OBJ, OBJ2}\rangle\text{)'} \\
\text{OBJ}_{\text{TO}} \text{ [PRED 'Mary']} \\
\text{OBJ} \begin{bmatrix} \text{PRED 'snake'} \\ \text{SPEC DEF} \end{bmatrix}
\end{bmatrix}
$$

Although these structures differ in choice of labels and style of presentation, they are essentially equivalent in their basic nature.

It is the grammatical relation labels rather than phrase-structural concepts of linear order and phrase membership that are relevant to subcategorization and semantic role assignment. Subcategorization is indicated explicitly in the LFG representation by the sequence of grammatical relation labels within the angle brackets following the PRED value of the clause structure. This 'lexical form' is also assumed to assign semantic roles to the NP of the sentence by means of a convention assigning semantic roles to the positions in the lexical form (first position=agent, second=recipient, third =theme, in this case). Although work in relational and arc-pair grammar does not seem to have produced any specific proposals about subcategorization, the same kind of approach could obviously be taken.

The grammatical relations of NP are coded in the overt form of sentences by their phrase-structure properties, their case marking, or both (and also by agreement properties). Subcategorization restrictions are then stated in terms of the grammatical relations. The resulting indirect connection between linear order and subcategorization provides another solution to the redundancy problem. For it is the grammar of the language that specifies the positions of subjects, objects, etc. relative to each other and the verb. The verb merely specifies what grammatical relations are present, and has no way to impose idiosyncratic orderings on the NPs that bear them.

Relational theories provide a straightforward account of the problem with multiple objects encountered by GB. One merely needs to posit two object-like grammatical relations (OBJ and OBJ2 in LFG), expressed by bare NPs after the verb, appearing in fixed or variable relative order, depending on the language. They likewise have no problem with the fact that verb-final languages tend to lack evidence for a VP. For the distinctions between subcategorized and non-subcategorized NPs are formulated in terms of types of grammatical relations rather than constituent structure configurations.

Bresnan (1982c:287) proposes a fundamental distinction between 'subcategorizable' and 'nonsubcategorizable' grammatical relations. Subcategorizable relations include subject, object, the 'oblique' grammatical relations associated with idiomatic prepositions, and certain others associated with complement clauses. The nonsubcategorizable relations are those borne by adjuncts of various kinds (ADJUNCT and XADJUNCT). The distinction can be understood in fundamentally semantic terms: NPs bearing subcategorizable relations are interpreted as arguments, and so must receive a semantic role from a predicate which subcategorizes them. Nonsubcategorizable relations are on the other hand borne by phrases that operate as semantic functors, applying to the interpretations of the remainder of their clause.

Since subcategorizability is a property of label types rather than of structural positions, there is no reason why subcategorizable and nonsubcategorizable grammatical relations cannot appear interspersed with each other in a constituent. There is therefore no need for a VP-like constituent to contain the verb and the subcategorized NP. The lack of evidence for such a constituent in verb-final languages is consequently not a problem. Furthermore, since there is no reason why subjects should not be in the domain of relationally based subcategorization, there is no fundamental basis for a distinction between external and internal arguments.

In fact, relationally based theories suffer from a problem which is essentially the converse of that faced by TG and by GB: in relationally based theories it is not clear why there is a substantial number of languages with SVOX word order, with an apparent VP and a tendency for the object and other arguments to directly follow the verb.

Relationally based theories also do not employ any component like Case marking as a derived-structure subcategorization method. In LFG, lexical items subcategorize for their 'surface' grammatical functions, rules such as passivization being located in the lexicon, deriving passive verb forms from active ones (Bresnan 1982b). In relational and arc-pair grammar, there are mechanisms such as strata and sponsor-erase relations between arcs that produce some of the effects of transformational rules.

Subcategorization in relational theories is thus simpler and more uniform in its structure than in GB. If one wants to give special properties to certain grammatical relations such as subject, one must achieve this with special stipulations in the theory.

Although their more uniform structure may cause relational theories to appear less promising from an explanatory point of view than GB, with its apparatus of internal and external arguments, etc., it should not be forgotten that the results of GB are achieved at the price of a considerable amount of rather stipulative machinery (for example, the principle that there can be zero or one external arguments), most of which has never been formulated in a rigorous way.

### 3.5. Montague grammar and categorial grammar

A rather different way of looking at lexical structure emerges in work derived from Montague's (1974) 'The proper treatment of quantification in English' (PTQ),[18] in which the theory of categorial grammar initiated by Ajdukiewicz (1935) plays a substantial role. There are a considerable number of proposals relevant to lexical structure in this work. I will here survey some of the main themes.

### 3.5.1. Basic Montague syntax

Most generative grammatical formalisms take a top-down, abstract-to-concrete approach in which rules of some kind define a set of grammatical

---

[18] Montague's approach is developed in a number of other papers, but PTQ is probably the most widely read.

structures, which then determines the set of grammatical strings. But in Montague's syntax one starts with a list of words, or 'basic expressions,' belonging to various categories. The set of basic expressions corresponds to the lexicon in other generative theories. There are then rules which determine how *n*-tuples of expressions of various categories can be combined to produce further expressions. One rule (rule 1) might specify that a noun and an adjective may be combined by putting the adjective before the noun to produce an expression of the category noun, while another (rule 2) would say that a noun phrase and an intransitive verb combine to produce a sentence.

The PTQ framework is quite permissive about the nature of the rules and operations allowed in syntax. The forms of the expressions being combined can be operated upon in complex ways, and there are no restrictions on the number and types of expressions that can be combined. For example, in PTQ (but not in much subsequent work) quantifiers such as *a* and *every* are treated as 'syncategorematic words' introduced by rules that convert nouns into noun phrases by prefixing a quantifier, say *every* (rule 3). A sentence such as *Every small dog barks* is then built up from the basic expressions *small*, *dog* and *barks* by the operations indicated in the following 'analysis tree':

(25)

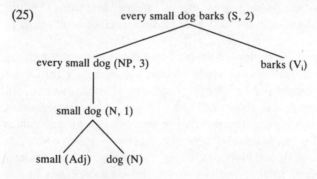

Each composite expression is followed by its category (in conventional linguistic notation rather than Montague's), and the number of the rule that licenses its production.

Aside from its 'bottom-up' nature, the other most significant feature of Montague's syntax is its close relation to semantics: each syntactic category corresponds to a semantic type, so that all expressions of that category must be of that type (several syntactic categories can however correspond to the same semantic type). Transitive verbs, being in effect two-place predicates, are of a different semantic type from intransitive verbs, which are one-place predicates. They are therefore of different syntactic categories.

Another feature is that there is no fundamental difference between a basic expression of a category, and one derived by operations. For example, when a transitive verb combines with its object, the resulting expression is of the same syntactic category as a basic intransitive verb such as *run* or *walk*. So it is customary to speak of these as being 'intransitive verb phrases' whether they are basic or derived, and similarly for other categories.

## 3.5.2. **Categories**

Montague presented his analyses in a notation based on the categorial grammar of Ajdukiewicz (1935). The fundamental idea of categorial grammar is that one starts with a small and finite set of basic categories, which includes the category of sentence (usually represented as 't,' representing 'truth value'), and at least one other. Montague's other basic categories were CN (common noun) and IV (intransitive verb (phrase)), these latter two being of the same semantic type (one-place predicates).

Further categories are defined as 'functors' that apply to some other category to produce a resultant. (Prenominal) adjectives, for example, apply to a CN to produce a CN. Functor categories can be designated with a 'slash notation,' whereby the 'argument category' is placed to the right of the slash, the resultant to the left. Prenominal adjectives would thus be of category CN/ CN. If noun phrases are taken to be a functor category that turns IVs into sentences, they will be of category t/IV. Determiners will then be of category (t/IV)/CN.

. The assignment of categories is furthermore linked to the semantics by the condition that if a category *A* applies as functor to *B* to yield *C*, the semantic type of *A* should also be a function applying to an argument of the type of *B* to yield a result of the type of *C*. In a simple extensional fragment of English, for example, where sentences have the semantic type of truth values (the set $\{1,0\}$, or $\{T, F\}$), the semantic type of noun phrases is thus a function that applies to the type of one-place predicates (essentially, sets of entities), yielding truth values as results. In other words, the semantic type of noun phrases is sets of (or characteristic functions of sets of) sets of entities.

In spite of Montague's use of the notion of categorial grammar, he does not seem to have allowed its concepts to constrain his practice in any serious way, so it is unclear that one can say that he really had a theory of categories. Rather than treating quantifiers as belonging to the category (t/IV)/CN, for example, he introduced each of them with a distinct *ad hoc* rule converting CNs into t/IVs. There is furthermore no indication that the choice of basic categories in a language was to be governed by anything more than convenience for that particular language. In addition, rather than seeking any generalizations connecting the categories of words and phrases to the nature of the operations employed in the syntactic combination rules (e.g. principles to the effect that functors precede what they operate on, or follow them), each of these rules is spelled out in full and often quite redundant detail (although morphology is treated informally). The theory is also reminiscent of *Syntactic structures* in lacking any mechanism to express the relationships between many categories that are clearly related, such as transitive and intransitive verbs.

But subsequent workers, especially Bach (1979) and Flynn (1981, 1983) have developed the ideas of categorial grammar into a substantive theory with significant consequences for lexical structure. The syntactic categories of lexical items are factored into two components, in Bach's terminology a 'major lexical category,' which is one of the symbols N, V or A, and a 'categorial index,' which determines the category's status as a functor, and also its semantic type. The fundamental categories are 't,' the type of sentences, and 'e,' which corresponds semantically to entities, but not to any actual class of natural language expressions. Nouns are of type [N, t/e], and intransitive verbs of type [V, t/e], prenominal adjectives of type [A, [N, t/e]/ [N, t/e], and so on. Transitive and intransitive verbs are linked by sharing the major lexical category V, but differ in their categorial index ((t/e)/[N, t/e] vs. t/e). The advantages of *Aspects* over *Syntactic structures* are thus recaptured.

Furthermore, if we insist that the only permissible syntactic combinations be those specified by the categories (disallowing, for example, Montague's quantifier introduction rules), the category of an item will determine most aspects of its syntax – virtually everything, in fact, except that exact nature of the grammatical operation (which direction of concatenation or what kind of intercalation) that is used for composing it with other categories.[19] It is even possible to code the syntactic operations in the category symbols: Lambrek (1961), for example, uses '\' to form the category of a functor that is placed after what it applies to, '/' to form one that is placed before it. One can imagine further generalizations of this, such as using 'O' in languages such as Latin or Warlpiri to form a functor whose words can be freely intermixed with those of what it applies to.

Flynn (1981, 1983), furthermore, has shown that to a large extent the operations used to combine two expressions can be predicted from their categories from rather general principles. For example, Flynn proposes for English a principle ((16) in Flynn 1983:145) which provides in effect that all lexical functors other than intransitive verbs precede what they apply to. This principle places quantifiers in front of what they quantify, verbs and propositions in front of their objects, attributive adjectives in front of their nouns, and much else besides. This version of Montague grammar, therefore, largely succeeds in reducing the syntax of a language to lexical structures.

[19] Curry (1963), cited in Dowty (1982), calls this aspect of grammatical structure 'tectogrammatical' structure, as opposed to 'phenogrammatical' structure, in which the effects of the syntactic operations used appears.

### 3.5.3. **Functional application and subcategorization**

Since predicates are treated as functors, the category of a predicate does the
work of a subcategorization frame or its equivalent in other generative
theories. But the nature of functional application leads to important differences in behavior. I will here mention two, which seem to me to be
empirically problematical.

In the first place, there is no clear reason in either 'classical' Montague
grammar or in theories such as those of Flynn and Bach why there shouldn't
be a grammatical category with the morphological features of verbs, but of
the category t ([V, t] in Bach's notation). Subjects are therefore in effect
subcategorized, and it is accidental (at least in terms of the basic structure of
the theory) that subjectless verbs seem to be lacking in many languages.
Note that since there are neither transformational derivations nor anything
like a relation between constituent structures and functional/relational
structures, one cannot say that subject is a structurally obligatory position
into which empty NPs are inserted when needed.

A second problem emerges in the treatment of multitransitive verbs. In
most generative theories, the two VP arguments of a ditransitive verb are
both approximately sisters (though in a VP such as *supply the children with
pencils*, one of the arguments is buried in a PP). In theories derived from
Montague's, on the other hand, an *n*-place predicate is treated as a function
that maps an argument onto an *n*−1-place predicate, with the result that the
arguments have to be semantically composed one at a time with the verb.
Therefore, the analysis tree of a sentence with a ditransitive verb should
have three nested phrasal levels. The subject is of course the argument that
is combined last, while it is generally assumed, and argued by Dowty (1982),
that the (first, or passivizable) object should be combined second-to-last.

Thus an analysis tree for *We supply the children with pencils* would look
roughly like this:

(26) We supply the children with pencils

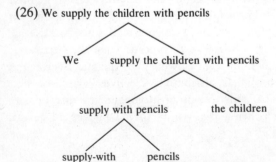

*Supply with pencils* is treated as a transitive verb (phrase), whose object is combined with it to form an intransitive verb phrase by an operation of 'right wrap' (Bach 1979:516) which consists of putting the object after the first constituent of the transitive verb phrase.

The effect of right-wrapping is to prevent multitransitive verbs from displaying the more deeply concentric structures they might be expected to have on the basis of their analysis trees. But there is no explanation for why right-wrapping is the overwhelmingly preferred option for combining transitive verb phrases with their objects in SVO languages: multitransitive verbs in such languages almost always have the direct (passivizable) object in the first position after the verb, with the additional arguments, which are composed with it earlier, coming second.

Other theories as they stand do not predict what appears to be the unmarked order pattern. But at least they don't predict that arguments other than the subject and object should be found making up some kind of composite unit with the verb.

## 3.6. Conclusion

The aspect of lexical structure that we have concentrated upon is how the lexical entries of predicators, especially verbs, constrain their syntactic environment and the semantic interpretation of surrounding NPs. Although the theories we have surveyed all provide some kind of solution to the redundancy problem of *Aspects*, they also all seem to suffer from a variety of less striking, but nonetheless real, problems.

Among the aspects of lexical structure about which we have said little, perhaps the most important is how to capture the generalizations about the relationships between semantic roles and grammatical relations that concerned Gruber and Fillmore. Why, for example, is there so often a grammatical relation, usually called 'subject,' that is associated with the semantic role of 'agent'? This kind of question can to a large extent be explored independently of the issues we have considered in this chapter, and raises some very difficult issues, such as how to define and individuate semantic roles, and the relationships of these roles to the semantic structures of predicates.

Perhaps the most widespread approach to these problems in recent work is what one might call 'linking theory,' which originated in work by Richard Carter (1977).[20] In linking theory one assumes some scheme of semantic representation for predicators that makes available a set of semantic roles (agent, theme, source, . . .), and also some theory of subcategorization (broadly construed) whereby one can refer to the subject, first (or last)

---

[20] Ostler (1980) provides one of the most extensive exemplifications of linking theory, while Zaenen, Maling & Thráinsson (1985) provide one of the more recent.

object, *to*-object, etc. of the predicator. A predicator's lexical entry is presumed to specify a set of semantic roles and a subcategorization frame, and the linking principles determine how the semantic roles are to be assigned to the positions in the subcategorization frame. These principles can be thought of either as rules for filling in partially specified lexical entries, or constraints on the form of fully specified entries. A typical linking principle might be:

(27) *Agent rule:*
   If there is an agent, link it to the subject.

Under a natural interpretation, this rule will require predicators that have agents to have subjects. Passivization and similar phenomena can be accommodated either by having rules that re-arrange linkings, or by making the linking principles more complex, and sensitive to a feature [+Pass].

Linking theory throws into prominence the contrast between grammatical relations such as subject and object, which express a wide variety of semantic roles, and arguments marked by prepositions such as *to* and *from*, which appear to be semantically more restricted. In most present accounts, this contrast can be noted and built into the theory in various ways, but not really explained. Carlson (1985) and Marantz (1984) suggest (formally quite different) approaches whereby the treatment of prepositionally marked grammatical relations can be strongly differentiated from those of subjects and objects. In effect, a preposition can assign a semantic role to its object independently of the verb. This semantic role then determines how the referent of the prepositional object participates in the event designated by the verb.

Semantic roles thus function as an essential intermediary between the syntactic environment of certain NPs and the way in which they are integrated into the semantic representation of the sentence. It remains to be seen whether these proposals will develop into a genuine and consistent alternative to the theories that are presently most widely accepted.

*REFERENCES*

Ajdukiewicz, K. 1935. Über die syntaktische Konnexität. *Studia Philosophica* 1: 1–27. Reprinted in English under the title 'Syntactic connection' in S. McCall (ed.) 1967. *Polish logic 1920–1939*. Oxford: Clarendon Press.
Anderson, S. R. & Kiparsky, P. (eds.) 1973. *A festschrift for Morris Halle*. Holt, Reinhart & Winston.
Andrews, A. D. 1982. The representation of case in modern Icelandic. In Bresnan (1982a).
Bach, E. 1979. Control in Montague grammar. *Linguistic Inquiry* 10: 515–31.
Bresnan, J. W. (ed.) 1982a. *The mental representation of grammatical relations*. Cambridge, MA: MIT Press.
Bresnan, J. W. 1982b. The passive in lexical theory. In Bresnan (1982a).

Bresnan, J. W. 1982c. Control and complementation. *Linguistic Inquiry* 13: 343–434. Reprinted in Bresnan (1982a).

Burzio, L. 1981. Intransitive verbs and Italian auxiliaries. Doctoral dissertation, MIT.

Carlson, G. N. 1985. Thematic roles and their role in semantic description. *Linguistics* 22: 259–79.

Carter, R. J. 1977. Some linking regularities. In *Recherches linquistiques* 5–6. Paris: Université de Vincennes.

Cattell, R. 1984. *Composite predicates in English.* New York: Academic Press.

Chomsky, N. A. 1957. *Syntactic structures.* The Hague: Mouton.

Chomsky, N. A. 1965. *Aspects of the theory of syntax.* Cambridge, MA: MIT Press.

Chomsky, N. A. 1970a. Remarks on nominalization. In R. A. Jacobs & P. S. Rosenbaum (eds.) *Readings in English transformational grammar.* Waltham: Ginn.

Chomsky, N. A. 1970b. Deep structure, surface structure and semantic interpretation. In R. Jakobson & S. Kawamoto (eds.) *Studies in general and oriental linguistics.* Tokyo: TEC Corporation. Also in Steinberg & Jakobovits (1971).

Chomsky, N. A. 1981. *Lectures on government and binding.* Dordrecht: Foris.

Curry, H. B. 1963. Some logical aspects of grammatical structure. In R. Jakobson (ed.) *Structure of language in its mathematical aspects. Proceedings of the Twelfth Symposium in Applied Mathematics.* Providence: American Mathematical Society.

Dowty, D. R. 1982. Grammatical relations and Montague grammar. In Jacobson & Pullum (1982).

Durie, M. 1985. *A grammar of Acehnese on the basis of a dialect of North Aceh.* Dordrecht: Foris.

Emonds, J. 1972. Evidence that indirect object movement is a structure preserving rule. *Foundations of Language* 8: 546–61. Reprinted in D. J. Napoli & E. N. Rando *Syntactic argumentation.* Washington: Georgetown University Press.

Emonds, J. 1976. *A transformational approach to English syntax.* New York: Academic Press.

Erguvanli, E. E. 1984. *The function of word order in Turkish.* Berkeley: University of California Press.

Fillmore, C. J. 1968. The case for case. In E. Bach & R. Harms (eds.) *Universals in linguistic theory.* Holt, Rinehart & Winston.

Flynn, M. 1981. Structure building operations and word order. Doctoral dissertation, University of Massachusetts.

Flynn, M. 1983. A categorial theory of structure building. In Gazdar *et al.* (1983).

Gazdar, G., Klein, E. & Pullum, G. K. (eds.) 1983. *Order, concord and constituency.* Dordrecht: Foris.

Gazdar, G., Klein, E., Pullum, G. K. & Sag, I. 1985. Generalized phrase structure grammar. Cambridge, MA: Harvard University Press.

Gruber, J. 1965. Studies in lexical relations. Doctoral dissertation, MIT. Revised and extended version published in 1976 as *Lexical structures in syntax and semantics.* New York: North-Holland.

Heny, F. 1979. Review of Noam Chomsky, *Logical structure of linguistic theory. Synthese* 40: 317–52.

Jackendoff, R. S. 1972. *Semantic interpretation in generative grammar.* Cambridge, MA: MIT Press.

Jackendoff, R. S. 1973. The base rules for prepositional phrases. In Anderson & Kiparsky (1973).

Jacobson, P. & Pullum, G. K. (eds.) 1982. *The nature of syntactic representation.* Dordrecht: Reidel.

Johnson, D. E. & Postal, P. M. 1980. *Arc-pair grammar.* Princeton: Princeton University Press.

Katz, J. J. & Fodor, J. A. 1964. The structure of a semantic theory. In J. R. Fodor & J. J. Katz (eds.) *The structure of language.* Englewood Cliffs: Prentice-Hall.

Katz, J. J. & Postal, P. M. 1964. *An integrated theory of linguistic descriptions.* Cambridge, MA: MIT Press.

Keyser, S. J. & Roeper, T. 1984. On the middle and ergative constructions in English. *Linguistic Inquiry* 15: 381–416.

Lakoff, G. P. 1970. Pronominalization, negation and the analysis of adverbs. In R. A. Jacobs & P. S. Rosenbaum (eds.) *Readings in English transformational grammar.* Waltham: Ginn.

Lambek, J. 1961. On the calculus of syntactic types. In R. Jakobson (ed.) *Structure of language in its mathematical aspects. Proceedings of the Twelfth Symposium in Applied Mathematics.* Providence: American Mathematical Society.

Levin, B. 1982. On the nature of ergativity. Doctoral dissertation, MIT.

Levin, B. 1983. Unaccusative verbs in Basque. In *NELS* 13.

Marantz, A. P. 1984. *On the nature of grammatical relations.* Cambridge, MA: MIT Press.

McCawley, J. D. 1968. Lexical insertion in a transformational grammar without deep structure. In *CLS* 4. Reprinted in McCawley (1973).

McCawley, J. D. 1973. *Grammar and meaning.* Tokyo: Taishukan Publishing Co.

Montague, R. 1974. The proper treatment of quantification in English. In R. Thomason (ed.) *Formal philosophy. Selected papers of Richard Montague.* New Haven: Yale University Press. First published in B. Visentini *et al.* (eds.) 1970. *Linguaggi nella societa e nella tecnica.* Milan: Edizione di Communità.

Newmeyer, F. 1986. *Linguistic theory in America.* 2nd edn. New York: Academic Press.

Ostler, N. 1980. A theory of case-linking and agreement. Distributed by the Indiana University Linguistics Club.

Perlmutter, D. M. 1978. Impersonal passives and the unaccusative hypothesis. In J. Jaeger *et al.* (eds.) *BLS* 4.

Perlmutter, D. M. 1983a. Personal vs. impersonal constructions. *Natural Language and Linguistic Theory* 1: 141–200.

Perlmutter, D. M. (ed.) 1983b. *Studies in relational grammar I.* Chicago: University of Chicago Press.

Perlmutter, D. M. & Postal, P. 1984. The 1-advancement exclusiveness law. In Perlmutter & Rosen (1984).

Perlmutter, D. M. & Rosen, Carol (eds.) 1984. *Studies in relational grammar 2.* Chicago: Chicago University Press.

Pesetsky, D. 1982. Paths and categories. Doctoral dissertation, MIT.

Rosen, C. 1981. The relational structure of reflexive clauses: evidence from Italian. Doctoral dissertation, Harvard University.

Rothstein, S. 1985. *On the syntactic forms of predication.* Published by the Indiana University Linguistics Club.

Shieber, S. M. 1984. Direct parsing of ID/LP grammars. *Linguistics and Philosophy* 7: 135–54.

Steinberg, D. & Jakobovits, L. (eds.) 1971. *Semantics: an interdisciplinary reader in philosophy, linguistics and psychology.* Cambridge: Cambridge University Press.

Stowell, T. A. 1981. Origins of phrase structure. Doctoral dissertation, MIT.

Williams, E. 1980. Predication. *Linguistic Inquiry* 11: 203–38.

Zaenen, A., Maling J. & Thráinsson, H. 1985. Case and grammatical function: the Icelandic passive. *Natural Language and Linguistic Theory* 3: 379–483.

Zubizarreta, M. L. 1985. Morphophonology and morphosyntax: Romance causatives. *Linguistic Inquiry* 16: 247–89.

Zubizarreta, M. L. & Vergnaud, J. R. 1982. On virtual categories. In A. P. Marantz & T. A. Stowell (eds.) *MIT Working Papers in Linguistics, 4. Papers in syntax.*

# 4 Semantic theory

*William A. Ladusaw*

## 4.1. Goals of semantic theory

The term *semantics* covers a wide range of issues involving the meaning, significance, interpretation, and understanding of language. This survey is a limited one[1] which examines the goals of semantics construed as a component of linguistic theory and surveys techniques, results, and issues emerging from current work in the area. We begin by discussing three goals of a linguistic semantic theory.

### 4.1.1. Semantic properties of sentences

The principal descriptive goal of semantic theory is an account of the semantic structure of a language, the properties and relations which hold of the expressions of a language in virtue of what they mean. On analogy with syntactic theory, it is an account of part of the native speaker's linguistic competence, namely, that knowledge underlying 'semantic competence.'[2] As such, it presumes an account of the syntax of a language and predicts judgements of semantic relations between its expressions based upon proposals about what they mean.

Chief among the relations to be accounted for are paraphrase (or semantic equivalence) and semantic consequence (or entailment). For example, an adequate semantic theory for English should derive the fact that the sentences in (1) are paraphrases of each other, that the sentences in (2) are logically equivalent,[3] and that the (a) sentences of the pairs in (3)–(4) have the (b) sentences as semantic consequences:

---

[1] For less limited discussions, see Fodor (1977), Kempson (1977), Lyons (1977), and Jackendoff (1983).

[2] This view of linguistic semantics is articulated in Katz & Fodor (1964), Katz (1972), and most later work. It is a perspective different from that of semantics as carried out within logic, in that it introduces an explicitly psychological interpretation of the theory. Cresswell (1978) presents the case for considering truth-conditional semantics as a plausible basis for such a theory of semantic competence.

[3] Synonymy and paraphrase are equivalence relations. It seems unlikely that there is one invariant, unitary intuition of such relations. Certainly pairs of active and passive sentences are generally truth-conditionally equivalent, though they have, for example, different potential for use in discourse. If

(1) a. John chased Fido
   b. Fido was chased by John
(2) a. John didn't eat the beans or cook the rice
   b. John didn't eat the beans and John didn't cook the rice
(3) a. John and Mary stayed in Vienna
   b. John stayed in Vienna
(4) a. That is a red book
   b. That is a book

Other semantic properties to be accounted for are the anomaly of sentences like the ones in (5), the fact that (6) is contradictory, and that (7) is necessarily true in virtue of what its parts mean:

(5) a. Colorless green ideas sleep furiously
   b. The theory of relativity is shiny
(6) My brother is an only child
(7) That bachelor isn't married

Semantic equivalence and entailment relations cannot be defined directly on their (surface) syntactic structures. For example, though the paired sentences in (8)–(11) are syntactically parallel to those in (1)–(4), the semantic relations between them are different:

(8) a. No one chased any of the dogs
   b. Any of the dogs was chased by no one
(9) a. John ate the beans or cooked the rice
   b. John ate the beans and John cooked the rice
(10) a. John and Mary met in Vienna
   b. John met in Vienna
(11) a. That is a fake book
   b. That is a book

In order to give an account of these relations, semantic theory must provide a mapping from expressions to objects which serve as their interpretations, which we will call *semantic representations*. The equivalence and consequence relations are defined on these representations. Expressions of the language are equivalent if the mapping from syntactic to semantic representations assigns them equivalent semantic representations.

## 4.1.2. Compositionality

Since languages are infinite sets of expressions, the mapping from sentences to their semantic representations cannot be a simple list. While the connec-

---

explaining such differences were considered part of the task of semantic theory, then the sentences in (1) would not be completely equivalent. Equivalence is always relative to some understood criterion, which in logical semantics is sameness of truth conditions.

tion between words like *cat, dog,* and *no* and their meanings is arbitrary, the interpretations of the noun phrases *no cat* and *no dog* are not arbitrary. This fact is reflected in the assumption of a principle of compositionality, which states that the meaning of a complex expression is determined by the meaning of its constituents and the manner in which they are combined. As in syntax the lexicon of a language is distinguished from the principles which determine the structure of its phrases and clauses, so one distinguishes in semantics between lexical semantics and compositional semantics. The former describes the semantic representations of words or other basic syntactic elements. The latter provides the principles which determine how lexical interpretations are combined to yield semantic representations for syntactically complex expressions.[4]

The term *compositionality* is used for constraints of varying strength on the mapping from syntactic structure to semantic representation; every theory, however, provides some account of how the meaning of an arbitrary complex expression can be systematically calculated from the meaning of its basic constituents and its syntactic structure.[5]

## 4.1.3. Aboutness

A semantic theory makes a claim, implicitly or explicitly, about the fundamental nature of semantic representations and their relation to what language is used to talk about. Semantic representations can be viewed as standing directly for aspects of the world, the things talked about. But linguistic semantics is assumed also to have a psychological aspect, and so, in some approaches, semantic representations are viewed as primarily mental objects. The tension between these two points of view has not yet been uniformly resolved and is responsible for major differences among semanticists.

Consideration of these three quite general points suggests the following four questions as useful diagnostics for particular theories of linguistic semantics:

---

[4] The distinction between lexical and compositional in semantics is not necessarily the same as that between lexical and phrasal in syntax. Polymorphemic words may have completely compositional meanings and apparently phrasal constituents may have idiomatic meanings. See Dowty (1978) and Hoeksema (1984) for a discussion of the relationship between compositionality and the lexical/syntactic distinction.

[5] For further discussion, see the chapters by Enç and ter Meulen in this volume. Partee (1984) discusses a number of issues concerning compositionality. Within semantic theory on the model of Montague's work (see below), compositionality has been taken to be a particularly strong constraint which rules out certain ways of associating syntactic representations with semantic representations in addition to having the weaker requirement that the interpretations of complex expressions must be calculable from the interpretations of their parts. Katz & Fodor (1964:493) appealed to the weaker sense of compositionality to justify a projection rule component in their theory. Jackendoff (1983) assumes the calculability requirement as a basic requirement for semantic theory and strengthens it with a 'grammatical principle' which preserves the constituent structure of syntactic representations in semantic representations (see section 4.4.3 below).

1. What is the formal characterization of the objects which serve as semantic representations?
2. How do these objects support the equivalence and consequence relations which are its descriptive goal?
3. How are expressions associated with their semantic representations?
4. What are semantic representations? Are they considered to be basically mental objects or real-world objects?

## 4.2. **Argument structure and semantic roles**

The semantic equivalence of two expressions can be represented in two ways. One is to allow the mapping from the syntax to assign them the same semantic representation. Alternatively, given an equivalence relation on semantic representations, they can be assigned different, but equivalent, semantic representations.

The manner in which intuitions of equivalence are represented is an important axis along which theories of the interface between syntax and semantics differ. In particular, they differ with respect to the prominence given to aspects of semantic representation and the consequence relation which is defined on them. For example, if semantic representations are formulas in a logical language with an explicit interpretation, like predicate logic, then equivalence of semantic representation is logical equivalence. Two sentences are thus equivalent just in case the formulas which serve as their semantic representations always have the same truth value in any given circumstance. So for example, the sentences in (12) would be predicted to be equivalent if they are assigned the two formulas in (13) respectively as their semantic representations, ignoring the internal semantics of the verb phrase:

(12) a. Not everyone likes brussels sprouts
     b. Some people don't like brussels sprouts
(13) a. $\neg(\forall x)[person(x) \rightarrow like\text{-}brussels\text{-}sprouts(x)]$
     b. $(\exists x)[person(x) \wedge \neg like\text{-}brussels\text{-}sprouts(x)]$

The assumption that semantic representations are logical formulas from an independently defined logic allows the theory to incorporate all of the familiar logical equivalences which guarantee that the two formulas in (13) are equivalent. There is no need to constrain the syntax–semantics mapping in such a way as to map (12a) and (12b) onto exactly the same formula. Their equivalence, the equivalence of the sentences in (2), and the non-equivalence of the sentences in (9) follow immediately from familiar laws of logic.

By assuming that semantic representations are sufficiently like logical languages to support set-theoretic interpretation or syntactic deductive systems, equivalences for which there are logical analyses (like those which depend upon 'logical constants' like *and, or,* negation and some determiners and modals) can be readily incorporated by providing an explicit mapping from the structure of the sentences to the structure of the formulas.

Consider now the equivalence of the active and passive sentences in (1), which is representative of a number of equivalences which follow from principles of clause structure. How are such equivalences to be represented? One option is to preserve the syntactic difference between the two sentences in their semantic representations by providing formulas like those in (14a) and (14b) respectively:

(14) a. *chase (John, Fido)*
    b. *be-chased-by (Fido, John)*

The equivalence between (1a) and (1b) is then reduced to the equivalence between (14a) and (14b), which is guaranteed by a requirement[6] that *chase* should hold of the ordered pair $\langle x,y \rangle$ if and only if *be-chased-by* holds of $\langle y,x \rangle$. This strategy preserves a fairly direct relation between the syntactic structure of the sentence and its semantic representation.

On the other hand, the synonymy of these pairs of sentences can be handled by a more indirect mapping between the syntax and the semantics which ensures that both sentences are mapped onto formula (14a). This strategy is frequently taken for the analysis of sentences which differ only with respect to how the 'logical arguments' of their predicates are related to the grammatical relations borne by the noun phrases which express them.[7]

Stating how the logical arguments of a predicate are associated with the complements of a verb in a sentence requires a grammatically neutral way of naming the logical arguments. The most common way of doing this is to assume a set of *semantic roles* or *thematic roles*. The sentences in (1) describe the same event, which involves two participants: John and Fido. Both sentences attribute the same role in the event to John and likewise to Fido. John is moving toward Fido with the intention of catching him and Fido is the moving goal of pursuit. The interpretation of these sentences should guarantee that despite the difference in grammatical relation of the two noun phrases (subject, direct object, object of preposition *by*), the roles played in the event by the referents are the same. Similarly, (15) should be interpreted as describing an event in which Fido and John have reversed roles from the situation described by (1).

(15) Fido chased John

[6] This requirement would be expressed by a 'meaning postulate,' i.e. a restriction on admissible interpretations for the semantic representation language. On this approach, the active–passive relation would be captured by meaning postulates which relate individual active transitive verb interpretations to interpretations for their passive participles.

[7] The standard theory assumption that deep structure is the only input to semantic interpretation, for example, represents this strategy.

Thus the semantic role played by John in (1a) can be called the *agent* role because John's intentions (and not the dog's) are crucial to the event's being a chase (as opposed to a flight from). The role played by the dog could be called *theme* because the dog is necessarily moving, or the *goal* because it is the target of the pursuit. Other commonly assumed semantic roles are *patient, source, experiencer,* and *location.* Semantic roles have played an important role in the study of lexical meaning, especially the meaning of verbs, by allowing finer distinctions to be made than those which are needed to determine the logical equivalence alone.[8] The sentences in (16), for example, are logically equivalent. The difference between *sold* and *bought* is in the assignment of the agent role to a participant. In both cases the subject noun phrase is the one which refers to the agent. However, in (16a) it is the volition of the source, John, which is highlighted, while in (16b) the volition of the goal, Mary, is highlighted:

(16) a. John sold a book to Mary
b. Mary bought a book from John

Semantic roles can also serve as a syntax-neutral way of naming the argument positions of predicates and relations which are used as lexical interpretations. They can be used in defining the mapping from syntax to semantic representation to state lexically specific mappings between argument positions and grammatical relations. For example, *like* can be described as differing from *please* in that the former maps its experiencer role onto its subject NP, while the latter maps it onto its direct object. Roles are also used to express restrictions on grammatical processes which cannot be viewed as sensitive only to structural information, such as the participle–adjective conversion rules discussed in Bresnan (1982:23).

## 4.3. Model-theoretic truth-conditional semantics

The most widely pursued approach to the construction of a theory of semantics for natural language has been based upon model-theoretic possible worlds accounts of truth-conditional meaning. This approach has a long history in the study of semantics within philosophy and logic (for discussion, see ter Meulen, Chapter 16 in this volume). The importation of logical semantics into linguistic semantics is attractive because it provides a theory which readily meets the goals sketched in section 4.1. The most widely

---

[8] Cf. Gruber (1976), Fillmore (1971), and Jackendoff (1972). The definitions for roles given below are paraphrased from Jackendoff (1972:29–32). Recently there has been increased interest in questions about the nature of semantic roles and their utility in formal semantic theory. See Carlson (1984), Chierchia (1984), Dowty (to appear) and the papers in Wilkins (to appear).

pursued program based on logical semantics has been termed 'Montague grammar,' which attempts to apply the methods used to interpret logical languages directly to natural languages.[9]

The goal is a theory which assigns to each sentence of a language an interpretation which represents the conditions under which it would be true. (Hence it is termed *truth-conditional*.) It does so by stating constraints on possible models which interpret the language, where a model is a consistent assignment of a denotation to every expression in the language. The denotation of a sentence in a model is a truth value: either 1 (true) or 0 (false) (Hence the term *model-theoretic*.) Here we briefly sketch how such a theory answers the questions given in section 4.1 before moving on to specific proposals.

*What are the semantic representations?* The interpretations for sentences and other expressions of the natural language are set-theoretic objects constructed from three basic sets: a set of entities $E$; the set $\{0,1\}$ of truth values, called $2$; and a set of indices or points of reference $I$, which index 'possible worlds.'

The interpretations of sentences are representations of their truth conditions in terms of models in which they denote a truth value. Constituents of the sentence are given interpretations of different types which represent the information they contribute to its interpretation. New types of semantic objects are recursively defined on the basic types $E$, $2$, and $I$ by taking the set of functions from one type to another type as a new type. The set of functions from $E$ to $2$ written as $(E \rightarrow 2)$, is the type of the denotation of one-place predicates. The set of functions from $E$ to $(E \rightarrow 2)$ is the denotational type of two-place relations. The set of functions from $(E \rightarrow 2)$ to $2$ is also a type, used in Montague's analysis for noun phrase denotations (see below). To every such denotational type corresponds an intensional type, which is a function from $I$ into the extensional type.

*How do these objects support equivalence and consequence relations?* This account of truth conditions is based upon the notion 'true in a model.' A model *satisfies* a sentence if and only if the sentence denotes 1 (true) in that model. Two sentences $\varphi$ and $\psi$ are semantically equivalent if and only if they always have the same truth value under the same circumstances (that is, they are satisfied by exactly the same models). Furthermore, $\varphi$ has $\psi$ as a consequence ($\varphi$ entails $\psi$) if and only if the circumstances under which $\varphi$ is true are a subset of those under which $\psi$ is true (i.e. if and only if every model

---

[9] See Dowty, Wall & Peters (1981), Partee (1974, 1976), and Montague (1974).

which satisfies $\varphi$ also satisfies $\psi$). Equivalence is consequently analyzed as mutual entailment. A sentence is contradictory if and only if no model satisfies it and a tautology if and only if every model satisfies it.[10]

*How is the syntax–semantics mapping compositional?* Senses, the function, from $I$ to denotational types, are assigned to lexical items. The interpretations of syntactically complex constituents are determined by associating semantic composition operations with the syntactic rules which generate the phrases. Assuming that *John* and *Fido* are both assigned objects in $E$ as their denotations, and that the transitive verb *chase* denotes a function equivalent to a set of ordered pairs of elements of $E$, then *chase Fido* will denote the set of entities which are the first members of ordered pairs in the denotation of *chase* whose second members are the entity denoted by *Fido*. *John chased Fido* will be true if and only if the entity denoted by *John* is in the set denoted by *chased Fido*. The denotation of the sentence is determined by the denotation of its parts and the operations associated with its phrasal construction.

*What are the semantic objects really?* The denotations assigned to expressions in the language are set-theoretic constructions. Models are constructed from sets of elements taken as primitive, the set of entities, the set of truth values, and the set of indices of possible worlds and times. Functions whose ranges and domains are these sets or sets of functions defined on them serve as denotations. The denotations associated with expressions are not mental objects, but are rather mathematical constructs which stand in for objects in the world.

Montague's theory implements Frege's (1892) distinction between the sense and the reference of an expression by distinguishing between the denotation assigned to expressions relative to a given point of reference and the sense of an expression which remains constant across points of reference. Like denotations, senses (the intensions of expressions) are set-theoretic objects as well: functions from points of reference to denotations. It might be possible to construe intensions as psychological objects, though Frege viewed them as independent of individuals who might grasp them.[11]

### 4.3.1. Montague's analysis

The use of first-order predicate logic as a means of explicating meaning admitting only variables and quantifiers over entity-denoting expressions is inadequate in a number of respects. Montague's seminal paper (1973, hereafter *PTQ*) proposed a solution to two of its problems.

---

[10] Compatible theories of anomaly can be found in Thomason (1972) and Waldo (1979).
[11] Cf. Partee (1979) and Carlson (1985) for further discussion of this point.

The first problem concerned the denotation of quantifier noun phrases. While proper names like *John* can be thought of as denoting particular entities, quantifier noun phrases like *every man* and *some woman* cannot. The customary logical translation of (17a) is (17b), which does not contain a subconstituent corresponding to the subject quantifier noun phrase:

(17) a. Every man walks
  b. $\forall x[man'(x) \rightarrow walk'(x)]$

In the *PTQ* analysis, Montague provided a type of denotation for such quantificational noun phrases. These denotations are sets of sets of entities, functions of the type $((E \rightarrow 2) \rightarrow 2)$, which are termed 'generalized quantifiers.'

The generalized quantifier denotation for such noun phrases provides the same account of the truth conditions of (17a) as does (17b). For example, the common noun *man* denotes a set of men at a given point of reference, which we name by *man'*, and the verb phrase *walk* also denotes a set of entities that walk at that point of reference, which we name by *walk'*. Note that (17b) will be true if and only if all of the members of the set of men are also members of the set of entities that walk. On the generalized quantifier analysis, the denotation of *every man* is a set of sets containing all the sets which contain the set of all men. The truth conditions of (17a) are equally well represented by the expression in (17c):

(17) c. *walk'* $\in$ *every-man'*

The set of walkers will be a member of the generalized quantifier denoted by *every man* just in case the set of men is a subset of the set of walkers, i.e. precisely in case (17b) is true.

Assuming that quantificational noun phrases denote sets of sets of entities gives every noun phrase a denotation. The type of denotation assigned to noun phrases can be made uniform for proper names and quantifier noun phrases by noting that for each entity *e* in *E*, a generalized quantifier can be generated which is defined as the set of those sets which contain *e*. Noun phrases, which on a first-order analysis denote entities directly, denote generalized quantifiers generated by an individual. Thus, the predictions of the first-order analysis are maintained. The provision of a uniform denotation for all noun phrases is an important feature of the *PTQ* analysis. Because Montague was attempting to provide a compositional model-theoretic interpretation for English which respects its syntactic structure, all noun phrases had to have a denotation. In order to preserve the syntactic unity of the category without complicating the syntax–semantics mapping, all noun phrases had to have the same type of denotation.

Further, a move away from the approach to quantification represented by formulas like (17b) is also necessary for empirical reasons, because quantifications like *most men are mortal* cannot be expressed in terms of the first-order quantifiers ( $\forall$ x) and ( $\exists$ x).[12] Montague further exploited the generalized quantifier denotation for noun phrases to expand the range of possible interpretations for relations and predicates. The arguments of predicates and relations in a first-order theory are basic entities. Montague raised the type of relations and predicates by taking their arguments to be generalized quantifiers. Doing so preserved the correct features of a first-order analysis, since every first-order relation has a corresponding relation between generalized quantifiers, and, in addition, made available a solution to one of the problems posed by the sentences in (18):

(18) a. John found a book on quark-theoretic semantics
    b. John sought a book on quark-theoretic semantics
(19) There is a book on quark-theoretic semantics

While (18a) entails (19), (18b) does not. This is predicted by treating *find* as equivalent to a first-order relation between entities, and by treating *seek* as a relation between generalized quantifiers not reducible to a relation between entities. Thus it might be true that John stands in the seek relation to the generalized quantifier denoted by *a book on quark-theoretic semantics* other than the generalized quantifier based on a single entity of *E*. Part of the difference in meaning between *seek* and *find* is that *find* must denote a relation between generalized quantifiers which is an extension of a first-order relation while *seek* need not. The syntactic parallel between the two sentences is preserved in the mapping from syntax to interpretation and the difference in their semantic consequences is located in the lexical semantics.

The second problem for a first-order theory which is addressed in the *PTQ* analysis concerns 'opaque' or 'intensional' contexts, in which the substitution of expressions which have the same denotation does not preserve the denotation of the whole expression. If the denotation of a complex expression is determined completely by the denotations of its parts, one would expect that constituents with the same denotation could be substituted without changing the denotation of the whole.

Frege (1892) proposed that in opaque contexts the denotation of some constituent depends upon the sense, rather than just the denotation, of at least one of its parts. Under his assumptions, sentences *denote* a truth value at a given point of reference, but they *express* their sense – a proposition. If the denotation of a sentence like *The Greeks believed that the world was round* (its truth value) depended on the truth value of the complement sentence, then the substitution of any true sentence in the complement would preserve

[12] See Barwise & Cooper (1981:213–16) for discussion.

the truth of the whole. Frege avoided this incorrect prediction by proposing that in such cases the constituent in question denoted its sense, rather than its customary denotation, i.e. its truth value.

Montague treated all denotations as functions of some type, and adopted Frege's treatment of intensional contexts by having the denotations of all function-denoting expressions apply to the senses of their arguments rather than their denotations. This allows the value of the function to differ even for arguments which have the same denotation. As in the case of higher-order generalized quantifier relations, the composition rules systematically allow for the most general case, and expressions which do not induce opacity effects are lexically specified as reducible to functions which apply to denotations.

## 4.3.2. Extensions of the program

A great deal of work has been done which extends the general program of Montague grammar.[13] Here we mention a few areas of research which follow this general approach.

*Generalization across types.* Montague tied his interpretations to the syntax of the language by requiring that each syntactic category have a particular semantic type. Maintaining this principle forces semantic distinctions to be replicated in the syntax and obscures cross-categorial generalizations. Several lines of work have been devoted to capturing cross-categorial and cross-typal generalizations.

The 'Boolean semantics' of Keenan & Faltz (1985) treats sets of possible denotations as Boolean algebras, that is, sets with operations defined on them which satisfy laws of generalized conjuction, disjunction, and negation. The approach shares most of the advantages that Montague's has with respect to first-order treatments, and provides additional structure in which many cross-categorial properties may be defined. For example, the class of first-order reducible relations in Montague's higher-order type are shown to be just the homomorphisms which preserve the Boolean structure of their domains. Because many different denotation sets are Boolean algebras, generalizations stated in terms of their Boolean structure are automatically cross-typal and cross-categorial. Hence a cross-categorial semantics of coordination is given for the categories which can be syntactically coordinated. Similarly, because adjectives and adverbs are functors over domains with similar Boolean structure, the semantic classes of modifiers, which are crucial to representing the contrast between (4) and (11), can be defined in a way which covers both.

There is a trade-off between the structure imposed by a strong type

---

[13] See the bibliography in Dowty *et al.* (1981:270–6).

structure and the ability to state cross-categorial generalizations. Partee and Rooth (1983; and Rooth and Partee 1982) have investigated loosening the connection between syntactic categories and their semantic types in a systematic way which allows expressions to float among several types. This is useful in capturing cross-categorial coordination and copular complements.

*Generalized quantifiers.* The generalized quantifier analysis of noun phrase denotations and the semantics of determiners has been one of the most intensively studied areas. If common noun phrases are extensionally set-denoting expressions and noun phrases have generalized quantifier denotations, determiners denote relations between sets. However, not just any relation between two sets can be the denotation of a natural language determiner. The seminal article on the semantics of determiners, Barwise & Cooper (1981), proposes several universals with respect to them and noun phrase denotations.[14]

*Adding structure in the ontology.* A number of proposals have been made to structure the basic ontology of the models used as interpretations beyond the simplest set $E$ of individuals. Most of these have concentrated on giving more structure to $E$. Among them are Carlson's (1977) influential treatment of generic bare plural nouns by sorting entities, predicates, and relations into kinds, objects, and stages of objects.

Several recent proposals about the semantics of singular, plural and mass term use a structured construction of $E$ – for example, those of ter Meulen (1980), Link (1983), and Hoeksema (1983). The general strategy is to partition $E$ into particular entities, groups and masses. The subdomains are connected by operations which relate groups to their constituent individuals and objects to the stuff of which they are made. Given this additional structure, analyses can be given, for example, for the difference between the determiners *each* and *all*, the meaning of conjoined NPs, and the difference between the distributive and collective readings of sentences like *The men lifted the piano*.

*Time and events.* On the model-theoretic approach to semantic analysis, the truth of a sentence is relativized to a point of reference. Crude analyses of temporal reference and aspectual distinctions in natural language can be constructed by making 'points of time' part of the definition of a point of reference and including in the language sentential tense operators interpreted on them. Current research has advanced far beyond this type of analysis for the verb tense and temporal anaphora of individual sentences and

---

[14] Cf. also Zwarts (1983), van Benthem & ter Meulen (1985), van Benthem (1986:3–54), and Keenan & Stavi (1986).

is seeking to relate sentence interpretation and the interpretation of stretches of discourse.

Just relativization to moments of time is inadequate to account for differences between the various aspectual types that sentences may have.[15] A more complex structure on time must be defined where interpretations are relative to intervals of time (see Dowty 1979). Another approach to the representation of aspectual distinctions takes events themselves to be the primitive objects, and views as derivative time as a set of moments.[16] The analysis of tense and aspect morphology in terms of operators on sentences is empirically inadequate on a number of counts, as argued in Enç (1981).

*Properties as functions and arguments.* In Montague's theory, properties, the senses of set-denoting expressions, are functions from possible worlds to sets of individuals. The close fit between syntactic category and semantic type that Montague assumed leads to a systematic duplication of types for verbal phrases that can be used both as predicates and arguments. Consider the sentences in (20):

(20) a. John is swimming
   b. Swimming is fun
   c. John is fun

(20a) suggests that swimming is a property which entities can have. Yet swimming itself can have properties as in (20b). Hence *fun* must represent a property of properties in (20b) and a property of entities in (20c). If the type hierarchy is consistent, *fun* (and many other expressions) will have to be of an infinite number of types. Relating properties to objects which themselves can have properties would enlarge the ontology while preserving the logical consistency of the system. This move is explored in Chierchia (1982, 1984).

*Pronouns and binding.* A logical formula which contains a free variable has an interpretation relative to an assignment of a value to the variable. For example, the formula which translates *he saw him* is *see* $(x,y)$, which contains two different variables. Here the variables $x$ and $y$ can be assigned, independently of each other, any individual as their interpretation. When the same variable is used in more than one argument place, the same value must be assigned to all of its occurrences. Hence the formula *see* $(x,x)$ is an appropriate translation for *he saw himself*. Bound variables, variables which occur in the scope of a binding operator like $(\exists x)$ or $(\forall y)$, have their

---

[15] The most commonly assumed typology of aspectual types is that referred to as the 'Aristotle–Ryle–Kenny–Vendler' verb classification by Dowty (1979:51), which distinguishes (in Vendler's terms) among states, activities, accomplishments, and achievements.
[16] Cf. Kamp (1979) and Hinrichs (1986). See ter Meulen (1984) and Bach (1986) for discussion of the parallels between the aspectual domain and the mass–count distinction in the nominal domain.

interpretations determined by the operator which binds them. Hence the interpretation of a formula like ( ∃ x)[*see* (x,x)] does not vary relative to an assignment of values to its variables.

The pronouns of natural languages are in many ways analogous to variables in a logic in that they have the syntax of referential terms and can have both a free referential and a bound interpretation. For example, the italicized pronoun in (21) can be construed in two different ways:

(21) Every man said that *he* had seen John

The pronoun can be interpreted as referring deictically to some particular individual of relevance in the context who had seen John. The interpretation of the pronoun is then independent of the interpretation of the other noun phrases in the sentence. Alternatively, the pronoun can be interpreted as bound by the quantifier noun phrase *every man*. In this case the value of the pronoun will depend on the interpretation of the binding quantifier noun phrase, so that each man's claim is that he himself had seen John.

A syntactic account of this difference between these two interpretations of the pronoun in (21) can be given by assuming that noun phrases are assigned indices to which the interpretation procedure is sensitive, making (26) structurally ambiguous, each structure having a different NP index. The bound interpretation of the pronoun in (21) would be represented by the indexing which gives the pronoun and the NP *every man* the same index, while in the referential interpretation, they have different indices.

A number of conditions on co-indexing must serve to limit the ability of quantifier noun phrases to bind pronouns. For example, reflexive pronouns cannot receive their interpretations arbitrarily but must be interpretationally dependent on another noun phrase which is syntactically 'close enough' to it. A nearly complementary condition of 'disjoint reference' requires that nonreflexive pronouns not be co-indexed if they are syntactically 'too close together.' So in *he saw him*, the two noun phrases cannot be interpreted as referring to the same entity, though in *he saw himself*, they must be (see Reinhart 1983 for more discussion and references).

Alternatively, one might consider dispensing with the syntactic indexing procedure in favor of stating these conditions within the interpretation procedure itself (see Bach & Partee 1980). The treatment of these conditions within a framework which directly interprets surface syntax is developed by Cooper (1979, 1983).[17] Engdahl (1986) presents further analysis of a number

---

[17] The 'Cooper storage' conventions developed in Cooper (1975) are the basis of a number of proposals for surface interpretation without syntactic disambiguation of quantifier scope or pronoun indexing. This storage mechanism allows quantifier noun phrases to be compositionally interpreted according to their syntactic position or else be given an interpretation with wider scope, and it thus handles scope ambiguities without requiring their disambiguation within the syntax. For more discussion, see Enç (Chapter 9, this volume).

of problems, including cases in which there does not seem to be any consistent way of satisfying the constraints on binding, as in a sentence like *Which picture of himself does every photographer admire most?* Sentences like these, in which a reflexive pronoun occurs in a displaced constituent present a problem on the interpretation in which the question phrase *which picture* is interpreted as having the quantifier phrase *every photographer* in its scope (i.e. the reading which could be answered by *His latest one*). The reflexive pronoun must occur in the scope of the quantifier noun phrase to get bound by it, and yet occur as a part of a constituent which has wide scope over the quantifier noun phrase.

More work in this area is carried out under one of the 'discourse representation' frameworks discussed below in section 4.4.1. The question of whether the conditions on pronoun interpretation are to be considered part of the theory of syntactic structure, sentence interpretation, discourse interpretation, pragmatics, or some combination, continues to be an important area of debate.

### 4.3.3. Some outstanding questions

The truth-conditional approach to semantics defines its equivalence relation as logical equivalence, i.e. having the same truth value in the same circumstances. The truth conditions of sentences are represented by functions from points of reference to truth values. These functions are called *propositions* and they play two roles in this type of semantic theory. First, they represent the senses of (declarative) sentences, the content that they express. Second, since sentential constituents can occur as complements to predicates (such as verbs of propositional attitude like *believe* and *doubt*), propositions must also serve as a semantic argument to this type of predicate. Each of these roles gives rise to problems whose solutions seem to demand a fundamental modification of the framework.

First, there is more to meaning than truth conditions. We should ask how natural a line the truth-theoretic account cuts across the broader domain of meaning. If sentences express propositions and propositions are representations of truth conditions, then all logically equivalent sentences express the same proposition. By definition, tautologies are logically equivalent, because they are necessarily always true, and similarly, contradictory sentences are also logically equivalent. But it seems wrong to say that all tautologies have the same meaning. Additional contributors to meaning must be sought outside the account of truth-conditional meaning. The utterance of a sentence in a certain context conveys information beyond what is conventionally associated with the elements of a sentence. Some aspects of meaning fall under the rubric of 'conversational implicature' in the sense of Grice (1975) and given their nonconventional nature, they are best excluded from the domain of semantics proper. There is also a need for an account of 'presuppositional' meaning, truth conditions which are conventionally reserved from focus in the assertion or denial or questioning uses of a sentence (see Wilson 1975; Gazdar 1979). Karttunen & Peters (1975, 1979) attempt to construct an account of this type of meaning within compositional truth-conditional semantics as an account of Gricean 'conventional implicature'.

The second problem arises from the treatment of 'propositional attitude' predicates like *believe* and *doubt*. If these verbs express relations between individuals and propositions are objects which represent the circumstances under which sentences are true, then logically equivalent sentences express the same proposition. It follows that if some individual *x* believes a proposition *p*, then every sentence of the form *x believes that S* where S expresses a proposition equivalent to *p* will have the same truth value and similarly for other attitudes like *assert* and *doubt*. Hence, believing one tautology or one contradiction entails believing all of them. This is generally considered a counterintuitive result.

The source of the problem is that propositions construed as representations of truth conditions in terms of possible worlds do not provide fine enough distinctions to give an adequate analysis of our intuitions about belief sentences. This problem is widely cited as the fundamental empirical problem with the possible-worlds semantics approach. Summary discussions of the issues involved can be found in Bigelow (1978) and Partee (1982). One can view this problem as an indication of the difficulty of moving from a 'semantics as mathematics' point of view to one of 'semantics as psychology' (cf. Partee 1979). Several approaches have been suggested that make the objects of propositional attitude verbs more distinct than functions from possible worlds to truth values allow (cf. Stalnaker 1978; von Stechow 1982; Cresswell 1985).

A major question for the model-theoretic, truth-conditional approach to semantics is how a more robust account of meaning can be constructed which avoids these problems while preserving the rich descriptive and deductive powers of the theory.

## 4.4. Some more recent approaches

Concerns about a foundational question, the suitability of model-theoretic semantics as a basis for a psychologically relevant semantics, and empirical shortcomings of the approach provide many points of departure for other current approaches to semantics. Here we will take up four quite briefly.

### 4.4.1. Discourse representations

Kamp (1981) and Heim (1982, 1983) propose theories of interpretation which supplement model-theoretic truth-conditional semantic theory with a theory of discourse representation and provide solutions for some problems involving the reference of definite and indefinite noun phrases and pronouns. Both theories make use of a level of semantic representation which mediates between the syntactic representations of sentences and the truth-theoretic interpretation.[18] The *discourse representations* constructed as part of the interpretation of discourses are sets of entities, namely the discourse referents available for the interpretation of pronouns, and conditions on them specified by the discourse. The discourse representation of (22a) would, for example, contain the information in (22b): two objects identified by the names *Robin* and *Fido* and that the former owns the latter:

(22) a.  Robin owns Fido         (23) a.  Robin owns a dog

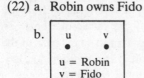

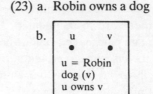

While (22b) can be viewed simply as a particular graphic representation of the information contained in a first-order logical translation, the innovation of this approach to interpretation can be seen in (23b), the discourse representation constructed for (23a), which contains an indefinite noun phrase direct object. Indefinite noun phrases are taken to be referential terms rather than quantificational expressions; their interpretation introduces an entity into the discourse representation which serves as its referent. Hence the conditions associated with the noun phrase *a dog* in (23a) trigger the introduction of the referent *v* and the requirement that *v* be a dog.

The principles of discourse representation construction unify information contained in successive sentences, so they allow intrasentential and intersentential pronominal reference to be represented in a unified way. Interpretation of the sentence *She beats him* following (22a) or (23a) involves extending the representations to include more information about the entities it contains. One of the ways in which (22b) and (23b) could be extended follows

---

[18] Here I use Kamp's term 'discourse representations.' The theory presented in Heim (1982), 'File change semantics,' views discourse representations as files of information opened and updated dynamically as sentences are interpreted. The comments in the text here attempt to represent the common features of the two proposals without claiming that they are equivalent.

from choosing to link the pronouns to the entities already in the discourse representation, yielding the representations in (24) and (25) respectively:

(24) a.  Robin owns Fido
She beats him

(25) a.  Robin owns a dog
She beats him

b.

Note the dynamic view of interpretation taken by these approaches. The connection between expressions and model-theoretic denotations is indirect, mediated by the discourse representations. Interpreting expressions consists of constructing and updating these discourse representations; the expressions being interpreted can guide this process by coding instructions on how the representations are to be updated. For example, the difference between indefinite noun phrases and definite noun phrases is expressed in terms of the change in the discourse representation which results from their evaluation: indefinites introduce new discourse referents and definites do not.

Mediating sentence interpretation through the construction and updating of structured collections of representations which include discourse entities and conditions on them provides analyses of the interpretation of pronouns in conditionals, modals, and so-called 'donkey sentences'[19] which are superior to those constructed within theories in which the sentences are interpreted directly or through the mediation of logical translations.

### 4.4.2. Situation semantics

Barwise & Perry (1983) develop 'situation semantics' as an alternative to the possible-worlds-based model-theoretic semantics. It shares some of the goals and techniques of possible-worlds-based model-theoretic semantics, but it seeks to avoid the problem with the account of propositional attitudes mentioned above and the foundational question of the precise nature of possible worlds.

On the view of situation semantics, the world consists of situations, which contain real individuals, properties, relations, and locations in space–time. Situations are set-theoretic constructions, but properties and relations are primitive, rather than constructed from individuals and points of reference. The situations in the world are classified by situation types which are collec-

---

[19] An example of a 'donkey sentence' is *Every man who owns a donkey beats it*, in which the pronoun must be construed as dependent upon the noun phrase *a donkey* without allowing *a donkey* to have wider scope than the universal quantification expressed by *every*.

tions of sequences of individuals, spatio-temporal locations, relations, and polarity values, all of which are ontologically basic. For example, (26) represents a situation of Fido chasing Felix and Felix not chasing Fido at location $l$.[20]

$$(26) \quad \begin{cases} \langle l, \text{chase}, \text{Fido}, \text{Felix}, 1 \rangle \\ \langle l, \text{chase}, \text{Felix}, \text{Fido}, 0 \rangle \end{cases}$$

Sequences like those in (26) can be built up as the interpretations of sentences by combining the situation types associated with parts of the sentence to provide a compositional account of sentence interpretation. The interpretations of sentences combined with a theory of constraints, allow equivalence and consequence relations to be defined.

The additional structure of situations in comparison to propositions offers possibilities for new solutions to the problem of propositional attitudes and suggests interesting accounts of the semantics of certain constructions. The agenda of situation semantics, however, is not exclusively devoted to linguistic semantics, but is an attempt to construct a general relational view of meaning. Linguistic meaning is viewed as a particular type of meaning, on a par with the sense of meaning reflected in statements like *Those spots mean that Mary has measles*. Meaning is a relation between different types of situations and the relation between situations involving linguistic events and other types of situations are not viewed as different in kind from relations between nonlinguistic situations.[21]

### 4.4.3. Jackendoff's 'conceptual structures'

Jackendoff (1983) views semantic representations as completely psychological. His semantic representations are 'conceptual structures' which are assumed to be mental objects. Jackendoff complements the goals for semantic theory outlined in section 4.1. with two constraints: the 'grammatical constraint' and the 'cognitive constraint.' The grammatical constraint says that, other things being equal, a semantic theory which explains otherwise arbitrary generalizations about the syntax or the lexicon is to be preferred. The cognitive constraint takes the form of a hypothesis that conceptual structures are the representations used by the sensory and motor systems as well as the linguistic system.

The notation used for conceptual structures are attribute-value trees. The constituents of these trees are assigned to one of the following ontological

---

[20] Sequences like those in (26) but without locations or without polarity (truth) values are also used in the theory. I cannot here present an account of all the distinctions which are drawn among situation-theoretic objects.

[21] For discussion and a critique of the program of situation semantics, cf. the papers in *Linguistics and Philosophy* 8, 1.

categories: THINGS, PLACES, DIRECTIONS, ACTIONS, EVENTS, MANNERS, and AMOUNTS. These conceptual structures are associated with sentences by 'correspondence rules' which preserve some of the constituent structure of sentences in the conceptual representation. For example, the conceptual structure associated with the sentence (27a) is given in (27b):

(27) a. The man put the book on the table

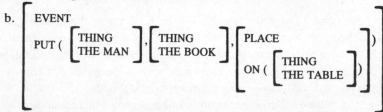

     Given the grammatical constraint, such representations, which preserve the surface constituent structure of the sentence, are preferable to, for example, first-order logical translations which do not contain constituents corresponding to the noun phrases. (It is interesting to note that the effect of the grammatical constraint in this case has an effect similar to Montague's attempt to provide direct interpretation of surface constituent structure.) These conceptual structures are the representations over which inference rules are stated as transformations and thus provide the desired definitions of equivalence and consequence.[22]

### 4.4.4. Cognitive semantics

Another developing approach to linguistic semantics, the 'cognitive semantics' of Lakoff (1986a), rejects meaning as a relationship between symbols and the world. It attempts to develop a theory of cognitive structures from basic level concepts, 'image-schemata' and operations which manipulate them. The image-schemata are structured objects which are intended to support analogs of some of the relations we have taken here as the core of a semantic theory.

     The transformations of schema-type representations are useful in representing structural parallels which can be exploited in a theory of the systematic polysemy of lexical items and metaphorical extension, particularly in the analysis of the semantics of prepositions and other items whose meanings concern the locational and spatial domain. As an example, consider the systematic polysemy of the prepositions in (28)–(29):

(28) a. John walked over the hill
    b. John lives over the hill

---

[22] Cf. the rule in Jackendoff (1983:73) and the comments on pp. 103–5.

(29) a. John walked through that doorway
　　b. The office is through that doorway

In the (a) sentences, the prepositional phrase specifies the path of John's walking, while in the (b) sentences it specifies a particular location. According to Lakoff (1986a:32) this polysemy follows from two things. First, it is a consequence of the assumption that the preposition's interpretation is done in terms of a PATH image schema consisting of four structural elements: a source, a destination, the path connecting them, and a direction (toward the destination). In the (a) sentences, the object of the preposition specifies information about the path of the image schema. Second, it follows from the fact that PATH schemata are generally transformable by a destination-focussing operation. The systematic polysemy of the prepositions is resolved in the (b) sentences since stative verbs are consistent only with the destination-focussed image schema, while the activities make use of the path-focussed schema. Presentation of the programs and analyses within this approach can be found in Lakoff (1986b) and Langacker (1986).

## 4.5. Residual questions

Each of the approaches to semantic theory mentioned here has its internally developed problems for further research. Each has areas in which it provides appealing analyses and each is in need of extension to wider ranges of phenomena. We conclude here with some questions which will no doubt remain under discussion for some time to come.

The question of what semantic representations really are is the thorniest. The application of model-theoretic semantics to linguistic semantics provided an immediate arsenal of techniques and a precision of formulation which has stimulated a great deal of research. While other approaches have attempted to avoid the problems with propositional attitudes, or have moved toward more psychologistic notions of meaning, they have not yet reached the coverage of model-theoretic semantics. As their coverage expands, the contrasting analyses should throw more light onto the more fundamental questions about the techniques used in semantic theory.

The mapping between syntax and semantics is another thorny problem, given its dependence upon assumptions made about its input and its target. The variety in current approaches to syntactic theory and the corresponding variety of assumptions about the range of the interpretation mapping produce many different proposals about the nature of the syntax–semantics interface. These differences keep open the question of the extent to which languages are compositional (cf. the discussion in Enç, Chapter 9 in this volume).

Another important group of questions on which some progress is being made concerns the relationship between semantics as it has been characterized here and pragmatics. We have presented semantics as a theory of the interpretation of sentence types, not sentence tokens, linguistic abstractions not actual utterances. Only utterances are understood and convey or ask for information. The theory of pragmatics takes utterances as its objects of study and the description of the understanding conveyed by language use as its goal (cf. Horn, Chapter 5 in this volume). If we take semantics as a description of linguistic competence, then this abstraction seems a reasonable one, since the distinction between semantics and pragmatics thus accords with that between competence and performance. It remains to be seen, however, how effectively the theories and analyses discussed here can be integrated with the most successful pragmatic theories.

*REFERENCES*

Bach, E. 1986. The algebra of events. *Linguistics and Philosophy* 9: 5–16.
Bach, E. and Partee, B. H. 1980. Anaphora and semantic structure. In J. Kreiman & A. Ojeda (eds.) *Papers from the parasession on pronouns and anaphora*. Chicago: Chicago Linguistic Society.
Barwise, J. & Cooper, R. 1981. Generalized quantifiers and natural language. *Linguistics and Philosophy* 4: 159–219.
Barwise, J. & Perry, J. 1983. *Situations and attitudes*. Cambridge, MA: MIT Press.
Bäuerle, R., Egli, U. & von Stechow, A. (eds.) 1979. *Semantics from different points of view*. Berlin, New York: Springer Verlag.
Bäuerle, R., Schwarze, C. & von Stechow, A. (eds.) 1983. *Meaning, use and interpretation*. Berlin, New York: de Gruyter.
Benthem, J. van. 1986. *Essays in logical semantics*. Dordrecht: Reidel.
Benthem, J. van & ter Meulen, A. 1985. *Generalized quantifiers in natural language*. Dordrecht: Foris.
Bigelow, J. C. 1978. Believing in semantics. *Linguistics and Philosophy* 2: 101–44.
Bresnan, J. 1982. The passive in lexical theory, In J. Bresnan (ed.) *The mental representation of grammatical relations*. Cambridge, MA: MIT Press.
Carlson, G. N. 1977. Reference to kinds in English. Doctoral dissertation, University of Massachusetts at Amherst.
Carlson, G. N. 1984. Thematic roles and their role in semantic interpretation. *Linguistics* 22, 3: 259–79.
Carlson, G. N. 1985. Review of *Semantics and cognition* by R. Jackendoff. *Linguistics and Philosophy* 8: 505–19.
Chierchia, G. 1982. Nominalization and Montague grammar: a semantics without types for natural languages. *Linguistics and Philosophy* 5: 303–54.
Chierchia, G. 1984. Topics in the semantics of infinitives and gerunds. Doctoral dissertation, University of Massachusetts at Amherst.
Cooper, R. 1975. Montague's semantic theory and transformational syntax. Doctoral dissertation, University of Massachusetts at Amherst.
Cooper, R. 1979. The interpretation of pronouns. In F. Heny & H. Schnelle (eds.) *Syntax and semantics, vol. 10: Selections from the Third Groningen Round Table*. New York: Academic Press.
Cooper, R. 1983. *Quantification and syntactic theory*. Dordrecht: Reidel.
Cresswell, M. J. 1978. Semantic competence. In F. Guenthner & M. Guenthner-Reutter (eds.) *Meaning and translation*. New York: New York University Press.
Cresswell, M. J. 1985. *Structured meanings*. Cambridge, MA: MIT Press.

Dowty, D. 1978. Applying Montague's views on linguistic metatheory to the structure of the lexicon. In D. Farkas, W. M. Jacobsen & K. W. Todrys (eds.) *Papers from the Parasession on the Lexicon*. Chicago: Chicago Linguistic Society.

Dowty, D. 1979. *Word meaning and Montague grammar*. Dordrecht. Reidel.

Dowty, D. To appear. On the semantic content of the notion 'thematic role.' In B. Partee, G. Chierchia & R. Turner (eds.) *Properties, types and meaning*. Dordrecht: Reidel.

Dowty, D., Wall, R. E. & Peters, S. 1981. *Introduction to Montague semantics*. Dordrecht: Reidel.

Enç, M. 1981. Tense without scope: an analysis of nouns as indexicals. Doctoral dissertation, University of Wisconsin, Madison.

Engdahl, E. 1986. *Constituent questions*. Dordrecht: Reidel.

Fillmore, C. F. 1971. Types of lexical information. In D. D. Steinberg & L. A. Jakobovits (eds.) *Semantics: an interdisciplinary reader in philosophy, linguistics and psychology*. Cambridge: Cambridge University Press.

Fodor, J. D. 1977. *Semantics: theories of meaning in generative grammar*. New York: Thomas Y. Cromwell.

Frege, G. 1982. Über Sinn und Bedeutung. *Zeitschrift für Philosophie und Philosophische Kritik*, 100: 25–50. Translated as: On sense and nominatum. In H. Feigl & W. Sellars (eds.) 1949. *Readings in philosophical analysis*. New York: Appleton-Century-Crofts.

Gazdar, G. 1979. *Pragmatics: implicature, presupposition and logical form*. New York: Academic Press.

Grice, H. P. 1975. Logic and conversation. In P. Cole & J. Morgan (eds.) *Syntax and semantics, vol. 3: Speech acts*. New York: Academic Press.

Gruber, J. S. 1976. *Lexical structures in syntax and semantics*. Amsterdam: North-Holland.

Heim, I. R. 1982. The semantics of definite and indefinite noun phrases. Doctoral dissertation, University of Massachusetts at Amherst.

Heim, I. R. 1983. File change semantics and the familiarity theory of definiteness. In Bäuerle, Schwarze & von Stechow (1983).

Hinrichs, E. 1986. Temporal anaphora in discourse. *Linguistics and Philosophy* 9: 63–82.

Hoeksema, J. 1983. Plurality and conjunction. In A. ter Meulen (ed.) (1983).

Hoeksema, J. 1984. *Categorial morphology*. Dordrecht: von Denderen.

Jackendoff, R. 1972. *Semantic interpretation in generative grammar*. Cambridge, MA: MIT Press.

Jackendoff, R. 1983. *Semantics and cognition*. Cambridge, MA: MIT Press.

Kamp, J. A. W. 1979. Events, instants, and temporal reference. In Bäuerle, Egli & von Stechow (1979).

Kamp, J. A. W. 1981. A theory of truth and semantic representation. In J. A. G. Groenendijk *et al.* (eds.) *Formal methods in the study of language*. Mathematical Centre Tracts 135. Amsterdam: Mathematisch Centrum.

Karttunen, L. & Peters, S. 1975. Conventional implicature in Montague grammar. In C. Cogen *et al.* (eds.) *Proceedings of the First Annual Meeting of the Berkeley Linguistics Society*. Berkeley: Berkeley Linguistics Society.

Karttunen, L. & Peters, S. 1979. Conventional implicature. In D. Dinneen & C.-K. Oh (eds.) *Syntax and semantics 11: Presupposition*. New York: Academic Press.

Katz, J. J. 1972. *Semantic theory*. New York: Harper & Row.

Katz, J. J. & Fodor, J. A. 1964. The structure of a semantic theory. In J. A. Fodor & J. J. Katz (eds.) *The structure of language*. Englewood Cliffs: Prentice-Hall.

Keenan, E. L. & Faltz, L. M. 1985. *Boolean semantics for natural language*. Dordrecht: Reidel.

Keenan, E. L. & Stavi, J. 1986. A semantic characterization of natural language determiners. *Linguistics and Philosophy* 9: 253–326.

Kempson, R. 1977. *Semantic theory*. Cambridge: Cambridge University Press.

Lakoff, G. 1986a. Cognitive semantics. *Berkeley Cognitive Science Report No. 36*. Berkeley: Institute of Cognitive Studies, University of California, Berkeley.

Lakoff, G. 1986b. *Women, fire and dangerous things: what categories reveal about the mind*. Chicago: University of Chicago Press.

Landman, F. & Veltman, F. (eds.) 1984. *Varieties of formal semantics*. Dordrecht: Foris.

Langacker, R. W. 1986. *Foundations of cognitive grammar, vol. 1*. Stanford: Stanford University Press.

Link, G. 1983. The logical analysis of plurals and mass terms. In Bäuerle, Schwarze & von Stechow (1983).

Lyons, J. 1977. *Semantics*, vols. 1 and 2. Cambridge: Cambridge University Press.

Meulen, A. ter 1980. Substances, quantities and individuals. Doctoral dissertation, Stanford University. Distributed by the Indiana University Linguistics Club.

Meulen, A. ter (ed.) 1983. *Studies in model theoretic semantics*. Dordrecht: Foris.

Meulen, A. ter 1984. Events, quantities and individuals. In Landman & Veltman (eds.) (1984).

Montague, R. 1973. The proper treatment of quantification in ordinary English. In K. J. J. Hintikka *et al.* (eds.) *Approaches to natural language*. Dordrecht: Reidel.

Montague, R. 1974. *Formal philosophy*. Ed. and with an introduction by R. H. Thomason. New Haven: Yale University Press.

Partee, B. H. 1974. Montague grammar and transformational grammar. *Linguistic Inquiry* 6: 203–300.

Partee, B. H. (ed.) 1976. *Montague grammar*. New York: Academic Press.

Partee, B. H. 1979. Semantics–mathematics or psychology? In Bäuerle, Egli & von Stechow (1979).

Partee, B. H. 1982. Belief-sentences and the limits of semantics. In S. Peters & E. Saarinen (eds.) *Processes, beliefs, and questions*. Dordrecht: Reidel.

Partee, B. H. 1984. Compositionality. In Landman & Veltman (eds.) (1984).

Partee, B. H. & Rooth, M. 1983. Generalized conjunction and type ambiguity. In Bäuerle *et al.* (eds.) (1983).

Reinhart, T. 1983. *Anaphora and semantic interpretation*. Chicago: University of Chicago Press.

Rooth, M. & Partee, B. H. 1982. Conjunction, type ambiguity, and wide scope *or*. In D. Flickinger, M. Macken & N. Wiegand (eds.) *Proceedings of the First West Coast Conference on Formal Linguistics*. Stanford: Department of Linguistics, Stanford University.

Stalnaker, R. 1978. Assertion. In P. Cole (ed.) *Syntax and semantics, vol. 9: Pragmatics*. New York: Academic Press.

von Stechow, A. 1984. Structured propositions and essential indexicals. In Landman & Veltman (1984).

Thomason, R. 1972. A semantic theory of sortal incorrectness. *Journal of Philosophical Logic* 1: 209–58.

Waldo, J. 1979. A PTQ semantics for sortal incorrectness. In S. Davis & M. Mithun (eds.) *Linguistics, philosophy and Montague grammar*. Austin: The University of Texas Press.

Wilkins, W. To appear. *Syntax and semantics*, vol. 21: *Thematic relations*. New York: Academic Press.

Wilson, D. 1975. *Presupposition and non-truth-conditional semantics*. London: Academic Press.

Zwarts, F. 1983. Determiners: a relational perspective. In ter Meulen (ed.) (1983).

# 5 Pragmatic theory
*Laurence R. Horn*

## 5.1. Pragmatics: internal constituency and foreign relations

The quandary of pragmatics as a subdiscipline within (or overlapping with) linguistics is illustrated by a recent circular announcing the foundation of the International Pragmatics Association. 'Today,' the pamphlet begins by conceding, 'pragmatics is a large, loose, and disorganized collection of research efforts.' Rather than throwing up his or her anonymous hands at such a situation, the author announces a new, comprehensive bibliography of the field scheduled to emerge at the end of 1986, which 'offers 2000 pages of information on the field of pragmatics in the widest sense.' What kind of field could possibly be deemed worthy, on the one hand, of a 2000-page annotated bibliography, loose and disorganized enough on the other hand to prevent the formulation of a precise definition or a widely accepted and rigorous formalism, and just serious and fundamental enough on the third hand to have begun to be included within the standard course offerings of linguistic programs within the United States and abroad?

If the coming of age of an academic discipline is at least partly conditioned on the emergence of a broad, comprehensive, intellectually honest, and pedagogically sound introductory textbook, pragmatics is in pretty good shape. With the publication of Levinson (1983), we have a text for pragmatics that is superior to any extant analog for its 'mother discipline' semantics, and compares favorably with standard texts in phonology and syntax (cf. also Bach & Harnish 1979 and Leech 1983 for useful, though less thorough, introductions to the field). Like other branches of linguistics of undoubted legitimacy, pragmatics has both its 'pure' theoretical side (although the notion 'hardcore pragmatics' may strike some as an oxymoron) and its applications: speech act theory has been successfully (and unsuccessfully) applied to the study of metaphor and fiction; presupposition and implicature are clearly relevant to the study of 'online' inferencing strategies; a good deal of recent and current work on language development has focussed on the acquisition of pragmatic rules (cf. Ochs &

Schieffelin 1979); and the interaction of maxims of conversation and politeness has even been applied to (if not blamed for) the breakdown of contemporary marriages (Tannen 1975). Yet the status of pragmatics as a field remains unsettled.

Part of the problem may be the disjunctive attitude toward the characterization of pragmatics on the part of mainstream theoretical linguistics. If a phenomenon can be shown to be too ill-behaved and variable to be treated coherently within the syntactic or semantic component, and if it doesn't seem to be quite arbitrary enough for the lexicon or quite phonological enough for the phonology, it must be pragmatic, i.e. (all too often) not worth worrying about. This is the flip side of Bar-Hillel's celebrated admonition (1971: 405), 'Be careful with forcing bits and pieces you find in the pragmatic wastebasket into your favorite syntactico-semantic theory. It would perhaps be preferable to first bring some order into the contents of this wastebasket.'

But just how does one go about ordering the contents of a wastebasket? We may begin by noting that pragmatics has become a repository for different types of extragrammatical considerations and the effects of these factors on grammatical and lexical form. If we were to compartmentalize the wastebasket, we would need at least two major separate compartments, one for what we might call *conversational pragmatics* (cf. Austin 1962; Grice 1967; Searle 1969; and papers in Cole & Morgan 1975 and in Cole 1978, 1981) and one for *functionalist pragmatics* (cf. Firbas 1964; Kuno 1972, 1976; Gundel 1974, 1985; Prince 1981; Reinhart 1981; and papers in Grossman, San & Vance 1975; Li 1976; Givón 1979b). We might also reserve a separate (sub)compartment (*psycholinguistic pragmatics*?) for a theory of perception and linguistic processing (cf. especially Grosu 1972, 1981; Bever 1975; and papers in Bever, Katz & Langendoen 1976).[1]

There remains a strong motivation for collecting all of these compartments under a single rubric, especially since each compartment has had its contents regularly extracted in the search for plausible, explanatory, and reductionist theories of superficially complex or recalcitrant phenomena within universal grammer or the grammar of a given language. Thus, attempts have been made to provide a functional basis for so-called 'island' phenomena (Ross 1967), so that the derivational constraints posited by Ross, or the equivalent mechanisms within competing syntactic theories, would no longer need to be stipulated (cf. Grosu 1972, 1981; Kuno 1976). Whether such reductionist programs can in fact succeed is a question to

[1] If we define functionalist pragmatics broadly enough (not restricting its scope to the 'packaging' of information into sentences, and resultant considerations of topic/comment, given/new, etc.), we might incorporate the perceptual and processing theories within the former compartment (indeed, Bever, Langendoen, and others are self-proclaimed 'neo-functionalists'), but this would obscure an important difference in the types of mechanism involved.

which we shall return below, but within the modular approach to language (cf. e.g. J. A. Fodor 1982; Newmeyer 1983; Harnish & Farmer 1984) it is reasonable to expect that an independently motivated pragmatic theory (or several such theories, on the compartmentalized view) should provide simplification and generalization elsewhere in the overall description of language.

Whether pragmatics constitutes a module in the strict sense of Fodor (1982) is, however, far from clear. Sperber & Wilson (1986) present a cogent argument that, unlike grammatical theory, but like scientific reasoning (Fodor's paradigm case of a nonmodular, 'horizontal' system), pragmatics – given the indeterminacy of the predictions and explanations it offers and the global knowledge it calls upon – cannot be a module. Leech (1983: 21ff) makes the same point in a different vocabulary: syntax and semantics are *rule-governed*, while pragmatics is *principle-controlled*. The point remains, however, that a regimented account of language *use* facilitates a simpler and more elegant description of language *structure*.

Pragmatics itself may be viewed as *internally* modular and interactionist, in the sense that the conceptually distinct subcomponents (suborientations?) of pragmatic analysis may be simultaneously called upon within a single explanatory account of a given phenomenon, just as autonomous but interacting grammatical systems may interact to yield the simplest, most general, and most comprehensive treatment of some linguistic phenomenon (cf. the deconstruction of passive in Chomsky 1982). Thus, Langendoen & Bever (1973) invoke a mixed perceptual and conversational account (one which also utilizes the controversial claim that there are pockets of acceptable ungrammaticality within a linguistic system) in their analysis of *A not unhappy* (\**not happy*, \**not sad*) *person entered the room*. Horn (1979) draws upon both Praguean functionalism and conversational pragmatics in order to predict the disappearance of a noncontradictory de re reading for comparatives like #*That he is stronger than he is was claimed* (cf. *It was claimed that he is stronger than he is*) in the same syntactic frame where equatives preserve their nontautologous dc re interpretation (*That he is as strong as he is surprising*). And Horn (1986) combines functional and perceptual considerations in a proposed explanation for the inability of topicalization to apply to the output of extraposition (\**That she resigned, it seems*; Fr. \**Les mensonges, il existe cela*).

While we shall touch on functionally and psychologically based pragmatic explanations,[2] the remainder of this overview will focus on conversa-

---

[2] There are important areas of pragmatic research which we shall leave entirely untouched, including conversation analysis (as represented in the work of Sacks, Schegloff, Jefferson, and others), discourse analysis, and text grammar; see Levinson (1983: ch. 6) for an excellent summary of the similarities and differences among these approaches, and for a suggestion of how CA might be linked more explicitly to Gricean conversational pragmatics than is standardly attempted by its practitioners.

tional pragmatics, partly because we do not have the space to cover all subfields of pragmatics even-handedly, partly because the other subfields are dealt with in other contributions to this *Survey*, and partly because it constitutes the area I deal with most in my own research.

But what is pragmatics, anyway? The standard place to look for the referent of a name (especially on the causal theory; cf. Kripke 1972) is in the original act of dubbing, which in this case takes us back to the trichotomy proposed by Morris, Carnap, Peirce, and their associates in the course of their rather ambitious program for an *International encyclopedia of unified science*. Morris (1938) takes *syntactics* to involve the purely formal study of the relations of signs to one another; *semantics* to involve the relation of signs to their designata and hence to the objects they denote (or may denote); and *pragmatics* to be 'the science of the relation of signs to their interpreters,' dealing with 'the psychological, biological, and sociological phenomena which occur in the functioning of signs.' That pragmatics has developed, half a century later, into a 'large, loose, and disorganized' enterprise should perhaps come as no surprise, given the breadth and vagueness inherent in this early definition.

If we adopt either Morris's definition, or Stalnaker's succinct characterization (1972: 383) of pragmatics as 'the study of linguistic acts and the contexts in which they are performed' (see Levinson 1983: 1–35 for other attempts at definitions, and their inherent difficulties), it follows that the study of pragmatics antedates the term by centuries if not millennia. (The same point can obviously be made about semantics.) The interaction between the context of utterance of an expression and the formal interpretation of elements within that expression constitutes a central domain within pragmatics, variously labelled *deixis*, *indexicality*, or *token-reflexivity* (see Lyons 1977 and Levinson 1983: ch. 2, for useful summaries of the literature).

Philosophers (Bar-Hillel 1954; Montague 1968; Stalnaker 1972) and linguists (Jakobson 1957; Fillmore 1975; Brown & Levinson 1978) have long recognized the importance of an account of shifters or indexicals, expressions whose meaning can best be viewed as a function from context to individual by assigning values to variables for speaker, hearer, time and place of utterance, style or register, purpose of speech act, etc. Typical examples of indexicals are *I*, *you*, *here*, *there*, *now*, *then*, *hereby*, and tense/aspect markers.[3] Stalnaker takes it as one of the central goals of pragmatics

[3] The centrality of pragmatic issues to any theory of reference emerges from such works as Donnellan (1966, 1978), Stalnaker (1972, 1978), Kripke (1977), Kaplan (1978), Nunberg (1978), and Enç (1981). Unfortunately, our brief survey of the field must pass over the extremely interesting but extremely thorny issues involved in the pragmatics of reference.

to 'characterize the features of the speech context which help determine which proposition is expressed by a given sentence.'

Beyond helping to determine the assignment of lexical and sentential meanings, the context provides a specification of the *universe of discourse* which implicitly restricts the range of the operators within a sentence. This notion was part of the analytical toolkit of the scholastic logician: the thirteenth-century philosopher William of Sherwood, for example, pointed out that *Only Socrates runs* entails not that nobody other than Socrates runs but that 'nothing other than Socrates *within the same genus* is running' (Kretzmann 1968: 72–3; emphasis mine). The factors which have recently led McCawley (1981) and others to opt generally for restricted quantification were also a concern of the scholastics. More recently, the semantic interpretation of other linguistic elements (besides shifters, performatives, and quantified variables) has been argued to incorporate crucial reference to the context of utterance; Partee (1973) points to analogs between tense and deictic pronouns, while Enç (1981) defends the view that all nouns must be treated as indexicals, thereby dispelling both scopal analyses of tense, modals, and descriptions and the scope paradoxes that can be shown inevitably to arise therefrom.

## 5.2. The pragmatics of implicature: beyond truth conditions

Let us take another case in point. The pragmatic principle which has yielded the most linguistic mileage (in terms of its generality, explanatory power, and consequences for simplifying grammatical and lexical description) is Grice's first maxim of quantity. Grice's 'first shot' at this principle (1961: 132) is the dictum: 'One should not make a weaker statement rather than a stronger one unless there is a good reason for so doing.' In later work, Grice (1975: 45) reformulates the same principle as the first submaxim of quantity: 'Make your contribution as informative as is required (for the current purposes of the exchange).'

This principle, which was apparently discovered independently by Ducrot (1972, 1973), whose 'loi d'exhaustivité[4] is a restatement of the maxim of quantity, is the foundation for a general theory of scalar implicature (Horn 1972, 1973; Gazdar 1979; Hirschberg 1985) which treats all scalar or gradable predicates (cf. Sapir 1944; Bolinger 1972; Horn 1972; Fauconnier 1975) as inherently *lower-bounded* by entailment or truth-conditional meaning and *upper-bounded* by pragmatic inference or implicature. But while Levinson's observation (1983: 100) that 'implicature does

---

[4] This law 'exige que le locuteur donne, sur le thème dont il parle, les renseignements les plus forts qu'il possède, et qui sont susceptibles d'interesser le destinataire' (Ducrot 1972: 134).

not have an extended history' may be literally true, the essential insight can be traced back at least to John Stuart Mill. In his response to the logic of Sir William Hamilton (1860), in which *some* is taken (on the default reading) as equivalent to *some only* (cf. Horn 1973), Mill observes:

> No shadow of justification is shown . . . for adopting into logic a mere *sous-entendu* of common conversation in its most unprecise form. If I say to any one, 'I saw some of your children to-day', he might be justified in inferring that I did not see them all, not because the words mean it, but because, if I had seen them all, it is most likely that I should have said so: even though this cannot be presumed unless it is presupposed that I must have known whether the children I saw were all or not. (Mill 1867: 501)

Notice both the proto-Gricean tenor of this argument and Mill's recognition of the epistemic rider on quantity-based inferences: the use of a weaker predicate suggests (implicates) that *for all the speaker knows*, the stronger predicate on the same scale could not have been substituted *salva veritate*.

While Grice may not have invented the notion of quantity-based inference, his contribution was essential, in situating both the principle and the inferencing strategy within a general theory (or, some would argue, a general *framework*) for describing the nature of pragmatic inference or *implicature*.[5] In his ground-breaking work on language use and the logic of conversation, Grice (1967, 1975, 1978) suggests a procedure whereby participants in a conversation may compute what was meant (by a given speaker's contributing a given utterance at a given point in the interaction) as a function of what was said (by that speaker, in that utterance, at that point). The governing dictum is an overarching *cooperative principle* ('Make your conversational contribution such as is required, at the stage [of the talk exchange] at which it occurs').

Within this basic guideline, Grice establishes four specific subprinciples, the general (indeed almost trivial-seeming) and presumably universal maxims of conversation which he takes to govern and essentially define all rational interchange (Grice 1975: 45–6):

(1) *Grice's maxims of conversation*
QUALITY:    Try to make your contribution one that is true.
           1. Do not say what you believe to be false.

---

[5] Strawson (1952: 178–9) offers a very similar 'general rule of linguistic conduct,' viz. that 'one should not make the (logically) lesser, when one could truthfully (and with equal or greater clarity) make the greater claim.' But as Strawson attributes the operation of his 'pragmatic rule' to 'Mr H. P. Grice,' we can safely continue to credit the latter with the development of the first full-blown theory of implicature. (In this same passage, Strawson foreshadows much of the vituperation of the next generation by defending his analysis against the objection that the considerations he raises are 'merely pragmatic.')

2. Do not say that for which you lack evidence.

QUANTITY:    1. Make your contribution as informative as is required (for the current purposes of the exchange),
2. Do not make your contribution more informative than is required.

RELATION:   Be relevant.

MANNER:     Be perspicuous.
1. Avoid obscurity of expression.
2. Avoid ambiguity.
3. Be brief. (Avoid unnecessary [*sic*] prolixity.)
4. Be orderly.

The mutual assumption that both speaker and hearer are observing the cooperative principle (CP) and its component maxims (even when surface appearances suggest the contrary) permits the exploitation of these maxims to generate *conversational implicata*, nonlogical inferences comprising conveyed meaning (what is meant without being, in the strict sense, said).[6]

But not all implicature is conversational. In his earliest published work on the (as yet unnamed) doctrine of implicature, Grice (1961: §3) distinguishes several separate species within the genus of non-entailment relations. He bids us consider the respective inferences drawn from the sentences in (2):

(2) a. Smith has left off beating his wife
   b. She was poor but honest
   c. Jones has beautiful handwriting and his English is grammatical
   d. My wife is either in the kitchen or in the bathroom

Part of the meaning of (2a) involves the *presupposition* that Smith has been beating his wife; Grice tentatively follows Strawson (1950) in assuming that the truth of this presupposition is a necessary condition on the truth-or-falsity of (2a). In any case, this inference is neither cancelable (\**Smith has left off beating his wife, but then he never beat her in the first place*) nor detachable (in the sense that any other means of asserting what (2a) asserts seems to induce the same presupposition; cf. *He has stopped/ceased beating her*,[7] *He no longer beats her*, etc.).

In (2b), the inference is that there is some contrast between her poverty and her honesty. As in the presupposition case of (2a), this inference is non-

---

[6] The Gricean mechanism (and its linguistic correlates) are elaborated further in Horn (1972), Walker (1975), Gazdar (1979), and Levinson (1983: ch. 3). (Cf. Cohen 1971 for a dissenting view, and the replies by Walker and Gazdar; a different form of criticism is offered by E. O. Keenan, and we shall return to her argument below.)

[7] The Megarians (third century BC) were partial to the question '*Have you stopped beating your father? Answer yes or no.*' The shift from this form to the *sophisma* of choice for the donkey-obsessed scholastics (*Do you still beat your ass?*) to the moderns' wife-beating example represents a discouraging commentary on 23 centuries of progress in social sensitivity.

cancelable – but it *is* detachable, since we can express the same truth-conditional content in a way that removes (detaches) the inference: *She is poor and honest.* The implication in (2b) also differs from that in (2a) by its irrelevance to truth-conditional considerations: (2b) is true if the referent is both poor and honest, and false otherwise. In later work (Grice 1975; Karttunen & Peters 1979), such detachable but non-cancelable inferences which are neither part of what is said (part of truth-conditional meaning) nor *deducible* in any general, natural way *from* what is said are termed *conventional* implicata.

If (2c) is uttered in the course of an evaluation of Jones by the philosophy faculty, there is 'a strong, even overwhelming implication that Jones is no good at philosophy.' As in the prior case, this implication is non-truth-conditional. But this time, the inference is *not* detachable (as in the case of (2a), any other way of expressing the literal content of (2c) in the same context would license the same inference) and it *is* cancelable (if the same sentences were uttered in reference to a secretary or a plumber no implication would be drawn as to Jones's competence at philosophy; nor would any inference go through if the speaker had added . . . *but I don't mean to suggest that he's no good at philosophy*).

The utterance of (2c) 'does not *standardly* involve the implication . . . attributed to it; it requires a special context to *attach* the implication to its utterance' (Grice 1961: 130). The case of (2d) is conceptually similar to that of (2c) in that once again, the inference – that the speaker did not know in *which* of the two rooms his wife was located – is non-truth-conditional, non-detachable and cancelable. Again as in (2c), it is not the *proposition* or the *sentence*, but the *speaker* (or the speaker's *utterance*) which induces the implication in the appropriate context. But this time we don't need to assume a special, marked context in order to derive the implication. In the language of his later work, (2c) is an instance of *particularized conversational implicature*, while (2d) represents the linguistically far more important concept of *generalized conversational implicature*.

We can represent Grice's model of implicature schematically as in Figure 1 on page 121. Within this model, as the annotations indicate, we can define the respective domains of semantics and pragmatics as either disjoint or overlapping. If semantics is essentially concerned with those aspects of meaning which affect truth or satisfaction conditions, then conventional implicata are outside its domain (and squarely within pragmatics). But if we take pragmatics to coincide with *natural* and semantics with *conventional* aspects of meaning, the domain of conventional implicature seems to fall within the semantics camp.

In the earlier days of formal pragmatics, the hope was entertained that the categories of truth-conditional semantics and Gricean conversational prag-

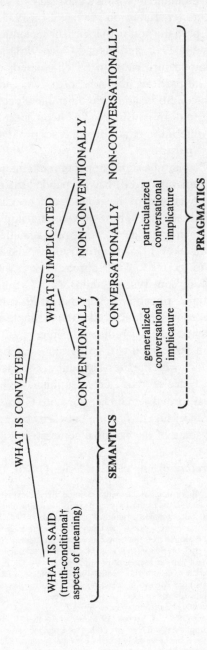

Figure 1.

† This should probably be generalized to some notion like *satisfaction*-conditional aspects of meaning, since Grice's model should not be restricted to declarative sentences (Searle's class of representatives). This does not affect the schematic model, however.

matics might eventually exhaust the entire area of inquiry; so-called 'presuppositions' or 'conventional implicata' could then be reassigned to the more coherent classes of semantic entailment (within a classical two-valued logic) and conversational implicature (cf. Kempson 1975; Wilson 1975; Wilson & Sperber 1979). On this view, both the notion of logical or semantic presupposition (cf. Frege 1892; Strawson 1950; and indeed Grice 1961) and Grice's category of conventional implicature were to be eliminated, or perhaps restricted to a few recalcitrant particles like *even*, *also*, *but*, and *therefore*, where the case for non-truth-conditional but unpredictable aspects of meaning seemed to be too strong to dismiss. But this heady prospect has largely dissipated with the rapid proliferation of additional cases profitably analyzable after the fashion of these particles.

Indeed, Karttunen and Peters, in a series of papers culminating in Karttunen & Peters (1979; henceforward K&P) have expanded the category of conventional implicature to cover most of the ground earlier occupied by the notion of presupposition. Their account of how conventional implicata affect the discourse context owes much to earlier accounts of pragmatic presuppositions (Karttunen 1974; Stalnaker 1974) as propositions whose truth the speaker (acts as if he) takes for granted.[8] This approach shares with the antipresuppositionalist line of Kempson, Wilson, and Boër & Lycan (1976) the conclusion that presuppositional phenomena[9] are non-truth-conditional in nature, when they cannot be reduced (à la Russell 1905) to simple entailment. But K&P accept the existence of an irreducible category of non-truth-conditional inferences whose association with expressions can be predicted (built up) compositionally along with the literal meaning of the same expressions. Their analysis marries Grice's notion of conventional implicature with Montague's truth-conditional formal semantics. For both Grice (1975) and K&P there is a systematic conceptual distinction between conventional and conversational implicature; some of the essential contrasts are indicated in Table 1:[10]

Besides the *but* and *therefore* examples from Grice (1975), the conven-

[8] On Stalnaker's account, pragmatic presupposition is not a mental attitude (like believing, wishing, or hoping) but a linguistic disposition: to act as if the truth of a given proposition is noncontroversial, accepted by speaker and hearer as part of the common ground. Cf. also Stalnaker (1978) for a valuable possible-worlds-based account of assertion, presupposition, and their effect on the context of conversation. The Oh & Dinneen (1979) anthology is the locus classicus on presupposition and its place within semantic and pragmatic theory; cf. J. D. Fodor (1979) and Martin (1979) for defenses of the currently unpopular notions of truth-value gaps and semantic presupposition.
[9] We shall employ this term nonprejudicially to refer to the constellation of phenomena which originally motivated the introduction of presuppositions into the linguistic literature, however they are to be accounted for: factive predicates, definite descriptions, category mistakes, etc., cf. E. L. Keenan (1971) and Levinson (1983: 177–85) for reasonably comprehensive inventories.
[10] The first five distinctions are due to Grice (1975); cf. Sadock (1978) on some of the difficulties with Grice's diagnostics for conversational implicata, and Nunberg (1981) for a reply to Sadock. Curiously, analogs of Grice's two types of implicature can be found in Ducrot's parallel system (1972). A *sous-entendu* (note Mill's usage, cited above!) is an inference located in the rhetorical component; it is

Table 1.

| CONVENTIONAL IMPLICATA | CONVERSATIONAL IMPLICATA |
| --- | --- |
| (a) Make no contribution to *truth conditions*, but constrain *appropriateness* of expressions with which they are associated. | |
| (b) *Unpredictable*, arbitrary part of meaning; must be learned *ad hoc*. | *Natural* concomitant of what is said or how it is said; *non-conventional* by definition. |
| (c) *Non-cancelable*; apply in all contexts of utterance. | *Cancelable*, either explicitly (by linguistic context) or implicitly (by extralinguistic context). |
| (d) *Detachable*: two synonyms may have different conventional implicatures. | *Non-detachable* if arising via one of the content maxims (quality, quantity, relation). *Detachable* if arising via maxim of manner. |
| (e) *Not calculable* through any procedure; must be stipulated. | *Calculable* through cooperative principle and the maxims of conversation. |
| (f) Akin to pragmatic presuppositions (non-controversial propositions speaker posits as part of common ground); cf. Stalnaker (1974). | Conceptually related to Mill's '*sous-entendu*' of common conversation' (see above) or Ducrot's '*sous-entendu*' as discourse or rhetorical notion. |
| (g) Exhibit a well-defined set of *projection properties* enabling the implicata of larger expressions to be computed from those of their subparts (Karttunen & Peters 1979). | Projection properties unclear, since conversational implicatures 'may be indeterminate'† (Grice); but cf. Gazdar (1979) and Hirschberg (1985) on the determination of implicata. |

*Note*: †To illustrate the indeterminacy of conversational implicature, consider the implicata drawn from the two tautologies *It ain't over till it's over* vs. *When it's over, it's over*.

tional implicature analysis has been extended (*inter alia*) to the italicized expressions in (3a, b):

(3) a. *Even* John passed the test
    b. John *managed to* pass the test

On K&P's account, (3a, b) not only *entail* but are in fact truth-conditionally *identical* to (4):

(4) John passed the test

but (3a) adds the conventional implicata (induced by *even*) that others (in the context set) passed the test and that John was the least likely member of this set to have done so, while (3b) brings in the conventional implicatum

context-dependent (i.e. cancelable or defeasible) and derivable via some sequence of reasoning (i.e. calculable). A *presupposé* is located in the semantic (linguistic) component, it is not context-dependent and cannot be derived by reasoning. *Sous-entendre* (lit. to 'undermean') is standardly glossed 'to make or let something be understood [i.e. to convey something] without saying it,' hence a *sous-entendu* is that which one conveys without saying (it). Mill's usage was perhaps more transparent in this regard than Grice's.

(contributed by *manage to*) that it was relatively difficult for him to pass (or something of the sort; the content of this implicatum, as of others, is notoriously hard to pin down).

While all of Grice's and most of K&P's candidates for conventional implicature involve simple lexical expressions,[11] this is by no means a necessary restriction. Working within the K&P paradigm, Halvorsen (1978) argues that a cleft sentence (e.g. *It is John that Mary loves*) both entails and conventionally implicates the corresponding existential proposition (*Mary loves somebody*); this is of course one of the classic presuppositional phenomena cited by, *inter alia*, E. L. Keenan (1971).

The category of conventional implicature extends naturally to tense and supersegmental phenomena, both of which contribute non-truth-conditional but non-calculable aspects of meaning to the sentences in which they occur. On such an account *John will leave yesterday* is a grammatical sentence which may even be true (if John did in fact leave yesterday), but it can never be uttered appropriately, since the conventional implicatum contributed by the tense clashes with the literal meaning of the adverb. The complex meanings associated with the contradiction and fall–rise contours (cf. Ladd 1980) might also best be viewed as conventional implicata.

The projection properties of presuppositions (cf. Morgan 1969; Langendoen & Savin 1971; Karttunen 1973, 1974) re-emerge within the K&P account as projection properties of conventional implicata. Notice in particular that the fact that presuppositions/implicata are transparent to ordinary negation – both (3b) and its negation (5):

(5) John didn't manage to pass the test

equally implicate (4) – are accounted for by treating negation as (in the terms of Karttunen's earlier work) a *hole*, rather than plug or filter. Factive predicates (*realize, regret, be surprising*; cf. Kiparsky & Kiparsky 1970) are also typical holes, letting presuppositions percolate through them to become inherited by the next highest expression. Verbs of speaking, on the other hand (*says, claims, mutters*), are in principle *plugs*, blocking the transmission of implicata (cf. Levinson 1983: 195–6 for a contrary view). Thus, (6a) but not (6b), implicates that there is a king of France:

(6) a. Kim regrets that Lee is dating the present king of France
    b. Kim said that Lee is dating the present king of France

[11] One class of phenomena involving lexical choice that is a prime candidate for this type of analysis is the T and V 2nd person singular pronouns in German, Romance, Slavic, and other language families. On this account, *Tu es heureux* and *Vous êtes heureux* express the same proposition and are true under the same circumstances (if the addressee is in fact happy), but differ with respect to their appropriateness conditions (cf. Levinson 1983 for discussion). It might also be maintained that both these sentences differ from their feminine analogs (. . . *heureuse*) by conventionally implicating that the addressee is male.

Two-place logical connectives are neither simple plugs nor holes, but *filters*, letting some presuppositions/implicata through but not others, depending on the internal content of the relevant clauses:

(7) a. Sam has a wife, and his wife is
    unhappy

   b. If Sam has a wife, his wife is     [implicature of second clause,
    unhappy                          viz. *Sam has a wife*, filtered out
                                       by first clause]

(8) a. Sam has a dog, and his wife is
    unhappy

   b. If Sam has a dog, his wife is     [implicature of second clause,
    unhappy                          viz. *Sam has a wife*, survives]

While much has been learned from K&P's attempt to incorporate a compositional account of presupposition/implicature inheritance within an explicit formal semantic model, there are both empirical and conceptual problems with the account they propose, as observed by Gazdar & Rogers (1978), Soames (1979), and especially Gazdar (1979).[12] Gazdar's own account of presupposition inheritance differs from the Karttunen and K&P models in at least two essential ways. First, his *pre-suppositions* (potential presuppositions), unlike Grice's and K&P's conventional implicata, are *cancelable* when they clash with propositions already in the discourse context. Secondly, potential presuppositions interact in a systematic way with two categories of *im-plicata* (potential conversational implicata), which have their own projection properties. While Gazdar's formal model of presupposition and implicature is not without problems of its own (cf. Landman 1981; Soames 1982; Levinson 1983), the fact that two explicit, comprehensive, falsifiable (and in some cases falsified) theories of formal pragmatics are now on the market casts doubt on the widespread view that pragmatics is inherently fuzzy and informal.

## 5.3. Implicature and the status of negation

One problem which has plagued both traditional theories of semantic presupposition and K&P-style formal models of pragmatic presupposition or conventional implicature is the interaction of presuppositional phenomena with negation. Kempson, Wilson, Boër & Lycan, Gazdar, and others have pointed out that no theory in which presuppositions – either semantic or

---

[12] Levinson (1983: ch. 4) provides a useful discussion of the issues involved in settling on an adequate theory of presuppositions and their projection properties, focussing on the K&P and Gazdar treatments. Levinson argues that an important distinction is lost if we assimilate all presuppositional phenomena to Grice's class of conventional implicata, as K&P bid us do.

pragmatic – are defined at least partly by constancy under negation can straightforwardly predict the acceptability of sentences like (9):

(9) a. The king of France isn't bald – there isn't any king of France
   b. Kepler didn't regret that the planetary orbits were round, because they're elliptical
   c. John didn't *manage* to pass the test – he passed it, but he was given the answers

The only solution (short of ignoring the existence of these sentences, as Frege 1982 and Strawson 1950 seem to have done) has been to acknowledge the need for two separate negation operators in language, one – a hole to presuppositions – for the ordinary negation in (7), the other – a plug, effectively outside the scope of the presupposed or implicated material – for the examples of (9). Yet this line (which Karttunen and Peters essentially adopt in embracing a 'contradiction negation' – see K&P: 46ff) seems to violate the metatheoretical desideratum known as 'Occam's razor': entities are not to be multiplied beyond necessity. In particular, senses or dictionary entries must not proliferate; this is the doctrine variously known as the 'modified Occam's razor' (Grice 1978: 118–19) and 'Occam's eraser' (Ziff 1960: 44). All things being equal, an analysis which posits two homophonous negative operators is to be rejected in favor of an analysis which does not. But *are* all things equal?

Evidence is presented in Horn (1985) that while the negation appearing in contexts like those in (9) does not represent a distinct semantic operator (external or plug negation), contra K&P and the multivalued logicians, neither can it be directly assimilated (contra Kempson, Gazdar *et al.*) to the ordinary negation of (7) which allows presuppositions or implicata to percolate through. Rather, it is an instance of a general phenomenon which (after Ducrot 1972) I have termed *metalinguistic* negation, a means for rejecting a previous utterance on any grounds whatever, including its morphosyntactic or phonetic form. The distinction between this metalinguistic operator and ordinary, truth-functional, propositional negation can be viewed as representing not a semantic ambiguity but what we might call (following Donnellan 1966 and Stalnaker 1972) a *pragmatic ambiguity*, a built-in duality of use, not meaning.

Another application for the notion of pragmatic ambiguity emerges from the realm of generalized conversational implicature. It has been recognized at least since Aristotle that words like *possible* are used in two systematically distinct ways: the 'two-sided', upper- and lower-bounded reading (=‘neither impossible nor necessary’) on which the possible refers to ‘that which is not necessary but, being assumed, results in nothing impossible,’ and the one-sided, lower-bounded reading, on which ‘we say ambiguously of the necessary that it is possible' (*Prior analytics* 32a18–28, *De interpretatione* 22b20; cf. Hintikka 1960 and Horn 1973 for elaboration). Assuming, as is plausible, that Aristotle is considering *possible*, and not *necessary*, to be the ambiguous item here, what sort of ambiguity is involved?

If *possible* is semantically or lexically ambiguous between a one-sided ('at least possible') reading and a two-sided ('exactly possible') reading, a consistent account of scalar operators would find analogous ambiguities in such sentences as:

|  |  | One-sided reading | Two-sided reading |
|---|---|---|---|
| (10) | a. He has three children | '. . . at least three . . .' | '. . . exactly three . . .' |
|  | b. You ate some of the cookies | '. . . some if not all . . .' | '. . . some but not all . . .' |
|  | c. It's possible she'll win | '. . . at least possible . . .' | '. . . possible but not certain . . .' |
|  | d. Maggie is patriotic or quixotic | '. . . and perhaps both' | '. . . but not both' |
|  | e. I'm happy | '. . . if not ecstatic' | '. . . but not ecstatic' |
|  | f. It's warm out | '. . . at least warm . . .' | '. . . but not hot' |

But we have an obvious violation of the aforementioned Occamistic principle here: if we follow this approach, the ambiguity of *possible* extends to *every* scalar predicate – including each of the $\aleph_0$-many cardinal numbers substitutable into the frame of (10a). The obvious alternative, urged in Horn (1972) and formalized in Gazdar (1979), is to generate just the one-sided readings directly from the logical forms of sentences like (10a–f), deriving the two-sided understandings as quantity-based implicata. All scalar operators are thus lower-bounded by their truth-conditional meaning, and upper-bounded by generalized conversational implicature. (In fact, as Mill noticed, what is implicated is that *for all the speaker knows* no stronger value on the same scale applies.) The ambiguity of the sentences of (10) will thus be pragmatic, rather than semantic or lexical.

Thus, a pragmatically based account utilizing an independently motivated principle, the maxim of quantity (whose domain, as Grice has observed, is not even purely linguistic, let alone restricted to the realm of the logical constants), offers an intuitively satisfying way of dealing with the apparent discrepancies between the standard logical characterizations of the operators (quantifiers, binary connectives, modals, negation) and their natural language equivalents.[13] This modular approach yields a simpler, more con-

[13] Another instance in which the motto 'Grice saves' might be readily invoked is that of conjunction. A sentence like *They had a baby and got married* would seem to be ambiguous between atemporal ('symmetric' or 'logical,' *and also*) and temporal (*and then*) readings. Evidence against this position

servative account of the semantics of these operators than a holistic treatment which either intermingles the semantic and pragmatic facts, ignores the latter entirely, or embraces an infinitude of lexical ambiguities.

But now negation once more rears its problematic head. While the negations of scalar predications like those in (10) are ordinarily understood as negating the one-sided values which are the putative logical forms of these sentences (cf. *He didn't eat three cookies* = 'less than three'); *It isn't possible she'll win* = 'impossible,' etc.), the so-called 'paradoxical' negations of (11) must be understood as negating the corresponding two-sided understandings:

(11) a. He doesn't have *three* children, he has *four*
     b. You didn't eat *some* of the cookies, you ate *all* of them
     c. It isn't *possible* she'll win, it's downright *certain* she will
     d. Maggie isn't patriotic *or* quixotic, she's both patriotic *and* quixotic
     e. I'm not *happy* – I'm *ecstatic*
     f. It's not *warm* out, it's downright *hot*

To take one case in more detail, consider the example involving *or*. On the standard pragmatic analysis, disjunction is always *in*clusive by meaning and sometimes *ex*clusive by implicature. Returning once more to Mill (1867: 501), we find the observation that 'If we assert that a man who acted in a particular way, must be either a knave or a fool, we by no means assert, or intend to assert, that he cannot be both'; indeed, many of us could nominate some favorite politician as a single-handed refuter of the necessary exclusivity of this particular disjunction. This approach to *or* as an unambiguously inclusive operator (cf. also Barrett & Stenner 1971) is supported by Gazdar (1977, 1979: 81–2), who cites the (putatively) unambiguous nature of the negative counterpart of sentences like Mill's or (10d); a negation like those in (12) is understood as a joint denial, i.e. an assertion that each disjunct is false, rather than as a negation of an exclusive *or*:

includes the following (i) On the two- *and* theory, conjunction in virtually every language would be described as ambiguous in just the same way as in English. (ii) No natural language contains a single conjunction ambiguous between 'and also' and 'and earlier' readings; i.e. no language could be just like English except for containing a conjunction *shmand* such that *They had a baby shmand got married* would be interpreted either atemporally or (asymmetrically) as 'They had a baby and, before that, they had gotten married.' (iii) The same 'ambiguity' exhibited by *and* arises in paratactic constructions in which two clauses describing related events are juxtaposed without any overt connective (*They had a baby. They got married.*)

Grice's alternative position, which I take to be correct, is that conjunctions are semantically univocal, but may conversationally implicate (through the exploitation of the manner submaxim 'Be orderly') that the events occurred in the order in which they were described. The impossibility of *shmand* on this account is pegged to the absence of any maxim enjoining the speaker to 'Be disorderly.' Notice that as with scalar implicature, the asymmetric implicatum may be canceled or suspended: *They had a baby and got married, but not necessarily in that order.* (Grice's line on asymmetric conjunction is supported by Schmerling 1975; Wilson 1975; Gazdar 1979; Levinson 1983; while it is rejected in favor of a semantic account by Bar-Lev & Palacas 1980 and McCawley 1981.)

(12) a. He isn't a knave or a fool
    b. Maggie isn't either patriotic or quixotic

But, as we have seen, we can – with the right intonation and continuation – get precisely the reading Gazdar predicts we cannot, viz. that of (11d).[14]

This dual character of negation with scalar predications has been recognized at least since Jespersen (1924: 325–6), but its resolution is crucial for a determination of the character of the division of labor between semantics and pragmatics. If there is only one negation in natural language, the truth-functional, one-place propositional connective of Fregean semantics, the well-formedness of the examples in (11) apparently indicates that the upper-bound must be built into the logical form, or at least the propositional content, associated with these scalar predications – contrary to the Gricean line just argued for.

This is precisely the conclusion reached by the practitioners of what I have elsewhere (Horn 1984a) called the 'London School of Parsimony'; cf. e.g. Kempson & Cormack (1979), Kempson (1979, 1980, 1982), Burton-Roberts (1984). They argue from the position that negation is not ambiguous (and from the existence of sentences like those in (11)) to the conclusion that scalar operators *do* result in ambiguity, although this ambiguity applies not at semantic interpretation or logical form but at the level where sentences together with contexts determine propositional form. For Kempson and her colleagues, semantic interpretation radically underdetermines propositional content, and there is vastly more (propositional or logical) ambiguity than has been recognized.

The alternative view, defended in Horn (1984a, 1985), is that the negation appearing in (11), like that of (9), is – as previously signalled – a metalinguistic operator which cannot be assimilated to ordinary negation.[15] If this view proves correct, the orthodox Mill–Grice view on scalar predications will be vindicated.[16] (Notice that the external (plug) semantic operator, con-

---

[14] Gazdar's argument *does* go through for the incorporated (*neither . . . nor*) version of these negated disjunctions: *He is neither a knave nor a fool* (*he's both*); *Maggie is neither patriotic nor quixotic* (* – *she's both patriotic and quixotic*). This reflects a general property of metalinguistic negation; cf. Horn (1985) for details.

[15] Evidence for this position comes from various phonological, morphosyntactic, and pragmatic parallels between the negative sentences of (11) and (13) and such sentences as (i)–(iii):
    (i) He didn't [mɪ́ʳənɨj] to pass the test – he [mǽnɨjd] to pass it
    (ii) I'm not a Trotsky*ite*, I'm a Trotsky*ist*!
    (iii) Grandma isn't 'feeling lousy,' Johnny, she's indisposed
where it is clear that the negative element does not 'negate' anything in logical form, but rather signifies the speaker's rejection of any aspect of some previous utterance from its phonetic form to its register.

[16] The same point applies to the conjunction case of note 13: given the possibility of (i), first pointed out by Wilson (1975: 151):
    (i) It's not true that they had a baby and got married – they got married and had a baby
we would either have to accept that this negation is metalinguistic (or otherwise unassimilable to ordinary propositional negation) or give up the elegant Gricean solution to the 'ambiguity' of *and*.

tradiction negation, invoked by K&P for the conventional implicature cases of (9) is not a live option for the conversational implicature-canceling negation of (11) – much less the examples involving phonetic form or register – since K&P exclude the possibility of incorporating *conversational* implicata into the logical form that contradiction negation takes wide scope over.)

### 5.4. Conversational inference: possible problems, possible solutions

We must leave this dispute unsettled and move on to a more general (but all too brief) survey of some problems associated with conversational implicature in the post-Gricean era of pragmatic theory. Grice's original framework is clearly at best incomplete and at worst inadequate beyond repair to the task of predicting sets of nonlogical inferences which are actually drawn from a given utterance in a given context. It is simultaneously too weak, in allowing the derivation of virtually anything by encompassing directly opposed maxims like the first quantity maxim on the one hand and the relation maxim (or, for that matter, the second quantity maxim) on the other, and too strong, in treating all calculable inferences monolithically. Kroch (1972) argues that the cooperative principle (CP) is in fact vacuous, and much of the subsequent work on the Gricean schema relying on the CP since the nonpublication of Grice (1967) has in fact constituted an attempt to put some teeth into that schema (cf. especially Gazdar 1979). We shall return below to the other major points of criticism, those involving the heterogeneity of conversational implicata and maxim clash. But another objection remains to be disposed of.

Given the general form of the Gricean maxims, it is tempting to misconstrue them as prescriptive statements or absolute edicts intended to be taken at face value by all self-respecting speakers, hearers, and 'behavers.' The conversational maxim would then be the modern heir of what has been known since the days of the Justinian code as the *pragmatic sanction* (*pragmatica sanctio*), a solemn imperial decree having the force of a fundamental and irrevocable law referring to the affairs of a community (see *OED* entry).

In fact, E. O. Keenan (1976) seems to assume just such a characterization of the Gricean program, and adduces evidence from the conversational behavior of Malagasy speakers to argue that Grice's maxims are culture-specific; the maxim of quantity, in particular, is alleged not to hold on the island of Madagascar. But, as pointed out by Brown & Levinson (1978: 298–9) and Prince (1982), the Malagasy facts as Keenan presents them are not just *consistent* with the maxim of quantity, they actually *require* this maxim in order to be understood. What Keenan does show is that the maxim of quantity may be overruled by some other conversational or nonconversational[17] principle, depending on the values assigned by the context for such variables as the importance of the information sought, the availability of that information outside the contribution of the responder, the avoidance of *tsiny* (a form of culture-specific guilt), and the sex and status of the speaker. The point is that in just those circumstances where the maxim of quantity does operate, the assumption that it does is necessary and sufficient to predict the nonlogical inferences that seem to be drawn. This is exactly as we should expect. (Cf. Prince for a description of the unlikely sorts of possible worlds we must assume in which the CP and maxims were truly irrelevant.)

What of the objection that the set of maxims is both internally redundant and internally inconsistent? The inconsistency is after all to be expected, given the indeterminacy of conversational implicature built into the system. This by no means rules out the possibility of coming up with a more adequate account of just when a given principle will take precedence over which other principle; indeed, as the research of Keenan (1976), and others, suggests, linguistic communities may differ precisely on the specific criteria for relative weighting of the maxims (cf. also Tannen 1975). It should not be surprising if pragmatic competence, like syntactic competence (*à la* Chomsky 1982), thus turns out partially to involve knowing how to set the parameters of variation: the principles set out by Grice and others might well be universal, but their relative strength in a given context might well vary across languages and cultures. (This perspective is inconsistent with the stance of Kempson 1975 and Cresswell 1978 that identifies pragmatics as the performance counterpart of semantic competence, i.e. semantics:pragmatics::competence:performance. See Green & Morgan 1981; Levinson 1983; Harnish & Farmer 1984 for additional problems with this proportion.)

The redundancy of the Gricean schema has provided more problems, or at least more challenges, for subsequent theorists. From the proposal in Harnish (1976) for a combined maxim of quality/quantity to Sperber & Wilson's (1986) attempt to reduce all inference schemata to a suitably elaborated all-encompassing principle of relevance,[18] reductionists have sought to boil down the maxims to a set of those rules which are truly indispensable and which do not constitute submaxims of other members of that set.

---

[17] One source of non-conversational maxims would seem to lie in the area of politeness phenomena (cf. R. Lakoff 1973; Brown & Levinson 1978). It is plausible that politeness maxims, akin to Grice's conversational maxims but often conflicting with them (and with each other), generate inferences which occupy the slot within Grice's overall schema (see Figure 1) for non-conventional but non-conversational implicata. (Another candidate for this slot might be the maxim of self-preservation; the silence of someone actually or metaphorically pleading the Fifth Amendment does not thereby indicate a lack of fuller relevant knowledge on the topic of inquiry.)

[18] For discussion of the principle of relevance, see Kempson, Chapter 8 in Volume II of this series; Carston, Chapter 2 in Volume III; Blakemore, Chapter 13 in Volume IV.

Table 2.

| THE Q PRINCIPLE | THE R PRINCIPLE |
|---|---|
| *Make your contribution sufficient; Say as much as you can* (given R) | *Make your contribution necessary; Say no more than you must* (given Q) |
| Lower-bounding principle, inducing upper-bounding implicata | Upper-bounding principle, inducing lower-bounding implicata |
| Collects Grice's quantity-1 maxim ('Be informative') and the 'Avoid ambiguity' & 'Avoid obscurity' submaxims of manner. | Collects Grice's relation maxim ('Be relevant') quantity-2, and the 'Avoid prolixity' ('Be brief') submaxim of manner. |
| Locus classicus: *scalar implicature* (cf. above) | Locus classicus: *indirect speech acts* |

One current proposal is sketched in Horn 1984b: there are two basic antinomic forces operative in all of language and related information systems, the R principle (a speaker-based economy for the minimization of form, akin to Zipf's (1949) 'principle of least effort') and the Q principle (a hearer-based economy for the maximization of informational content, akin to Grice's (first) maxim of quantity). R is intended to invoke relation, and Q quantity, but the principles themselves, outlined in Table 2, are intended to have far wider scope.

The dialectic tension between these two antinomic forces, and the various resolutions of this tension, motivate a variety of phenomena in pragmatic inferencing, grammatical and lexical structure, and language change ranging from conversational implicature and politeness strategies to the interpretation of pronouns and gaps, from lexical blocking and distributional constraints to indirect speech acts, from case marking to lexical change.

Among the factors influencing the relative power of Q- and R-based inference patterns in a particular case are the availability of a quantitative scale (Horn 1972; Ducrot 1972; Fauconnier 1975; Gazdar 1979) tending to reinforce the former pattern, and the availability of a particular stereotype narrowed or strengthened reading tending to reinforce the latter (cf. Atlas & Levinson 1981; Horn 1984b). To see that these are not the only factors involved, notice that while we tend to take an assertion like *I slept in a car yesterday* as Q-implicating that the car was not mine (if it were, I should have said so), we contrarily take the assertion *I broke a finger yesterday* as R-implicating the (stereotypic) situation in which the finger *was* mine (unless you knew that I was an enforcer for the mob). It seems relevant here that while nothing would have prevented me from using the more informative genitive construction in the former case if I were in an epistemic position to do so, the employment of the *my finger* form in the latter case might suggest wrongly that I have but one finger.

Similar approaches, albeit less reductionist than my dualistic model (which is in turn less reductionist than the monist relevance-driven theory of Sperber & Wilson), have been offered by Atlas & Levinson (1981; cf. Levinson 1983: ch. 3 for a summary); Leech (1983), whose 'principles of clarity and economy' correspond roughly to the Q and R principles respectively, and Levinson (1985, 1986). Whether the pragmatic maxims Grice identified (along with those he did not identify, but implicitly allowed for) can be reduced to the three forces of Levinson's work, the two of mine, or the one of Sperber & Wilson's remains a question for (it is devoutly hoped) further illuminating research.

## 5.5. Pragmatics, grammar, lexicon: frozen effects

Whatever set(s) of maxims may eventually be adopted, a principal focus of linguists' interest in the conversational schema has been, and will continue to be, the interface of pragmatic inference and grammar. One locus of the interaction of pragmatics and grammar is situated not in the syntactic component but in the lexicon. It was argued in Horn (1972: ch. 4) that a systematic series of lexical gaps in the natural language realizations of quantificational, modal, and allied notions can be pegged to the operation of quantity-based implicature. The negative values of the southeast, O, corner of the traditional logical square – *some not* (=*not all*), *possible not*, *not obligatory*, *not always*, *or not* – tend not to become lexicalized in natural language, since they are Q-implicated by the corresponding positive (I-corner) subcontrary – *some*, *possible*, *permitted*, *or*. Assuming that a language in general provides lexicalizations only for expressions which cannot otherwise be simply conveyed, the generalized implicature we discussed in connection with the examples of (10) makes it possible to dispense with lexical equivalents for one of the two subcontraries; given the markedness of negative statements (cf. Givón 1979 and Horn In preparation, for details), it is predictably the negative values which are blocked from lexicalizing. (Since the strong negative E values are not inferrable by generalized conversational implicature, nothing prevents them from lexicalizing, as in e.g. *none*, *nobody*, *impossible*, *forbidden*, *never*, *neither . . . nor*.)

Another set of pragmatically motivated lexical constraints has been discussed in McCawley (1978), Horn (1978a), Kempson (1980), and Horn (1984a, b): the existence or denotative range of a given lexical item or expression may be constrained by the availability of a simpler, more informative alternative item. Thus, for example, the range of application of *cause to die* may be pragmatically restricted by the existence of a simple lexical item *kill* which applies to a subset of situations to which *cause to die* is in principle applicable; similarly for *pink* in relation to *pale red*. Given the principle variously formulated as the 'law of differentiation' (Bréal 1900) and the 'avoid synonymy principle' (Kiparsky 1983), which can in turn be viewed as the lexical analog of the even more general (and more ancient, by two millennia) 'elsewhere condition,' the appropriate use of the less lexicalized expression tends to be barred from the specific niche of the wider meaning which has been carved out by the more lexicalized alternative. In Horn (1984b), these examples and others are taken to exemplify a 'division of pragmatic labor' resulting from the dialectic of R-based and Q-based inference patterns.

By the same token, we can account pragmatically for the fact that while thumbs are fingers and squares rectangles, we tend not to report an abrasion of the thumb as a bruised finger, or describe an equilateral four-sided figure as a rectangle. This represents a straightforward working out of Q-based implicature: if you knew that it was a thumb (square), and this information was relevant, it would have been misleading to describe it as a finger (rectangle); your choice of the less informative item licenses the (pragmatic) inference that the more informative, denotatively narrower, item does not apply.

But in the lexical domains, as in the syntactic, it must be recognized that a pragmatically motivated explicans may not tell the whole story about the explicandum. Grice himself acknowledges (1975: 58) the nondiscrete nature of the natural/conventional boundary in the realm of implicature: 'It may not be impossible for what starts life, so to speak, as a conversational implicature to become conventionalized.' Grice goes on to point out that 'to suppose that this is so in a given case would require special justification.' Much recent work in the semantics/pragmatics border country has been devoted precisely to providing such justification. One relatively detailed example may be in order here to demonstrate the point.

One phenomenon that would seem eminently deserving of a pragmatically oriented account is the restriction on subjects in imperative sentences to 2nd person. The behavior of tags, reflexives, possessives with *own*, and fixed constructions (*crane one's neck*, *nod one's head*) provided the motivation for one of the classic results in early transformational grammar: to capture the generalization governing the distribution of these items in both declarative and imperative sentences, we need to assume that imperative sentences are generated in deep structure with a 2nd person subject and that this subject is (optionally) deleted after determining the acceptability (or unacceptability) of the various constructions involved. Thus, sentences (13)–(16), *inter alia*, will be ruled out essentially at the level of deep structure:

(13)   Shave{*myself/*herself}     (√yourself)

(14) *Shave you!                 (√me, √him)
(15) Nod{*my/*her}head           (√your)
(16) Wash{*my/*their}own car     (√your)

While this approach continues to be offered to introductory syntax students (it is reproduced, for example, in such standard texts as Akmajian & Heny 1975), it is not with the same clear conscience as in 1964. For one thing, it strikes us as unsatisfying that it must be *stipulated* that imperative sentences have *you* as underlying subject. Could there in fact be a language just like English except that imperative sentences had *they*, or *syntacticians*, as underlying subject, so that we would get *Shave {themselves/*them/*yourself/you}*, etc.? Given the implausibility of such a situation, it would be desirable to offer a principled account for this restriction.

Within the generative semantics model of the 1960s, it was pointed out (by J. R. Ross, George Lakoff and James McCawley) that with the adoption of the 'performative hypothesis' (Ross 1970), in which illocutionary force is represented directly in the underlying structures of sentences, the restriction on imperative subjects falls out as a subcase of equi (coreferential complement subject deletion): imperative sentences all contain an abstract [I ORDER YOU . . .] clause atop their deep structure, and the 2nd person object of this structure causes the deletion of the subject of the next highest clause (i.e. of the eventual main clause of imperative sentences) just in case it is coreferential to it. Non-2nd person subjects fail to satisfy the coreferentiality condition on equi, and the derivation (of e.g. [I ORDER YOU [I pres shave myself]]) blocks. (13) is thus ruled out for the same reason as *I {ordered/forced} you for me to shave myself*, which has the virtue of reducing two separate stipulations to one.

This approach, unfortunately, can be no more compelling than the performative hypothesis on which it is grounded, and the years have not been kind to that hypothesis, nor indeed to any of its contemporary analogs in which some distributional parallel in surface morpho-syntax was accounted for by making the remote structure of the relevant sentences much more abstract, incorporating whatever seemed necessary to account for the meaning or normal use of the surface sentences displaying the distributional parallel. Notice that the derivation of imperative sentences from structures incorporating an abstract performative clause which never surfaces directly (here, [I ORDER YOU]) requires an obligatory deletion rule to remove that clause; difficulties with this assumption, and a wide range of both empirical and conceptual problems, have doomed the performative hypothesis (cf. Anderson 1971; Fraser 1971; Boër & Lycan 1976; Gazdar 1979: ch. 2; Levinson 1983: ch. 5).[19]

---

[19] For discussion of the performative hypothesis, see Sadock, Chapter 10 in Volume II of this series.

On the standard theory approach, it is an accident that English imperative sentences have 2nd person subjects in their deep syntactic structure. On the generative semantics approach, it is an accident that imperative sentences have 2nd person *objects* in the abstract highest clause of their deep syntactico –semantic structure. Obviously, neither solution is ideal. The way is thus open for a *non*syntactic account which exploits the undeniable *pragmatic* fact that any appropriately uttered imperative sentence is directed at the addressee, who is thereby asked to perform some action (of which he or she is the intended agent and hence the active subject); cf. e.g. Searle (1969) for an account of this fact within speech act theory. In fact, Harnish & Farmer (1984: 264–7) have recently offered just such a theory of the imperative subject restriction, designed to disburden the syntactic component (and indeed the grammar *per se*) of the responsibility of ruling out sentences like (13)–(16).

If such an account, exploiting natural, independently motivated pragmatic principles governing the use of imperative sentences, semantic principles governing the distribution of reflexives and related structures, and lexical 'facts' defining the literal use of pronouns, could be made to work successfully, we will have succeeded in ruling out (13)–(16) as *pragmatically* ill-formed, without complicating the grammar with an *ad hoc* stipulation that only sentences with a specified kind of subject (*you*) can under certain conditions delete that subject – and, even more crucially, without weakening the *theory* of grammar by allowing such stipulations.

Unfortunately, however, Harnish & Farmer's account – and indeed any such pragmatically grounded approach – is fatally flawed, and it is instructive to see why. The 'strong modular' view, on which the ill-formedness of (13)–(16) is *purely* a matter of pragmatics (although resulting from the interaction of pragmatic with grammatical principles and rules), is incapable of ruling out these sentences when their subjects happen to refer to the addressee. While it is true that the 2nd person pronoun is conventionally associated with the addressee, this association is not absolute. But if I look at myself in the mirror at 7am and blearily order myself to shave, I can only use the form *Shave yourself!*. Despite the fact that (13) will not be ruled out *pragmatically* in this context, where speaker and hearer happen to coincide in the same individual, I still cannot utter *\*Shave myself!* grammatically. By the same token, if I am exasperated with myself for hesitating when you pop the question, I can mutter to myself *Nod your head, you idiot*, but hardly *\*Nod my head, you/me idiot!*

These facts fall out from the standard theory approach, but not from the model urged by Harnish & Farmer (1984), in which the unacceptability of (13)–(16) is reduced to a property of the implausibility of a situation in which a 1st (or 3rd) person object can co-refer with the addressee.

(Similarly, it might be noted that not *every* sentence with imperative syntax is used only for actual requests or orders. A razor-blade manufacturer sponsoring 'Miami Vice' might well shout at the Don Johnson character *Shave yourself!* (*himself*) without it being the case that the (unexpressed) subject of the imperative refers in any direct sense to a possible addressee or hearer.)

Evidently, an additional constraint is required to assure that the agent in an imperative sentence, whether or not it is overtly represented, must somehow not just denote the addressee, but count as 2nd person; this stipulation, however, involves abandoning the strong modularity claim motivating Harnish & Farmer's position. What we seem to need is a version of the facts on which the restriction of imperatives to 2nd person subjects is pragmatically motivated, through the principles invoked by Searle and by Harnish & Farmer, but has become fossilized or conventionalized as a fact about the grammar of English (see also Leech 1983: 25).

While this result forces a weakening of the theory, it turns out to epitomize a widely repeated pattern emerging from research into the pragmatics–grammar interface: almost invariably, some phenomenon which is pragmatic in origin – grounded in principles from the realms of functional sentence perspective, linguistic processing, speech act theory, and/or conversational pragmatics, as the case may be – is ultimately conventionalized, grammaticized, frozen, or fossilized (according to one's terminological preference) and must be dealt with *per se* in the syntax or lexicon of the language. A pragmatic theory may *motivate* and *explain* (or contribute to explaining) a syntactic fact, but it does not obviate the incorporation of that fact within the grammar. (Grice saves, but there's no free lunch.)

Grammars and lexicons are rife with instances in which a pragmatogenic process has become partially conventionalized. One area which has come under recent investigation in these terms is anaphora (cf. Chomsky 1982; Horn 1984b; Kempson 1984; Levinson 1986). The need to acknowledge an irreducibly formal, grammaticized stratum for functionally motivated constraints and rules (contra the approach of Givón 1979a and other practitioners of what we might call, after Lightfoot 1979, the 'California School') has been stressed by Kuno (1976), Horn (1986), and especially Newmeyer (1983). And Sadock (1984) scores some telling points against the practitioners of the so-called 'radical pragmatics' line (cf. Cole 1981), prominent among whom is one J. Sadock!

## 5.6. Indirect speech acts and the inferential short-circuit

A related issue emerges from the consideration of indirect speech acts (cf. Sadock 1971, 1972, 1974; the entries in Cole & Morgan 1975; Morgan 1978;

van der Auwera 1980). While we cannot discuss indirect (or direct) speech acts in detail (and needn't, given Jerry Sadock's contribution to this *Survey*), one question is worth addressing here: how can we explain the fact that apparently synonymous expressions can differ in their illocutionary act potential and associated morphosyntactic and phonological correlates? For example, the request in (17) can be, and standardly is, indirectly conveyed by asking the question in (18a), but not (at least not without several additional degrees of indirectness) by asking the questions in (18b, c):

(17) Close the window
(18) a. Can you close the window?
    b. Are you able to close the window?
    c. Do you have the ability to close the window?

If, as the Gricean line on indirect speech acts spelled out by Searle (1975) posits, (18a) conversationally (R-)implicates (17) (requesting, like other speech acts, can be indirectly performed by questioning the satisfaction of a hearer-based preparatory condition), this implicature should be non-detachable; its disappearance when we move from (18a) to the essentially synonymous (18b, c) is thus a mystery. It is just this mystery which prompted Sadock (1972) to reject the pure conversationalist line on indirect speech acts (as embodied in, for example, Gordon & Lakoff 1971) in favor of a theory which posits a semantic ambiguity for (18a), with the request reading constituting a *speech act idiom*.

But Searle (1975: 76) rejects this approach on descriptive and metatheoretical grounds, observing that 'there can be conventions of usage which are not meaning conventions,' and that by these conventions 'certain forms will tend to become conversationally established as the standard idiomatic forms for indirect speech acts,' e.g. (18a) but not (18b, c) for indirect requests. Extending this notion, Morgan (1978) motivates the concept of the *short-circuited (conversational) implicature* (SCI) for such cases as that in (18a), where the implicature is in principle *calculable* (as are all conversational implicata by definition) but is not in practice actually *calculated* by participants familiar with the relevant convention of usage. The key linguistic correlate of the request SCI is the possibility of inserting preverbal *please* ({*Can you*/\**Are you able to*} *please close the window?*), a morpheme whose distribution can now be tied to a conventionally signalled request, whether the relevant convention is one of meaning, as in (17), or of usage, as in (18a).

While a pragmatic (usage) convention in this sense is conceptually distinct from a conventional implicature – which can never be calculated – Morgan cites a plethora of instances showing that SCIs constitute halfway houses on the road to conventionalization, including *Goodbye* (from *God be with you*, where the conventionalization had become complete the first time an atheist could utter the valedictory sincerely) and *Go to the bathroom* (whose shift in literal meaning is attested by the possibility of a dog doing so on the living room rug). Crucially, then, SCIs undergo further conventionalization or fossilization – from usage convention to meaning convention, metaphor to idiom, rhetoric to grammar.

Since the short-circuiting of implicata is itself a matter of convention, we can expect to find crosslinguistic (and cross-idiolectal) differences as to just which conventions of usage are operative. And indeed, the standard use of *Would you . . .* and *Can you . . .* questions to convey orders and requests is subject to a wide range of variation across languages, as Searle (1975: 76) and Green (1975) amply demonstrate. But the most indirect requests, e.g. *It's freezing in here* as a hint to close the window, do not exhibit the same variation, as Green observes; this is precisely to be expected if hints involve *non*-short-circuited, and hence non-detachable, implicata: only the literal meaning and extralinguistic context can be relevant for determining what is hinted, not the choice of expression used to express that meaning.

It is argued in Horn (1978b) that the so-called 'neg-raising' phenomenon (the lower-clause understanding of higher-clause negation in contexts like *I don't think he'll come, He doesn't want to come*) must be analyzed synchronically in English as an instance in which a fundamentally pragmatic or functional process has become conventionalized. But this case can in fact be subsumed under the SCI category, as noted in Horn & Bayer (1984) as in the case of the *Can you . . .* questions conventionally used for indirect requests, the higher-neg version is semantically unambiguous but is conventionally strengthened, via an essentially euphemistic R-based inferencing process, to convey the stronger proposition roughly equivalent to the literal meaning of the corresponding lower-neg sentence, e.g. *I think he won't come, He wants not to come*).[20]

The extension of the distribution of strict negative polarity items like *until* and *in weeks* from environments containing a tautoclausal negation to those in which a so-called neg-raising predicate intervenes between trigger and polarity item (cf. Horn 1978b) correlates directly with the presence of the SCI associated with such a predicate, in the same way that preverbal *please* extends from direct to short-circuited indirect requests. Given that all English

[20] A related instance of conventionalization of R-based implicata is discussed in Horn (1972), although not under that rubric. If I say that Ralph was *tall enough to play basketball*, I may (depending on the context) R-implicate that he did in fact play; if I say he was *clever enough to have written that letter*, the parallel implicature is short-circuited. Finally, if I say he was *kind enough to invite me to his party*, the conventionalization is complete; here (as in the request *Please be kind enough to open the window*) the *X enough to* formation is – as with *manage to*, discussed above – effectively *transparent* to content (what is said). *Be kind enough to* serves merely to adverbialize the real content expressed in the sentence (*Ralph invited me to his party, Please open the window*), which is now entailed rather than merely implicated.

speakers conventionally use *think* and *suppose* so as to transmit their negation downstairs, while only some speakers operate with the analogous convention for *guess*, and none do for *hope*,[21] the distribution of polarity items follows accordingly:

(19) I don't{think/%guess/*hope}he'll arrive until Sunday

Whether a given predicate will be transparent to negation thus depends on the availability of an SCI; the acceptability of the polarity item in contexts like (19) depends in turn on this transparency. While conversational implicature is essentially (for Grice and subsequent pragmaticists) a matter of *parole*, the short-circuiting of implicature into a usage convention takes place, as it were, on the boundary between *parole* and *langue*; it is this feature which enables SCIs to trigger various linguistic correlates, including preverbal *please* in conventionally signalled indirect requests, and polarity *until* in the so-called neg-raising environment of (19).

Further evidence is provided in Horn & Bayer (1984) and Horn (in preparation) for the conclusion that the determination of the acceptability of a given item regularly involves whether a given expression not only can be but *is conventionally* used to convey something not literally expressed. Searle's non-meaning conventions, Morgan's short-circuited implicatures, or some more precise and explanatory refinements of these notions, may well play an increasingly central role not only for neg-raising and (other) indirect speech acts, but wherever we find pragmatically or functionally based phenomena which are less than fully productive and regular across a given syntactic construction type or semantic class. (Other instances illustrating the stages by which 'what starts life as a conversational implicature' becomes conventionalized – cf. Grice 1975: 58, cited above – are discussed insightfully by Cole 1975; Schmerling 1975; Sadock 1984.)

While an appreciation of the proper role of pragmatics has turned out to be crucial for philosophical, sociolinguistic, psycholinguistic, ethnographic, and AI-oriented approaches to meaning and use, it is not clear that the same notion of pragmatics is involved in these different endeavors. For linguists, the inspection and ordering of the contents of the pragmatic wastebasket has already provided considerable insight and simplification *en route* to the construction of a modular theory of language, and promises to contribute further to our understanding as we develop more tools for the formalization of linguistic pragmatics. Whatever the resolution of the semantics/pragmatics and natural/conventional border wars and of the debates over the proper

---

[21] German *hoffen* and other Germanic cognates of *hope* do allow a lower-clause understanding for negation; the well-known crosslinguistic and idiolectal variation in the raisability of negs (cf. Horn 1978 for discussion) is naturally accounted for if neg-raising involves the presence of an operating convention, whether semantic or (as assumed here) pragmatic.

schema for the representation of implicature and presupposition, it is clear that we have come a long way since the days when pragmatics were busybodies, and Milton could proclaim in his defense of divorce (as we may occasionally still wish to do in other connections), 'These matters are not for pragmatics . . . to babble in' (Milton 1645: 369).

## REFERENCES

Akmajian, A. & Heny, F. 1975. *Introduction to the principles of transformational syntax.* Cambridge, MA: MIT Press.

Anderson, S. 1971. On the linguistic status of the performative/constative distinction. Distributed by IULC.

Atlas, J. & Levinson, S. 1981. *It*-clefts, informativeness, and logical form. In Cole (1981).

Austin, J. L. 1962. *How to do things with words.* New York: Oxford University Press.

Auwera, J. van der 1980. Indirect speech acts revisited. Distributed by IULC.

Bach, K. & Harnish, R. 1979. *Linguistic communication and speech acts.* Cambridge, MA: MIT Press.

Bar-Hillel, Y. 1954. Indexical expressions. Reprinted in Y. Bar-Hillel *Aspects of language.* Jerusalem: Magnes (1970).

Bar-Hillel, Y. 1971. Out of the pragmatic wastebasket. *Linguistic Inquiry* 2: 401–7.

Bar-Lev, Z. & Palacas, A. 1980. Semantic command over pragmatic priority. *Lingua* 51: 137–46.

Barrett, R. & Stenner, A. 1971. On the myth of exclusive 'or'. *Mind* 79: 116–21.

Bever, T. G. 1975. Functional explanations require independently motivated functional theories. In Grossman, San & Vance (1975).

Bever, T. G., Katz, J. & Langendoen, D. T. (eds.) 1976. *An integrated theory of linguistic ability.* New York: Crowell.

Boër, S. & Lycan, W. 1976. The myth of semantic presupposition. Distributed by IULC.

Bolinger, D. 1972. *Degree words.* The Hague: Mouton.

Bréal, M. 1900. *Semantics.* Trans. Mrs H. Cust. New York: Henry Holt.

Brown, P. & Levinson, S. 1978. Universals in language usage: politeness phenomena. In E. Goody (ed.) *Questions and politeness.* Cambridge: Cambridge University Press.

Burton-Roberts, N. 1984. Modality and implicature. *Linguistics and Philosophy* 7: 181–206.

Chomsky, N. 1982. *Lectures on government and binding.* 2d edn. Dordrecht: Foris.

Cohen, L. J. 1971. The logical particles of natural language. In Y. Bar-Hillel (ed.) *Pragmatics of natural language.* Dordrecht: Reidel.

Cole, P. 1975. The synchronic and diachronic status of conversational implicature. In Cole & Morgan (1975).

Cole, P. (ed.) 1978. *Syntax and semantics.* Vol. 9: *Pragmatics.* New York: Academic Press.

Cole, P. (ed.) 1981. *Radical pragmatics.* New York: Academic Press.

Cole, P. & Morgan, J. (eds.) 1975. *Syntax and semantics.* Vol. 3: *Speech Acts.* New York: Academic Press.

Cresswell, M. 1978. Semantic competence. In M. Guenther-Reutter & F. Guenther (eds.) *Meaning and translation.* London: Duckworth.

Davidson, D. & Harman, G. (eds.) 1972. *Semantics of natural language.* Cambridge: Cambridge University Press.

Donnellan, K. 1966. Reference and definite descriptions. *Philosophical Review* 75: 281–304. Reprinted in Steinberg & Jakobovits (1971).

Donnellan, K. 1978. Speaker reference, descriptions, and anaphora. In Cole (1978).

Ducrot, O. 1972. *Dire et ne pas dire.* Paris: Hermann.

Ducrot, O. 1973. *La preuve et le dire.* Paris: Maison Mame.

Enç, M. 1981. Tense without scope: an analysis of nouns as indexicals. Doctoral dissertation, University of Wisconsin.

Fauconnier, G. 1975. Pragmatic scales and logical structures. *Linguistic Inquiry* 6: 353–75.

Fillmore, C. 1975. Santa Cruz lectures on deixis. Distributed by IULC.

Firbas, J. 1964. On defining the theme in functional sentence perspective. In *Travaux Linguistiques de Prague* 1. University of Alabama Press.

Fodor, J. A. 1982. *The modularity of mind.* Cambridge, MA: MIT Press.

Fodor, J. D. 1979. In defense of the truth-value gap. In Oh & Dinneen (1981).

Fraser, B. 1971. An examination of the performative hypothesis. Distributed by IULC.

Frege, G. 1892. On sense and reference. Reprinted in P. T. Geach & M. Black (eds.) *Translations from the philosophical writings of Gottlob Frege.* Oxford: Blackwell.

Gazdar, G. 1977. Univocal *or.* In S. Fox *et al.* (eds.) *Chicago Linguistic Society book of squibs.*

Gazdar, G. 1979. *Pragmatics: implicature, presupposition and logical form.* New York: Academic Press.

Gazdar, G. & Rogers, A. 1978. Conventional implicature: a critical problem. University of Texas. ms.

Givón, T. 1979a. *On understanding grammar.* New York: Academic Press.

Givón, T. (ed.) 1979b. *Syntax and semantics.* Vol. 12: *Discourse and syntax.* New York: Academic Press.

Gordon, D. & Lakoff, G. 1971. Conversational Postulates. In *CLS* 7. Reprinted in Cole & Morgan (1975).

Green, G. 1975. How to get people to do things with words: the whimperative question. In Cole & Morgan (1975).

Green, G. & Morgan, J. 1981. Pragmatics, grammar, and discourse. In Cole (1981).

Grice, H. P. 1961. The causal theory of perception. *Proceedings of the Aristotelian Society,* supp. vol. 35: 121–52.

Grice, H. P. 1967. Logic and conversation. Unpublished ms. (William James lectures at Harvard).

Grice, H. P. 1975. Logic and conversation. In Cole & Morgan (1975) (Lecture 2 of Grice 1967).

Grice, H. P. 1978. Further notes on logic and conversation. In Cole (1978) (Lecture 3 of Grice 1967).

Grossman, R., San, L. & Vance, T. (eds.) 1975. *Functionalism: papers from the parasession on functionalism.* Chicago: Chicago Linguistic Society.

Grosu, A. 1972. The strategic content of island constraints. *Ohio State University Working Papers in Linguistics* 13.

Grosu, A. 1981. *Approaches to island phenomena.* Amsterdam: North-Holland.

Gundel, J. 1974. Role of topic and comment in linguistic theory. Distributed by IULC (1977).

Gundel, J. 1985. 'Shared knowledge' and topicality. *Journal of Pragmatics* 9: 83–107.

Halvorsen, P.-K. 1978. The syntax and semantics of cleft constructions. *Texas Linguistic Forum* 11.

Hamilton, Sir W. 1860. *Lectures on logic.* Edinburgh: Blackwood & Sons.

Harnish, R. 1976. Logical form and implicature. In Bever, Katz & Langendoen (1976).

Harnish, R. & Farmer, A. 1984. Pragmatics and the modularity of the linguistic system. *Lingua* 63: 255–77.

Hintikka, J. 1960. Aristotle's different possibilities. *Analysis* 3: 18–28.

Hirschberg, J. 1985. A theory of scalar implicature. Doctoral dissertation, University of Pennsylvania. Distributed by Dept. of Computer and Information Science, Moore School of Electrical Engineering.

Horn, L. 1972. On the semantic properties of logical operators in English. Doctoral dissertation, UCLA. Distributed (1976) by IULC.

Horn, L. 1973. Greek Grice: a brief survey of proto-conversational rules in the history of logic. *CLS* 9: 205–14.

Horn, L. 1978a. Lexical incorporation, implicature, and the least effort hypothesis. In *Papers from the parasession on the lexicon.* Chicago: Chicago Linguistic Society.

Horn, L. 1978b. Remarks on neg-raising. In Cole (1978).

Horn, L. 1979. A pragmatic approach to certain ambiguities. *Linguistics and Philosophy* 4: 321–58.

Horn, L. 1984a. Ambiguity, negation, and the London School of Parsimony. *NELS* 14: 108–31.

Horn, L. 1984b. Toward a new taxonomy for pragmatic inference: Q-based and R-based implicature. In Schiffrin (1984).

Horn, L. 1985. Metalinguistic negation and pragmatic ambiguity. *Language* 61: 121–74.

Horn, L. 1986. Presupposition, themes and variations. In A. M. Farley *et al.* (eds.) *Papers from the parasession on pragmatics and grammatical theory*. Chicago: Chicago Linguistic Society.

Horn, L. In preparation. *A natural history of negation*. Chicago: University of Chicago Press.

Horn, L. & Bayer, S. 1984. Short-circuited implicature; a negative contribution. *Linguistics and Philosophy* 7: 397–414.

Jakobson, R. 1957. *Shifters, verbal categories, and the Russian verb*. Cambridge, MA: Harvard University Dept. of Slavic Languages and Literature.

Jespersen, O. 1924. *The philosophy of grammar*. London: Allen & Unwin.

Kaplan, D. 1978. DTHAT. In Cole (1978).

Karttunen, L. 1973. Presuppositions of compound sentences. *Linguistic Inquiry* 4: 169–93.

Karttunen, L. 1974. Presupposition and linguistic context. *Theoretical Linguistics* 1: 181–93.

Karttunen, L. & Peters, S. 1977. Requiem for presupposition. *BLS* 3: 360–71.

Karttunen, L. & Peters, S. 1979. Conventional implicature. In Oh & Dinneen (1979).

Katz, J. J. & Langendoen, D. T. 1976. Pragmatics and presupposition. *Language* 52: 1–17.

Keenan, E. L. 1971. Two kinds of presupposition in natural language. In C. Fillmore & D. T. Langendoen (eds.) *Studies in linguistic semantics*. New York: Holt, Rinehart & Winston.

Keenan, E. O. [=E. Ochs] 1976. The universality of conversational postulates. *Language in Society* 5: 67–80.

Kempson, R. 1975. *Presupposition and the delimitation of semantics*. Cambridge: Cambridge University Press.

Kempson, R. 1979. Presupposition, opacity, and ambiguity. In Oh & Dinneen (1979).

Kempson, R. 1980. Ambiguity and word meaning. In S. Greenbaum, G. Leech & J. Svartvik (eds.) *Studies in English linguistics*. London: Longman.

Kempson, R. 1982. Negation, ambiguity, and the semantics–pragmatics distinction. Paper presented at the Annual Meeting of the Linguistic Society of America, San Diego.

Kempson, R. 1984. Pragmatics, anaphora, and logical form. In Schiffrin (1984).

Kempson, R. & Cormack, A. 1979. Ambiguity and quantification. *Linguistics and Philosophy* 4: 259–309.

Kiparsky, C. & Kiparsky, P. 1970. Fact. In M. Bierwisch & K. Heidolph (eds.) *Progress in linguistics*. The Hague: Mouton. Also in Steinberg & Jakobovits (1971).

Kiparsky, P. 1983. Word-formation and the lexicon. In F. Ingemann (ed.) *Proceedings from the 1982 Mid-America Linguistics Conference*. Lawrence: University of Kansas Dept. of Linguistics.

Kretzmann, N. 1968. *William of Sherwood's treatise on syncategorematic words*. Minneapolis: University of Minnesota Press.

Kripke, S. 1972. Naming and necessity. In Davidson & Harman (1972).

Kripke, S. 1977. Speaker's reference and semantic reference. In *Midwest Studies in Philosophy* II: 255–76.

Kroch, A. 1972. *The semantics of scope in English*. Doctoral dissertation, MIT. Reprinted New York: Garland.

Kuno, S. 1972. Functional sentence perspective. *Linguistic Inquiry* 3: 269–320.

Kuno, S. 1976. Subject, theme, and the speaker's empathy: a reexamination of relativization phenomena. In Li (1976).

Ladd, R. 1980. *The structure of intonational meaning*. Bloomington: Indiana University Press.

Lakoff, R. 1973. The logic of politeness. *CLS* 9: 292–305.

Landman, F. 1981. A note on the projection problem. *Linguistic Inquiry* 12: 467–71.

Langendoen, D. T. & Bever, T. G. 1973. Can a not unhappy person be called a not sad one? In S. Anderson and P. Kiparsky (eds.) *A festschrift for Morris Halle*. New York: Holt, Rinehart & Winston.

Langendoen, D. T. & Savin, H. 1971. The projection problem for presuppositions. In C. Fillmore & D. T. Langendoen (eds.) *Studies in linguistic semantics*. New York: Holt, Rinehart & Winston.

Leech, G. 1983. *Principles of pragmatics*. London: Longman.

Levinson, S. 1983. *Pragmatics*. Cambridge: Cambridge University Press.

Levinson, S. 1985. Minimization and conversational inference. To appear in M. Papi & J. Verschueren (eds.) *Proceedings of the International Pragmatics Conference at Viareggio*.

Levinson, S. 1986. Pragmatics and the grammar of anaphora. University of Cambridge. ms.

Li, C. (ed.) 1976. *Subject and topic.* New York: Academic Press.
Lightfoot, D. 1979. Review of C. Li (ed.) *Mechanisms of syntactic change. Language* 55: 381–95.
Lyons, J. 1977. *Semantics 2*, ch. 15. Cambridge: Cambridge University Press.
McCawley, J. 1978. Conversational implicature and the lexicon. In Cole (1978).
McCawley, J. 1981. *Everything that linguists always wanted to know about logic (but were ashamed to ask).* Chicago: University of Chicago Press.
Martin, J. 1979. Some misconceptions in the critique of semantic presupposition. Distributed by IULC.
Mill, J. S. 1867. *An examination of Sir William Hamilton's philosophy.* 3rd edn. London: Longman.
Milton, J. 1645. Colasterion: a reply to a nameless answer against 'the doctrine and discipline of divorce'. In J. A. St. John (ed.) *The prose works of John Milton.* vol. III. London: H. C. Bohm, 1848.
Montague, R. 1968. Pragmatics. In R. Montague *Formal philosophy: selected papers*, ed. (1974) by R. Thomason. Yale University Press.
Morgan, J. 1969. On the treatment of presupposition in transformational grammar. *CLS* 5: 167–77.
Morgan, J. 1978. Two types of convention in indirect speech acts. In Cole (1978).
Morris, C. W. 1938. *Foundations of the theory of signs.* Chicago: University of Chicago Press.
Newmeyer, F. 1983. *Grammatical theory.* Chicago: University of Chicago Press.
Nunberg, G. 1978. The pragmatics of reference. Doctoral dissertation, CUNY. Distributed by IULC.
Nunberg, G. 1981. Validating pragmatic explanations. In Cole (1981).
Ochs, E. & Schieffelin, B. (eds.) 1979. *Developmental pragmatics.* New York: Academic Press.
Oh, C.-K. & Dinneen, D. (eds.) 1979. *Syntax and Semantics.* Vol. 11: *Presupposition.* New York: Academic Press.
Partee, B. H. 1973. Some structural analogies between tenses and pronouns in English. *Journal of Philosophy* 70: 601–10.
Prince, E. 1981. Toward a taxonomy of given–new information. In Cole (1981).
Prince, E. 1982. Grice and universality: a reappraisal. University of Pennsylvania. ms.
Reinhart, T. 1981. Pragmatics and linguistics: an analysis of sentence topics. *Philosophica* 27: 53–94.
Ross, J. R. 1967. Constraints on variables in syntax. Doctoral dissertation, MIT.
Ross, J. R. 1970. On declarative sentences. In R. Jacobs & P. Rosenbaum (eds.) *Reading in English transformational grammar.* Waltham: Ginn.
Russell, B. 1905. On denoting. *Mind* 14: 479–93.
Sadock, J. 1971. Queclaratives. *CLS* 7: 223–31.
Sadock, J. 1972. Speech act idioms. *CLS* 8: 329–39.
Sadock, J. 1974. *Toward a linguistic theory of speech acts.* New York: Academic Press.
Sadock, J. 1978. On testing for conversational implicature. In Cole (1978).
Sadock, J. 1984. Whither radical pragmatics? In Schiffrin (1984).
Sag, I. & Prince, E. 1979. Bibliography of works dealing with presupposition. In Oh & Dinneen (1979).
Sapir, E. 1944. Grading: a study in semantics. In *Selected writings*, ed. (1951) by D. Mandelbaum. Berkeley: University of California Press.
Schiffrin, D. (ed.) 1984. *Meaning, form, and use in context: linguistic applications (GURT '84).* Washington: Georgetown University Press.
Schmerling, S. 1975. Asymmetric conjunction and rules of conversation. In Cole & Morgan (1975).
Searle, J. 1969. *Speech acts.* Cambridge: Cambridge University Press.
Searle, J. 1975. Indirect speech acts. In Cole & Morgan (1975).
Soames, S. 1979. A projection problem for speaker presuppositions. *Linguistic Inquiry* 10: 623–66.
Soames, S. 1982. How presuppositions are inherited: a solution to the projection problem. *Linguistic Inquiry* 13: 483–545.
Sperber, D. & Wilson, D. 1986. *Relevance: communication and cognition.* Cambridge, MA: Harvard University Press.
Stalnaker, R. 1972. Pragmatics. In Davidson & Harman (1972).

Stalnaker, R. 1974. Pragmatic presuppositions. In M. Munitz & P. Unger (eds.) *Semantics and philosophy*. New York: NYU Press.

Stalnaker, R. 1978. Assertion. In Cole (1978).

Steinberg, D. & Jakobovits, L. (eds.) 1971. *Semantics: an interdisciplinary reader . . .* Cambridge: Cambridge University Press.

Strawson, P. F. 1950. On referring. *Mind* 59: 320–44.

Strawson, P. F. 1962. *Introduction to logical theory*. London: Methuen.

Tannen, D. 1975. Communication mix and mixup, or how linguistics can ruin a marriage. *San Jose State Occasional Papers in Linguistics*.

Walker, R. 1975. Conversational implicatures. In S. Blackburn (ed.) *Meaning, reference, and necessity*. Cambridge: Cambridge University Press.

Wilson, D. 1975. *Presupposition and non-truth-conditional semantics*. London: Academic Press.

Wilson, D. & Sperber, D. 1979. Ordered entailments: an alternative to presuppositional theories. In Oh & Dinneen (1979).

Ziff, P. 1960. *Semantic analysis*. Ithaca: Cornell University Press.

Zipf, G. K. 1949. *Human behavior and the principle of least effort*. Cambridge, MA: Addison-Wesley.

# 6 Morphological theory*

*Stephen R. Anderson*

## 6.0. Introduction

Morphology is the study of the structure of words, and of the ways in which their structure reflects their relation to other words – both within some larger construction such as a sentence and across the total vocabulary of the language. Traditional grammars saw the study of words and their relations as the context in which most of the problems we now call 'syntax' and 'phonology' arise, and in many ways as the foundation of linguistics.

During the past 125 years or so, a concern for morphology has been particularly characteristic of the 'mature' phase of theoretical currents in the study of language. For example, while the early excitement and sense of revolution associated with neogrammarian work (and historical Indo-European studies, more generally) arose from novel ideas about phonological structure and change, subsequent developments brought attention back to essentially morphological questions in the work of de Saussure, and later Hjelmslev, Kuryłowicz, and Benveniste; and it is arguable that the most active continuation of that paradigm (in the work of Calvert Watkins, Warren Cowgill, and their students) focusses most clearly on morphology.

Similarly, synchronic structuralist theory (especially in America) began by dropping the question of word structure – indeed, denying that there was anything of interest to study there – and concentrating on phonology to the exclusion of all else. Later, though, when the basic results of phonemic phonology were considered to have been achieved, the methods developed there were applied to the study of morphology, and morphological issues gradually assumed a more and more central position in later structuralist discussion (in America, in the work of Harris, Hockett, Nida and others),

Perhaps the (re)discovery that problems of word structure have a character and interest of their own is a sign of the maturity of an approach to language (or perhaps a sign of its senescence!), but in any event the same development can be traced in the relatively short history of generative

* This work was supported in part by grant #BNS-84-18277 from the National Science Foundation.

linguistics since the 1950s. The remainder of this section sketches this history, and notes some of the motivations for the emerging recognition starting in the mid 1970s of morphology as an irreducible subpart of linguistics. Subsequent sections will first develop the foundational problems of what sort of structure words should be assumed to have, and then focus on the relation of morphology to the various components of a grammar in turn: the syntax, the phonology, and the lexicon.

### 6.0.1. Some history

In American structuralist terms, the enterprise of morphology can be divided into the study of *morphotactics* (the arrangement of morphological elements into larger structures) and *allomorphy* (variations in the shape of the 'same' unit). Early generative views, typified by Chomsky (1957) or Lees (1960), assigned the arrangement of all items into larger constructions to the syntax, whether the structures involved were above or below the level of the word – which effectively eliminated the independent study of morphotactics. The program of classical generative phonology, on the other hand, as summed up in Chomsky & Halle (1968), was to reduce all variation in shape of unitary linguistic elements to a common base form as this might be affected by a set of phonological rules – which effectively reduced the study of allomorphy to the listing of arbitrary suppletions. With nothing of substance left to do in morphology, generative linguists had to be either phonologists or syntacticians.

By the early 1970s, however, both of these reductive attacks on morphology were losing ground. The reaction to the program of generative semantics, on which even submorphemic semantic constituents were organized into larger structures by syntactic operations, was largely focussed on the 'lexicalist hypothesis,' according to which, words were to be treated as minimal, indivisible entities from the point of view of the syntax. The seminal work in establishing the importance of this claim was Chomsky (1970), though the actual assertion of that work was considerably more modest. The lexicalist hypothesis brought with it the realization that if the syntax cannot combine morphemes into words, some other, independent mechanism must be available to do so. This re-establishment of the charter of the field of morphology was taken up in Halle (1973), the first work to establish the outlines of a generative approach to morphology as a distinct discipline, and in Jackendoff (1975), where the relation between the lexicon and the syntax was made explicit.

## .0.2. Why have a (distinct) morphology?

As this area of investigation developed, it became clear that the principles governing the internal structure of words are quite different from those determining the internal structure of phrases. This can often be seen on a language-particular basis, in languages where rigid principles of sentential structure are systematically contradicted by the organization of superficially similar elements within the word. An example of this is provided by the Wakashan language Kʷakʷʼʷala. In this language, strict principles govern most aspects of intrasentential constituent ordering (see Anderson 1984a for details and discussion). Syntactically represented NP objects of verbs, for example, always follow both the verb and its subject NP. Word-internally, however, one portion of a word may correspond to a 'verb' and another portion to the 'object' of that 'verb.' In a sentence such as (1), the apparently 'verbal' element (necessarily) follows its apparent 'object,' which in turn (necessarily) precedes the subject NP:

(1)  ina-gil-ida      ts'idaq
     oil-make-DEM    women
     'The women are making (fish) oil'

The point is that in Kʷakʷʼʷala there is a richly detailed set of principles governing the internal structure of words, as well as an equally detailed set of principles governing the structure of phrases, and the two sets are quite distinct. It follows that in this language, at least, morphotactics cannot be reduced to syntax. Such a language would also appear to pose problems for the program of autolexical syntax (for which see Sadock 1985), where syntactic and morphological structure are imposed as two parallel but independent organizations of the same surface material. On that theory, the syntax does not respect (or even know about) the boundaries of words; but in Kʷakʷʼʷala at least, it is clear that the syntax must organize exactly the independent words of the language into phrases, with a quite different system being responsible for the internal structure of words.

The same conclusion can also be argued more generally (Wasow 1977). Taking up the position of Chomsky (1970) and Jackendoff (1975) that rules distinct from those of the syntax operate in the lexicon to describe words, Wasow examined the properties of these lexical rules. Incorporating the collateral comments of Anderson (1977a), there seem to be at least the following differences between syntactic and lexical rules:

(i) Lexical rules, but not syntactic rules, are necessarily 'structure preserving' (in roughly the sense of Emonds 1976), since all lexical items – whether basic or derived by lexical rule – must be inserted into the same set of base structures.

(ii) Lexical rules may relate items from distinct lexical classes (e.g. deriving nouns from verbs), while there is no reason to give syntactic rules the power to change category.

(iii) Lexical rules are *local* in the sense that they can only refer to material within the subcategorization frame of a single item. Syntactic rules, on the other hand, can relate positions not within a single item's subcategorization frame, as for instance in the case of 'subject to subject raising'.

(iv) Lexical rules have access to the thematic relations (θ-roles) associated with particular arguments, while there is no reason to believe a syntactic rule could ever affect, say, exactly *agents* (as opposed to affecting exactly *subjects*).

(v) Lexical rules apply to one another's outputs, but not to the output of syntactic rules.

(vi) Lexical rules can have arbitrary, lexical exceptions, while syntactic rules are structurally general.

Rules for the internal structure of words, thus, are distinct in type (as well as in language-particular content) from rules that organize words into phrases and larger constructions. A similar conclusion can probably be derived from the nature of the structural possibilities we find in the two areas of grammar. Syntactic constructions often involve essentially free recursion both on the left and on the right (as well as center-embedding) within the same language, and thus grammars for the syntactic structure of natural languages must have (at least) the power of context-free phrase structure grammars (Chomsky 1963). Word-internal structure, on the other hand, where it is not strictly finite, is generally recursive in only one direction. In fact, the only known systems that apparently exhibit genuinely free recursion are those in which the addition of suffixes – hence, recursion on the left – is unbounded. This suggests that the set of morphological systems may fall within the (much narrower) class of finite-state languages. The only potential counterexamples to this generalization (cf. e.g. Langendoen 1981; Carden 1983; Culy 1985) come from the domain of compound-formation, and it is precisely such processes whose assignment to the morphology (as opposed to the syntax) is most questionable, as we will argue below on page 187, under the heading 'Compounding'.

Just as the construction of theories based on the lexicalist hypothesis (in various forms) led to the need to treat morphotactics as distinct from syntax, other developments led to the conclusion that allomorphy cannot be reduced to the operation of rules of the phonology. As conditions of the sort introduced in Chomsky & Halle (1968) were studied in more detail, it became apparent that rules governing variation in phonological shape observe somewhat different principles, depending on whether their conditioning factors are morphological or purely phonological in nature. An early study of these differences is Anderson (1975); the subsequent literature has established a number of other differences, though not always with explicit attention to this issue. Among the factors which could be cited are:

(i) Rules which effect a complete and exact *exchange* of two segments in a single environment are apparently always governed by a morphological category, not by purely phonological conditions (Anderson & Browne 1973).

(ii) Variables occurring in rules are interpreted disjunctively if the rule is purely phonological: that is, only the application of the rule corresponding to a maximal interpretation of the variable is admitted. For morphologically conditioned rules, on the other hand, the interpretation of variables is conjunctive: *any* application corresponding to a possible interpretation of the variable is admitted.

(iii) Disjunctive ordering of phonological rules is apparently governed entirely by a formal condition (known usually as the 'elsewhere' condition, following Kiparsky 1973). Disjunctive ordering among morphologically conditioned rules, on the other hand, is governed by related but distinct conditions. Further, disjunction among morphological (but not phonological) rules may under certain conditions be stipulated on a language-particular basis (Anderson 1986b).

We conclude that just as lexical rules obey different conditions from those governing syntactic rules, morphologically conditioned rules governing variation in shape obey different conditions from those governing sound structure alone. As we will see below in section 6.2.2, the theory of 'lexical phonology' is based on an intricate and highly structured interaction of morphological and purely phonological rules of a sort that can only be studied in the context of a distinction between the two types; and current research assumes a distinction between rules of 'phonology' and rules of 'allomorphy' virtually without comment.

Both in syntax and in phonology, then, the development of the field has seen the re-emergence of a distinct concern with issues of word structure: morphotactics in word formation, and allomorphy in the realization of morphological material. If there is thus something to study in morphology after all, an appropriate place to begin is with the foundational issue of the nature and status of 'morphemes'.

## 6.1. **What are words made of?**

Partly for historical reasons, the origins of contemporary thought about word structure are in the position developed by American structuralist morphologists. In the early days of generative phonology and syntax, the assumptions of structuralists about the nature of words and their component parts were not so much attacked as ignored; and when morphology came to be studied again, these basic notions were simply taken over unexamined as defining the subject matter. In fact, however, the structuralist ontology was not just a simple and obvious set of postulates, but rather a carefully constructed theory of word structure, arrived at after a great deal of discussion; and this theory presented notable problems, as recognized explicitly by its developers. We sketch its premises here for this reason, as well as because of the exemplary explicitness of structuralist theorizing about morphology.

### 6.1.1. **Classical morphemes**

The starting point for the structuralist discussion is Bloomfield (1933), whose goal was to provide a firm procedural basis for the analyses linguists arrive at. These procedures were to be based (at least in principle) on a notion of 'contrast' and on the study of the distribution of linguistic elements. In analyzing a language, one was supposed to collect a large corpus of utterances, and then identify the similarities among them, as well as determine which utterances 'contrast' with one another. The fundamental principle of such analysis was that non-identical utterances may still be *partially* similar to one another in form and meaning. The task of linguistic analysis (and of morphology in particular) is thus to characterize these similarities precisely.

The elemental unit of morphological analysis is the *morpheme* – 'a linguistic form which bears no partial phonetic-semantic resemblance to any other form' (Bloomfield 1933: 161). The thrust of this definition is the requirement that phonetic and semantic resemblances be correlated. In other words, it is at the point where further division of the form would destroy the correlation of phonetic with semantic resemblances that the analyst has arrived at its constituent morphemes. A problem which this approach leaves unsolved (but which was noted in the literature of the period) was the status of 'phonesthetic' elements, such as the *gl* sequence in English *glitter, gleam, glow*, etc. Most linguists have resisted calling these elements 'morphemes,' but they certainly meet the criterion of constituting a minimal phonetic-semantic unit within larger forms. Nonetheless, it was (and still is) assumed that the extension of the term 'morpheme' can somehow be appropriately restricted.

151

A postulate of morphological analysis was (and continues to be, for many) that every form is made up entirely of morphemes. In consequence, when we identify a morpheme within (but not coextensive with) some word, it should follow that the residue after extracting this morpheme is another morpheme (or sequence of morphemes). If this residue occurs nowhere else (as for example *huckle*, *boysen*, etc. in the infamous English *-berry* words *huckleberry*, *boysenberry*, etc.) the result is a so-called 'bound morph'.

A morpheme is to be a 'minimal same of form and meaning' – an indivisible stretch of phonetic (or phonological) material with a unitary meaning. While this notion is often identified with that of the Saussurean *sign*, it is in fact a particularly limited view of the sign relation, as compared with that of de Saussure (cf. Anderson 1985). De Saussure himself apparently held that the domain of the sign relation (the minimal scope within which phonological form is consistently associated with its semantic content) was the word or complex form, not the morpheme or simple form; but this subtlety went essentially unnoticed in developing the observation that correlations can exist between parts of a form and parts of its meaning.

Bloomfield's own use of the notion of 'morpheme' assumes a determinate phonological content, so it is actually closer to later use of the term *morph* or *allomorph*, though his actual practice is often at variance with his definitions in allowing diverse phonological content to be ascribed to the same morpheme (in cases like *duke/duchess* for example). A series of subsequent papers (Harris 1942; Hockett 1947; Nida 1948, among others) developed and refined this notion to the form in which it is familiar today. For them, a morpheme was actually an abstraction: a class of 'morpheme alternants' or 'allomorphs,' each with a determinate phonological form, having the same meaning and occurring in complementary (or at least noncontrastive) distribution with one another. Some of these 'morphs' were allowed to be rather abstract objects themselves: phonologically null ('zero morphs'), substituting one content for another ('replacive morphs,' as in *ablaut* phenomena), deleting phonological material (as in Bloomfield's analysis of French adjectives, in which the masculine is derived from the more basic feminine by the addition of a 'subtractive' morph which removes the final consonant), grammatically significant metathesis (re-ordering without change of phonological content), copying phonological material (as in reduplication), etc.

The basic properties of the classical morpheme were the following:

Morphemes are homogeneous and indivisible atomic units of linguistic form.

Words are exhaustively composed of morphemes.

Each morpheme in a given form is phonologically represented by

exactly one morph, and each morph represents exactly one
morpheme.

The morphs themselves are consistently and uniquely (though not
necessarily bi-uniquely) related to surface phonemic form.

The morphemes are arranged into a structure of immediate
constituents, which yields a sort of phrase marker as the analysis of
a word's internal structure.

The morphology, on this account, was a set of statements about how
these abstract elements are distributed with respect to one another and
organized into immediate constituent structures (the morphotactics); and
about how each is realized, in terms of its morphological and/or phonological environment (the statements of allomorphy). Argumentation generally
accepted this picture of the relevant units, and focussed on issues such as
how the statements were to be organized with respect to each other, and
how to define procedures for discovering morphological units. While the
assumptions of structuralists about these latter issues have generally been
disregarded, their underlying ontology was adopted with surprisingly little
discussion in initial generative treatments.

### 6.1.2. Classical problems with morphemes

American structuralist linguists realized that the consensus picture of morphological structure presented in the preceding subsection poses a number
of residual problems.[1] One difficulty, of course, is that the identification of
zero, subtractive, replacive, metathesizing, and other 'ill-behaved' morphs
in a corpus by any sort of mechanical procedure is obviously a 'a difficult
maneuver, however desirable' (Hockett 1947: 323f). An approach to linguistic structure not based on the formulation of discovery procedures does
not encounter the same difficulties, but these entities are still puzzlingly at
variance with the overall notion of what morphemes are like. A variety of
other problems flow from the principles of morphemic structure cited
above, which include:

*Infixes*, as in Latin *rumpō* 'I break,' where the nasal infix interrupts
the continuous substring of the form corresponding to the root
√*rup*; cf. *rūpī* 'I broke'.

*Empty morphs*, or subparts of a form that lack any content
whatsoever, such as the thematic vowels that occur in some (but not

---

[1] Both the overall structuralist account and much of the critical commentary here are insightfully
presented in Matthews (1972).

all) forms of verbs in Romance languages, where all of the categories expressed by the verb are marked by some other part of the form and the theme vowel is simply necessary 'morphological glue'.

*Superfluous morphs*, redundant or even inappropriate as markers of categories expressed by a given form, such as the feminine marker in French adverbs in *-ment* (e.g. *doucement* 'softly;' cf. *doux* 'soft (adj)').

*Cumulative morphs*, where more than one apparently independent dimension of a paradigm is expressed by a single formative, as when . the *-ō* in Latin *ferō* 'I carry' marks both 1st person singular subject and present tense (cf. *feram* 'I will carry,' etc.).

*Reciprocal conditioning*, as in Icelandic *tek-ur* 'you (sg.) take' vs. *tók-st* 'you (sg.) took,' where each of the two components of the form (the stem and the ending) simultaneously depends both on the tense and on the person and number of the subject.

*Structure without meaningful morphemes*, as in English prefix plus stem combinations like *refer, receive, defer, deceive*, etc. where (as shown in detail by Aronoff 1976) all of the conditions for a formal analysis into morphemes are present, but no sensible meaning can be assigned to the component parts.

*Overlapping or portmanteau morphs*, as in French *du* 'of the (=de+le),' or Breton *e dad* 'his father' vs. *e zad* 'her father' vs. *tad* 'father,' where the portions of the form corresponding to two distinct morphemes exhibit a relation of overlap or inclusion rather than being disjoint.

This is of course a rather heterogeneous collection of problems, but the frequency with which such situations are met with in the languages of the world suggests that the principles underlying the structuralist notion of the morpheme must be at least revised, if not abandoned.

### 6.1.3. Generalizing the phonological structure of the morpheme

A number of the problems cited in the previous subsection revolve around cases in which some apparent 'morpheme' does not correspond to a consistent and continuous substring of the segments making up forms in which it apparently occurs. This is the case, for example, with reduplication (where the content of the same element varies completely or partially from form to form), with infixes (where the infix itself breaks up the string of segments corresponding to whatever other element it is infixed into), and with overlapping or portmanteau morphs. Some cases of superfluous morphs could be analyzed as discontinuous morphs as well: for example, negation in Choctaw verbs is marked by (a) a suffix -*o* at the end of the verb; (b) glottalization of the penultimate vowel; and (c) choice of a special set of pronominal agreement prefixes. If we regard these as independent morphemes, some are clearly superfluous from the point of view of marking negation; but if we regard them as a single combined marker of negation, the resulting morpheme is not a continuous one.

In an important paper for the development of generative morphology (McCarthy 1981), it was suggested that the appropriate way to approach such problems was by revising the fundamental notion of what constitutes a morphological analysis of a form. The classical model sees morphemes as units, composed of phonological material and concatenated to create full forms. McCarthy proposed instead that we should view the morphological and phonological representations of a form as coordinate but independent analyses of it. That is, instead of representing the morphological decomposition of a word by a series of internal boundary elements that delimit its constituent morphemes, we give its phonological material a simultaneous analysis as a collection (possibly, but not necessarily, sequentially ordered) of morphological units. Parallel to the theory of autosegmental phonology, McCarthy suggested that each such morphological unit (represented as a $\mu$ on the morphological tier of the representation) is linked by lines of association to some of the phonological material in the form. In these terms, the classical model of morphological structure corresponds to a strong form of the well-formedness conditions on autosegmental representations (Goldsmith 1979). Assuming all of the morphological elements (the $\mu$'s) appear on the same autosegmental tier, the association of these units with phonological material in a language with only 'classical' morphemes would satisfy the following:

(i) Lines of association do not cross (i.e. no morpheme is interrupted by any part of another).

(ii) Every phonological element is associated with exactly one morphological element (i.e. the form is exhaustively composed of non-overlapping morphemes).

McCarthy's insight was (in essence) that many of the problems confronted by traditional views of the morpheme could be seen as relaxations of these conditions. For example, one of the classic puzzles for morphological analysis is the verbal system of Semitic languages, in which roots apparently consisting only of consonants are 'interdigitated' with patterns consisting only of vowels which mark categories such as tense and aspect, and the whole is related to a canonical syllabic structure which serves (in part) to identify categories such as voice, transitivity and/or causativity, etc. With the exception of a small number of prefixes and suffixes, virtually none of the morphological structure of such forms conforms to the classical picture of continuous, discrete morphemes.

If we view the morphemes making up a Semitic verb as each constituting a distinct representational tier, however, rather than all occurring on the same tier, the nature of the interdigitation of vocalic and consonantal elements no longer violates the requirement that lines of association from elements on one tier (that corresponding to a given morpheme, for example) to another (the phonological representation) must not cross. If we further recognize that the syllabic structure of a form may constitute an aspect (or tier) of its representation that is distinct from the tiers where its actual phonological feature content appears, the association of one morphemic tier (that corresponding to the 'binyan' or derivational category, in traditional terminology) with this syllabic structure while others (the root morpheme tier and the vowel pattern tier) are linked to the segmental material no longer presents a formal problem. The unusual aspect of Semitic structure, then, consists in the fact that (some of) its morphemic elements appear on distinct tiers of representation. From this, together with (a) the independently motivated autosegmental phonological structure of the form; and (b) the well-formedness conditions, the rest of the properties of Semitic verbal inflection can be made to follow.

An influential series of subsequent papers by McCarthy and others (e.g. McCarthy 1982, 1983, 1986; Yip 1982; Archangeli 1983) have pursued the analytic possibilities opened up by this approach to what has come to be known as *non-concatenative* morphology (as opposed to traditional, purely affixational or 'concatenative' morphology). Most of this work has focussed on the analysis of discontinuous elements in morphology, but it has also extended to some other problems as well. A particular area of activity has been the treatment of reduplication.

The problem posed for the traditional view of morphemes by reduplication is simply that the content of reduplicated material is apparently not constant: it is rather a copy of (some portion of) the material to which it is attached. Thus, the reduplicated syllables (in boldface) in the Tagalog verbs *mag**la**lakbay* 'to travel (intensive),' from *maglakbay* 'to travel,' and *pag**bu**buksan* 'to open (intensive),' from *buksan* 'to open' have no actual phonological segments in common, but nonetheless represent the same morphological element: the 'intensive'.

The advantage of an autosegmental approach to describing reduplication is that it admits an association of a particular morphological element μ with only some components of the phonological content of the form. In particular, by analogy with the recognition that Semitic syllabic structure templates may themselves constitute morphological markers (of the binyan of a given verb) in a way that is independent of their featural content, it is possible to propose that it is precisely the segmental (or syllabic) structure of the reduplicated material which is the content of a reduplication morpheme, with the associated phonological feature 'melody' supplied by convention. The Tagalog intensive marker is simply the skeletal pattern 'CV,' added to the stem (after an initial prefix such as *mag-* or *pag-*). The process by which the melodic material of the stem's first consonant and vowel comes to be associated with the C and the V of the affix is not, strictly speaking, a part of the affix itself, which can thus be assigned a constant form. An analysis of reduplication phenomena which derives from McCarthy's is pursued in Marantz (1982), and this sort of account has become more or less standard in current work.

The autosegmental approach to morphology thus revises the traditional view of the phonological structure of the morpheme, allowing morphological elements to be associated with discontinuous parts of a form and/or subparts of the phonological content of individual segments. By interpreting the relation between morphological and phonological content as a matter of associations among the tiers of a complex representation (rather than as the concatenation of phonologically instantiated morphological units), at least some of the morphological problems noted by, for example, Hockett (1947) and Matthews (1972) find a satisfying account.

### 6.1.4. Items vs. processes in morphology

If we generalize the relation between morphemes and their phonological content along the lines of the preceding subsection, do we therefore evade all of the difficulties for the structuralist notion of morpheme noted earlier? Manifestly this approach accommodates infixation and related problems; and by further relaxing the well-formedness conditions we can describe portmanteau morphs (if phonological material is required merely to be linked to 'at least one' μ rather than to 'exactly one') and empty morphs (representing morphologically unlinked phonological material analogous, perhaps, to floating tones in phonology). Other problems, however, do not have obvious solutions along parallel lines.

Consider one of the classic chestnuts of morphological analysis: *ablaut* (vowel change) relations, such as that between English *sit* and *sat* or *mouse* and *mice*, Assuming that the morphological analysis of *sat* involves a morpheme {PAST}, and that *mice* involves {PLURAL}, what is the phonological content of each of these morphemes?

It is possible to construct an autosegmental analysis, in which the small subset of English in which such apophonic relations appear is treated as analogous to e.g. Classical Arabic. On this line, the verb *sit* involves a consonantal root morpheme ($\sqrt{}$s-V-t) which occurs with one of two vocalic patterns (/ɪ/ marking 'present' and /æ/ marking 'past'), while the noun *mouse* contains another consonantal root ($\sqrt{}$m-V-s) that occurs with vocalic patterns /aw/ 'singular' and /aj/ 'plural.'

This analysis is not obviously wrong (in that there is no reason to believe it cannot describe the facts), but it is noteworthy that there does not appear to be any substantive evidence in its favor (as there clearly is, for example, for something like McCarthy's analysis of Arabic and other Semitic languages). Most analysts find it counterintuitive, though that hardly constitutes evidence. If we are required to provide an analysis that consists in enumerating the morphemes that make up a form, however, and associating each of these with determinate phonological content (as on the classical view, augmented by McCarthy's enriched notion of the nature of this correspondence), this or something very like it is what we must come up with (as structuralist morphologists like Bloch, Hockett, and Nida recognized).

Consider another possible account of the relation, however. Suppose that instead of saying, for example, '/æ/ is the realization of {PAST} in *sat*' we say 'the PAST form of *sit* is formed by replacing /ɪ/ with /æ/.' On this description, what represents {PAST} in *sat* is not the segment /æ/ but rather the relation between *sat* and *sit*, expressed as the *process* by which one is formed from the other.

The choice between these two modes of description is a familiar one, raised (in one form) in Hockett (1954). The standard view of morphemes, inherited from structuralism, treats them as (phonologically realized) entities or (lexical) items. The alternative of the preceding paragraph, however, treats morphological material as represented by relations (between word forms) or processes (by which one word form can be constructed from another). How might we decide between these two accounts, other than on the basis of an *a priori* preference or commitment to one over the other (the basis on which the issue is posed in Hockett 1954)?

On grounds of descriptive coverage, it seems clear that the process view is (potentially) less restrictive than the item-based view. This is because the presence of any given formative marking a particular category can always be described as a process that adds the relevant phonological material to a more basic stem in the presence of that category; but the opposite does not hold. Admitting morphological processes of other than this limited sort (simple affixation) thus runs the risk of weakening the theory, and calls for further investigation of the precise formal limits of morphological systems. One response to this might be to impose maximally narrow constraints on the expressive power of the rule formalism, so as to exclude rule types that are not attested in natural languages; but there are other ways to approach these problems as well. See my 'Morphological change' chapter in this volume for further discussion of this issue.

If a morphological process necessarily involves some change in the phonological content of a form other than the addition of some (possibly discontinuous) phonological material, it cannot naturally be reformulated as an item whose positive presence in the form marks the category in question. Another way of posing the theoretical problem is the following: is it possible to reduce all of morphology to affixation (admitting the rich notion of 'affix' that follows from autosegmental accounts of the nature of morphemes)? If not, the item-based theory should probably be rejected.

Phenomena such as *ablaut* in English do not really resolve this issue either way. An affixational analysis is possible; but in the absence of positive evidence it is not obviously correct, and seems (to many, at least) to do violence to the facts. Another area in which traditional views saw an argument for non-affixational morphology was reduplication, but as we have seen above, reduplication is argued in McCarthy (1981) and Marantz (1982) to be fundamentally affixational rather than processual in character, when correctly viewed. We can note that there remain some objections to the claim that a comprehensive affixational account of reduplication in, for example, Tagalog is available (cf. Carrier-Duncan 1984); and also that the reduction of reduplication to affixation is not complete even on the view of, for example, Marantz (1982), since the (non-trivial) mechanism by which melodic content is associated with the skeletal reduplicative affix must still be specified. Nonetheless, reduplication cannot be said clearly to falsify the claim that all morphology is affixation. Among the problems (traditional and otherwise) for an item-based view of morphemes, however, there are others for which an affixational analysis seems unlikely.

Some languages for example exhibit 'subtractive' morphs, or categories which are marked by the *deletion* of phonological material. Although Bloomfield's proposed example of this situation, gender marking in French adjectives, is surely not valid (virtually all analyses of French agree that there is no morphologically determined deletion of final consonants to form the masculine), other cases are known. One such is the formation of imperatives in Danish from the infinitive by the truncation of a final schwa (cf. Anderson 1975 and references cited there). Crucially, Danish imperatives show phonological properties which follow from general rules if the infinitive is taken as the basic form, but which require that the rule marking the imperative consist not in the addition but in the deletion of phonological content. Similarly, there is a class of action nouns in Icelandic which are derived from verbs by deletion of the *-a* of the infinitive (e.g. *hamr* 'hammering,' from *hamra* 'to hammer,' itself from *hamar* '(a) hammer'). A number of clear phonological criteria (e.g. the distribution of vowel length, the failure of *u*-epenthesis in final *-Cr* clusters, the preservation of final post-consonantal *-j*, etc. – cf. Orešnik & Pétursson 1977 and Kiparsky 1984, for details and discussion) show these nouns to be formed by a completely morphological rule whose sole content is the truncation of the final vowel from the base infinitive. Obviously, if the 'content' of a putative morpheme is the loss (rather than the addition) of phonological material, there is no way to parse the surface form of a word containing this category so that some (possibly discontinuous) subpart of its structure constitutes the morph in question.

Similarly, if the content of a proposed morph consists not in some subset of the features of a form, but rather in an aspect of their arrangement, there is no obvious way to provide an affixational analysis for it. This is the case with proposed cases of (morphologically motivated) metathesis. Such rules were discussed in Thompson & Thompson (1969), where a central example was the formation of the 'actual' form of verbs from the 'non-actual' in the Salish language Clallam. The content of the former category (a sort of progressive) is not relevant, but its form is: it is apparently derived for roots of the form **CCV** by interchanging the second consonant with the vowel (cf. *čkʷú-t* 'shoot,' *čúkʷ-t* 'shooting'). As far as the available facts about Clallam morphology and phonology show, the account of this category as derived by a metathesis rule seems correct; but alternatives may exist. The corresponding category in the related language Lummi is shown by Demers (1974) not to be derived by a metathesis rule. Rather, the relevant roots contain two vowels, and stress is assigned to the first of these in the 'actual' forms but to the second in the 'non-actual.' Whichever of the two vowels remains without stress is subsequently deleted by independently needed rules of the phonology. On a corresponding analysis of Clallam, the root for 'shoot' would have the form /čukʷu/, and assignment of stress to either the first (in the 'actual') or the second (in the 'non-actual') would result in the deletion of the other vowel to yield the observed forms.

On present information, it is not clear whether an analysis similar to Demers' account of Lummi could also be sustained (and equally important, motivated) for Clallam. A recent description (Montler 1986) of another Salish language, Saanich, however, makes it clear that in this language a rule of metathesis is indeed responsible for forming the 'actual' of verbs. Montler demonstrates that (a) phonological rules of the sort crucial to Demers' account of Lummi are not motivated in Saanich (and in fact could not apply there); and (b) the roots showing metathesis in Saanich must actually be underlyingly vowel-less. The stressed vowel position which undergoes metathesis with a root consonant is either epenthetic or belongs to an immediately following suffix. The view on which these roots have vowels in both of the relevant positions, and stress falls on one or the other resulting in the loss of the unstressed one, is thus excluded. Independently of the structure of the metathesizing roots, Saanich in fact preserves unstressed vowels (including schwa), rather than deleting them. The metathesis account of the formation of the 'actual' in this language thus seems assured.

If some morphological categories are marked by deletion or re-ordering of phonological material, rather than by its presence, it is surely not possible to reduce all of morphology to affixation except by trivializing the problem, as by treating such elements as phonological zeros with the property of triggering pseudo-phonological rules of deletion or metathesis. Other problems, too, appear for that program. For example, it is by now fairly well established (cf. Anderson & Browne 1973) that morphologically conditioned rules (and only such rules) can effect an exact exchange of two segment types in comparable environments (e.g. making long vowels short and short vowels long without any differentiation of the environments in which the two possibilities occur). Obviously, such a case poses a problem for an affixational analysis, because whatever phonological content is appropriate for such a putative affix in one class of cases will be precisely *in*appropriate for the same affix in the other class. An extension of this line of argument applies in the case of morphological categories marked by a sort of 'chain-shifting' process. Given a category which is marked by (a) voicing or spirantizing a single stop, but (b) degeminating a geminate stop (as in the morphologized residue of formerly phonological consonant gradation in some Uralic languages such as Lappish), there seems to be no consistent phonological content that can be assigned to the hypothesized affix, even on the rather rich notions of what such content can be that are associated with autosegmental views.

If we accept the conclusion that morphology (in the general case) is more adequately represented by relations or processes than by discrete lexical-item affixes, the consequences are far-reaching. Instead of a lexicon of affixes, the morphology of a language would then be better seen as a set of rules, each describing some modification of an existing form that would relate it to other forms. If this is the case, some other facts also seem to fall into place. For example, on the view of lexical phonology (cf. 6.2.2 below), the rules of the lexical phonology ought to apply to every lexical item. It appears, however, that affixal material must be specifically prohibited from having a phonological cycle of its own (cf. Kiparsky 1982b), being subject to the lexical rules only in so far as it forms a cyclic domain with some other material. This is exactly what we expect, however, if the lexical rules apply to the *lexicon*, and affixal material appears only by virtue of a modification made by some morphological rule to the shape of a form. Similarly, the notion of a derived environment, important to an understanding of the conditions under which lexical rules may apply, can be unified if we regard both morphological changes (such as the addition of affixal material) and phonological ones as rules modifying the shape of a form.

## 6.1.5. **Word-based vs. morpheme-based morphology**

The notion that morphology is represented by a set of rules rather than by an inventory of items also makes contact with another important foundational issue: the claim of Aronoff (1976) that morphology is based on (whole) words rather than on morphemes as the domain of the sign relation. Aronoff noted that in the general case, it is only at the level of whole words that form is associated with meaning. Another way of putting this is to observe that both the forms and the meanings of words are potentially internally divisible (disregarding the purely phonological division of word forms into segments, features, etc.); but the relation between categories of meaning and aspects of form is often many-to-many rather than one-to-one. This is also the conclusion drawn in Matthews (1972) from the points made above in section 6.1.2. Empty morphs are formatives unassociated with any morphemic content; superfluous morphs are cases where more than one formative is associated with the same category; cumulative and portmanteau morphs involve more than one category associated with the same formative; and reciprocal conditioning and structure without meaningful morphemes are cases in which a (possibly complex) content is irreducibly linked to several distinct and separable formatives within the complex word. In all of these cases, the one-to-one relation between components of meaning and components of form which is essential to the classical morpheme is violated.

Accepting the conclusion that the basic sign is the word, not the morpheme, Aronoff proposes that morphological rules are also relations between these entities. These *word formation rules*, on his view, relate one word to another in terms of some specifiable set of changes in properties. A change in the form of the word (perhaps, but not necessarily, the addition of affixal material) is correlated with some change in the syntax (e.g. a change of word class, or of subcategorization requirements, etc.) and/or some change in the semantics of the word. Since the relation between form and meaning exists only at the level of the word, no difficulty is entailed by cases in which a single word formation rule introduces multiple changes into a form (as in the case of negation in Choctaw noted above).

The notion that it is words (not morphemes) that constitute lexical entries makes sense of the fact that it is with words (not morphemes) that idiosyncrasies must be associated. Thus, the English word *appreciable* is a perfectly regular formation from the verb *appreciate* by way of the rule forming adjectives in *-able* from transitive verbs; but the meaning is not the expected one ('capable of being appreciated'), but rather 'substantial, considerable.' One of the most common forms of historical change, in fact, is the accretion of individual, idiosyncratic meaning to particular words, without regard to whether these words are morphologically complex or not.

The claim that words and not morphemes constitute the terms of morphological relations has been rejected by some authors (cf. Bauer 1979; Selkirk 1982; Lieber 1983b; and discussion in Scalise 1984). At least one class of objections to this position can be disposed of fairly directly. If the relevant notion of 'word' for a word-based morphology is in fact an existing surface word, it is not hard to find abundant counterexamples to such a principle. Consider, for example, formation of adjectives from nouns in Latin according to the pattern illustrated by the pair *vir* 'man,' *virīlis* 'manly'. In this case, the suffix meaning roughly 'belonging or pertaining to (noun)' can be added directly to the occurring nominative singular of the noun to form the adjective. But what of other pairs, such as those in (2)?

(2) a. vulgus 'common people'; vulg-āris 'commonplace'
  b. rēx 'king'; rēg-ius 'royal'
  c. mors 'death'; mort-ālis 'mortal'

In these cases the base from which the adjective is derived never shows up as a word by itself: in every occurrence, it is followed by some ending marking case and number. Of course, the correct move here is to say that it is not words but *stems* that function as the base of word formation rules. An appropriately constrained notion of stem, in turn, seems to be 'word minus (productive) inflectional affixation'. If correct, this provides at least the skeleton of an argument to the effect that the class of (possibly complex) forms representing the output of rules of derivation but prior to the operation of productive inflection has a special status in the grammar: essentially, these are the 'lexical items' that are entered in a language's dictionary and thus available to its word formation rules. We will discuss below the implication that inflectional rules are separable from derivation, in that the latter apply to form lexical items while the former apply to convert these into surface inflected words.

With this modification, then, we accept here the proposition that the morphology of a language consists of a set of word formation rules which operate on lexical stems to produce other lexical stems (which, if fully inflected, will be surface words). On this view, the morphological structure of a word is given as a derivation, showing the set of rules by which it is related to other words (and ultimately to a basic lexical entry). Considerations of space preclude a reasoned comparison of this view with the more traditional one (represented in the generative literature by work such as that of Williams 1981; Selkirk 1982; Lieber 1983b, and others) according to which a word's structure is given in the form of a phrase marker indicating constituency relations among its component morphemes. If some aspects of a word's formal structure cannot in principle be represented as concrete morphemes, however, as we have argued above, it is clear that the traditional account cannot be adequate in general.

## 6.2. The organization of morphology

There is a tendency in linguistics, once having identified a category of rules, to assign these to a 'component' of grammars and then to represent the interaction of these components by a block diagram which treats each as an autonomous and insulated part of the grammar, having an internal structure independent of that of other components, and related to other components in a purely external way. It is often at least as important to ask how a given set of rules is related to those of other types, though, as it is to ask how they are separated. In the case of word structure, it is clear that morphological rules have important and intimate relations with virtually every part of the grammar: the phonology, the syntax, the semantics, and certainly with the lexicon. The following subsections explore some of these connections (omitting a discussion of the relation of morphology to semantics with the usual plea that 'too little is known about this area').

It is also important to ask about the degree to which the system of morphological rules displays an internal structure of its own. Traditionally, morphology is divided into three distinct areas: *inflection*, *derivation*, and *compounding*. The nature of this division is fairly clear on intuitive grounds, but has proven frustratingly difficult to define in explicit, formal terms. The discussion of the place of morphological operations with respect to the rest of the grammar helps to clarify this matter of the internal organization of the morphology.

## 6.2.1. Morphology and the syntax[2]

The question of what relation morphology should bear to syntax revolves around the question of the correctness of (some version of) the lexicalist hypothesis, referred to above in 6.0.1. While the original proposal in Chomsky (1970) was limited to the narrow claim that, in English, the 'base rules might be extended to accommodate derived nominals directly,' this was widely interpreted as the proposal that morphologically complex words

---

[2] This section summarizes the discussion in Anderson (1986c), which provides further details of the positions expounded here.

ought in general to be treated syntactically as atoms, and assigned their structure in some other component of the grammar (the lexicon). A concrete formulation of this understanding would be roughly as in (3):

(3) *Lexicalist hypothesis*:
   The syntax neither manipulates nor has access to the internal form of words.

The elegance of this attempt at intercomponential insulation is somewhat marred by the obviousness of the apparent counterexamples to it. While the status of derived categories like the English nominalizations Chomsky was concerned with might be in doubt, other aspects of linguistic structure seem manifestly to be interconnected with the syntax in a way inconsistent with (3). The two most prominent areas of difficulty for this view would seem to be those of clitics and of inflectional morphology.

## Clitics

Clitics form a particularly obvious area in which part of a 'word' is apparently a syntactically functional element. Following the spirit of an extensive series of recent works (most prominently, Zwicky 1977; Klavans 1980, 1985; Kaisse 1985), we can distinguish two broad classes of clitics. A *simple* clitic is an element of some basic word class whose position relative to the rest of its clause is one in which it would (or at least could) be put by the normal rules of the syntax applying to other words of its class. For example, the English auxiliary elements *is* and *has* have a reduced form *'s* which forms part of a 'word' with preceding material:

(4) a. Who's on first? (cf. Who is on first?)
   b. Who's got the ball? (cf. Who has got the ball?)

The position of *'s* in these examples is the same as that of the corresponding unreduced elements, and their behavior is thus accounted for by the same syntactic rules as those applying to non-clitics. Their only peculiarity, indeed, is the fact that they form a phonological unit with their 'host' (in the terminology of Zwicky 1977).

Recent developments in phonology, especially the elaboration of metrical theories of stress, provide us with a fairly direct account of this property of simple clitics. Metrical phonology proposes that segmental structure is not all there is to phonological organization: segments are themselves organized into syllables, which are in turn organized into metrical feet, and (perhaps with still further layers of intermediate organization) these are in turn organized into phonological words and phrases. Some phonological properties (notably stress) are not actually properties of segmental elements at all, but rather aspects of the relation among such metrical constituents. On this basis, we can say that the difference between (simple) clitics and corresponding non-clitic elements is that the former are lexically deficient in prosodic structure. Normal words, that is, have a metrical structure up to the level of the phonological word, but clitics are metrical fragments (segments, possibly syllables or even feet, but not words). As such, they must be incorporated into the metrical structure of an adjoining element, and it is this incorporation that constitutes their cliticization. The (language-particular) rule that performs this function can be called *stray adjunction*, and may be constrained to operate either leftward or rightward (yielding enclitics or proclitics, respectively).

Note, incidentally, that this view does not entail the claim that clitics are never stressed: it has been noted (cf. Klavans 1985) that a clitic may sometimes bear stress, but only as part of a larger constituent within which the language happens to locate stress in such a way as to make it fall on the clitic. What is implied, rather, is the claim that properties like stress (which are logically aspects of the orgnization of the phonological word or phrase) are not *autonomously* assigned within the domain of the clitic.

The lesson presented by simple clitics is not that (3) is too strong, but rather that the notion of 'word' it refers to is not that given by phonological criteria alone. If the massive traditional literature on defining the word yields any conclusion, it is that several distinct sets of criteria (phonological, morphological, syntactic, semantic, etc.) do not converge on the same unit. It would of course be a happier result if the notion of 'word' were a unitary one, but recognition that it is not need not preclude an appeal to particular notions of 'word' in particular areas of the grammar.

More interesting than the simple clitics are the *special* clitics: elements whose position within some larger phrasal unit is specified by principles other than those of the non-clitic syntax. Again following the literature (especially Klavans 1985 and Nevis 1985), the principles governing clitic location can be rather narrowly constrained. Such principles locate a clitic with respect to its position in some constituent that constitutes its domain; and the position in which it is located can be limited to one of the following: (a) initial in the domain; (b) final; (c) 'second-position' (i.e. immediately following the first item of some appropriate type in the domain); (d) penultimate; (e) immediately preceding the head of the domain constituent; or (f) immediately following the head. These possibilities can in turn be reduced to a set of parameters for possible cliticization rules:

(5) a. the *scope* of the clitic (NP, VP, S, etc.);
   b. the *anchor* of the clitic as the beginning, the head, or the end of its domain;
   and

   c. whether the clitic precedes or follows its anchor.

In addition, Klavans (1980) shows that the question of which direction a clitic attaches phonologically (to the left or to the right) is independent of these factors. By a direct extension of the account given above of simple clitics, however, we can say that this last factor is expressed as the direction-ality of the language's (phonological) rule of stray adjunction, and is not *per se* an additional parameter of clitic position.

Of course, narrowing down the principles of special cliticization does not make the problem special clitics pose for the syntax go away. The behavior of simple clitics can be reduced to the interaction of the non-clitic syntax with the phonology; but special clitics demand special rules. Nonetheless, we can assume that the phenomenon can be identified and isolated; and that the problem they pose for (3) is no more serious than that posed by simple clitics. In both cases, the crux of the matter as far as (3) is concerned is the need to distinguish phonological or prosodic words from other kinds. Once this is done, the morphology (as a theory of the structure of lexical or syntactic words) can ignore clitics. We will see below that there is more to say on this matter, but for the present we will simply assume the irrelevance of clitics to (3).

## Inflection

The real problem for (3) is not the existence of clitics (of both the simple and the special sort), but rather that there seem to be some irreducibly morpho-logical properties of words which are not independent of the syntactic structures in which they occur, and which must not be invisible to syntactic rules.[3] Among the kinds of properties which illustrate this problem are the following:

> *Configurational properties* such as (overt) case in nouns, special forms of verbs used exactly in relative clauses, etc., which are assigned on the basis of the larger structure in which the word appears.

> *Agreement properties* which are aspects of a word's form that are determined by reference to the properties of some other word(s) in the same structure

> *Inherent properties* such as gender in nouns which must be accessible to whatever rule assigns agreement properties to other (agreeing) words

---

[3] Of course, one issue that needs to be resolved is just what counts as a 'syntactic' rule, but we take the somewhat rough and ready view here that this is really the same issue as the one of what 'words' are: any rule that applies entirely within a word-level domain is thereby morphological, as opposed to syntactic rules which operate within domains that are necessarily phrasal. In practice, the status of rules on this basis is seldom in doubt.

> *Phrasal properties* which are ascribed to larger, phrasal domains but realized on particular words within those domains. Some of these are responsible for determining the way these domains behave syntactically (as when, e.g. the assignment of tense to a clausal domain causes it to delimit the scope of binding principles), while others represent properties assigned configurationally from outside, as when case is assigned to NP but realized on the last word of the NP.

All of these properties appear to have something in common: they are aspects of 'inflectional' as opposed to 'derivational' morphology. Unfortunately, this observation does not get us any further forward, since there is no satisfactory established basis for this traditional categorization. A number of candidates for such a definition are surveyed in Matthews (1972) and Anderson (1982), and are found to be deficient in one way or another. The conclusion is that the distinction between inflectional and non-inflectional morphology can apparently be made only on theory-internal grounds: inflectional morphology consists exactly of those aspects of word structure that are syntactically relevant, in the sense of being determined by or accessible to essentially syntactic rules. On this view, a theory of 'inflectional morphology' becomes precisely a theory of the qualifications that need to be made to (3).

Merely determining the lexical insertion potential of an item does not make a morphological category syntactically 'relevant' in this sense. Thus, a derivational operation such as the formation of causatives from non-causative verbs certainly is relevant to determining the syntactic environment in which the resulting verb can occur (by virtue of its effect on the subcategorization frame of the item); but the intent of (3) is precisely to make such manipulations of subcategorization frame (as well as lexical category) take place in the lexicon, and therefore not referred to by a rule of the syntax.

An alternative way of conceptualizing the distinction between inflectional and non-inflectional morphology is proposed in Borer (1984), where it is suggested that some morphological formations obey the *projection principle* (and thus are allowed to take place in the syntax, where this principle obtains) while others do not (and are thus blocked from applying in the syntax by this principle). We could thus refer to the former class of morphology as 'inflectional' and the latter as 'derivational'; and the actual basis of the distinction would be quite similar to that proposed above.

This would be an extremely appealing program if it turned out to provide an adequate basis for distinguishing inflection from derivation, since it would make the nature (and indeed the existence) of such a distinction follow entirely from other principles of grammar (namely, the role of the projection principle as a constraint in the syntax). This depends, however, on finding an adequate version of the projection principle. In Borer's formulation, this principle is the requirement that syntactic operations preserve the lexical features of an item, including its subcategorization requirements, semantic properties, etc. Unfortunately, if operations in the syntax are required to preserve the semantics (and arbitrary lexical features) of words, this effectively prevents us from considering as 'inflectional' the marking of words for their inherent (or base-generated) features. That is, *cats* differs from *cat* just as *reread* differs from *read*; and if the latter formation is to be assigned to the lexicon by virtue of its lack of semantic neutrality (as Borer assumes), the former must also. In so far as the category of inflectional morphology seems to have any significance, however, it appears that the productive marking of English nouns for plurality is just as much inflectional as the productive marking of finite verbs for the plurality of their subjects (a property Borer clearly considers inflectional). In the absence of a refinement of the relevant principle, then, the scope of inflectional morphology will be taken to be given by the reference syntactic rules make to morphological properties and *vice versa*, rather than as a theorem within the syntax.

Of course, it remains to be shown that it makes any difference whatsoever how we choose to define inflectional morphology. Just because this is a traditional term hardly means that it is also a significant one which should find a basis in any grammatical theory. Only if it can be shown that the status of a morphological formation as inflectional or not has consequences for its behavior in the grammar will there be any necessity to clarify its boundaries in a principled way. A number of recent proposals about morphological theory, indeed, deny explicitly that there is any significant difference between inflectional and derivational morphology.

The picture of morphological structure presented in Lapointe (1980), for example, assigns the formation of all inflected as well as derived forms to the lexicon. Rather than being handled by a syntactic rule that determines the correct member of an inflectional paradigm, agreement is described by a semantic mechanism that assimilates it to selectional restrictions. Plural (as opposed to singular) verbs, for example, have a semantic representation that results in an incoherent (or inconsistent) interpretation if they are combined in a reading with a singular subject NP.

An immediate objection to such a view is the fact that it requires us to assign to the semantics properties such as arbitrary gender or noun class whose content would appear to be purely grammatical. Additionally, it is not immediately clear how such a treatment of agreement could be extended to accommodate the properties called configurational and phrasal above. More important, however, would be a demonstration that in fact inflection and derivation cannot be described in a completely homogeneous way without loss of generalization.

Another view on which inflection and derivation are assimilated is that of lexical phonology (for which see section 6.2.2 below). Following Lieber (1983b), the lexical phonological literature has generally assumed that both inflection and derivation are 'in the lexicon,' on the basis of the observation that both deploy the same set of formal operations. Both inflection and derivation, that is, can be indicated by prefixes, suffixes, infixes, *ablaut*, etc., and there is apparently no formal operation which is unique to one domain, suggesting that the two belong together in the grammar.

It is surely true that the structural changes performed by word formation rules realizing inflectional and derivational categories constitute a unitary class. This does not at all entail the conclusion, however, that it is unnecessary (or wrong) to distinguish inflection from derivation. Such a conclusion is already suspect in an intellectual atmosphere in which it is assumed that the same basic syntactic operation ('move α') applies in several separate components of the grammar – in the syntax, in logical form, and even in the 'phonology' (broadly enough construed) without compromising the distinctness of these components. But there are more important reasons to believe that such an argument from the similarity of formal operations underestimates the degree of internal structure of the field of morphology.

The issue here hinges on an equivocation which is quite pervasive in the literature about what constitutes a 'morphological operation'. For a morphology based on the morpheme as a minimal sign, a word bears a given signification exactly in so far as it contains the particular (formal) morpheme with that signification. Since the attachment of morphemes is a unitary process, it would follow that a word acquires both its form and its corresponding sense at some single determinate point in the grammar, as many assume. If morphological structure is (potentially) a many-to-many relation between the categories expressed by a word and the formal markers of those categories, however, it is possible that words acquire their significant categories in very different parts of the grammar from the component responsible for assigning them an appropriate surface form. On that view, the interaction of different modules of grammar could well have the consequence that significant differences exist between the domain of inflection, which is *ex hypothesi* syntactically relevant, and that of derivation, which (if (3) is correct) is invisible to and not manipulated by the syntax.

Within lexical phonology, there is already an indication that some further relevant structure remains to be uncovered. In descriptions of particular languages within this framework, individual formal morphological operations are assigned to designated strata or levels of the lexicon (cf. section 6.2.2). Now in fact, in all cases it appears to be true that the class of productive inflectional rules (as opposed to derivation or to unproductive, lexically idiosyncratic markers of inflection) constitute the last (clearly non-phrasal) level of the lexical phonology. If this is indeed a general result, and not simply an accident of the languages described thus far, it ought to follow as a theorem from the organization of grammars, rather than as a stipulation; but if inflection and derivation are assimilated as a single homogeneous class, it is not clear that the apparatus is available to support even a stipulative account of the generalization, let alone an explanatory one. We will argue below, however, that there is a basis for distinguishing inflection from derivation other than that of the formal content of the structural change performed by a word formation rule, such that this result (a version of the familiar observation that inflectional material comes 'outside of' derivational material) follows from the structure of the grammar.

Aside from this consideration, there are other hints that inflection and derivation enjoy different status within the grammar. We have already mentioned, for instance, the fact that a coherent theory of word-based morphology must rest not on surface word forms as the bases of word formation rules, but rather on *stems* – surface words minus their purely inflectional marking. In order for this picture to be principled, it requires the inflectional material which is disregarded to be distinguishable in some way. Other lines of argument tending in the same direction include the following:

(i) Aphasia of the type called *agrammatism* seems to involve (for at least one class of patients) a deficiency in ability to construct and manipulate syntactic structure and inflectional morphology, while the rest of the lexicon (including derivational morphology) remains relatively intact.

(ii) Portmanteau morphs generally involve the conflation of two or more otherwise independent inflectional categories in a single formative. They apparently never involve combinations of derivational material with inflectional. Indeed, cases in which two or more independent derivational categories in a single language are combined in a portmanteau (as opposed to mere internally complex derivational categories) are difficult or impossible to find.

(iii) It is shown in Bat-El (1986) that Modern Hebrew word formation is often based on a process of 'extraction,' in which the consonants in an existing word are abstracted from it and associated with another **CV**-pattern. Interestingly, consonants that are part of derivational material may be extracted along with root consonantism as part of a single pattern; but inflectional material is never extracted.

We conclude, then, that there are some reasons to imagine that inflection and derivation differ in some way in their grammatical status. On the basis of the considerations adduced above, we will take inflection to be that mor-phology which is visible to and/or manipulated by rules of the syntax. We have also already observed that 'morphology' in the relevant sense involves both the assignment of morphological categories and their phonological realization by word formation rules; and this suggests that the complete set of processes relevant to inflection may be distributed across more than one part of the grammar. If we take the set of apparent problems for (3) enumerated at the beginning of this subsection as the content of inflectional morphology, it appears that a theory of inflection actually involves several distinguishable subtheories.

### The theory of morphosyntactic representations

An initial requirement is an account of the informational interface between the rules of the syntax and the rules of inflectional word formation. What, that is, is the formal structure of the representation of a word's inflectional properties which can be constructed, referred to, and manipulated by the syntax, and which controls the relevant word formation rules that effect the formal realization of the categories a word signals? In so far as this question is ever addressed (in the literature on computer parsing of natural language, for example) it is generally assumed that the relevant representation is simply a division of the word into its constituent morphemes, where these are perhaps organized into a labeled constituent structure tree. Taken literally, however, this theory can be seen to be simultaneously too strong and too weak to be adequate.

It is too strong in the sense that an accurate representation of the organization of words into formatives must necessarily contain information which is never *in principle* available to the rules of the syntax. For example, the morphology must obviously specify the linear ordering of formatives with respect to one another, but there is no reason to believe that the syntax can ever be sensitive to (or determine *qua* syntax) whether a given category is represented by a prefix, a suffix, or an infix.[4] Similarly, the same category may be represented by a single formative or by more than one aspect of the structure of the word (recall the Choctaw negative verbs, for example); but there is no reason to believe that such differences are visible to or manipulated by the syntax.

---

[4] This does not deny the claim that, in general, the order of formatives in a complex word will reflect the order of processes in its lexical derivation. Such a relation is referred to as the 'mirror principle' in Baker (1985), and undoubtedly is substantially correct. This result follows directly, however, for lexical processes, since the word formation rules that operate in the lexicon simultaneously effect a syntactic and semantic change, such as the addition or absorption of arguments, change in assignment of θ-roles, etc., and a phonological change such as affixation. The order in which affixes appear will thus reflect the order in which the corresponding changes were made, *ceteris paribus*. There is little or no reason to believe, however, that the same is true for the relation between the ordering of inflectional material and the syntactic processes to which it corresponds (see Durie 1986 for refutation of Baker's most apparently persuasive example, plural 'agreement' in Chamorro). Since if (3) is at all correct, the syntax could at most have access to the final result of all derivation, the correctness of the mirror principle for derivation within the lexicon has no bearing on the present issue.

The view that what the syntax sees and manipulates is an organization of the word into formatives is too weak, on the other hand, because this representation does not bear all of the relevant information. Some necessary information may be carried not by the presence but rather by the *absence* of certain grammatical formatives. A particularly banal case is the fact that in English the singular is indicated by the absence of plural marking; the general point can be supported with more interesting examples. A similar problem is posed by portmanteau morphs: when a single, indivisible formative carries information about two distinct paradigmatic dimensions (indicating '2nd person subject acting on 3rd person object,' for instance), the internal organization of the word does not have enough structure to support the syntactic principles (here, those of agreement with the two arguments). Another problem involves the status of morphological processes which are not affixational in character. In so far as these determinants of a word's form carry information about the category it expresses, there is no obvious way to indicate their presence in such a constituent structure representation (other than by trivializing the notion that it is the word's component formatives that make up this structure).

The *morphosyntactic representation* of a word should thus be formally distinct from its structure as a collection of phonological formatives. What seems to constitute the minimal interface between the syntax and the part of the grammar responsible for realizing inflectional categories is simply an indication of the relevant categories – minimally, in the form of an unordered complex of feature values. This, indeed, was the theory of morphosyntactic representations presented in Chomsky (1965), where they constitute the complex symbols that function as the terminal nodes of phrase markers and are subject to lexical insertion.

Unfortunately, a completely unstructured feature complex cannot serve in general as a word's morphosyntactic representation. This is because in some instances, more than one independent value must be specified for the same inflectional feature on a single word, and the various feature specifications must be kept distinct. In many languages, for instance, a verb can show agreement not only with its subject but also with its object(s); and if the feature of agreement with these various arguments are the same ('person' and 'number,' for example) we must clearly provide a way to distinguish e.g. 'you hit him' from 'he hits you.' If all of the agreement features form elements of an unstructured 'soup,' however, this will not be done.

In several works (including Anderson 1977b, 1982, 1984b), a solution to this problem has been suggested that involves the admission of a minimal internal structure for morphosyntactic representations. This consists in allowing the elements of the morphosyntactic representation to be not only single features but also lists of features (and lists of lists, etc.), so that a given features specification may occur at various levels of hierarchical subordination within the feature complex. Concretely, this allows the features corresponding to (say) the subject and the object of a transitive verb to be distinguished, as in (6):

(6) a. Transitive verb morphosyntactic representation: [Tense, etc., $F_i$, $[F_j]$ ]
   b. Intransitive verb morphosyntactic representation: [Tense, etc., $F_i$]

In (6), $F_i$ stands for the agreement features corresponding to the subject NP, while $F_j$ stands for the features of the object NP. A rule referring to these representations can distinguish subject features from object features by their structural position in the feature complex.

This structure is certainly not the only way to allow for the needed differentiation (for an alternative, see Zwicky 1986a, b), but it seems to be both adequate to the known facts in this area, and minimal in the amount of structure it allows. We can in fact regard this structure as created in only one circumstance, namely by convention:

(7) *Layering principle*:
When a rule assigns features from a paradigmatic dimension $D$ into a morphosyntactic representation $R$ that already contains values from $D$, the result is that the existing values are made hierarchically subordinate to the new values.

If (7) is indeed the only source of hierarchical structure in morphosyntactic representations, it is possible to suggest that the syntax performs only minimal manipulation of these representations:

(8) *Conservation of features*:
The only change a syntactic rule can make in a morphosyntactic representation is to add feature specifications to it.

The extent to which further constraints can be imposed on the access both of the syntax and of the morphology to the content and structure of the morphosyntactic representation remains a topic for further investigation. For example, it is proposed in Anderson (1984b) that the morphology of Georgian contains a rule, responsible for the peculiarities of the 'inversion' construction in this language which rearranges the internal structure of certain morphosyntactic representations. In the analysis ultimately arrived at there, however, the rule in question applies in the lexicon, not in the syntax, and so does not violate (8); and it results in the application of a 'structure-preserving movement rule' in the phonology. This analysis achieves certain advantages over an alternative which treats Georgian inversion as primarily a syntactic, rather than a morphological phenomenon; but it is only possible in the presence of a developed and explicit theory of the nature of morphosyntactic representations.

## The theory of configurational assignment

The next area within the study of inflection is an account of the way in which properties such as (overt) case are assigned to the phrases that bear them. We do not attempt to provide such a theory here in any detail, since this is obviously a part of syntactic theory. It can be observed, however, that the assignment of configurational properties can be divided into two subcases: *structural* assignments and *lexically governed* assignments. The first sort (typified by the assignment of accusative case to direct objects purely on the basis of their structural position in many languages) is evidently the domain of what is called the theory of 'Case' in the syntactic literature, with the proviso that it is overt morphological case that is in question, and not simply the covert property called 'abstract Case'. Indeed, most of the literature on 'abstract Case' is based essentially on the properties of languages like English and French, where morphological case is highly restricted or even entirely absent. This construct may well be motivated for such languages; but when one studies languages with richly developed systems of overt case, it soon becomes clear that much or all of the work done by the abstract notion in a language like English can be formulated in terms of the principles (obviously necessary in any event) which determine overt case. A difference between languages with 'abstract Case' (perhaps augmented by some degenerate overt case distinctions in restricted environments) and languages with genuinely morphological case may well be a parameter of syntactic systems.

The category of lexically governed assignment of configurational properties is typified by languages like Icelandic, where many verbs require a case on their objects (and/or their subjects) which is other than that which would be assigned on structural bases alone. One account of such languages involves rules that actually assign a case feature to NPs on the basis of a reference to the lexical properties of their governing verb. Such a rule would appear to involve a reference to the internal structure of lexical items, however, contrary to the spirit of (3). An alternative is simply to allow for the free generation of case in certain positions, and then allow the verbs in question to subcategorize their arguments for this feature. The question then arises of whether verbs should be allowed to subcategorize their subjects, as this requires; but in fact the same question arises on the other view, where it is necessary to allow verbs to assign case to an NP which appears in subject position (a position not governed by the verb, on most views). We assume that whatever solution is motivated within the one framework can be translated into the other; and thus that a subcategorization account of lexically governed (or 'quirky') case and similar properties is available.

## The theory of agreement

This area is also clearly syntactic in nature, and will not be treated here at length. Again, it is possible to distinguish two sub-cases: the agreement of modifiers with their heads, and the agreement of predicates with their arguments. The former (e.g. agreement of adjectives in gender, number, case, etc. with the N they modify) can be described as a matter of the inheritance by non-head elements within a structure $\overline{X}$ of features assigned to the parent phrasal node. These features may be either ones assigned from the outside (e.g. case is assigned to NPs, from which position it can be transferred to their constituent words), or ones which are projected up from the head X to its phrasal node $\overline{X}$. The study of these projections and inheritances obviously falls within the domain of $\overline{X}$-theory.[5] The most extensive proposals in this domain have come from syntacticians working within the framework of generalized phrase structure grammar (see Gazdar *et al*. 1985).

The agreement of predicates (e.g. verbs) with their arguments (e.g. the subject and object NPs) turns out to have a number of syntactically interesting properties. For example, it appears always to be local, in the sense that the agreeing elements can be found within the same clausal or 'predicational' domain. Apparent counterexamples to this generalization, where the elements are widely separated syntactically, can always be reduced to instances in which a chain of individually local relations (involving the traces of movement, for example, or relations of control, where some or all of the intermediate elements are phonologically null) stand between the two superficially distant elements. Further, as argued by a number of writers, agreement relations involve not simply the registration on the agreeing element of the presence (and features) of what it agrees with, but also the establishment of a relation of co-indexation between the two. As a result of these properties, much if not all of the theory of this kind of agreement actually falls under the syntactic theory of anaphora and binding.

## The theory of phrasal properties

As we noted above, some properties that are assigned to phrases are inherited by (and thus realized on) the constituent words of these phrases (typically, on the head, but sometimes on the last element of the phrase). In other cases, however, a property which is assigned to a phrase is apparently realized not as part of a morphological word within the phrase, but rather in the form of a special clitic whose domain (in the sense of (5) above) is the phrase. For example, the possessive genitive -'s in English clearly represents a property of the entire NP, but it appears as a clitic on the last word of the NP regardless of the word class or syntactic role of this word.

[5] Assuming, as pointed out in Pullum (1985), that we had one.

This suggests that in fact the theory of special clitics (or at least a part of it) is actually a theory of affixes on phrases (as opposed to words). In substantive terms, there is quite a close parallel between the properties of clitics and those of affixes: the kinds of properties affixes and clitics represent (case marking, definiteness, gender, person, and number of arguments, tense, etc.) are all marked by affixes as well. But in fact, the similarity is quite close on formal grounds also.

As argued in Anderson (1986a), the set of parameters governing the placement of affixes by word formation rules is exactly the same as those governing the placement of clitics (e.g. initial clitics correspond to prefixes, second-position clitics to post-initial infixes, etc.). Just as some word formation rules perform non-affixational changes, some 'clitics' consist of non-affixational changes: for instance, the element that indicates a sort of definiteness in Tongan NPs is a shift of stress from penultimate to final vowel mora on the last word of the NP (see Churchward 1953; Poser 1985). This change does not involve the addition of an affix, but rather a change in the form; and like the English genitive, it affects the last word of the NP, regardless of the word class or structural role of this word. In fact, though considerations of space preclude a detailed demonstration of this point, it is probably possible to construct a unified theory of the structural descriptions of word formation rules which applies as well to specify the formal effect of 'cliticization.' This unity, in turn, further undermines the argument from the formal similarity of inflectional and derivational morphology for the absence of a difference between them. In fact, a single set of formal possibilities seems to exist for rules of morphology (broadly construed, to include inflection, derivation, and clitic insertion) which cuts across the different functions served by the relevant rules.

The analogy between clitics and word formation rules can be drawn even more closely if we distinguish two sort of special clitics. One set is analogous to inflectional morphology, and represents the realization of phrasal properties of their domain. This includes auxiliaries and tense markers (whose presence clearly participates in determining the syntactic behavior of phrasal domains for the purposes of, for example, the binding theory); pronominal clitics representing arguments of the verb (in a way analogous to the representation of these same arguments through agreement); and determiners and possessive markers in NPs.

The other set of clitics is analogous, we suggest, to derivational morphology. These are the elements loosely called 'particles' in common usage, which bear concrete semantic content of their own (often, but not always, related to discourse functions). We therefore propose that a grammar contain a set of *phrase formation rules* closely parallel to word formation rules: rules that effect some change in the shape of a phrase (typically, the introduction of affix-like phonological material at some designated position). Some of the phrase formation rules also effect a change in the semantics (and perhaps also the syntax) of their associated phrase: these are the derivational phrase formation rules. Others are responsible for realizing grammatical features assigned to the phrase: these are the inflectional phrase formation rules.

Somewhat remarkably, when languages involve extensive systems of both kinds of clitics at once, the 'inflectional' ones come outside of (i.e. after if enclitic, before if proclitic) the 'derivational' ones – just as inflectional morphology in words is known to appear outside of derivational morphology. For example, in Ngiyambaa, Klavans (1983) argues that 'particle (en)clitics' systematically precede 'pronominal (en)clitics.' Furthermore, in languages where it would be relevant, a sort of cyclic principle governs clitic placement. When the same word can bear clitic elements derived from more than one domain (e.g. a sentence-initial noun can have clitics both from its NP and from the entire S), the clitics associated with the inner domain appear inside those associated with the outer domain. The conclusion which seems to be indicated is that phrasal constituents undergo a set of phrase formation rules analogous to the word formation rules that apply to words, with clitics being the phrasal equivalent of affixes. This is a parallel which has been suggested by various authors (e.g. Klavans 1980), and questioned by others (e.g. Nevis 1985); but the extent of the similarity between the two categories has not been drawn out as far as it can be.

We can note that this view of the realization of phrasal properties also suggests a theory of the syntax of clausal inflection, or INFL. This can be viewed as the set of features assigned to the clause as a whole, including tense, agreement (with various arguments), etc. These properties (like other phrasal properties), instead of forming a syntactically autonomous constituent (as in most current versions of the theory of government and binding), are properties of S constituents which are realized formally by phrase formation rules either assigning them to the verb (as head of the clause) or else to some special clitic position. The famous 'verb-second' phenomenon then results if the features of INFL are assigned to second position, but not to a lexical item. When this happens, the verb (in fact, the only verb not already inflected as a result of the requirements of some auxiliary element) must move to the same position to bear the features of INFL – both so that it can be inflected itself, and so that the features of INFL will not be stranded. A natural extension of this view would be to see VSO languages (in so far as they can be argued to involve some non-initial position of the verb in underlying structure) as exactly parallel, but with INFL realized as an initial special clitic, rather than in second position.

## The phonological realization of morphological properties

The final subpart of a theory of inflection concerns the way in which inflectional material is introduced into words to reflect the featural content of their morphosyntactic representation. Much of the recent literature on the 'extended word and paradigm' theory (see Thomas-Flinders 1981; Anderson 1982, 1986b; and others) addresses this issue specifically. The formal realizations of inflectionally relevant properties arise in two distinguishable ways within the grammar. On the one hand, in so far as the realizations of such properties are idiosyncratic to particular lexical items and not predictable by general rule, they must be present in the lexical representation of the corresponding stem. For instance, it is not possible to predict from the singular *foot* that its plural is *feet*, and so *feet* must appear in the lexicon as the [+PLURAL] member of the paradigm of *foot*. Similarly, *crept* must be listed lexically as the [+PAST] member of the paradigm of *creep*: even though there is probably a rule of English that forms *crept* from *creep*, it is a lexically idiosyncratic rule, since it is not possible to tell from other properties of *creep* that it applies to this word.

A principle of disjunctive ordering governs the choice among such lexically related forms, and also between lexically listed items and others constructed by general rule. Some skepticism has been expressed in the literature about the applicability of such a principle in morphology (Janda & Sandoval 1984), but many of the apparent criticisms raised against it can in fact be answered (Anderson 1986b), and its explanatory value seems significant enough to warrant further pursuit of a fully adequate formulation.

Unpredictable inflected forms are listed in the lexicon, with their stems assigned a partially completed morphosyntactic representation. Predictable forms, in contrast, are built from stems whose morphosyntactic representation is not intrinsically specified for the relevant features by the operation of word formation rules. Inflectional word formation rules operate on a pair $\{S, M\}$ consisting of a stem $S$ chosen from the lexicon (and perhaps already modified by the operation of other word formation rules), and the morphosyntactic representation $M$ of the syntactic position in which the word is inserted. These rules are in principle productive, but again disjunctive ordering may intervene to prevent their application in particular cases, either because of the prior application of more specific inflectional rules, or because the stem is already (lexically) characterized for the features the rule would mark.

The difference between inflectional and derivational word formation rules is now apparent: inflectional rules operate on a pair consisting of a lexical stem and a morphosyntactic representation corresponding to the position of lexical insertion; while derivational rules operate entirely within the lexicon, applying to a lexical item (including not only its stem, but other lexical properties such as its subcategorization frame, semantics, etc.). From this difference, we can derive the important result in (9):

(9) '*Inflection follows derivation*';
Material introduced by inflectional rule (not lexically) on the basis of properties assigned in the syntax to the morphosyntactic representation of the word may presuppose, but is not presupposed by, material that is present in the lexical form.

In other words, all derivational rules precede all (productive) inflectional rules.[6] This result follows from the fact that lexical insertion into a syntactic structure depends on the full range of lexical properties of an item: thus, derivational operations must all be completed prior to lexical insertion. It is only *after* an item undergoes lexical insertion, however, that it is associated with the morphosyntactic representation which is necessary for it to undergo inflectional rules.

Note that non-regular (hence lexical) morphology, on the organization proposed above, ought to behave formally as 'derivational,'[7] corresponding to the observation in lexical phonology that unproductive inflection typically occurs at deeper levels of the lexicon than productive inflection. Similarly, material which corresponds not to the requirements of the syntactic structure into which the item is inserted, but rather to the internal structure of the item, is also formally 'derivational,' regardless of the fact that the same material (bearing much the same meaning) may also have 'inflectional' uses in the language. Thus, in modern (Khalkha) Mongolian, the derivational suffix -*xi* forms adjectives from adverbials, and can be added to the dative/locative form of nouns. In the adjective *gertəxi* 'domestic,' from the locative form *gertə* of *ger* 'house,' we appear to have a derivational suffix added after an inflectional one; but the crucial point here is that the locative suffix in this form is not functionally inflectional. That is, the rule introducing it does not refer to the morphosyntactic representation of the position in which the adjective is to be inserted. The appearance of even fully productive 'inflectional' formatives inside other derivation in such non-inflectional uses is thus predicted. The claim in (9) is a rather precise one, and since it follows as a theorem from the proposed organization of the grammar, it represents a significant result.[8]

---

[6] This is essentially the same as the claim appearing in Perlmutter (1986) under the name of the 'split morphology hypothesis'.

[7] A similar prediction is made by Lieber (1983b).

[8] Bochner (1984) reviews several cases in which he argues that inflectional material precedes derivation. Each of these has interesting consequences, but they do not in fact falsify (9). His example from Georgian demonstrates that in this language, a preverb plus verb combination has an internal structure, and the regular inflectional morphology applies to the head of this structure rather than to the entire form. Such cases are discussed in Anderson (1986a): the appearance that inflectional affixes are 'inside'

## 6.2.2. **Morphology and the phonology**

We turn now to the relations among rules belonging to the two broadly distinguishable classes that determine sound structure: word formation rules and phonological rules. We have already argued above (in section 6.0.2) that purely phonological rules have properties that are distinguishable from those sensitive to morphological categories – a conclusion that is probably uncontroversial for the set of clear word formation rules that actually create the markings for such categories. An issue arises with regard to the existence of an intermediate class of rules: 'morphologically conditioned phonological rules,' if they exist, would be rules of the phonology which do not themselves mark a category, but are nonetheless sensitive to its presence. On a view of morphology based on minimal sign morphemes, such rules must obviously be invoked in many cases, but with a shift in conception to a morphology based on word formation rules, their motivation becomes much less secure. This is because it is generally possible to incorporate all of the phonological 'side effects' of a given category into the word formation rule that creates the category in the first place. If this conclusion is indeed correct, it is probably desirable to eliminate reference to morphological categories from phonological rules altogether. Further research is obviously called for to determine this point.

Assuming that there are just two classes of rules, phonological rules and word formation rules, the question to be addressed is the manner in which these interact. The classical answer, as given in Chomsky & Halle (1968), is based on the overall structure of the grammar. On the view espoused there, the syntax constructs a lexically interpreted phrase marker containing all of the morphemes (hence, all of the formatives) that occur in the surface structure of the sentence. This representation is then subject to a class of *readjustment rules*, which effect idiosyncratic changes in the shapes of particular formatives in the presence of certain others. The output of the readjustment rules then serves as the input to the phonology proper. This organization thus requires that all of the rules determining the shapes of

the derivational prefixes is based on linear sequence rather than the logical structure of the derivation. In Bochner's Yiddish case, it is precisely the genuinely irregular plural formations that appear within derivation, as predicted here; see also Perlmutter (1986). In his Tagalog example, the 'inflectional' process he refers to is one deriving object focus verbs from subject focus forms. While this is surely 'relevant to the syntax' in the broad sense, the definition given here attempts to make clear that such manipulations of subcategorization frames fall within derivation rather than inflection in the present sense. Finally, the fascinating example of verbs of possession in Maliseet discussed in Sherwood (1983) involves a case in which the apparently inflectional material found inside of the incorporation-like structure of possessive verbs does not in fact bear inflectional import. This is shown for instance, by the fact that the form 'I have a canoe,' like all other possessives, is built on a base inflected for a *3rd person* possessor. This example, like the Khalkha case discussed in the text, shows that it is not particular *formatives* but rather particular *applications of rules* that are 'inflectional' or 'derivational' for the purposes of (9). Of course, the mechanisms by which such formally (but not functionally) inflected forms become available to word formation rules must still be specified.

particular formatives (the morphology itself and the readjustment rules) come before all of the phonological rules.

Now in fact, a number of examples appeared in the literature after the publication of Chomsky & Halle (1968) in which it was necessary to assume that at least some phonological rules can apply before at least some morphological rules (see Anderson 1975; Dressler 1976; and others). If these examples are valid (and the number of well-established cases is by now quite large), it follows that the phonology and the morphology are intermixed to some extent. It is obviously undesirable to conclude from this, however, that there is simply one large collection of rules, morphological and phonological, whose interactions with one another are unconstrained by principles other than language-particular orderings.

The guiding intuition of the traditional view is that morphology (whether construed as a set of morphotactic rules that specify the set of well-formed combinations of morphemes, or as word formation rules) serves to create new meaningful combinations of phonological material, while the phonology serves to 'adjust' the results of such combinations to the sound system of the language. But within contemporary views, the set of word formation rules are taken (as argued above) to operate on words[9] rather than on minimal building blocks of words (morphemes). Since it is also words (not morphemes) that constitute the domain of the phonology, this suggests a revision of the picture as presented in Chomsky & Halle (1968). Where a word formation rule produces a result which is subject to phonological adjustment, it would seem reasonable to say that it is in this adjusted form that the output of the rule becomes available as the input of other rules. If so, the interaction of rules is somewhat more complicated, but nonetheless constrained by the organization of the grammar. A set of phonologically adjusted forms constitute the lexical items of the language. These can serve as the input to word formation rules; when they do, the result is submitted to the phonology for adjustment to create a new lexical item – which is in turn available to other word formation rules, etc. In consequence, phonological operations will sometimes be found to have applied prior to the operation of morphological ones, precisely in the case where the phonological operation applied to the form which constitutes the base of the morphological process.

The model of lexical phonology and morphology (Pesetsky 1979; Kiparsky 1982a; Mohanan 1982; and other recent works – for a lucid overview, see Kaisse & Shaw 1985) is based directly on this insight: that much of the phonology operates together with the word formation rules in such a cyclic fashion to define the class of lexical items within a given language. Considerations of space prevent anything like a full treatment of the

---

[9] Actually, as we have seen, on stems – but the difference is not significant at this point.

principles of this theory here, but one other fundamental feature of it with foundations in the morphological literature must be mentioned.

It has long been noted (see especially Chomsky & Halle 1968; Siegel 1974; Rotenberg 1978) that there are (grossly) two sorts of affix in English. Some affixes (e.g. *-ity* in *profundity*) form an integral part of the phonological word with the material they are added to, interacting extensively with this material in determining the stress pattern and segmental shape of the word. Others, however (e.g. *-ness* as in *profoundness*), are more loosely connected with their bases, and the addition of these affixes causes little or no alteration of their stress pattern or shape.

In Chomsky & Halle (1968) the difference between these two classes of affix was described by the use of different boundary elements to separate them from the base to which they were added: '#' for the first class, and '+' for the second. An extensive theory of boundaries developed in the phonological literature to support the principle that the applicability of rules is controlled by such distinctions. Various aspects of the boundary theory were seen as less than satisfactory, but one generalization arising from it drew particular attention: in the general case, all '# boundary' (or loosely attached) affixes in a given word appear outside of all '+ boundary' (or closely attached) affixes. If this is indeed the case, it is in no way predicted by the boundary theory, since # and + in themselves are simply two distinct quasi-segmental units.

As an improvement on the boundary theory, it was proposed that the morphology should be 'level-ordered'. That is, instead of differentiating affixes by boundaries, they can be divided into distinct subsets or levels within the lexicon, where the division of the word formation rules corresponds to a division among the phonological rules. Some rules of each type belong to level 1, some to level 2, and so on. The operation of the lexical rules, then, follows the cyclic mode described above, but in a way that respects the organization into levels. Word formation rules of level 1 apply, with the results being subject to the level 1 phonology, producing items that can undergo further level 1 morphology, etc. Then, when no further processes at level 1 apply, the resulting forms serve as input to level 2 morphology, then level 2 phonology, then more level 2 phonology, and so on until phonologically well-formed items at the last level of lexical structure are obtained.

The hypothesis of a level-ordered organization of the lexicon is not unproblematic. For one thing, the generalization that all 'level 1' affixes are attached before any 'level 2' affixes is by no means a secure one (see Aronoff & Sridhar 1983). In addition, a number of words seem to demand a morphological structure on this view which is at variance with their semantic structure. For example, in the word *ungrammaticality*, the affix *-ity* can be shown to be at level 1 by its phonological behavior, and thus attached before the level 2 prefix *un-*, but the meaning of this item is clearly better represented as [[*un-grammatical*]-*ity*] than as [*un-*[*grammatical-ity*]], as the morphology would seem to demand. The literature on such 'bracketing paradoxes' is by now quite considerable (see Pesetsky 1985), but inconclusive.

The two principles of (a) level-ordering of the rules, and (b) cyclic interaction of the word formation rules and the phonology at each level, constitute the foundations of the theory of lexical phonology and morphology. Other points within this theory, such as the positing of rules applying after all of the lexical rules have operated and having properties distinct in important ways from the lexical rules, belong more to the study of phonology than morphology. For reasons of space we therefore confine the presentation of this influential current view to the remarks above, which represent an understanding of the relation between morphological processes and the rules of the phonology.

### 6.2.3. Morphology and the lexicon

Much of what has already been said above has strong implications for the place of the lexicon in relation to the overall morphological description. In particular, from the discussion of the word-based nature of morphology, and of the interaction of morphology with the syntax and with the phonology, the internal organization of the lexicon is fairly clear. As is traditional, we assume that the lexicon is primarily the locus of what is arbitrary and unpredictable about the words of a language. This does not at all entail the conclusion that the lexicon is simply a list of items, however. In fact, even when a language has a rich set of general principles for forming new words, it is typically the case that the question of whether or not a given possible word is also an actual one remains a lexical issue. The lexicon must thus contain ways of relating existing words, in so far as these are (at least partially) systematic, and also for describing the formation of new words. In traditional terms, the principles of such word formation can be divided into two areas: derivation, and compounding.

### Derivation

From the remarks above, it will be seen that this category refers to the operation of word formation rules within the lexicon: specifically, to the operation of those word formation rules whose structural descriptions do not involve a reference to the morphosyntactic representation of the position into which the word is to be inserted. These rules may refer to (and manipulate) the lexical category, syntactic subcategorization frame, semantics and argument frame, etc. of the stems to which they apply. They also typically perform some phonological change such as the addition of an affix (though some word formation rules make no change in the shape of the stem, in the case of 'zero derived' forms such as denominal *to hoe*, *to rake*, *to shovel*, etc.).

A question arises concerning the role of derivational rules in the lexicon. Is it appropriate to list those words that are formed by a word formation rule, or should these rather be considered implicit in the set of unpredictable words that clearly must be listed, taken together with the set of rules? For instance, what is the correct treatment of patterns such as the one that makes adverbs in *-ly* from adjectives in English? Essentially any adjective has such a corresponding adverb, except for (a) adjectives whose stems end in *-ly*, such as *silly*; and (b) adjectives for which a corresponding irregular adverb appears in the lexicon (e.g. *\*goodly* is not available as the adverb corresponding to *good* because of the existence of *well*). Essentially by definition, it is necessary to list those items which are in some way idiosyncratic. The possibility of omitting a word can thus only arise in the case of words formed by rules that are fully productive. But in that case, it is necessary to explore the question of what it means for a rule to be 'productive'.

The notion of productivity is often appealed to in the sense of the sheer number of forms accounted for by a given rule, but this is surely not a significant parameter of linguistic structure. What interests us is not how many forms exist, but rather how many of the ones a rule might predict to exist are real possibilities. Thus, both the suffixes *-ment* and *-ion* form nouns from verbs in English (*detachment*, *inversion*), but *-ion* only applies to verb stems in the latinate class: cf. *wonderment*, *settlement*, *amazement*, etc., for which no corresponding froms in *-ion* exist. Since the latinate verbs are a proper subset of the total class of verbs, it is misleading to take a simple count of the number of *-ion* forms vs. the number of *-ment* forms in assessing the relative productivity of these rules.

The problem centers on what we should say about forms predicted to exist by a given rule, but which are not in fact possible. An early approach to this problem was that of Halle (1973). He allowed the rules to generate forms freely, and then marked non-occurring forms in the lexicon with a feature [−LEXICAL INSERTION]. While formally possible, such a device has little to recommend it: aside from the extent to which it removes virtually all constraints from the description, it is hard to imagine how a language learner could ever acquire the fact that a given 'word' bears this feature.

Many non-occurring words can be blocked by conditions that are systematic parts of the structural description of a rule. For instance, requiring a verb stem that undergoes the *-ion* rule to bear the feature [+LATINATE] will account directly for the absence of *\*amazion*, etc. Of course, if we have no constraints on the inventory of features that can be appealed to in this way, this position is not significantly more interesting than the use of [−LEXICAL INSERTION], but this is a problem which must be faced in any event.

Sometimes the property of a rule's structural description which excludes certain potential applications is a phonological one. Thus, we have causative verbs in *-en* from some adjectives (e.g. *blacken*, *redden*, *madden*, *quicken* etc.) but not others (e.g. *\*bluen*, *\*lilacen*, *\*pooren*, etc.). As was pointed out by Siegel (1974), there is a phonological generalization here: only monosyllabic stems that end in an obstruent (preferably a dental) at the appropriate level of their derivation are eligible to undergo this rule. Some other apparent exceptions (*\*gooden*, *\*badden*, *\*muchen*) which apparently do end in a dental obstruent actually point to another fact about the rule: these are just the adjectives with irregular comparatives. In fact, when we look at the only one of these comparatives which itself meets the description of the rule, we find it actually undergoes it: *worsen* shows us that it is really the comparative and not the absolute form of the adjective which serves as the input to the rule, with the suffix *-er* truncated if this is present before *-en* is added. The moral of this is that once the conditions on the structural description of a rule are completely understood apparent exceptions often turn out to be systematic.

Still other forms can be argued to be blocked by a semantically based extension of the principle of disjunctive ordering (e.g. *\*goodly* 'in a good way,' because of *well*; *\*cooker* 'person who cooks,' because of the existence of *cook* with that sense; cf. Kiparsky 1982b), but there remain words which are predicted but whose non-existence seems arbitrary. How are we to block, for example *\*scrupulosity* from *scrupulous* without an appeal to an arbitrary feature?

A proposal of Aronoff (1976) is to reduce the issue of productivity to that of compositionality. Any word whose properties can be exhaustively predicted from the properties of existing words plus the set of word formation rules is implicitly possible, on this view, and need not be explicitly listed. In so far as the word formation rule is systematically incomplete, though, or the word has some idiosyncrasy of form, meaning, or syntax, it must be explicitly given in the lexicon. The more idiosyncratic a given formation is, the less information can be extracted in the formulation of a rule for it, and hence the less productive it will be. For instance, there are a number of English adjectives with a prefix *a-*: *afield*, *afoot*, *afire*, *abroad*, *ajar*, *aground*, etc. It is quite impossible to add to this class, however – because, on this view, the sense of these formations is totally unpredictable. If a new form were created, the rule would give no information about how it is related to its base beyond its shape. This suggests that the accretion of particular, idiosyncratic senses attached to instances of a given formation leads to a state in which speakers (and language learners) trust it less, and thus its productivity reduces. It would indeed be quite elegant if the problem of productivity could be reduced in such a way, but this is still a programmatic goal rather than a demonstrated result.

Importantly for present purposes, the notion of a word formation rule that is basic to this program is that of a relation between words in the lexicon which may be only partial. In fact, the suggestions of Jackendoff (1975) along these lines probably represent as strong a position as can be maintained. On that view, a word formation rule is actually a sort of 'redundancy rule' over the items in the lexicon, specifying the amount of independent information present in a given lexical entry – and only superficially a process by which forms are created. Instead, the words of the language are all part of its lexicon, and the word formation rules exist to specify the partially (but not entirely) systematic relations that exist among them. In so far as a word's properties are entirely predictable from the rules, we can say that the amount of additional information carried by its lexical entry is minimal. Furthermore, if a word does not exist but its properties can be entirely predicted, the rules can be employed productively to add it to the lexicon. In the general case, however, word formation rules exist to specify partially systematic relations among lexical items rather than to carry out active 'derivation'.

## Compounding

Compounding differs from derivation in a way that is straightforward and traditional: it consists in the combination of (two or more) existing words into a new word, while derivation consists in the application of a word formation rule to a single existing word. In terms of a theory based on the morphotactic combination of morphemes, the differences between them seem minimal. Both involve the combining of morphemes; but the elements combined in a compound happen to enjoy independent status while, at most, one of the elements combined in derivation is autonomous; this, however, seems more of a convenient division in terminology than an essential difference of type.

In a word-based theory employing word formation rules, in contrast, the difference seems much more prominent. A word formation rule, recall, operates on a single word (or stem) to manipulate its phonological form (typically, by affixation) and other properties. Compounding, in contrast, involves the combining of stems from the lexicon into a quasi-syntactic structure. This word-internal structure seems to be unique to compounds, in fact: the only structure which seems motivated internal to non-compound words is a metrical one, based on the phonological rather than the syntactic properties of their subparts. The formation of compounds seems to involve a genuinely syntactic combination of lexical elements below the level of the word (perhaps along lines like those explored in Selkirk 1982), while non-compounds have only a phonological structure (in contrast to the efforts of Selkirk and others to extend syntactic structure to the level of formatives, parallel to the views of American structuralist morphotactics).

Other arguments support the suggestion that compounding is really more a process of word-internal syntax than of morphology. For example, the elements of compounds typically fill (rather than merely absorb) argument positions in the semantics of other elements: cf. *cutthroat, dogcatcher*. The relation between compound elements and the argument frames of their co-constituents has been studied by Roeper & Siegel (1978), Lieber (1983a), and others. It is clear that whatever the principles governing the internal relations of these elements, they are syntactic in a way which is quite different from other morphology.

Finally, it is precisely when compounding is involved that it seems necessary to invoke the device of 'looping back' in the lexical phonology of a language. This refers to the necessity of allowing forms that have undergone rules at a late level of the lexicon to serve as input to rules of earlier levels (see Mohanan 1982; Halle & Mohanan 1985). Such a notion obviously evacuates the strong claim of a level-ordered morphology, and as such should be resisted. If compounding in fact involves the combining of lexical stems into new word structures, however, this is what we might expect. There is every reason to believe that the stems combined, as lexical items, will already have undergone rules at various levels, but a newly formed compound might itself be subject to phonological adjustments appropriate to all levels of the lexicon, including comparatively deep ones. The point is that the mechanism of compounding is unlike that of (other) word formation in that it involves the combining of lexical stems into a syntactic structure rather than an operation on the stem itself.

There is obviously much more to be said about how compounds are formed. The purpose of these remarks has simply been to suggest that the assimilation of compounding to other mechanisms of word formation has perhaps been exaggerated, under the influence of a morpheme-based model which sees all word formation as the combining of minimal signs to make complex ones.

## 6.3. Conclusion

This concludes our survey of the constituents of a theory of word structure. There are many areas left untreated (or underplayed) which other authors would no doubt consider central to their work in the field. The present essay has been based on an understanding of a 'theory' of a given domain as a framework of assumptions and propositions within which it is possible to bring order and coherence to particular facts within that domain. As such, it has concentrated on the ontological and epistemological underpinnings of our understanding of word structure, and especially on the ways in which morphology is related to other aspects of linguistic structure. It is undoubtedly the case that most 'working morphologists' spend the bulk of their time on the concrete and explicit analysis of actual sets of facts about word structure in natural language(s), rather than on such foundational issues. Nevertheless, it is only in the context of an understanding of the fundamental content of a field that its results are intelligible, or have consequences for our broader understanding of language. Since morphology is a field whose interrelations with the rest of language are particularly intricate, it follows that it is especially important to be clear about its nature if particular analyses and proposals are to have significance.

## REFERENCES

Anderson, S. R. 1975. On the interaction of phonological rules of various types. *Journal of Linguistics* 11: 39–63.

Anderson, S. R. 1977a. Comments on Wasow: the role of the theme in lexical rules. In P. W. Culicover, T. Wasow & A. Akmajian (eds.) *Formal syntax*. New York: Academic Press.

Anderson, S. R. 1977b. On the formal description of inflection. *CLS* 13: 15–44.

Anderson, S. R. 1982. Where's morphology? *Linguistic Inquiry* 13: 571–612.

Anderson, S. R. 1984a. Kwakwala syntax and the government–binding theory. In E.-D. Cook & D. B. Gerdts (eds.) *The syntax of native American languages*. New York: Academic Press.

Anderson S. R. 1984b. On representations in morphology: case, agreement and inversion in Georgian. *Natural Language and Linguistic Theory* 2: 157–218.

Anderson, S. R. 1985. *Phonology in the twentieth century*. Chicago: University of Chicago Press.

Anderson, S. R. 1986a. Clitics are phrasal affixes. Paper read at 2nd International Conference on Word Formation, Veszprém, Hungary.

Anderson, S. R. 1986b. Disjunctive ordering in inflectional morphology. *Natural Language and Linguistic Theory* 4: 1–32.

Anderson, S. R. 1986c. Inflection. Paper read at Milwaukee Morphology Meeting. To appear in M. Hammond & N. Noonan (eds.) *Theoretical morphology*. Orlando: Academic Press.

Anderson, S. R. & Browne, W. 1973. On keeping exchange rules in Czech. *Papers in Linguistics* 6: 445–82.

Archangeli, D. 1983. The root CV-template as a property of the affix: evidence from Yawelmani. *Natural Language and Linguistic Theory* 1: 347–84.

Aronoff, M. 1976. *Word formation in generative grammar*. Cambridge, MA: MIT Press.

Aronoff, M. & Sridhar, S. N. 1983. Morphological levels in English and Kannada, or atarizing Reagan. In *Interplay*, Parasession volume for *CLS* 19, pp. 3–16.

Baker, M. 1985. The mirror principle and morphosyntactic explanation. *Linguistic Inquiry* 16: 373–415.

Bat-El, O. 1986. Extraction in Modern Hebrew morphology. Master's thesis, UCLA.

Bauer, L. 1979. Against word-based morphology. *Linguistic Inquiry*, 10: 508–9.

Bloomfield, L. 1933. *Language*. New York: Holt.

Bochner, H. 1984. Inflection within derivation. *The Linguistic Review* 3: 411–21.

Borer, H. 1984. The projection principle and rules of morphology. *NELS* 14: 16–33.

Carden, G. 1983. The non-finite = state-ness of the word formation component. *Linguistic Inquiry* 14: 537–41.

Carrier-Duncan, J. 1984. Some problems with prosodic accounts of reduplication. In M. Aronoff & R. T. Oehrle (eds.) *Language sound structure*. Cambridge, MA: MIT Press.

Chomsky, N. 1957. *Syntactic structures*. The Hague: Mouton.

Chomsky, N. 1963. Formal properties of grammars. In R. D. Bush, R. R. Bush & E. Galanter (eds.) *Handbook of mathematical psychology*. New York: Wiley.

Chomsky, N. 1965. *Aspects of the theory of syntax*. Cambridge, MA: MIT Press.

Chomsky, N. 1970. Remarks on nominalizations. In R. A. Jacobs & P. S. Rosenbaum (eds.) *Readings in English transformational grammar*. Waltham: Ginn & Co.

Chomsky, N. & Halle, M. 1968. *The sound pattern of English*. New York: Harper & Row.

Churchward, C. M. 1953. *Tongan grammar*. London: Oxford University Press.

Culy, C. 1985. The complexity of the vocabulary of Bambara. *Linguistics and Philosophy* 8: 345–51.

Demers, R. 1974. Alternating roots in Lummi. *International Journal of American Linguistics* 40: 15–21.

Dressler, W. 1976. Morphologization of phonological processes (are there distinct morphonological processes?). In A. Juilland (ed.) *Linguistic studies offered to Joseph Greenberg*. Saratoga: Anma Libri.

Durie, M. 1986. The grammaticalization of number as a verbal category. *BLS* 12.

Emonds, J. 1976. *A transformational approach to English syntax*. New York: Plenum.

Gazdar, G., Klein, E., Pullum, G. & Sag, I. 1985. *Generalized phrase structure grammar*. Cambridge, MA: Harvard University Press.

Goldsmith, J. 1979. *Autosegmental phonology*. New York: Garland.

Halle, M. 1973. Prolegomena to a theory of word formation. *Linguistic Inquiry* 4: 3–16.

Halle, M. & Mohanan, K. P. 1985. Segmental phonology of modern English. *Linguistic Inquiry* 16: 57–116.

Harris, Z. 1942. Morpheme alternants in linguistic analysis. *Language* 18: 169–80.

Hockett, C. F. 1947. Problems of morphemic analysis. *Language* 23: 321–43.

Hockett, C. F. 1954. Two models of grammatical description. *Word* 10: 210–34.

Jackendoff, R. S. 1975. Morphological and semantic regularities in the lexicon. *Language* 51: 639–71.

Janda, R. & Sandoval, M. 1984. *'Elsewhere' in morphology*. Indiana University Linguistics Club.

Kaisse, E. 1985. *Connected speech*. New York: Academic Press.

Kaisse, E. & Shaw, P. 1985. On the theory of lexical phonology. *Phonology Yearbook* 2: 1–30.

Kiparsky, P. 1973. 'Elsewhere' in phonology. In S. R. Anderson & P. Kiparsky (eds.) *A festschrift for Morris Halle*. New York: Holt, Rinehart & Winston.

Kiparsky, P. 1982a. Lexical morphology and phonology. In *Linguistics in the morning calm*. Seoul: Hanshin Publishing Company.

Kiparsky, P. 1982b. Word formation and the lexicon. In F. Ingemann, (ed.) *Proceedings of the 1982 Mid-America Linguistics Conference*. Lawrence: University of Kansas.

Kiparsky, P. 1984. On the lexical phonology of Icelandic. In C.-C. Elert, I. Johansson & E. Strangert (eds.) *Nordic Prosody III*, University of Umeå. Stockholm: Almqvist & Wiksell.

Klavans, J. L. 1980. *Some problems in a theory of clitics*. Indiana University Linguistics Club.

Klavans, J. L. 1983. The morphology of cliticization. In *Interplay*, parasession volume for *CLS* 19: 103–21.

Klavans, J. L. 1985. The independence of syntax and phonology in cliticization. *Language* 61: 95–120.

Langendoen, D. T. 1981. The generative capacity of word-formation components. *Linguistic Inquiry* 12: 320–2.

Lapointe, S. 1980. A theory of grammatical agreement. Doctoral dissertation, University of Massachusetts.

Lees, R. B. 1960. *The grammar of English nominalizations*. The Hague: Mouton.

Lieber, R. 1983a. Argument linking and compounds in English. *Linguistic Inquiry* 14: 251–85.

Lieber, R. 1983b. *On the organization of the lexicon*. Doctoral dissertation, MIT. Published by Indiana University Linguistics Club.

Marantz, A. 1982. Re reduplication. *Linguistic Inquiry* 13: 435–82.

Matthews, P. H. 1972. *Inflectional morphology*. Cambridge: Cambridge University Press.

McCarthy, J. 1981. A prosodic theory of non-concatenative morphology. *Linguistic Inquiry* 12: 373–418.

McCarthy, J. 1982. Prosodic templates, morphemic templates, and morphemic tiers. In H. van der Hulst & N. Smith (eds.) *The structure of phonological representations, I.* Dordrecht. Foris.

McCarthy, J. 1983. Consonantal morphology in the Chaha verb. *West Coast Conference on Formal Linguistics* 2: 176–88.

McCarthy, J. 1986. OCP effects: gemination and antigemination. *Linguistic Inquiry* 17: 207–63.

Mohanan, K. P. 1982. *Lexical phonology.* Doctoral dissertation, MIT. Published by Indiana University Linguistics Club.

Montler, T. 1986. *An outline of the morphology and phonology of Saanich, North Straits Salish.* Occasional Papers in Linguistics 4, University of Montana.

Nevis, J. A. 1985. Finnish particle clitics and general clitic theory. Doctoral dissertation, Ohio State University.

Nida, E. 1948. The identification of morphemes. *Language* 24: 414–41.

Orešnik, J. & Pétursson, M. 1977. Quantity in modern Icelandic. *Arkiv för Nordisk Filologi* 92: 155–71.

Perlmutter, D. 1986. The split morphology hypothesis: evidence from Yiddish. Paper presented at Milwaukee Morphology Meeting; to appear in the *Proceedings*.

Pesetsky, D. 1979. Russian morphology and lexical theory. Dept of Linguistics, MIT ms.

Pesetsky, D. 1985. Morphology and logical form. *Linguistic Inquiry* 16: 193–246.

Poser, W. 1985. Cliticization to NP and lexical phonology. *West Coast Conference on Formal Linguistics*, 4: 262–72.

Pullum, G. K. 1985. Assuming some version of X-bar theory. *CLS* 21: 323–53.

Roeper, T. & Siegel, M. 1978. A lexical transformation for verbal compounds. *Linguistic Inquiry* 9: 199–260.

Rotenberg, J. 1978. The syntax of phonology. Doctoral dissertation, MIT.

Sadock, J. 1985. Autolexical syntax: a proposal for the treatment of noun incorporation and similar phenomena. *Natural Language and Linguistic Theory* 3: 379–439.

Scalise, S. 1984. *Generative morphology.* Dordrecht: Foris.

Selkirk, E. 1982. *The syntax of words.* Cambridge MA: MIT Press.

Sherwood, D. 1983. Maliseet verbs of possession. *Linguistic Inquiry* 14: 351–6.

Siegel, D. L. 1974. Topics in English morphology. Doctoral dissertation, MIT.

Thomas-Flinders, T. 1981. *Inflectional morphology: introduction to the extended word and paradigm theory.* Occasional Papers in Linguistics 4. UCLA Dept. of Linguistics.

Thompson, L. C. & M. T. Thompson 1969. Metathesis as a grammatical device. *International Journal of American Linguistics* 35: 213–19.

Wasow, T. 1977. Transformations and the lexicon. In P. Culicover, T. Wasow & A. Akmajian (eds.) *Formal syntax.* New York: Academic Press.

Williams, E. 1981. On the notions 'lexically related' and 'head of a word'. *Linguistic Inquiry* 12: 245–74.

Yip, M. 1982. Reduplication and CV-skeleta in Chinese secret languages. *Linguistic Inquiry* 13: 637–61.

Zwicky, A. 1977. *On clitics.* Indiana University Linguistics Club.

Zwicky, A. 1986a. Agreement features: layers or tags? *Ohio State University Working Papers in Linguistics* 32: 146–8.

Zwicky, A. 1986b. Imposed vs. inherent feature specifications, and other multiple feature markings. Unpublished paper submitted to IULC.

# 7 Phonological theory*

*Hans Basbøll*

## 7.0. Introduction: some recent developments and basic concepts in phonology

### 7.0.1. Phonology in the last decade

From about the middle of the 1960s to the middle of the 1970s, the dominant phonological paradigm was 'classical' or 'orthodox' generative phonology, the standard work of which is Chomsky & Halle (1968) *The sound pattern of English* (*SPE*), and which is presented in introductions by Dell (1973), Schane (1973), and Kenstowicz & Kisseberth (1979).[1] The main focus of interest of *SPE* phonology was the construction of a rule component in which morphologically related word forms could be derived from a set of morpheme-invariant underlying forms.[2] Favorite topics of discussion were how to constrain this type of grammar by placing conditions on abstractness of underlying representations, on application of rules, and so forth. This discussion may be said to have culminated in the work by Kiparsky and others in lexical phonology (cf. 7.4.1).

The most notable feature in the evolution of phonology in the last decade, as I see it, has been a positive widening of the issues treated within the generative paradigm, and a new openness to the idea of a general synthesis between generative phonology and other schools of thought with different roots and traditions (cf. 7.5).

A number of phonological phenomena that could not be dealt with adequately in the *SPE* model have found more adequate treatment in other

---

* I am indebted to Mike Davenport, Eli Fischer-Jørgensen, and Ellen Kaisse for numerous valuable remarks on the manuscript, concerning both content and style.

[1] Which is not to say that for the past half-century, at least, there have not been a number of other schools of phonology (for discussion, see Makkai 1972; Fischer-Jørgensen 1975; Sommerstein 1977; Dinnsen 1979; and Basbøll 1980). General and comprehensive introductions to phonology are provided by Hyman (1975), Lass (1983), and Hawkins (1984).

[2] In this sense, *SPE* phonology was a direct outgrowth of Bloomfieldian item-and-process phonology. For discussion of this point, see Rischel (1974: 361–5). *SPE*'s explicitly defined goal was to describe mental realities, but, as Linell (1979a) notes, most of the general work carried out within that framework was surprisingly independent of such goals.

approaches. For example, uniform processes like vowel raising and lowering, which defied adequate treatment in *SPE*, have been handled (in quite different ways) in the multivalued parameter approach (7.1.3) and in dependency phonology and particle phonology (7.1.4). The most elaborate of these approaches is dependency phonology, which operates with gestures and subgestures below the segment and makes use of a sophisticated notational system (with emphasis on different logical types of relations between elements) to account for inventories of segments and the processes they enter into.

But an even more radical enlarging of the subject of inquiry has been undertaken within the field of prosody, which seeks to represent phonological structuring above the segment. In the last decade, the syllable has regained its importance (7.2), and phonological domains (7.3.1) and stress (7.3.2) have been fruitfully investigated. It would be untrue to claim that stress was not within the field of interest of *SPE* phonology, since a great part of that volume was concerned with the description of English stress; but in *SPE*, stress was treated in a fashion almost exactly parallel to segmental phenomena. Not surprisingly, therefore, one of the most influential models within generative phonology since *SPE*, metrical phonology, has dealt with stress and other prosodic phenomena in a more structured way. This model will be taken up in 7.3.2. Another very influential model within the same paradigm is autosegmental phonology, which has been especially effective in dealing with tonal phenomena. This model will be discussed in 7.2.4.

A further important trend is natural phonology, within which the emphasis is laid on those phonological processes that might be said to be 'natural'. This trend began with Stampe (1969) and has been subject to a major integrative effort in Dressler (1985) (see 7.4.2). Natural generative phonology (Vennemann 1974; Hooper 1976), in which the role of the syllable, the word, and the utterance was emphasized, will be mentioned only in passing here, due to lack of space. Bailey's so-called 'phonetology' (1983), which lays particular weight on variational aspects of phonology and phonetics, as well as Vennemann's (1981) 'phonology as nonfunctional nonphonetics,' will, for the same reason, not be dealt with at all.[3]

## 7.0.2. On phonological data and the notion of contrast

One essential aspect of phonology is the reduction of the infinitely varying speech signal to a limited number of recurring elements. Some such phonological analysis, perhaps in a very rudimentary, and certainly implicit, form

---

[3] A number of phonological trends rooted mainly in the structuralist tradition (in the broad sense of the term) have continued to exist, including Martinet's functionalism, Pike's tagmemics, and Lamb's stratificational grammar (for discussion, see Fischer-Jørgensen 1975).

not only underlies normal speech behavior, but is one prerequisite for the invention and use of alphabetic writing systems.

A special type of alphabet is the so-called 'phonetic' one, i.e. an inventory of symbols used in phonetic transcription. If we look, for example, at a phonetic transcription in a pronunciation dictionary or, in fact, in the majority of phonological transcriptions, we note that they are abstractions from a whole class of individual, and thus non-identical, pronunciations. That is, a transcription ignores a lot of phonetic detail, and the way in which the continuum of sound is rendered into such a discrete notation necessarily implies phonology. In short, there exists no such thing as a phonetic transcription wholly independent of phonological considerations. Even during field work on a language that is completely unknown to a phonologist, the phonetic transcriptions used in the beginning are bound to be revised during the work, due to the analyst's increased knowledge of which phonetic traits are linguistically relevant in the language in question.

Now, what does 'linguistically relevant' mean in this context? First of all, 'linguistically relevant' may be taken to mean 'contrastive': if two utterances are systematically distinguished in meaning as well as in sound, they are said to be 'in contrast'; and if two utterances in contrast are phonetically identical except for one place where they have two different sounds, these sounds are said to be 'contrastive'. If only the sounds that can be contrastive (under this definition) in the language in question are rendered with different symbols, a rather narrow transcription will result. Secondly, noncontrastive phonetic differences may be 'linguistically relevant' in the sense that they signal e.g. sociological or stylistic information that can be very important to native speakers of the language.

Thus the input data that are used in most phonological analyses are themselves of a phonological nature as they involve abstraction from linguistically irrelevant traits; they are thus never 'purely phonetic' in the sense of nonphonological, even in the case of the most narrow transcriptions made by highly trained phonologists.

The notion of contrast has often been taken in a more restricted sense, however, by being applied solely to utterances consisting of isolated words or words pronounced distinctly. The phonological contrasts covering such a restricted material have most often been established, explicitly or implicitly, by means of the so-called 'commutation test,' using minimal pairs (cf. Fischer-Jørgensen 1956). This test has both a syntagmatic and a paradigmatic function, namely to establish the number of positions, and the inventory of contrastive segments in each position, respectively. The commutation test, however, gives no hint as to how to identify contrastive segments in different positions, nor to whether one or the other segment is contrastive in the case where two consecutive segments condition one another mutually.

### 7.0.3. Positions, phonemes, and segments

Which criteria could or should be used for the phonological identification of contrastive segments in different positions? Within the influential (post-) Bloomfieldian paradigm the motto was 'Once a phoneme, always a phoneme,' i.e. the same speech sound represents the same phoneme everywhere. Thus in a case like German *Rade, Rat* [ʁaːdə, ʁaːt] 'wheel' (dat. sg., nom. sg.), the dental stop would represent the phonemes /d/ and /t/ respectively, in these two caseforms of 'wheel' (cf. *Rate, Rat* [ʁaːtə, ʁaːt] 'councilor' (dat. sg., nom. sg.) with /t/ in both these caseforms of 'councilor').

But it is exactly from the point of view of contrast that such a theory may be unrevealing, since it identifies phonologically the same sound (e.g. [t]) with the same phoneme, /t/, everywhere, regardless of whether it is in contrast with /d/ or not. Within the Prague School of phonology (whose main work is Trubetzkoy 1939), the [t] in word-final position, for example, would be taken to represent an archiphoneme (say T) which represents the 'neutralization product' (i.e. the suspension of the distinction) between the phonemes /t/ and /d/, both of which are found in intervocalic position.[4]

That the segment is a significant phonological unit has been taken for granted throughout the present section. But at least one framework, Griffen's 'nonsegmental phonology' (1976), does not subscribe to the reality of the segment, which it sees as a convenient fiction. Instead, Griffen argues for a 'syllable in which the vowel is considered to be the articulatory base and consonants are constraints carried out on the vowel and concurrently with it' (1977: 375). In response, I would say that although the segment may be, *phonetically* speaking, just a convenient fiction, particularly in cases of reduced speech, I find the *phonological* arguments for the segment convincing: insertion, deletion, and interchange ('metathesis') of whole segments are well-attested, both as synchronic phonological rules and as diachronic processes. It would be very strange indeed to describe metathesis as a simultaneous interchange of all distinctive features of the two columns involved. And there even seems to be direct psychological evidence for the segment (see Chapter 7, by Fromkin, in Volume II of this survey). Even if phonological processes *could* be described without the use of segments, at the cost of extra complexities in the account, this fact would not mean that segments are not significant phonological entities. It appears that segments are simply there to be observed, just like (as we will soon see) syllables and distinctive features.

---

[4] For discussion of the concepts 'archiphoneme' and 'neutralization,' see Davidsen-Nielsen (1978). The related notion 'archisegment' has been introduced in natural generative phonology (Hooper 1976: 122ff). For general discussion of these concepts, see Fischer-Jørgensen (1975: 284–96).

## 7.1. Below the segment: features and gestures[5]

### 7.1.1. Distinctive features and natural classes

Consider a phonological rule whereby /p, t, k/ turns into (or corresponds to) /ɸ, θ, x/ (cf. the Germanic sound change). No phonologist would state the process involved as three independent changes or correspondences: /p/→ /ɸ/, /t/→/θ/, /k/→/x/. This is because these changes are identical in the sense that a voiceless stop is turned into (or corresponds to) a fricative in all cases. Both the input and the output segments to the rule are *natural classes*. As soon as we operate with natural classes of segments, we in fact also operate with distinctive features characterizing these classes, at least implicitly. The abovementioned change, for example, might be given an initial formulation as follows:

$$(1) \quad \begin{bmatrix} - \text{sonorant} \\ - \text{voiced} \\ - \text{continuant} \end{bmatrix} \rightarrow \begin{bmatrix} - \text{sonorant} \\ - \text{voiced} \\ + \text{continuant} \end{bmatrix}$$

When redundant features are removed from the formula, it can be reduced to (2):

$$(2) \quad \begin{bmatrix} - \text{sonorant}^6 \\ - \text{voiced} \end{bmatrix} \rightarrow [+ \text{continuant}]$$

Any description of a phonological process in terms of natural classes like 'high vowels,' 'fricatives,' 'nasals,' etc. constitutes at least an implicit use of some sort of distinctive features. That is, the processes would be unformulable unless the structures (represented by the natural classes of categories) were there to support them. Stated somewhat differently, rules entail phonological structures that permit them to capture the linguistically significant generalizations involved. The task of the phonologist is to devise a set of distinctive features that makes the notion of natural class explicit and formalizable.

### 7.1.2. What is described by distinctive features?

In the preceding section, I have argued as if distinctive features simply codified different but simultaneous classifications of segments, for example by characterizing /p/ as obstruent, noncontinuant, oral, labial, and voiceless

---

[5] For more detailed discussion of distinctive features, see Chapters 8 and 11, by Beckman and Keating, in this volume.

[6] If feature-interpreting conventions demand that sonorants necessarily be voiced, then [−sonorant] need not be explicitly stated in the rule.

at the same time. This was in fact Trubetzkoy's position, but the greatest figure in the theory of distinctive features, Roman Jakobson (co-founder of Prague School phonology), took the features to be the very building blocks of phonology, thereby ascribing to the segment a less important role. Although notations in terms of segments still abound in phonological descriptions, mainly for practical reasons, Jakobson's position has won in phonological theory, in the sense that the features, which may be said to function as 'phonological atoms,' so to speak, have an existence of their own: they may spread over several segments, and, according to such frameworks as autosegmental phonology, their boundaries need not co-occur with those between segments. They may even follow one another within the segment, as in the case of prenasalized stops and certain other segments (cf. Anderson 1976; Ewen 1982). Even many phonologists whose very (traditional) definition of a distinctive feature excludes consecutive ones within a segment operate with features like 'delayed release' (in the characterization of affricates) which in reality include the time dimension within the single segment (cf. Ladefoged 1971). And anyone who observes reduced speech must recognize that what would be a segment – e.g. a nasal or /r/ – in more formal speech is sometimes reduced to a feature – e.g. nasalization or retroflection – in a neighboring segment, often a vowel.

In the following, I shall compare briefly the three dominant systems of distinctive features, namely those of Jakobson, *SPE*, and Ladefoged, without going into a discussion of individual features proposed. Jakobson (see Jakobson, Fant & Halle 1952; Jakobson & Halle 1956) uses about a dozen universal distinctive features, prosodic features not included, to build up the phonemes of all languages. This small number is possible only because oppositions that are acoustically related and which, according to Jakobson, never occur as contrastive in the same language, are reduced to one 'distinctive feature'. An example is pharyngealization, rounding, and retroflection, which are seen as representatives of the distinctive feature 'flat' (vs. 'plain'). In principle, the distinctive features receive a definition in three realms: production, acoustics, and perception. But whereas a single feature might involve different articulatory mechanisms, the acoustic and perceptual characterizations are necessarily more unified. This unity is in accord with Jakobson's views on the centrality of communicative function to language, i.e. since speech is transmitted via perception, perception has priority over production.[7]

According to *SPE*, distinctive features should be used to define all 'systematic phonemic' segments in all languages, as well as all phonetic distinctions (the latter case by supplementing binary feature values with

[7] For discussion of the role of perception in language acquisition and language change, see Andersen (1973).

nonbinary ones). Chomsky & Halle's distinctive features are defined on the basis of production, which leads to a much larger number of features than in Jakobson's system.

Ladefoged (1971) (also Williamson 1977 and Lindau 1978 within the same basic paradigm) wants to characterize phonetically all distinctions between segments that in any language can be contrastive (at the phonetic level). He uses both articulatory and acoustically defined features: those features that can be given at least as uniform a definition on an articulatory as on an acoustic basis are defined on the former basis (e.g. 'labial,' 'nasal'); others can be much more easily characterized acoustically (e.g. 'grave'), and they are defined on that basis. Ladefoged's inventory of distinctive features and their definitions are superior from a phonetic point of view to all earlier feature systems (but it does not, of course, follow from this that the basic characteristics of the system must then be superior too).

In my view, it is not the case that the Jakobsonian feature system has been made obsolete by the later proposals by Chomsky & Halle, by Ladefoged, or by anyone else, since it had its own unique, and still important, goal, namely to define the types of contrasts possible in phonemic (sub)systems of the world's languages.[8] Jakobson's system is thus still of interest for those investigating the human capacity for phonological distinctions. I find it suggestive, for example, that Kean (1981), who departed from the *SPE* feature system, was able to group the features together, by external evidence (from aphasic patients) in function groups reminiscent of Jakobson's much earlier inventory of features.

### 7.1.3. Binarism, ordering, and scalarity

Jakobson maintains strict binarism: all distinctive features must be binary, since they express that the segment in question either belongs to or does not belong to, a given category. Notice that binarism or nonbinarism is not an empirical issue according to this view. *SPE* also advocates binarism for the distinctive features in the phonological component (except for prosodic ones like 'stress'). Ladefoged uses both binary and multivalued features: e.g. 'nasal' is binary but 'constriction' is not.

I think that the debate for and against binarism has sometimes been less clear than necessary because there is more than one alternative to 'binary'. The three main possibilities of feature values that I think should be distinguished are these:

(3) a. Binary      (divalent)

---

[8] Phonological typology, while of great interest to the field of phonology, will not be treated here. The reader is referred to Chapter 17, by Comrie, in this volume and to some standard works on the topic: Trubetzkoy (1939), Hockett (1955), Greenberg (1978), and Maddieson (1983).

b. Polyvalent (multivalued, i.e. discrete nonbinary)
c. Scalar    (continuously varying within certain limits)

It is clear that (3c) is not an option for the *phonological* function of distinctive features. As far as (3a) is concerned, it is consistent to choose binarism by means of a Jakobsonian argument, but if binarism (in the sense of exclusively binary features) is taken as an empirical issue, I think that it is wrong. Natural phonological rules, for example, may lower vowels by one degree in a certain environment, and such a rule can be captured in an insightful way only by a nonbinary system. The same might also be said for consonantal strengthening and other processes.

As for the relation between the universal and language-specific function of distinctive features, the following three options, which are not mutually exclusive, seem relevant.

(i)  Every language picks its own selection from the universal inventory of distinctive features, the other features always assuming their unmarked value. At the phonetic level, features may take nonbinary values. This seems to be the *SPE* position.

(ii)  Languages may define 'second-order features' or 'cover features' (Lass 1976; cf. Anderson 1974 on glottal features), i.e. particular configurations of the universally available distinctive features. Such second-order features may be relevant in the phonology of one or a group of related languages.

(iii)  The distinctive features represent universal phonetic parameters (such as the one from [i] to [ɑ] ) on which each language defines its own values and limits. This phonetically oriented approach (cf. Fischer-Jørgensen 1984) takes phonological features to be discrete, but not necessarily binary, though they end up phonetically as nondiscrete.

## 7.1.4. Feature hierarchies, gestures, and particles

It has so far been an implicit premise of the discussion that distinctive features constitute an unordered set whose members are of equal status. This premise is by no means self-evident, however. According to Postal (1968: 190), the order of the universal marking conventions establishes what he calls the 'feature hierarchy'. Several phonologists since Postal's work have put forward other proposals of language-specific ordering (or ranking) of features. Andersen (1975, 1978) and Bailey (1977) have proposed accounting for certain diachronic and synchronic phonological facts of typological relevance by a hierarchy, for example (in the latter case) by positing that p> f> v in Germanic and p> b> v in Romance is due to the relative weight of [continuant] and [voiced] in these two language families. This issue is quite unsettled. Also Fant (1973) has operated with crucially different orderings of features in different languages. Van der Broecke (1976) has shown that different criteria for one language, and the same criteria for different languages, will lead to different (but often related) hierarchies. Consonantal hierarchies in relation to syllable structure are considered in 7.2.3.

The other relevant question in this context is whether features occur in 'bundles,' 'types,' or the like within the individual segments. The standard approaches to distinctive features (mentioned above) classify these features into 'tonality features,' 'major class features,' etc., but they in general make little use of such classifications. An interesting attempt at such a classification is a recent one from dependency phonology.[9] Ewen (1986: 207) proposes (4) below as the internal structure of the segment:

(4)

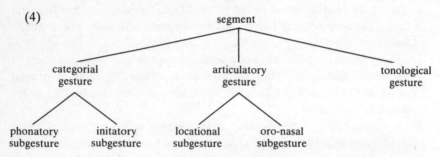

The four subgestures cover (from the left) sonorancy, voicedness, backness, and nasality. Phonological rules are expected to make reference to the features of one gesture or whole gestures only.

As for the structure below the subgesture within dependency phonology, one brief example must suffice. According to this theory, the end points of the vowel triangle, *a*, *i*, *u*, may occur alone, manifesting the [ɑ], [i], [u], respectively, or may act as features of more complex vowels. Thus [e] could be seen as the surface manifestation of *i* governing *a*, and [æ] as *a* governing *i*. This part of dependency phonology strikingly resembles Schane's (1984) 'particle phonology,' where *i*, *a*, and *u* are considered as vowel 'particles,' so that *i* represents [i], *ai* [e], and *aii* [ɛ] or [æ]. A related approach is put forward by Kaye, Lowenstamm & Vergnaud (1985). An even more highly structured model of the internal structure of segments is Clements (1985), which considers feature representations to be multi-tiered hierarchical structures (the phonetic content of segments being arrayed on two different types of tiers, namely feature tiers and class tiers, the latter including laryngeal, supralaryngeal, manner, and place tiers) – cf. 7.2.4. Such detailed representations of segments are generally supported by the argument that rules such

---

[9] For an introduction to dependency phonology (which makes use of the general principles of dependency grammar), see Lass (1983: 271–93).

as umlaut, vowel harmony, assimilation, and others need the proposed hierarchical structure.

## 7.2. Above the segment: syllabic rules and syllable structure

### 7.2.1. Syllabic rules

It is, of course, an old insight in both phonetics and phonology that segments are organized in syllables (cf. Bell & Hooper 1978). In large parts of the phonological tradition, this insight was never lost (cf. Hjelmslev 1939; Pike & Pike 1947; Kuryłowicz 1948; Fudge 1969; Pulgram 1970; Allen 1973; to mention just a few). But in *SPE*, there was no syllable. Since generative phonology has traditionally been rule-oriented rather than structure-oriented, the arguments for the reintroduction of the syllable within this paradigm are based on the idea that rules must refer to syllabic structure. In 1972, three papers of this type on the syllable appeared, by Vennemann, Hooper, and Basbøll (the latter of which develops ideas introduced in an important but often overlooked dissertation by McCawley 1968, cf. 7.3.1).

Hooper concentrated on the effect of syllable boundaries (symbolized by $) in the structural description of phonological rules. A typical example (1972: 533) is a rule nasalizing a high vowel before a nasal consonant in the same syllable, with would traditionally be stated as in (5):

$$(5) \begin{bmatrix} V \\ +\text{high} \end{bmatrix} \rightarrow [+\text{nasal}]/\underline{\hspace{1em}} [+\text{nasal}] \begin{Bmatrix} C \\ \# \end{Bmatrix}$$

(The environment in curly brackets is taken to imply that the preceding nasal is syllable-final.)

Hooper claims that the rule should instead be stated as in (6):

$$(6) \begin{bmatrix} V \\ +\text{high} \end{bmatrix} \rightarrow [+\text{nasal}]/\underline{\hspace{1em}} [+\text{nasal}] \, \$$$

But this formulation predicts incorrectly that a consonant occurring between the nasal and the syllable boundary would block the rule (see Basbøll 1974). This could be remedied by inserting a (not very revealing) $C_0$ before $. The correct solution, however, is that the *domain* of the rule is the syllable, and hence it can be formulated simply as (7):

$$(7) \begin{bmatrix} V \\ +\text{high} \end{bmatrix} \rightarrow [+\text{nasal}]/\underline{\hspace{1em}} [+\text{nasal}]$$

That rules occur with the syllable as their domain is the normal case, I would claim, as far as feature copying from consonants to adjacent vowels is concerned. Likewise, the syllable may occur as a unit in the structural description of phonological rules (for discussion, see McCawley 1968: 36). This is typical of prosodic phenomena such as stress, tone, and the Danish stød. For a general defense of the necessity of the syllable in phonological theory, see Basbøll (1974: 48ff).

## 7.2.2. Syllabification

The existence of rules which refer to syllables presupposes a method for organizing segments into syllables. Most work on this topic has been concerned with the proper division and distribution of consonant clusters. It is widely agreed, for instance, that clusters should be syllabified in agreement with the phonotactics of the language in question, a medial cluster being divided into a possible word-final cluster plus a possible word-initial one. But there are principles of syllabification which have little to do with consonants. It is often the case that grammatical boundaries override the phonologically motivated rules of syllabification in a given language. And a language may choose to syllabify one and the same cluster of consonants leftward or rightward depending on the strength of adjacent vowels – stressed or full vowels being more attractive than unstressed or reduced ones. Finally, all things being equal, the vowel following a consonant or consonant cluster tends to attract those consonants more strongly than the vowel preceding.

## 7.2.3. Consonantal hierarchies and syllable structure

Vennemann (1982) combines the phonotactic criterion for the syllabification of consonants with a hierarchy of consonantal strength to establish an interesting set of 'preferential principles' of syllabification. A number of different proposals regarding consonantal hierarchies have been made, including those by Drachman (1977), Hooper (1976: 195ff), Foley (1977), and Vennemann (1982). Such hierarchies all resemble Jespersen's (1897–9), which was rooted in 'sonority'. However, this notion has never to my knowledge been operationalized and is at best a handy cover term. A typical example of such a hierarchy is vowels > glides > liquids > nasals > obstruents. As far as the relation of hierarchies to syllable structure is concerned, a particularly difficult point is where voice and continuancy fall within the obstruents: is fricatives > plosives or voiced obstruents > voiceless obstruents the last step of the hierarchy? Both options seem to make sense and have in fact been proposed.

The claim that fricatives are systematically higher than plosives on a hierarchy intended to account for syllable structure makes the prediction that voicing need not be continuous within the syllable, so that, for example, a syllable ending in [-esb] with voiceless [s] and voiced [b] should be a possibility. This seems a very daring hypothesis to me, and the burden of proof certainly lies with those claiming a non-exceptional status for such syllables.

The alternative claim, namely that voiced segments are systematically higher than voiceless ones in a hierarchy intended to account for syllable structure makes a different prediction: that fricatives sometimes occur farther from the center of the syllable than plosives (though not of course if the fricative is voiced and the plosive voiceless). And this situation is in fact well-attested in many languages, for example, the much discussed cases of sibilants occurring at the uttermost margin of the syllable, separated from the center by a plosive (e.g. English *spill*, *ax*).

Consonantal hierarchies have been set up with many purposes in mind besides syllable structure. Naturally then, in order to evaluate such general hierarchies many different types of criteria are necessary besides their adequacy in handling syllable structure alone. But as far as syllable structure is concerned, I have no doubts that voicing is part of the hierarchy and that the distinction between fricatives and plosives is not. For a model that predicts this result, see Basbøll (1974).

I shall now briefly consider proposals about the internal structure of syllables in general, independent of the nature of the segments involved. Different proposals have been advanced, though it is not always clear (to me at least) what kind of evidence will decide between them, or if they do not simply follow from some particular aspect of the theory in which they are embedded. Selkirk (1982) proposes the following model, which seems to embody the traditional view within phonology:

(8)

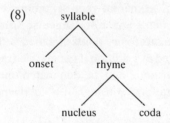

Note that this model predicts that rhymes may be prosodically relevant without regard to their onset, and that there are in general tighter phonotactic constraints between nucleus and coda than between nucleus and onset. The model also allows one to visualize clearly the traditional distinction between 'heavy' and 'light' syllables: heavy syllables have more than one segment in the rhyme. Some interesting approaches to the constituency of the syllable will be discussed in the next section.

## 7.2.4. Autosegmental phonology, CV phonology, and 'phonological weight'

I shall end this section by considering the framework of autosegmental phonology and two interesting proposals on syllable structure that have been advanced departing from this model: the so-called 'CV phonology' of Clements & Keyser (1983) and Hyman's theory of 'phonological weight' (1985).

Autosegmental phonology was first advanced in order to account for tonal phenomena (see Goldsmith 1979). Tones in many ways seem to act independently of the segments that they are associated with. If a segment is deleted, for example, the tonal contour, rather than being changed, is normally spread over the now smaller segmental chain. Autosegmental phonology accounts for such phenomena by recognizing separate *tiers* (layers) for segments and tones, the latter acting as *autosegments*, i.e. segments in their own right, independent of the 'normal' segments. This approach allows a different number of elements in each tier and does not require that the boundaries between them coincide. Thus the process of associating the elements of the different tiers is a crucial one; one might consider the mapping of autosegments to be a kind of 'blank filling'. The autosegmental approach has also been applied (often successfully, in my view) to vowel and consonant harmony, where harmonic elements are considered to be autosegments, and to Icelandic preaspiration, where a laryngeal tier has been posited (Thráinsson 1978).[10]

At the same time that autosegmental phonology was being developed to deal with tonal phenomena, Kahn (1976) began to apply its insights to the study of syllable-dependent processes, concentrating on the phonology of English. Capitalizing on the ability of autosegmental representations to permit a one-to-many relation between segments and autosegments, Kahn formalized the notion of ambisyllabic consonants (consonants affiliated with two adjacent syllables), a relation not allowed in traditional generative tree structure representations, where a particular node may be dominated only by one single node.[11] By way of illustration, consider the following

---

[10] For further discussion of autosegmental phonology, see this volume, Chapter 6, section 6.2.3 and Chapter 13, section 13.2.2. Its basic idea is strongly reminiscent of Firthian 'prosodic analysis' (cf. Palmer 1970). Metrical phonology (7.3.2) also represents viewpoints of an earlier structuralist framework, in this case, for example, that of Rischel (1964). Historically speaking, it seems to be the general case that what appear to be independent evolutions within the dominant paradigm result in solutions, which, though in general more highly structured, are nevertheless reminiscent of much earlier frameworks.

   At present, there is an interesting discussion devoted to integrating insights from autosegmental phonology and metrical phonology into one basic framework (see the important anthologies edited by van der Hulst & Smith 1982, 1985, with excellent introductions to these two influential nonlinear approaches).

[11] Ambisyllabic consonants have also been proposed within dependency phonology (Anderson & Jones 1974).

representation of the word *Jennifer* from Clements & Keyser (1983: 3), in which /n/ and /f/ are ambisyllabic ('S' stands for 'syllable'):

(9)
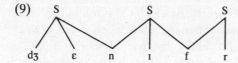

Kahn (1976) is an important precursor to Clements & Keyser's CV phonology, whose novelty lies in the addition of a CV-tier to the segmental and syllabic tiers already accepted within autosegmental phonology. *Jennifer* is rendered as follows by Clements & Keyser (1983: 8), where 'σ' stands for 'syllable,' 'V' for 'syllabic peak' and 'C' for 'syllabic nonpeak (or margin)':[12]

(10)
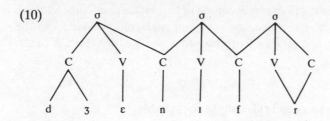

The CV-tier removes the need for the feature [syllabic], which, as Ladefoged (1971: 94) pointed out, was difficult to define phonetically and, unlike other segmental features, had prosodic properties in the sense that, like stress, it indicated a sort of culmination. On the other hand, the CV model fails to express the high degree of predictability of the feature [syllabic] from the sonority of the segments in question.

The existence of the CV-tier allows Clements & Keyser to exploit further the one-to-many and many-to-one relationships permitted by autosegmental representations. In the illustration above, /r/ functions both as a syllable peak and as a 'normal consonant,' and the affricate [dʒ] is seen simultaneously as two segments and as only one (on the 'CV-tier'); the same device may be used for other tightly connected segments, e.g. certain diphthongs. But once again we must be cautious: if this device is to be more than a trick (corresponding to the vague statement that, for example, affricates can function both as one and as two elements), it must be shown by *independent* criteria that in all cases where they function as one element it is the CV-tier that is relevant, and that

---

[12] Note that Clements & Keyser do not consider the syllable internally structured into onset, rhyme, etc. (cf. 7.2.3). Thus the syllable structure is flat, despite the addition of a CV-tier and a nucleus tier. The latter is not a level interposed between syllable and CV, but an independent projection.

in all cases where they function as two elements it is the segmental tier. Also where the dual behavior of long vowels and geminates, as one or two elements, is accounted for by one segment associated to two slots (on the CV-tier), there should be independent criteria for which tier is relevant.

Instead of CV-slots as timing units, Hyman (1985) operates with a 'weight tier' with 'weight units' (WUs), recalling the use of morae in Prague phonology. The maximal expansion of a single WU (=x) is hypothesized to be as follows (1985: 119):

(11)

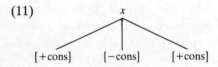

This means that heavy syllables will consist of two morae; and since all three segments in the above expansion are optional, all syllables can be exhaustively composed of WUs (for discussion, see van der Hulst & Smith 1985: 41ff).

## 7.3. Phonological structures and rules above the syllable

### 7.3.1. Boundaries and domains

In *SPE* (364–71), boundaries were considered units with the feature [−segment] in the phonological string, whereas segments were considered units with the feature [+segment]. Three types of boundaries were proposed: '+' (the 'formative boundary'); '#' (the word boundary, which was posited to occur before certain suffixes as well); and '=' (a special boundary posited to occur in certain words involving foreign morphemes, e.g. in *per=mit*). Phonological rules were assumed to ignore instances of + unless that boundary was specifically required in the structural description of the rule in question. Other boundaries, however, in order to be involved in a rule, needed to be mentioned explicitly in the structural description.

This system, complicated as it was, was adhered to and developed in the decade following the publication of *SPE*. Interestingly, however, another late 1960s proposal, McCawley (1968), was both more elegant and more descriptively adequate than the *SPE* view, and corresponds better to current views of prosody. McCawley proposed a ranking of the boundaries in a language, the syllable boundary having the lowest rank. The function of such boundaries was to delimit the domain of phonological rules, so that, for example, a rule with the syllable as its domain, is, by definition, a rule ranked by the syllable boundary. Rules, by convention, ignore boundaries that are lower than their ranking.[13]

## 7.3.2. Stress and metrical phonology

One of the most influential articles from the last decade within generative phonology is Liberman & Prince (1977), which proposes to account for stress and 'linguistic rhythm' by means of a rather complicated formal system involving crucially *metrical trees*, *metrical grids*, and a +/− stress distinction in the basic strings. The metrical trees have (until quite recently, see below) been considered the central type of structure in metrical phonology. Metrical trees are partly used to account for phrasal stress, and in that function they are basically syntactic trees with a particular labeling (cf. Selkirk 1984: 155ff). In (12) is an example (where 'R' stands for 'root'; 'w' for 'weak'; and 's' for strong):

(12)

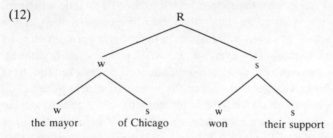

The same types of metrical tree structures have been extended to account also for accentual word structure and even for syllable structure, as in Kiparsky (1981), where syllabic peaks are considered a culminative structuring on a par with accentual peaks, or stresses.[14]

A number of formal aspects of metrical trees may be distinguished (cf. Hayes 1981, 1984):

**(i)**   Only tree structures of the traditional type in generative phonology are

---

[13] In Basbøll (1978) I attempt to eliminate the mention of boundaries in rules. A word-final vowel-tensing rule would be formalized as follows:

(i) If    X V
          ↓
    Then  [+tense]
    Rank: #

(where the variable X is interpreted according to Stanley 1973, its absence to the right of V being significant)

The constrained nature of this view of boundaries as delimiters of domains should find support in the types of processes one finds in natural language. Combined with the proposal that such domains can also occur as units in rules, this view brings us close both to the traditional view of hierarchical units in phonology (syllable, phonological phrase, etc.) and to recent proposals such as Selkirk (1981).

[14] For an earlier view, see Rischel (1964) and his references to glossematics.

allowed. This means that the sort of syllable structures proposed within dependency phonology or autosegmental phonology (with ambisyllabic consonants) will not be allowed as parts of the metrical tree.

(ii)   Only binary branchings are allowed. Thus an intonational phrase cannot have three immediate constituents, nor can ternary feet exist, assuming that the foot is the node label immediately above the syllable (for discussion, see Dogil 1984).

(iii)   Each branching node has one strong branch (labeled 's') and one weak branch (labeled 'w'). This idea of strong (or dominant) and weak (or dependent) branches has no parallel within traditional generative syntax, though it is akin to ideas of dependency grammar and other grammatical models using notions like 'head' and 'modifier'.

(iv)   All nodes have exactly one label.

(v)   The node labels are strictly ordered paradigmatically from weak to strong.

The metrical trees, with their close relationship to syntactic structure, account for obviously structure-dependent stress phenomena such as the reduction of the stress of *eleven* with respect to that of *men* in *eleven men*, by the nuclear stress rule. However, it is well-known that rhythmical phenomena may go counter to structure-dependent stress, as when the stress of the first syllable is stronger than that of the second (compare *thirteén* and *thìrteen mén*). While some such rhythmic phenomena might be accountable for by rules changing the metrical trees involved (by inverting s and w branches, or whatever), Liberman & Prince (1977) posited another structure to account for 'avoidance of clashes of stress,' namely the *metrical grid*. The metrical grid is a sequence of columns (one for each syllable), each column consisting of a number of 'beats,' as in the following example from Selkirk (1984: 44):

(13)                       x
       x                   x
       x     x       x     x
       x  x  x  x    x  x  x  x  x
       Abernathy gesticulated

Rhythmically conditioned stress alternations are seen as movements of the beats involved (see Prince 1983; Selkirk 1984), recalling in a sense the 'floating tones' of autosegmental phonology.

This complete structure with trees, grids, and +/− stress is extremely complex, and often admits to various alternative options (e.g. trees vs. grids). A number of attempts have therefore been made to constrain the theory, both by constraining the tree structures themselves (for example by predicting the distribution of s and w branches), by concentrating on the tree structures at the expense of the grid (cf. Kiparsky 1981), or by giving more precise principles for when which structures can be used.

One of the most interesting proposals to reduce and ameliorate the descriptive apparatus within the metrical theory of stress and rhythm is Selkirk (1984), which builds upon Prince (1983) in particular. The proposal is to account for stress by means of the metrical grid, disposing entirely of the metrical trees, and other aspects of the prosody are described in terms of a syntactic hierarchy. Selkirk further argues that the metrical grid itself is derived from the intonated surface structure. The relations between such hierarchies is still controversial, but the reduction to one phonological and one kind of surface syntactic hierarchy seems conceptually advantageous when compared to intermediate hierarchies like metrical trees.[15]

## 7.4. Phonological processes and morphonological rules

### 7.4.1. Lexical phonology: derivations reconsidered

The theory of lexical phonology (Kiparsky 1982, 1985; Mohanan 1982; Rubach 1984; Booij & Rubach 1984; Kaisse & Shaw 1985), while developed within the tradition of mainstream generative phonology, presents a radically different view of the interaction of phonological rules from that of *SPE*. In particular, it makes crucial use of the (traditional pre-generative) distinction between word-phonology and phonology above the word. Morphological and word-phonological rules are interspersed, and apply together cyclically within the lexicon, in the following way (from Kaisse & Shaw 1985: 9):

(14)

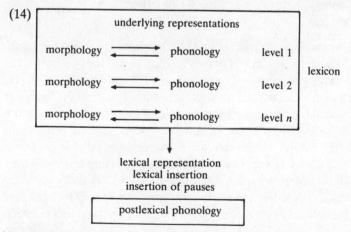

---

[15] Metrical phonology is discussed further by Hayes, in Chapter 12, Volume II of this survey. For an interesting theory of stress that is less highly structured than metrical phonology, see Schane's (1979) 'linear theory'.

Lexical phonology uses no boundary symbols; instead the brackets provided by the morphology delimit cyclic domains and are then erased at the end of each level. The interspersing of morphological and phonological rules means, for example, that stress on *arríve* is part of the information to which the word formation rule giving rise to *arríval* has access.

Phonological rules that apply above the word level are supposed to apply only after the word-level rules and they apply noncyclically: they are justly termed 'postcyclical' or 'postlexical' rules and they apply across-the-board (an example is flapping in North American English). According to lexical phonology, then, a large part of what had earlier been described within the phonological component of a grammar is now taken care of within the lexical component, including internal sandhi.[16] The descriptive interest within lexical phonology still, to a large extent, lies in the same sort of phonological rules and regularities, in part of a rather abstract type, which constituted the main field of interest for earlier types of generative phonology (cf. Kiparsky 1973). But it constitutes a great step forward when compared to *SPE*, since a number of classical problems within generative phonology have come closer to a solution (e.g. constraints on abstractness by means of cyclicity, principles for rule application, and the elimination of morpheme structure conditions). Within generative phonology, lexical phonology may be considered the main theory accounting for the 'derivational aspect,' whereas autosegmental and metrical phonology account for the (nonlinear) 'representational aspect' (cf. van der Hulst & Smith 1985).[17]

### 7.4.2. Natural phonology: naturalness, semiotic function, and substantive evidence

A short programmatic paper by Stampe (1969) presented the main points of the evolving trend of 'natural phonology' (not to be confused with the 'natural generative phonology' of Vennemann 1974 and Hooper 1976). He posited that a number of natural processes are innate, and during language acquisition the child learns to suppress the natural process in question if it is not present in his or her language, or to restrict it in some particular way. For example, the natural process devoicing obstruents in syllable-final position would end up being suppressed by French and Hungarian children, whereas children acquiring certain other languages, like Russian and most types of German, would learn to restrict it, for example, only to word-final position, or to some set of obstruents. The role of such natural processes has

---

[16] Sandhi may in general be considered a symptom, or signal, of the structuring of complex signs, cf. Andersen (1986).

[17] For more discussion of lexical phonology, see sections 14.3.3., 14.3.4. of Chapter 14 in this volume, and section 6.3.2. of Chapter 6.

remained the crucial feature of natural phonology ever since (cf. Stampe 1973, 1980; Donegan 1978; Donegan & Stampe 1979).

Natural phonology has been elaborated in great detail in Wolfgang Dressler's important book *Morphonology: the dynamics of derivation* (1985), which represents an integrative effort in many senses. First, it categorizes a wide class of rules with respect to their naturalness, from universal phonological processes with their language-specific restrictions, to (mor)phonological rules like the English vowel shift rule, to morphological rules (also cf. Linell 1979b; Dressler 1984). In this framework, 'morphonology' emerges as the field of interaction between (natural) phonology and (natural) morphology. Second, it attempts to ground natural phonology and morphology in Peircian semiotics, utilizing such notions as 'plurifunctionality' and conflicting goals. Third, it derives a large number of predictions of a quantitative nature, such as whether a phonological phenomenon will be rare or common. It also predicts correlations between processes and levels of formality and delineates possible vs. impossible changes. These predictions are derived from an examination of highly diversified material from the literature and from fieldwork to a greater extent than is normal in phonology. Fourth, it bases its predictions to a great extent on substantive evidence from language acquisition, aphasia, socio-phonological variation, contrastive phonology, and loan phonology. Rightly, it considers such evidence central, rather than merely 'external.'

Phonological processes in Dressler's approach fall into two basic types: foregrounding and backgrounding (fortitions and lenitions, respectively, according to the terminology of Donegan & Stampe 1979). Foregrounding and backgrounding processes are rooted in the demands of the perceiver and producer, respectively, and encompass, for example, dissimilations and assimilations. Foregrounding processes are predicted to occur relatively frequently in certain styles, as, for example, when adults talk to small children, and in formal style; backgrounding processes more frequently in casual speech.

## 7.5. Prospects for the future: towards a new synthesis?

The introduction to this chapter called attention to the degree to which phonological theory is fragmented into a number of more or less isolated schools of thought. I have, however, alluded in several places to a positive evolution away from the danger of extreme fragmentation, and shall end the chapter by summarizing the positive signs pointing to a synthesis. To begin with, it should be noted that the individual schools of phonology largely investigate different issues; one might hope and expect, then, that the particular findings of one school will ultimately be relevant to the others. Indeed, as we have seen, this is already happening.

At the institutional plane, two symptoms of an inchoate synthesis should be mentioned. First, there is the tradition of International Phonology Meetings (*Phonologietagungen*), organized by the Institut für Sprachwissenschaft an der Universität Wien every fourth year, starting with 1968. These meetings are organized very broadly, in the sense that all different approaches to phonology are included, and in fact they have been attended by a large and increasing number of phonologists from the most diversified backgrounds. The publications from the meetings are entitled *Phonologica 1972, 1976*, etc. (though the first was entitled *Phonologie der Gegenwart*). They are useful comprehensive anthologies of current work in phonology.

The other encouraging institutional fact is the publication by the Cambridge University Press of an international *Phonology Yearbook* (volume 1, 1984), edited by Colin J. Ewen and John M. Anderson. The *Yearbook* is both of high scientific standard and theoretically pluralistic.

I shall close by mentioning three other areas where a certain open-mindedness seems already to be present, and where its increase could only contribute further to the advancement of phonological theory. First, within the generative paradigm, I find encouraging the attempts to synthesize metrical and autosegmental phonology. Second, the increased interest in sentence prosody (intonation, phrasal and rhythmical stress, and so on) is resulting in a welcome integration of work in phonetics, phonology, syntax, semantics, pragmatics (including discourse analysis), and psycholinguistics. Third, the study of natural spoken language and approaches to phonological typology have resulted in an encouraging expansion of the database. Likewise, appeal to a variety of types of substantive evidence has resulted in the increasing use of a broad spectrum of such additional but crucial data.

In short, I think that the discipline of phonology is in a more thriving state than it has ever been. Let us hope that it will continue in its current health.

REFERENCES

Allen, W. S. 1973. *Accent and rhythm*. Cambridge: Cambridge University Press.
Andersen, H. 1973. Abductive and deductive change. *Language* 49: 567–95.
Andersen, H. 1975. Markedness in vowel systems. *Proceedings of the 11th International Congress of Linguists* II: 891–7.
Andersen, H. 1978. Vocalic and consonantal languages. In H. Birnbaum *et al.* (eds.) *Studia linguistica A. V. Issatschenko a collegis amicisque oblata*. Lisse: Peter de Ridder.
Andersen, H. (ed.) 1986. *Sandhi phenomena in the languages of Europe*. Trends in Linguistics no. 33. Berlin: Gruyter.

Anderson, J. M. & Jones, C. 1974. Three theses concerning phonological representations. *Journal of Linguistics* 10: 1–26.

Anderson, S. R. 1974. *The organization of phonology*. New York: Academic Press.

Anderson, S. R. 1976. Nasal consonants and the internal structure of segments. *Language* 52: 326–44.

Bailey, C.-J. N. 1977. Linguistic change, naturalness, mixture, and structural principles. *Papiere zur Linguistik* 16: 6–73.

Bailey, C.-J. N. 1983. *Grundzüge der englischen Phonetologie. Allgemeine Systematik*. Berlin: Technische Universität.

Basbøll, Hans. 1972. Some conditioning factors for the pronunciation of short vowels in Danish with special reference to syllabification. *Annual Report of the Institute of Phonetics, University of Copenhagen* 6: 185–210.

Basbøll, H. 1974. The phonological syllable with special reference to Danish. *Annual Report of the Institute of Phonetics, University of Copenhagen* 8: 39–128.

Basbøll, H. 1978. On the use of 'domains' in phonology. *Proceedings of the 12th International Congress of Linguists*: 763–6.

Basbøll, H. 1980. Phonology. *Language and Speech* 23: 91–113.

Bell, A. & Hooper, J. B. (eds.) 1978. *Syllables and segments*. Amsterdam: North-Holland.

Booij, G. & Rubach, J. 1984. Morphological and prosodic domains in lexical phonology. *Phonology Yearbook* 1: 1–27.

Broecke, M. van der 1976. *Hierarchies and rank orders in distinctive features*. Assen/ Amsterdam: Van Gorcum.

Chomsky, N. & Halle, M. 1968. *The sound pattern of English*. New York: Harper & Row.

Clements, G. N. 1985. The geometry of phonological features. *Phonology Yearbook* 2: 225–52.

Clements, G. N. & Keyser, S. J. 1983. *CV phonology: a generative theory of the syllable*. Cambridge, MA: MIT Press.

Davidsen-Nielsen, N. 1978. *Neutralization and archiphoneme*. Copenhagen: Akademisk Forlag.

Dell, François. 1973. *Les règles et les sons*. Paris: Hermann. Translated (1980) as *Generative phonology*. Cambridge: Cambridge University Press.

Dinnsen, D. A. (ed.) 1979. *Current approaches to phonological theory*. Bloomington: Indiana University Press.

Dogil, G. 1984. Review article of van der Hulst & Smith (1982). *Phonology Yearbook* 1: 157–73.

Donegan, P. J. 1978. *On the natural phonology of vowels*. Working Papers in Linguistics 23, Ohio State University.

Donegan, P. J. & Stampe, D. 1979. The study of natural phonology. In Dinnsen (1979).

Drachman, G. 1977. On the notion 'phonological hierarchy'. In W. U. Dressler *et al.* (eds.) *Phonologica 1976*. Innsbruck: Innsbrucker Beiträge zur Sprachwissenschaft.

Dressler, W. U. 1984. Explaining natural phonology. *Phonology Yearbook* 1: 29–51.

Dressler, W. U. 1985. *Morphonology: the dynamics of derivation*. Linguistica Extranea, Studia 12. Ann Arbor: Karoma.

Ewen, C. J. 1982. The internal structure of complex segments. In van der Hulst & Smith (1982, II).

Ewen, C. J. 1986. Segmental and suprasegmental structure. In J. Durand (ed.) *Dependency and nonlinear phonology*. London: Croom Helm.

Fant, G. M. 1973. *Speech sounds and features*. Cambridge, MA: MIT Press.

Firth, J. R. 1957. *Papers in linguistics 1934–51*. Oxford: Oxford University Press.

Fischer-Jørgensen, E. 1956. The commutation test and its application to phonemic analysis. *For Roman Jakobson. Essays on the occasion of his sixtieth birthday*. The Hague: Mouton.

Fischer-Jørgensen, E. 1975. *Trends in phonological theory*. Copenhagen: Akademisk Forlag.

Fischer-Jørgensen, E. 1984. Some basic vowel features, their articulatory correlates and their explanatory power in phonology. *Annual Report of the Institute of Phonetics, University of Copehagen* 18: 255–76.

Foley, J. 1977. *Foundations of theoretical phonology*. Cambridge: Cambridge University Press.

Fudge, E. C. 1969. Syllables. *Journal of Linguistics* 5: 253–86.

Goldsmith, J. 1979. *Autosegmental phonology*. New York: Garland.

Greenberg, J. (ed.) 1978. *Universals of human language*. Vol. 2: *Phonology*. Stanford: Stanford University Press.

Griffen, T. D. 1976. Toward a nonsegmental phonology. *Lingua* 40: 1–20.

Griffen, T. D. 1977. German [x]. *Lingua* 43: 375–90.

Hawkins, P. 1984. *Introducing phonology*. London: Hutchinson.

Hayes, B. 1981. *A metrical theory of stress rules*. Bloomington: Indiana University Linguistics Club.

Hayes, B. 1984. The phonology of rhythm in English. *Linguistic Inquiry* 15: 33–74.

Hjelmslev, L. 1939. The syllable as a structural unit. *Proceedings of the Third International Congress of Phonetic Sciences*.

Hockett, C. F. 1955. *A manual of phonology*. *IJAL* Memoir 11. Baltimore: Waverly Press.

Hooper, J. B. 1972. The syllable in phonological theory. *Language* 48: 525–40.

Hooper, J. B. 1976. *An introduction to natural generative phonology*. New York: Academic Press.

Hulst, H. van der & Smith, N. (eds.) 1982. *The structure of phonological representations* I, II. Dordrecht: Foris.

Hulst, H. van der & Smith, N. (eds.) 1985. *Advances in non-linear phonology*. Dordrecht: Foris.

Hyman, L. M. 1975. *Phonology. Theory and analysis*. New York: Holt, Rinehart & Winston.

Hyman, L. M. 1985. *A theory of phonological weight*. Dordrecht: Foris.

Jakobson, R., Fant, G. & Halle, M. 1952. *Preliminaries to speech analysis*. Cambridge, MA: MIT Press.

Jakobson, R. & Halle, M. 1956. *Fundamentals of language*. The Hague: Mouton.

Jespersen, O. 1897–9. *Fonetik*. Copenhagen: Det Schubotheske Forlag.

Kahn, D. 1976. *Syllable-based generalizations in English phonology*. Bloomington: IULC.

Kaisse, E. M. & Shaw, P. A. 1985. On the theory of lexical phonology. *Phonology Yearbook* 2: 1–30.

Kaye, J., Lowenstamm, J. & Vergnaud, J.-R. 1985. The internal structure of phonological elements: a theory of charm and government. *Phonology Yearbook* 2: 305–28.

Kean, M. L. 1981. On a theory of markedness: some general considerations and a case in point. In A. Belletti *et al.* (eds.) *Theory of markedness in generative grammar*. Pisa: Scuola Normale Superiore.

Kenstowicz, M. & Kisseberth, C. 1979. *Generative phonology*. New York: Academic Press.

Kiparsky, P. 1973. Abstractness, opacity, and global rules. In O. Fujimura (ed.) *Three dimensions of linguistic theory*. Tokyo: TEC.

Kiparsky, P. 1981. Remarks on the metrical structure of the syllable. In W. U. Dressler *et al.* (eds.) *Phonologica 1980*. Innsbruck: Innsbrucker Beiträge zur Sprachwissenschaft.

Kiparsky, P. 1982. From cyclic phonology to lexical phonology. In van der Hulst & Smith (1982, I).

Kiparsky, P. 1985. Some consequences of lexical phonology. *Phonology Yearbook* 2: 85–138.

Kuryłowicz, J. 1948. Contribution à la théorie de la syllabe. *Biuletyn polskiego towarzystwa jezykoznawczego* 8: 80–114. Reprinted (1973) *Esquisses linguistiques I*, 2nd edn. München: Wilhelm Fink.

Ladefoged, P. 1971. *Preliminaries to linguistic phonetics*. Chicago: University of Chicago Press.

Lass, R. 1976. *English phonology and phonological theory. Synchronic and diachronic studies*. Cambridge: Cambridge University Press.

Lass, R. 1983. *Phonology. An introduction to basic concepts*. Cambridge: Cambridge University Press.

Liberman, M. & Prince, A. S. 1977. On stress and linguistic rhythm. *Linguistic Inquiry* 8: 249–336.

Lindau, M. 1978. Vowel features. *Language* 54: 541–63.

Linell, P. 1979a. *Psychological reality in phonology*. Cambridge: Cambridge University Press.

Linell, P. 1979b. Evidence for a functionally-based typology of phonological rules. *Communication and Cognition* 12: 53–106.

Maddieson, I. 1983. *Patterns of sounds*. Cambridge: Cambridge University Press.

Makkai, V. B. (ed.) 1972. *Phonological theory. Evolution and current practice*. New York: Holt, Rinehart & Winston.

McCawley, J. D. 1968. *The phonological component of a grammar of Japanese*. The Hague: Mouton.

Mohanan, K. P. 1982. *Lexical phonology*. Bloomington: Indiana University Linguistics Club.

Palmer, F. R. 1970. *Prosodic analysis*. Oxford: Oxford University Press.

Pike, K. L. & Pike, E. 1947. Immediate constituents of Mazateco syllables. *International Journal of American Linguistics* 13: 78–91.

Postal, P. 1968. *Aspects of phonological theory*. New York: Harper & Row.

Prince, A. S. 1983. Relating to the grid. *Linguistic Inquiry* 14: 19–100.

Pulgram, E. 1970. *Syllable, word, nexus, cursus*. The Hague: Mouton.

Rischel, J. 1964. Stress, juncture and syllabification in phonemic description. *Proceedings of the 9th International Congress of Linguists*.

Rischel, J. 1974. *Topics in West Greenlandic phonology*. Copenhagen: Akademisk Forlag.

Rubach, J. 1984. *Cyclic and lexical phonology: the structure of Polish*. Dordrecht: Foris.

Schane, S. A. 1973. *Generative phonology*. Englewood Cliffs: Prentice-Hall.

Schane, S. A. 1979. The rhythmic nature of English word accentuation. *Language* 55: 559–602.

Schane, S. A. 1984. The fundamentals of particle phonology. *Phonology Yearbook* 1: 129–55.

Selkirk, E. O. 1981. On the nature of phonological representation. In J. Anderson, J. Laver & T. Meyers (eds.) *The cognitive representation of speech*. Amsterdam: North-Holland.

Selkirk, E. O. 1982. The syllable. In van der Hulst & Smith (1982, ii).

Selkirk, E. O. 1984. *Phonology and syntax. The relation between sound and structure*. Cambridge, MA: MIT Press.

Sommerstein, A. H. 1977. *Modern phonology*. London: Arnold.

Stampe, D. 1969. The acquisition of phonetic representation. *CLS* 5: 443–54.

Stampe, D. 1973. On chapter nine. In M. Kenstowicz & C. Kisseberth (eds.), *Issues in phonological theory*. The Hague: Mouton.

Stampe, D. 1980. *A dissertation on natural phonology*. New York: Garland.

Stanley, R. 1973. Boundaries in phonology. In S. R. Anderson & P. Kiparsky (eds.) *A festschrift for Morris Halle*. New York: Holt, Rinehart & Winston.

Thráinsson, H. 1978. On the phonology of Icelandic preaspiration. *Nordic Journal of Linguistics* 1: 3–54.

Trubetzkoy, N. S. 1939. *Grundzüge der Phonologie*. Travaux du Cercle linguistique de Prague 7.

Vennemann, T. 1972. On the theory of syllabic phonology. *Linguistische Berichte* 18: 1–18.

Vennemann, T. 1974. Words and syllables in natural generative grammar. In A. Bruck *et al.* (eds.) *Papers from the parasession of natural phonology*. Chicago: Chicago Linguistic Society.

Vennemann, T. 1981. Phonology as non-functional non-phonetics. In W. U. Dressler *et al.* (eds.) *Phonologica 1980*. Innsbruck: Innsbrucker Beiträge zur Sprachwissenschaft.

Vennemann, T. 1982. Zur Silbenstruktur der deutschen Standardsprache. In T. Vennemann (ed.) *Silben, Segmente, Akzente*. Tübingen: Niemeyer.

Williamson, K. 1977. Multivalued features for consonants. *Language* 53: 843–71.

# 8 Phonetic theory
*Mary E. Beckman*

## 8.0. Introduction

Phonetics is the study of speech, of its production by the human articulatory apparatus, of its characteristics as an acoustic signal, and of its processing by the human auditory and cognitive systems. More than any other area of study encompassed by linguistics, speech is an interdisciplinary science. We can contrast it, for example, with the study of syntax. While there are many different theories of syntax, it is still possible to identify a common thread of 'syntactic theory' because the different specific theories are all formulated from the single perspective of the linguist; when scientists from other disciplines address questions of syntax, they adopt the terminology and attendant assumptions of the linguist's approach. Similarly, everyone who addresses questions in speech shares the International Phonetic Alphabet or some provincial derivative of it, a legacy of the time when phonetics was synonymous with phonology; but this shared representation and its attendant assumptions about the size and shape of basic speech units no longer constitute the bulk of 'phonetic theory' in the way that they did in the late nineteenth and early twentieth century. Instead, there are as many different phonetic theories as there are reasons for studying speech. The engineer studies the speech signal as an application of a more general theory of signal processing; the psychologist studies speech perception and organization as part of the search for a general theory of perception and cognition; the physiologist studies speech production as a complex example of the general problem of motor control; and so on.

The lack of a single dominant perspective makes it impossible to provide an encyclopedic overview of phonetics that would not make it seem as if this field of study is too splintered to allow much cumulative progress. Such an impression would be inaccurate. Often, an issue or a set of results from one approach to speech has relevance to others. Then, the questions and debates come to be couched in the terminology of more than one discipline, which can lead to a hybrid approach to the problem and an advance toward a more

216

unified general theory of speech. Instead of attempting a sketchy coverage of the major issues in all subfields of phonetics, therefore, I will cover three broad areas in which a hybrid approach has developed or seems about to develop, displaying the interdisciplinary nature of phonetics to its best advantage. The three areas are the specification of acoustic properties for distinctive features, the determination of auditory and phonological bases for categorical perception, and the characterization of segmentation and coarticulation in speech production.

## 8.1. Acoustic invariants for phonetic features

A major landmark in the emergence of a modern interdisciplinary science of phonetics was the proposal of a system of distinctive phonetic features based on the application of information theory, electrical engineering, and recent advances in acoustics (Jakobson, Fant & Halle 1952). The debt to each of these areas is evident in the insistence on discrete binary features and the notion of redundancy, in the use of a source-filter transmission network model, and in the proposal of an acoustic definition for each feature. None of these aspects of the new feature system was novel in itself. Other linguists were exploring the implications for phonology of the newly emerging field of information science (e.g. Hockett 1953), and the definition of acoustic properties would have been sketchy indeed if there had not already been a great deal of work on a source-filter model for speech acoustics (e.g. Chiba & Kajiyama 1941). What was different about the new feature system was rather the change in value assigned to the physical and perceptual content of the elements in phonological opposition. The earlier attitude is exemplified by Bloch's (1948) axioms for phonological analysis, which included the postulate that no observation of articulatory and auditory properties was necessary other than phonetic transcription. The authors of *Preliminaries to speech analysis*, by contrast, called for 'experimental verification and further elaboration' of the articulatory, acoustic, and perceptual specifications for the distinctive features in a program of 'coordinated research by linguists, psychologists, experts in the physiology of speech and hearing, physicists, communications and electronics engineers, mathematicians, students in symbolic logic and semiotics, and neurologists dealing with language disturbances.' (Jakobson *et al.* 1952: v).

This description of an interdisciplinary program for studying distinctive features characterized a great deal of work done on speech for the next three decades. Acoustic patterns were isolated by synthesis so as to determine their salience as perceptual cues (e.g. Delattre *et al.* 1952; Delattre, Liberman & Cooper 1955). Articulatory prerequisites for the acoustic patterns were explored in programs for calculating formants from vocal tract area functions (e.g. Stevens & House 1955; Fant 1960). Auditory correlates of the resonances were tested in models that incorporated emerging knowledge of the relevant psychophysical functions for perception of timbre (e.g. Carlson, Fant & Granstrom 1975; Chistovich & Lublinskaya 1979). Articulatory correlates of vowel features were studied when new technology such as electromyography and cinefluorography was applied to speech (e.g. MacNeilage & Sholes 1964; Perkell 1969). More accurate phonetic characterizations of problematic consonant features such as [tense] and [voiced] were achieved as their acoustic and physiological correlates were discovered (e.g. Lisker & Abramson 1964; Ohala & Ohala 1972). The list could be extended *ad infinitem* to illustrate how much has come to be known about speech articulation, acoustics, and perception because speech scientists from many different disciplines were engaged in research that assumed a set of paradigmatically contrasting primitive sound qualities and searched for corresponding quantifiable properties at each level of the speech chain.

A recurrent question in this research is the issue of invariance. One aspect of this problem is contextual variability. A major tenet of phonological theory has been that gross differences in the realization of a segment from one context to another can be described by changes in redundant phonetic features for a given phonemic opposition. For example, the different places of closure for the initial stops in Japanese *kimi* 'sensation' vs. *kumi* 'class' might be explained as a change in the feature [back], which is redundant for stop consonants in Japanese. However, place of contact for the tongue dorsum on the soft palate can be varied continuously, and cineradiographic studies show it to be progressively further back in the series /ki, ke, ku, ka, ko/ (Wada *et al.* 1970). This articulatory variability cannot be captured by a phonological rule assimilating the phonetic features of the velar stop to those of the following vowel. A related problem is that the formant transitions after the stop's release, which have been shown to be a reliable cue to place, also differ depending on the following vowel.

Another aspect of the problem of invariance is variability in the realization of a distinctive feature from one language to another. Early generative phonology described such cross-language variability as a sort of phonetic redundancy resulting from language-specific rules for implementing each binary-valued distinctive feature along a multivalued physical scale (Chomsky & Halle 1968). For example, in languages that contrast rounded and unrounded front vowels, such as Swedish or Cantonese, [i] and [y] tend to be produced with a more front lingual constriction than the midpalatal tongue position typical of [i] in languages like English (Wood 1986), with a consequently higher third formant value for [i] (Fant 1960). Also, the high back vowel [u] is produced with the lips considerably more protruded and more closely approximated in these languages, with a consequently much lower second formant value. In traditional phonological theories, these two facts might be attributed to differences in the specification of a phonetic value along the physical scale for the features [back] and [round], differences which should be irrelevant to the general phonological function of contrasting the vowels [i] and [u]. However, the phonetic detail is not just language-specific. It is phoneme-specific as well. An [y] typically does not have the very rounded pattern of the [u] in the same language, but rather has the less protruded, less approximated articulation of the [u] in a language with no front rounded vowel. The notion of a language-specific value along a phonetic scale for a feature cannot account for this. Nor does it explain the phonetic generalities; why is it just those languages that have [y] that make [i] more front and [u] more round?

Because of such evidence for phonetic variability of several types, some phoneticians (e.g. Lindau & Ladefoged 1986) have argued against the proposed isomorphism between distinctive features and physical properties. Others have chosen instead to maintain the isomorphism by reinterpreting the variability so as to ascribe much of it to some nonlinguistic factor that can be incorporated into the mapping between phonological qualities and physical quantities. For example, any algorithm for interspeaker normalization of formant frequencies amounts to a claim that the isomorphism between vowel features and vowel spectra involve some unit other than hertz, that variation in formant frequency must be reinterpreted so as to ignore variability due to differences in vocal tract size as irrelevant to the issue of invariance.

One large-scale reinterpretation of articulatory variation that has greatly influenced subsequent research is Stevens's (1972) proposal that much gross variability in articulatory correlates of distinctive features is linguistically irrelevant because of nonlinearities in the mapping between the relevant articulatory and acoustic parameters. These nonlinearities quantize the articulatory parameter into regions of acoustic stability that are bounded by regions of instability. For values at the boundary regions, small changes in the articulatory parameter produce large changes in the acoustic parameter. For values within the stable 'quantal' regions, on the other hand, even the largest changes in the articulatory parameter produce little or no change in the acoustic parameter. The acoustic properties associated with such quantal regions would be natural candidates for use in distinguishing phonemes.

The articulatory-to-acoustic nonlinearities might also explain some classes of contextual variation. For example, the continuous articulatory parameter for the place of constriction of an obstruent is quantized into regions defined by the intersections of the lower resonance frequencies for the cavities behind and in front of the constriction. One intersection point is about two-thirds of the way from the larynx to the lips, where the first resonance of the back cavity crosses that of the front cavity. Moving the constriction location from one side of this boundary to the other shifts the cavity affinities for the second and third formants. Therefore, noise from turbulence at the constriction will be accentuated in the frequencies of the third formant or the second formant, depending on whether a fricative is articulated in front of or behind the boundary region. The spectral peak in a stop burst likewise will be higher or lower, and the 'velar pinch' that is characteristic of formant transitions for front vowels around velars will be present or absent. These different acoustic patterns might be correlates for two different phonemes in languages like Salish, where uvular stops contrast with velar stops, but they also make two acoustically distinct contextual variants for velar stops in languages like Japanese, where continuous coarticulatory variation for the velar place of constriction spans the region of instability.

The exploitation of such nonlinearities also seems to motivate some cross-language differences in phonetic detail. For example, Wood (1986) shows that extreme labial protrusion or approximation makes the second formant extremely sensitive to variations in degree of constriction in the palatal region. The more moderate rounding in [y] than in [u] in languages like Swedish and Cantonese, on the other hand, optimizes insensitivity, and in effect produces a quantal region of stability at the palate in this articulatory dimension. The extreme rounding for the [u] also can be thought of as an optimizing feature of another sort. It lowers the second formant for the [u] and thus maximizes its difference from [y]. Stevens, Keyser & Kawasaki (1986) have described extreme protrusion and approximation of the lips in an [u] as the enhancement of the distinctive feature [+back] by the addition of redundant features [+round] and [+labial]. The difference between the very round [u] in languages like Swedish and Cantonese and the much less rounded [u] in languages like English and Japanese suggests that the occurrence of such enhancements might be highly correlated with the structural requisites of contrasting front and back rounded vowels, in which case it may be necessary to reformulate the notion of redundancy so as to distinguish such cases from redundant features in contextual variants within a language.

The suggestion that seemingly redundant features are controlled to enhance phonological distinctions means that the quantal nature of speech should be much more than a passive artifact of the physical nonlinearities. Wood's (1986) explanation of the articulation of [y] emphasizes a purposeful coordination among palatal constriction, labial configuration, and larynx height that seems specially designed to optimize the mapping from vocal tract shape to stable second formant value. The resulting quantal region makes it seem unlikely that this coordination is a passive mechanical coupling among the articulators. Instead, there seems to be an active linguistically motivated organization among the separate articulations. Further evidence for the active linguistic nature of such coordinative structures is seen in their response to perturbation. For example, labial closure for a [b] is achieved by coordinated movements of the jaw, the lower lip, and the upper lip. When an artificial load is applied to perturb the movement of the jaw, the lower and upper lip movements adjust to preserve the phonological goal of complete closure and its attendant acoustic effects. It is clear that the adjustments are compensations to preserve linguistic structure, because the upper lip adjustment is not present if the load is applied during the production of an [f] (Abbs, Gracco & Cole 1984), and because the tongue responds instead of either lip when the load is applied during a [z] (Kelso *et al*. 1984). The same sorts of coordinative mechanisms are seen also in compensation for coarticulatory variation in jaw height during normal speech production (Edwards 1985; Macchi 1985).

One final aspect of Stevens's quantal theory that is important for the issue of invariance is that by making the acoustic patterns produced in quantal regions isomorphic with distinctive features, it requires that the acoustic correlate of a phonetic feature be relatively invariant and consistently present at all occurrences of that feature. For stop place features, for example, this implies that, despite their attested perceptual adequacy, the variable formant transition patterns into the vowel are not the most relevant property, that some less context-dependent pattern must be present in the preceding burst portion. Stevens & Blumstein (1978, 1981) and Kewley-Port (1983) have independently had some success in isolating such acoustic invariants in the bursts for syllable-initial stops. However, the acoustic properties do not generalize to syllable-final stops without bursts (see Kewley-Port 1986), and there is some evidence that these burst invariants may be less powerful in cueing the consonant's place of articulation than are the context-dependent vowel formant transitions (Walley & Carrell 1983).

## 8.2. The auditory and phonological bases of categorical perception

Stevens's proposals about articulatory quanta and invariant acoustic correlates for distinctive features are in marked contrast to previously widespread assumptions about phonetic variability. A common view among the American structuralists, for example, was that the human articulatory apparatus is capable of producing an infinite variety of speech sounds, which the phonological system of a language arbitrarily divides into acceptable variation about phonemic norms. Any apparent invariance was assumed to stem from the phonemic categorization itself, which shapes the perceptual capabilities of a native speaker who has not undergone artificial training to hear differences that are not distinctive in the native language (e.g. Gleason 1961: 239, 257–61). Both of these assumptions are now open to question. The first is contradicted if nonlinearities in the mapping from articulation to acoustics do indeed divide articulatory parameters into a few discontinuous regions corresponding to universal phonetic categories. The second is also open to doubt, since any corresponding discontinuities in human speech perception might then be byproducts of the same discretization that defines the phonetic categories. There is a large body of research relevant to the second question, most of which begins with the issue of the interpretation of categorical perception.

*Categorical perception* refers to a class of discontinuities in the labeling and discrimination of items along acoustic continua, for which the archetype is results from a study by Liberman *et al.* (1957). The stimuli in this study were two-formant syllables synthesized with second formant onset frequencies varying in equal sized steps from a transition suitable for a bilabial stop to one suitable for a velar. Liberman and his colleagues first obtained an identification function for the series by asking subjects to label the randomly presented stimuli as tokens of /ba/, /da/, or /ga/, and then plotting the percentage of each response against the stimulus number in the continuum. The same subjects then participated in a discrimination test using an ABX paradigm. They were asked to identify the X test stimulus with either the A or the B comparison stimulus. In each triplet, X was always the same as either A or B, and the two comparison stimuli differed by some given number of steps along the continuum. A discrimination function was obtained by plotting the percent correct responses against the A stimulus number. Comparison of the two functions showed that both had abrupt changes, and that these changes occurred in the same places. In the identification function there were two sharp transitions around stimuli 4 and 9 (F2 onset frequencies of about 1700 and 2100 Hz) as subjects went from 100% labeling as /ba/ to 100% labeling as /da/ and then from /da/ to /ga/. In the discrimination function, also, there were sharp peaks with perfect (100% correct) discrimination around stimuli 4 and 9 and generally much worse discrimination (near 50% chance level) elsewhere. These results were interpreted to mean that subjects could perceive differences only between items that were labeled as belonging to different categories, hence the term 'categorical perception'.

It should be noted that this original hypothesis of categorical perception does not necessarily imply that the categories be linguistic. For example, later experiments tested continua of musical chords and intervals, with results suggesting categorical perception by musicians but not by nonmusicians (Locke & Kellar 1973; Siegel & Siegel 1977). Originally, however, the effect was thought to be specific to speech categories. A strictly phonological interpretation was given by Fry (1960), who took the results for the [ba]–[ga] continuum to mean that language-specific phonemic categories define perceptual capabilities, as in the common assumption of the structuralists. He recognized, however, that the crucial experiments for this interpretation must test speakers of languages having different phonemic categorization along a given acoustic continuum. Phonetic continua that have been tested crosslinguistically using this paradigm include voice onset time (VOT) continua (e.g. Abramson & Lisker 1970), [l] to [r] formant continua (Miyakawa *et al*. 1975), and [i]–[ɛ]–[æ] and [i]–[y]–[ʉ] vowel formant continua (Stevens *et al*. 1969). The perception of the consonant continua in these experiments tends to support Fry's interpretation. Identification functions for the VOT continuum show three sharply differentiated categories for Thai speakers, but only two categories for English speakers, and discrimination functions using the ABX paradigm show the appropriately placed troughs and peaks for the two different languages. Discrimination along the [l] to [r] continuum, similarly, has a sharp peak corresponding to the phoneme boundary for American English speakers, but is uniformly poor for Japanese speakers. The vowel continua, on the other hand, show much less effect of linguistic experience. English speakers discriminate items all along the [i]–[y]–[ʉ] second formant continuum as well as the Swedish speakers do, even though English has only two phonemic categories /i/ and /u/ along this dimension.

In fact, vowel formant continua in general have yielded continuous rather than categorical discrimination (e.g. Fry *et al*. 1962). Results from some experiments suggest that this difference between vowels and consonants may be due in part to the different processing times afforded by the durations of the relevant acoustic cues. Stop bursts and transitions are by definition transient events. The stimuli used in most experiments on vowel continua, by contrast, are relatively long steady-state formant patterns. When shorter vowel stimuli are used, they are perceived more categorically (e.g. Pisoni 1975).

The difference between consonants and long steady-state vowels receives an interesting explanation in the *motor theory* of speech perception (Liberman *et al*. 1967; Liberman & Mattingly 1985). This theory proposes the existence of a special mode of perception for speech, in which the hearer's knowledge of articulation mediates between the acoustic signal and phonetic percepts. Roughly summarized, the main argument for the motor theory is that the acoustic patterns that cue a phonetic segment in speech generally overlap with those that cue adjacent segments and are extremely context-dependent. For example, the formant transitions that can cue the place of articulation of a syllable-initial stop consonant (as in the original experiment on categorical perception) occur after the release of the stop into the following vowel. These transitions vary greatly in overall shape and direction of movement, depending on the phonetic value of the vowel. Despite this complex overlap and context dependency, the consonant is perceived as an invariant unitary phonetic percept. Phonetic percepts, therefore, must be products of a separate *phonetic mode*, in which general auditory processing of the acoustic events is bypassed to produce a more direct perception of the invariant articulatory events underlying the phonetic category. When acoustic continua are processed in this phonetic mode, categorical perception results. Long-steady-state vowel formant shapes, on the other hand, might allow processing in the general auditory mode, producing intermediate nonspeech auditory percepts like those of complex tones, thus explaining their continuous perception.

This interpretation of categorical perception has been challenged on several grounds. One problem with attributing it to a special phonetic mode is that categorical perception of some consonant continua may hinge on short-term memory limitations resulting from the ABX discrimination task itself. When other less memory-taxing discrimination tasks are used, VOT differences within a phoneme category can be distinguished as well as are differences across the phoneme boundary (Carney, Widin & Viemeister 1977). However, the argument that such results show categorical perception to be an artifact of memory limitations imposed by the ABX discrimination task might be countered by the claim that the alternative discrimination tasks are conducive to processing in the auditory mode. Another more serious problem with the posited phonetic mode is that categorical perception may not be specific to phonetic categories, as demonstrated by the experiments on musical categories mentioned above.

The observation that it is not limited to speech-like stimuli has led to an important alternative explanation of categorical perception. In what might be called an *auditory theory* of perception, the perceptual discontinuities at category boundaries are explained in terms of more general psycho-acoustic nonlinearities in the mapping between acoustics and auditory qualities. For example, the categorical perception of VOT continua may be a result of limitations on the ability to discriminate the relative timing of onsets of two components of a complex stimulus. When the components begin within 20 ms of each other, they are perceived as beginning simultaneously (Hirsh 1959). Applied to the onset of periodicity relative to the noise of a stop burst, this general psychophysical effect would predict a peak in discrimination functions for VOT values around the crossover point between simultaneous and sequential perception, independent of any language-specific boundary between aspirated and unaspirated stops. Discrimination functions for nonspeech stimuli with component onset time differences like those seen in VOT continua should also show pronounced peaks at this crossover point. Such categorical perception has been demonstrated for the relative onset times of periodic and noisy components by Miller *et al.* (1976) and for two pure tones by Pisoni (1977).

Further evidence for this general auditory theory for categorical perception is drawn from experience with human infants (see the review by Jusczyk 1981) and nonhuman mammals (Kuhl & Miller 1978; Kuhl & Padden 1983). The tests of infant discrimination are typically done by recording sucking rate or head turning responses to items along an acoustic continuum. A baseline response pattern is established by the repeated presentation of one item, and then presentation is switched to a new test item from either the same or a different adult phonetic category. For example, typical experiments along a VOT continuum might use baseline/test stimuli pairs at $-20/0$ ms, $+20/+40$ ms, and $+60/+80$ ms. Infants in the $+20/+40$ ms test group show a sudden increase in sucking rate or number of head turns when presentation switches to the new stimulus, where those in the other test groups tend to respond not much differently from a control group that hears only a baseline stimulus. The techniques used with the chinchillas and macaques are somewhat different but show similar response patterns. Proponents of auditory theories of speech perception interpret such results to mean that the infants and nonhuman mammals distinguish only the items from different speech categories because the category boundaries coincide with psychoacoustic discontinuities common to all mammalian auditory systems.

Stevens (1972, 1981) discusses the phonological implications of this auditory explanation for categorical perception. He proposes that such coincidences between general psychoacoustic discontinuities and speech category boundaries are not accidents. Rather the acoustic-to-auditory nonlinearities accentuate articulatory-to-acoustic nonlinearities to constitute a biological basis for the speech categories. A weak form of this proposal is that the nonlinearities are implicated in the ontogeny of distinctive features and patterns of markedness. Stevens, however, adopts a strong form of the proposal in which speech perception proceeds through the differential response of the auditory system to the acoustic correlates of phonetic features. For example, the psychophysical nonlinearities which have been implicated in categorical response to VOT continua not only would provide a psychophysical basis for an unmarked phonetic implementation of the features [voiced] and [aspirated], but they would also mediate directly in the perception of words containing these features. In addition to the apparent connection between voicing features and psychologically discrete VOT categories, Stevens (1981) cites features involving various rate-of-change continua. For example, formant transition rate is a cue for the contrast between stops and glides (Liberman *et al*. 1956). A model built by Goldhor (1983) suggests that nonlinearities at the auditory periphery, such as the adaptation of neural firing rates to sustained stimulation, accentuate the distinction between a short abrupt transition in [ba] and a long gradual transition in [wa] (Goldhor 1985), providing a likely psychoacoustic basis for the categorical perception of formant transition rate continua. Amplitude rise time, similarly, is a cue in the contrast between affricates and fricatives. It also cues a contrast between 'plucked' and 'bowed' musical sounds. Cutting & Rosner (1974) have shown categorical perception for a [ʃa] to [tʃa] rise time continuum with a phoneme boundary at 40 ms and also for a 'plucked' to 'bowed' rise time continuum that yields a 40 ms category boundary between the two nonspeech sounds, which suggests a similar psychoacoustic basis for the perception of both the nonspeech and the speech categories and thus provides further evidence for a general auditory theory of speech perception. (However, see Howell & Rosen 1983).

Proponents of the motor theory of speech perception have countered that this auditory theory cannot explain why certain sorts of acoustic continua are perceived categorically or continuously depending on whether the subjects are instructed to hear the stimuli as speech or as nonspeech. For example, Mann & Liberman (1983) report an experiment in which they divided synthetic CV syllables along a [da]–[ga] continuum into a variable third formant transition shape and an invariant everything else. When the two pieces of such a stimulus are presented dichotically, the transition shape is heard as a nonspeech 'chirp' and also, at the same time, is fused perceptually with the invariant base to be heard as a CV syllable. When subjects presented with these duplex sensations were told that they were being tested for their ability to discriminate speech sounds in the face of distracting nonspeech chirps, the discrimination function showed the appropriate peak at the category boundary and troughs elsewhere, but when they were tested using the same stimuli for their ability to discriminate nonspeech chirps in the presence of distracting speech sounds, the discrimination function was flat.

A further argument against an explanation of categorical perception in terms of general psychoacoustic effects is that such an explanation implies a coincidence between the posited auditory nonlinearities and the attested categorization functions which must occur consistently across all context-dependent variation in the categorization functions (Liberman & Mattingly 1985: 6). For example, the slopes of formant transitions by CV syllables depend on overall speech rate (Gay 1978). When the overall duration of the synthetic syllables in a [ba] to [wa] transition rate continuum is changed to simulate a different speech rate, the location of the category boundary also shifts accordingly, and so does the peak in the ABX discrimination function (Miller 1980). If the categorical perception of these continua is a result of general auditory nonlinearities, then the nonlinearities must also be dependent on overall stimulus duration in a way that mirrors the articulatory dependency on speech rate. On the other hand, since the shift in discrimination under changes in stimulus duration is seen also in infant responses (Miller & Eimas 1983), this argument against a general auditory explanation for categorical perception implies a strong version of the motor theory in which the perceptual processes of the phonetic mode are not learned by association during the acquisition of speech but are innate. This strong version of the motor theory has difficulty explaining the categorical responses to nonspeech stimuli and the cross-language differences outlined above. However, the cross-language differences are a problem also for the strong version of the auditory theory, since they contradict the strict equation between categorical perception and more general psychoacoustic nonlinearities.

As the above discussion should make clear, there is at present no consensus about the meaning of categorical perception. Rather, the ongoing competition between two general classes of explanation has engaged ever increasing areas of study. There are two promising directions for future research in categorical perception. One is to extend the research on possible psychoacoustic bases. This includes the devising of more sophisticated simulations of seemingly speech-specific effects with nonspeech stimuli. For example, the shifts in discrimination peaks with differences in overall stimulus duration have been duplicated using sinewave analogs of the [ba]–[wa] formant transition continuum (Carrell, Pisoni & Gans 1980), suggesting that the effect of syllable duration on the [ba]–[wa] responses is not an adjustment to speech rate. Sinewave analogs have also been used to explore possible psychoacoustic bases for the trading relationship between VOT and first formant transition in the perception of stop voicing (Summerfield 1982; Hillenbrand 1984). The search for psychoacoustic bases for categorical perception will probably also begin to include the application of more general models from audiology and psychoacoustics to speech perception. For example, there has been a great deal of research in the last five years on the peripheral processing of speech signals (e.g. Delgutte 1984; Delgutte & Kiang 1984a, b). The discovery of nonlinearities introduced at the auditory periphery could not explain the categorical perception of dichotically presented stimuli (Mann & Liberman 1983), but it would delimit those effects that must be explained more centrally. There has also been increasing research on central auditory memory processes and their relationship to perception. For example, Braida *et al.* (1984) have developed a model of auditory memory in intensity resolution tasks that they have recently begun to extend to the perception of vowel formant continua (Goldberg, Macmillan & Braida 1985). An interesting aspect of this model is that it posits internal *perceptual anchors* which are derived from a composite of internal and external factors including intrinsic landmarks from the sensory system and properties of the stimulus set. The latter may eventually explain certain stimulus range effects in the perception of some phonetic continua. For example, Howell & Rosen (1983) showd that both the [ʃa]–[tʃa] phonetic category boundary and the 'plucked'–'bowed' musical category boundary depend on the range of rise times covered in amplitude rise time continua. Keating, Mikos & Ganong (1981) demonstrated a similar effect of range for the prevoiced–voiceless boundary for Polish speakers along VOT continua. Other research on general auditory memory and perception that shows potential applicability to understanding categorical perception is the investigation of the limits imposed by learning rates and informational complexity on the discrimination of complex sounds (Watson & Foyle 1985). This research may eventually explain why some non-native distinctions, such as [l] vs. [r] for Japanese speakers, seem impervious to training (MacKain, Best & Strange 1980), whereas others, such as negative VOT distinctions for English speakers, are less so (Pisoni *et al.* 1982; see also Tees & Werker 1984).

The second promising direction of research is the large amount of work being done on the development of categorical perception. There are several findings of special interest in this area. One is that the discrimination of phonetic categories in early infancy is not limited to categories that are phonemically distinct in the native language of adults in the infant's environment, as demonstrated by Werker & Tees (1984a). This is not a recent finding. For example, Streeter (1976) showed that infants in a Kikuyu-speaking environment discriminate initial stops with +10 and +40 ms VOT even though Kikuyu does not distinguish aspirated and unaspirated stops. What is novel about the study by Werker and Tees is that it tests such discriminative abilities longitudinally, and pinpoints the time when the 'non-native' phonetic distinctions begin to be no longer discriminated. This is surprisingly early, somewhere between 8 months and a year. There have also been studies with older children in which items all along a given continuum are tested, as in the classic categorical perception experiments. An interesting result from these studies is that identification functions are much smoother (i.e. less categorical) for small children than for adults, and become increasingly abrupt for older and older children (Zlatin & Koenigsknecht 1975; Simon & Fourcin 1978). From these experiments, it is now beginning to seem less likely that categorical perception is a single unified phenomenon. Werker & Tees (1984b) have proposed that the original experiments and the cross-language experiments with adult subjects may be tapping phonological processing strategies that are so highly practiced on language-specific categories that they affect attentional capabilities, whereas the infant studies may be tapping more general psychoacoustic (phonetic) capabilities that underlie possible phonological categories. Thus, neither the motor theory nor the strict auditory theory may be true in their strong versions, but each may be describing a different stage of the ontogeny of speech perception. Jusczyk (1986) proposes a developmental model along these lines. Kuhl (1986), on the other hand, says such models are premature, in part because they do not take into account the infant's ability to relate speech sounds to pictures of faces articulating the sounds (Kuhl & Meltzoff 1984).

## 8.3. Coarticulation and timing in speech production

Another major issue that ties together the research on the physical properties and perception of distinctive features is the question of how the features are realized in time, and how they can be realized invariantly in the variable time scales of different speech rates or prosodic structures. It is a common observation that although the acoustic record of an utterance provides boundary events sufficient to divide it into discrete segments in time such acoustic segments do not correspond exactly to the sequence of phonetic segments defined by the distinctive features. The lack of correspondence is partly a problem of number; there are more acoustic segments than phonetic segments. Phoneticians have developed conventions for grouping the acoustic segments into as many composite units as there are phonemes in order to make observations about durational properties. But no grouping resolves the lack of correspondence, because no grouping results in acoustic segments that show properties of only one phoneme. In the first place, articulators cannot move instantaneously, so that portions of the signal must show the overlapping influence of any two adjacent segments as the relevant articulators move from a vocal tract configuration that produces the acoustic properties for one set of features to that for another. Moreover, even if this ubiquitous manifestation of transition is disregarded, there still is overlap, because the segments that are not discounted as transitional segments also show influence from neighboring phonemes. For example, the noise spectrum in the voiceless portion of a prevocalic [s] differs enough from one context to another that the context vowel can be identified from the frication excised from the following voiced formant transitions at levels well above chance in forced choice listening tasks (Soli 1981). Such contextual variability, or *coarticulation*, exists in all fluent speech, and its explanation has become an increasingly controversial issue in the last two decades.

There are two accounts of coarticulation that are compatible with representations of phonetic segments as linear strings of discrete feature bundles, as is assumed in most existing phonological theories. The older of these is a purely mechanistic account in terms of *target undershoot* (Lindblom 1963; Stevens & House 1963). According to this model, coarticulation occurs because of physiological and neurological limitations on the speed with which an articulatory parameter can change from the value appropriate for one vocal tract configuration to that for another. Actualization of a particular sequence of phonetic segments includes a schedule of commands to assume a configuration appropriate to each successive feature bundle, but the target values may not always be achieved before the scheduled onset of change toward the next configuration. This explanation was soon demonstrated to be untenable as a universal account of coarticulation by evidence that some coarticulation occurs even at very slow rates, and that the influence of a phoneme can extend well beyond the acoustic segments associated with adjacent phonemes. The alternative, therefore, is to view much or all of coarticulation as a more active assimilatory process that occurs at a higher level in the programming of the sequence of target configurations. Henke (1966), for example, proposes a look-ahead procedure that is an early phonetic version of autosegmental *feature spreading*; a feature specified for a later segment is copied onto all preceding segments until it is blocked by an opposing feature specification for some segment. (Since the input to this feature-spreading process is the sequence of phonetic segments output by the phonology, the model also is in effect an early proposal for surface underspecification. See Keating 1985 for a discussion of this fact.)

Both target undershoot accounts and feature-spreading accounts have been criticized extensively on several grounds by proponents of what has come to be known as *action theory* (Fowler *et al.* 1980). One major criticism is that these accounts separate the input plan of specifications for the linear string of target articulatory configurations from the schedule of commands for executing the specifications sequentially in time. Fowler (1980) argues against this *extrinsic timing* because it cannot provide any natural means for generating certain problematic timing relationships. For example, it has been shown both for Swedish (Lindblom, Lyberg & Holbrem 1981) and for English (Fowler 1983) that measured durations of acoustic segments for vowels vary inversely with the number of consonants in the syllable. This variation can be generated in a linear model only by unmotivated *post hoc* modifications to the extrinsic schedule for the execution of the sequence of consonant and vowel segments. Fowler also argues that target undershoot and feature-spreading accounts cannot model attested patterns of vowel-to-vowel coarticulation during VÇV sequences. In languages such as Swedish and English, the formant transitions out of the first vowel and into the second vowel are strongly influenced by the vowel on the other side of the intervening consonant, slightly interrupted by the transition into and out of the intervening consonant (Öhman 1966), and the tongue body moves from a configuration appropriate for the first vowel toward that appropriate for the second even when the intervening consonant requires a lingual constriction (e.g. Carney & Moll 1971), almost as if the vowels are participating in a VV transition that 'ignores' the consonant. Bell-Berti & Harris (1981) have also criticized linear sequential models, because neither target undershoot nor feature spreading is compatible with their results showing that, when a varying number of consonants unspecified for rounding intervenes between an unrounded and a rounded vowel, the onset of muscular activity in the orbicularis oris occurs at a fixed time before the onset of voicing in the rounded vowel rather than at the offset of the unrounded vowel.

Proponents of action theory claim that these patterns can be accounted for only in a model that does not assume certain problematic aspects of traditional phonological representations. They consider the major source of problems to be the separation of the executor, with its extrinsic specification of the timing, from the plan, with its timeless specification of a sequence of static feature configurations. The plan must instead be equated with the execution of the articulation in time. Consequently, the underlying phonetic segments must be represented as dynamic and overlapping articulatory gestures. For example, the representation of a [b] must include a specification not just of the labial closure, but also of the movement into and out of the closure. Central to the model is the notion of the vowel-to-vowel cycle, a periodic spacing of successive vowels that governs the timing of large-scale opening and closing gestures for the relevant articulators, thus providing an intrinsic specification for the coarser-grained metrical patterns of rate and stress. The articulation of consonants then constitutes a minor rhythm that rides on top of the large vowel-to-vowel rhythm, a smaller-grained timing pattern which is defined intrinsically by an invariant phase specification for the onset of the consonant closing gesture in the vowel-to-vowel period. This relationship has been shown to be invariant for CV syllables under changes in rate and stress (Harris, Tuller & Kelso 1986; Kelso, Saltzman & Tuller 1986), a result which is interpreted as support for the vowel-to-vowel cycle. The picture of vowel-to-vowel coarticulation across intervening consonants falls out naturally from this notion of the vowel cycle as a carrier wave for the consonants, and the shortening effects of adding consonants within a syllable also fall out as an acoustic artifact of the greater portion of the vowel period occupied by consonant gestures (Fowler 1983). Thus, by doing away with the notion of a strictly linear sequence of segments, the action theory model provides an elegant account of these otherwise problematic patterns.

Other aspects of the model are less convincing, however, in particular the claim that phonetic segments are underlyingly dynamic. As presently formulated, this aspect of the model amounts to an insistence that the functional units of speech production be equated with the physics of articulatory dynamics rather than with any more direct specification of linguistic intent, such as target configurations for distinctive features. This insistence tends to make the theory incompatible with the needs of phonological description. One important need that is not met is the description of certain language-specific patterns of coarticulation and timing. For example, Öhman (1966) shows that the vowel-to-vowel coarticulation patterns considered typical of VCV sequences do not occur in Russian; distinctive palatalization of the intervening consonant blocks any effect from the other vowel on the formant transition patterns. Keating (1985) proposes to describe the Russian pattern by providing separate autosegmental tiers for consonant and vowel features. In English and Swedish there is a complementary underspecification between these tiers; vowel segments are left unspecified for consonant features and *vice versa*, and the pattern of smooth transitions from vowel to vowel in VCV sequences comes about because the phonetic rules for interpolating between target specifications apply locally to each tier. The Russian pattern differs, then, because the intervening consonant is specified for the vowel feature [back], which introduces an intervening target for the interpolation rules on the vowel feature tier. It is difficult to see how this difference might be captured in a model that looks for the functional units of the vowel cycle in the dynamics of the vowel-to-vowel gesture so as to avoid reference to future targets.

Another potential problem centers around the interpretation of invariant phase relationships for consonant and vowel onset gestures. Action theory interprets the attested invariance over changes in rate and stress as evidence that the invariant phase angle itself defines the timing pattern without reference to time *per se*. Lindblom & MacNeilage (1986), however, point out that a more abstract extrinsic representation of time will be necessary if perturbation of the timing of a closing or opening gesture results in readjustments that preserve acoustic segment durations at the expense of maintaining constant phase. It also remains to be seen whether an invariant phase angle will adequately describe the articulation of consonant clusters, of distinctive length in consonants and vowels, or of interactions between stress pattern and syllable structure. The scaling of other large-scale prosodic patterns such as the durational correlates of intonational prominence and phrasing should also be examined.

On the other hand, certain aspects of the action theory model may prove useful in the development of modern nonlinear phonological theories. The vowel-to-vowel cycle, for example, suggests itself as one way to relate the coarser-grained timing patterns that metrical theory represents in the grid with the finer-grained timing patterns of the articulation of individual segments. Phonologists might do well to explore ways of incorporating this notion of temporal overlap between consonants and vowels into autosegmental representations, not only as an explanation for coarticulation, but also to understand the phonetics of such phenomena as syllable weight. One possibility is suggested by treatments of the alignment between intonation patterns and text. For example, Pierrehumbert & Beckman (forthcoming) have shown that certain aspects of Japanese intonation contours can be captured elegantly if the temporal locations of tones are determined in some cases by rules of autosegmental association to minimal tone-bearing units and in other cases only from their properties of belonging to higher-level nodes in the prosodic hierarchy of an utterance. If the same notion were applied to segmental timing, syllable weight in a given language might be represented by the way that segments on a consonant tier are aligned to a prosodic structure tier whose terminal nodes are slots in a timing pattern regulated by the vowel-to-vowel period. The fact that syllable-initial consonants do not count in determining syllable weight might then be described as a constraint stating that their alignment is always governed by the property of belonging to a particular syllable node and never by autosegmental association to a terminal mora slot in the prosodic structure.

## 8.4. Summary

The discussion in the three previous sections is by no means a digest of all lasting issues in phonetic theory. It is not even an exhaustive catalog of the results and ideas that have contributed in important ways to the general issue covered in each section. The section on coarticulation and timing, for example, does not mention quantitative models of 'effort' (Lindblom 1983; Nelson, Perkell & Westbury 1984), although these may ultimately explain problematic variations in articulatory velocity without resorting to underlying dynamic phonetic segments. Omissions such as this should not be taken as any indication of a lack of relevance to phonetic theory. The decision to include or exclude a particular set of results or a particular model was based as much on ease of exposition as it was on any measure of importance to the field as a whole. As was stated in the introduction, the goal of this chapter cannot be to cover all important issues in phonetic theory; rather, I have tried to give a sense of phonetics as being an interdisciplinary field of research which relies heavily on laboratory experiments and quantitative models. If phonetic theory can be unified in any neat summarizing statement, that statement will be just the general principle that underlies all scientific theory – namely, that knowledge advances when many different ways of looking at the world are available, and that it advances cumulatively only when it is driven by the scientific method of reducing competing ways of looking to testable hypotheses and then designing and performing the appropriate experiments to test them.

*REFERENCES*

Abbs, J. H., Gracco, V. L. & Cole, K. J. 1984. Control of multimovement coordination: sensorimotor mechanisms in speech motor programming. *Journal of Motor Behavior* 16: 195–231.
Abramson, A. S. & Lisker, L. 1970. Discriminability along the voicing continuum. In *Proceedings of the Sixth International Congress of Phonetic Sciences*. Prague: Academia.
Bell-Berti, F. & Harris, K. S. 1981. A temporal model of speech production. *Phonetica* 38: 9–20.
Bloch, B. 1948. A set of postulates for phonemic analysis. *Language* 24: 3–46.
Braida, L. D., Lim, J. S., Berliner, J. E., Durlach, N. I., Rabinowitz, W. M. & Purks, S. R. 1984. Intensity perception. xiii. Perceptual anchor model of context-coding. *Journal of the Acoustical Society of America* 76: 722–31.
Carlson, R., Fant, G. & Granström, B. 1975. Two-formant models, pitch, and vowel perception. In G. Fant & M. A. A. Tatham (eds.) *Auditory analysis and perception of speech*. New York: Academic Press.
Carney, P. & Moll, K. 1971. A cinefluorographic investigation of fricative consonant–vowel coarticulation. *Phonetica* 23: 193–202.
Carney, A. E., Widin, G. P. & Viemeister, N. F. 1977. Noncategorical perception of stop consonants differing in VOT. *Journal of the Acoustical Society of America* 62: 961–70.
Carrell, T. D., Pisoni, D. B. & Gans, S. J. 1980. Perception of the duration of rapid spectrum changes: evidence for context effects with speech and nonspeech signals. *Journal of the Acoustical Society of America*. 68, Suppl. 1 (Abstract).
Chiba, T. & Kajiyama, M. 1941. *The vowel – its nature and structure*. Tokyo: Kaiseikan.
Chistovich, L. A. & Lublinskaya, V. V. 1979. The 'center of gravity' effect in vowel spectra and critical distance between the formants: psychoacoustical study of the perception of vowel-like stimuli. *Hearing Research* 1: 185–95.
Chomsky, N. & Halle, M. 1968. *The sound pattern of English*. New York: Harper & Row.
Cutting, J. & Rosner, B. S. 1974. Categories and boundaries in speech and music. *Perception and Psychophysics* 16: 564–70.
Delattre, P., Liberman, A. M. & Cooper, F. S. 1955. Acoustic loci and transitional cues for consonants. *Journal of the Acoustical Society of America* 27: 769–73.
Delattre, P., Liberman, A. M., Cooper, F. S. & Gerstman, L. J. 1952. An experimental study of the acoustic determinants of vowel color: observations on one- and two-formant vowels synthesized from spectrographic patterns. *Word* 8: 195–210.
Delgutte, B. 1984. Speech coding in the auditory nerve: ii. Processing schemes for vowel-like sounds. *Journal of the Acoustical Society of America* 75: 879–86.
Delgutte, B. & Kiang, N. Y. S. 1984a. Speech coding in the auditory nerve: iii. Voiceless fricative consonants. *Journal of the Acoustical Society of America* 75: 887–96.
Delgutte, B. & Kiang, N. Y. S. 1984b. Speech coding in the auditory nerve: iv. Sounds with

consonant-like dynamic characteristics. *Journal of the Acoustical Society of America* 75: 897–907.

Edwards, J. 1985. Contextual effects on lingual-mandibular coordination. *Journal of the Acoustical Society of America* 76: 1944–8.

Fant, G. 1960. *Acoustic theory of speech production*. The Hague: Mouton.

Fowler, C. A. 1980. Coarticulation and theories of extrinsic timing. *Journal of Phonetics* 8: 113–33.

Fowler, C. A. 1983. Converging sources of evidence on spoken and perceived rhythms of speech: cyclic production of vowels in monosyllabic stress feet. *Journal of Experimental Psychology: General* 112: 386–412.

Fowler, C. A., Rubin, P., Remez, R. E. & Turvey, M. E. 1980. Implications for speech production of a general theory of action. In B. Butterworth (ed.) *Language production*, vol. 1. London: Academic Press.

Fry, D. B. 1960. Linguistic theory and experimental research. *Transactions of the Philological Society* pp. 13–39. Reprinted in W. E. Jones & J. Laver (eds.) 1973. *Phonetics in linguistics*. London: Longman.

Fry, D. B., Abramson, A. S., Eimas, P. D. & Liberman, A. M. 1962. The identification and discrimination of synthetic vowels. *Language and Speech* 5: 171–89.

Gay, T. 1978. Effect of speaking rate on vowel formant transitions. *Journal of the Acoustical Society of America* 63: 223–30.

Gleason, H. G. 1961. *An introduction to descriptive linguistics*. Rev. edn. New York: Holt, Rinehart & Winston.

Goldberg, R., Macmillan, N. A. & Braida, L. D. 1985. A perceptual-anchor interpretation of categorical phenomena on a vowel continuum. *Journal of the Acoustical Society of America* 77, Suppl. 1. (Abstract).

Goldhor, R. 1983. A speech signal processing system based on a peripheral auditory model. In *Proceedings of the IEEE International Conference on Acoustics, Speech, and Signal Processing*. New York: IEEE.

Goldhor, R. 1985. Auditory correlates to phonetic features: results of a modeling study. *Journal of the Acoustical Society of America* 77, Suppl. 1. (Abstract).

Harris, K. S., Tuller, B. & Kelso, J. A. S. 1986. Temporal invariance in the production of speech. In Perkell & Klatt (1986).

Henke, W. L. 1966. Dynamic articulatory model of speech production using computer simulation. Doctoral dissertation, MIT.

Hillenbrand, J. 1984. Perception of sine-wave analogs of voice onset time stimuli. *Journal of the Acoustical Society of America* 75: 231–40.

Hirsh, I. J. 1959. Auditory perception of temporal order. *Journal of the Acoustical Society of America* 31: 759–67.

Hockett, C. F. 1953. Review of *The mathematical theory of communication* by Shannon & Weaver. *Language* 29: 69–93.

Howell, P. & Rosen, S. 1983. Production and perception of rise time in the voiceless affricate/fricative distinction. *Journal of the Acoustical Society of America* 83: 976–84.

Jakobson, R., Fant, C. G. M. & Halle, M. 1952. *Preliminaries to speech analysis: the distinctive features and the correlates*. Cambridge, MA: MIT Press.

Jusczyk, P. W. 1981. Infant speech perception: A critical appraisal. In P. D. Eimas & J. L. Miller (eds.) *Perspectives on the study of speech*. Hillsdale: Erlbaum.

Jusczyk, P. W. 1986. Toward a model for the development of speech perception. In Perkell & Klatt (1986).

Keating, P. A. 1985. CV phonology, experimental phonetics, and coarticulation. *UCLA Working Papers in Phonetics* 62: 1–13.

Keating, P. A., Mikos, M. J. & Ganong, W. F. 1981. A cross-language study of range of voice onset time in the perception of initial stop voicing. *Journal of the Acoustical Society of America* 70: 1251–71.

Kelso, J. A. S., Saltzman, E. L. & Tuller, B. 1986. The dynamical perspective on speech production: data and theory. *Journal of Phonetics* 14: 29–59.

Kelso, J. A. S., Tuller, B., Vatikiotis-Bateson, E. & Fowler, C. A. 1984. Functionally specific articulatory cooperation following jaw perturbation during speech: evidence for coordinative structures. *Journal of Experimental Psychology: Human Perception and Performance* 10: 812–32.

Kewley-Port, D. 1983. Time varying features as correlates of place of articulation in stop consonants. *Journal of the Acoustical Society of America* 73: 322–35.

Kewley-Port, D. 1986. Converging approaches towards establishing invariant acoustic correlates of stop consonants. In Perkell & Klatt (1986).

Kuhl, P. K. 1986. Reflections on infants' perception and representation of speech. In Perkell & Klatt (1986).

Kuhl, P. K. & Meltzoff, A. N. 1984. The intermodel representation of speech in infants. *Infant Behavior and Development* 7: 361–81.

Kuhl, P. K. & Miller, J. D. 1978. Speech perception by the chinchilla: identification functions for synthetic VOT continua. *Journal of the Acoustical Society of America* 63: 905–17.

Kuhl, P. K. & Padden, D. M. 1983. Enhanced discriminability at the phonetic boundaries for the place feature in macaques. *Journal of the Acoustical Society of America* 73: 1003–10.

Liberman, A. M. & Mattingly, I. 1985. The motor theory of speech perception revised. *Cognition* 21: 1–36.

Liberman, A. M., Delattre, P. C., Gerstman, L. J. & Cooper, F. S. 1956. Tempo of frequency change as a cue for distinguishing classes of speech sounds. *Journal of Experimental Psychology* 52: 127–37.

Liberman, A. M., Cooper, F. S., Shanwiler, D. P. & Studdert-Kennedy, M. 1967. Perception of the speech code. *Psychological Review* 74: 431–61.

Liberman, A. M., Harris, K. S., Hoffman, H. S. & Griffith, B. C. 1957. The discrimination of speech sounds within and across phoneme boundaries. *Journal of Experimental Psychology* 54: 358–68.

Lindau, M. & Ladefoged, P. 1986. Variability of feature specifications. In Perkell & Klatt (1986).

Lindblom, B. 1963. Spectrographic study of vowel reduction. *Journal of the Acoustical Society of America* 35: 1773–81.

Lindblom, B. 1983. Economy of speech gestures. In P. F. MacNeilage (ed.) *The production of speech*. New York: Springer.

Lindblom, B. & MacNeilage, P. 1986. Action theory: problems and alternative approaches. *Journal of Phonetics* 14: 117–32.

Lindblom, B., Lyberg, B. & Holmgren, K. 1981. *Durational patterns of Swedish phonology: do they reflect short-term motor memory processes?* Monograph distributed by Indiana University Linguistics Club.

Lisker, L. & Abramson, A. S. 1964. A cross-language study of voicing in initial stops: acoustical measurements. *Word* 20: 384–422.

Locke, S. & Kellar, L. 1973. Categorical perception in a non-linguistic mode. *Cortex* 9: 355–69.

Macchi, M. J. 1985. Segmental and suprasegmental features and lip and jaw articulators. Doctoral dissertation, New York University.

MacKain, K. S., Best, C. T. & Strange, W. 1980. Native language effects on the perception of liquids. *Journal of the Acoustical Society of America* 67, Suppl. 1. (Abstract).

MacNeilage, P. & Sholes, G. 1964. An electromyographic study of the tongue during vowel production. *Journal of Speech and Hearing Research* 7: 209–32.

Mann, V. A. & Liberman, A. M. 1983. Some differences between phonetic and auditory modes of perception. *Cognition* 14: 211–35.

Miller, J. D., Wier, C. C., Pastore, R. E., Kelly, W. J. & Dooling, R. J. 1976. Discrimination and labeling of noise-buzz sequences with varying noise-lead times: an example of categorical perception. *Journal of the Acoustical Society of America* 60: 410–17.

Miller, J. L. 1980. Contextual effects in the discrimination of stop consonant and semivowel. *Perception and Psychophysics* 28: 93–5.

Miller, J. L. & Eimas, P. D. 1983. Studies in the categorization of speech by infants. *Cognition* 13: 135–65.

Miyakawa, K., Strange, W., Verbrugge, R. R., Liberman, A. M., Jenkins, J. J. & Fujimura, O. 1975. An effect of linguistic experience: the discrimination of [r] and [l] by native speakers of Japanese and English. *Perception and Psychophysics* 18: 331–40.

Nelson, W. L., Perkell, J. S. & Westbury, J. R. 1984. Mandible movements during increasingly rapid articulations of single syllables: preliminary observations. *Journal of the Acoustical Society of America* 75: 945–51.

Ohala, J. & Ohala, M. 1972. The problem of aspiration in Hindi phonetics. *Annual Bulletin, Research Institute of Logopedics and Phoniatrics, University of Tokyo* 6: 39–46.

Öhman, S. E. G. 1966. Coarticulation in VCV utterances: spectrographic measurements. *Journal of the Acoustical Society of America* 39: 151–68.

Perkell, J. S. 1969. *Physiology of speech production: results and implications of a quantitative cineradiographic study.* Research Monograph no. 53. Cambridge, MA: MIT Press.

Perkell, J. S. & Klatt, D. H. (eds.) 1986. *Invariance and variability in speech processes.* Hillsdale: Erlbaum.

Pierrehumbert, J. B. & Beckman, M. E. Forthcoming. Japanese tone structure. *Linguistic Inquiry* monograph.

Pisoni, D. B. 1975. Auditory short-term memory and vowel perception. *Memory and Cognition* 3: 7–18.

Pisoni, D. B. 1977. Identification and discrimination of the relative onset of two component tones: implications for voicing perception in stops. *Journal of the Acoustical Society of America* 61: 1352–61.

Pisoni, D. B., Aslin, R. N., Perey, A. J. & Hennessy, B. L. 1982. Some effects of laboratory training on identification and discrimination of voicing contrasts in stop consonants. *Journal of Experimental Psychology: Human Perception and Performance* 8: 297–314.

Siegel, J. A. & Siegel, W. 1977. Categorical perception of tonal intervals: musicians can't tell *sharp* from *flat. Perception and Psychophysics* 21: 399–407.

Simon, C. & Fourcin, A. J. 1978. Cross-language study of speech-pattern learning. *Journal of the Acoustical Society of America* 63: 925–35.

Soli, S. D. 1981. Second formants in fricatives: acoustic consequences of fricative–vowel coarticulation. *Journal of the Acoustical Society of America* 70: 976–84.

Stevens, K. N. 1972. The quantal nature of speech: evidence from articulatory–acoustic data. In E. E. David & P. B. Denes (eds.) *Human communication: a unified view.* New York: McGraw-Hill.

Stevens, K. N. 1981. Constraints imposed by the auditory system on the properties used to classify speech sounds: data from phonology, acoustics, and psychophysics. In T. Myers, J. Laver & J. Anderson (eds.) *The cognitive representation of speech.* Amsterdam: North-Holland.

Stevens, K. N. & Blumstein, S. E. 1978. Invariant cues for place of articulation in stop consonants. *Journal of the Acoustical Society of America* 64: 1358–68.

Stevens, K. N. & Blumstein, S. E. 1981. The search for invariant acoustic correlates of phonetic features. In P. Eimas & J. Miller (eds.) *Perspectives on the study of speech.* Hillsdale: Erlbaum.

Stevens, K. N. & House, A. S. 1955. Development of a quantitative description of vowel articulation. *Journal of the Acoustical Society of America* 27: 484–93.

Stevens, K. N. & House, A. S. 1963. Perturbation of vowel articulations by consonantal context: an acoustical study. *Journal of Speech and Hearing Research* 6: 111–28.

Stevens, K. N., Keyser, S. J. & Kawasaki, H. 1986. Toward a phonetic and phonological theory of redundant features. In Perkell & Klatt (1986).

Stevens, K. N., Liberman, A. M., Studdert-Kennedy, M. & Öhman, S. 1969. Cross-language study of vowel perception. *Language and Speech* 12: 1–23.

Streeter, L. A. 1976. Kikuyu labial and apical stop discrimination. *Journal of Phonetics* 4: 43–9.

Summerfield, Q. 1982. Differences between spectral dependencies in auditory and phonetic temporal processing: relevance to the perception of voicing in initial stops. *Journal of the Acoustical Society of America* 72: 51–61.

Tees, R. C. & Werker, J. F. 1984. Perceptual flexibility: maintenance or recovery of the ability to discriminate non-native speech sounds. *Canadian Journal of Psychology* 38: 579–90.

Wada, T., Yasumoto, M., Ikeoka, N., Fujiki, Y. & Yoshinaga, R. 1970. An approach for the cinefluorographic study of articulatory movements. *Cleft Palate Journal* 7: 506–22.

Walley, A. C. & Carrell, T. D. 1983. Onset spectra and formant transitions in the adult's and child's perception of place of articulation in stop consonants. *Journal of the Acoustical Society of America* 73: 1011–22.

Watson, C. S. & Foyle, D. C. 1985. Central factors in the discrimination and identification of complex sounds. *Journal of the Acoustical Society of America* 78: 375–80.

Werker, J. F. & Tees, R. C. 1984a. Cross-language speech perception: evidence for perceptual reorganization during the first year of life. *Infant Behavior and Development* 7: 49–63.

Werker, J. F. & Tees, R. C. 1984b. Phonemic and phonetic factors in adult cross-language speech perception. *Journal of the Acoustical Society of America* 75: 1866–78.

Wood, S. 1986. The acoustical significance of tongue, lip, and larynx maneuvers in rounded palatal vowels. *Journal of the Acoustical Society of America* 80: 391–401.

Zlatin, M. & Koenigsknecht, R. A. 1975. Development of the voicing contrast: perception of stop consonants. *Journal of Speech and Hearing Research* 18: 541–53.

# 9 The syntax–semantics interface
*Mürvet Enç*

## 9.0. Introduction

The relation between syntax and semantics is a central issue in linguistic theory, and assumptions about this relation hinge on assumptions about the properties of the syntax and the semantics. However, although the nature of this relation is controversial, it remains uncontroversial that there is a relation. To see why this is so, let us look at the interpretation of a simple sentence of English.

(1) Mary kissed John

First of all, the interpretation of the sentence in (1) depends on the interpretation of the lexical elements contained in it. We want (1) to be true just in case the individual denoted by the name *Mary* kissed the individual denoted by the name *John*. We cannot tolerate a semantic theory which specifies that (1) is true just in case the cow jumps over the moon, no matter how general and principled such a theory might be. Although this point may seem obvious, it illustrates the fact that the interpretation of a sentence must be constructed out of the interpretation of its parts.

Lexical information alone is not sufficient for determining the meaning of the sentence, and semantics needs access to other kinds of information. Consider (2):

(2) John kissed Mary

Sentence (2) contains exactly the same lexical elements as (1), yet the two sentences have different interpretations. We will make the simple assumption that in (1) and (2), the verb *kiss* yields a relation between two individuals, and that the NPs yield individuals. It is not sufficient for the semantics to specify that the individuals denoted by the NPs stand in the relation denoted by the verb, because the relation here is not symmetric. In other words, the semantic role of *Mary* in (1) is different from that of *John*. What is the difference between (1) and (2) due to? Intuitively, *Mary* is the subject in (1), whereas it is the object in (2). But 'subject' and 'object' are syntactic notions, which we assume to be defined in terms of syntactic configuration.[1] Therefore the semantic role of the NPs depends on their syntactic properties.

(1) and (2) show that certain syntactic differences lead to differences in the assignment of semantic roles, and hence to differences in truth conditions. However, not all syntactic differences between sentences have this consequence. For example, the semantic roles of the NPs in (3) and (4) are the same as in (1) and these three sentences have equivalent truth conditions:

(3) John was kissed by Mary
(4) John, Mary kissed

The fact that the passive sentence in (3) and the sentence with a topicalized NP in (4) have the same truth conditions as the simple active sentence in (1) is not accidental. If we substitute other names for *John* and *Mary*, and another transitive verb for *kiss*, the active, the passive and the topicalized versions would remain equivalent. Therefore the grammar must guarantee that the assignment of semantic roles to NPs remains constant under these particular syntactic differences.

We saw that the interpretation of a sentence is a function of the interpretation of its parts and of the syntactic relations holding between the parts. This generalization is one of the most fundamental principles of semantics and is usually called *the principle of compositionality* or *Frege's principle*, assumed to originate with Frege (see, e.g. Frege 1977). Thus an inquiry into the relation between syntax and semantics is an inquiry into the nature of compositionality, and one of the major tasks facing linguists is determining what properties of the syntax are relevant to determining interpretations. In this chapter we will confine ourselves to a discussion of the role of syntax in two areas of semantics, the predicate–argument relation and variable binding.

## 9.1. Type assignment

We noted that in (1) the verb *kiss* yields a relation between individuals, that is to say, it is a predicate of individuals. In this sentence, the arguments of the predicate are provided by the NPs *John* and *Mary*. Similarly, the verbs in (5) and (6) denote relations between individuals, and are predicated to hold between the individuals denoted by the NPs:

(5) Richard loves Kathy
(6) Sally saw Peter

[1] Within certain frameworks such as relational grammar (RG), 'subject' and 'object' are syntactic primitives, but this difference is not relevant to the discussion at hand.

Intransitive verbs do not take direct objects, and occur with one obligatory argument:

(7) Danny slept

The verb *sleep* is a one-place predicate and yields a property of individuals, in contrast to *see* and *love*, which are two-place predicates. The individual that the property of sleeping is attributed to in (7) is the denotation of the subject NP. These sentences illustrate a generalization that holds about the relation between syntactic categories and semantic objects. Verbs provide predicates of individuals, and NPs provide their arguments.[2] This is true no matter which lexical items are dominated by the NPs and the verb. We could capture this generalization by stating that all verbs denote functions which take at least one individual argument. We thus associate with the syntactic category V a semantic type which specifies the possible denotations of V. To capture the differences between various classes of verbs we have to further refine type assignment. Intransitive verbs like *sleep* denote functions which take one individual argument, whereas transitive verbs like *see* denote functions which take two individual arguments. Some transitive verbs like *believe* and *hope* take sentential complements, and they denote functions with two arguments, one of them an individual and the other a proposition. Thus these three classes of verbs are assigned different types. In frameworks such as the government–binding theory (GB) where the number and nature of the arguments are specified in the lexicon these differences will be due to their lexical properties. That is to say, type assignment to verbs cannot be predicted solely in terms of the syntactic category but also depends on lexical entries, and the syntactic category V is not assigned a unique semantic type. In categorial frameworks such as Montague (1974), the differences between verbs discussed above are encoded in the syntactic category, e.g. transitive verbs are of a different *syntactic* category from intransitive verbs. In such frameworks, type assignment is a function and each syntactic category is assigned a unique semantic type. There is a trade-off here between the simplicity of type assignment and capturing the generalization that syntactically verbs form a natural class in spite of their differences.

Various issues in type assignment are discussed in Montague (1974), Rooth & Partee (1982), Kempson & Cormack (1983), Williams (1983), Moortgat (1984), Chierchia (1985), and Dowty (1985). Type assignment, however it is to be accomplished, provides one of the links between syntax and semantics.

---

[2] For ease of exposition, we are ignoring sentential arguments at this point.

## 9.2. **The assignment of θ-roles**

Type assignment allows us to get at the right sorts of semantic objects which will be combined to get the interpretation of the sentence. We now need mechanisms that determine how these objects are to be combined. We noted that the difference in meaning in (1) and (2) stemmed from the difference in the syntactic relations between the NPs and the verb. We assume that the lexicon specifies for each verb the semantic roles, also called *theta-roles* (θ-roles), that the verb assigns to its arguments.[3] Thus the entry for *kiss* will specify that two θ-roles are assigned. We need to ensure that in (1), the agent θ-role is assigned to the subject, and the patient to the object. However, there is no simple one-to-one correlation between grammatical relations and θ-roles. In the passive sentence in (3), the agent role is not assigned to the subject. The grammar must specify a systematic way of assigning θ-roles to the arguments. This is done in various ways in various frameworks. In GB, the correct argument structure is ensured by an interaction of various sub-theories, mainly by the *projection principle* (which requires the argument structure of the verb to be preserved at every level of representation), θ-theory (which requires each argument to bear a unique θ-role and each θ-role to be assigned to a unique argument), the theory of government, and assumptions about how the roles are assigned (cf. Williams 1980, 1984; Chomsky 1981). In Williams's work, one semantic argument is designated as the external argument, and its θ-role is assigned to an NP outside the maximal projection of the verb, in case the syntactic subject–predicate relation holds between the NP and the VP. The internal argument, on the other hand, is assigned under the government relation. Thus the external argument of *kiss* (agent) in (1) is assigned to the subject NP, and the internal argument (patient) is assigned to the object NP governed by the verb. In the passive (3), it is assumed that the NP which is in the object position at D-structure has moved to the subject position at S-structure, leaving a trace in its original position. The trace is assigned the patient role in the usual way. The agent role is absorbed by the passive morphology and transmitted to the *by*-phrase if there is one.

In rule-driven, nontransformational frameworks such as Montague grammar and generalized phrase structure grammar (GPSG), the approach is somewhat different. For example, in Montague (1974), Dowty (1979), and Gazdar (1982), active sentences like (1) are generated by the application of two rules. The semantic arguments of the verb are ordered in such a way that when the VP rule combines the verb with an NP, the NP supplies the internal argument (sometimes referred to as 'the second argument'). The S-rule

---

[3] See the discussion of grids in Stowell (1981).

combines the VP with an NP which then provides the external argument (or the first argument). These rule-based approaches diverge sharply from GB in the case of passives, topicalizations, etc. Since they do not admit movement rules, the surface subject of the passive in (3), for example, cannot get its θ-role through its trace. Here the solution lies in the semantic rule corresponding to the syntactic passive rule. The semantic rule specifies lambda abstraction over the second argument, and when the passivized VP combines with the subject NP, this NP now provides the second argument. The rule also specifies that the first argument comes from the *by*-phrase if there is one, and is existentially closed otherwise (see Dowty 1982; Gazdar 1982). Dowty (1982) remarks that in such treatments, the passive changes the verbs or the verb phrase, rather than the NP, by reversing the relation. A similar treatment is given in Keenan & Faltz (1985).[4] In such rule-driven approaches, then, the correct assignment of θ-roles relies on stipulations in semantic rules, whereas in GB the burden shifts to the syntax. Thus, although the assignment of θ-roles depends on properties of the syntax in all approaches, for certain aspects of the phenomenon the explanation can be either syntactic or semantic. This is also illustrated in the next issue we will discuss, the scope of quantifiers.

## 9.3. Scope assignment

Quantificational NPs such as *every man* need to have their scope specified. (8) is ambiguous:

(8) Every man interviewed some child

On one reading, the sentence is true if for every man there is some child (possibly different) that the man interviews. On the other reading, the sentence is true if there is some child that is interviewed by every man. In most approaches, such sentences are disambiguated at some syntactic level.[5] The two readings are assigned different syntactic representations, leading to differences in the scope of the NPs. In Montague (1974), this is accomplished by allowing variables to be generated in NP positions, and introducing the quantifiers that bind the variables at a higher point in the tree. The GB analog of this 'quantifying-in rule' is the movement of NPs at logical form (LF), proposed in May (1977) and dubbed *quantifier raising* (QR).[6] At LF, the scope of the quantifier is defined as its c-command domain. Differences in the relative scope of the quantifiers give rise to differences in interpretation.[7]

---

[4] See Dowty (1982) and Keenan & Faltz (1985) for other relation-changing rules, and Bach (1980) for a nonlexical treatment of passive.

[5] Cooper (1979, 1982, 1983), May (1985) are exceptions.

[6] We emphasize here that LF is a level of *syntactic* representation, in spite of its name.

[7] In May (1985), sentences like (8) are not disambiguated at LF, although the NPs undergo QR.

In Cooper's work (Cooper 1979, 1982, 1983), scope differences are accounted for in the course of semantic interpretation and have no reflexes in the syntax. Cooper proposes a storage mechanism, together with rules for retrieving stored items. (8) has a single syntactic representation, with *every man* in subject position and *some child* in object position. Sentences are interpreted from the bottom up, and if the interpretation of *some child* is not stored, it combines with the interpretation of the verb directly, eventually yielding the reading where the subject has wide scope over the object. However, the interpretation of the object NP may be put in storage, and a variable substituted in its place. The store consists of the interpretation of the stored item with the specification of the variable it is to bind. Interpretation proceeds up the tree until the node over which the NP is to take scope. At that point, the operator is retrieved from the store and binds the variable. Cooper argues that sentences like (8) are not *syntactically* ambiguous, and that therefore the scopes of quantifiers should be accounted for in the semantics, not in the syntax. Note that the objects stored are the interpretations of phrases, i.e. semantic objects. His account achieves a simplicity in the syntax by enriching semantic structures.

## 9.4. Constraints on interpretation

Perhaps the most controversial issue in the relation between syntax and semantics is the nature of constraints on interpretation. Linguists differ as to whether such constraints are syntactic or semantic. We will discuss briefly some constraints on reference and on variable binding.

### 9.4.1. Constraints on reference

It is a well-known fact about natural languages that the interpretation of anaphors (such as reflexives and reciprocals) and pronouns is constrained in certain ways. A reflexive needs an antecedent, therefore (9a) is ungrammatical whereas (9b) and (9c) are grammatical:

(9) a. *Himself is here
    b. John told Mary about himself
    c. John told Mary about herself

However, (10) shows that not every NP in a sentence is a possible antecedent:

(10) a. *John's mother likes himself
     b. *The fact that John is flunking bothers himself
     c. *John thinks that Mary likes himself
     d. *John called the girl that himself met last week

Note that there is no semantic incoherence involved here. The sentences would have had perfectly coherent interpretations if *John* could bind the reflexive. For example, (10a) would have meant that John's mother loves him.[8] Therefore some grammatical principle must block *John* as the antecedent in (10).

One requirement for anaphors seems to be that their antecedents c-command them. In GB, the c-command requirement is part of the definition of (syntactic) binding (cf. Chomsky 1981).[9] If we require that anaphors be bound, it follows that their antecedents must c-command them. Then the ungrammaticality of (10a) and (10b) is explained, since *John* does not c-command the reflexive.

The c-command requirement is satisfied in (10c) and (10d), yet the sentences are ungrammatical. In these sentences, the antecedent is too far away, in some sense, to bind the reflexive. Therefore a locality requirement must be imposed on the binding of anaphors.[10] In GB, this locality requirement is captured in condition A of the binding theory, which stipulates that anaphors must be bound in their minimal governing category. The minimal governing category of an expression is defined as the minimal domain containing that expression, its governor, and a subject accessible to it (cf. Chomsky 1981). In (10c), the governing category of the anaphor is the complement clause, and in (10d) it is the relative clause. Neither of these clauses contains a possible antecedent, therefore the sentences are ungrammatical.

There are constraints on the reference of pronominals and names as well:

(11) a. *John$_i$ likes him$_i$
    b. John$_i$ said that Bill$_j$ would shave him$_{i/*j}$
(12) a John$_i$ said that he$_i$ is smart
    b. *He$_i$ said that John$_i$ is smart

We will assume that co-indexed elements are coreferential. Sentence (11) shows that a pronominal cannot be too close to its antecedent. This property of pronominals is captured in condition B of the binding theory, which states that pronominals must be free (i.e. not co-indexed with a c-commanding NP) in their governing category.[11]

Given the indexing, the two sentences in (12) would have been equivalent if (12b) were grammatical. In the binding theory, such sentences are accoun-

---

[8] See Higginbotham (1985) for remarks on the interpretability of ungrammatical sentences.
[9] There are several issues about the relevant definition of c-command, especially concerning PPs (see Reinhart 1979; Chomsky 1981).
[10] We discuss here only reflexives, but the behavior of reciprocals is similar in many respects; for differences, see Lebeaux (1983).
[11] This is a constraint on the *presupposed* coreference of pronominals (see Postal 1971; Chomsky 1980; Heim 1982).

ted for by a constraint on R-expressions (names and variables), which states that R-expressions must always be free, thus barring R-expressions from being c-commanded by any other argument (condition C of the binding theory).[12]

The account sketched above constrains reference *syntactically*. It appeals to the configurational notion of c-command and states locality in terms of syntactic domains. In the transformational tradition, although the particulars of the treatment of such constraints have changed, the approach has remained syntactical (Lasnik 1976; Reinhart 1979; Chomsky 1980, 1981; Aoun 1985).

A different approach to constraints on reference can be seen in the semantic literature. Keenan (1974) states that the reference of an argument must be determinable independently of the meaning or the reference of the function. This is a semantic constraint, stated in terms of semantic objects: functions and arguments.[13] Semantically, VPs yield functions which take as argument the value of the subject NP. It follows from Keenan's general principle that no NP inside a VP can serve as the antecedent of an anaphoric or pronominal subject. This takes care of the ungrammaticality of sentences like (12b), although it allows sentences like (13), since both NPs are names:

(13) *John$_i$ said that John$_i$ is smart

In contrast, condition C of the binding theory treats (12b) and (13) alike, the ungrammaticality of (13) being explained by the fact that the name in the complement is c-commanded by a coreferential NP.

Keenan's principle ensures that anaphoric subjects cannot take as their antecedent NPs inside VPs. In syntactic treatments, this is ensured by the c-command requirement. However, Keenan's account does not extend to cases where the locality requirements for anaphors and pronominals are violated, as in (10) and (11).

Bach & Partee (1980) and Partee & Bach (1981) propose an analysis within the Montague grammar framework, utilizing Cooper's storage mechanism.[14] In order to capture the locality requirements, they propose a *local pronoun store* (LPST) where the translations of pronouns can be stored, and they place constraints on LPSTs. For example, the intersection of the LPSTs of the constituents of NPs and Ss must be empty. As a result, a pronominal subject cannot be coreferential with a pronominal object. In addition, they state that LPSTs of NPs and Ss do not inherit the LPSTs of their constituents, whereas the LPSTs of other nodes do. Because the LPSTs

---

[12] The notion of binding here is clearly syntactic, since names are not the sorts of objects that can be bound semantically.

[13] The syntactic notion of argument in GB is not to be confused with semantic argument (see Safir 1984).

[14] Bach & Partee's analysis is not purely semantic, and relies on references to the translations of expressions into intensional logic.

of NPs and Ss are emptied in this way, a pronominal in an NP or an S can be coreferential with a pronominal outside the NP or the S.

In Bach & Partee's analysis, a number of facts about antecedence are captured in nonsyntactic ways. For example, the determination of the antecedents of anaphors does not rely on c-command, but on semantic rules and semantic function/argument structures. However, as noted in Bach & Partee (1980), in a great many instances this makes the same predictions as the c-command requirement, and this is because the function/argument structure is largely mirrored in the syntactic structure. The syntax dependence of the constraints on LPSTs is more obvious. Bach & Partee follow the rule-by-rule approach, where the grammar consists of a set of syntactic rules paired with semantic rules. As noted above, the content of the LPSTs depends crucially on the relevant syntactic constituents translated. In effect, the NP- and S-nodes are singled out as syntactic constituents whose LPSTs differ in systematic ways from other constituents. In that sense, the constraints are partly specified in syntactic terms.[15]

One area where Bach & Partee's analysis makes different predictions from the binding theory is NPs. In the binding theory of Chomsky (1981) NPs and Ss are not singled out as binding domains. Rather, it is proposed that any category that has a subject will function as a binding domain. Ss and small clauses always have subjects, but NPs do not require subjects, and can be governing categories only if they do have a subject. This approach is supported by the sentences in (14) and (15):

(14) a.  John read a book about himself
   b. *John read Mary's book about himself
(15) a.  John$_i$ saw Sally's picture of him$_i$
   b. *Sally saw John's$_i$ picture of him$_i$

In these examples, only the NP containing a subject is the governing category of the reflexive or the pronoun in the NP. If this generalization about the role of subjects is correct, as it seems to be, then Bach & Partee's analysis needs to be modified in a way that requires accessing even more syntactic information.[16]

## 9.4.2. Constraints on variable binding

Natural languages contain a number of variable binding operators, among them quantifiers and *wh*-phrases. In this section, we will briefly discuss some

---

[15] Landman & Moerdijk (1983), also within the framework of Montague grammar, argue for a syntactic treatment of the constraints on reference.
[16] See Pollard & Sag (1983) for an alternative account.

constraints on these operators, and compare syntactic approaches to such constraints with semantic approaches.

In some languages like English, the *wh*-phrases are dislocated at surface structure. It is well-known that there are constraints on the domains within which the *wh*-phrase can bind its variable.[17]

(16) a.  Who did John say [e loves Mary]
    b. *Who did John say [that e loves Mary]
    c.  Who did John say [that Mary loves e]
    d. *Who did John believe the claim [that Mary loves e]
    e. *What did John see the girl [that Bill gave e to e]

Such structures are generated by *wh*-movement in transformational frameworks, and base-generated in mono-level frameworks such as GPSG and Montague grammar. For ease of exposition, we will confine ourselves to the discussion of movement analyses.

In the transformational framework, the differences in the grammaticality of the sentences in (16) have always been accounted for syntactically, although the accounts have varied. For example, Ross (1967) stated that certain structures such as relative clauses and complex NPs were islands, and that no *wh*-phrase could be moved out of islands. More recently, certain aspects of the grammaticality of *wh*-structures have been accounted for not by constraints on movement, but by constraints on the occurrence of empty categories, in particular by the *empty category principle* (ECP) which states that all nonpronominal empty categories must be properly governed (cf. Chomsky 1981; Lasnik & Saito 1984).[18]

It has also been observed that the scope of quantifiers in natural languages is constrained.

(17) Guinevere has a bone that is in every corner of the house

Sentence (17) is an example from Rodman (1976), and shows that *every corner*, which is inside a relative clause, cannot take scope over *a bone*. That is to say, the sentence does not have a reading where every corner of the house has one of Guinevere's bones. It has been suggested in Postal (1974), Rodman (1976), and Cooper (1979) that the scope of quantifiers is constrained by precisely the same principles which constrain *wh*-operators. On this view, for example, relative clauses are islands for both *wh*-operators and quantifiers.

It seems, however, that quantifiers are more restricted than *wh*-operators. Consider (18):

(18) Some student believes [that John loves every women]

---

[17] In (16), the gaps are marked [e] (empty category).
[18] For the definition of proper government, see Chomsky (1981).

The direct object of the complement, *every woman*, cannot take scope over the matrix subject. Sentence (18) does not have a reading where for every woman there is some student (possibly different) who believes that John loves her. It seems to be a fact about natural languages that quantifiers are clause-bounded, i.e. their scope cannot extend beyond the minimal S in which they are generated. This contrasts with *wh*-movement, where NPs can move to the matrix COMP from complements, as shown in (16a) and (16c). Therefore, some extra stipulation is necessary for quantifiers.

As mentioned before, the GB treatment of quantifiers involves movement of quantifiers at LF. Their scope is defined as the domain they c-command at LF, and some of the restrictions on their scope (e.g. their clause-boundedness) are achieved by restrictions on their movement. In May (1977), it is stipulated that quantifiers adjoin to the first S up, and in May (1985) they are also allowed to adjoin the NPs and VPs inside this minimal S. Thus in GB the scope of all operators is determined syntactically. In some very fundamental way, quantification and variable binding are semantic phenomena. The significance of the GB approach is the assumption that the semantics of quantification and variable binding is syntactically constrained, just as semantic reference is syntactically constrained as discussed above.

In spite of differences in their movement possibilities, quantifiers and *wh*-phrases share a number properties. This is not surprising, since they are both variable binding operators. We will now discuss one such similarity in order to illustrate yet another case where the semantics is assumed to be constrained by the syntax: the phenomenon of weak crossover.

Pronouns can function like bound variables in natural languages, as shown in (19):

(19) Every child$_i$ thought that his$_i$ mother was tough

The pronoun in (19) can function as a variable bound to the quantifier *every child*, resulting in a reading which is true if for every x, x a child, x thought x's mother was tough. We will assume that a pronoun can have a bound-variable reading only if it is (syntactically) bound by the operator, i.e. only if the operator is co-indexed with the pronoun and c-commands it at LF. However, this condition is not sufficient, since it does not account for the ungrammaticality of (20) and (21):

(20) *Who$_i$ did his$_i$ mother see [e$_i$]
(21) *His$_i$ mother saw every child$_i$
(22)  His$_i$ mother saw John$_i$

The binding of the pronoun in (20) and (21) results in ungrammaticality. That is to say, (20) does not mean 'whose mother saw him,' and (21) does not mean 'every child's mother saw him.' Both sentences are grammatical if the pronoun is not co-indexed with the operator, i.e. if not bound by it. As frequently observed, the binding theory does not rule out (20) and (21). Nor should it, given the grammaticality of (22). The contrast between (20) and (21) on the one hand and (22) on the other hand indicate that the constraint ruling out (20) and (21) applies to variables and variable binding operators.

Now note that the c-command condition does not account for the unavailability of the bound reading for the pronoun in these sentences. In (20), the operator already c-commands the pronoun, and this relation will not be altered at LF. The quantifier in (20) will undergo raising at LF, and will also c-command the pronoun. The LF representation of (20) will be as in (23):

(23) [every child$_i$ [his$_i$ mother saw e$_i$]]

Therefore, for pronouns to function as bound variables, they must satisfy some additional condition.

(20) and (21) illustrate cases of weak crossover.[19] Early works account for weak crossover by a condition on *wh*-movement (Postal 1971). The parallelism between *wh*-operators and quantifiers is noted in Chomsky (1977), where the *leftness condition* is proposed which states that a variable cannot be the antecedent of a pronoun to its left. Higginbotham (1980) provides evidence against the leftness condition, and proposes instead that a pronoun can be bound to an operator only if c-commanded by the variable left behind the operator, and this proposal is further supported in Jaeggli (1984).

We are less concerned here with the differences between proposals than with their nature. That pronouns are sometimes interpreted as bound variables rather than as deictic elements is a *semantic* phenomenon. The treatments cited above share an important property. They propose *syntactic* constraints on this semantic phenomenon.[20]

Cooper's treatment of constraints on binding are in sharp contrast to the approaches mentioned above (Cooper 1979, 1982, 1983). We noted that the scope of quantifiers is not represented in the syntax in Cooper's work. Instead, it depends on whether or not the interpretation of the quantifier has been stored. Similarly, the binding of variables by *wh*-operators is accomplished through storage. Cooper argues that constraints on variable binding operations can be and should be captured in semantic ways. He discusses in detail Ross's *complex noun phrase constraint*, and proposes a semantic alternative in terms of the properties of the store.[21] He considers the possibility of requiring that the store of any NP must be empty before it can be further processed (Cooper 1982). This statement refers to the syntactic

---

[19] See Postal (1971), Wasow (1972, 1979), Chomsky (1977, 1982), Higginbotham (1980), Koopman & Sportiche (1983), Jaeggli (1984), Safir (1984), Williams (1986), among others.

[20] In fact, crossover facts are usually used to argue for the syntactic level LF; Williams (1986) is an exception.

[21] This is also the strategy adopted in Partee & Bach (1981).

category NP and is therefore not cast solely in semantic terms. Cooper points out that Montague's characterization of all NPs as quantifiers allows a statement in semantic terms. He then proposes (24):

(24) If the interpretation is a quantifier (i.e. NP-interpretation), then the store must be empty before the derivation can continue.

In fact, Cooper proposes that all semantic constraints be stated in semantic terms, a restriction that he characterizes as a semantic autonomy condition.

We have seen, however, that the scope of quantifiers is limited to the minimal S in which they are generated, whereas *wh*-operators are not so restricted. Therefore, something extra needs to be stipulated in the semantic rules which allow quantifier interpretations in the store to be passed up the tree. The complex NPs discussed by Cooper which motivate (24) are NPs containing relative clauses and sentential complements; but if the scope of a quantifier is already restricted to its minimal S, then (24) is not needed to prevent quantifiers from having wider scope than these complex NPs, and perhaps (24) does not capture a true generalization about both quantifiers and *wh*-operators.

Cooper (1982) argues that a semantic account of the conditions on binding automatically constrains the kind of conditions one may impose. He notes that although the complex NP constraint can be cast in semantic terms, the *nominative island condition* in Chomsky (1980) cannot. It then remains to be seen whether an adequate grammar can be constructed where all constraints on variable binding are stated in the semantics. One case that seems particularly difficult for a semantic treatment is the so-called *that trace* (*that-t*) effect.

(25) a. John said Bill loves Mary
     b. John said that Bill loves Mary

The two sentences in (25) differ only in that one contains the complementizer *that* and the other does not, and the sentences are semantically equivalent. However, we saw earlier that *wh*-movement from the subject position of the complement is possible only if the complementizer is absent. The relevant examples are repeated here:

(16) a.   Who did John say [e loves Mary]
     b. *Who did John say [that e loves Mary]
     c.   Who did John say [that Mary loves e]

In most current analyses within GB, these extraction facts are explained by the syntactic *empty category principle*, which is a principle governing all structures and is not stipulated merely to account for the facts in (16a–c) (Chomsky 1981). How would a semantic account of these facts proceed? It would be necessary to stipulate that the interpretation of the complements in (16a–b) are distinct, and that one kind of interpretation requires the store to be empty, and the other allows the store to be passed on. How the interpretations can be distinguished is not obvious. Furthermore, the complementizer blocks only the extraction of the subject, and not the object, as (16c) shows. However the interpretations of the complements are distinguished, the distinction has to be sensitive to the *syntactic position* that the variable is in.

It is hard to see a plausible and elegant account of the *that-t* effects in semantic terms, and it is very probable that an adequate analysis of this phenomenon will be in syntactic terms. If so, at least some constraints on variable binding will be syntactic, a conclusion not ruled out in Cooper (1982). Are there principled differences between the cases explained by semantic constraints and the cases explained by syntactic constraints? One possible approach is to appeal to the distinction in Cooper (1983) between controlled quantification (e.g. *wh*-movement) which has a syntactic reflex, and free quantification (e.g. quantified NPs) which does not in his treatments. One could suggest that constraints on controlled quantification are syntactic and those on free quantification are semantic. This approach would run into problems with languages such as Chinese and Japanese where *wh*-phrases do not move at S-structures but remain in situ, although they obey the same sorts of constraints as in English (Aoun, Hornstein & Sportiche 1981; Huang 1982; Lasnik & Saito 1984). Furthermore, the weak crossover cases discussed earlier indicate that some conditions on binding (in this case the binding of pronouns) apply to both *wh*-operators and to quantifiers, indicating that conditions on these operations cannot always be distinct. If there are some cases where semantic operations are syntactically constrained, and if we cannot propose principles which determine whether a generalization should be captured in syntactic or semantic terms, then the preferability of stating some constraints in semantic terms is cast in doubt.

## 9.5. Conclusion

The *compositionality principle*, which states that the interpretation of a phrase is a function of the interpretation of its constituents and the syntactic relation that holds between them, is a fundamental tenet of semantic theories. The exact nature and role of compositionality is a matter of debate.[22] It is hard to see compositionality itself as a significant constraint on grammars. It can make no interesting empirical predictions on its own, since it does not constrain what kind of constituents an expression can have, nor how their meanings are to be combined. In fact, Partee (1979) acknowledges

---

[22] See Partee (1984) for extensive discussion.

that compositionality does not limit the choice of analysis, and Landman & Moerdijk (1983) claim that it has no empirical content. It is perhaps nothing more than an acknowledgement of the need to assign interpretations recursively in a systematic way, to the output of the syntax.

Montague stated that he 'fail[ed] to see any great interest in syntax except as a preliminary to semantics' (Montague 1974: 223, fn 2). However, linguistic research indicates that certain generalizations about human language are syntactic and cannot be reduced to the properties of the semantics, thus lending support to the thesis of the autonomy of syntax. The assignment of interpretations depends on the theory of syntax, the theory of semantics and the relation between them. We have seen various treatments of the link between syntactic categories and semantic types, the assignment of θ-roles, the constraints on reference and variable binding. In some, the generalizations were captured in the semantics, in others in the syntax. Ultimately, the choice between these treatments is an empirical issue and rests on the adequacy of the linguistic theory as a whole.

*REFERENCES*

Aoun, J. 1985. *A grammar of anaphora*. Cambridge, MA: MIT Press.
Aoun, J., Hornstein, N. & Sportiche, D. 1981. Some aspects of wide scope quantification. *Journal of Linguistic Research* 1: 69–93.
Bach, E. 1980. In defense of passive. *Linguistics and Philosophy* 3: 297–342.
Bach, E. & Partee, B. 1980. Anaphora and semantic structure. In J. Kreiman & A. E. Ojeda (eds.) *Papers from the parasession on pronouns and anaphora*. Chicago: Chicago Linguistic Society.
Chierchia, G. 1985. Formal semantics and the grammar of predication. *Linguistic Inquiry* 16: 417–43.
Chomsky, N. 1977. Conditions on rules of grammar. In *Essays on form and interpretation*. Amsterdam: North-Holland.
Chomsky, N. 1980. On binding. *Linguistic Inquiry* 11: 1–46.
Chomsky, N. 1981. *Lectures on government and binding*. Dordrecht: Foris.
Cooper, R. 1979. Variable binding and relative clauses. In F. Guenthner & S. J. Schmidt (eds.) *Formal semantics and pragmatics for natural languages*. Dordrecht: Reidel.
Cooper, R. 1982. Binding in wholewheat* syntax (*unenriched with inaudibilia). In Jacobson & Pullum (1982).
Cooper, R. 1983. *Quantification and syntactic theory*. Dordrecht: Reidel.
Dowty, D. 1979. *Word meaning and Montague grammar*. Dordrecht: Reidel.
Dowty, D. 1982. Grammatical relations and Montague grammar. In Jacobson & Pullum (1982).
Dowty, D. 1985. Type raising, functional composition, and non-constituent conjunction. Paper presented at the Tucson Conference on Categorial Grammar.
Frege, G. 1977. On sense and reference. In P. Geach & M. Black (eds.) *Philosophical writings of Gottlob Frege*. Oxford: Blackwell.
Gazdar, G. 1982. Phrase structure grammar. In Jacobson & Pullum (1982).
Heim, I. 1982. The semantics of definite and indefinite noun phrases. Doctoral dissertation, University of Massachusetts/Amherst.
Higginbotham, J. 1980. Pronouns and bound variables. *Linguistic Inquiry* 11: 679–708.
Higginbotham, J. 1985. On semantics. *Linguistic Inquiry*. 16: 547–93.
Huang, C.T. J. 1982. Logical relations in Chinese and the theory of grammar. Doctoral dissertation, MIT.

Jacobson, P. & Pullum, G. (eds.). 1982. *The nature of syntactic representation*. Dordrecht: Reidel.
Jaeggli, O. 1984. Subject extraction and the null subject parameter. In C. Jones & P. Sells (eds.) *NELS* 14. Amherst: GLSA.
Keenan, E. 1974. The functional principle: generalizing the notion of 'subject of'. *CLS* 10: 298–309.
Keenan, E. & Faltz, L. 1985. *Boolean semantics for natural language*. Dordrecht: Reidel.
Kempson, R. & Cormack, A. 1983. Type lifting rules and VP anaphora. In M. Barlow, D. Flickinger & M. Wescoat (eds.) *Proceedings of the West Coast Conference on Formal Linguistics* 2. Stanford.
Koopman, H. & Sportiche, D. 1983. Variables and the bijection principle. *The Linguistic Review* 2: 139–60.
Landman, F. & Moerdijk, I. 1983. Compositionality and the analysis of anaphora. *Linguistics and Philosophy* 6: 89–114.
Lasnik, H. 1976. Remarks on coreference. *Linguistic Analysis* 2: 1–22.
Lasnik, H. & Saito, M. 1984. On the nature of proper government. *Linguistic Inquiry* 15: 235–89.
Lebeaux, D. 1983. A distributional difference between reciprocals and reflexives. *Linguistic Inquiry* 14: 723–30.
May, R. 1977. The grammar of quantification. Doctoral dissertation, MIT.
May, R. 1985. *Logical form: its structure and derivation*. Cambridge, MA: MIT Press.
Montague, R. 1974. *Formal philosophy*. New Haven: Yale University Press.
Moortgat, M. 1984. A Fregean restriction on metarules. In C. Jones & P. Sells (eds.) *NELS* 14. Amherst: GLSA.
Partee, B. 1979. Montague grammar and the well-formedness constraint. In F. Heny & H. Schnelle (eds.) *Syntax and semantics*. Vol. 10. New York: Academic Press.
Partee, B. 1984. Compositionality. In F. Landman & F. Veltman (eds.) *Varieties of formal semantics: Proceedings of the Fourth Amsterdam Colloquium*. Dordrecht: Foris.
Partee, B. & Bach, E. 1981. Quantification, pronouns, and VP anaphora. In J. Groenendijk, T. Janssen & M. Stokhof (eds.) *Formal methods in the study of language*. Amsterdam: Mathematical Center Tracts.
Pollard, C. & Sag, I. 1983. Reflexives and reciprocals in English: an alternative to the binding theory. In M. Barlow, D. Flickinger & M. Wescoat (eds.) *Proceedings of the West Coast Conference on Formal Linguistics* 2. Stanford.
Postal, P. 1971. *Crossover phenomena*. New York: Academic Press.
Postal, P. 1974. On certain ambiguities. *Linguistic Inquiry* 5: 367–424.
Reinhart, T. 1979. Syntactic domains for semantic rules. In F. Guenthner & S. J. Schmidt (eds.) *Formal semantics and pragmatics for natural languages*. Dordrecht: Reidel.
Rodman, R. 1976. Scope phenomena, 'movement transformations', and relative clauses. In B. Partee (ed.) *Montague grammar*. New York: Academic Press.
Rooth, M. & Partee, B. 1982. Conjunction, type ambiguity, and wide scope 'or'. In D. Flickinger, M. Macken & N. Wiegand (eds.) *Proceedings of the West Coast Conference on Formal Linguistics* 1. Stanford.
Ross, J. 1967. Constraints on variables in syntax. Doctoral dissertation, MIT.
Safir, K. 1984. Multiple variable binding. *Linguistic Inquiry* 15: 603–38.
Stowell, T. 1981. Origins of phrase structure. Doctoral dissertation, MIT.
Wasow, T. 1972. Anaphoric relations in English. Doctoral dissertation, MIT.
Wasow, T. 1979. *Anaphora in generative grammar*. Ghent: E. Story-Scientia.
Williams, E. 1980. Predication. *Linguistic Inquiry* 11: 203–38.
Williams, E. 1983. Semantic vs. syntactic categories. *Linguistics and Philosophy* 6: 423–46.
Williams, E. 1984. Grammatical relations. *Linguistic Inquiry* 15: 639–73.
Williams, E. 1986. A reassignment of the functions of LF. *Linguistic Inquiry* 17: 265–99.

# 10 The syntax–phonology interface

*Geoffrey K. Pullum and Arnold M. Zwicky*

## 10.0. Introduction

It is not in dispute that syntax and phonology are interconnected to some extent. Though syntax and phonology are certainly distinct levels, nonetheless the grammar and pronunciation of a language cannot be fully described in disjoint vocabularies with neither description making any reference to the categories employed in the other. The issues discussed here are how far each domain is relevant to generalizations in the other, and in what specific ways. One *a priori* possibility would be that there was unlimited scope for interconnections and cross-references. Another would be that there were certain specific types of information from each domain available to the other. We believe that neither of these positions is the actual one. We hold that there is an asymmetry: certain specific types of syntactic information are indeed available to phonology, but no phonological information is available to syntax. This chapter will be to some extent a brief for this position, as well as a sampler of the recent literature on the syntax–phonology interface.

## 10.1. Phonology, morphology, and syntax

We take it as established that it is common, perhaps even universal, in the languages of the world for the phonological form of certain linguistic units to depend on nonphonological properties, either of these units or of the constructions they occur in. Certainly the phonological form of a morpheme can depend on nonphonological properties of its own as well as of the morphemes it combines with; for examples and discussion, see Chapters 6 and 7 in this volume, on 'Morphological theory' and 'Phonological theory'. It is also true that the phonological form of a word or phrase can depend on nonphonological properties of its own or of the sentences it occurs in.

In Welsh, for instance, an NP like *cath* [kaθ] 'a cat' or *pob cath* [pobkaθ] 'every cat' in combination with a preposition will have different phonemic forms, depending idiosyncratically on the preposition: *wedi pob cath* [wɛdipobkaθ] 'after every cat' and *mewn cath* [mɛunkaθ] 'in a cat' (with NP-initial /p/ and /k/, respectively); *i bob cath* [ibobkaθ] 'to every cat' and *gan gath* (gangaθ) 'by means of a cat' (with /b/ and /g/); *yn nghath* [əŋŋaθ] 'in a cat' (with initial /ŋ/); *gyda chath* [gədaxaθ] 'together with a cat' (with initial /x/). Word order is relevant: an adjective preceding a noun affects it phonologically (*hen gath* [hɛngaθ] 'an old cat') but one following it does not (*cath od* [kaθod] 'a strange cat'). Grammatical categories are also relevant: an adjective following a noun is itself affected, but only by a feminine singular noun and not by a plural or a masculine (*cath goch* [kaθgox] 'a red cat,' *cathod coch* [kaθodkox] 'red cats,' *ci coch* [kikox] 'a red dog'). Syntactic function is also relevant: vocative NPs are affected (*Gath!* [gaθ] 'Cat!', *Gathod!* [gaθod] 'Cats!'), and so are bare NP adverbials (*pob dydd* [pobdið] 'every day' as subject or object, but *bob dydd* [bobdið] as an adverb).

This is a considerable range of syntactic properties to be involved in a matter of phonological realization. The first question, then, to be asked about the way in which syntax and phonology interface with one another is (A) below.

(A) What syntactic information is accessible to phonological rules?

Question A naturally suggests a converse question, about whether non-phonological properties of a syntactic unit can depend on the phonological form of its parts or of the units with which it combines:

(B) What phonological information is accessible to syntactic rules?

Questions like (A) and (B) cannot be usefully explored in a theoretical vacuum. They make sense only against a considerable background of assumptions about the architecture of grammar – about the components of grammar, about the types of representations available in a grammar, and about the nature of the rules within particular components.

We will assume from the outset that grammatical theory will distinguish (one or more components of) phonology from (one or more components of) morphology and from (one or more components of) syntax. It follows that (A) is a distinct question from (A') and (A") below, and that (B) is distinct from (B') and (B").

(A') What morphological information is accessible to phonological rules?
(A") What syntactic information is accessible to morphological rules?
(B') What phonological information is accessible to morphological rules?
(B") What morphological information is accessible to syntactic rules?

Only (A) and (B) fall within the scope of this chapter. However, the other four questions, which concern morphology rather than syntax or morphology rather than phonology, are easily confused with (A) and (B).

In speaking of 'syntactic information' in (A) and 'phonological information' in (B), we made no commitment as to the number of types of syntactic and phonological representations that might be relevant, nor as to the relationship between such representations and the 'information' referred to in (A) and (B). In part, such matters are simply what is at issue in questions like (A) and (B). But they are also determined to some extent by the choice of theoretical framework, so that (A) and (B) become somewhat different questions in different theoretical contexts.

Consider question (A) with respect to classical transformational grammar, that is, the kind of work that flourished in the period after Chomsky (1965) was published, in which deep structures representing function–argument relations and participant roles for NP referents in basic simple clause types are linked by transformations to surface structures representing linear order and phonologically relevant constituent structure. Classical TG distinguishes several types of syntactic representations. Deep structures are the structures defined prior to any transformational operations. Cyclic structures (Pullum 1979: 154) are the output of the set of cyclic transformations applying within a given cyclic domain. Shallow structures (*ibid.*) are the output of the entire set of cyclic transformations in all cyclic domains. Surface structures are the structures defined after all transformational operations. In addition, since the syntactic framework is derivational, with different levels of representation related to one another via a series of intermediate representations (corresponding to the application of individual transformations), a host of unnamed intermediate representations is also made available by the framework. In principle, any one of these types of representations might incorporate information relevant to the applicability of a phonological rule.

In fact, it has been suggested by a number of different linguists that information from any of these representations might condition or constrain phonological rules; viz. the espousal of 'global rules' by Lakoff (1970), the suggestion of Baker & Brame (1972: 54) that the classical theory might be 'incorrect in maintaining a strict separation between syntactic rules on the one hand vs. morphological and phonological rules on the other,' the claim by Hetzron (1972: 251–2) that 'there is no clearcut boundary between syntax and phonology,' the echoing of this by Tegey's assertion (1975: 571) that 'a strict separation of phonological from syntactic processes is not possible,' and many other statements quoted in Zwicky & Pullum (1986).

In contrast, in a monostratal syntactic framework, such as that of generalized phrase structure grammar (GPSG) (Gazdar *et al.* 1985, henceforth GKPS), only one type of syntactic representation, corresponding to the surface structure level of classical TG, is available. Since a tree is defined as well-formed if it meets all the clauses of a single, static definition of admissibility (GKPS: 104), the notion that syntactic and phonological rules might

257

be interspersed, as some have suggested, does not even make sense. It is a notion that only arises under the classical theory's assumption, shared by current variants of government–binding (GB) theory, of a sequential derivation through a series of transformations, after any of which some phonological rule might in principle apply.

With respect to the representations they posit, standard TG and GPSG share at least one important assumption, however: that syntactic representations are *constituent structures*; they indicate the way in which contiguous constituents, belonging to specified categories, are grouped into constructs of specified categories. Such representations indicate the boundaries and category membership of syntactic constituents, but do not indicate, directly at least, many types of information that could in principle be relevant for the operation of phonological rules and which are represented explicitly in some other grammatical frameworks. Among these types of information are: (1) which constituent in a construct is the head; (2) among non-head constituents, which are modifiers of the head and which are complements to the head; and (3) for a particular complement, which grammatical relation it bears to its head. We might add that many linguists assume that pure constituent structure frameworks have to be modified to allow not only for the representation of semantically needed constituents that are syntactically absent (examples might be the determiner in *Birds have wings*, the head noun in *the very rich*, or the implicit subject and object pronouns in languages such as Japanese), but also for at least two types of syntactically present but phonologically null constituents: empty anaphoric ones, as in *We tried to 0*, and traces, as in *Who did you see 0?*. Constituent structure-based frameworks are not obviously adequate for linguistic description, therefore. Clear evidence of the phonological relevance of the kinds of information they fail to represent, under conditions that did not allow for constituent structure surrogates to serve the purpose, would provide an interesting kind of evidence from phonology about the character of syntactic theory. We regard many questions in this area as still open.

## 10.2. Rule types in morphology and phonology

Question (A) potentially has a number of different answers, depending upon what is meant by 'phonological rules'. In virtually every extant theory about how phonological shapes are associated with linguistic units, the task of making this association is divided between the lexicon and the grammar proper, and within the grammar proper the task is parceled out among several components.

Some aspects of pronunciation belong idiosyncratically to particular words, of course. No sort of generalization predicts that the base form of the verb *go* is /gō/, that the past tense form of *go* is *went* rather than *\*goed*, or that the base form of the causative verb related to *die* is *kill* rather than *die*. Some aspects of the pronunciation of words, on the other hand, can be predicted from other of their properties. The dividing line between aspects of pronunciation that are predicted by rule and aspects that are stipulated in lexical entries is a matter on which phonological theories diverge dramatically.

Moreover, the very far-reaching changes in phonological theory that have emerged over the past ten years (since the publication of such works as, for example, Goldsmith 1976; Kahn 1976; Liberman & Prince 1977) have introduced a vast range of relevant new questions about different aspects of phonological structure. Morris Halle has presented in various public lectures the notion of a structural representation for a sentence as an object with the topology of a spiral-bound notebook, the string of phonetic segments being set out along the spine and the different pages providing structural descriptions of that string in different descriptive vocabularies (metrical structure, autosegmental tone representation, CV skeletal structure, morphological structure, syntactic structure, and so on). Ultimately we have to understand, for the entire *n*-dimensional cartesian product, which pages of the notebook can make reference to which information on which other pages.

Thinking on these questions within the TG investigative paradigm has traditionally been oriented toward thinking about derivations. Process-oriented derivational metaphors have been extremely potent and long-lived, but in our view they have obscured matters as often as they have illuminated them. We regard the limited (but still insufficient) move toward nonderivational thinking in generative linguistics as eminently desirable and long overdue. The issue of syntactic influence in phonological rules, for example, is not about whether a 'late' rule in the phonology may 'look back' at the syntactic description to 'see what was there,' but whether allocation of phonological properties may be contingent on facts about the syntactic environment. Likewise, the issue of phonological influence in syntactic rules is not about 'peeking ahead' at the phonology, notwithstanding the many places in the literature where this phraseology has been used; see Cornulier (1972) for one example of alleged 'peeking', and Sadock (1985: 436) for a hint of how the portmanteau morphs discussed by Cornulier might be analyzed.

In the next five subsections we will very briefly review our conception of the phonological and morphological parts of the grammar. The theory we sketch is not known from the literature; it draws distinctions that have not hitherto been drawn consistently, or at all. We present it here, however, because we have found the framework it provides to be very valuable in clarifying the ways in which syntax and phonology mesh together.

## 10.2.1. Regularities in the lexicon

The lexicon is the repository of unpredictable phonological information about words. But it does not, we suggest, contain *only* unpredictable information. Rather, a lexical entry contains a phonological base and also a list of word forms. Thus the entry for GO will contain not only a phonological base /gō/ but also a list of word forms: *goes* (3rd sg. pres.), *went* (past), *gone* (past ptcpl.), *going* (pres. ptcpl.), *go* (default).

Some aspects of the shape of word forms are predictable via general principles, at least in so far as special idiosyncrasies do not interpose themselves. There will doubtless be principles of derivational morphology, i.e. word formation, though we will say nothing about them here. There may also be *lexical implication principles* (more usually known as lexical redundancy rules). Lexical implication principles state correlations between properties of lexical items, and we tentatively assume that they may mention phonological properties; for example, if there were a language where all verb stems had the shape CVC, a lexical implication principle could express the generalization that the morphosyntactic feature 'verb' implies the phonological form CVC. We suspect that clear cases of this sort are rare to the point of being non-existent, but we do not entirely rule out the possibility of phonological reference in the special case of generalizations about the form of classes of words. Accidents of history could in principle have a language with generalizations of this sort holding of its lexicon (for example, as C. E. Bazell once pointed out, none of the monosyllabic verbs of English that are phonologically palindromic have irregular morphology; this looks like a coincidence to us, but it is exceptionlessly true). Conceivably, a descriptive linguist might want to incorporate such a generalization into the description of the lexicon. This would not, we submit, constitute a challenge to the claim that syntactic rules do not refer to phonology.

## 10.2.2. Inflectional allomorphy statements

It is uncontroversial, almost definitional, to say that inflectional allomorphy rules are rules of *realization*: they are statements about the phonological form that is associated with certain elements characterized in morphosyntactic terms. But we propose that two basic types of rule should be recognized: rules of *exponence* and rules of *referral*. Rules of exponence state correspondences between morphosyntactic categories and morphophonological operations; a typical example from English morphology would be (informally): 'the category FINITE VERB, PAST TENSE is realized by the operation of adding the suffix /d/.' Rules of referral state correspondences between morphosyntactic categories and stipulate that they have the same rule of exponence; a typical example would be: 'the category VERB, PAST PARTICIPLE has the same realization as the category FINITE VERB, PAST TENSE.'

As should be obvious (since the foregoing examples do not express exceptionless claims about English), all realization rules are *defaults* rather than absolute conditions. Rules imposing more specific conditions override them.

## 10.2.3. Conditions on shape

Quite distinct from the realization rules of inflectional allomorphy are *shape conditions*, which are sensitive to more than just the internal feature composition of words. Shape conditions override not only other phonological rules but even lexical entries. We distinguish three types of shape condition, involving (1) filtering, (2) realization, and (3) referral.

*Filtering shape conditions* are a proper subset of the well-known class of constraints referred to in the transformational literature as 'filters' (Chomsky & Lasnik 1977), 'surface structure constraints' (Perlmutter 1971), or 'output conditions' (Ross 1967: ch. 3). They state local constraints on permissible morphological and phonological realizations of word sequences in ways that have often been cited as illustrative of phonological conditions on syntactic structure (Perlmutter 1971: ch. 3; Hetzron 1972: section 4.2; Schachter 1974; Rivero & Walker 1976; and many others works). We assume that they may be sensitive to the superficial syntactic properties and the basic (underlying) phonological form of more than just one word, which is why they cannot be regarded as a part of the morphology, with which they otherwise have something in common. (Clear evidence that underlying phonology is the level referenced, rather than some more superficial 'phonemic' level, is not available, incidentally; we consider this to be a topic that needs further investigation.)

Our position is essentially identical to the one defended by Perlmutter (1971: esp. ch. 3), though we will ignore the question of whether linguistic theory countenances positive filters, negative filters, or both, to which Perlmutter devotes some attention. It seems very likely to us that this issue has no content: a positive filter requiring structures to meet condition $C$ is equivalent to a negative filter blocking structures that meet $\sim C$, and given only that $C$ is a recursive predicate in the sense of recursive function theory, any filter could be phrased either way.

Filtering shape conditions appear to be needed to capture some generalizations, such as the ill-formedness of strings with sequence of articles in English (\**a the Hague shipping company*, \**an 'A Chorus Line' performance*, \**the 'The Gables' on Main Street*), the prohibition against sequences of adjacent identical clitic pronouns in many languages, the constraint against sequences of adjacent infinitives in Italian (Longobardi 1980), and so on. For a particularly clear case, see the study of Tagalog clitic order by Schachter (1974).

Filters are strictly local (i.e. they do not make reference to variables over infinite classes of strings); in fact all the cases we are aware of refer to nothing more than two adjacent lexical items. Because of this, there is a very large part of the domain of syntax that filters (in our sense) cannot in principle express. Nonetheless, some have assigned a wider role to filters than we would. Thus some claimed examples of filters discussed in the literature certainly do not meet the definition of filtering shape conditions. The filter '*[V adjunct NP], NP lexical' in Chomsky & Lasnik (1977: 479) does not, for example (it is a constraint on constituent order intended to claim that a lexically filled direct object NP cannot be legally separated from the preceding verb by an adjunct such as an adverb or PP). We are concerned here solely with filters that state conditions on the morphological and phonological composition of word sequences.

Other alleged filters may not be rules of grammar at all. For example, the 'doubl-*ing* constraint' of Ross (1972), relevant because Ross argues that several distinct suffixes pronounced *ing* cause ungrammaticality if they appear on adjacent words, has been argued by Bolinger (1979) to be an illusion. The phonetically ugly effect of two adjacent words with similar endings can, if the rhythmic structure enhances the ugliness, sound strikingly unacceptable, but no grammatical condition need be postulated, he suggested. *It is continuing raining* is no more ungrammatical that *It's rotten to have gotten forgotten*, though both are phonesthetically inept.

It may turn out that no filters are genuinely needed in syntax, in which case the relative autonomy and non-uniformity of the components of grammar would be even clearer; but at present we assume at least a small amount of evidence supports them.

*Realizational shape conditions* can be illustrated by reference to the familiar fact of English that the indefinite article is *a* when followed by a consonant but *an* when followed by a vowel. This is not part of the lexical entry for the word, because it refers to the following syntactic context. It is not a phonological rule of English, for it applies only to the indefinite article and has no general applicability to phonological domains. It is a condition on shape that overrides the lexical entry for the indefinite article and stipulates that another shape is called for.

*Referral shape conditions* can also be illustrated with a fact about the phonological form of articles. In Spanish, when the definite article is adjacent to a feminine singular noun that begins with a vowel, its normal shape, *la*, is discarded, and the shape assigned instead is that of the masculine article, *el*. Clearly syntactic factors are at work here; for example, a prenominal adjective beginning with a vowel does not trigger the referral even though a homonymous noun does (cf. *la alta torre*, 'the high tower,' but *dar el alta* '(re)assign to military service' not \**dar la alta*, even though the noun *alta* is feminine). Thus although it is conceivable that a phonological account could be given of these facts, it seems to us that an account in terms of a referral shape condition is more plausible.

Summarizing, we observe that there is some support for directly stated conditions governing the allowable shapes of particular sequences of adjacent words, and we regard these as evidence of conditions stated *on* the interface of syntactic structure and phonological realization, not as evidence of intermingling or interaction *across* the boundary.

### 10.2.4. Morphonology

The allomorphy rules and shape conditions mentioned so far can all be thought of as stating constraints on the phonological form an item can take. Clearly, morphological and morphosyntactic rules make reference to, and determine, phonological facts. However, Dressler (1985) has clarified at length a very important distinction between phonological aspects of morphological statements on the one hand, and rules of what he calls *morphonology* on the other.

Morphonology embraces those aspects of phonology that are concerned solely with the phonological realization of morphemes in phonological contexts but are nonetheless conditioned in part by morphological or syntactic factors. Vowel harmony alternations seem in general to be governed by morphonological rules, as are the Finnish consonant gradations. Dressler's extended examples (1985: chs. 6, 7) are certain palatalizations of velars in Italian and Polish. One difference between morphonology and morphology/morphosyntax is that we assume that rules of morphonology may well be formalized as processes converting one phonologically defined shape into another, whereas in our view morphological rules should not be.

A defining characteristic of morphonological rules is that although they operate on phonological inputs they are not blindly applicable to items of the appropriate shape in the appropriate contexts; lexical properties conferring exceptional status may cause some apparently eligible items to be ineligible, so there may be items whose phonetic form appears to contradict a morphonological rule. Morphonological rules are, in a word, non-automatic (see Kiparsky 1973: 68, for an explicit definition of this term).

The morphonological rules that apply in phrasal domains are the *rules of connected speech* or *rules of external sandhi* of Kaisse (1985): they are non-automatic, morphosyntactically sensitive rules of phrase phonology. Kaisse's own examples (ch. 7) are French liaison, Ewe tone sandhi, Italian syntactic doubling (*raddoppiamento sintattico*), Mandarin tone sandhi, and Kimatuumbi vowel shortening.

## 10.2.5. Phonology

We shall reserve the word *phonology* for the remainder of the rules mapping syntactic and lexical representations into phonetic. A more explicit term would be *automatic phonology*, but it seems preferable to use a one-word term if confusion will not result. To some extent, our usage represents a return to an earlier tradition in American linguistics, when phonology (or phonemics) was assumed to be purely automatic and not morphosyntactically conditioned. Phonology, then, consists of the rules which have effects only on phonetically defined material and which are automatic in Kiparsky's sense.

This class of rules is heterogeneous. It includes the automatic morphophonemic rules (like the one governing the /s/~/z/ alternation in English *cats* and *dogs*), i.e. the rules that may neutralize surface contrasts but nonetheless do this in a way that does not depend on membership in morphological or syntactic exception classes. It includes allophonic rules, both obligatory and optional. The familiar argument given by Halle (1959: 22–3) against the level of autonomous phonemics is thus no paradox for this conception of phonology; Russian devoicing is a phonological rule in our technical sense, though sometimes morphophonemic and sometimes allophonic.

A defining feature of phonological rules is that they have *prosodic*, not morphosyntactic, domains of application. In so far as they apply across word boundaries, they coincide with what are referred to as *fast speech rules* by Kaisse (1985); an example is the rule of American English that turns intervocalic /t/ into a voiced apico-alveolar flap (Kaisse 1985: 25ff).

## 10.3. Syntax in morphology and phonology

Given the articulated theory of the mapping between syntax/lexicon and phonetics that we have sketched, a question about syntactic influence on phonology is likely to split into a number of distinct questions with differing answers. To agree that shape conditions make reference to syntactic structure is not by any means to admit that allophonic rules can do the same, for example.

Some things are almost indisputable. One sort of syntactic information that is certainly necessary for morphonological and even strictly phonological rules is the location of word boundaries; that this much is needed is a view that goes back at least to Pike (1947). But other matters are less clear. And because generative phonologists have not in general assented to a strict articulation into components such as the one we advocate, the literature on syntax–phonology relations over the past thirty years can be somewhat frustrating to someone seriously interested in this topic. For example, Postal (1968: ch. 6) has an extended discussion headed 'Nonphonetic properties in phonology' arguing emphatically that there is syntactic influence on phonology, but he does not provide much of a basis for characterizing such influence.

Postal asserts that underlying phonological representation must contain the full surface syntactic structure of the sentence because some phonological rules are sensitive to such 'categorial properties,' and in English 'the rules of stress assignment are largely of this character . . .' But a close examination of the stress rules in Chomsky & Halle (1968) reveals very little that actually depends on syntactic category or constituent structure (as opposed to broader notions like 'beginning of a word' or 'end of a stressable constituent'), and in some reanalyses, e.g. that by Fudge (1975), this is even clearer, morphological conditions being abundant but syntactic ones virtually non-existent.

Some generalizations abstracted from Chomsky & Halle's work that related English stress to syntactic category are cited by Kenstowicz & Kisseberth (1977: 77–8); for example, in verbs and adjective but not nouns, 'stress appears on the final syllable if it . . . ends in more than one consonant.' Kenstowicz & Kisseberth cite pairs like *ásterisk* (N) vs. *eléct* (V) to illustrate this. Now, of course, linguists use the word *asterisk* as a verb (sentences are asterisked to indicate ungrammaticality), and the stress pattern is not changed to the expected verbal stress pattern *\*asterísk*. There is some very insightful and well-supported discussion of facts of this sort in Kiparsky (1982: 11–12ff), the upshot being that surface syntactic structure is exactly what the stress rule does *not* look at; stress is sensitive (in a fairly exception-ridden way) to *lexical* classes of words, in a way that we might wish to analyze using lexical implication statements (and which for Kiparsky is the domain of level 1 word stress rules). The summary by Kenstowicz & Kisseberth oversimplifies; just because some syntactic category membership is relevant to some stress assignment rule, that does not imply that the phonological rules have access to surface syntax. The access to the relevant information could be entirely mediated by the lexicon, as it is in Kiparsky's theory.

After mentioning English stress, Postal gives two Mohawk examples as further illustrations of syntactic reference in phonology. He claims that 'no *Verb* may have less than two vowels in its phonetic representation' (p. 116) and that 'word initial glides drop in nouns' (p. 118); but it is not at all clear that these are morphonological rules in our sense rather than, as we suspect, rules of allomorphy. The rest of this chapter pertains exclusively to non-phonetic lexical features, and not to syntax.

We do not wish to claim that morphonological rules *cannot* make reference to syntactic category. Kenstowicz & Kisseberth (1977: 78–83) cite several examples that suggest that they can: a tonal downstep rule in Igbo that applies only to nouns, a vowel shortening rule in Hausa that applies only to a verb followed by a direct object noun, a palatalization rule in Dakota that applies only to a lexical subclass called the 'active' verbs, an accent retraction rule in Russian that applies only to feminine and neuter plural nouns, and a voicing rule in Rundi that applies only in a morpheme immediately preceding a root. We suggest, however, that such rules are not as common as some accounts would imply, and that some of Kenstowicz & Kisseberth's cases may turn out on closer analysis to be allomorphy rules or shape conditions rather than morphonological rules in Dressler's and our sense.

Placement of sentential accent is a topic that has led some linguists to postulate much more extensive integration of syntactic and phonological information than has been established elsewhere. Bresnan (1971a) is a particularly interesting example, allowing phonological rules to apply interspersed between transformational cycles in the syntax. However, we have criticized the reasoning that led Bresnan to regard sentence stress as syntactically predictable (Pullum & Zwicky 1984; see also Berman & Szamosi 1972 and Bolinger 1972 for earlier critiques), and Culicover & Rochemont (1983) have recently provided an important reanalysis of this domain. The Culicover & Rochemont analysis does not postulate Bresnan's interleaving of syntactic and phonological rule applications, and thus does not carry the implication that phonological properties of subordinate clauses are in principle accessible to syntactic rules on later cycles (cf. Lakoff 1972: 301 on this point).

It is clear that assignment of stress and intonation contours to sentences will refer in certain ways to the surface constituent structure of sentences. But we do not believe that the non-surface strata of syntactic representation that various theories postulate (be they the functional structures of lexical–functional grammar, the D-structures or other strata of GB, the initial grammatical relations of relational grammar, or 'logical form' representations of whatever sort) have been clearly shown to play any role in phonological rule systems.

Two celebrated cases from the *non*-prosodic phonology of English have often been argued to provide evidence that at least some information from syntactic representations at non-surface strata has relevance to phonology. These are the phenomena of 'auxiliary reduction' (the pattern of strong and weak phonetic forms of function words such as auxiliary verbs and prepositions) and *to*-contraction (the encliticization of infinitive-marking *to* onto certain verbs. The literature on these two sets of facts (wrongly implied to be a unified class of facts in some works, e.g. Lakoff 1970) is now enormous, and we cannot review it thoroughly here. We have space only to provide a rough sketch of the competing lines of theoretical attack, which we do in the next two subsections.

### 10.3.1. Strong and weak phonetic forms in English

As Selkirk (1972: 160, n. 1) observes, the fact that English has strong and weak phonetic forms for certain minor grammatical elements was noted as early as 1890 by Henry Sweet in his *Primer of spoken English*, and all careful phonetic descriptions of English pay some attention to them. The full description of the phenomenon is a complex business, involving automatic morphophonemic rules like assimilation of voice in fricative suffixes, allomorphy rules for the various auxiliary verbs, and syntactic conditions on a pre-phonological cliticization (see Selkirk 1972: 22ff; Kaisse 1985: 40ff). The facts that have been of most interest to generative grammarians concern the syntactic conditions, and were pointed out by King (1970); they involve contrasts like *I know where it is* and *\*I know where it's*, and the acceptability judgements involved are extremely clear in most cases. Selkirk notes (22–37) that not only auxiliaries like *is* are involved; pairs like *Who are you looking at?* and *Look at that!* show a clear difference in the phonetic form of *at* under analogous syntactic conditions. The descriptive problem we are concerned with is how to characterize the conditions.

Five main lines of analysis are represented in the literature. The first is informally suggested by King (1970), and more explicitly endorsed by Lakoff (1970). It claims that if the constituent immediately following an auxiliary verb is moved or deleted by a transformation, the auxiliary in question is *ipso facto* forbidden to contract. The arbitrariness of this approach should be apparent: linguistic theory offers no reason whatever to suppose that deletion or movement of a constituent would affect the phonological behavior of some adjacent constituent. Moreover, it incorrectly predicts that contraction will be blocked in *Where's the party?*, since *where* is immediately after *is* at an earlier stage of the derivation in all transformational accounts.

The hypothesis of Bresnan (1971b) is something of an improvement. Bresnan proposes that a procliticization rule applying during the syntactic cycle attaches auxiliaries to their immediately following constituents. The inability of the auxiliary to contract in *I know where it is* to yield *\*I know where it's* is explained under the assumption that once *'s* has cliticized onto *where*, the structural description of *wh*-movement is not met. However, Selkirk (1972: 74–93) provides convincing arguments that this counterintuitive but ingenious analysis does not work correctly. (The arguments are complicated, and we omit them here.)

Selkirk's own proposal is that word boundary symbols are placed in syntactic terminal strings at deep structure and remain when transformations move or delete elements. A rule called the 'monosyllable rule' that weakens stress level on auxiliaries (and also other 'dependents' that Selkirk incorporates into her account) is blocked by a following sequence of two or more word boundary symbols, so moving or deleting a constituent (or inserting a parenthetical constituent) immediately after such an element prevents the monosyllable rule from applying.

There is no crucial support for Selkirk's assumption that deep structure is the level at which word boundaries are inserted. Cyclic rules like *there*-insertion do not disrupt auxiliary reduction (cf. *There's a moon out tonight*, with deep structure [*a moon is out tonight*], but *\*He's, I think, out tonight*). Her account would have the same consequences if modified in such a way as to have word boundaries inserted at the end of each syntactic cycle (Pullum 1979: 162–8), which would mesh well with the hypothesis of Bresnan (1971a, b) that there is a class of phonology-related rules that apply at the end of each transformational cycle in the syntax.

An account along the lines of Selkirk's achieves a very considerable measure of success in accounting for the facts. Moreover, Kaisse (1983) shows that it continues to do well when a range of new facts about auxiliary reduction are considered. But Selkirk herself has described the actual mechanical details of her (1972) analysis as involving 'a certain amount of formal legerdemain' (1984: 446, n. 41), and it must be acknowledged that her rejection of the view that an encliticization rule is involved, and the dependence of her analysis on the peculiar assumption that constituent boundary markers can be stranded by movement rules, have probably stimulated the search for a more elegant and unified account of the facts.

That search is not over. Selkirk (1984: 401) now accepts that a cliticization rule brings auxiliaries and other dependent items 'juncturally . . . closer to what precedes,' agreeing with most work on the topic, and argues for a 'rhythmic restructuring' rule, which 'alters only the metrical grid alignment of the sentence, affecting syntactic relations not at all' (1984: 405). Selkirk leans toward a purely prosodic explanation, in other words.

Some significant ongoing work based on the assumption that there is a syntactic principle involved is that of Karen Zagona and others at the University of Washington (see Kaisse 1985: ch. 3, for some details and references). The line of attack is related to an idea put forward by Wood (1979), namely that what is wrong with a string like *\*I know where it's* is that it has a wholly empty VP in its surface syntactic structure, the cliticization of *is* having shifted out the VP's only member. The strategy they are pursuing is to attempt to make Wood's idea follow from a more general principle, viz. the 'empty category principle' of GB (see Chapter 2, on 'Syntactic theory' in this volume).

We have insufficient space to review the recent literature in detail here, but we wish to make one observation about the trend we observe. Selkirk (1984), Kaisse (1985), and other recent works seem to share the assumption that only surface syntax is relevant to the solution of the auxiliary reduction puzzle. In Selkirk's view, this is because of a more elaborate and highly structured conception of phonology; in that of Kaisse and others, it is because of a conception of surface structure that embraces empty categories. But both confirm the generalization that phonology accesses only surface syntactic form.

## 10.3.2. Contraction of the infinitival marker

A large literature has developed around the phenomenon we will call *to*-contraction, found in pronunciations like the one graphically represented as *wanna* (for *want to*). (At least the forms *wanna*, *gonna*, *hafta/hasta*, *gotta*, *oughta*, *usta*, and *supposta/sposta* are relevant; some writers claim that there are others.) Again, the situation is complex, involving fast speech rules of English (the relation between [wanttə] and [wānə] can clearly be connected to the reduction of [wɪntər] 'winter' to [wĩnɾ]) but also special lexical and syntactic conditions. The discussion in the literature rarely touches on the phonological rules involved, concentrating on the syntactic conditioning. Much of the literature has been predominantly polemical in its aims; the argument of Lightfoot (1976) that *to*-contraction has relevance to claims about 'trace' and 'PRO' to syntactic theory stimulated a long series of papers arguing for or against this conclusion, and analyzing the facts of *to*-contraction only in passing. (The debate up to that point is summarized, from a standpoint opposed to Lightfoot's conclusions, by Postal & Pullum 1982. The dispute continued until the winter of 1986, when as three more papers on the topic appeared, the editor of *Linguistic Inquiry* took the unprecedented step of declaring a moratorium.)

The descriptive problem that is involved can be encapsulated in this observation: while the *want to* in *Who do you want to see?* can be contracted to *wanna*, the same word sequence in *Who do you want to see this memo?* cannot. (A large percentage of English speakers agree on this judgement, though the percentage is by no means one hundred.) Why the difference? There have been at least six basic proposals around which specific answers to this question have been developed.

First, there are analyses which in effect state global conditions. Lakoff (1970) implies such an account. The idea is, roughly, to say that the presence of *who* between *want* and *to* at an earlier point in the derivation blocks the pronunciation of *want to* as *wanna*: the phonology is sensitive not just to the string being phonetically interpreted but also to the representation of it that is found at a distinct and less superficial stratum of the derivation. A problem arises in that classical derivations of *I wanna leave* from [sI want [sI leave]] make it unclear why *wanna* is not forbidden here too; but Pullum (1979: 161) offers a version of this sort of account that covers the facts correctly in classical TG terms, by identifying the stratum that must be referred to (the end of the transformational cycle on the clause most immediately containing the crucial verb).

Second, Bresnan (1971b) offered a solution that depended on ordering of rules: a rule joining *want* and *to* together syntactically was stipulated as applying at the end of each transformational cycle. Crucially, even if *you want to see . . .* is assumed to be derived from a structure like *you want you to see . . .* by 'equi-NP deletion,' *want* and *to* will be adjacent by the end of the cycle on the *want* clause in *Who do you wanna see?*, whereas in *Who do you want to see this memo?*, the NP *who* would still intervene at the corresponding stage, and the structural description of the rule would not be met. The proposal of van Riemsdijk & Williams (1981) is in effect a theoretical rephrasing of Bresnan's approach.

Third, numerous authors (too many to cite here) have maintained that the inhibiting factor for *to*-contraction is the presence of a 'trace' between *want* and *to*. This idea originates with Baker & Brame (1972), and was first worked out in detail by Selkirk (1972), though the (essentially phonological) form it took in Selkirk's work was very different from the form it took in later works such as Lightfoot (1976) and Chomsky & Lasnik (1977). The problems with the idea have always been of the same sort: under assumptions that were needed for other purposes, there always turned out to be additional traces that blocked contraction incorrectly in some environments (see Postal & Pullum 1982 and previous works cited there).

Fourth, there have been several proposals that *to*-contraction is sensitive to the relation of *government*: the verb (*want*, or whatever) must govern *to* if contraction is to take place, where 'governs' is not the traditional notion of that name but is a technical notion usually explicated in terms of a relation between nodes such as c-command (see Pullum 1986). The first such proposal seems to be that of Bouchard (1982). Given a carefully phrased definition of the government relation (many different definitions have been offered, and many are poorly drafted) and appropriate ancillary assumptions, a close approach to covering all the relevant facts can be achieved in these terms.

Fifth, it has been suggested (first by Frantz 1977) that *to*-contraction takes place in precisely the contexts where 'clause union' (also known as 'verb raising,' 'restructuring,' etc.) is observed in many languages. Taken together with the claim that the correct analysis of *to* is as an auxiliary verb (independently argued in Pullum 1983), the claim could be strengthened to make *to*-contraction actually an instance of clause union, with a matrix verb like *want* uniting syntactically with the verb (*to*) of its object complement clause.

Finally, it has been repeatedly suggested that lexical rather than syntactic uniting might be in evidence, i.e. that *wanna*, *gonna*, etc. might be lexical items. However, this has never been more than a brief aside on the part of those suggesting it. No one has worked out in detail a defensible analysis in such terms that it overcomes the morphological problems it raises – problems that seem to us insuperable (the alleged lexical item *wanna* in *I wanna* lacks all the word forms that are found in *she wants to*, *we wanted to*, *wanting to*, etc. – precisely because it is not really a word at all, we would claim).

We draw from this bewildering profusion of analytical proposals just a single point: more recent analyses almost uniformly agree on one thing, namely that it is *surface* syntactic structure (moreover, a very small portion of the surface syntactic context, local in terms of both adjacency and bracketing) that is relevant for the determination of whether a given word sequence can have the contracted pronunciation.

## 10.3.3. Other cases

The two *causes célèbres* from English morphology and phonology that we have just reviewed are not in any sense more important or instructive than dozens of other cases we could have discussed.

Selkirk (1972) has an extended discussion of the phenomenon of 'liaison' in French. For certain speakers in certain styles, normally elided final consonants are retained; thus we find phrases like *elle est oubliée* [ɛlɛtublije] 'she is forgotten' with *est* pronounced [ɛt] before the vowel [u], but *ce qu'elle est ou ce qu'elle a fait* [skɛlɛuskɛlafɛ] 'what she is or what she has done' with *est* pronounced as [ɛ] before the same vowel. Selkirk analyzes liaison using mechanisms identical to those she employs for English phonological reduction rules; the intuition is that a following major boundary inhibits liaison (or reduction), and a following weak boundary permits it.

Napoli & Nespor (1979) argue that the rule of initial consonant gemination in Italian is sensitive to the syntactic notion 'left branch' (but in the surface constituent structure, as our general position would predict).

The Celtic mutation phenomenon, mentioned in 10.1 above, is highly sensitive to aspects of syntactic structure (but see Zwicky 1986 for an analysis reducing the syntactic reference somewhat).

Numerous other syntactically conditioned phenomena (tone sandhi rules, for example, which we do not treat here at all) could be cited, and many important questions remain open about the exact nature of the fit between syntax and phonology that these phenomena imply. What we believe to be true of them, however, is that recent trends in linguistics have somewhat decreased the emphasis on syntactic involvement in phonology, somewhat increasing the role of phonologically defined prosodic structures of various sorts, and that the syntactic reference that linguists can generally agree to be necessary is to superficial, not more abstract, syntactic structures.

## 10.4. **Phonology in syntax**

In this section we consider question (B), the question of what syntactic phonological information is available to syntactic rules. Large numbers of published arguments have attempted to establish that there can be phonological influence on syntactic rules. Hetzron (1972) and Rivero & Walker (1976), for example, are independent (and non-overlapping) reviews of several such putative cases. However, after close examination of every case that has been brought to our attention over the past fifteen years, we remain convinced that the extent of truly phonological influence on truly syntactic rules is zero. The cases that have been put forward are of extraordinarily diverse sorts, but fall into clear categories. We will attempt to give a brief overview here.

We will assume that it is fairly straightforward to identify information as phonological: if it is phonological information it will have a direct correspondence to an interpretation in phonetic (articulatory, auditory, or acoustic) predicates. Phonological information will thus include information about properties like voicing, nasality, stridency, vowel height, tone, stress level, syllable count, syllable structure, and so on. (We ignore here certain attested types of human language, in particular the sign languages of deaf communities, not because of a policy decision but simply because we know too little about the analogous issues for those languages.)

A genuine violation of the *principle of phonology-free syntax* would be a generalization about a specific language which is correctly expressed as a syntactic rule referring to phonological constructs. An apparent violation could thus fail to be genuine in any of the following five ways.

(i) The generalization might be spurious.

(ii) A real generalization might involve not a rule, but rather a preference or tendency.

(iii) A real generalization might involve a rule not of grammar, but rather of some extragrammatical domain.

(iv) A rule of grammar might be located not in the syntactic component, but rather in one of the other components: for example, it might be a morphological rule.

(v) A rule of grammar might be subject to a phonological condition or constraint that is universal, and therefore is not to be stated as part of the rule.

We have encountered many examples of each of these in the literature. We will try to illustrate each mode of failure briefly, or at least clarify what would count as an instance of it.

## 10.4.1. Spurious generalizations

In a number of cases we have examined, alleged generalizations involving phonological conditions in syntax simply turn out to be spurious: there is no generalization to capture. An example would be the occasionally encountered suggestion that the dative movement rule in English is subject to the phonological condition that the triggering verb should be monosyllabic (thus we have *give someone something* but not *\*donate someone something*, *send someone something* but not *\*contribute someone something*, and so on). Of course, in current grammatical frameworks there is no syntactic rule corresponding to dative movement anyway; under GB theory movement into object position is impossible, so that the relationship in question would be a lexical one concerning multiple subcategorizations, and under GPSG and LFG the same would be true *a fortiori*. But even when we consider a framework like RG, which would certainly state the analog of dative movement as a syntactic rule, we find that the generalization evaporates. Dative movement verbs include *promise*, *offer*, *cable*, *advance*, *permit*, *deliver*, *telephone*, and *guarantee*, none of which are monosyllabic, and, on the other hand, the dative movement construction is not found with *lift*, *raise*, *lisp*, *yell*, *prove*, or *voice*, which are monosyllabic and do permit the construction V NP *to* NP. Monosyllabicity is neither a necessary condition nor a sufficient one for a verb to admit the dative movement construction.

The proposed analysis of some interesting facts of Somali agreement discussed in Hetzron (1972: section 5) seems to represent another case of a spurious generalization. Hetzron notes there are Somali sentences in which a subject noun, the article in the subject NP, and the obligatory resumptive

273

subject pronoun are masculine plural but all happen to 'look' feminine singular, through accidents of (i) irregular noun plural formation, (ii) morphological ambiguity in pronouns, and (iii) gender polarity-switching in articles and in the gender-indicating tone patterns of nouns. In such sentences, the verb may optionally show feminine singular agreement form instead of the expected masculine plural. Under Hetzron's interpretation of these facts, the verb agreement is a 'playful' reflection of the superficially feminine-looking phonology of the sentence, and a syntactic account deprived of access to phonological properties cannot capture what is going on. Zwicky & Pullum (1983b) shows in detail why this is not so. Phonological references in a syntactic rule would come nowhere near what would be needed to formalize what Hetzron suggests is going on. The phonology of distinct sentences with feminine nouns (feminine nouns that do not exist in the language, moreover) would have to influence the syntax of sentences with masculine plural nouns. Such a trans-sentential constraint is not countenanced in any current accepted theory of grammar, and no theories in which they can be stated seem to have been seriously developed. Our own description of Somali agreement is simple and unsurprising: an optional rule assigns the feminine singular agreement form to verbs whose subject NPs contain irregular masculine plural nouns. The fact that there are suggestions of feminine-like phonology in the sentence where this occurs may be part of the explanation of how this rule developed historically, but in our account it is not (and could not be) part of the synchronic grammar. Our description makes verb agreement depend on morphological properties of subject nouns (as it does in many languages, e.g. the Bantu languages), but it does not involve reference to phonology in the syntax. Such reference not only is not needed, but apparently could not do what needs to be done.

### 10.4.2. Preferences and tendencies

Some putative cases of phonological influence on a syntactic rule illustrate in fact only a phonetic aspect of a preference for some form of expression over another, or a tendency for some collection of properties to cluster. Thus we find Chomsky & Lasnik (1977: 433) remarking that they assume 'stylistic rules' apply after phonological rules have applied, and 'may refer to phonetic properties.' No basis for this surprising assumption is cited, but it seems likely to us that what Chomsky and Lasnik have in mind is the well-known group of phenomena involving apparent 'heaviness' effects in syntax (first discussed by Ross 1967: ch. 3). We note also that Fiengo (1974: 85) claims that it is more felicitous to right-shift the position of a long word than a short one (his examples – none too convincing – are *I found in the dictionary the word flaucinaucinihilipilification* vs. *I found in the dictionary the word amah*). He concludes that 'Heavy-NP Shift is not a transformation' because the crucially phonetic length property 'cannot be stated as a Boolean condition on analyzability.' Thus Fiengo appears to agree with Chomsky and Lasnik: there are phonetically sensitive movement rules that are not 'transformations' in the strict sense.

The view that there are both movement transformations that cannot refer to phonology and later movement rules that are not transformations but can refer to phonology is highly permissive. It is hard to imagine what interactions of phonology and syntax it rules out. Certainly, imaginary rules like 'A verb moves to sentence-initial position if it contains a liquid' (Perlmutter 1971: 87) or a rule fronting time adverbial phrases if the first segment of the head adverb is not [b] (Zwicky 1969: 413) would appear to be permitted by it. This seems both undesirable and unnecessary.

Suppose it were the case (which we do not think it is to any significant extent) that passive sentences were judged to sound better than corresponding actives if the agent phrase was phonetically long and the patient NP was short (e.g. if *The Llanfihangel-y-Creuddyn rugby team beat Rhyl* were consistently judged less acceptable than *Rhyl was beaten by the Llanfihangel-y-Creuddyn rugby team* regardless of discourse context.) The obvious conclusion, we submit, would be that the choice of syntactic construction could affect the prosodic properties of the sentence and thus the stylistic acceptability, but that no syntactic condition was involved, since presumably even Chomsky, Lasnik, and Fiengo would not suggest that a construction as centrally syntactic as the passive is defined in partly phonetic or phonological terms. Exactly the same can be said about the rightward shifting construction referred to as 'heavy NP shift', so the postulation of a class of 'stylistic rules' that can move constituents but can also access phonetic properties is quite unmotivated.

We note that Fiengo himself, rejecting his earlier position, has since argued (1977: 48–9) that whatever phonetic heaviness condition there may be on the heavy NP shift construction, it cannot be on the rule itself, but must be a surface-structure 'filter that evaluates the output for relative heaviness' of VP constituents. This is exactly as argued by Ross (1967), not cited by Fiengo. We would simply add that we do not think the evaluation of relative heaviness is the work of a component of grammar at all. What is correct is that the crucial factor influencing the acceptability is simply whether a long and complicated constituent has been placed at the end of the sentence or not, and no syntactic rule needs to deal in issues of 'relative heaviness'. What is not correct is that the stylistically poorer sentences with nonfinal heavy constituents are **linguistically ill-formed**; they are simply not preferred by speakers, probably for processing reasons (crudely, it is easier to complete a lengthy processing chore if there is nothing left on the stack to return to when it is done).

### 10.4.3. Extragrammatical domains

Some cases of alleged syntax–phonology interpenetration that linguists have cited involve rules that are perfectly genuine but simply do not belong to the grammar of the language concerned. The domain that is confused with grammar most frequently seems to us to be that of verbal art and play. To cite just one example from a fairly rich field, we believe that the infixing of expletive forms inside English compound words (*Santa-bloody-Cruz*) or even morphemes (*Kalama-goddam-zoo*) is better understood as a kind of verbal game than as a grammatical rule of English. This is not to say that there are not intricate connections between the phonological structure of English and the ways in which expletives can be inserted; attempts like *?Los-bloody-Angeles* and *?Abi-goddam-lene* sound thoroughly lame, for thoroughly phonological reasons (see McCarthy 1982 for an interesting metrical study). Nonetheless, the word coinage involved here looks to us like a verbal game, at which some speakers will be much better and more creative than others (see McCawley 1978 for some informal experimental evidence that this is indeed the case). It is not a part of the syntax of English, but rather, it is something verbal that (some) English speakers do with their language. (See Zwicky & Pullum 1987 for further discussion.)

### 10.4.4. Nonsyntactic rules

Where a rule of grammar *is* involved, it is not necessarily a syntactic rule, even if it has been discussed as such in the literature. Plainly morphological facts were often treated syntactically in the earlier transformational literature. For example, both Cook (1971), on Sarcee, and Brandon (1975), on Swahili, discuss interesting facts about deletion rules being blocked when the deletion would leave too few remaining syllables, and both assume they have discovered a phonological constraint on syntax. But an examination of the facts reveal that the rules involved are purely morphological; they operate entirely in a word-internal domain, and the phonological conditions are just such as would be expected in realization rules, making reference to disyllabic and monosyllabic stems, and so on. We have discussed these and several similar cases in Zwicky & Pullum (1983a).

To say that the phenomena belong to morphology is not to say the facts do not pose intricate descriptive problems; we only wish to point out that our claims are about sentence structure and cannot in general be extended to become claims about word structure. Early transformational studies that treated morphology and syntax as something of a seamless web, attaching derivational affixes with transformations and so on, may have blurred the syntax/morphology distinction during part of the last thirty years, but it was traditionally taken to be an important distinction in the theory of grammar, and we believe that the tradition in question is correct.

## 10.4.5. Universal conditions

Our claim about phonological influence in syntax is that there is no direct reference to phonology by the syntactic rules of any language. This does not exclude the possibility that there are universally based interconnections between syntactic and phonological form. Relevant here are the several cases of allegedly showing phonological identity affecting omissibility of constituents in coordinate ellipsis and coordination of subsentential constituents of various sorts. Phonology can clearly be ignored in some constructions: in *I haven't yet done my homework, but I will ∅*, the ellipted material is (or means) *do my homework*, and in *John absented himself and so did Susan*, it is *absent herself* that is missing; in neither case would the ellipted material have been phonologically identical to any other constituent if it had been overtly realized. However, in other cases, phonology seems to matter. *He has not spoken and he will not speak* cannot reduce to either *\*He has not and will not spoken* or *\*He has not and will not speak*. (Many speakers will find the latter preferable to the former because the offending sequence *\*has not. . . speak* is interrupted, but most speakers reject both options.) What is crucial is that *has* governs the past participle and *will* governs the bare infinitive, and these are phonologically distinct for the verb *speak*.

But now note that there are verbs where the past participle and the infinitive are accidentally identical; *come* is one such irregular verb. When we use one of this class of verbs, we find that we get a sentence that most speakers will accept: *He has not and will not come.*

We do believe that phonological facts are crucial here. Moreover, there is evidence from German and Xhosa (reviewed in Pullum & Zwicky 1986) that it is a superficial level of phonology that is relevant, the level at which contrasts are perceptible to the native speaker and available for purposes like rhyme (something like the level that is input to natural processes in David Stampe's theory of natural phonology, probably the same as the lexical level of Paul Kiparsky's theory of lexical phonology). The position taken in Pullum & Zwicky (1986) is that the outlines of how phonology may contribute to ellipsis possibilities in natural languages are given by general linguistic theory. This position is not entirely secure; we discuss some problematic facts indicating variation between speakers regarding what they will and will not tolerate on the grounds of phonological identity between forms. However, we set forth a framework for the description of such variation, and circumscribe the range of facts as narrowly as possible in universal terms. Whether our account is fully successful or not, we hope the strategy is clear: we aim to substantiate the claim that if there are systematic phonological influences on syntactic phenomena at all, they do not vary idiosyncratically from language to language.

## 10.5. Conclusion

We have tried to make two major points, and to indicate, while elaborating them, something of the content of the research that is currently going on at the syntax–phonology interface. The two major points are these:

(1) While many have suggested that the influence of syntax on phonology is complex and pervasive and can involve nonsuperficial aspects of syntax, this is turning out not to be the case; superficial syntax seems likely to suffice as a basis for phonological description.

(2) While it has often been suggested that there is phonological influence of various kinds on syntactic rules, this does not appear to be the case. Many different types of phenomena have been taken for phonological conditions on syntactic rules, but no indisputably genuine cases have been attested as far as we know.

We continue to think, therefore, that the generalizations we have referred to as the *principle of superficial constraints in phonology* and the *principle of phonology-free syntax* (Zwicky 1969, 1970) represent strongly confirmed hypotheses about the organizational principles of grammars for natural languages. In this regard, we think it is promising that some recent developments in syntactic theory have come closer to making these two principles consequences of the theory of grammar as opposed to mere stipulations. This point is discussed further in Pullum & Zwicky (1984) and in Zwicky & Pullum (forthcoming).

*REFERENCES*

Baker, C. L. & Brame, Michael K. 1972. 'Global rules': a rejoinder. *Language* 48: 51–75.
Berman, Arlene & Szamosi, Michael 1972. Observations on sentential stress. *Language* 48: 304–25.
Bolinger, Dwight 1972. Accent is predictable (if you're a mindreader). *Language* 48: 633–44.
Bolinger, Dwight 1979. The jingle theory of double -*ing*. In D. J. Allerton, Edward Carney, & David Holdcroft (eds.) *Function and context in linguistic analysis: a Festschrift for William Haas*. Cambridge: Cambridge University Press.
Bouchard, Denis 1982. *On the content of empty categories*. Doctoral dissertation, MIT. Published 1984 by Foris, Dordrecht.

Brandon, Frank Roberts 1975. A constraint on deletion in Swahili. *Working Papers in Linguistics* 20: 241–59. Ohio State University.

Bresnan, Joan W. 1971a. Sentence stress and syntactic transformations. *Language* 47: 257–81.

Bresnan, Joan W. 1971b. *Contraction and the transformational cycle in English.* Unpublished paper, MIT. Published 1978 by Indiana University Linguistics Club, Bloomington.

Chomsky, Noam 1965. *Aspects of the theory of syntax.* Cambridge, MA: MIT Press.

Chomsky, Noam & Halle, Morris 1968. *The sound pattern of English.* New York: Harper & Row.

Chomsky, Noam & Lasnik, Howard 1977. Filters and control. *Linguistic Inquiry* 8: 425–504.

Cook, Eung-Do 1971. Phonological constraint and syntactic rule. *Linguistic Inquiry* 2: 465–78.

Cornulier, Benoit de. 1972. A peeking rule in French. *Linguistic Inquiry* 3: 226.

Culicover, Peter W. & Rochemont, Michael 1983. Stress and focus in English. *Language* 59: 123–65.

Dressler, Wolfgang U. 1985. *Morphology: the dynamics of derivation.* Ann Arbor: Karoma.

Fiengo, Robert W. 1974. Semantic conditions on surface structure. Doctoral dissertation, MIT.

Fiengo, Robert W. 1977. On trace theory. *Linguistic Inquiry* 8: 35–61.

Frantz, Donald G. 1977. A new view of *to*-contraction. In John P. Daly (ed.) *Workpapers of the Summer Institute of Linguistics, University of North Dakota.* Huntingdon Beach: Summer Institute of Linguistics.

Fudge, Erik 1975. English word stress: an examination of some basic assumptions. In Didier L. Goyvaerts & Geoffrey K. Pullum (eds.) *Essays on The sound pattern of English.* Ghent: Story-Scientia.

Gazdar, Gerald, Klein, Ewan, Pullum, Geoffrey K. & Sag, Ivan A. 1985. *Generalized phrase structure grammar.* Cambridge, MA: Harvard University Press.

Goldsmith, John A. 1976. *Autosegmental phonology.* Bloomington: Indiana University Linguistics Club.

Halle, Morris 1959. *The sound pattern of Russian.* The Hague: Mouton.

Hetzron, Robert 1972. Phonology in syntax. *Journal of Linguistics* 8: 251–65.

Kahn, Daniel 1976. *Syllable-based generalizations in English phonology.* Bloomington: Indiana University Linguistics Club.

Kaisse, Ellen M. 1983. The syntax of auxiliary reduction in English. *Language* 59: 93–122.

Kaisse, Ellen M. 1985. *Connected speech: the interaction of syntax and phonology.* Orlando: Academic Press.

Kenstowicz, Michael & Kisseberth, Charles 1977. *Topics in phonological theory.* New York: Academic Press.

King, Harold V. 1970. On blocking the rules for contraction in English. *Linguistic Inquiry* 1: 134–6.

Kiparsky, Paul 1973. Phonological representations. In Osamu Fujimura (ed.) *Three dimensions of linguistic theory.* Tokyo: Tokyo Institute for Advanced Studies of Language.

Kiparsky, Paul 1982. Lexical morphology and phonology. In The Linguistic Society of Korea (ed.) *Linguistics in the morning calm.* Seoul: Hanshin.

Lakoff, George 1970. Global rules. *Language* 46: 627–39.

Lakoff, George 1972. The arbitrary basis of transformational grammar. *Language* 48: 76–87.

Liberman, Mark & Prince, Alan 1977. On stress and linguistic rhythm. *Linguistic Inquiry* 8: 249–336.

Lightfoot, David 1976. Trace theory and twice-moved NPs. *Linguistic Inquiry* 7: 559–82.

Longobardi, G. 1980. Remarks on infinitives: a case for a filter. *Journal of Italian Linguistics* 5: 101–5.

McCarthy, John J. 1981. Prosodic structure and expletive infixation. *Language* 58: 574–90.

McCawley, James D. 1978. Where you can shove infixes. In A. Bell & J. B. Hooper (eds.) *Syllables and segments.* Amsterdam: North-Holland.

Napoli, Donna Jo & Nespor, Marina 1979. The syntax of word-initial consonant gemination in Italian. *Language* 55: 812–41.

Perlmutter, David M. 1971. *Deep and surface structure constraints in syntax.* New York: Holt, Rinehart & Winston.

Pike, Kenneth Lee 1947. Grammatical prerequisites to phonemic analysis. *Word* 3: 155–72.

Postal, Paul M. 1968. *Aspects of phonological theory.* New York: Harper & Row.

Postal, Paul M. & Pullum, Geoffrey K. 1982. The contraction debate. *Linguistic Inquiry* 13: 122–38.

Pullum, Geoffrey K. 1979. *Rule interaction and the organization of a grammar*. New York: Garland.

Pullum, Geoffrey K. 1983. Syncategorematicity and English infinitival *to*. *Glossa* 16: 181–215.

Pullum, Geoffrey K. 1986. On the relations of IDC-command and government. *Proceedings of the Fifth West Coast Conference on Formal Linguistics*, pp. 192–206. Stanford: Stanford Linguistics Association.

Pullum, Geoffrey K. & Zwicky, Arnold M. 1984. The syntax–phonology boundary and current syntactic theories. *Working Papers in Linguistics* 29: 105–16. Ohio State University.

Pullum, Geoffrey K. & Zwicky, Arnold M. 1986. Phonological resolution of syntactic feature conflict. *Language* 62: 751–75.

Riemsdijk, Henk van & Williams, Edwin 1981. NP-structure. *Linguistic Review* 1: 171–217.

Rivero, Maria-Luisa & Walker, Douglas C. 1976. Surface structure and the centrality of syntax. *Theoretical Linguistics* 3: 99–124.

Ross, John Robert 1967. *Constraints on variables in syntax*. Doctoral dissertation, MIT. Published 1968 by Indiana University Linguistics Club, Bloomington.

Ross, John Robert 1972. Doubl-ing. *Linguistic Inquiry* 3: 61–86.

Sadock, Jerrold M. 1985. Autolexical syntax: a proposal for the treatment of noun incorporation and similar phenomena. *Natural Language and Linguistic Theory* 3: 379–439.

Schachter, Paul 1974. Constraints on clitic order in Tagalog. In A. Gonzalez (ed.) *Parangal kay Cecilio Lopez* (*Philippine Journal of Linguistics* Special Monograph 4). Also in *UCLA Working Papers in Syntax* 5: 96–118.

Selkirk, Elizabeth O. 1972. *The phrase phonology of English and French*. Doctoral dissertation, MIT. Published 1980 by Garland, New York.

Selkirk, Elizabeth O. 1984. *Phonology and syntax: the relation between sound and structure*. Cambridge, MA: MIT Press.

Sweet, H. 1890. *A primer of spoken English*. Oxford: Clarendon Press.

Tegey, Habibullah 1975. The interaction of syntactic and phonological processes: examples from Pashto. In Paul R. Clyne, William F. Hanks & Carol L. Hofbauen (eds.) *CLS* 11.

Wood, Winifred J. 1979. Auxiliary reduction in English: a unified account. In Paul R. Clyne, William F. Hanks & Carol L. Hofbauen (eds.) *CLS* 15: 366–77.

Zwicky, Arnold M. 1969. Phonological constraints in syntactic descriptions. *Papers in Linguistics* 1: 411–63.

Zwicky, Arnold M. 1970. Auxiliary reduction in English. *Linguistic Inquiry* 1: 323–36.

Zwicky, Arnold M. 1986. The general case: basic form versus default form. *BLS* 12: 305–14.

Zwicky, Arnold M. & Pullum, Geoffrey K. 1983a. Deleting named morphemes. *Lingua* 59: 155–75.

Zwicky, Arnold M. & Pullum, Geoffrey K. 1983b. Phonology in syntax: the Somali optional agreement rule. *Natural Language and Linguistic Theory* 1: 385–402.

Zwicky, Arnold M. & Pullum, Geoffrey K. 1986. The principle of phonology-free syntax: introductory remarks. *Working Papers in Linguistics* 32: 63–91. Ohio State University. To appear as part of Zwicky & Pullum (forthcoming).

Zwicky, Arnold M. & Pullum, Geoffrey K. 1987. Plain morphology and expressive morphology. *BLS* 13: 330–40.

Zwicky, Arnold M. & Pullum, Geoffrey K. Forthcoming. *The syntax–phonology interface*. New York: Academic Press.

# 11 The phonology–phonetics interface*

*Patricia A. Keating*

## 11.0. Introduction

Both phonetics and phonology are concerned with the sounds of human language: phonetics with their physical properties, and phonology with their patterning. Because the two fields share this domain of inquiry, there are many areas in which they should interface. However, historically that interface has been somewhat limited, mainly devoted to distinctive feature theory (e.g. Jakobson & Halle 1968, 'Phonology in relation to phonetics'). Since Chomsky & Halle (1968), the scope of inquiry has broadened to include questions of grammatical organization (e.g. Fromkin 1975, 'The interface between phonetics and phonology'), and in addition, questions of naturalness and phonetic explanation (e.g. Ohala 1979, 'The contribution of acoustic phonetics to phonology'). As these titles show, attention has been paid to the relation between the two fields; despite this fact, each field has developed largely independently, as was recently discussed by Liberman (1983). However, there is a heartening tendency these days for more and more cooperation between phoneticians and phonologists, and I predict that in the future each field will influence the other in more substantive ways than has previously been the case. In this chapter I will selectively survey the current state of this interaction and point out some interesting issues, with special attention to those where the activity is likely to be high in the next few years.

## 11.1. Feature theory

In considering the relation between phonetics and phonology, we begin with feature theory, in particular developments since Chomsky & Halle (1968, hereafter *SPE*). *SPE* served to maintain the interest of phoneticians and

* Preparation of this chapter was supported by the National Science Foundation under Grant No. BNS-8418580. I thank the members of the UCLA Phonetics Lab for on-going discussions of all matters phonetic, S. Jay Keyser for some helpful observations, and Bruce Hayes for comments on the manuscript.

phonologists in questions of the proper set and definitions of features, by proposing that a feature theory be responsible for describing the details of a wide range of phonetic categories, as opposed to the highly abstract set of features due to Jakobson. Some overviews of features in the *SPE* framework include Anderson (1974), Hyman (1975), Sommerstein (1977), and Kenstowicz & Kisseberth (1979).

### 11.1.1. What are features for?

Features are linguistically significant phonetic aspects of sounds: they express the crucial fact that speech sounds can be organized as phonetic classes. Many issues surrounding the proper choice and definition of features remain open. I will discuss some of these in terms of various criteria or goals for feature theory (taken in part from Kenstowicz & Kisseberth 1979 and Fromkin 1979).

Phonologists usually want binary-valued, classificatory features to do two things: to characterize segment contrasts so that lexical entries will be distinct, and to group segments together into classes for writing phonological rules. The first task by itself would be trivial if there were no constraints; it would always be possible to add some new feature to the inventory to distinguish two sounds. The second task makes the first more interesting. Considering that the main use for a feature theory is to appropriately characterize natural classes and express generalizations about what classes occur in rules, it is somewhat surprising that feature theory has yet to be based on a really systematic survey of phonological natural classes. After the fact, certain features have been modified because the classes they identified were not attested. For example, the feature [strident], carried over from Jakobson, Fant & Halle (1963) into *SPE*, and originally defined to apply to a variety of fricatives, was then found to define natural classes only for coronal consonants. Halle & Stevens (1979) therefore redefined [strident] so that it is now equivalent to traditional features like grooved or sibilant; [strident] now picks out only coronal fricatives, and therefore identifies the natural class needed for such rules as the English plural epenthesis rule. However, it would be extremely valuable if a large-scale survey of groups of segments in rules were done to establish, independently of any particular feature system, what generalizations need to be expressed by such a system. While this would be an enormous undertaking, the success of Maddieson's (1984) survey of phoneme inventories may well encourage someone to begin.

Decisions about features in their distinctive function are often decided in conjunction with another goal for feature systems, namely, that they be phonetically grounded. Presumably, what makes natural classes natural is their phonetic basis, i.e. their unitary nature in some articulatory or perceptual domain. Again, this requirement places interesting constraints on the choice of features. However, it is sometimes assumed that phonetics is the ultimate source of evidence about the proper set of phonetic features. In a sense, this is correct, if one intends the set of features to represent, for example, independent dimensions of articulatory control, or salient auditory properties. Nonetheless, I think it impossible to begin one's search for features with phonetic data. Phonetic studies provide an overwhelming number of feature candidates that can only be useful in the light of additional, phonological, evidence. As has traditionally been noted (see also Anderson 1974: ch. 1, 1981), precisely what is interesting about features is that only a subset of the abundant available phonetic dimensions is chosen for use in formal phonological computation. Consider some examples of feature candidates based on blind examination of some phonetic data.

*Example A*: On spectrograms, we can observe changes in formant frequencies – for example, fall or lowering (over short time intervals) in second formants. We might hypothesize that such lowering is a crucial phonetic property. Data on Swedish VCV utterances in Öhman (1966) reveals that the second formant falls in a large number of cases both into and out of vowels: between high front vowels and labial consonants, between high or mid front vowels and alveolar consonants, between high or mid front vowels and back velars, between high back vowels and back velars, between velars and following vowels after front vowels, and many other cases. A phonetic theory should account for the long list of contexts in which a falling second formant is observed, but should a phonological feature theory look to posit a common feature? This example is presented as a patently absurd case, to show that some phonetic properties are irrelevant to decisions about features.

*Example B*: In X-rays, we can observe the position of the tongue root and the general area of the lower pharynx. The following sounds: (a) low vowels in any language, (b) [constricted pharynx] vowels in languages with vowel harmony sets, (c) English 'bunched /r/,' and (d) pharyngeal (but not pharyngealized) consonants, all involve articulations in the lower pharynx (Delattre 1971; Ghazeli 1977; Lindau 1979). Does this information by itself motivate a shared feature? *A priori*, this seems unlikely, though we cannot rule it out without further investigation. The point is that such further study will not be phonetic; it will be to determine if the observed articulation is phonologically relevant.

The reverse kind of case is also found. Phonetic study will provide a range of candidates when we know a feature is needed to provide a distinction. For example, contrasts between dental and alveolar stops and nasals are found (Ladefoged 1971). A traditional account of these contrasts might

283

be based on the location of the constriction (the 'place of articulation'), with a feature such as [±dental], but another option is to consider the positioning of the active articulator: Chomsky & Halle's feature [distributed] distinguishes laminal from apical articulations. Still other options are to consider the shape or position of the tongue as a whole (possibly, more back vs. less back), as Stevens, Keyser & Kawasaki (1986) suggest, or to look for acoustic distinctions (Lahiri, Gewirth & Blumstein 1984). Again, it is most likely that not all of these identifiable phonetic dimensions are phonologically relevant. Phonological evidence in favor of identifying the feature as [distributed] comes from Lardil (Hale 1973), in which a class of laminal dentals plus palatoalveolars ([+distributed]) can be opposed to a class of apical alveolars plus retroflexes ([−distributed]) in a final-consonant deletion rule.

There is another reason why phonetic data are not sufficient to determine a set of features: phonetic evidence is technology-driven and -bound. I suggest that changes in technology to date have had a great impact on proposals for feature inventories, especially in changing preferences for articulatory vs. acoustic feature definitions. Thus, the availability of the spectrograph and other methods of acoustic analysis made possible the general acoustic-based theory of features presented in Jakobson, Fant & Halle (1963), a major shift away from traditional articulatory descriptions. The change back to articulatory features in *SPE* followed a decade of work at Haskins Laboratories arguing that acoustic variation as revealed in spectrograms was much greater than the variation in the underlying articulations, and use of improved techniques for studying physiology, such as electromyography. Then in the 70s new computer-based acoustic displays became widely available, which, taken together with developments in neuroscience suggesting the possibility of neural detectors for phonetic features, led to further acoustically based proposals such as invariance theory (Stevens & Blumstein 1981). By now, a shift back to articulation is underway, as phoneticians begin to use speech gestures as the basis for phonetic description. Of course I do not mean to imply that technology is the only factor shaping feature theory; but it does shape our impression of the available phonetic dimensions. Phonetics is on the verge of widespread availability of technology that will greatly increase the amount of articulatory information available: both X-ray data from the microbeam system (Fujimura, Kiritani & Ishida 1973; Nadler, Abbs & Thompson 1985) and alternative technologies to X-ray (Perkell & Cohen 1985, also ongoing work at Stockholm University) will provide still more candidates for features and feature definitions. In the future it will continue to be important to bear in mind the distinction between the sum total of phonetic dimensions and the ways in which language exploits some of these for its own uses.

## 11.1.2. Issues and directions in feature theory

The criterion that features have a phonetic basis can be taken to mean that each feature should represent some intrinsic phonetic property of segments. More specifically, in the *SPE* framework features are intended to represent the set of independently controllable articulations available for speech, with each feature representing control of some articulatory dimension. This position is spelled out clearly in Halle (1983). Recent developments in phonological theory have resulted in some profound continuing changes in feature theory that bear more or less directly on these notions.

Views on what is the inherent phonetic content of segments have been affected by the addition of hierarchical and other multi-level structure to phonological theory. Several features proposed in or since *SPE* have been replaced in effect by structure, such that they are now treated as relational properties or timing effects. Thus the feature [stress], always problematic because it was not binary, is no longer a feature assigned to individual segments, but now is expressed in metrical theory (Hayes 1981) as strong–weak relations between syllables. Similarly, the feature [syllabic] was always recognized as a variable across languages, rather than an intrinsic property of segments; Kiparsky (1979), however, has argued that syllabicity is encoded in hierarchical tree structure built over segments, and is thus a relation between segments within a syllable. Of course, for both of these features, the exact nature of the posited structure differs across particular proposals, but the general effect of such theoretical developments with respect to these features seems agreed upon. Furthermore, some phonologists propose replacing the binary feature [sonorant] with the notion of a sonority hierarchy or continuum, so that this feature also will encode a relative property (Hankamer & Aissen 1974). This continuous feature would then be referred to by syllable structure constraints (Kiparsky 1979; Steriade 1982). The effect of thus recasting some features as structural relations is that the remaining features can be expected to refer to more specific articulatory properties intrinsic to segments.

Another way in which features are being replaced by structure concerns features encoding timing relations. Certain features were problematic because they existed only to represent temporal effects within segments. Thus [delayed release] represented the sequence of phonetic events within affricates, and later features such as [prenasalized] and [preaspirated] represented other sequences of manners mainly within stops. After *SPE*, various phonologists proposed complex segment representations to allow sequences of feature values within a single segment (e.g. Campbell 1974; Anderson 1976; Williamson 1977). In CV theory (McCarthy 1979, 1981; Halle & Vergnaud 1980; Steriade 1982) such complex segments are represented as a sequence of two feature matrices both linked to a single segment position, eliminating the need for such features of timing relations. Similarly, long or geminate segments were earlier represented as a single segment bearing a feature [+long]; in CV theory they may be represented as a single feature matrix linked simultaneously to two segment positions. Thus the total number of features is reduced under CV theory, and we can expect that future developments in the theory will effect further changes in the inventory or the definitions of features.

In the *SPE* theory, the inventory of features represents all linguistically controllable aspects of articulation. Further, every feature in the inventory is claimed to be available for distinguishing phonemes in underlying representation. However, earlier discussions of the phonology–phonetics interface by Fromkin (1975, 1979) suggested that some systematic phonetic distinctions are never used contrastively. This would mean either that in addition to the features there are other dimensions that function linguistically, or that there are two types of features. Fromkin based such suggestions on cross-language comparisons of phonetic detail being made by Ladefoged and colleagues (e.g. Ladefoged 1983a). The changes in feature inventories due to CV phonology provide new evidence that not all features are used contrastively. Consider the feature [length] as discussed by Stevens *et al.* (1986). They discuss a theory of redundant features in which every feature is available for contrastive use but may in a given language be merely redundant. In their theory the redundant features accompany particular contrastive features to enhance or accentuate their inherent properties. The feature [length] may redundantly accompany and enhance the contrastive feature [voice] in an adjacent segment, as appears to be the case in English. However, we have just seen that under CV theory no contrastive feature [length] is needed. Thus if the added duration encoded by a phonetic feature [length] really has a phonological function, as Stevens *et al.* claim for their enhancing features, then there must be linguistic features that are not used contrastively.

This point takes us back to the earlier discussion of the abundance of phonetic dimensions relative to formal features. There are also independently controllable aspects of articulation which do not get used contrastively, as features or as structure, but which presumably should be included in a phonetic description. One such example is tension of the vocal tract walls. This dimension has measurable aerodynamic and acoustic effects on sounds, but by itself probably does not produce large enough effects to be the basis of linguistic contrasts (e.g. Keating 1984b). However, it appears to be systematically controlled in the production of some sounds, for example obstruents traditionally characterized as [fortis] in Korean. Dart (1984) made aerodynamic and acoustic measurements of such stop contrasts in Korean, and then compared these measurements with the outputs of an aerodynamic model to see what articulations might be involved. She found that a combination of vocal cord setting, wall tension, and increased subglottal pressure was required to simulate the observed data for the fortis stops. We can hypothesize that this complex interaction of control dimensions is needed to effect an adequate difference between the classes of Korean stops; and further, that it is precisely this degree of complexity that makes this contrast relatively rare. At the same time, wall tension (and also subglottal pressure) by itself is not distinctive; it is in this case simply associated with the glottal feature. Thus we do not want to define a theory of linguistic features *per se* as enumerating independent articulatory capabilities; rather, a feature theory must be supplemented by an account of the various parameters that underlie it. Though not developed to date, such an account will be given by the low-level rules of phonetic implementation; we turn now to questions about this part of the grammar.

## 11.2. Phonetic rules and derivations

Since phonetic rules interpret the output of the phonology, their exact form and function obviously depends on the nature of that output. In the theory advanced in *SPE*, the output of the phonology was taken to be a complete feature matrix in which each feature had a numerical (rather than binary) value for each segment, so that the matrix was essentially equivalent to an allophonic transcription. The provision of such numerical values was done in the phonological, not the phonetic, component. Recall also that all controllable articulatory dimensions were available as features, so were listed in the matrix and received values as part of the phonology. The phonetic component consisted of mostly automatic, universal rules for implementing these feature matrices as continuous physical events.

Much of the interest in generative phonetics was occasioned by the *SPE* proposals centered on the idea of a universal phonetics (e.g. Fromkin 1979; Keating 1985a). Phoneticians were encouraged to look for cross-language phonetic generalizations and for effects of articulatory biomechanics that could serve as the universal phonetic rules. However, the more phoneticians looked, the more exceptions they found to possible phonetic generalizations. The view that somehow phonetic processes are more regular, automatic, and hence trivial, than other linguistic processes, seems unjustified. Rather, phonetic rules appear to be at least partly language-specific and of linguistic interest. However, they may well derive from a basic set of preferences (called 'default options' in Keating 1985a) in, for example, speech production, which languages may incorporate into their grammars. On this view, cross-language patterns, and the phonetic rules that generate them, reflect universal 'conveniences' of the various physical phonetic systems. However, a language need not include rules that reflect a particular default pattern; non-default options are often chosen instead. Furthermore, even if a default pattern is used, it need not manifest itself as a purely 'phonetic' rule; it may hold at a more abstract phonological level than the surface output. As an example, vowel duration before voiced vs. voiceless consonants appears to be a patterning available to languages; some use it and some do not, and those that do, do so either as an opaque phonological rule, or in the phonetics (Chen 1970; Dinnsen 1985; Keating 1985a). The fact that the same types of patterns can occur at different levels of representation suggests that phonetic implementation is not something divorced from the rest of the grammar, but something controlled as part of the grammar. More and more, the phonetics is being viewed as largely the same sort of creature as the phonology, that is, a formal system of rules.

Since *SPE*, ideas about phonetic rules have been affected by several crucial changes in views as to the output of the phonology. These changes include proposals on autosegmental representations and underspecification of features. Also of great importance has been work on intonation, particularly at Bell Labs (Pierrehumbert 1980; Liberman 1983; Liberman & Pierrehumbert 1984; see also Cutler & Ladd 1983). The major presentation of this work is Pierrehumbert (1980), in which English intonation is analyzed as an autosegmental linking of tone units to text according to metrical theory. The importance of this work for phonetics is that it provides explicit rules for implementing sequences of phonologically motivated discrete tone units as continuous intonation contours. These rules distinguish the process of converting tones to actual pitch levels, from the process of constructing a contour between such discrete pitch levels; this distinction is likely to be influential in future work on segmental phonetic rules.

Let us consider the nature of such proposals as relevant to a model of interaction between phonology and phonetics. It should be noted that, given these proposals, it is too early to decide the exact division of labor between phonological and phonetic rules; in fact, it is no longer clear what is at stake in positing such a division, or what arguments would be relevant in deciding. Nonetheless, it is possible to suggest what tasks might be accomplished by one component or the other during a derivation.

Both in classical phonetic theory (Pike 1943) and in generative phonology (Anderson 1974, 1976) it has been proposed that each articulator's activities can be represented simultaneously but independently. This idea has been elaborated within the framework of autosegmental phonology (Goldsmith 1979), where tones and segments are represented on separate tiers but linked by association lines, which denote simultaneity of utterance. In the extension of autosegmental phonology to CV phonology, the segments themselves were decomposed into separate tiers, including a separate 'timing tier,' or 'skeleton,' consisting only of the elements C and V, and a featural specification, or 'melody'. However, the segmental melodies themselves may be further decomposed into component features. Some recent work in CV phonology (for example, Clements 1985) has addressed Goldsmith's original suggestion that such autosegmental representation could be used phonetically. The tiers of the phonological representation can be related to the control of individual articulators; by spreading and realignment of autosegmentalized features, segmental representations can be converted into coordinated 'orchestral scores' at the phonetic level. The CV tier remains as the core of the representation, controlling gross aspects of timing and serving as the skeleton to which all the articulatory tiers are (at least indirectly) linked.

At some point in this process the representation must come to include all the potentially independent articulatory parameters, not just those used as features. These parameters are controlled by features that are used contrastively. Following the orchestral score analogy, additional parameters may act more like double basses, doubling the cello part, than like separate parts in the score. Examples we have seen above include wall tension controlled by a glottal feature in Korean, length controlled by voicing in English, and activity of all lower pharyngeal articulators controlled by the features [low, back] for pharyngeal consonants in Arabic. It remains to be seen how many features can control a parameter, and how many parameters can be associated with a feature, in a given language.

Phonological rules operating on autosegmental representations may add association lines between tiers, in doing so sometimes also delinking existing associations. The added lines spread features associated with one segment to other segments, providing a mechanism for expressing assimilation processes. Such spreading is also one mechanism for filling in unspecified feature values for segments: with spreading, such an underspecified segment receives a value from the context. (For discussion of underspecification, see Kiparsky 1982; Archangeli 1984). This filling in of unspecified feature values is one of the tasks of a derivation. The other major way of accomplishing that task is by various sorts of table look-up, including default, rules. In Stevens *et al.* (1986), the focus is on look-up rules, in particular, rules which refer to the specified feature values of a segment to determine the unspecified values of that same segment. In Keating (1985b), the focus is on rules that spread values from context and equally on segments that receive no fill-in value at all. However it is that particular segments receive their redundant feature values, we want to know, first, when the phonology is sensitive to such values, and second, whether, once supplied, they have the same status as underlyingly specified values. On the first point, Stevens *et al.*

(1986) give a case from Lardil in which a redundant value for [back] supplied to certain consonants by one of their look-up rules, is then referred to by a phonological rule for consonant alternations. On the second point, Keating (1985b) suggests that a redundant value for [high] supplied to [s] may behave exactly like underlying [high] values in later phonetic rules. However, these questions obviously require more study.

After decomposition and redundant feature value fill-in, features are provided with quantitative values (Pierrehumbert 1980). At certain key points in an utterance (those endowed with feature values) articulatory targets that may be sensitive to the context are supplied. Thus a feature value for phonetic voicing will distribute control specifications to the vocal cords, to the pharynx (to vary size), and to wall tension (etc.) as a function of the other features of the segment in question, and of the context in which it is found. How are decisions made about balancing conflicting demands both within segments, and across segments within a span? The available evidence suggests that not all feature specifications provide equally important targets. At the point where evaluation is done, certain articulatory requirements are given a special status as organizing points or 'phonetic anchors' for a sequence of articulations. Phonetic anchors are the feature (or parameter) values which are evaluated first, regardless of context, with other features evaluated in terms of any nearby anchors. The anchor points resist coarticulation with their context, while requiring coarticulation on the part of neighboring segments. One example of a phonetic anchor, from Vaissière (1983), concerns the feature [nasal]. Here, syllable-initial consonants may serve as anchors, controlling velum height for neighboring segments. Another example, from Keating (1983), is the segment [s], which serves as an anchor for jaw height.

The final step of a derivation must be interpolation between specifications (Pierrehumbert 1980). What shapes the interpolating functions may have, and whether these can vary across languages is not yet known. What is known is that some segments appear to have no specifications of their own, even after all the fill-in rules have applied. It is clear from both acoustic data (Keating 1985b) and articulatory data (Vaissière 1983) that some segments instead simply lie along the 'path' from a value specified in a previous segment to a value specified in a later segment.

Note that in this proposal phonological feature values are never numerical. The rules of quantitative evaluation (target assignment) are phonetic rather than phonological – the numerical values assigned to features as interpretations of the binary values are to be construed as fairly concrete entities. Pierrehumbert (1980) suggested that rules of evaluation have much in common with rules of interpolation between values, in that both must refer to quantitative scales, and so should be found in the same component.

Furthermore, the thrust of Pierrehumbert's analysis of English intonation was that such phonetic rules are linguistic, not physical, in nature, and so should be considered part of the grammar, like the phonology. The extent to which her treatment of intonation, with no discrete level of representation corresponding to a phonetic transcription, will carry over to treatments of segmental phonetics, is unclear, but should be a very interesting focus of research in the near future.

## 11.3. Phonetic naturalness and explanation

The final topic to be addressed concerns the explanatory value of phonetics for phonology – that is, the role of phonetics in providing substance-based theories. Much of the interest of phoneticians and phonologists in each others' disciplines relates to questions of phonetic naturalness. Phoneticians look to phonology for phenomena to be explained, and phonologists look to phonetics for explanations in general and for support for particular analyses. Feature theory, which has already been discussed, can be viewed as a special instance of this theme. The phonetic correlates of features can be thought of as explanations for why certain sounds should naturally group together. In this section other instances of such explanation are considered: definitions of units, and motivations for rules. Phonologists often look to phonetics for evidence that a particular unit of analysis posited by a theory has some physical basis; they may also look for evidence that a proposed rule is plausible or natural.

### 11.3.1. Phonetic basis of phonological units

Segments

Although all of traditional phonetics (e.g. Ladefoged 1982) has been based on the notion of segment, some phoneticians are ready to abandon the segment as a phonetic entity, leaving the segment to phonologists without any phonetic justification. Ladefoged (1983b) and Lindblom (1983b) can be read in this way. Browman & Goldstein (1986) go still further to say that segments are not used even in lexical representations; rather, articulatory gestures are taken as the only basis of representation. Neither of these positions, as they stand, is likely to lead to an integrated theory of phonetics and phonology. A different tack is taken by Fowler and colleagues (e.g. Fowler *et al.* 1980): there are phonetic segments, but they are hard to see because they include a temporal dimension. This temporal dimension is present even in lexical representations, that is, phonetic segments can be used as phonological segments. Thus Ladefoged says that both phonological segments and phonetic representations exist but there is no relation between them; Browman & Goldstein say that phonological segments do not exist; Fowler says that phonological segments are just like phonetic segments. Finally, many phoneticians have posited intermediate rules of some sort to relate phonological and phonetic segments via some form of derivation: much of the traditional coarticulation literature, the older Haskins theories, Perkell (1980), Keating (1984a). Obviously the field is in some disarray on this point.

The most likely outcome, in my opinion, would be abandoning the claim that segments are directly attested in the phonetic signal as anything resembling discrete units. Rather, the component features of segments can be identified in the signal, misaligned with each other in time. This does not mean that there are no phonetic segments, but only that discrete segments are abstract, operating as a sort of control over or organizer of articulation. This view has already been outlined above, in the discussion of rules of phonetic implementation.

## Syllables

*SPE* assumed that syllables play no role in the grammar, making syllables only a surface phonetic phenomenon. However, this view somewhat overestimates the extent to which syllables have received any coherent phonetic definition. The phonetic literature is quite inconclusive as to either what a syllable is, or how to define properties, such as sonority, that might be exploited to define syllables, although phonologists have been happy to assume that such questions are nearly settled. Thus, for example, Kahn (1976), in his discussion of syllables in generative phonology, repeats the idea that syllables are phonetically understood, and rather misleadingly concludes that there is as much evidence for phonetic syllables as for phonetic segments.

Kahn relies mainly on some hopeful general remarks by Ladefoged (1971), and on the hypothesis that each syllable is defined by a single respiratory muscular gesture. Ladefoged himself refuted this hypothesis, which was due to Stetson (1951), in his earlier work (summarized in Ladefoged 1967). Stetson had claimed that syllables can be defined by 'chest pulses,' but Ladefoged showed that respiratory muscular activity occurs for stressed syllables, and before voiceless fricatives, that is, in contexts requiring high airflow. Thus there is no special relation between syllables and respiration.

However, Ladefoged does believe that syllables act as units of organization for articulation. Kozhevnikov & Chistovich (1965) are often cited as phonetic evidence for such a claim. They proposed the syllable as an articulatory domain on the basis of coarticulation of lip rounding in Russian. However, their proposal should not be taken as support for a phonological unit. The syllables they found bear no relation to phonological syllables; they are defined as any number of consonants plus a following vowel. Also, Kozhevnikov & Chistovich looked only at lip rounding, whereas studies of other articulations have tentatively suggested other articulatory units. Furthermore, as Maddieson (1985: 217) points out, coarticulatory studies referring to syllables generally do not directly compare minimal differences in syllabification. In a related vein, the papers in Bell & Hooper (1978) on the role of syllables in phonetics attribute little phonetic role to an entire phonological syllable. However, the contribution of Fujimura & Lovins (1978) does rely on syllable components as an articulatory domain. A more recent and very promising study implicating syllable position as an articulatory organizer is Vaissière (1983), in which velum height is shown in some cases to depend on a consonant's syllable position.

Another result in this area concerns the role of the syllable in phonetic timing. Maddieson (1985) examined whether syllable membership, or the syllabification of a string of segments, can be determined from vowel durations, which are affected by a common phonetic rule shortening vowels in closed syllables. On the basis of a cross-language study, he argues that the application of such a rule indicates tautosyllabic membership of consonants after a vowel. The generality of closed syllable vowel shortening means that in at least some cases syllable membership can be read directly off the acoustic representations. Such results should be of interest to phonologists, and lead to further cooperation between experimentalists and theoreticians. In general, currently the phonological evidence for syllables is much more convincing than the phonetic evidence, but we can expect progress to be made in the phonetic directions charted by Vaissière and Maddieson.

## The sonority hierarchy

In the discussion of features within new phonological theories, the sonority hierarchy was mentioned as a basis of (phonological) syllable structure representation. The basic notion is that stop consonants and open vowels are at opposite ends of a continuous dimension, with other segment classes ordered in between. Classes at the more sonorous end are used as syllabic nuclei, while syllable margins are supposed to be less sonorous than nuclei. However, the point along the hierarchy at which nuclei are distinguished from margins is not fixed in advance; this is determined by individual languages (or other proposals such as Steriade 1982). Thus, languages may differ in how they use the hierarchy to determine syllable structure. Hankamer & Aissen (1974) note that there is no phonetic definition for the

293

hierarchy available, but they do want it to have one: phonetically different segments across languages should be ordered differently along the hierarchy. So far no one has provided a phonetic definition that would work across languages; and if they did, there are still intralanguage discrepancies. Thus Ladefoged (1975/1982) rejects the hypothesis that syllables can be defined phonetically by peaks in sonority (defined as relative loudness), because of the many counterexamples encountered in actual syllables.

A view that seems worth pursuing is that no single physical dimension entirely determines the sonority hierarchy or syllabicity. Rather, various properties of syllables can be distinguished, and together may provide a definition of syllables while still allowing the ambiguities and discrepancies observed across languages. Such an approach is discussed by Price (1980), Keating (1983), Ohala & Kawasaki (1985), and indirectly by Lindblom (1983a). Syllables can be seen as single cycles along various dimensions such as jaw movement, glottal gestures, first formant frequency, and acoustic energy, that is, physical dimensions largely relating to slow-moving articulators and their acoustic effects. While these dimensions are largely correlated and define similar 'sonority' hierarchies, there are at the same time subtle differences giving individual segments more than one position in an overall ordering of segments. Thus English alveolar obstruents have high jaw positions and so might favor positions in syllable margins when syllables are defined by a jaw movement cycle; but in a syllable defined by an intensity cycle a fricative like [s] will be more 'sonorous'. The large degree of overlap between hierarchies defined along these various dimensions gives the impression of a single sonority hierarchy, but really there is only a coincidental overall 'sonority look' to segment organization in syllables.

## Feet

A foot consists of a stressed syllable, and optionally one or more stressless syllables; the exact nature of a foot depends on the particular phonological proposal. Generally in phonetics the topic of feet arises in connection with investigations of isochrony, meaning equal timing of some unit, usually the syllable or the stress foot (Lehiste 1977; Dauer 1983). Thus there have been many phonetic studies of syllable vs. stress timing across languages. However, most such studies do not draw in any way on recent theoretical proposals in the area of metrical phonology, and do not aim to offer any phonetic basis for the varied, and often abstract, feet posited by metrical phonologists. An exception is Nakatani, O'Connor & Aston (1981), who looked at stress timing using several kinds of feet, including feet headed by syllables with secondary stress. They found that foot duration depended on foot size (type); furthermore, syllables with secondary stress were shorter than syllables with main stress, making any temporal definition of inter-stress intervals unlikely. However, studies of isochrony in both the acoustic and the perceptual domains continue, and may perhaps be related to concerns of phonological theory.

Of course the phenomenon of stress itself has been much studied (though a summary of that literature is beyond the scope of this chapter), and therefore the actual stressed syllables may be identified phonetically. But the question of whether the phonological unit plays any other role in determining phonetic form is more difficult. Öhman (1966) is often cited as showing that tongue body coarticulation goes from stressed vowel to stressed vowel – which might look like a foot basis for coarticulation. But in fact he only looked at VCV sequences in which both vowels were stressed, so his work shows only that coarticulation may extend at least that far; it does not define the foot as a coarticulatory unit.

Thus again we see that phonetics has yet to provide a physical basis for a useful theoretical construct. As more phonetics labs become equipped for a variety of experimental techniques, and as phoneticians try to formulate precise rules of quantitative implementation, we can expect more attention to the role of suprasegmental domains like syllables and syllable constituents in determining phonetic patterns. Phonetic evidence may then become clear enough to provide physical corroboration for theoretical constructs. But if past experience is any guide, we should not expect the phonetic evidence to be superficially direct.

## 11.3.2. Phonetic bases of inventory structure

Even though acoustic support for discrete segments has not been forthcoming, segments are still used as the basis of descriptions of languages' inventories of sounds. Furthermore, segmental phonemic descriptions allow comparisons across languages of segment occurrence; from such comparisons, many generalizations about distributions within inventories are found. Most recently, Maddieson (1984) has provided a statistical study of phoneme inventories that supersedes earlier accounts of cross-language generalizations and patterns. Some results are perhaps unsurprising. For example, languages are most likely to have two manner series of stop consonants, and those two series are most likely to be plain voiceless and plain voiced. Also, most languages have at least one nasal, and that nasal is usually dental or alveolar. However, the value of the statistical analysis lies equally in determining which cases are not themselves additional patterns but instead the result of the interactions of more basic patterns. Thus no special explanation is required for the lack of voiced velar stops in some languages; this gap can be attributed to a general lack of velars, plus a general preference for voiceless over voiced stops.

The fact that unrelated languages show recurring patterns of sounds suggests that there is some general or universal basis that is physiological or cognitive, or both, in nature. Thus the explanation of such generalizations may fall within the domains of both phonetics and phonology. Phonology may focus on structural principles such as maximal exploitation of a given feature contrast, or symmetry of inventories; phonetics will consider principles such as perceptual distinctiveness and articulatory ease. Phonetic explanations may be particularly likely for common gaps and asymmetries in inventories, which overall structural principles will not address.

Some of the best-known work in phonetics has been addressed to the issue of explaining segment inventory generalizations. Ohala (1983a and earlier work) considers certain individual generalizations from the point of view of articulation and perception. He briefly discusses, for example, sounds that never occur, the ratio of obstruents to sonorants within a language, and obstruent voicing patterns, including voicing of geminates and of different places of articulation. Especially noteworthy is his reliance on articulatory modeling as a technique for developing hypotheses.

Others have aimed at more general theories accounting for overall properties of segment inventories. Stevens's (1972) 'quantal theory' held that segment inventories are formed from a finite set of discrete phonetic categories; these categories in turn are based on discontinuities in the relation between articulation and acoustics, and between acoustics and perception. Similar categories are to be expected across languages because there is only a certain set of categories made available by physiology. However, quantal theory does not necessarily explain why particular subsets of categories occur more frequently than others. Another well-known theory is that of Liljencrants & Lindblom (1972; also Lindblom 1978), generally called 'dispersion theory'. Unlike quantal theory, dispersion theory focusses on the overall distribution of segments in an inventory without positing pre-existing phonetic categories. Thus unrounded front vowels, and rounded back vowels, are preferred because such vowels maximize the dispersion of vowels in the phonetic vowel space. The theory allows specific formulations of how a criterion of perceptual distance between sounds can be used to provide a distribution in a phonetic space. For further discussion and comparison of these two theories, see Disner (1983); she shows that neither theory by itself is adequate to account for all the facts she presents.

A more recent theory (Stevens et al. 1986), which can be called 'enhancement theory,' is presented in that paper from the viewpoint of phonology, as a theory of fill-in rules for redundant feature values. However, the theory can also be considered from the viewpoint of phonetics, as a theory of segment inventory construction based on phonetic features. Enhancement theory holds that segments are chosen so that the value of one feature acoustically enhances or emphasizes the value of another feature; that is, particular combinations of feature values are preferred. This theory describes the example of back vowels being rounded as the enhancement of an acoustic correlate of backness, namely a low second formant, by an acoustic correlate of rounding, namely lowering of formant values. These correlates are complementary rather than contradictory, hence the enhancement relation. The theory attempts to extend this description to other cases besides vowel rounding. The notion of acoustic enhancement incorporates the idea of perceptual distinctiveness, while its formulation in terms of distinctive features retains the categorial basis of quantal theory. However, it remains to be seen just how generally the rules of enhancement can be formulated.

Although there is no phonetic theory of inventories that is currently widely accepted, it can be expected that in the future more work will be devoted to this question. More and better models of various aspects of both perception and articulation are being developed, and these models should lend themselves to formulating and testing explanations for inventory patterns.

### 11.3.3. Phonetic basis of rules

In *SPE* it was observed (pp. 400–2) that its formal theory provides no explanation for why some phonological rules are more plausible or natural than others. Since then phonetic naturalness has, for at least some phonologists, been a criterion for evaluating proposed rules (for example, Schane 1972; Hooper 1976; Stampe 1979). Many phonologists seem to take it for granted that metrics for phonetic naturalness have been or could easily be provided. Given this focus, it is perhaps surprising that relatively little attention has been given by phoneticians to phonetic motivations for particular phonological rules, or, more generally, to elaborating a general framework for evaluating rule naturalness. Ohala and his students have stood out for their interest in physiological explanations for phonological rules, both synchronic and diachronic. Ohala (1983a) is a recent statement of his views and results from articulatory modeling, with special attention to the effects of oral pressure variation on consonant voicing, affrication, and aspiration. He shows that certain synchronic and diachronic rules have plausible articulatory motivations. Another valuable piece of work in this

297

direction is Beddor (1982), which provides a unified phonetic account of various synchronic and diachronic effects of nasalization on vowel quality, again using articulatory modeling techniques.

Westbury & Keating (1986) use such articulatory modeling to explore the limits of phonetic explanation by examining systematically a related set of phonetic patterns involving stop consonant voicing. Some of the patterns are indeed generated by the articulatory model, but others are counter-examples. This work shows how articulatory modeling can help identify cases where other, non-articulatory, bases for rule naturalness must be posited.

Phonetic explanations for phonological rules have been criticized by Dinnsen (1980) on the grounds that articulatory constraints never motivate a particular phonological rule. At best they define a 'problem' for articulation, and one or more possible solutions to the problem. For example, a problem sequence of two obstruents that disagree in voicing can be solved by a devoicing rule, by a voicing rule, by a directional assimilation rule, by a vowel epenthesis rule, or by a consonant deletion rule. Individual languages may deal with the situation differently, in ways that reflect the phonetic situation but do not spring directly from it. Thus the phonology cannot simply be reduced to such phonetic considerations. Similarly, Anderson (1981) and Keating (1985a) stress that even phonetically natural phonological rules may be more or less arbitrary in their instantiation in a given language; they may be ordered opaquely with other rules, and so have surface exceptions, or they may apply to a domain different from the phonetically most natural one. For example, final devoicing of obstruents can be motivated physically by aerodynamic considerations, but only for utterance-final position; languages that employ devoicing rules in word- or syllable-final positions are no longer responding only to physical considerations.

Such insistence on a distinction between physiology and phonology does not of course vitiate attempts to document the range of phonetic variation available for re-encoding as higher-level phonological rules. Study of low-level variation may be especially interesting in the area of diachronic phonology, as Ohala (e.g. 1983a, b, 1984) has shown. He proceeds from the point that the phonetic source of sound change is cross-language allophonic variation. Ohala (1983b) and Goldstein (1983) consider why changes proceed in one direction rather than another. Perhaps the best-known example of this kind of research is that on tonogenesis due to consonant voicing, discussed by Hombert, Ohala & Ewan (1979). In this case, an originally allophonic variation in vowel fundamental frequency becomes phonemic when the triggering consonant voicing distinction is lost, and in this sense we can say that the consonant voicing is the cause of the tonal development.

Thus at a certain point in time an originally phonetic pattern of variation ceases to be phonetically controlled.

The mechanism behind such sound changes is of great interest in terms of how grammars work. One sound induces a phonetic effect on another sound, and then disappears; but the allophonic effect on the second sound is preserved even without the surface trigger. The new surface pattern is now a synchronic counterexample to the cross-language phonetic pattern. Thus after the tonogenesis process it will not be the case that vowel fundamental frequency will depend on consonant voicing. To me, the interesting point about this process is that grammars allow suppression of phonetic patterning in this way, apparently without regrets for the abandoned surface generalization.

Phonological systems across languages have many things in common, from their basic constituent units to particular rules, that seem to both phonologists and phoneticians to warrant at least indirect grounding in phonetic substance. However, as we have seen, progress to date has not been equal to expectations, though some interesting approaches have been suggested.

## 11.4. Conclusion

The apparent complexity of the relation between phonological and phonetic descriptions of speech underscores the need for cooperative research strategies in both fields. Fortunately, prospects for progress are greatly enhanced by recent proposals within phonological theory and by new approaches to phonetic research. Both phonologists and phoneticians are interested in pursuing phonetic aspects of phonological derivations, treating phonetics as an integral part of the grammar that can provide evidence about formal representations and rules. Such cooperative research will benefit linguistic theory in general, and the study of linguistic sound systems in particular. It seems to me a very exciting time to be working in the area of generative phonetics.

*REFERENCES*

Anderson, S. 1974. *The organization of phonology*. New York: Academic Press.
Anderson, S. 1976. Nasal consonants and the internal structure of segments. *Language* 52: 326–44.
Anderson, S. 1981. Why phonology isn't 'natural'. *Linguistic Inquiry* 12: 493–539.
Archangeli, D. 1984. Underspecification in Yawelmani phonology and morphology. Doctoral dissertation, MIT.
Beddor, P. S. 1982. Phonological and phonetic effects of nasalization on vowel height. Doctoral dissertation, University of Minnesota.
Bell, A. & Hooper, J. B. (eds.) 1978. *Syllables and segments*. Amsterdam: North-Holland.

Browman, C. & Goldstein, L. 1986. Towards an articulatory phonology. *Phonology Yearbook* 3: 219–52.

Campbell, L. 1974. Phonological features: problems and proposals. *Language* 50: 52–65.

Chen, M. 1970. Vowel length variation as a function of the voicing of consonant environment. *Phonetica* 22: 129–59.

Chomsky, N. & Halle, M. 1968. *The sound pattern of English*. New York: Harper & Row.

Clements, G. N. 1985. The geometry of phonological features. *Phonology Yearbook* 2: 225–52.

Cutler, A. & Ladd, D. R. (eds.) 1983. *Prosody: models and measurements*. Heidelberg: Springer.

Dart, S. 1984. Testing an aerodynamic model with measured data from Korean. *UCLA Working Papers in Phonetics* 59: 1–18.

Dauer, R. 1983. Stress-timing and syllable timing reanalyzed. *Journal of Phonetics* 11: 51–62.

Delattre, P. 1971. Pharyngeal features in the consonants of Arabic, German, Spanish, French, and American English. *Phonetica* 23: 129–55.

Dinnsen, D. 1980. Phonological rules and phonetic explanation. *Journal of Linguistics* 16: 171–91.

Dinnsen, D. 1985. A re-examination of phonological neutralization. *Journal of Linguistics* 21: 265–79.

Disner, S. F. 1983. Vowel quality: the relation between universal and language-specific factors. *UCLA Working Papers in Phonetics* 58.

Fowler, C., Rubin, P., Remez, R. & Turvey, M. 1980. Implications for speech production of a general theory of action. In B. Butterworth (ed.) *Language production*, vol. I. New York: Academic Press.

Fromkin, V. 1975. The interface between phonetics and phonology. 8th International Congress of Phonetic Sciences, Leeds. Also in *UCLA Working Papers in Phonetics* 31: 104–7.

Fromkin, V. 1979. Persistent questions concerning distinctive features. In B. Lindblom & S. Öhman (eds.), *Frontiers of speech communication research*. London: Academic Press.

Fujimura, O., Kiritani, S. & Ishida, H. 1973. Computer-controlled radiography for observation of movements of articulatory and other human organs. *Computers in Biology and Medicine* 3: 371–84.

Fujimura, O. & Lovins, J. 1978. Syllables as concatenative phonetic units. In Bell & Hooper (1978).

Ghazeli, S. 1977. Back consonants and backing coarticulation in Arabic. Doctoral dissertation, University of Texas.

Goldsmith, J. 1979. *Autosegmental phonology*. New York: Garland Press.

Goldstein, L. 1983. Vowel shifts and articulatory–acoustic relations. Symposium 5: Phonetic explanation in phonology. In A. Cohen & M. P. R. van der Broecke (eds.), *Abstracts of the Tenth International Congress of Phonetic Sciences*. Dordrecht: Foris.

Hale, K. 1973. Deep–surface canonical disparities in relation to analysis and change: an Australian example. *Current Trends in Linguistics* II: 401–58.

Halle, M. 1983. On distinctive features and their articulatory implementation. *Natural Language and Linguistic Theory* 1: 91–105.

Halle, M. & Stevens, K. 1979. Some reflections on the theoretical bases of phonology. In B. Lindblom & S. Ohman (eds.) *Frontiers of speech communication research*. London: Academic Press.

Halle, M. & Vergnaud, J. -R. 1980. Three dimensional phonology. *Journal of Linguistic Research* 1: 83–105.

Hankamer, J. & Aissen, J. 1974. The sonority hierarchy. *Papers from the Parasession on natural phonology*. Chicago Linguistic Society.

Hayes, B. 1981. A metrical theory of stress rules. Doctoral dissertation, MIT. Distributed by IULC.

Hombert, J. -M., Ohala, J. & Ewan, W. 1979. Phonetic explanations for the development of tones. *Language* 55, 1: 37–58.

Hooper, J. B. 1976. *An introduction to natural generative phonology*. New York: Academic Press.

Hyman, L. 1975. *Phonology: theory and analysis*. New York: Holt, Rinehart & Winston.

Jakobson, R., Fant, G. & Halle, M. 1963. *Preliminaries to speech analysis*. Cambridge, MA: MIT Press. Fourth printing. First published 1951.

Jakobson, R. & Halle, M. 1968. Phonology in relation to phonetics. In B. Malmberg (ed.), *Manual of phonetics*. Amsterdam: North-Holland.

Kahn, D. 1976. Syllable-based generalizations in English phonology. Doctoral dissertation, MIT. Distributed by IULC.

Keating, P. 1983. Comments on the jaw and syllable structure. *Journal of Phonetics* 11: 401–6.

Keating, P. 1984a. Phonetic and phonological representation of stop consonant voicing. *Language* 60, 2: 286–319.

Keating, P. 1984b. Physiological effects on stop consonant voicing. *UCLA Working Papers in Phonetics* 59: 29–34.

Keating, P. 1985a. Universal phonetics and the organization of grammars. In V. Fromkin (ed.), *Phonetic linguistics: essays in honor of Peter Ladefoged*. Orlando: Academic Press.

Keating, P. 1985b. CV phonology, experimental phonetics, and coarticulation. Paper presented at the Colloque 'Phonologie Pluri-Linéaire,' June 1985, Lyons, France. To appear in conference *Proceedings*. Also to appear in *UCLA Working Papers in Phonetics* 62.

Kenstowicz, M. & Kisseberth, C. 1979. *Generative phonology: description and theory*. New York: Academic Press.

Kiparsky, P. 1979. Metrical structure assignment is cyclic. *Linguistic Inquiry* 10: 421–41.

Kiparsky, P. 1982. Lexical morphology and phonology. In The Linguistic Society of Korea (ed.) *Linguistics in the morning calm*. Seoul: Hanshin.

Kozhevnikov, V. & Chistovich, L. 1965. *Speech: articulation and perception*. Translated and distributed by Joint Publications Research Service, Washington, DC.

Ladefoged, P. 1967. Stress and respiratory activity. In *Three areas of experimental phonetics*. Oxford: Oxford University Press.

Ladefoged, P. 1971. *Preliminaries to linguistic phonetics*. Chicago: University of Chicago Press.

Ladefoged, P. 1975, 1982. *A course in phonetics*. New York: Harcourt Brace Jovanovich. 2nd edn. 1st edn. 1975.

Ladefoged, P. 1983a. Cross-linguistic studies of speech production. In P. MacNeilage (ed.) *The production of speech*. New York: Springer.

Ladefoged, P. 1983b. The limits of biological explanation in phonetics. In A. Cohen & M. P. R. van der Broecke (eds.) *Abstracts of the Tenth International Congress of Phonetic Sciences*. Dordrecht: Foris.

Lahiri, A., Gewirth, L. & Blumstein, S. 1984. A reconsideration of acoustic invariance for place of articulation in diffuse stop consonants: evidence from a cross-language study. *Journal of the Acoustic Society of America* 76, 2: 391–404.

Lehiste, I. 1977. Isochrony reconsidered. *Journal of Phonetics* 5: 253–63.

Liberman, M. 1983. In favor of some uncommon approaches to the study of speech. In P. MacNeilage (ed.) *The production of speech*. New York: Springer.

Liberman, M. & Pierrehumbert, J. B. 1984. Intonational invariance under changes in pitch range and length. In M. Aronoff & R. Oehrle (eds.) *Language sound structure*. Cambridge, MA: MIT Press.

Liljencrantz, J., & Lindblom, B. 1972. Numerical simulation of vowel quality systems: the role of perceptual contrast. *Language* 48, 4: 839–62.

Lindau, M. 1979. The feature expanded. *Journal of Phonetics* 7: 163–76.

Lindblom, B. 1978. Phonetic aspects of linguistic explanation. *Studia Linguistica* XXXII I–II: 137–53.

Lindblom, B. 1983a. Economy of speech gestures. In P. MacNeilage (ed.) *The production of speech*. New York: Springer.

Lindblom, B. 1983b. Can the models of evolutionary biology be applied to phonetic problems? In A. Cohen & M. P. R. van der Broecke (eds.) *Abstracts of the Tenth International Congress of Phonetic Sciences*. Dordrecht: Foris.

McCarthy, J. 1979. Formal problems in Semitic phonology and morphology. Doctoral dissertation, MIT.

McCarthy, J. 1981. A prosodic theory of nonconcatenative morphology. *Linguistic Inquiry* 12: 373–418.

Maddieson, I. 1984. *Patterns of sounds*. Cambridge: Cambridge University Press.

Maddieson, I. 1985. Phonetic cues to syllabification. In V. Fromkin (ed.) *Phonetic linguistics: essays in honor of Peter Ladefoged*. Orlando: Academic Press.

301

Nadler, R., Abbs, J. & Thompson, M. 1985. The new nationally shared x-ray microbeam facility: status report. *Journal of the Acoustical Society of America* 78, Suppl. 1: 538–9.

Nakatani, L., O'Connor, K. & Aston, C. 1981. Prosodic aspects of American English speech rhythm. *Phonetica* 38: 84–106.

Ohala, J. 1979. The contribution of acoustic phonetics to phonology. In B. Lindblom & S. Öhman (eds.) *Frontiers of speech communication research*. London: Academic Press.

Ohala, J. 1983a. The origin of sound patterns in vocal tract constraints. In P. MacNeilage (ed.) *The production of speech*. New York: Springer.

Ohala, J. 1983b. The direction of sound change. Symposium 5: Phonetic explanation in phonology. In A. Cohen & M. P. R. van der Broecke (eds.) *Abstracts of the Tenth International Congress of Phonetic Sciences*. Dordrecht: Foris.

Ohala, J. 1984. Symposium 5: Phonetic explanation in phonology, discussion. In A. Cohen & M. P. R. van der Broecke (eds.) *Proceedings of the Tenth International Congress of Phonetic Sciences*. Dordrecht: Foris.

Ohala, J. & Kawasaki, H. 1985. Prosodic phonology and phonetics. *Phonology Yearbook* 1: 113–27.

Öhman, S. 1966. Coarticulation in VCV utterances: spectrographic measurements. *Journal of the Acoustical Society of America* 39: 151–68.

Perkell, J. 1980. Phonetic features and the physiology of speech production. In B. Butterworth (ed.) *Language production*, vol. I. New York: Academic Press.

Perkell, J. & Cohen, M. 1985. Design and construction of an alternating magnetic field system for transducing articulatory movements in the midsagittal plane. *Journal of the Acoustical Society of America* 77, Suppl. 1: 599.

Pierrehumbert, J. B. 1980. The phonology and phonetics of English intonation. Doctoral dissertation, MIT.

Pike, K. L. 1943. *Phonetics*. Ann Arbor: University of Michigan Press.

Price, P. 1980. Sonority and syllabicity: acoustic correlates of perception. *Phonetica* 37: 327–43.

Schane, S. 1972. Natural rules in phonology. In R. Stockwell & R. Macauley (eds.) *Linguistic change and generative theory*. Bloomington: Indiana University Press.

Sommerstein, A. 1977. *Modern phonology*. Baltimore: University Park Press.

Stampe, D. 1979. A dissertation on natural phonology. Doctoral dissertation, University of Chicago. Distributed by IULC.

Steriade, D. 1982. Greek prosodies and the nature of syllabification. Doctoral dissertation, MIT.

Stetson, R. 1951. *Motor phonetics*. Amsterdam: North-Holland.

Stevens, K. 1972. The quantal nature of speech: evidence from articulatory-acoustic data. In P. Denes & E. David (eds.) *Human communication: a unified view*. New York: McGraw-Hill.

Stevens, K. & Blumstein, S. 1981. The search for invariant acoustic correlates of phonetic features. In P. Eimas & J. Miller (eds.) *Perspectives on the study of speech*. Hillsdale: Erlbaum.

Stevens, K., Keyser, S. J. & Kawasaki, H. 1986. Toward a phonetic and phonological theory of redundant features. In J. Perkell & D. Klatt (eds.) *Symposium on invariance and variability of speech processes*. Hillsdale: Erlbaum.

Vaissière, J. 1983. Prediction of articulatory movement of the velum from phonetic input. ms. Abstract published as: Suprasegmental effect on the velum movements in sentences. In A. Cohen & M. P. R. van der Broecke (eds.) *Abstracts of the Tenth International Congress of Phonetic Sciences*. Dordrecht: Foris.

Westbury, J. & Keating, P. 1986. On the naturalness of stop consonant voicing. *Journal of Linguistics* 22: 145–66.

Williamson, K. 1977. Multi-valued features for consonants. *Language* 53: 843–71.

# 12 Syntactic change*

*David Lightfoot*

## 12.0. Introduction

People don't speak the way they used to. A middle-aged person who has
kept letters or tape-recordings from 20 years ago can often see and hear that
there are changes in the kinds of expressions used and sometimes in aspects
of pronunciation. The most striking changes in an individual's speech
involve the use of idiomatic phrases, which may change substantially in
one's lifetime. More generally, the speech of Margaret Thatcher is different
from that of William Shakespeare, more different from that of Geoffrey
Chaucer, and even more different from what one finds in *Beowulf*. Linguistic change affects individuals and languages quite generally, and its
generality formed the basis of the beginning of modern linguistics. The
nineteenth-century linguists aimed to formulate principles which governed
the way in which sound systems and morphology changed, but they
recognized also that syntax changed in the course of time, although they had
no very clear ideas about how change operated in this area.

This article will ask what kinds of things one can and cannot hope to
explain about how and why syntactic systems change in an individual and in
a language, and what kinds of things we can learn from such work for other
purposes. These two questions are closely related because one will learn
something from language change only if one understands it in some way,
and conversely one will achieve explanations only if one relates language
change to something else. Let us first describe as theory-neutrally as possible some fundamental aspects of how language changes, in the hope of
clarifying certain points which are more controversial than they should be.

Some sort of linguistic system develops in children exposed to a range of
linguistic expressions. At least some basic aspects of the system are 'fixed'
by about the age of puberty and after that age simple exposure to an
equivalent range of expressions in another linguistic setting does not lead to
the development of such a system in the same way. Certain aspects of the

* Thanks to Anthony Warner and Gary Miller for helpful comments on an earlier version.

system may change after puberty, depending on the person's subsequent circumstances: particularly, new kinds of expressions may be used, new pronunciations and new morphological forms, albeit within limits. If the range of linguistic expressions to which a pre-puberty child is exposed is changed somewhat, this may have the effect of yielding a different productive system in maturity. These differences may be fairly minimal, but nonetheless quite distinctive: witness the systems which emerge in two children raised in Liverpool and London. In current parlance, one might say that certain parameters are fixed differently in the children, so that they attain different grammars, where by 'grammar' one means the system of representation which grows in an individual on exposure to some range of linguistic expressions.

Under this perspective, an explanatory model along the lines of (1) is appropriate. The triggering experience consists of those expressions that a person hears and which permit the growth of the relevant grammar. Universal grammar (henceforth, UG) consists of a set of genotypical principles and parameters which are relevant for the growth of grammars in children, and the grammar is a representation of a person's linguistic capacity in maturity:

(1) Triggering experience (UG→ grammar).

It is natural to assume initially that UG does not vary in its central components from one individual to the next, although future work may require some revision to that working assumption; but, of course, triggering experiences and grammars most certainly do vary. Consequently, examining triggering experiences which differ fairly minimally and seeing how they trigger different grammars may cast light on the nature of UG.

Grammars do not simply mirror triggering experiences; their growth is mediated by UG. Examining the ways in which individuals' mature capacities, their grammars, go well beyond what they experienced in childhood leads one to suppose that UG must include a rich set of principles and parameters to provide the necessary bridge (see Lightfoot 1982 for extensive discussion of the logic of the 'poverty of the stimulus' and how this shapes theories of UG). The triggering experience that effects the growth of some linguistic capacity in a child consists only of a haphazard set of simple and readily occurring expressions made in an appropriate context. This means that when historical records show that construction-types ceased to occur at certain stages, there is something to explain. At a certain stage speakers must have heard the relevant construction-type while not uttering it. The fact that speakers fail to produce a class of construction-types that they heard would need to be explained, could not be attributed simply to environmental factors, and would need to be attributed to some new grammatical property which was itself triggered presumably by new expressions in a child's linguistic environment. Similarly, major changes in the meaning of certain expressions would require explanation and would need to be attributed to some aspect of a person's grammar which was triggered by environmental factors. We shall see that these basic factors shape the possible descriptions and explanations that can be invoked for historical change.

## 12.1. Some history

Before turning to particular changes, let us consider first how the scope of discussion for syntactic change has been modified over the years. The nineteenth-century linguists, while formulating general laws and principles of sound and morphological change, compiled lists of construction-types for various languages and made no attempt to posit general principles of syntactic change. While it made sense for them to think of some Latin word as 'corresponding to' some French word (so *frater* and *frère*), it made no analogous sense to think of some Latin sentence as corresponding to some sentence of modern French; at least such a notion of correspondence does not appear in their syntactic writings, although ubiquitous in their work on sound change. They did not agree what 'syntax' was and had no notion of an abstract grammar which 'generated' structures or sentences. Lightfoot (1979a: ch. 1) argued that they did not have the means to do coherent work on syntactic change and that it is not an accident that there is no neogrammarian legacy for syntacticians remotely comparable to what they left for subsequent phonologists. Certainly there was no tradition of work on syntactic change, and, despite isolated discussions, it was not until the 1970s that syntactic change became an area of communal work among linguists.

The earliest examples of a communal interest in syntactic change (e.g. the anthologies of Li 1975, 1977; Steever, Walker & Mufwene 1976) were also conducted independently of the notion of a grammar, and often were based instead on the notion of 'language types,' where languages might be consistently of a certain type or mixed; mixed languages were said to be transitional and moving necessarily toward some new consistent type, although it was never clear why. The types were defined in terms of clusters of harmonic surface properties, based on the findings of Greenberg (1966), who formulated universals of the form: if a language has surface feature $p$, then it will tend with a certain degree of probability also to have surface feature $q$. This approach to language description had internal problems which led to its demise (see Smith 1981; Coopmans 1983, 1984); for historical work it could only invoke autonomous principles of change and, because it was not associated with any account of language acquisition by children, it was unable to offer any form of explanation for the changes discussed (Lightfoot 1979b).[1]

An autonomous law of history would satisfy a researcher who felt that a particular change (say, the fact that some 'SOV language' developed *pre*positions) is explained by saying that there is a universal tendency for 'SOV languages' to turn into 'SVO languages' and that in doing so they acquire prepositions instead of postpositions. But this is just an inductive generalization and not really an explanation, unless one accepts laws of history and believes that Clio or some other muse is directing changes in the affairs and language of human beings and in a principled and consistent way. Such a general tendency for SOV languages to become SVO, if it exists (and there is virtually no evidence for it), would be an explicandum rather than an explicans. The same holds for the often invoked 'simplification': to say that a grammar was simplified does not explain a change unless one also explains how the earlier, less simple, grammar was also attained by earlier generations (O'Neil 1982). The view that explanations for historical changes must be grounded elsewhere and presumably in human psychology is a traditional one, held by many nineteenth-century linguists. Grimm (1848) explained the sound changes described by his 'law' by saying that they were 'connected with the Germans' mighty progress and struggle for freedom . . . Does there not lie a certain courage and pride in the strengthening of voiced stop into voiceless stop and voiceless stop into fricative?' Jespersen (1928) claimed that the change in the meaning of *like* in Middle English (to be discussed below) 'was brought about by the greater interest taken in persons than things.' They did not always presuppose a very sophisticated or even plausible psychology, but it is clear that historians have looked to psychology for their explanations.

Perhaps as a reaction to the implausible psychological notions of earlier historians, this traditional concern for explanation has been lost somewhat in recent years. In fact, it has even been forgotten in some quarters. Lass (1980) shows that autonomous approaches to language change are undermined by narrowly circular reasoning. Rather than considering the non-autonomous approaches which the earliest historians had adopted, his solution is to view work on language change as a 'metaphysical research program.'

The first grammatically oriented work on syntactic change also took some false steps. One error ignored the idealization involved in the notion of a grammar of, say, Old English, and people sought to write 'grammars' which captured all the known facts of Old English and even to write 'diachronic grammars,' which were intended to encompass facts about various stages of a

---

[1] One of the more bizarre aspects of most historical work based on this approach was that it dealt often with changes between reconstructed proto-languages and attested daughter languages, sometimes over vast time spans (Lehmann 1974; Friedrich 1975; etc.), and never spelled out the method of reconstruction despite obvious and frequently discussed dissimilarities with the reconstruction of phonological systems (see Lightfoot 1980).

language and the transitions among those stages (Traugott 1969). In this work a grammar was taken as a means of cataloging and inter-relating a fairly arbitrary range of linguistic facts and included some complex and quite unnatural rules. But there is no such thing as 'the grammar of OE'; rather, there were thousands of speakers all of whom had internalized grammars, some differing from others. That *set* of grammars generated most of the OE corpus and much more that went unrecorded.

Another false step was to focus on defining the formal relationship between the grammars of adjacent generations of speakers, as if those grammars would be more closely related *formally*. This turned out to be a wild goose chase, which led only to a sterile debate about the 'gradualness' of grammatical change and to the notion that grammars could not be radically restructured from one generation to the next (for discussion, see Lightfoot 1981b).[2]

## 12.2. Case study I

If we take our psychological perspective seriously and view individual grammars as emerging by virtue of the linguistic environment fixing parameters defined by the theory of grammar, then theories of grammar which have been available over the last ten years permit nice explanations for some changes, particularly the way that superficially unrelated changes occur in clusters. Conversely, we can gain some insight into the nature of grammars from the study of certain kinds of changes. Of course, a prerequisite is that one writes at least partial grammars of the earlier and later stages under investigation, as was first recognized by Klima (1964a, b). I shall first take two examples which have been discussed extensively and show how different explanations have been offered and what kinds of debates arise.

A change which is now quite well understood concerns the shift in meaning of a class of English verbs such as *like*, *ail*, and *repent*, and a corresponding change in their syntax. *Like* used to mean 'please' in one of its uses, and frequently used to occur in this sense in an [object ___ subject] frame

---

[2] So, Harris's (1980) concern for gradualness led her to analyze early Middle English sentences like *þam wife* (DAT) *þa word* (NOM) *wel licodon* (pl.), which she glossed as 'the woman liked these words well,' with *wife* as the underlying subject and *word* as the underlying object. An 'inversion' rule demotes the subject to indirect object and an 'unaccusative' rule advances the direct object to subject. She offered no evidence for this analysis of these ME sentences, considered no alternatives, and, most strikingly, did not mention the semantic change in the verbs which occur in these contexts, nor did she ask why the change took place. Instead, the goal was to discuss the gradualness of the loss of the putative inversion rule, as if this took place independently.

Elsewhere, much of the discussion of gradualness really concerns the gradual spread of some phenomenon through a speech community, but it is couched misleadingly in terms of a gradual grammatical change. This confusion stems, I suspect, from forgetting that 'the grammar of OE' is an idealization along the lines of the French liver, and other such convenient fictions. It often leads to adopting 'lexical' grammars, popular with historians because they are powerful enough to state even the narrowest generalization.

in Middle English. One might argue that the subject was moved to a postverbal position, as in (2) below (Lightfoot 1979a); or one might adopt an analysis along the lines of Rizzi's (1982) treatment of Italian ergatives, whereby the subject is base-generated in the V″, as in (3) (sometimes being moved to the preverbal position). Choosing between these analyses has consequences for the treatment of impersonals like *him hungers* and *rains*, which I shall not discuss here.

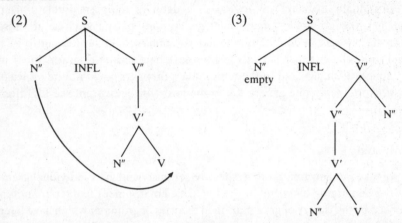

At a certain stage children started acquiring a new phrase structure rule for the expansion of V′, whereby it consisted of a V followed by a direct object, whereas earlier generations had the reverse order. How and why that change took place need not concern us here (see Lightfoot 1982: ch. 8). A child with the new PS rule would most easily analyze a sentence like *The king liked the pears* as subject–verb–object, whereas the generation with the earlier PS rule treated it as object–verb–subject. Notice that by the fifteenth century the case system was so dysfunctional that it would not have indicated that *king* must be construed as an object. Sentences such as *Him liked the pears*, *The king like pears*, etc., which do indicate the need for an object–verb–subject analysis were not robust enough to trigger that analysis; we know this because such sentences eventually dropped out of the language and were neither heard nor produced by later generations. A child with the verb–object PS rule would analyze *The king liked the pears* as subject–verb–object easily and in conformity with the projection principle of Chomsky (1981), which requires a verb's subcategorization frame to be honored at all levels of derivation. Another logically possible analysis which conforms to the projection principle would move *the king* to a clitic position before the verb (analogously to French pronouns), but there is no independent motivation for such a position in grammars at this stage of English, and in any case a non-pronominal would not be treated as a clitic:[3]

---

[3] In (4) *the king* must be in an A′ position, and the trace [e_i] is required at S-structure by the *projection principle*.

(4) [e$_j$] INFL $_{V''}$[[the king$_i$] liked [e$_i$] [pears$_j$]]]

The fact of the matter is that although children with the new PS rule would have heard phrases like *him like pears*, they were ignored and did not make up part of the triggering experience, i.e. did not trigger a grammatical device which would ensure that they could be generated. Such sentences therefore became obsolescent, and cases of this type tell us something about the limits to triggering experiences. Sentences like *Him like pears* are simple and of a type that any child would be likely to hear. We have no way of knowing with any accuracy what percentage of a child's input they would have made up, nor for analogous sentences for children in London in the 1980s. We can only assume that although children heard such sentences, they were not part of the triggering experience; and we should bear in mind that a sentence which is heard, even heard with some frequency, is not necessarily part of a person's triggering experience.[4]

However, *The king liked pears* was part of triggering experiences at this time, even though it did not receive the same analysis as in earlier generations. It was heard in an appropriate context and, when analyzed as subject–verb–object, required an interpretation under which *like* could only mean 'derive pleasure from,' unlike the earlier sense of 'cause pleasure for.' Given such a shift in meaning, the sentence was used by each generation with the same cognitive import. Older speakers might have noticed some new agreement patterns, such as *The king likes pears*, and younger speakers might have noticed antiquated forms as *The king like pears*, but these were not enough to disturb communication, one assumes, although they might have led a 'purist' ancestor of Edwin Newman to beseech the king to set up an academy of proper speech.

The first grammatical account of the correlation between the new word order and the loss of the old sense of *like* etc. (Lightfoot 1979a: ch. 5) did not offer an explanation. It noted that a derivation involving a permutation of subject and object seemed to be opaque in some undefined sense, and argued that the fact that certain structures became obsolete indicated that the theory of grammar should be stated in such a way as to forbid such opacity.[5] It also argued that the analysis of such diachronic changes might provide some insight on the limits to opacity. This hope was realized soon afterwards, when Dresher & Hornstein's (1979) 'trace erasure principle' provided a specific

---

[4] I am assuming, surely uncontroversially, that the kinds of things which occur frequently in the historical record are the kinds of things that children of the time would have heard, i.e. the set of expressions from which the trigger experience was drawn. There is much that is not yet known about the *limits* to the triggering experience, but we can still draw some conclusions about central elements of the experience of the Middle English child; furthermore, I am arguing that historical data, properly analyzed, can tell us something about the limits to triggering experiences. For some discussion of those limits see Lightfoot (1985).

[5] For discussion of the *transparency principle* and some misunderstandings that it led to, see Lightfoot (1981c). Bennett (1979) pointed out correctly that the transparency principle covered different kinds of complexity and that it was unlikely that one principle, when properly formulated, would cover them all.

constraint which would eliminate permutation processes which had the effect of erasing traces (Lightfoot 1981b). The trace erasure principle, in turn, was soon subsumed under the new projection principle. Clearly the precision of the trace erasure principle improved on the earlier hope for a limit to acceptable opacity, but, similarly, keying the explanation to the more general and more natural projection principle represents an advance in that it raises new questions about the analysis of the language at the time of the change. Similarly, the success of Rizzi's ergative analysis for Italian postverbal subjects raises new issues for the analysis of postverbal subjects in Middle English. Consequently, debates about the appropriateness of the projection principle and the ergative analysis are integrated with questions about the proper analysis of *The king liked pears* in late Middle English, if one adopts this view of syntactic change, taking a theory of grammar as a central component of explanations for diachronic changes. This is mutually enriching: changes in Middle English now have a wider significance and diachronic explanations are more readily refinable because their components have wider empirical effects. That is, the analysis of the Middle English changes might have to be changed if the projection principle is revised in the light of work on Chamorro or Chinese. So debates about analyses of Middle English phenomena become more lively and more productive as they are keyed to a wider empirical domain. For more discussion of this change, see Fischer & van der Leek (1981, 1983), Leffel & Miller (1985), Warner (1983).

Current theories of grammar, incorporating something along the lines of the projection principle, can explain the demise of the old sense of *like* and the fact that this coincided fairly closely with new word order patterns associated with the new V' PS rule. This is a striking and nontrivial correlation. It is also the kind of change which demands a linguistic explanation and cannot simply be attributed to accident or to a new fashion among some prestige group to use the verb *like* differently, in the reverse of its previous sense. Notice that there is no 'prediction' here that all speakers underwent the changes at the same time, nor even that a speaker with the new PS rule would never utter a sentence of the old form; speakers may have used the old forms from time to time in the same way that modern speakers say *by and large, me thinks, if I were you*, and many other less extremely antiquated forms, or even adopt expressions of other dialect groups occasionally. Consequently, there is no reason to expect the historical record to show the old forms in full profusion in 1350 and totally vanished in 1351 . . . although I am often struck by how clearly the transitions are manifested in the records. All of this does not mean that our account is unfalsifiable in some vicious sense; the projection principle, on which it centers, has consequences for the analysis of myriad facts and phenomena, and can be refined, revised or 'falsified' in many ways.

## 12.3. **Case study II**

The scope for debate and for alternative analyses is wide, as can be seen clearly if one considers the history of the English modals. This constitutes one of the first and clearest arguments for the proposition that the syntactic component of a grammar can be restructured fairly radically from one generation to the next. Lightfoot (1974, revised in 1979a) argued that certain expressions, given in (5), dropped out of the language simultaneously, revealing that *can, could, do, did, may, might, must, shall, should, will, would*, formerly treated as main verbs, were now being treated as manifestations of Aux (=INFL) and were 'auxiliary verbs'. Hence, in current terminology, some parameter had been fixed differently:

(5) a. I shall can do it
   b. I am canning do it
   c. I have could do it
   d. I want to can do it

Again, no real explanation was offered, but the change was keyed to a mounting 'opacity' in the grammars of earlier generations, whereby those verbs steadily became more and more exceptional as they developed the characteristics given in (6). As their exceptionality reached a certain point, children attained a different grammar, which assigned these 'verbs' to a new category. Again, if the theory of grammar could define acceptable levels of exceptionality, it would explain why a new grammar was triggered at a certain stage.

(6) i.  These verbs lost their ability to take direct objects.
  ii.  They became inflectionally distinct after the loss of other preterite-present verbs.
  iii.  With the loss of the subjunctive mood, the relation between their present and past tenses became nontemporal in certain senses.
  iv.  They were never followed by the *to* form of the infinitive.

There has been extensive discussion of this and analogous changes, most usefully by Warner (1983), and some revision seems called for. A curious feature of the treatment of Lightfoot (1974, 1979a) was that the reanalysis of these verbs was dated as complete by the early sixteenth century, the cluster of simultaneous changes in (5) providing the evidence, but that the old inversion and negative forms (*Came John?* and *John came not*) persisted much later, being robust and productive until the late seventeenth century. Warner argues that (6 i) probably belongs with the changes of (5) and was not a causal factor; and he suggests that the simultaneity of (5) was less extensive than supposed by Lightfoot (1979a). Warner (1982) argues for a lexical treatment and for placing the reanalysis earlier. However, the persistence of the old inversion and negative forms suggests the opposite, that at least some critical part of the reanalysis took place later, towards the end of the seventeenth century, with the new inversion and negative forms showing the new analysis.

Warner's discussion suggests that there were two crucial stages to the change: first the modal verbs acquire the properties (6 ii–iv) and lose their nonfinite forms (5), and their direct objects (6 i), and later the new inversion and negative forms come in. The first stage was completed in the sixteenth century, but it may not have been as cataclysmic as Lightfoot (1979a) suggested. Nonfinite forms of *can*, *may* and *will* are found in the sixteenth century, but it seems that nonfinite forms of *must* and *shall* were absent earlier. Arguments *ex tacito* must always be treated cautiously and we must await the publication of the second half of the *Middle English dictionary* for definitive information on this point. If indeed the nonfinite forms of *shall* and *must* disappeared earlier, that will argue for a lexical treatment of the early changes and for placing the structural reanalysis later, being completed at the end of the seventeenth century, when the old inversion and negative forms are no longer recorded, and when the last inflected forms disappear (*can(e)st*, *could(e)st*, etc.).

If one defines INFL as the head of a clause, then it is the key element for inversion and negation processes: inversion applies to INFL and negatives occur immediately to the right of INFL. If, as a result of changes in the tense and mood system, modal verbs became morphologically distinct and gradually acquired the ability to manifest INFL directly at D-structure (7), then the seventeenth-century structural change would consist of the fact that nonmodal verbs lose the ability to move up to INFL and thus to interact with inversion and negation properties. Roberts (1985) has developed one account along these general lines. The attraction of verbs to INFL has been a persistent notion in studies of Germanic syntax (Safir 1981; den Besten 1983; Evers 1984; Koopman 1984, etc.), but there is still no entirely satisfactory treatment; a good analysis of verb movement in Old and Middle English (which will presumably reflect or entail good analyses of comparable phenomena in modern Dutch and German) is a prerequisite to understanding the early Modern English changes. However, it is clear that Modern English has become unusual with regard to the other Germanic languages in not allowing regular verbs to move to INFL and to participate in inversion and negation processes. This strongly suggests that the parametric change, or what used to be called reanalysis, should be keyed to the development of the periphrastic *do*; for relevant discussion see Lightfoot (1979a: ch. 2, app.) and I hope to return to this in future work. The net result of the seventeenth-century change was that the INFL position was appropriated by a subclass of verbs (the premodals and *do*) and other verbs could no longer occur here; such distributional differences usually motivate a category distinction (although it is also possible, as Warner suggests, that the category change took place earlier as the modals became morphologically distinct, but this raises some difficulties).

(7)

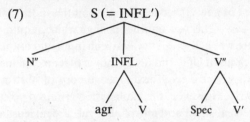

As with the earlier example, when the reanalysis took place, there was a discrepancy between experience and production. Some children heard the old forms (*Came John?*, etc.) but did not accommodate them; so, these forms were not part of the triggering experience, despite being simple and presumably quite frequent and robust. If *can* and *come* were now assigned to different categories, INFL and V respectively, what sort of inversion rule would be triggered? Notice first that the old forms could be perpetuated quite simply under the new grammar if the inversion rule were formulated with a disjunction as in (8):

(8) $N'' \left\{ \begin{array}{c} \text{INFL} \\ \text{V} \end{array} \right\}$ /permute

With such a rule, there would be no discrepancy between input and output for the inversion data. However, we know that there was a discrepancy, which means that (8) was not triggered despite available data. This suggests quite strongly that (8) is not an attainable rule of grammar, that disjunctions of this sort do not exist. If the theory of grammar does not have this effect, it is hard to see why the change should have taken place and why there should have been a discrepancy between input and output; that discrepancy *requires* an explanation and that is one reason why a purely lexical account is inadequate. Again we learn something about the limits to triggering experiences, about the nature of UG, and about the interaction between the two entities, and we learn by carefully distinguishing a child's input and output. Perhaps ironically, we can learn about a child's input from earlier stages of a language, despite limited records.

## 12.4. Morphological influences

If a rethinking along these lines proves fruitful for the English modals, it will be another instance of a syntactic reanalysis being stimulated by earlier morphological changes, i.e. loss of the nonfinite forms of the premodals. The change involving *like* etc. illustrates the conditioning effect of morphology in that it would never have taken place if the nominal inflectional system had not been dysfunctional. Moreover, morphology can sometimes play a more critical role. Lightfoot (1981a), modifying ideas of Bennett (1980) and Lieber (1979), linked the development of new N" movement possibilities in English to the loss of a distinct dative case. This was another change which required an explanation, i.e. where there was a discrepancy between input and output which required appeal to principles of UG, and it was shown that an explanation could be offered in terms of the newly developed theory of abstract (syntactic) Case (Chomsky 1981). However, the explanation required positing in UG a relationship between abstract and morphological case, at least at the level of markedness. So, three distinct abstract Cases may be posited if there are three (or more) morphological cases. If this idea is correct, one would expect the new syntactic phenomena to occur first in those dialect areas where the dative case was first lost (on the loss of morphological case in English, see O'Neil 1982). There have been several studies in recent years arguing for a change in category membership, where a class of items is assigned to a new category along the lines of the English modals, and almost invariably morphological changes played a key role (Carlson 1978; Spamer 1979; see also Janda 1981).

Lightfoot (1981a) differed from Bennett (1980) and Lieber (1979) in entailing the non-occurrence of 'indirect passives' (*John was given the book*, where the subject of the passive corresponds to an indirect object) until the loss of oblique case in Middle English. Lieber claimed to have found four earlier indirect passives:

(9) a. . . . he cuað ðæt he haten wæs. (Ælfred, Bede (Miller) 388, line 29) 'he said what he was commanded (to say).'

b. . . . swa ic eom forgifen fram þam ælmihtigan gode nu þyssere byrig siracusanan eow to geþingienne . . . (*Aelfric's Lives of saints* (EETS nos. 76, 82) and ch. ix lines 136–8) 'so now am I given by the almighty God to this city of Syracuse, to intercede for you.'

c. . . . he was iȝefen Arþure to halden to ȝisle . . . (Laȝamon *Brut* (Brook & Leslie edition, line 11372 (EETS no. 277)) 'he was given to Arthur to hold as hostage.'

However, Russom (1982) argued that none of these were indirect passives. In active sentences with *hatan*, the person commanded is regularly in the accusative; consequently the passive in (9a) does not involve a passivized indirect object. Lieber cites (9b) twice, confused by the fact that secondary sources cite OE examples sometimes by volume and page, sometimes by chapter and line. It is actually just one sentence. Russom examined its context: noting that *forgiefan* 'give' subcategorizes a direct object (the thing given) and an indirect object which is usually a person, she found that here the person *ic* was the thing given to the city, hence the underlying direct object. In (9c) Russom shows that Lieber (and Visser 1973) omitted the macron over the final *r* of *Arþur*, which indicates inflectional endings in the Madden edition; the EETS edition spells the macron out as a dative ending. Consequently *he* represents an underlying accusative and (9c) is no indirect passive. More generally, Mitchell (1979: 539) argued that 'none of the OE examples cited by Visser in his discussion of the passive (iii, §1905–2000) breaks the general rule that only verbs which can take an accusative object in the active voice are used personally in the passive,' despite Visser's claims to the contrary. So Russom demonstrates that one cannot simply go uncritically to the handbooks to gather raw data, and the debate illustrates the productive interaction of philology and theory.

## 12.5. Idealizations

This point is worth emphasizing because it reflects on the idealizations used in historical work. Having claimed that there were a few indirect passives in Old English, Lieber conceded that there was a significant increase in their frequency in the fifteenth century but this was not important for her. 'Even a single example from the 13th century of a construction such as the pseudo-passive is significant . . . There is therefore little basis for the claim that the prepositional passive is a 15–16th century innovation' (p. 672). Taking 'a single example from the 13th century' as evidence that such sentences were grammatical for all speakers of the language may allow one to suppose that there was no change in grammars and hence nothing to explain, but the conclusion is extravagant. If some constructions occur much more frequently in fifteenth-century texts, then presumably there was a change in many individual grammars. There is no reason to suppose that there was 'a grammar of Middle English' which generated all the sentences found in the texts and changed uniformly and simultaneously for all speakers of English, although it is often convenient to work in terms of such an idealization. One should not forget that it is an idealization and it should not take precedence over the philological care and skill which is needed to interpret the texts properly. (For an imaginative application, see Pintzuk & Kroch's 1985 use of metrical patterns to reveal syntactic units.)

A similar moral emerges from the analysis of changes affecting the English modals. The identification of a change in the *grammars* of English speakers led Warner to ask new questions about the history of the modals and his answers in turn lead to revised accounts of the grammatical change. Similarly, Rivero (1984) offered a detailed analysis of free relatives in Spanish, seeking to provide learnable structures for all stages and to explain changes taking place between the thirteenth and sixteenth centuries. She argued that thirteenth-century Spanish manifested structures where the *wh*-item was in COMP (as in modern Spanish) and structures where the *wh*-item was in the head NP position with another *wh*-word in COMP. The second type, Rivero argued, was lost by the sixteenth century. This analysis led Posner (1985) to re-examine the data discussed by Rivero. Posner claimed that Rivero's thirteenth-century data were based largely on 'texts with a Navarro-Aragonese flavour, whereas the 16th-century and modern evidence is Castilian. Navarro-Aragonese dialects are spoken today in only a few areas, and in many cases have been subject to Castilian influence, so it is hard to say whether a "change" has really taken place, or whether there has been replacement of one dialect by another' (p. 184). Posner reinterpreted some of Rivero's data and sketched the outlines of another analysis, whereby *wh*-items occur in the head N″ position and may be followed by an empty or overt complementizer. This analysis entails *structural* differences between thirteenth-century dialects and raises new questions about thirteenth-century Spanish: were Rivero's examples specific to one dialect, or were all thirteenth-century dialects more or less uniform in relevant respects, and can the dialect differences be treated rather as lexical variation? Meanwhile Posner (p. 188) concluded correctly:

> Clearly more research is required into these problems, and we must be grateful to Rivero for bringing them into the context of more general linguistic discussion. The more we can match the detailed work done by old-time philologists with the theoretical speculations of modern linguistics the greater will be our understanding of language history.

Productive debates of this kind are a recent phenomenon and they increase our understanding of why grammars change, what the limits are to available grammars and to trigger experiences, and how the data should be interpreted and analyzed at various stages in the history of a language. They illustrate an important point, which is often made and rarely appreciated: the 'data' do not lie prestine pure in a well-organized supermarket awaiting collection by a conscientious scholar. Often it is not enough simply to go to the handbooks and look up the facts, as if they exist independent of interpretation, analysis, and debate. In the case of illuminating changes, things are rarely that simple.

This commonplace idea, unfortunately, is less well entrenched amongst historians of language than what I have dubbed the 'Ebeling principle'

(Lightfoot 1979b): the more exotic a language and the fewer the linguists who have analyzed it, the more tractable and self-evident its grammar. This powerful and damaging principle has misled historians to invest significant energy in studying reconstructed languages, which have very shaky and largely undiscussed foundations, which in turn leave them free to concoct analyses unconstrained by empirical limitations. See Szemerényi (1985) for more on the tendency to reconstruct by fiat.[6]

## 12.6. Creoles

The charm of the Ebeling principle has also led historians to turn to creolists for the keys to understanding language change, on the assumption that creolization processes provide some special insight on the nature of historical change. Again, the difficulty concerns the basis for hypothesizing reliable grammars. Given the perspective adopted here, particularly the biological conception of grammars, the interest of creoles is that sometimes children develop productive grammars despite an especially heterogeneous triggering experience, consisting of expressions from various languages, including perhaps a 'pidgin' language. Of course, creoles are as interesting as any other language and work by Derek Bickerton, Francis Byrne, Hilda Koopman, Claire Lefebvre, Pieter Muysken, Donald Winford, and others has brought them into the empirical range of the generative research program; this work is as important as work on Chinese, French and Hopi, and no doubt it will eventually lead to revisions and refinements of UG in the usual way when a body of analytical work is established.

However, creoles are acquired, at least in their early stages, under unusual conditions, where the linguistic experience of one generation of children is quite different from that of a generation earlier, and, more importantly, where the linguistic input for that generation differs quite dramatically from the capacity the children eventually attain. If we can discover some properties of the grammars which emerge in these people, and if we know something of their childhood experience which acted as a triggering experience, we may be able to learn something about triggers in general and about the limiting cases. The particularly dramatic contrast

[6] I refer here to the reconstruction of proto-*syntaxes*, which cannot be postulated by the same methods as sound systems, as has often been noted. Even if a reliable method is found for reconstructing a proto-syntax, it will necessarily be based on what we know about the nature of syntactic change as a result of examining changes in attested stages of language. It is hard to imagine how one could learn anything new about the nature of change from a reconstructed system. This, of course, is not to argue that there is no point in doing reconstruction. One can still reconstruct a proto-system, as Meillet did, as a means of expressing precisely the relationship between languages. In that case, the empirical limitations will concern whether one's formula captures the various forms of the related languages neatly and completely. Questions of historical reality will not arise, as Meillet (1937) noted, and therefore there would be no basis for seeking a grammar of the proto-language, under the sense of 'grammar' adopted here.

317

between the input and the mature capacity of the first creole speakers might make it easier to identify which elements of their experience acted as triggers for the emerging grammars.

In the usual case, the *relevant* input for the child, i.e. the trigger experience, is a subset of the total experience, perhaps consisting only of simple main clauses (Lightfoot 1985), and the total experience includes much redundant information. Under that perspective, the restrictedness of the input to creole-speaking children does not look as dramatic as when one is concerned with the total experience that children have. The question now arises: to what extent does the creole child lack relevant input for fixing the parameters provided by UG? If the lack is not extensive, this would explain how children with apparently impoverished input nonetheless attain a mature capacity more or less as rich structurally as that of children with a more extensive and more uniform input; it would simply mean that they have less redundant information. Answering this question will require fairly detailed knowledge of the input to the first creole speakers, which is why Sankoff's work on Tok Pisin is so important (see Sankoff & Laberge 1973, etc.). Usually, however, the trigger experience of original creole speakers is shrouded in the mists of history and written records are meagre. Hence imaginative detective work is needed, of the kind that Bickerton (1984) has done for the early history of Saramaccan; see also Singler's (1984) discussion of relevant demographic material for other creole languages, which indicates roughly which languages were available as potential trigger experiences and to what degree.

Under a research program seeking to find how children acquire their mature linguistic capacity, creole languages can be studied profitably in the context of unusual trigger experiences, and one can expect the sharp contrast between input and eventual mature capacity to provide a useful probe into the nature of trigger experiences in general. However, one sometimes finds claims that one cannot expect to understand the nature of linguistic change without studying creolization processes, and claims that creoles uniquely manifest properties of UG. These claims seem very premature, unlikely to be true, and certainly not justified by current published work (Koopman 1985). On the contrary, the sparseness of the historical record for early stages of creoles entails special difficulties for the analysis of the *origins* of these languages, which are related to some extent to the difficulties in working with reconstructed languages. Rather than expecting creolization to provide the key to understanding language change, it seems more likely that efforts to understand creolization will benefit from what we learn about the nature of syntactic change, working with the richest possible historical records. Where the data are relatively plentiful, there will be debates about the proper analysis of the English modals and Spanish free relatives and the like; where the data are sparse, the debates will be thin and insubstantial, and likewise the conclusions.[7]

## 12.7. **Where grammatical explanation stops**

There is more to linguistic change than what I have discussed here and not all changes demand the kind of explanation offered by (1). Consider the changes which occur in our speech as we move through adolescence and middle age. Typically these changes are not subject to the model of (1) and are often induced by contact with other languages and dialects or introduced for stylistic reasons – some are novel forms which achieve stylistic effect purely through their novelty, and these are an important and often underestimated source of change. In each case these innovations either mimic or are in a sense self-standing, but they do not involve poverty of stimulus properties whereby elements of the input are not accommodated into a person's output. For such changes we have no systematic explanations and, as far as the grammarian is concerned, they may as well be attributed to chance: they are unlikely to tell us much about the nature of grammars, grammatical theory, or trigger experiences (except perhaps illustrating the structural limits within which borrowing takes place), and it is hard to see how grammatical theory could explain why English speakers borrowed expressions from French in the Middle Ages.

This, however, is not to say that such changes are unimportant. They have the effect of changing trigger experiences for future generations and this may entail a new fixing of some parameter. So, for example, it is quite possible that some English speakers, perhaps monastic scribes, began using new accusative+infinitive forms in Middle English, imitating Latin texts: *I believe Jay to be happy*. If such forms spread beyond the monastery, they might have become robust enough to trigger in some children a general process of exceptional case marking (ECM), permitting *believe* etc. to assign Case to an infinitival subject. This may raise interesting sociological or political questions about how the new forms spread through the community eventually triggering ECM processes in all speakers of English, while analogous forms did not spread in Dutch, French, German, Italian, etc. However, historical records are seldom rich enough in a way that would enable us to pursue such questions meaningfully. In any case, it is unlikely that grammatical theory will cast much light on this development, and conversely, unlikely that the development will tell us anything new about grammatical theory. (Of course, the fact that the new process occurred in 20% of the texts in, say, 1386 does not indicate that Geoffrey Chaucer

[7] For further discussion on creoles, see Chapter 14, I and II, by Bickerton and Muysken, in Volume II of this series, and Chapter 9, by Foley, in Volume IV.

would use the process in one out of five opportunities – whatever that might mean – because grammars are properties of individuals and not of countries or speech communities and such statistics tell us nothing about the internal properties of individual grammars; for some discussion of these issues see Romaine 1982, but also Kroch's cautionary review in 1985.) Such innovation, however, takes place constantly and a person's speech changes through adulthood. Some of these innovations may 'catch on' and in some cases may even affect triggering experiences in such a way as to entail new parameter fixings. These changes, then, are grist to the mill of historical change and without them linguistic change would be a less interesting and probably non-existent phenomenon. They certainly show the folly of trying to construct lengthy 'drag chains,' whereby the development of a language over millennia is construed as an inevitable consequence of some single innovation or property which set it all off. Drag chains may involve two or three links (so the new expansion of V' entailed a new analysis of *like*), but there are no lengthy drag chains recorded so far which do not depend on the intervention of language-specific novelties. These phenomena are ubiquitous and indispensable to keep the mill of linguistic change turning, but they do not necessarily cast light on grammatical theory and are probably beyond grammatical explanation.

## 12.8. Conclusion

I have discussed some issues which arise as syntactic change is viewed as manifesting changes in individual grammars, where a grammar is a representation of a person's mature linguistic capacity: these debates concern the nature of the parametric change and how the new parameter setting might have been triggered. For some changes, particularly in the history of English, there is now a substantial body of literature, much of it in journals like *Linguistic Inquiry* and *Natural Language and Linguistic Theory* alongside articles about the implications of Chinese anaphors for the binding theory; this is quite appropriate, but a recent development. Our database has been greatly enriched to include Old Iranian (Haider & Zwanziger 1984), Irish (Disterheft 1984), Swedish (Platzack 1982), Medieval and Modern Greek (Joseph 1983), Kru (Marchese 1984), and much more. There is much scope for work along these lines on the history of various Romance languages, given a rich historical record and detailed accounts of parametric variation among Modern French, Italian, Portuguese, Spanish etc.; studies like Pearce (1985) provide a good foundation. There are also particular areas of grammar which have provoked interesting cross-language diachronic work, such as clitics (Steele 1977; Jeffers & Zwicky

1980; Kempchinsky 1983, etc.). The study of syntactic change is an emerging field, beginning to yield implications for theories of UG and explanations for the kind of clusters of phenomena that are being discovered in the history of many languages.

The nature of the debates has changed enormously over the last ten years, and now diachronic syntax can be viewed as a particular form of comparative syntax, casting light on the ways in which linguistic systems can vary. The particular interest of diachronic work lies in the minimality of the variation, by which a small change in trigger experiences leads sometimes to a new parameter fixing. This potentially allows some insight on the nature of the trigger experience, the least studied of the three components of models of language acquisition (1). This in turn has cast new light on the history of the languages investigated. However, progress has been possible only where hypotheses are based on adequate and properly interpreted records, and there is no reason to expect that to change.

*REFERENCES*

Bennett, P. 1979. Observations on the transparency principle. *Linguistics* 17: 843–61.
Bennett, P. 1980. English passives: a study in syntactic change and relational grammar. *Lingua* 51: 101–14.
Besten, H. den 1983. On the interaction of root transformations and lexical deletive rules. In W. Abraham (ed.) *On the formal syntax of the Westgermania.* Amsterdam: Benjamins.
Bickerton, D. 1984. The language bioprogram hypothesis. *Behavioral and Brain Sciences* 7, 2: 173–203.
Carlson, A. 1978. A diachronic treatment of English quantifiers. *Lingua* 46: 295–328.
Chomsky, N. 1981. *Lectures on government and binding.* Dordrecht: Foris.
Coopmans, P. 1983. Review article on B. Comrie (1981) *Language universals and linguistic typology. Journal of Linguistics* 19: 455–73.
Coopmans, P. 1984. Surface word order typology and universal grammar. *Language* 60: 55–69.
Disterheft, D. 1984. Irish complementation: a case study in two types of syntactic change. In Fisiak (1984).
Dresher, B. E. & Hornstein, N. 1979. Trace theory and NP movement rules. *Linguistic Inquiry* 10: 65–82.
Evers, A. 1984. Clause union in French and German. Rijksuniversiteit Utrecht. ms.
Fischer, O. C. M. 1983. The demise of the OE impersonal construction. *Journal of Linguistics* 19: 337–68.
Fischer, O. C. M. & van der Leek, F. C. 1981. Optional vs radical reanalysis: mechanisms of syntactic change. *Lingua* 55: 301–49.
Fisiak, J. (ed.) 1984. *Historical syntax.* Trends in Linguistics, no. 23. The Hague: Mouton.
Friedrich, P. 1975. *Proto-Indo-European syntax. Journal of Indo-European Studies* monograph no. 1. Hattiesburg.
Greenberg, J. H. 1966. Some universals of grammar with particular reference to the order of meaningful elements. In J. H. Greenberg (ed.) *Universals of language.* Cambridge, MA: MIT Press.
Grimm, J. 1848. *Geschichte der deutchen Sprache*, vol. 1. Leipzig: Weidmannsche Buchhandlung.
Haider, H. & Zwanziger, R. 1984. Relatively attributive: the 'ezāfe'-construction from Old Iranian to Modern Persian. In Fisiak (1984).

321

Harris, A. 1980. On the loss of a rule of syntax. In Traugott, Lebrum & Shepherd (1980).

Janda, R. 1981. A case of liberation from morphology into syntax: the fate of the English genitive marker *-(e)s*. In B. B. Johns & D. R. Strong (eds.) *Syntactic change*. Natural Language Studies, no. 25, Department of Linguistics, University of Michigan.

Jeffers, R. & Zwicky, A. 1980. The evolution of clitics. In Traugott, Lebrum & Shepherd (1980).

Jespersen, O. 1928. *A modern English grammar*, part III. London: Allen & Unwin.

Joseph, B. 1983. *The synchrony and diachrony of the Balkan infinitive: a study in areal, general, and historical linguistics*. London: Cambridge University Press.

Kempchinsky, P. 1983. Some considerations on the evolution of the Spanish clitics. UCLA. ms.

Klima, E. 1964a. Studies in diachronic transformational syntax. Doctoral dissertation, Harvard University.

Klima, E. 1964b. Relatedness between grammatical systems. *Language* 40: 1–20.

Koopman, H. 1984. *The syntax of verbs*. Dordrecht: Foris.

Koopman, H. 1985. The genesis of Haitian: implications of a comparison of some features of the syntax of Haitian, French and West-African languages. Université du Québec à Montréal. ms.

Kroch, A. 1985. Review of Romaine (1982). *Language* 61: 698–704.

Lass, R. 1980. *On explaining language change*. London: Cambridge University Press.

Leffel, K. G. & Miller, D. G. 1985. Personalization in Old and Middle English: some implications of and for government and binding. University of Florida. ms.

Lehmann, W. P. 1974. *Proto-Indo-European syntax*. Austin: University of Texas Press.

Li, C. N. (ed.) 1975. *Word order and word order change*. Austin: University of Texas Press.

Li, C. N. (ed.) 1977. *Mechanisms of syntactic change*. Austin: University of Texas Press.

Lieber, R. 1979. The English passive: an argument for historical rule stability. *Linguistic Inquiry* 10: 667–88.

Lightfoot, D. W. 1974. The diachronic analysis of English modals. In J. M. Anderson & C. Jones (eds.) *Historical linguistics: proceedings of the First International Conference on Historical Linguistics*. Amsterdam: North-Holland.

Lightfoot, D. W. 1979a. *Principles of diachronic syntax*. London: Cambridge University Press.

Lightfoot, D. W. 1979b. Review article on Li (1977). *Language* 55: 381–95.

Lightfoot, D. W. 1980. Sur la reconstruction d'une proto-syntaxe. *Langages* 60. English version in P. Ramat (ed.) 1980. *Linguistic reconstruction and Indo-European syntax*. Amsterdam: Benjamins; also in I. Rauch & G. F. Carr (eds.) 1983. *Language change*. Bloomington: Indiana University Press.

Lightfoot, D. W. 1981a. A history of NP movement. In C. L. Baker & J. McCarthy (eds.) *The logical problem of language acquisition*. Cambridge, MA: MIT Press.

Lightfoot, D. W. 1981b. Explaining syntactic change. In N. Hornstein & D. W. Lightfoot (eds.) *Explanation in linguistics*. London: Longman.

Lightfoot, D. W. 1981c. A reply to some critics. *Lingua* 55: 351–68.

Lightfoot, D. W. 1982. *The language lottery: toward a biology of grammars*. Cambridge, MA: MIT Press.

Lightfoot, D. W. 1985. The child's trigger experience. University of Maryland. ms.

Lightfoot, D. W. 1986. Creoles, triggers and universal grammar. In C. Duncan-Rose *et al.* (eds.) *Rhetorica, pragmatica, syntactica: a festschrift for R. P. Stockwell*. London: Croom Helm.

Marchese, L. 1984. Exbraciation in the Kru language family. In Fisiak (1984).

Meillet, A. 1937. *Introduction à l'étude des langues indo-européennes*. Paris: Hachette.

Mitchell, B. 1979. F. Th. Visser, *An historical syntax of the English language*: some caveats concerning Old English. *English Studies* 60: 537–42.

O'Neil, W. 1982. Simplifying the grammar of English. In J. Anderson (ed.) *Language form and language variation: papers dedicated to Angus McIntosh*. Amsterdam Studies in the Theory and History of Linguistic Science, vol. 15. Amsterdam: Benjamins.

Pearce, E. 1985. Language change and infinitival complements in Old French. Doctoral dissertation, University of Illinois.

Pintzuk, S. & Kroch, A. 1985. Reconciling an exceptional feature of Old English clause structure. In J. Faarland (ed.) *Germanic linguistics: papers from a symposium at the University of Chicago*. Indiana University Linguistics Club.

Platzack, C. 1982. Three syntactic changes in the grammar of written Swedish around 1700. University of Stockholm. ms.

Posner, R. 1985. Diachronic syntax – free relatives in Romance. *Journal of Linguistics* 21: 181–9.

Rivero, M.-L. 1984. Diachronic syntax and learnability: free relatives in thirteenth-century Spanish. *Journal of Linguistics* 20: 81–129.

Rizzi, L. 1982. *Issues in Italian syntax*. Dordrecht: Foris.

Roberts, I. G. 1985. Agreement parameters and the development of English modal auxiliaries. *Natural Language and Linguistic Theory* 3, 1: 21–58.

Romaine, S. 1982. *Socio-historical linguistics: its status and methodology*. London: Cambridge University Press.

Russom, J. H. 1982. An examination of the evidence for OE indirect passives. *Linguistic Inquiry* 13: 677–80.

Safir, K. 1981. Inflection-government and inversion. *The Linguistic Review* 1:417–67.

Sankoff, G. & Laberge, S. 1973. On the acquisition of speakers by a native language. *Kivung* 6: 32–47.

Singler, J. 1984. Comments on Bickerton's 'Creoles and UG: the unmarked case?' Paper presented at winter meeting of the Linguistic Society of America, Baltimore.

Smith, N. 1981. Consistency, markedness and language change: on the notion 'consistent language'. *Journal of Linguistics* 17: 39–54.

Spamer, J. B. 1979. The development of the definite article in English. *Glossa* 13: 241–50.

Steele, S. 1977. Clisis and diachrony. In Li (1977).

Steever, S., Walker, C. & Mufwene, S. (eds.) 1976. *Diachronic syntax*. Chicago: Chicago Linguistic Society.

Szemerényi, O. 1985. Recent developments in Indo-European linguistics. *Transactions of the Philological Society* 1–71.

Traugott, E. 1969. Toward a grammar of syntactic change. *Lingua* 23: 1–27.

Traugott, E., Lebrum, R. & Shepherd, S. 1980. (eds.) *Papers from the 4th International Conference on Historical Linguistics*. Amsterdam: Benjamins.

Visser, F. Th. 1973. *An historical syntax of the English language*, Part 3, second half. Leiden: Brill.

Warner, A. 1982. *Complementation in Middle English and the methodology of historical syntax*. University Park: Pennsylvania State University Press.

Warner, A. 1983. Review article on Lightfoot (1979a). *Journal of Linguistics* 19: 187–209.

# 13 Morphological change*

*Stephen R. Anderson*

## 13.0. Introduction

Only a few years ago, Lightfoot (1979) could correctly note that a very substantial part of what passes for the study of syntactic change in the generative literature is really concerned with change in morphological rather than syntactic properties. A complementary observation could also be defended: much of the literature on phonological change is similarly devoted to essentially morphological problems. This state of affairs doubtless derives from the early generative program of reducing word structure either to syntax or to phonology, but in any case, the revival of synchronic morphology as a viable object of enquiry calls for corresponding study of the nature of change in morphological systems. There is, furthermore, the possibility, familiar from the study of change in phonology and in syntax, that our understanding of the internal dynamics of morphological systems will be enhanced by a study of the paths along which they change. Like an animal standing against the background of a forest, the outlines of a grammar can be thrown into sudden relief when something changes.

### 13.0.1. Morphological change and synchronic morphology

An understanding of change in the word formation principles of language can serve another function as well, assisting in the development of a genuinely explanatory theory of synchronic morphology.

Contemporary linguists are concerned (probably as never before) to find theories of linguistic structure that are not only adequate to the description of all possible human languages, but sufficiently constrained to provide an interesting and substantive understanding of just what systems are possible. On the other hand, recent developments (especially in the study of syntax) make it clear that explanatory theories of a particular domain are often to be derived not solely from the properties of that domain in itself, but also

* This work was supported in part by grant #BNS-84-18277 from the National Science Foundation.

324

from the way its facts and principles interact with the content of other domains. Allowing one part of the grammar to 'overgenerate' in the context of constraints imposed by its interaction with other areas often makes it possible to bring order and coherence to each independently – order and coherence that would be impossible if the principles determining the range of possible phenomena in each part of the grammar had to be limited to statements internal to that domain alone. Such a modular conception of grammar thus seems in many cases the only path to a constrained account.

In the study of morphology, we can apply this insight to a fundamental question: what formal realizations can morphological categories have? An adequate theory should limit the class of morphological operations to those actually possible in natural languages; and one widely advocated program for attaining this goal claims that all morphology can be described as affixation. If true, this would be a very substantial result, but there is good evidence that some morphological categories in some languages are expressed by replacements (*ablaut*), deletion, metathesis, and other non-affixal operations on word form (see Chapter 6 in this volume). If this conclusion entails the full power of 'the extremely rich transformational notation' (McCarthy 1981: 373), we are left without an account of why only a rather limited subset of possibilities is in fact attested. It would of course be possible to impose some set of constraints on a transformational formalism to exclude non-occurring rule types, but there is little ground for the hope that these would be especially interesting or reducible to some common underlying principle.

That synchronic morphology ought actually to admit of a wide range of rule types, however, is suggested by the fact that many of the sorts of permutations, deletions, counting operations, etc. which every morphologist feels the theory ought to prohibit actually arise in the rules of secret languages or language games. Language game evidence is quite generally appealed to in phonological and morphological discussion, for the reason that it often illustrates phonological circumstances that do not arise under 'normal' conditions. The rules of such systems can evidently be embedded into the morphological and phonological system of a language; and since this occurs in a wide range of literate and nonliterate linguistic communities alike, it is not possible simply to write it off as an artificial, secondary phenomenon. But if the range of possible word formation rules must accommodate those illustrated by language games, it is clear that constraints stopping much short of a 'transformational' formalism will not suffice.

Faced with a conflict between the apparent observational inadequacy of a purely affixational theory of morphology and the apparent over-richness of an unconstrained transformational theory, the possibility arises that the solution to the problem of accounting for what is found in the morphology of natural languages does not lie entirely within the synchronic theory of morphology itself. Following lines first made explicit by Baudouin de Courtenay and Kruszewski (Anderson 1985), we can see the various types of rule within a grammar as related historically. Many phonological rules are historical reflexes of earlier phonetic rules; and much morphology reflects earlier 'pure' phonology.[1] If such evolution is in fact characteristic of natural language development, it might be illuminating to view the set of possible morphological rules as constrained in an indirect way: as a function of the set of processes in other parts of the grammar which could potentially be morphologized, together with the set of possible morphologizations.

From this point of view, a process which, for example, exactly interchanges the first and last consonant of a word, no doubt a possible rule in a language game, need not be ruled out by synchronic morphological theory, if it can be shown that there is no way for such a rule to arise naturally in a language. The failure of such rules to occur in the morphologies of natural languages would then be attributed to the fact that there is no possible phonological (or syntactic) rule that could give rise to it, in light of the kind of transformations that morphologization effects. Exactly such an explanation is suggested, indeed, by Janda (1984) for the comparative rarity of morphologically conditioned rules of metathesis. If the most nearly 'explanatory' theory of the content of synchronic morphologies is thus to be found in their inter-relation with diachronic processes, the study of morphological change acquires an importance well beyond its interest as an object in itself.

## 13.0.2. Aspects of change in morphology

The conventional division of morphological structure into questions of morphotactics and allomorphy provides a convenient point of departure for organizing the study of morphological change. If morphological properties of individual languages are at least in part the end products of changes affecting regularities that originate elsewhere in the grammar, facts about allomorphy are readily seen as stemming from the phonology of earlier stages of a language. In parallel fashion, facts about morphotactics can be seen as the morphological reflexes of originally syntactic structures: indeed, morphotactics is often referred to precisely as '(word-)internal syntax'. Of course, we have by no means demonstrated that all of morphology can be traced back ultimately either to phonetics/phonology or to syntax,[2] and

---

[1] Consider the evolution of *umlaut* in Germanic languages, for example, from an original low-level assimilation of vowel quality to a phonologized change of vocalic identity, at one point a predictable concomitant of certain suffix vowels but later a morphologized effect which serves in some cases as the sole marker of a category (e.g. German *Vater* 'father'; pl. *Väter*).

[2] Although that reduction is not completely implausible, considered as a long-term program which would consolidate the explanatory value of the results that can be achieved in this area.

morphologization of such facts certainly does not exhaust the set of morphological changes. Morphological systems, once established, are not static, but can themselves evolve into new systems. We can therefore identify at least three distinguishable sources for changes leading to morphological regularities: the phonology, the syntax, and the morphology itself. Accordingly, the sections that follow will be concerned with the morphologization of phonological rules, the morphologization of syntactic structures, and change within the morphology itself. First, however, the assumptions about synchronic morphological organization that underlie the present chapter must be briefly outlined.

## 13.0.3. Synchronic assumptions

For the sake of explicitness, we sketch here without justification a set of assumptions about morphology which will be adopted in the discussion to follow, though little in succeeding sections depends crucially on the specifics of this picture. For further details and justification, see Chapter 6 of this volume, and references there.

The central component of a grammar for the purposes of its morphology is the *lexicon*. This contains a list of stems (uninflected words); for greater precision we can refer to this list as the *dictionary*, to distinguish it from other aspects of the lexicon. The stems in the dictionary each have a phonological form, semantic properties, and syntactic properties of various sorts (word class, subcategorization features, and perhaps others). The entries in the dictionary are further organized into paradigms, or *lexemes* (in the terminology of Matthews 1972 and others). In the simplest case, a lexeme will consist of a single stem, identified simply by word class; but often (when some inflected forms of a word or their properties cannot be predicted from a single stem, taken together with the rules of the language) more than one stem will appear as part of the same lexeme. In that case, each stem will be associated with a specification of its morphosyntactic properties, and the operation of lexical insertion is constrained to choose that stem from within the paradigm which is most specifically characterized, consistent with the requirements of the position in which it is to appear. The semantic and syntactic properties of stems that are part of the same lexeme are shared across the lexeme.

In addition to the dictionary, the lexicon also contains several sets of rules. Two of these are specifically morphological in character. A set of 'redundancy rules' (in the sense of Jackendoff 1975) relate lexical items to one another, describing the derivational or incompletely productive morphology. These rules characterize the relations among items listed individually in the dictionary; they also serve as the basis for the productive creation of new words. In addition, a set of inflectional rules operate on pairs $\{S, M\}$ consisting of a stem $S$ (either taken from the dictionary or the result of applying previous rules) and the morphosyntactic representation $M$ of the position in a syntactic structure where it is to appear. These rules develop the (productive) inflection of lexical stems.

Finally, the lexicon contains a set of phonological rules which apply as suggested in the theory of lexical phonology (Kiparsky 1982; Kaisse & Shaw 1985): stems in the dictionary are subject to phonological modification by word formation rules in so far as their properties are partially predictable, and words resulting from the application of morphological processes are subject to adjustment by phonological rules to the extent morphological processes create configurations meeting their structural descriptions. The morphological and the phonological rules may be further organized into a series of levels or strata, with the rules of each level applying fully before the rules of later levels.

A further relevant property of the morphology is the possibility that not only words, but also phrases have 'morphological' properties that are realized by rule. The phrasal properties in question include syntactically determined ones, such as the features of verbal arguments, tense, definiteness or possessors of NPs, etc., as well as less syntactic, more 'meaningful' ones. As a class, the phonological realizations of these phrasal properties are referred to as the (special) clitics of a language. The formal similarities between word affixes (as well as other kinds of word level morphology) and special clitics will play a role in the discussion below.

## 13.1. The morphologization of phonological rules

Principles of allomorphy, governing the appearance of the 'same' morphological element in phonologically distinct forms in different words, can be divided into several types. Sometimes the factors influencing the choice of one variant over another are purely phonological (as in the variants of the English regular plural ending); sometimes they depend on the identity of specific neighboring formatives (as when the final segment of *evade* is devoiced before *-ive* in *evasive*); and sometimes they are matters of arbitrary lexical suppletion (as in the case of *were* as the past form of *are*). It is hardly a novel suggestion that most if not all cases of morphologically or lexically determined variation can be traced historically to the effects of originally phonological rules.[3] The reanalysis of phonological rules as morphologically

---

[3] Among the exceptions to the claim that 'allomorphic' variation has diachronic phonological origins are (a) instances in which analogical reformation internal to the morphology has resulted in variation; and (b) instances in which the paradigms of two or more originally distinct forms have been blended into a single internally suppletive paradigm. It is at least worth exploring the possibility that the range of such exceptions can be narrowly limited, and the individual subtypes studied substantively enough to avoid

determined is thus a fundamental kind of change affecting morphology. In discussing such changes, we need to clarify two aspects: the mechanisms and motivations underlying the change itself, and its consequences for the properties of the rule.

## 13.1.1. The mechanism of morphologization

A hundred years ago, the Polish linguists Jan Baudouin de Courtenay and Mikołaj Kruszewski (Anderson 1985: ch. 3) hypothesized that phonological alternation has its origins in low-level, largely mechanical 'anthropophonic' (or as we would say today, purely phonetic) variations. These variations may at some point assume sufficient prominence for speakers as to be interpreted as governed by the system of the language rather than by the exigencies of articulation and acoustics, and as a result become phonological rules. As new phonological rules arise within the same language, obscuring the effects of others, the extent to which earlier ones remain phonetically motivated generalizations about the structure of surface forms declines: the earlier rules become increasingly *opaque* (in the sense of Kiparsky 1973 and elsewhere). As new generations of speakers confront the task of learning the language, they continue to look for phonological bases for variation, but increasing opacity may obscure this sufficiently that a set of morphological conditions is more accessible. At this point, the change effected by the rule may remain the same, but it is now interpreted as a fact about morphological categories rather than about phonological configurations. Morphologization of the rule has taken place.

On this view, the study of the process of morphologization is largely concerned with the development of opacity in phonological rules. The literature on this topic is considerable, and considerations of space preclude a serious review of it here. Several instructive examples are discussed in Wurzel (1980), specifically in connection with the conditions of morphologization; we summarize one of them here.

One of the nominal declensions of proto-Germanic was the class of *s*-stem, which displayed a paradigm like that of (1):

(1)      *Singular*       *Plural*

| | *Singular* | *Plural* |
|---|---|---|
| *Nom.* | lamb+iz | lamb+iz+ō |
| *Gen.* | lamb+iz+aza | lamb+iz+om |
| *Dat.* | lamb+iz+ai | lambz+iz+omoz |
| *Acc.* | lamb+iz | lamb+iz+ō |

In this paradigm, the element /+iz/ appears as a stem extension, present

evacuating the explanatory value which the theory of morphological change has for an understanding of the nature of synchronic systems.

in the lexical entry of such nouns as a characteristic of their membership in the set of *s*-stems.

A number of phonological changes affected these forms. Final /z/ was lost after unstressed syllables, affecting the nominative and accusative singular forms in (1). Later, final short /i/ was lost after heavy syllables (i.e. those containing a long vowel or ending in a cluster). Other changes yield the following paradigm for the pre-Old High German period:

(2)      *Singular*      *Plural*

| | *Singular* | *Plural* |
|---|---|---|
| *Nom.* | lamb | lamb+ir+u |
| *Gen.* | lamb+ir+as | lamb+ir+o |
| *Dat.* | lamb+ir+a | lamb+ir+um |
| *Acc.* | lamb | lamb+ir+u |

In (2), the stem formant (now /+ir/) only appears in some of the surface forms of the paradigm, due to the operation of phonological rules. Among these is the rule dropping final short /i/, which is rendered opaque by a subsequent process that shortens final long /ī/ to yield e.g. *gasti* from earlier *gastī*. The rule dropping final short /i/ also generalized to apply after light syllables as well as heavy syllables, which made it seriously opaque, since short /i/'s were thus lost in so many places as to be difficult to recover. Many of the forms originally involving such loss were simply reanalyzed with no underlying /i/. The /i/-loss rule is still involved in the paradigm of (2), but it applies in the same set of cases as the rule deleting final /z/ (now /r/). As a result, the motivation for separating the two rules disappears, and they are replaced by a single rule:

(3) $ir \rightarrow \emptyset / VC_0 \underline{\quad} \#$

Such a reduction of two rules to a single rule that achieves the same effect in one step is called 'rule telescoping' (Wang 1968). It contributes to the opacity of a rule to the extent that it takes it further from its phonological basis, and renders it applicable only to a limited set of specific morphological elements.

Further changes affecting the forms of interest here involved the loss of final short /u/ and the reduction of certain unstressed vowels to schwa (usually written *e*). This resulted in the following early Old High German forms:

(4)      *Singular*      *Plural*

| | *Singular* | *Plural* |
|---|---|---|
| *Nom.* | lamb | lamb+ir |
| *Gen.* | lamb+ir+es | lamb+ir+o |
| *Dat.* | lamb+ir+e | lamb+ir+um |
| *Acc.* | lamb | lamb+ir |

In this paradigm, application of rule (3) is no longer transparent, since final

/ir/ now appears in the nominative and accusative plural (where it was formerly protected from loss by the /u/'s that have now disappeared from the surface form). Since there is no longer an evident phonological generalization to appeal to, it is simpler to state the generalization as a morphological one describing where /ir/ appears:

$$(5)\quad \emptyset \rightarrow ir \left[ \begin{array}{l} +\text{Plural} \\ \left\{ \begin{array}{l} +\text{Genitive} \\ +\text{Dative} \end{array} \right\} \end{array} \right] \text{ (in certain nouns)}$$

The replacement of a rule like (3) by one like (5), which performs the inverse change in a set of environments that are effectively the complement of those of the first rule, is called 'rule inversion' (Vennemann 1972), a process which contributes to the opacity of a (phonological) rule by making its change phonologically more arbitrary. In the present case, the inversion accompanies a reanalysis of the rule's environment as morphological. The morphologization of the rule at this stage is confirmed by its subsequent evolution: the complex disjunction in (5) is simplified to insert /ir/ only in plurals, yielding the following Old High German paradigm:[4]

(6)

| | Singular | Plural |
|------|----------|--------------|
| Nom. | lamb | lemb+ir |
| Gen. | lamb+es | lemb+ir+o |
| Dat. | lamb+e | lemb+ir+um |
| Acc. | lamb | lemb+ir |

The loss of /ir/ from the genitive and dative singular forms has no purely phonological explanation, but constitutes a simplification on the view that the rules affecting this formative have been morphologized.

The general mechanisms illustrated here include rule telescoping and inversion, and the development of opacity in phonological processes through their interaction with other rules. All of these make an originally phonological condition more arbitrary and difficult for the learner to discover, and thus increase the appeal of a morphologically based rule. As such, they contribute to the morphologization of rules in numerous cases.

Accepting morphologization as a type of change, we can ask whether such changes are always categorial and complete or whether they are sometimes only partial. There are two senses in which morphologization might be partial: it might simply involve the addition of some morphological conditions to the rule, resulting in a 'morphologically conditioned phonological rule'; or it might involve the division of the rule into two (or more)

---

[4] The appearance of umlauted *e* from *a* in the plural forms in (6) is an additional innovation at this point which is not directly relevant to the matters under discussion here.

separate processes, some affecting morphologically characterized environments and some remaining purely phonological. We will reject the first possibility in the following section; but there is good reason to believe that a phonological environment for a given change may persist even after some instances of the rule's application have been reanalyzed as morphologically determined.

The rule of *u*-umlaut in Icelandic, for example, was originally purely phonological in character:[5]

(7) $a \rightarrow \ddot{o} /$ ___ $C_0 u$

This rule still applies in Modern Icelandic in all instances where its phonological environment would be satisfied, except for forms in which the *u* which might trigger it is itself epenthetic (cf. Anderson 1974; Kiparsky 1984).

A number of *u*'s which originally triggered the rule were lost, in categories where their original presence is subsequently indicated only by the occurrence of umlauted stem vowels. Since there is no other evidence for these original *u*'s, they have been eliminated, and their effects produced by a new umlaut rule effecting the same change as that in (7) in certain morphological categories: the nominative and accusative plural of strong neuter nouns (e.g. *barn* 'child' pl. *börn*) and adjectives, and all cases except the genitive of singular feminine strong nouns (e.g. *öxl* 'shoulder,' gen. *axlar*, pl. *axlir*), among others. The fact that these cases have been morphologized is indicated by the fact that the umlauted vowel has spread into the genitives of some strong feminine nouns (e.g. *verzlun* 'shop,' gen. *verzlunar*, pl. *verzlanir*), where the ending *-ar* precludes phonological conditioning of (7). We can also note that a very few masculine nouns, whose singular endings are normally inconsistent with the operation of (7), also show the effects of a morphologized umlaut rule (e.g. *söfnuður* 'congregation,' gen. *safnaðar*, dat. *söfnuði*, acc. *söfnuð*). These are exactly the masculine nouns that might be expected to show a morphologically based similarity to the feminine paradigms, since they are all ones characterized by the (normally feminine) genitive ending *-ar* instead of the usual masculine genitive ending *-s*. Modern Icelandic thus has two distinct kinds of *u*-umlaut: purely phonological instances, governed by rule (7), and morphologized ones governed by rules not based on phonological form. The process of morphologization has affected only those cases in which the degree of opacity of a phonological solution was too great: those where the conditioning desinential *-u* could never surface, and thus was lost. Among the remaining cases, some phonological

---

[5] This rule originally had the effect of rounding the vowel *a* when a *u* followed in the next syllable. The product of this change is a vowel which is written *ö* in the modern Icelandic orthography. Note also that the product of *u*-umlaut in unstressed syllables undergoes a rule of vowel reduction to become *u* – which can in its turn cause the umlaut of a preceding syllable.

environments make (7) partially opaque (since it must apply before the insertion of epenthetic /u/ in forms like *hattur* 'hat' from underlying /hatt+r/), but not sufficiently so to provoke a more widespread morphologization.

Phonological rules are morphologized when other aspects of the grammar render them sufficiently opaque, or when they lose their basis as generalizations about phonological structure and come to describe the behavior of a few specific morphological elements instead. In this case, a morphological formulation of the conditions for an alternation is evidently highly accessible in language acquisition. Phonological rules can remain phonological even in the face of some limited amounts of opacity, however; and even when morphological conditions come to determine some applications of a rule, a parallel phonologically based generalization may remain part of the grammar.

### 13.1.2. The consequences of morphologization

When a phonological environment for a rule is replaced by a morphological one, this might have other consequences as well. In particular, in so far as we can establish differences in the formal properties of phonological and morphological rules, we might expect that a rule whose status changes would also change with respect to whatever relevant properties it displays. In fact, there is reason to believe that this is the case.

One difference between phonological and morphological rules concerns the interpretation of variables in their structural description. Though an adequate formulation has never been achieved, most phonologists would agree that phonological rules are subject to a constraint by which only the 'nearest' part of a form that is potentially subject to phonological change under the influence of some other part of the form can be directly affected by a rule: the effects of a change can propagate further across a form only in a stepwise fashion. One way of formulating this constraint is to require that the 'focus' and the 'determinant' of the rule be strictly adjacent on the relevant projection of the phonological content of the form.[6] Morphological rules, in contrast, typically affect segments in a form without regard to their 'adjacency' to some conditioning factor. We might expect, therefore, that when a rule becomes morphological it could thereby come to apply to segments in positions within a form that were inaccessible to the antecedent phonological rule.

Instances of such a situation can indeed be found. For example, in the early history of the Southern Bantu languages, there was evidently a rule dissimilating labials to palatals or velars before a following /w/ (Doke 1954). In the modern languages, however, this rule has been morphologized in

---

[6] For the terminology of this discussion, as well as a brief review of the issues, see Anderson (1982) and other literature cited there.

association with a few particular categories in which it was originally motivated phonologically – most commonly the passive, marked by the suffix *-wa*. As a result of this morphologization of the environment, the rule might now apply to some labial consonants that are not strictly adjacent to the suffix; and indeed, in Xhosa it applies to all non-root-initial labials within the stem to which the passive is attached (Howard 1972). Thus, from the stem *nqumamisa* 'bring to a stop,' the derivation of the passive form *nqunyanyiswa* involves the palatalization of two separate /m/'s, neither of which is adjacent to the 'determinant' passive suffix (or its constituent /w/). The extension of palatalization to such non-adjacent segments is apparently a concomitant of the rule's morphologization.

An interesting example is furnished by the pattern of vowel harmony principles in various dialects of Maltese (Puech 1978). In this language, original consonantal distinctions of pharyngealization have been neutralized, giving rise to vowel quality distinctions that have been propagated across words as a system of vowel harmony. Puech notes that the harmony systems vary subtly from dialect to dialect. Two parameters of these systems are of interest to us here. First, in some dialects the harmony is purely phonological, in that certain phonological vowels trigger it regardless of morphological factors. In other dialects, however, it is morphologically conditioned in that only root vowels are allowed to trigger harmony. Second, some dialects require the harmony to affect only vowels in syllables adjacent to ones containing a triggering segment, while in other dialects it is possible for a non-harmonizing vowel to intervene. Crucially, it is precisely in the dialects in which the harmony has been morphologized that non-adjacent vowels are allowed to be affected, in accord with the claim under examination here.

Let us now return to the question, raised above, of whether it is possible for the morphologization of a rule to be 'partial' in the sense of consisting simply of adding morphological conditions to a phonological rule. The implicit answer provided by most of the phonological literature, which makes generous use of 'morphologically conditioned phonological rules,' is that such a change is possible. Suppose we were to claim, in contrast, that rules must be categorically either phonological or morphological: what consequences could we expect? On the picture of morphology sketched in section 13.0.3 above, morphological (or word formation) rules specify unitary (if complex) structural changes that determine the formal reflections of morphological categories. Thus, if the same formal marker is found in several distinct categories, it is on this view introduced by distinct word formation rules. Consequently, if a change were morphologized so as to apply in a number of distinct morphological categories instead of in a unitary phonological environment, this would result in its formal fragmentation into a number of distinct rules, in so far as there is no property unifying the categories involved.

We might then expect that the fragmented morphologized reflexes of an originally unitary alternation could develop individual idiosyncrasies. Of course, such a development is not obligatory as a consequence of morphologization: in so far as the reflexes of a phonological rule continue to be formally uniform, this is simply a result of their uniform source coupled with lack of change. But if changes in the formal character of the rule occur in its application to individual categories, without generalizing across all of the related cases, this implies that the rule has in fact been divided into a number of distinct rules.

This is exactly what we find. The most extensively studied morphologized reflex of an originally phonological rule is surely German umlaut; and as has been noted (Robinson 1975; Janda 1982), this rule shows a clear tendency to develop individual peculiarities in its various instantiating categories which argue for the presence of a number of distinct, category-specific rules of umlaut. The same result can also be demonstrated from other systems in which a morphologized rule applies in diverse categories (Anderson 1986): each category corresponds, in principle, to a distinct word formation rule, and in consequence historical change can affect them individually. This is exactly what is predicted if we claim that morphologization involves replacement of a phonological environment by a morphological one (rather than merely adding morphological conditions to phonological ones), since that claim entails the fragmentation of morphologized alternations.

This conclusion goes directly counter to the scientific instincts of most linguists, but it is important not to let one's esthetics interfere with the appreciation of fact. If there are indeed a dozen or more distinct rules in German that involve the change called umlaut, we naturally want to capture what they have in common – and the pre-eminent way to do this is by having a single rule, triggered in a variety of environments. If there is no single rule of umlaut, however, as now seems clear, we must look to some other device to express what is common to umlaut. Of course, the similarities have a historical foundation, as noted above, but there is also a synchronic uniformity (even if only a partial one) to be described.

One way to describe such facts would be to admit a notion of 'metarules' which formalize redundancies over the word formation rules of a language. A rule of this sort would be a specification not of some particular word formation rule in the language, but rather of the type of possible change a word formation rule might perform: something with the content of 'the SD of a rule may involve the fronting of back vowels according to the following pattern: . . .' Such a theory of morphological metarules remains to be developed, but the class of process-like changes performed by word formation rules is not the only possible domain for their application. A language's discrete affixes may also fall into quite regular patterns, without thereby constituting a single rule. No one would be tempted to say that the English regular plural, 3rd person singular present, and possessive, or even the regular past and past participle, are instances of the 'same' rule, but the fact remains that all regular nominal and verbal inflection in English is carried out by means of affixes with the form /z/ or /d/ – a uniformity that ought perhaps to be expressed as a fact about the language's structure.

To return to the central topic, once a rule is morphologized in some environment, the result is a rule whose formal properties are those of a word formation rule, and not those of a purely phonological rule. The differences in the character of these two types of rule may thus effect additional changes in an alternation which undergoes morphologization.

## 13.2. The morphologization of syntactic structures

It is a commonplace of historical change that many morphological elements can be derived historically from originally independent words. Thus, the English ending *-hood* that forms nouns like *childhood*, *manhood*, *neighborhood*, etc. from other nouns was an independent word in Old English (*hād* 'state, rank, character'), which could be used as the second part of compounds. An originally syntactic collocation developed into a pattern of compounds, and the recurrent second element of these compounds was then reanalyzed as a derivational suffix. An originally syntactic structure has been morphologized, and the rule which describes the addition of this affix to certain stems is a historical reflex of that syntactic structure.

There are many differences, of course, between the morphologization of a phonological alternation and that of a syntactic construction. One is that in the phonological case, what changes is the formal expression of an existing category: by developing a rule $X \rightarrow Y/[+F_i]$ the formal expression of the category $[+F_i]$ is changed, but the morphological system (the set of morphological categories of the language) is not. The antecedent existence of $[+F_i]$, in fact, is usually essential if morphologization is to be possible at all. In contrast, the morphologization of syntactic constructions typically creates new morphological categories.

A straightforward example cited by Comrie (1980) is the expression of the notion 'along with (NP)' in several Uralic languages. In Finnish, this is expressed by the postposition *kanssa* added to the genitive form of the NP: *hyvän pojan kanssa* 'good-GEN boy-GEN with.' In this structure, the word *kanssa* immediately follows the head noun, but is clearly external to the NP: a modifying adjective agrees with the genitive case, and *kanssa* itself is not subject to vowel harmony (cf. *tytön kanssa* 'girl-GEN with,' not *\*tytön känssä*). In some related languages, however, the cognate of this word has been reanalyzed as a suffix. Thus, in the Kukkosi dialect of Veps, the suffix is *-kä* as in *lahse-ka* 'with the child,' which is also subject to vowel harmony (cf. *lehmä-kä* 'with the cow'). Finally, in some dialects of Karelian, the cognate element *-kela/kelä* has not only been reduced from an independent word to a suffix, but has also become a category in the case system, such that modifying adjectives agree with their head noun in the presence of this element (cf. *kolme-n-kela lapše-n-kela* 'with three children'). The grammatical category of the *comitative* has thus arisen from the reanalysis of an originally syntactic construction as a marker of inflectional morphology.

From the perspective either of American structuralism or of early generative grammar, a change from syntactic to morphological structure is no real change at all, since these theories treated morphology and syntax as essentially the same domain. The recognition that morphological structure has properties of its own, however, is as important in the area of the internal construction of words (internal 'syntax') as it is in the study of morphologically determined aspects of phonological form. It is thus important to clarify the nature and consequences of transitions from syntactic to morphological status.

### 13.2.1. Morphology as 'yesterday's syntax'

Undoubtedly, the strongest statement of the position that principles of the internal structure of words derive from earlier syntactic constructions is that of Givón (1971). Givón's aphorism that 'today's morphology is yesterday's syntax' was intended to provide a tool for syntactic reconstruction: if morphological structure provides a faithful but fossilized representation of earlier syntactic structure, that earlier syntax can be recovered directly. For example, while most of the modern Bantu languages have SVO as the dominant word order, they exhibit extensive systems of preverbal pronominal prefixes, including ones that refer to objects. Givón interprets this as evidence that the system of prefixes arose through cliticization of pronominal NPs to the verb – at a point when the dominant word order of the language was SOV. This claim is said to be confirmed by various other aspects of the morphology of modern Bantu languages, and leads Givón to reconstruct an earlier stage of Bantu syntax with SOV order instead of today's SVO.

The form of this argument is as follows: where a morphological pattern is at variance with the synchronic syntax of a language, it is to be interpreted as a relic of the syntax of an earlier stage. Note that it is a synchronically anomalous *pattern* which is claimed to represent an archaic state of affairs, not necessarily its particular current instantiations. Thus, it has been argued that English compounds like *nut cracker*, *truck driver*, etc. reflect an early OV stage of the language, but this certainly does not entail the assertion that *sky scraper*, *line printer*, *fuel injector*, etc. are Old English formations. The pattern of NV compounds is a synchronic fact of English, whatever its source, and it is used productively to form new compounds as well as to analyze lexical ones.

Unfortunately, it is impossible to identify all of 'today's morphology' with 'yesterday's syntax.' For one thing, not all affixes have a (relevant) source in syntactic material: for example, the ending *-ir* which marks plurality in the Old High German paradigm in (6) above is the reflex of material restructured for phonological and morphological reasons through rule inversion and simplification, rather than an original independent word meaning 'plural' or the like.

Even when we have reason to suspect that a morphological element does originate as a separate word, it may be that its present position does not reflect the earlier position of that word. In Fula (Anderson 1976a) for example, nouns are followed by a suffixed marker of their noun class, which we can see as going back to earlier pronominal elements that may have served as determiners. This is not because Fula comes from an earlier stage in which NPs had an internal N-DET (or N-PRO) structure, however. There are two indications of this: first, the noun class markers in modern Fula have a phonological effect on the *initial* consonant of the noun to which they are attached; and second, most of the cognate languages in the West Atlantic family have noun class prefixes, not suffixes. In fact, the historical development seems to have been as follows: an original set of prefixes (perhaps reflecting cliticized prenominal determiners) induced phonological changes in the stem-initial consonants. Later, as an innovation entirely within the morphology, the prefixal elements were duplicated at the end of the noun (a development attested in other noun class systems in Africa); and subsequently the prefixal copies in the CL-N-CL structure were reduced, leaving as a trace only their (now morphologized) phonological effects on the root-initial consonant. The result is a structure N'-CL (where N' is the noun stem N with the proper initial consonantal mutation) in which the linear position of the classifier element does not reflect the position of a syntactically independent word at any stage of its history. From such examples we can see that developments internal to the morphology can alter the relations among morphological elements within a word, thus obscuring their bearing on earlier syntactic states of affairs.

Even where the morphology does reflect earlier syntax without change, the construction thus reflected may not be *basic* syntax. Indeed, it would be amazing if morphological facts did give us privileged access to features such as (earlier) basic word order, given the difficulty of establishing this from a full complement of surface data concerning the synchronic state of an existing language. Since it is surely surface syntactic patterns that undergo morphologization if any do, our inferences about properties such as basic word order could never be any better than the rather uncertain guide this source of evidence can provide. Most significantly, however, a morphologized structure may have had specialized and non-'basic' properties even at the point it was reanalyzed, so that no inference from it to the properties of more general structures in earlier stages of the language is possible. A case of this sort is analyzed in Comrie (1980), where it is shown that the postverbal agreement markers of Buryat Mongolian reflect not an earlier VS order, but rather the fact that precisely unstressed dependents of a head (from which agreement markers as cliticized pronouns must be assumed to derive) can appear in post-head position in the language. The suffixed position of the agreement markers derives from the properties of a specialized structure, used when a dependent is unstressed, rather than from the syntactically motivated S(O)V order of basic sentence elements (which is clearly attested since well before the development of the verbal affixes in question).

An example relevant to this situation can be provided from the structure of several modern Polynesian languages (Chung 1978). Some of these, like Sāmoan, have a set of preverbal subject clitics, which appear as clitic elements following the sentence-initial tense marker and preceding the verb. On the other hand, full NP subjects appear strictly following the verb: often finally, and often directly after the verb, but never in preverbal position. Can we infer from this pattern, however, that Sāmoan once went through a stage with preverbal subjects, of which the pronominal clitic pattern is a historical remnant? Surely this would be unwarranted – and in any case, it is probably quite incorrect, since we have no reason to doubt that Sāmoan (or the language ancestral to it) was verb-initial at the point the subject pronoun pattern developed. Rather, what is going on in this instance is that the subject pronouns have been reanalyzed as sentential clitics, and as such have taken on the positional possibilities of such elements. It is well-known that 'second position' is a very common location for clitic elements, and this is precisely where we find the subject pronominal element. Its appearance in second position does not indicate that subject NPs were once preverbal: rather, once pronominal subjects had been interpreted as sentential clitics and not autonomous NPs, the position immediately following a sentence-initial element (i.e. second position within the clause) was one in which they could be realized. The properties of this special construction (exactly the type which is typically ancestral to affixes as the reflexes of independent words) show us nothing about the basic word order of verb and subject in earlier stages of the language.

These reservations make it clear that we cannot accept morphological structure uncritically as reflecting (earlier) syntactic structure. This does not at all mean we should abandon the search for syntactic bases for morphological form, however: in fact, exactly the opposite is true. There is every reason to believe that much morphology does in fact represent the reanalysis of earlier syntactic complexity, but since the relation between the two sorts of structure is not simple and direct, it is important to explore the principles involved in the process of morphologization. We take up this problem in one concrete domain in the following subsections. While this hardly exhausts the subject, it will reveal some important principles relevant to the theory of morphologization.

## The development of ergative morphology

A classical anomaly in the relation between morphology and syntax is the existence of *ergative* languages, in which the same morphological category (the *absolutive*) appears to characterize the (notional) objects of transitive verbs and the subjects of intransitive verbs, as opposed to a distinct category (the *ergative*) which characterizes the subjects of transitive verbs only. In the examples below from Avar, the verbal agreement marker shows concord with the intransitive subject in (8a) and with the transitive object in (8b), but not with the transitive subject. The distinction between an unmarked absolutive and an overtly marked ergative NP follows the same lines:

(8) a. $\text{emen}_i$      roqove      $v_i$-us:ana
  $\text{father}_i(\text{ABS})$      home      $\text{he}_i$-returns
  'Father returns home'
  b. $\text{ins:u}_i\text{-c:a}$      $\text{ebel}_j$      $j_j$-ec:ula
  $\text{father}_i\text{-}(\text{ERG})$      $\text{mother}_j(\text{ABS})$      $\text{her}_j$-praised
  'Father praised mother'

The problem posed by such languages, of course, is that the categories apparently established by the morphology (absolutive and ergative) do not match those we expect to find in the syntax (subject and object). There seem to be two main alternatives: either the correspondence between syntactic and morphological categories is not one to one, or the syntactic relations relevant for ergative languages are not the familiar ones.

Once the appropriate domains of 'syntax,' 'morphoplogy,' and 'semantics' are properly delimited, it is reasonably clear (cf. Anderson 1976b) that with the important exception of a few Australian languages (notably Dyirbal), the syntactic evidence overwhelmingly favors the first of these possibilities. Genuinely syntactic principles, that is, systematically treat the NPs we expect to be subjects as constituting a unitary category regardless of the transitivity of the verb. These are the NPs that are possible antecedents for reflexives (and which cannot be reflexive themselves); it is this position in which the controlled PRO (or missing NP) of 'equi' constructions occupies; conjunction formation treats subjects as grammatically parallel (and distinct from objects) despite case-marking differences; switch-reference systems depend on identity of subjects, etc. We must conclude that the syntactic categories of ergative languages are like those of accusative languages, and that it is the morphology–syntax correspondence which is unusual.

There are a number of ways we could describe ergative morphology formally, but for concreteness let us assume the following account. Assume that 'agreement' is a rule of the syntax which copies the relevant set of features (in Avar, gender and number) from an agreeing NP into the morphosyntactic representation of the verb. Assume further that in languages with both subject and object agreement, the rule applies to these two positions in some determinate order: say object agreement first, then subject agreement. As a result, the (relevant parts of the) morphosyntactic representations[7] of (8a) and (8b) above will be:

(9) a. $\left[ +V, \begin{array}{c} +\text{masc.} \\ +\text{sg.} \\ i \end{array} \right]$

b. $\left[ +V, \begin{array}{c} +\text{masc.} \\ +\text{sg.} \\ i \end{array} \left[ \begin{array}{c} +\text{fem.} \\ +\text{sg.} \\ j \end{array} \right] \right]$

On the basis of these representations, we could say that the absolutive case is unmarked, and the ergative arises by the operation of a case-marking rule like (10):

(10) $NP_i \rightarrow [+\text{ERGATIVE}]$ (when properly governed[8] by) $[i[X]]$

By this rule, an NP which is co-indexed with the outer layer of a two (or more)-layer representation (i.e. a transitive subject) is marked ergative. The rule of agreement, on the other hand, operates on the inner layer of the representation: a marker ($v$- for masculine, $j$- for feminine, etc.) is introduced into the verb on the basis of the features present in the innermost layer of structure of its morphosyntactic representation. This will be the layer agreeing with the subject, if the verb is intransitive, or with the object, if transitive.

---

[7] The notion of a morphosyntactic representation is discussed in Chapter 6 of this volume. The internal structure of (9b) is a consequence of the layering principle suggested there.

[8] 'Proper government' may or may not be the correct way to refer to the relevant relation, which should be obvious in the current context. This depends on whether or not the agreement representation is actually constructed as a set of features on the phrasal node, and later inherited by the verb (as head of this constituent). These issues are orthogonal to our present concerns, and we ignore them here by simply calling the relation between an agreement representation and the NPs it indexes 'proper government'.

The point of this apparatus is to treat ergativity as a morphological phenomenon, rather than as syntactic.

We can now ask how such a system could arise. In principle, the generalization leading to a rule of ergative case marking could even result from a phonological change, it appears. Suppose a language with basic VSO order has a rule marking subjects with an ending *-s*, leaving objects unmarked. If this language now undergoes a phonological change by which final obstruents are lost before pause, this might affect (many) final *-s* markers on intransitive subjects, because these would also be sentence-final, but not on transitive subjects, where they would be followed by the object NP. The result might well lead to a reanalysis by which only transitive subjects are marked with *-s*, which would thus become an ergative marker rather than a nominative. We know of no example which exactly fits this scenario, though the historical development of ergativity in Chinook agreement comes close (Anderson 1977a).

A well-attested source for the development of ergative morphology, however, is in the reanalysis of earlier (syntactic) passive constructions. Note that in a passive sentence like *They were accosted by him on the way to the underground* we have all of the characteristics of 'ergative' morphology: the notional object of the (lexically) transitive verb *accost* bears the same case mark as an intransitive subject; the notional subject of *accost* has a special marker (the preposition *by* plus objective case); and the verb agrees with the notional object rather than with the subject. If we do not describe passive sentences in this way, it is because they are to be derived from active sentences by means of a rule which alters the grammatical relations of the argument NPs of the verb, making the notional object into the grammatical subject, etc. If we were to lose motivation for such a derivation, and still wanted to say that verbs like *accost* are transitive, the pattern of such passive sentences would no longer be distinguishable from that found in an ergative language. In essence, this is exactly what has happened in several unrelated language families: originally passive constructions have lost their relation to the putative underlying active forms, and as a result their surface form has been reanalyzed as ergative morphology rather than passive syntax.

A particularly well-documented case of this is found in Polynesian, as analyzed in Chung (1978). A language of this family displaying an ergative pattern is Tongan, whose sentences typically show the following pattern: transitive verbs, which may end in the suffix *-Cia* (for some lexically determined consonant C), mark their subject with the ergative particle *'e*. In conservative dialects, transitive objects and intransitive subjects are marked with the absolutive particle *'a*. There is no syntactically derived passive construction. In contrast, some related languages such as Maori show an accusative pattern of morphological marking, with a derived passive construction. Here active transitive sentences mark their objects with the particle *i*. Subjects, whether transitive or intransitive, are unmarked. In passive sentences, the verb is suffixed with (a form of) *-Cia*, the agent has the preposition *e*, and the notional object is the grammatical subject. The question for the history of Polynesian is whether the Tongan type or the Maori type is original. Chung (1978) shows clearly that it is the Maori pattern, since the following features can be reconstructed for proto-Polynesian:

(a) *-Cia* was originally a passive suffix for verbs.
(b) *i* was originally an accusative case marker, not a preposition.
(c) *e* was originally an agentive preposition, not a case marker.

Each of these points can be established by sound comparative technique, independent of the question of the evolution of case marking. Jointly, they establish that the properties of the Maori structural type are original; those of Tongan represent an innovation, consisting in the reanalysis of a passive structure as syntactically active. Note that transitive sentences are not *synchronically* passives: Chung shows that the verbs of such sentences are indeed transitive, not passive, and their agents are subjects, not oblique agent phrases.

The explanation of what has happened is apparently to be found in properties of the passive construction in Polynesian accusative languages like Maori. This has a much wider distribution than the English passive: it is much more common than the active in sheer numerical terms; it is obligatory in certain contexts, such as (nonreflexive) imperatives; and it is commonly used to mark the object of a transitive verb as 'affected' by the action. Apparently there is a strong preference for having the affected object (semantically, the *theme*) as the surface subject. If we imagine that this preference is quite old, and that in the history of languages like Tongan it rendered the passive effectively obligatory for a large class of structures, the corresponding active bases from which these passives were derived would simply have ceased to occur as surface forms. When that happened, the syntactically derived status of the 'passives' became opaque, and the formal markers of the construction were simply reinterpreted as the morphology of certain verbs and of case marking in transitive clauses.

## The correlation of case marking with aspect as a product of change

The development of ergative case marking from the reanalysis of an earlier passive construction reinterprets in diachronic terms the claim, common in traditional accounts of ergativity but now thoroughly discredited (cf. Anderson 1976b and references cited there), that ergative languages have (synchronically) 'passive' syntactic structures while only accusative languages have active ones. The temptation is to assume that such developments are always the source of ergative morphology, but this generalization would surely be an exaggeration: we have no evidence indicative of such an origin for many languages of this type, and some reasons for skepticism (such as the existence of productive passive constructions in ergative languages like Georgian). On the other hand, the historical source of ergativity in Polynesian is not an isolated case; and that provides us with the possibility of a historical account of a correlation which is (at least superficially) puzzling in purely synchronic terms.

As is well-known, many 'ergative' languages display ergative case marking only under some circumstances, with accusative patterns obtaining elsewhere. A particularly common variety of such 'split ergativity' is illustrated by languages in which ergative marking is confined to clauses whose main verb is marked for perfect aspect (or in some cases, for a tense form derived from an earlier perfect, as in many Indic languages where a modern past/nonpast distinction derives from an earlier perfect/imperfect one). From this frequently observed correlation, some have argued that the surface case-marking pattern of ergative languages is somehow especially suited or appropriate to the semantics of the perfect; but the nature of the connection remains elusive and essentially stipulative.

We would like to claim that the search for such a connection is based on a fundamental misunderstanding of the nature of the correlation to be explained. Ergativity shows up in perfects (or the reflexes of earlier perfects), not because of a particular synchronic affinity between the two, but rather because there are several ways in which aspectual distinctions between perfects and nonperfects tend to be created, and all of these happen to involve the generalization of constructions whose formal properties are 'ergative' in a new perfect, or 'accusative' in an innovated imperfect.

One example of languages with aspectually based split ergative systems is the Indic family. Originally, Indic (as represented by Sanskrit) had a full range of verbal inflectional marking for tense, aspect, and person. In particular, a set of personally inflected perfect aspect verbal forms was found. As an overall generalization about the development of verbal inflection in Indic, however (Bloch 1965), the personal forms were lost and replaced by alternative constructions. In the case of the perfect, the lost forms were supplied by a generalization of the originally passive periphrastic construction with the auxiliary verb 'be' and the participle in -*ta*. In this structure the 'goal' of a transitive verb appears not as object but as subject, and the verb's agent appears as an instrumental (hence oblique) phrase.

We may be in doubt about the semantic basis of a correlation between perfect aspect and ergativity, but there is no difficulty in seeing passives as semantically close to perfects. A passive presents the action from the perspective of the affected object, and thus, like a perfect, as already having taken place or been completed. As the original personally inflected verbal perfect forms disappeared from use, it was thus natural that their sense was supplied by passives. This generalization and alignment with an aspectual category, however, coupled with the simultaneous decline in the use of the personal active forms, led to a loss of the syntactic connection between actives and passives, and the opacity of a synchronic derivation of the (original) passive from active was increased. As a result, just as in the Polynesian case, the formal properties of the 'passive' construction came to be regarded not as indicative of its derivation from something else, but simply as surface markers of structures containing a transitive verb – here with the added significance of marking perfect aspect. The result is a morphologically ergative pattern of case marking superimposed on an ordinary, underived active syntactic structure for the purpose of marking perfect aspect. This was thereby opposed to the morphologically accusative pattern found in the reflexes of the nonpassive constructions that gave rise to the imperfect forms of transitive verbs.

In languages like Hindi, the resulting aspectual distinction was reinterpreted as one of tense, and thus modern Hindi displays an ergative pattern in past tense clauses: the subject is marked with the particle *ne* (the reflex of an earlier agent marker), and the verb agrees with its object if transitive or with its subject if intransitive. This agreement pattern is exactly that of participle agreement in the pair of structures 'I am beaten (by him),' 'I am come' which historically underlie the past tense forms. That the NP not marked with *ne* in transitive clauses is indeed the object, however, and not the subject, is shown both by its syntactic behavior and by the fact that it is marked with the same particle *ko* when definite as appears with transitive objects in nonpast clauses. Similar (but not identical) facts obtain in a number of other modern Indic languages.

The development here is quite parallel to that in Polynesian: an original syntactically derived passive construction loses (or has reinterpreted) its connection with its presumptive syntactic source. Once it becomes isolated in this way, the morphological markers of the construction are analyzed *de novo* as merely the surface marking of the relevant structure. In Tongan, the structure is simply that of a transitive verb, while in Hindi and similar languages it is that of a past tense (*né* perfect) verb. The case marker is thus assigned by a rule like (11):[9]

(11) $[NP_i \rightarrow [+\text{ERGATIVE}]$ (when properly governed by) $[v+\text{perfect}, i[X]]$

---

[9] The agreement rule for this structure operates over representations like those in (8) above, causing a verb whose aspect is perfect (or in Hindi, whose tense is past) to show agreement with the NP whose features appear in the innermost layer of its morphosyntactic representation.

The important point is that there is no direct and intrinsic connection between ergativity and perfect aspect shown by this construction. It is simply the case that both are aspects of the passive, and when this is the source of an innovated perfect, it brings along its morphological characteristics as more or less incidental baggage.

In fact, there is another source for new perfects in other languages. While this source is completely unrelated to the passive, it happens coincidentally to be the case that it, too, leads to ergative morphology when reanalyzed as a perfect marker. As stressed by Benveniste (1952) and others, a language's verb expressing possession is frequently employed in the formation of a new perfect, as is indeed the case in the English construction *I have solved the problem of the origin of life.* Perhaps this development passes by way of a construction like *I have (got) the problem of the origin of life solved*, but in any event there seems to be an intrinsic connection between possession and perfectivity.

Now in fact, in many languages the expression of possession is by means of a periphrastic construction of the 'at me is a book' type found in Russian and elsewhere. When this structure serves as the basis for the creation of a new perfect (as in e.g., Breton), we would expect something like 'at me is the problem solved' to express 'I have solved the problem'; and of course the properties of this structure are precisely those of an ergative construction. The transitive subject appears in an oblique form (perhaps governed by a preposition); the transitive object appears in the subject (or nominative) case; and the inflected verb agrees with the transitive object. Benveniste argues that this is exactly the origin of ergative case marking in the (innovated) perfects of Old Persian, Classical Armenian, Egyptian, and some other languages.

When the derived or periphrastic status of this structure becomes obscured, the change that results is parallel to that deriving perfects from passives. If the original properties of the oblique possessor construction, once this comes to be employed for the expression of perfect aspect in non-possessive clauses, become opaque, the formal marks of the construction are reanalyzed as simply the morphological apparatus of the perfect. The importance of this development for our purposes is the fact that it is completely independent of the possibility of generalizing a passive to make a new perfect, but 'conspires' with that alternative in that both have the result of assigning ergative morphology precisely to the newly created perfect forms. In neither case, however, must we interpret this as resulting from some supposed affinity of perfect and ergative *per se*.

This conclusion becomes even clearer when we consider a third possible way by which languages can develop a distinction between perfect and imperfect, which has nothing whatsoever to do with the two sources considered thus far, but which happens to produce the same sort of morphological result. The development in question is attested in the history of Georgian. Here it was a new set of imperfect forms rather than a new perfect that was created; the newly created imperfects were associated with a morphological pattern of the accusative type, but since this took place in a language whose basic case-marking pattern was ergative, the result was again an aspectually based split ergative system of much the same (superficial) type as that of e.g. Hindi.

In Georgian, the verb can appear in one of a large number of tenses, divided according to their associated case-marking pattern (among other things) into three series. One of these, the misleadingly named 'perfect' series (actually a set of 'reportive' tenses, distinguished from the others in terms of source of information rather than aspect), we disregard here. What is of interest to us is the fact that case marking in the 'present' series of tenses is of the accusative type, while in the 'aorist' series it is usually described as being ergative. The distinction between the tenses of the 'present' and 'aorist' series is not presently reducible to a single semantic dimension of aspect (or anything else), but the facts of Old Georgian give us good reason to believe that these originally differed in that the 'present' tenses were imperfective while the 'aorist' tenses were perfective. In this case, the split ergative system cannot apparently be accounted for by deriving the pattern of the 'aorist' tenses from an earlier passive (or possessive) construction, since comparative evidence shows that the pattern associated with these tenses is in fact original, and it is the accusative pattern of the 'present' series that is an innovation.

In a paper of some years ago (Anderson 1977a), it was suggested (echoing earlier proposals in the traditional literature) that the construction found in the present series should be derived from original 'object demotion' structures. Many languages have a secondary construction for transitive verbs (sometimes, when this option is systematic, labeled 'antipassive') in which their direct objects appear in an oblique case (or in a prepositional phrase), and the verb is treated as intransitive. This structure indicates that the action referred to by the sentence was incompletely carried out, or that it affected the object only partially, etc. In English we have only lexicalized pairs (such as *John shot at his neighbor* vs. *John shot his neighbor*; *My wife likes to drink from my glass of wine* vs. *My wife likes to drink my glass of wine*, etc.), but in other languages this relation is quite systematically carried through. In some, indeed (e.g. Finnish), the distinction between such *partitive* marking of direct objects and normal accusative marking is (interestingly for our purposes here) used as a way to express the difference between imperfective and perfective aspect.

Let us imagine that Georgian was originally fully ergative, and that it had such an object demotion (or antipassive) construction. Now suppose that this construction came to be analyzed as the expression of imperfective aspect, as a consequence of its being used to describe incompletely carried out actions. In the resulting imperfectives, the subject of transitive verbs would be treated exactly as the subject of an intransitive, since detransitivization is exactly one of the properties of object demotion constructions. Furthermore, the notional direct object of such a detransitivized verb would be assigned a distinct marker (the appropriate oblique case or preposition), which could be interpreted as an accusative case. If the morphological properties of an object demotion construction were then reinterpreted as assigned to basic transitive clauses to mark imperfective aspect, the result would be that these clauses would be assigned an accusative pattern, in the context of a prevailing ergative pattern in perfective clauses.

Harris shows in considerable detail in a recent book (Harris 1985) that this scenario is essentially correct, but considerably oversimplified. For one thing, the actual case-marking pattern of the modern Georgian 'aorist' series is not ergative but 'active'; for another, marking objects as oblique (or deleting them) in Old Georgian did not result in detransitivizing the verb. Nonetheless, it can be shown that the 'active' pattern of Modern Georgian is itself an innovation, based on an original pattern that was ergative; and the absence of detransitivization is a concomitant of the innovated active system, not the original ergative one. When we place it correctly in time, the development hypothesized above from a (detransitivizing) object demotion construction to an accusative system for the marking of imperfective aspect is well supported. Harris shows that this development explains a wide variety of idiosyncratic and very specific properties of the morphological structure of the present series of tenses, and not only its broad outlines. As a result, there is little remaining doubt that split ergativity can arise (and has in fact arisen, in Georgian) through the reinterpretation of object demotion (antipassive) structures as the imperfective aspectual forms of normal clauses.

Such creation of accusatively marked imperfective forms in a language otherwise displaying ergative marking is obviously quite distinct from the creation of ergatively marked perfects in accusative languages; but the resulting split along aspectual lines is superficially the same. We have now seen three distinct ways of creating new aspectual forms (generalizing either passive or possessive structures to make a perfect; or generalizing object demotion structures to make an imperfect). For reasons internal to each of the three, the result in each case is a split in case marking by which ergativity is associated with the perfect and accusativity with the imperfect. The historical account makes the real basis of this correlation clear, however, and makes it unnecessary to hypothesize some intrinsic connection between the semantics of aspect and a semantic interpretation of case marking. The result is a much clearer focus on those properties of synchronic systems that may actually have a semantic basis.

## Opacity and the conditions for morphologization

In the discussion above we have seen several instances of a single development, consisting of the reinterpretation of originally derived or syntactically complex constructions, in which the morphological markers were straightforwardly correlated with syntactic categories, as syntactically simple, basic structures in which the original morphology is preserved but bears a more complex relationship to syntactic categories. Such changes, and the states they result in, make an important point: morphological evidence alone is insufficient to establish the 'basic' or 'derived' status of a construction, or the categories of syntactic structure to which its elements belong.

Traditional grammar viewed 'syntax' as a sort of 'applied morphology,' in which the (apparent) morphological categories were primary and the (covert) categories of syntactic structure were associated with these rather directly, as 'the uses of the nominative,' etc. Much subsequent discussion continues the implicit assumption that the correspondence between morphological and syntactic categories is a simple one, and it is thus quite important to emphasize that this is not true in the general case. Morphological marking often represents the accretion of complexity from many sources over time: the fact that these markers are assigned by rule on the basis of syntactic and lexical structure does not mean that the rules involved are simple ones.

In section 13.1.1 above, we suggested (following Baudouin de Courtenay and Kruszewski) that the principal mechanism involved in the morphologization of phonological rules is the development of opacity, or the loss of motivation for deriving a surface form from a more abstract underlying form by phonologically motivated principles alone. When the properties of surface forms are no longer manifestly correlated with apparent phonological generalizations, but are better aligned with morphological categories, it seems that linguistic change tends to emphasize this by replacing originally phonological rules (which happened to apply in some morphological categories and not others) with ones that operate directly in terms of the morphology. The morphologization of syntactic rules is in fact based on essentially the same principle.

In the examples we have seen above, and others, what happens is the following: originally, two constructions (active and passive, directly vs. obliquely transitive, etc.) are correlated in such a way as to motivate a syntactic derivation of one from the other or a lexical relation between two syntactically distinct structures. Subsequently, however, one construction comes to be used systematically (and the other systematically excluded) under conditions that define some structural category: the passive in (some) Polynesian languages is used wherever there is a directly affected object; the Indic periphrastic passive indicated perfect aspect; the oblique object construction in early Georgian was a marker of incompleted action (hence imperfective aspect), etc. The result is that in the relevant circumstances, the complementarity of the two (originally related) structures makes the syntactic derivation of one from the other less transparent. The resulting development consists in interpreting the surface form of one structure not as reflecting its derivation from the other, but rather as the overt marker of the category with which it is correlated – applied to a syntactic structure which is no longer motivated as derived from a non-basic source. This is simply the syntactic analog of morphologization as it results from the development of opacity.

Taking the account above quite literally, however, it would appear to predict that whenever a syntactic rule is obligatory (and thus excludes the related, underived structure from the environments in which it applies) this ought to lead to its morphologization – clearly just as wrong as a corresponding claim that any phonological rule which is not completely transparent must be morphologized.[10] In fact, both syntax and phonology appear to involve at least some rules that are obligatory and partially opaque; and while this character may indeed be a necessary condition for morphologization, it surely cannot be a sufficient one as well.

In order for some distribution of markers to be interpreted as assigned to a morphological category (rather than to a syntactically derived structure), there must be some category available to serve as the basis of morphologized rule. As a result, we would expect morphologization only in those cases where the obligatoriness of an originally derived structure coincides with some possible morphological category.

The significance of this condition can be seen by comparing similar linguistic systems, where morphologization has taken place in some but not others. In Anderson (1980) several families of American Indian languages are cited, in each of which a passive construction has become obligatory under certain circumstances. In some of these, the result has been morphologized. For instance in the Algonquian languages, an original passive has been reinterpreted either as part of the system of agreement marking in active clauses (as in Potawatomi: cf. Anderson 1977b) or as a marker of indefinite or inanimate subject forms. In Navajo, in contrast, there is no reason to believe that the obligatoriness of passivization under determinate conditions has

---

[10] This is essentially the position of 'natural generative phonology,' an extreme limitation on the possibility of abstract phonological structure which is generally regarded today as implausible. See Anderson (1985: ch. 13) for discussion.

provoked a reanalysis of the rule so that it no longer relates two distinct syntactic structures.

The key to the difference between these two cases lies in the conditions which govern passive in each language. In Algonquian, passive became obligatory for certain combinations of subject and object person and excluded for others: when 3rd person acts on 1st, for example, passive was required, while when 1st person acts on 3rd it was not possible. Since the circumstances in which the morphology of passive appeared to align straight-forwardly with the morphological categories of agreement, it was easy to reinterpret the morphology as simply part of the apparatus marking subject and object agreement. In Navajo, in contrast, the conditions of obligatory passivization are vastly more involved, and depend on an extensive cate-gorization of beings as relatively more autonomous in action or relatively less autonomous. Passive is required when a relatively lower actor on this hierarchy (an insect, for example) acts on a relatively higher being (a large animal or a human, for example). The intricacy of this classification defies reduction to a unitary morphological category, and thus morphologization has not taken place.

Some examples suggest that the category with which a morphologized rule is associated must be one which is already established in the language. Thus, in Nihtinat passive is obligatory for certain combinations of subject and object NPs in a way reminiscent of the Algonquian and Navajo systems. The Nihtinat classification of NPs apparently requires passive when the subject is inanimate and the object animate (as well as in certain person combinations), but does not further subdivide the class of animates in a quasi-continuous fashion as in Navajo. In order for passive to be morphologized, Nihtinat would only have to recognize a categorial distinction between animates and inanimates, which is certainly a possible morphological category, but one which does not otherwise function in this language. The rule has not in fact been morphologized (that is, clauses with passive form actually undergo a passive rule, rather than simply having appropriate morphology assigned to them), and we could attribute that to the absence of the relevant category of animacy in the language's morphology.

While plausible, however, this further strong requirement that the cate-gory in question be a pre-existing one cannot be correct, since in some cases the morphologization of a syntactic construction is precisely the mechanism by which a new category is created, as in the case of Indic perfects or Georgian imperfectives. The strongest absolute constraint on morphologiza-tion that seems tenable is that it must be possible to interpret the conditions of obligatoriness as at least a *potential* morphological category in order for morphologization to occur. This suggests the significance of research into the substantive range of possible morphological categories in natural languages, and on the extent to which parameters of an existing system determine the directions in which it can be extended.

## 13.2.2. Clitics and morphologization

The cases we considered above all involved fairly radical reinterpretations of the syntactic structure of a construction. Morphologization in these examples has preserved the surface form of words in the construction, but reinterpreted its structure as syntactically less opaque. A much more commonly cited type of change involving morphologization is rather less extreme, however. This is the reduction of originally independent words to the status of affixes, generally assumed to pass through a stage of cliticization.

The example of the comitative in Karelian, taken from Comrie (1980) and cited at the beginning of this section, is typical. In the form *kolme-n-kela lapše-n-kela* 'with three children,' the ending *-kela/-kelä*, originally an independent word meaning 'along with,' was argued to have become an inflectional affix on two grounds. First, since it is subject to word-internal vowel harmony, it has evidently lost its autonomy as a word; and second, since modifiers of nouns with this suffix take it as well, it is evidently functioning as the marker of a category determining modifier head agreement, a prototypical inflectional function. We must keep these two aspects of the development separate, since cliticization does not by itself imply reanalysis as an inflectional affix. English *is* and *has*, to take a trivial example, are clitic in examples such as *John's the one that's got a banana in his ear*, without our having any reason to believe that they have somehow become inflections on *John* and *that* respectively.

In the framework espoused here (see Chapter 6 of this volume), English *'s* representing *is* or *has*, is a *simple* clitic, whose clitic property is the purely phonological one of lacking the prosodic structure of an independent word. Indicative of this status is the fact that its position in the sentence is exactly the position of the related auxiliary verb. Other clitics, however, display syntactically unusual positioning, and must be accorded a different status. These *special* clitics we treat as 'phrasal affixes': material introduced into phrases by rules that are highly parallel to the affixation rules that operate on words.

On this basis, we can provide a straightforward account of the development of words into affixes through cliticization. Let us take as an example the (rather surprising) case of modern English *-n't*, which is argued in Zwicky & Pullum (1983) to have become an inflectional affix. Though its alternation with the full form *not* certainly predisposes us to treat this as at most a simple clitic form, Zwicky and Pullum show that it displays all of the characteristics of a word-internal affix: formal and semantic idiosyncrasy, defective paradigms, syntactic solidarity with its base, etc. On the other hand, it is equally clear that this element originates as the full word *not*, and thus can serve to exemplify the transition from one status to the other.

What appears to have happened is as follows. For reasons connected with the prosody of sentence particles like *not*, this word originally developed a simple clitic form in (some subset of) the positions available to the full word form, which was prosodically dependent on a preceding word and subject to vowel reduction and loss. This resulted in the form *-n't* which attached to whatever word the word order rules of the language placed it adjacent to. However, the range of positions in which *not* appears is limited by its function as a sentence adverbial: especially when unstressed, these typically appear after the first auxiliary within the verb phrase. This position is thus the one in which *-n't* would generally be found: in second-position within the VP. Second position within a given phrase, however, is a common position for the location of clitics, and the (originally simple) clitic form *-n't* would thus be eligible for reinterpretation as a second position (special) VP clitic instead. The result is not a change in surface form, but rather in the underlying grammar: negation is thereby reanalyzed as (at least potentially) a phrasal property of VP, and not exclusively as the meaning of the lexical item *not*. This phrasal property would then be realized by a rule of affixation introducing the affix *-n't* in second position in [+NEGATIVE] VPs.

Other phrasal properties of English VPs, however, such as agreement and tense marking (inherited from the phrasal properties of the clauses in which they appear), are in fact reassigned to the word that constitutes the head of the relevant VP; i.e. the initial verb, where they are realized as word-level morphological properties. Since special clitic *-n't* in second position would in fact always follow a verb, it might be reinterpreted as a word-level affix, rather than phrasal. As Zwicky and Pullum show, this is essentially the stage reached in modern English. Descriptively, verb phrases can be treated as bearing a property [±NEGATIVE]. The phrasal value [+NEGATIVE] can be realized as the element *not* in second position; but if the head (i.e. the first verb) of the VP is an auxiliary, the value [+NEGATIVE] may be reassigned from the phrasal node to its head (a common treatment of phrasal properties, as the literature on generalized phrase structure grammars makes clear). In this position, its realization is determined by principles of word (rather than phrase) formation, and the properties cited in Zwicky & Pullum (1983) represent the expected behavior of what is effectively an 'inflectional' property of the auxiliary verb.

If such an apparently inflectional property were further reanalyzed as originally assigned to verbs (rather than being inherited from the phrase node that dominates them), we might find further changes. In the Karelian example, the originally independent word, having passed through the stages of simple clitic and special clitic which is final in its NP to be treated as a morphological property of nouns, is now the marker of a property which can in its turn be passed from the head noun of its NP to other elements (modifiers) within it.

The operative mechanism here is a simple one. When (some form of) an element becomes specialized in use in a way that limits its positional freedom to some location which is possible for special clitics, it may be morphologized as the marker of a phrasal property, introduced by a special clitic rule. If the host with which a special clitic typically occurs belongs to some specific word class, it may further be reanalyzed as introduced by a word formation rule applying to that class. Other factors, especially semantic and prosodic ones, are of course relevant to the treatment of individual examples, but the primary role in this development is played by rules of special cliticization construed as intermediate between word formation rules and fully independent words.

## 13.3 Analogy, or changes in morphological rules

To this point we have been discussing cases in which some aspect of the morphology has its origins in another area of the grammar: the phonology or the syntax. Under the heading of 'morphological change,' however, we must also include instances in which it is the morphology itself that undergoes change, without involving extra-morphological material. It might be expected that this kind of example would constitute the bulk of the present chapter; if that is not the case, it is because real results or established principles are hard to find. Explicit theories of morphological structure within the context of a full formal grammar are still comparatively new, and the literature devoted to change in such systems is quite limited. The discussion here thus focusses on the central category of morphological change in traditional descriptions: *analogy*.

### 13.3.1. Classical analogy

As a category, 'analogy' arose through the study of its opposite: sound change. In order to sustain the claim that linguistic change affects sounds, independent of the words they appear in, and thus proceeds without (lexical) exception, it was necessary to recognize two other ways in which languages in fact change: through borrowing, and through analogy. As an example of an analogical change, we take the development of the Old English Noun *bōk* 'book,' plural (nom. and acc.) *bēc*. The umlaut in this plural form is quite regular for nouns of this class, and still appears in modern English in the word *goose/geese*: we would expect the Old English plural form to develop into modern *beech*, by palatalization of /k/ following the front vowel /ē/ and vowel shift (as in the isolated *pluralia tantum* noun *breeches*, from OE *brēc* beside singular *brōc*). In Middle English, however, the form *bēc* was replaced by *bōkes*, obviously not as the result of some hypothetical sounds change shifting /ēc/ to /ōkes/ but rather, on the *analogy* of other ME plural forms with /-(e)s/ and no umlaut: *stōn/stōnes*, etc. Such extensions of a regular pattern to cover new cases form the core of the class of changes known as analogies in traditional historical linguistics.

The mechanism of change often proposed as a formal account of analogy is the device of the analogical proportion: one establishes a sort of equation, such as (12), and 'solves for $X$' to arrive at the analogically created form:

(12) stōn : stōnes = bōk:X
    X = bōkes

Actually, there is a certain amount of confusion in the literature between the set(s) of actual forms involved in such a proportion as (12) and the explanatory mechanism underlying the change. If proportional analogy is to 'explain' such changes as the replacement of *bēc* by *bōkes*, we must determine the extent to which it provides an account of exactly what analogical changes are possible. Manifestly, not every set of three terms makes up a relevant proportional base for an analogy:

(13) a.  book : shoe  = Fred : X
     b.  book : look  = bomb : X
     c.  book : cover = house : X

The 'proportion' in (13a) is clearly linguistically meaningless, since we have no possible way of solving it for $X$. This shows us that, at minimum, the terms of a proportion must be related in form and meaning. Note that neither is sufficient in complete isolation: we can certainly solve (13b) for $X=lomb$, but once we have done so we have no idea what the resulting form might mean, and thus no idea what to do with the solution. In (13c), on the other hand, it is clear that a value for $X$ would mean something like 'outer surface of a house,' but the proportion provides no basis for predicting what form this item might take. Clearly, then, a valid proportional analogy must be based on cases where a regular relation in sound reflects a regular relation in meaning.

While clearly necessary, this is not a sufficient condition, however. From the proportion in (14) below, it is not possible to create the form *heye* 'see,' since the relation between the two terms on the left is totally isolated in the language.

(14) ear : hear = eye : X

355

Similarly, the creation of *spice* as the plural of *spouse* on the analogy of *louse/lice* seems merely a joke. Even the morphologically motivated connection between *louse* and *lice*, while not totally isolated, is too marginal to serve as the basis of a valid analogy.

## 13.3.2. Structural interpretations of analogy

These points were generally understood, and the underlying mechanism of proportional analogy was appreciated by many earlier writers. Bloomfield, for example, speaks of analogy as the 'displacement' (by which, in context, he means 'extension') of 'analogic habits' – i.e. of the regular patterns of the language (Bloomfield 1933: 405). A valid analogy is thus always based on a valid and (reasonably) general *rule* of the language. Where no rule relates two forms (as in the case of (14) above), they cannot serve as the base of an analogical proportion. Of course, for Bloomfield the notion of a rule was limited to patterns of association among surface forms; and hence the only rules that could serve as bases for analogy were similarly relations among surface forms. In principle, however, what is crucial is that analogies must be based on the grammatical structure of the language, not on (possibly adventitious) resemblances between actual forms (whether surface forms or more abstract representations). As conceptions of what constitutes this structure have changed, so have the boundaries of potential analogies.

Earlier, de Saussure had also seen the dependence of analogy on the rules constituting a language's grammatical system. In fact, it is essential to understand this in order to make sense of his superficially dramatic claim that analogical change is no change at all, from the point of view of *langue*. On de Saussure's view, forms that we see as analogically created actually existed all along, as potentialities of the system. Thus, in so far as English at the time of the creation of *bōkes* contained a rule forming plurals in /-(e)s/, and a noun *bōk*, the form *bōkes* was thereby implicit. If it was not actually used, this was for reasons Saussure ascribed to usage: the alternate form *bēc* was used instead, but this was not really a fact about the *system* of the language, which is constituted by its rules and not by its patterns of usage (or *parôle*). Accordingly, so-called analogical 'change' is equally a matter of *parôle*: the old, nonregular form goes out of use, and the 'new,' regular form comes to be used more.

On these views, the basic mechanism of analogy is the extension of an existing rule to cover new forms. The rule can be instantiated by a proportion among surface forms, but it is the rule itself (not the forms that make up the proportion) that govern the change.

Consider now the replacement of older *kine* by *cows* as the plural of *cow*. On the picture of the lexicon adopted here, the form *kine* had lost its regular status and become a lexically listed idiosyncrasy as a result of the decline of earlier *-n* stems. The lexicon of early Modern English thus contained this form as the overtly listed [+PLURAL] form of *cow* (while words with regular plurals in /-(e)s/ needed no lexical listing for their plurals). The absence of the word *cows* at this point follows from disjunctive ordering, since a lexically listed form takes precedence over one created by rule (Anderson 1986). When the form *kine* was subsequently lost – perhaps through simple failure of a later generation of speakers to acquire the irregular item – the result was that the lexical entry for *cow* no longer contained a listed plural. The plural produced by rule (*cows*) would thus occur where required, since there would no longer be another form to block it by disjunction. Similarly, if *kine* were to develop a special sense (as it arguably has, in so far as it occurs at all in English today), parallel to the specialization of *brethren* as no longer simply the plural of *brother*, this would dissociate it from the lexical entry for *cow* and again allow the form *cows* to surface.

In many instances, analogy involves simply the loss of an irregular form, or perhaps a minor and restricted subregularity. The replacement of *bēc* by *bōkes* is of this latter sort. The umlaut rule was originally quite general, and probably phonological in character; but by the time of early Middle English, the rule had been morphologized and only applied to a few noun plurals. Simply losing the (arbitrary and unpredictable) property of forming the plural by umlaut would cause *bōk* to lose *bēc* as its plural. This would then entail its replacement by *bōkes*, as the (now regular) rule of plural formation was no longer blocked by a more specific form in this word.

Such cases are rather straightforwardly matters of simplification of the grammar through the loss of irregularity, as urged some years ago by Kiparsky (1965). Most valid instances of 'proportional analogy' result simply from the omission of morphological complexity, principally through the loss of irregular or idiosyncratic formations. In Saussurean terms, the system of *langue* is induced on the basis of observation of acts of *parôle*, and if speakers simply fail to learn (or adopt) some point of arbitrary usage, the result is that its place is filled by the product of the language's regular patterns. Such 'analogy' is not a primitive notion of change *per se*: it is simply the extension of an antecedent rule-governed relationship between form and meaning to new cases.

The most extensive attempt in the traditional literature to provide a genuinely theoretical understanding of the operation of analogical change is that associated with Kuryłowicz (1949, 1964, and elsewhere) whose goal was to find principles that govern the cases in which analogy could (or could not) operate. In part, the principles he proposes follow definitionally from his understanding of analogy; in part they constitute (essentially unexplained) empirical generalizations about circumstances in which such change can be seen to have taken place. Such observations, in so far as they can be shown to be valid, form a natural domain for further research on morphological change, since it clearly ought to be possible to establish them as theorems that follow from the nature of linguistic structure.

Kuryłowicz's theory is based on the model of proportional analogy, but he makes it abundantly clear that not all proportionals are well-formed, even if they involve related terms. Thus, *write : writer = receive : receiver* is valid, but *write : receive = writer:receiver* is 'nonsensical, as between *write* and *receive* there is not only no grammatical relation but not even a lexical one' (Kuryłowicz 1964: 37). In other words, one side of a proportion must be an instantiation of a relation between two (classes of) forms which is governed by some rule of grammar; and the other side represents the extension of this rule to another form. A proportion relates 'basic' forms to forms 'founded' on them, and a relation of foundation $a \rightarrow b$ must exist in order for $a : b = c : d$ to be admissible as a proportion.

Relations between founding and founded forms play much the same role in Kuryłowicz's system that rules play in a generative grammar, but there are also important differences. Most interestingly, if *b* is founded on *a*, this means that the existence of *b* presupposes the existence of *a*, rather than that *b* is constructed by starting with *a* and adding something. Thus, the stem of a paradigm is founded on the various fully inflected forms, rather than *vice versa*. Kuryłowicz regards the grammar as a set of relations among full surface forms (much as de Saussure did: cf. Anderson 1985), rather than as a set of rules specifying the construction of complex forms from simple components. In fact, the difficulties that arise in views of morphology based strictly on morphemes construed as minimal signs (see Chapter 6 of this volume) suggest that this picture may merit more consideration than it has sometimes received.

In terms of his notion of the relation between founding and founded forms as representing rules of grammar, Kuryłowicz proposes a number of interesting generalizations about morphological change, whose interpretation in other frameworks can be illuminating. One of the more significant of these proposed 'laws of analogy' is the fourth, given in (15):

(15) When a form undergoes differentiation as a consequence of a
     morphological change, the new form corresponds to its primary
     function and the original form is reserved for the secondary function.
     (Kuryłowicz 1949; my translation)

This includes the case of old inflectional patterns that remain in fossilized form, corresponding to some secondary sense or derived function of the original use. English examples include *straight* (originally a past participle of *stretch*), *brethren*, *elder* (originally the comparative of *old*, but now specialized as a noun or an attributive adjective referring to persons having priority over others by virtue of age), etc. The content of (15) is the claim that in pairs like *stretched/straight*, *brothers/brethren*, *older/elder*, etc., where one form is an analogical innovation, it is the new form that will carry the primary function (participle, plural, comparative, etc.), with the original form preserved (if at all) only in some secondary, specialized use.

In terms of the morphological theory adopted here, we can describe these cases as follows. In forms such as *straight* and (the noun) *elder*, what happened was that the secondary use (the past participle used as an adjective, the comparative adjective used as a noun) became autonomous lexical entries as they developed semantic specializations not applicable to the entire lexical entry from which they were (originally) derived. This lexical autonomy was not noticeable as long as they remained homophonous with the productively derived forms from which they came. When the grammatical system of the language changed, however (generalizing the 'weak' past formation in *-ed* for verbs, eliminating umlaut as a concomitant of comparative formation for adjectives, etc.), the changes in the relevant rules had no effect on these separate lexical items, since they were no longer synchronically derived. The replacement of past participle *straight* by *stretched*, that is, had no effect on the adjective *straight*. Forms such as *brethren* or *elder* (in adjectival usage) are similar: again, the association of a specialized sense with only one (or at least a proper subset) of the forms built on a lexical base results in lexical autonomy for the relevant form in that sense. As it acquired its distinct interpretation, *brethren* became a (morphologically underived) *pluralia tantum* noun distinct from *brother*; and when the plural form of *brother* became *brothers*, this change had no effect on *brethren*.

The lexical autonomy of such secondary uses follows from a strict interpretation of what it means to be a lexical entry. In particular, in so far as only some (grammatically characterized) uses of a lexical item are associated with a specialized sense, the implication is that these forms together with that sense constitute a lexical item distinct from the original, unspecialized item – typically, as in the case of *pluralia tantum* nouns like *brethren*, one with a defective paradigm, but sometimes (as with *straight*) one assigned to a different word class. From this we can conclude that when an inflected form develops such a specialized sense, not predictable from the semantics of its base form together with the category in which it appears, the result is that this surface form is separately lexicalized, even when its shape is predictable from the language's regular morphology. As a consequence, changes in regular morphology have no effect on the new item, in so far as the rules in question are no longer involved in its formation.

We can contrast these cases with others (Kiparsky 1974) which might appear to falsify (15). Specialized expressions such as *Toronto Maple Leafs*, *saber-tooths*, *still-lifes*, etc., built on formally irregular words (cf. *leaves*, *teeth*, *lives*, etc.) are clearly innovations, but here the regular form is associated with the secondary, not the primary function. Again what has happened is the creation of a new lexical entry. In this case, though, it is not some grammatically characterized member of a word's paradigm that is involved in the new formation, but the basic, unspecified form. Simply by failing to transfer the entire paradigm (with its specific, irregular forms) to the new lexical entry, morphologically derived forms of the new item will be produced by the regular rules of morphology. The difference between the two sorts of case is that in the first type (*straight*, etc.) a morphological change has taken place: the rules for forming past participles, etc. have changed, leaving unaffected the lexically idiosyncratic forms that were etymologically but not synchronically derived by those rules. In the second class of cases (*Toronto Maple Leafs*, etc.), the new lexical entry has been created *after* a change in morphology that left some irregular residual forms. In so far as the irregularity involved is not also incorporated into the new form, the result is a regularly inflected 'secondary' form – which, however, would not fall under (15) since the differentiation follows, rather than being brought about by, the morphological change.

The evidence provided by this example about the conditions and consequences of lexicalization illustrates the sort of information we can obtain about the structure of synchronic morphologies through the study of regularities of morphological change. The literature dealing with the historical morphology of the Indo-European family is rich in such changes, grouped into apparently natural classes designated by purported 'laws of analogy' such as (15). The analysis of these cases, and their explanation on the basis of principles of morphological structure, remains a potentially fruitful source of illumination concerning the nature of such principles.

## 13.4. Conclusion

The study of how language changes is of considerable interest in its own right, as has been realized ever since it was first observed that linguistic change is systematic in its nature. In the case of morphological change, this study involves consideration not only of changes in the system of word formation rules of a language, but also of changes that consist in the reanalysis of originally phonological alternations or syntactic constructions as morphological in character.

This chapter has also urged the position that there is another important reason to study morphological change. Especially in the domain of morphology, where much that we find is the product of historical change operating on originally nonmorphological material, it is important to recognize that what we find is the product not only of what can possibly exist, but also of what can come into existence. A proper appreciation of the way in which linguistic structure is a product of the interaction of its parts thus cannot omit an understanding of the possible mechanisms and channels of historical change. It may not be possible to understand the range of possible systems that are instantiated by the languages of the world in terms of their synchronic character alone.

## REFERENCES

Anderson, S. R. 1974. *The organization of phonology*. New York: Academic Press.
Anderson, S. R. 1976a. On the description of consonant gradation in Fula. *Studies in African Linguistics* 7: 93–136.
Anderson, S. R. 1976b. On the notion of subject in ergative languages. In C. Li (ed.) *Subject and topic*. New York: Academic Press.
Anderson, S. R. 1977a. On mechanisms by which languages become ergative. In C. Li (ed.) *Mechanisms of syntactic change*. Austin: University of Texas Press.
Anderson, S. R. 1977b. On the formal description of inflection. *CLS* 13: 15–44.
Anderson, S. R. 1980. On the development of morphology from syntax. In J. Fisiak (ed.) *Historical morphology*. The Hague: Mouton.
Anderson, S. R. 1982. Differences in rule types and their structural basis. In H. van der Hulst & N. Smith (eds.) *The structure of phonological representations II*. Dordrecht: Foris.
Anderson, S. R. 1985. *Phonology in the twentieth century*. Chicago: University of Chicago Press.
Anderson, S. R. 1986. Disjunctive ordering in inflectional morphology. *Natural Language and Linguistic Theory* 4: 1–32.
Benveniste, E. 1952. La construction passive du parfait transitif. *Bulletin de la Société de Linguistique de Paris* 48: 52–62.
Bloch, J. 1965. *Indo-Aryan*. Paris: Maisonneuve. English edn. by A. Master.
Bloomfield, L. 1933. *Language*. New York: Holt.
Chung, S. 1978. *Case marking and grammatical relations in Polynesian*. Austin: University of Texas Press.
Comrie, B. 1980. Morphology and word order reconstruction: problems and prospects. In J. Fisiak (ed.) *Historical morphology*. The Hague: Mouton.
Doke, C. M. 1954. *The Southern Bantu languages*. London: Oxford University Press.
Givón T. 1971. Historical syntax and synchronic morphology: an archeologist's fieldtrip. *CLS* 7: 394–415.
Harris, A. 1985. *Syntax and semantics*. Vol. 18: *Diachronic syntax: the Kartvelian case*. Orlando: Academic Press.
Howard, I. 1972. *A directional theory of rule application in phonology*. Doctoral thesis, MIT. Published as *Working Papers in Linguistics* 4, 7. University of Hawaii.
Jackendoff, R. S. 1975. Morphological and semantic regularities in the lexicon. *Language* 51: 639–71.
Janda, R. 1982. On limiting the form of morphological rules: German umlaut, diacritics, and the 'cluster constraint.' *NELS* 12: 140–52.
Janda, R. 1984. Why morphological metathesis rules are rare: on the possibility of historical explanation in linguistics. *BLS* 10: 87–103.
Kaisse, E. & Shaw, B. 1985. On the theory of lexical phonology. *Phonology Yearbook* 2: 1–30.
Kiparsky, P. 1965. *Phonological change*. Doctoral thesis, MIT. Published by Indiana University Linguistics Club.
Kiparsky, P. 1973. Phonological representations. In O. Fujimura (ed.) *Three dimensions of linguistic theory*. Tokyo: TEC Co.

Kiparsky, P. 1974. Remarks on analogical change. In J. M. Anderson & C. Jones (eds.) *Historical linguistics II*. Amsterdam: North-Holland.

Kiparsky, P. 1982. Lexical morphology and phonology. In *Linguistics in the morning calm*. Seoul: Hanshin Publishing Company.

Kiparsky, P. 1984. On the lexical phonology of Icelandic. In C.-C. Elert, I. Johansson & E. Strangert (eds.) *Nordic prosody III*. Stockholm: University of Umeå/Almqvist & Wiksell.

Kuryłowicz, J. 1949. La nature des procès dits 'analogiques'. *Acta Linguistica Hafniensa* 5: 15–37.

Kuryłowicz, J. 1964. *The inflectional categories of Indo-European*. Heidelberg: Carl Winter.

Lightfoot, D. 1979. Review of C. Li (ed.) *Mechanisms of syntactic change. Language* 55: 381–95.

Matthews, P. H. 1972. *Inflectional morphology*. Cambridge: Cambridge University Press.

McCarthy, J. J. 1981. A prosodic theory of non-concatenative morphology. *Linguistic Inquiry* 12: 373–418.

Puech, G. 1978. A cross dialectal study of vowel harmony in Maltese. *CLS* 14: 377–90.

Robinson, O. 1975. Abstract phonology and the history of umlaut. *Lingua* 37: 1–29.

Vennemann, T. 1972. Rule inversion. *Lingua* 29: 209–42.

Wang, W. S. Y. 1968. Vowel features, paired variables, and the English vowel shift. *Language* 44: 695–708.

Wurzel, W. 1980. Ways of morphologizing phonological rules. In J. Fisiak (ed.) *Historical morphology*. The Hague: Mouton.

Zwicky, A. & Pullum, G. 1983. Cliticization vs. inflection: English *n't. Language* 59: 502–13.

# 14 Phonological change*

*Paul Kiparsky*

We will begin with some classical and relatively well-understood issues of historical phonology and proceed to newer and more controversial ones. Section 14.1 reviews the neogrammarian exceptionlessness hypothesis. Section 14.2 outlines a theory of sound change, and surveys some currently active areas of investigation relevant to filling in that outline. Section 14.3 deals with issues of phonetic and phonological analogy, and section 14.4 with lexical diffusion. Our focus throughout will be as much on the theoretical background and implications of these ideas as on the question of their empirical validity.

## 14.1. The exceptionlessness hypothesis: conceptual and empirical issues

### 14.1.1. The neogrammarian argument for the EH

One of the principal issues in the theory of sound change remains the neogrammarian exceptionlessness hypothesis (EH), according to which sound changes are subject only to phonetic conditioning and have no exceptions. Although the EH has never commanded universal assent, its truth is assumed by much of the comparative method (Hoenigswald 1960, 1973) and important consequences have been drawn from it in synchronic linguistics. Specifically, the structuralist theory of autonomous phonology was largely motivated by the desire to derive the putative exceptionlessness of sound change from more basic assumptions about the organization of language.

The EH was first explicitly stated by Leskien (1876), but the way for it was paved by earlier methodological advances due primarily to Scherer (1868). According to Brugmann, '. . . it is Scherer's achievement to have effectively broached the question of how changes and innovations take place in a language' (Osthoff & Brugmann 1878). Scherer's key idea is the

* Thanks to W. van Lessen Kloeke, John Rickford, and W. S.-Y. Wang for bringing some relevant material to my attention, and to Keith Denning and William Poser for comments on a draft.

*uniformitarian principle*, viz. that 'the mental and physical activity of man must have been at all times essentially the same.' The uniformitarian principle had two important consequences: first, that properties of language change can and should be investigated not on the basis of hypothetical reconstructions but on the basis of known languages and known historical changes; second, that reconstructed proto-languages are constrained by the same principles as are valid for actual languages.[1]

Research based on these premises indicated that sound change is substantially regular:

> In all living dialects the shapes of sounds peculiar to the dialect always appear much more consistently implemented throughout the entire linguistic material and maintained by the members of the linguistic community than one would expect from the study of the older languages accessible merely through the medium of writing; this consistency often extends into the finest nuances of a sound. Whoever is not in the position to make this observation in his native dialect or elsewhere may refer to the excellent work by J. Winteler, *Die Kerenzer Mundart des Kantons Glarus* (1876), where he can convince himself of the accuracy of what has been said. And should not this fact be taken to heart now by those who so willingly and so often admit of unmotivated exceptions of the mechanical sound laws? (Osthoff & Brugmann 1878)

The uniformitarian principle also legitimized the postulation of analogical changes of the sort found in contemporary languages even for earlier stages of Indo-European:

> To the horror of not a few fellow investigators, but luckily for the field itself, Scherer made ample use of the principle of analogical leveling in his explanations in the abovementioned book. Suddenly many forms of even the oldest historically accessible stages were, according to him, nothing other than formations by false analogy . . . (*Ibid*)

A corollary of this new realism was that sound changes are language-specific historical processes situated in space and time, rather than simply general tendencies of 'phonetic erosion,' as they had previously been thought to be. This not only raised new questions about their phonetic interpretation, but also provided a basis for investigating their relative chronology. Thus, the statement of correspondences between the Germanic and Sanskrit obstruents, whose formulation by Grimm countenanced many exceptions, was replaced through Grassmann's and Verner's discoveries by a richer but

---

[1] See Christy (1983) for the history of the uniformitarian principle.

virtually exceptionless set of sound changes which related the two branches to a common Indo-European phonological system that differed significantly from both its descendants. Within a few years after this crucial conceptual shift to sound changes as potentially interacting historical processes, virtually all the major problems in Indo-European vowel and consonant phonology were solved, often by several linguists independently.

The EH was in essence a radicalization of the insight that sound changes are rule-governed historical processes: not only are sound changes rule-governed, they are governed by rules of a very special and restricted sort. Apparent exceptions or nonphonetic conditions, it was claimed, are *always* due either to analogy, or to borrowing, or to other interacting sound changes. A neogrammarian historical phonology accordingly consists of a list of sound changes together with an account of the apparent exceptions to each by means of these three factors. The considerable success with which the history of a wide range of languages could be covered in this constrained framework was an impressive argument for the correctness of the EH.

In addition to their empirical evidence, proponents of the EH claimed support for their theory on purely methodological grounds, holding either that the EH was necessary if linguistics was to be a scientific field at all,[2] or at least that the successes of historical phonology depended on it.[3] But this methodological argument is obviously worthless, since it depends on the false identification of exceptionlessness and regularity. Historical linguistics is viable because there are regularities, and does not depend at all on exceptionlessness or on the absence of nonphonetic conditioning.[4] In fact, the sound changes discovered by linguists who did *not* assume the exceptionlessness thesis – Verner, Grassmann, Ascoli, Collitz, Johannes Schmidt, to name five – were fully as important as any that the neogrammarians discovered.

## 14.1.2. The EH and autonomous phonology

The EH thus having come to be widely accepted, the question naturally arose of *why* it should hold. In order to provide a theoretical basis for exceptionlessness of sound change, it is necessary to postulate in one or another way that phonological representations are strictly independent of morphology and lexicon. The first attempt to formulate such a view of phonological representation was that of Paul (1880). Paul supposed that the acoustic and articulatory properties of words are mentally stored as 'memory images'. These

---

[2] Leskien (1876:xxiv); Osthoff & Brugmann (1878: xiv–xv). These and other classics of the debate on the EH are collected in Wilbur (1977), with an interesting and engaging introduction by the editor. See also Vennemann & Wilbur 1972.
[3] Bloomfield (1933: 355, 359).
[4] As implied by Verner himself in the article that presented his famous discovery (1877), and by Hugo Schuchardt (1928:78) in a polemic against the neogrammarians.

memory images are independent of the grammatical structure of language and can therefore be subject only to purely phonologically conditioned changes.

The eventual outcome of this line of thinking is the theory of autonomous phonemics. It would be an interesting matter to trace its development from this perspective in the works of Saussure and other theoreticians contemporary with the neogrammarians, but we will here look only at the carefully considered formulation that Bloomfield (1933) gave to it.

First, Bloomfield was able to add a simple and powerful argument in support of the EH: if sound changes were lexically idiosyncratic, then languages would have assorted 'stray sounds' left over from the previous stages of their history. English, for example, would have various relics of the Middle English, Old English, Germanic and Indo-European phonological inventories (say, [ü, ö, x, bh]) – much as, in morphology, *oxen* and *children* are residues left behind by the analogical change that eliminated plurals in *-en*. In reality, of course, languages always have concise phonemic inventories, and where marginal segments exist they are normally the result of borrowing or of expressive processes, not residues left behind by supposedly sporadic sound change.

Having reasoned that the EH must be true on the empirical grounds that otherwise there would be no coherent phonemic systems, Bloomfield recast this connection as causal: it is *because* phonemics is autonomous that sound change is regular. This yields a new version of Paul's theoretical deduction of the EH (1933: 364–5):

> Theoretically, we can understand the regular change of phonemes if we suppose that language consists of two layers of habit. One layer is phonemic: the speakers have certain habits of voicing, tongue-movement, and so on. These habits make up the phonetic system of the language. The other layer consists of formal-semantic habits: the speakers habitually utter certain combinations of phonemes in response to certain types of stimuli, and respond appropriately when they hear these same combinations. These habits make up the grammar and lexicon of the language.

There is an unspoken further assumption here which is needed to complete the argument: not only will there have to be two 'layers of habit' (levels of representation), but they must be mutually independent. Only if the 'phonetic system' is independent of the grammar and lexicon will it follow that the phonological structure of utterances cannot be determined by their grammatical-lexical structure.

The assumption that phonology is independent of higher-level structure is however extremely problematic. It is known that the pronunciation of words

366

can depend on certain morphological and lexical factors. Bloomfield himself acknowledged this fact on the next page of his book, in noting that some speakers of American English use:

> . . . a shorter variant of the phoneme [a] . . . before the clusters [rd, rt] followed by a primary suffix [-r, -n] as in *barter*, *Carter*, *garden*, *marten*, *Martin*. Before a secondary suffix [-r, -n], however, the longer variant is used, as in *starter*, *carter* ('one who carts'), *harden*. Here the existence of the simple words (*start*, *cart*, *hard*), whose [a] is not subject to shortening, has led to the favoring of the normal, longer variant. The word *larder* (not part of the colloquial vocabulary) could be read with the shorter variant, but the agent-noun *larder* ('one who lards') could be formed only with the longer type of the [a]-phoneme. (Bloomfield 1933: 366)[5]

Bloomfield considered [ă] and [ā] to be 'subphonemic variants,' being predictable from the nature of the suffix, and hence in spite of such minimal pairs, not distinctive. Given his acceptance of the EH, Bloomfield could not interpret this length difference as the result of a sound change that was sensitive to the category of secondary suffixes, and was therefore committed to an interpretation in terms of one of the other factors, in this case analogy. He assumed that the sound change was a shortening of *all* disyllables, and that an analogical change later reintroduced the longer allophone before secondary suffixes:

(1) *read : reader = stārt* : X     (X = *stārter*)

But while this interpretation saves the letter of the neogrammarian thesis, it quite undermines Bloomfield's deduction of that thesis from the phonemic principle. For once it is admitted that the distribution of 'subphonemic variants' can depend upon *grammatical* factors such as the categorization of *-er* as a secondary suffix, it is simply no longer the case that the 'phonetic system' is independent of the 'grammatical-lexical system,' and so there is no longer any reason to expect the neogrammarian exceptionlessness thesis to hold in the first place.

One way out of this dilemma is to *define* the phonetic system in such a way that it *cannot* be dependent on the grammatical-lexical system. This was the step taken by post-Bloomfieldian, so-called autonomous or taxonomic phonemic theory, which redefines the phonemic level as a strictly autonomous level obtained from phonetic representations by certain procedures

---

[5] The particular contrast described by Bloomfield does not appear to be very common, but quite a few formally identical cases in various regional dialects of English will be found in Wells (1982). In each of these cases, a vowel nucleus characteristic of monosyllables is also found before level 2 suffixes ('#'-suffixes).

of segmentation and classification. If the *ā* of *cãrt*, *cãrter* and the *ă* of *Cărter* contrast in minimal pairs they must then *eo ipso* represent different phonemes, in which case there is no longer any question of grammatical conditioning of subphonemic variants in the example at hand.

However, this redefinition of the phonemic level does not salvage the deduction of the EH from the doctrine of strict separation of levels. Recall that, on Bloomfield's assumption, there first occurred a sound change that shortened the vocalic nuclei of polysyllabic words (*cãrt* vs. *cărter*, *Cărter*), and afterwards an analogical change transferred the length from monosyllables (*cãrt*) to polysyllabic words formed from them by secondary suffixes (*cãr-ter*→ *cãrter*). From the viewpoint of autonomous phonemics, the *sound change* introduced two *allophones* for vocalic nuclei, with their distribution determined by the number of syllables in the word, and the subsequent *analogical* change made those allophones into independent *phonemes*. But if we have transfer of *allophones* (entities of the *phonetic* system) by *analogy* (a process operating in the *grammatical-lexical* system), then once again there can be no question of strict separation of levels as Bloomfield intended. The upshot is that the autonomy of the phonetic and gramatical-lexical systems has been achieved for sound change only to be abandoned again for analogical change. The facts thus preclude the kind of independence between the levels of representation that Bloomfield's deduction of the EH requires. The physical and mental aspects of language cannot be insulated from each other.[6]

We will return to the relation between change and levels of representation in connection with analogy in section 14.3 below. To summarize our story so far: the EH, originating as a methodological advance on older techniques of linguistic reconstruction, was formulated as an empirical hypothesis about sound change in the 1870s, and came to be widely regarded as empirically confirmed. Attempts to derive it in a principled manner from the basic organization of language began with Paul (1880) and culminated in the theory of autonomous phonemics, whose dubious status unfortunately compromises the proposed explanation.

## 14.1.3. The EH is consistent with every word having its own history

*Prima facie* counterexamples to the EH are easily found in any historical grammar. Advocates of the EH are of course well aware of their existence, precisely because the restrictive theory of change which they adopted first brought their problematic status to light. The controversy has turned on the question whether the relevant cases can be accommodated within the con-

---

[6] See Hockett (1965), Postal (1968), Bhat (1972), and Miranda (1974) for further discussion of the EH and its theoretical implications.

straints of neogrammarian theory. One group of linguists thought this impossible and consequently rejected the neogrammarian theory, under the slogan 'every word has its own history.' The neogrammarians and their successors for their part maintained that the remaining recalcitrant cases could be accounted for in their framework by certain less obvious mechanisms of borrowing and analogy. In the relevant kind of borrowing, called 'dialect mixture,' a dialect which has undergone a sound change borrows words from a related dialect which has not undergone that sound change (or *vice versa*), or two dialects with different phonologies are conflated, resulting in the appearance of lexically idiosyncratic sound change. A similar effect can be produced by a combination of borrowing and analogy called 'hypercorrection' or 'hyperurbanism'. In this process a prestigious speech trait is adopted in overgeneralized form by speakers who do not have it natively, as when speakers striving to replace their [uw] by [yuw] in words like *news* do it also in words like *noon*.

Advocates of the EH thus ended up claiming that certain historical processes which *look* like sound changes are in reality not sound changes in the technical sense at all, but arise by other mechanisms. This position can certainly not be dismissed out of hand, and so the outright rejection of the EH by many linguists was premature. Linguistic changes do not come neatly labeled in advance, so 'sound changes' cannot be pretheoretically identified as such. It is only through a specific framework of assumptions about linguistic change that they fall into that category. Hence the EH cannot be judged in isolation or refuted directly by apparent contrary data, but must be taken in conjunction with the other proposed mechanisms of change and their specific properties. The question is whether those mechanisms together adequately characterize the totality of change, and in particular whether analogy and borrowing can legitimately accommodate the residue of changes of an ostensibly phonological character which do not qualify as 'sound changes' in neogrammarian theory.

The neogrammarians argued that the EH was supported by the detailed dialect descriptions which were then beginning to become available. For example, J. Winteler's monograph on the Swiss German dialect of the village of Kerenzen (1876) showed that sound changes have indeed been carried out in this dialect with remarkable consistency. This seemed to them good evidence that as we approach the conditions of a homogeneous and isolated speech community, and the effects of dialect mixture and hypercorrection are thereby minimized, sound change indeed stands out as patently exceptionless.

It soon turned out that the remote and isolated Alpine valley studied by Winteler was in no way representative. Numerous dialect monographs and large-scale atlas projects showed that, by and large, 'the local dialects were no more consistent than the standard language in their relation to older speech-forms' (Bloomfield 1933: 322). While taking the self-contained homogeneous speech community as a theoretical idealization, the neogrammarians had grossly overestimated the extent to which this idealization approximates sociolinguistic reality. Dialect geography showed that heterogeneity and variation are not abnormalities but part of the normal condition of language.

However, the prevalence of language contact and diversity in no way disconfirms the EH, specifically not the *causal* claim which lies at the heart of it, namely that exceptions do not develop internally to a system but only through the interference between systems.[7] On the contrary, it makes that hypothesis more defensible by justifying the very assumptions of heterogeneity which must be invoked to explain away apparent contrary evidence. But by the same token it substantially insulates the EH from the actual data of change, and so makes it harder to put to an empirical test.

## 14.1.4. The EH is an empirical hypothesis

In view of the above, it can legitimately be asked whether the EH retains any testable empirical content at all. Hoenigswald (1978a) claims that it does not, and that it should be regarded simply as a matter of conventional definition, so that the question whether it is true or false does not arise. Commenting on the lexically idiosyncratic split of the Indo-European voiced palatals into Old Persian *z* and *d*, he remarks:

> We are free to consider these replacements either as examples of sound change along two lines of descent (true Persian and Median), or as an example of dialect borrowing interfering with the true line of descent for Old Persian. If this is how we reason, there is no occasion for surprise in Leskien's formula that sound change occurs without exception, since it is a tautology . . .

> Advocates of 'sporadic' sound change . . . will have their claim neither proved nor faulted until they can specify the circumstances under which competing regularities are to be interpreted neither as (a) 'analogic' . . . nor as (b) representing different channels of transmission, including the one dubbed the main channel, but instead as (c) 'sporadic' sound change. If this is only a case of labelling, in all

---

[7] Some introductory discussions of sound change forget this point in their ritual denunciation of the neogrammarians. For example, von Wartburg (1943/1969: 20) adduces some lexically idiosyncratic phonological developments as evidence against the EH – and then proceeds to show how they originate through dialect contact and hypercorrection, that is, in exactly the way envisaged by the neogrammarians.

sobriety, regularities of nonanalogical origin for which we cannot name or care to construct a reasonable historical background (the Medes or the Scandinavians) 'sporadic' means no more than 'somehow competing' and is noncommittal . . . It seems that sporadic sound change is either a contradiction in terms or merely a traditional and not particularly well chosen collective designation for other than main-channel material.

Hoenigswald goes so far as to express surprise that Leonard Bloomfield, among others, 'may have continued to regard this "assumption" [the EH] as material rather than definitional.'

Bloomfield accepted both the EH (as being *contingently* true) and the thesis (which he attributes to Jaberg) that 'every word has its own history' (p. 328). On his view they are not incompatible at all: they are reconcilable by means of the classical dialect-geographical concepts of fine-grained dialectal differentiation by intersecting isoglosses and shifting waves of cultural expansion emanating from centers of prestige. By way of illustration he cites the sociolinguistic situation of the dialect mixture which led to the lexical split of Germanic /u:/ into /u:/ and /y:/ in Dutch, summarizing Kloeke's argument that the dialect mixture hypothesis explains the distribution of the vowels across lexical items, and is confirmed both by areas where [u:] currently varies with the prestige pronunciation [y:], and by the occurrence of hypercorrect [y:] in words that have [u:] in the prestige dialect.[8]

So the answer to Hoenigswald's challenge is that any borrowing hypothesis must fit the known dialectological and sociolinguistic realities. The possibility of borrowing may perhaps never be categorically excluded, but it would certainly be highly suspect if dialects had to be invented *ad hoc* just for the sake of 'explaining' irregular correspondences. For example, the mixed [y:]/[u:] dialects would falsify the exceptionlessness thesis if there were no evidence of consistent [y:] and [u:] dialects out of which they could have been formed. Of course, for dead languages such as Old Persian the EH is not testable in practice because their dialectology is irrecoverable. This does not mean that the EH is definitional, but simply that the neogrammarians were right in insisting on evidence from living languages as the basis for the theory of change.

---

[8] The essentials of the analysis are confirmed by more recent work on Dutch dialectology, except that the likelihood of borrowing is not correlated with word frequency, as Kloeke apparently thought (Gerritsen & Jansen 1979). Bloomfield in any case relates the likelihood of borrowing not to frequency but to the learned vs. familiar status of a word. In any case, such a correlation is not even essential to the dialect borrowing hypothesis, although its existence would, of course, give independent support for it. We do not agree, then, with the view that 'discrepancies of the type [hy:s]/[mu:s] . . . dent, or even breach, Neogrammarian doctrine' (Malkiel 1967: 143), or that Bloomfield's 'chapter on dialectology was never reconciled with his chapters on phonetic change' (Malkiel 1967: 141; Labov 1981: 273).

Secondly, dialect mixture is only plausible if many dialectal traits are shared: 'It is highly implausible that the borrowing dialect (or language) will accept from the lending dialect only those morphemes which share a given phonetic or phonological characteristic' (Cheng & Wang 1977: 91).

## 14.1.5. The EH is false

There are a number of types of conditions on sound change which have a well-motivated theoretical interpretation that cannot be reconciled with the EH. These constitute a far more compelling refutation of the EH than any list of sporadic sound changes. In this section we will review some types of cases belonging in this category.

### Structural constraints on sound change

The first problem for the EH is that the phonological system of a language places constraints on the sound changes that language can undergo. This was pointed out by Jakobson (1929), in what amounted to a revolutionary departure from Saussure's basically neogrammarian conception of sound change (Halle 1984). Jakobson held that particular sound changes implement certain general structural principles in a language. For example, he analyzed the phonological evolution of Russian in terms of the establishment and subsequent dismantling of a system of 'syllabic synharmonism,' according to which palatality is a property of an entire syllable. Still more importantly, Jakobson argued that sound change is governed by principles of universal grammar. These principles include *implicational universals*, that is, universals which state that the presence (or absence) of property A in a language requires the presence (or absence) of property B. One of Jakobson's implicational universals was that free dynamic word stress and distinctive quantity are incompatible.[9] He showed how phonological changes in Slavic languages were governed by this constraint in that dynamic stress only developed in languages where the original quantity oppositions were lost. This is crucial to the sound change issue in that the very existence of nontrivial implicational universals referring to such things as distinctive quantity immediately refutes the EH: if sound changes were purely *phonetically* conditioned they should be blind to what was *distinctive* in the language, and should be capable of applying in such a way as to produce phonological systems that violate implicational universals framed in terms of those notions.

[9] See Anderson (1984) for an attempt to derive this principle from metrical theory.

## Morphological conditions

Sound changes, typically the loss of inflectional affixes, can be initiated in or restricted to certain morphological categories (see Johnson 1982 for a review, and Cerrón-Palomino 1974) or blocked by morphological boundaries (Timberlake 1978). In some cases this could be attributed to analogical restoration in mid-change, on the basis of categories where the ending was regularly retained (Anttila 1972). But, as pointed out by Sihler (1977), there are cases where this interpretation is impossible. Moreover, morphological conditions of a very similar type are known to be among the factors governing the inherent variability of postlexical optional rules. In the view of sound change presented below, morphological conditions on sound change originate as variable constraints at the postlexical stage; they become conditions on rules only when the rules enter the lexical phonology.

## Frequency

Sound changes sometimes apply just to frequent words of the language (Mańczak 1968, 1969, 1978, 1980; Leslau 1969; Fidelholtz 1975; Hooper 1976b; Phillips 1984). Frequency itself could hardly be the conditioning factor, or the 'cause,' of the change.[10] More plausibly, the causal link between frequency and change is redundancy: frequent items are more easily guessed by the hearer, so the speaker can afford more reduced pronunciations of them, which then may be lexicalized (Jespersen 1886/1933; Nyman 1978).

## Lexical diffusion

The word-by-word spread of sound change through the lexicon within a dialect, its *lexical diffusion*, is another kind of phenomenon which is incompatible with the EH.[11] Lexical diffusion need not imply that the change is sporadic: in due course, all words might be affected by the change, though the protracted course of the change allows for interruption, reversal, and interference with other changes in mid-course. We will deal with lexical diffusion in some detail in section 14.4.

---

[10] The old metaphor of words 'wearing down' from much circulation, like coins, is rather misleading: what is the psychological analog of friction by which just uttering a word would cause any change in its mental representation?

[11] See Chen & Hsieh (1973), Chen & Wang (1975), Robinson (1976, 1977), Janson (1977), Wang & Cheng (1977), Krishnamurti (1978), Bauer (1979, 1983), Wang (1979, 1982), Reighard (1980), Wanner & Cravens (1980), Hashimoto (1981). The Chao-zhou case (Cheng & Wang 1977) is most impressive but is apparently flawed (Chan 1982; Egerod 1982; Pulleyblank 1982). The term 'lexical diffusion' is sometimes also used to mean interdialectal borrowing of vocabulary, as in Gerritsen & Jansen (1979), Heath (1981); this lexical confusion is better avoided.

## 14.2. Towards a theory of sound change

The discussion we have reviewed so far follows a certain classical pattern. The argumentation turns either directly on data of the sort found in historical grammars or in dialect descriptions (e.g. evidence for nonphonetic conditioning), or on quite general conceptual points (e.g. the issue of separation of levels); it is of a rather straightforward sort in either case. In this section we will encounter theories of broader scope and more problematic import, engendering a very different sort of debate which spans many branches of linguistics, from phonetics to sociolinguistics and phonological theory.[12]

### 14.2.1. Causes of sound change

Linguistic changes are often thought to originate and spread like new fashions, by speakers of nonstandard varieties striving to emulate the speech of a prestige group, which for its part constantly innovates to keep its linguistic distance as a mark of its privileged position (Bloomfield 1933: 476ff; Joos 1952). On this view, one would expect innovations to originate usually in the speech of the upper class, and spread from there to other classes, perhaps in proportion to their desire for upward mobility. Sociolinguistic investigations have shown that this is not the case. Rather, innovations initiated by an elite tend to be borrowings from some external prestige group; otherwise linguistic innovations are evidently initiated in working-class and lower-middle-class speech (Labov 1965; Labov, Yaeger & Steiner 1972). In his earlier work, Labov attempted to reconcile this discovery with the traditional theory of sound change as adaptations to a prestige norm by positing hypercorrection by the lower middle class as the basic mechanism of sound change. More recently, he has come to a 'pluralist' view according to which any form of speech, including the vernacular, may have its own prestige (perhaps marking local, ethnic, or class identity[13]) which may attract linguistic change in its direction. Change can, on this view, be initiated in any social group:

> Studies of current sound changes in progress show that a linguistic innovation can begin with any particular group and spread outward and that this is the normal development; this one group can be the highest-status group, but not necessarily or even frequently so. (1972a: 286)

---

[12] For general surveys of the issues from various points of view, see Sieberer (1964), Weinreich, Herzog & Labov (1968), Koch (1970), Bluhme (1980), Habick (1980).

[13] For example, the degree to which speakers in Martha's Vineyard centralized their diphthongs was found to be correlated with their identification with the island community (Labov 1965).

Kroch (1978) emphasizes that, on the contrary, the empirical evidence 'universally points to the working class and lower middle class as the originators of sound change in contemporary American English,' and proposes to resolve the apparent paradox in a different way. Recalling the familiar observation that sound changes are 'natural' phonetic and phonological processes, in the sense that they 'are widespread in the languages of the world and appear to have some motivation in articulatory, perceptual or processing efficiency' (see, e.g. Stampe 1972/80; Rubach 1978), Kroch theorizes as follows:

1. The prestige social dialect of a language in a stratified society resists and suppresses certain phonetic and phonological processes that would result in a more 'economical' or 'natural' pronunciation. By contrast, the vernacular speech of the working class and other non-elite strata undergoes such processes quite freely and regularly.

2. The cause of the differential phonological behavior of prestige and vernacular dialects is to be sought not in purely linguistic factors but in ideology. Dominant social groups tends to mark themselves off symbolically as distinct from the groups they dominate and to interpret their symbols of distinctiveness as evidence of superior moral and intellectual qualities . . . In the case of pronunciation the easiest way for a dominant group to mark itself off is for it to inhibit natural phonological processes that the common people use, particularly as these processes are generally of variable application and so admit readily of non-linguistic influences. (Kroch, *Language and Society* 7: 17–18)

From this perspective, the causes of sound change are not so much social as inherent in the use of language itself. What needs to be explained by social factors is not why language changes but why change is sometimes impeded. More generally, it follows that the theory of sound change is not an autonomous theory but is built on, and in large part derivative of, other sub-theories of linguistics.[14] They include: (1) phonetics, whose subject matter is the relation between phonological representations and the physical implementation and perception of speech; (2) phonology, which deals with the form of phonological rules and representations, and with the organization of the phonology and its place in the grammar; (3) the theory of language processing; (4) sociolinguistics; and (5) the theory of language acquisition (in real time). Note that one corollary of this approach is that the theory of historical linguistics will have to give up the convenient idealizations of the ideal speaker–hearer and of instantaneous acquisition familiar from the

---

[14] See Lightfoot (1979) for a defense of this poistion in the domain of syntactic change.

formal theory of grammar. This is because language use and processing, and the actual course of language acquisition, will enter crucially into the explanation of historical change.

With this as background we will review in the next sections some of the contributions towards the understanding of sound change which can be derived from the study of natural phonological processes (section 14.2.2), variation (14.2.3), and the organization of the phonological component (14.2.4).

## 14.2.2. Types of sound change: natural phonological processes

### Approaches to phonological processes

Phonological processes have been studied in several research traditions: typology, phonetics, and phonology (synchronic and historical). Their separation is due to the fragmented past of the field, not to any incompatibility between them.[15]

A. *Typology*. A typological perspective is traditional in structural phonology (e.g. the typology of phonemic systems in Trubetzkoy (1939) and – in a 'parametric' form – is also characteristic of current work in generative phonological theory (e.g. the typology of stress systems in Hayes 1981). Typological studies, then, are simply part of the normal activity of linguistics. Recent decades have, in addition, seen the emergence of a more or less self-contained 'typological method,' which seeks generalizations (categorical, implicational, or statistical) through large-scale crosslinguistic studies (Comrie, in Chapter 17 of this volume; see Greenberg 1966, 1969, 1978a and Crothers 1978 for applications to phonology). One of the strengths of this approach is its 'processual' point of view which explicitly addresses both synchronic and diachronic phenomena. It concentrates on superficial structural features and processes,[16] and looks for inductive generalizations rather than abstract principles, Still, its results are of great interest for theoretical and historical linguistics.

B. *Phonetics*. The program of explaining phonological processes by the physical constraints of the vocal tract goes back to the beginnings of phonetics

---

[15] What Rischel (1986: 90) says about the importance of integrating general phonetics and historical linguistics holds for all these areas including phonological theory: 'It is of paramount importance both for the progress of historical linguistics and for the progress of general phonetic theory that these disciplines be coupled together. Well attested cases of sound change provided an excellent testing ground for general phonetics, and conversely, historical linguistics should employ the most recent advances in phonetic theory (rather than some 19th century notions about phonetics) to ensure lasting progress.'

[16] In part because of practical necessity, in part because of the empiricist orientation of its practitioners.

and flourished especially around the turn of the century (Passy 1890; Rous-
selot 1891; Sievers 1901; Grammont 1933). Ohala and his associates (Ohala
1974, 1983; Hombert, Ohala & Ewen 1979) have recently revived a more
sophisticated form of this line of research which brings in the entire speech
mechanism, including perception:

> . . . the pronunciation intended by the speaker may get distorted by
> the time it is perceived by the listener – either by the action of
> articulatory constraints which affect the way the sounds are uttered,
> or by the action of auditory constraints which affect the way the
> sounds are analysed by the listener's ear. Since the listener does not
> have independent access to the mind of the speaker, and thus may be
> unable to determine what parts of the received signal were intended
> and what were not, he may intentionally reproduce and probably
> exaggerate these distortions when he repeats the same utterances.
> Thus an intrinsic perturbation will come to be used extrinsically.
> (Hombert, Ohala & Ewan 1979: 37)

C. *Phonology.* Most ongoing work in phonological theory represents
some variety of generative phonology and has as its goal the development of
models of (1) phonological representations, (2) phonological rules, (3) the
organization of the phonology and its relation to other modules of grammar.
The characterization of phonological processes has been a particular concern
of natural phonology (Stampe, 1972/80, 1985; Dressler 1984; Donegan 1985)
and of autosegmental phonology (Goldsmith 1979; Pulleyblank 1986).

No-one as yet has a comprehensive theory of natural phonological processes to offer. However, there are some promising beginnings which we will
survey in the following sections. We will adopt a traditional taxonomy, as
interestingly interpreted by Donegan & Stampe (1979),[17] which distinguishes
three basic types:

1. *Prosodic processes*, accounting for the timing of speech by mapping
   feature bundles onto prosodic structures. These structures can be
   thought of as skeletal timing slots with a hierarchic prosodic
   organization.
2. *Weakening processes*, usually context-sensitive and favored in
   unstressed position, in the syllable coda, and in casual speech. These
   processes make things easier to say, but (in so far as they reduce or
   neutralize contrasts) harder to understand. Typical examples are:
   assimilation, vowel reduction, consonant lenition, deletion.

[17] See also Straka (1964), Schane (1971, 1972), Lüdtke (1982), Bluhme (1982). Ferguson (1978) is a
crosslinguistic study of the lenition process d → δ and the converse fortition process δ → d, which nicely
illustrates all the contrasting characteristics mentioned below.

3. *Strengthening processes* ('polarization'), usually independent of segmental context and favored in stressed position, in the syllable onset, and in explicit speech. They make (or are intended to make) things easier to understand, and usually demand extra articulatory effort from the speaker. Typical examples are vowel shifts and consonant fortition.

One unsatisfactory aspect of this classification is that the category of prosodic processes overlaps with both weakening and strengthening. For example, assimilations are characteristically weakenings (deletion of feature bundles) with concomitant prosodic spreading of features from a nearby segment onto the vacated slot (Poser 1982). With these reservations kept in mind, the classification will provide us with a serviceable way of organizing the material.

## Prosodic processes

There is a long tradition of descriptive studies in which tone is treated not as a feature of vowels but as a quasi-independent melody which is superimposed on the segmental material. The contribution of autosegmental phonology was to formulate general principles by which this superimposition, or association, is governed, and to show that autosegmental representations together with those principles make sense of a number of characteristic properties of tone which have no explanation as long as tone is considered a feature of vowels (Clements & Ford 1979; Goldsmith 1979). One of the crucial properties of autosegmental representations is that they permit one tone-bearing unit to be associated with more than one tone and the converse, thereby allowing a natural representation of contour tones on the one hand and of the spread of tones over longer spans on the other. Autosegmental representations also permit tones to be unassociated to any tone-bearing unit, and conversely tone-bearing units to be unassociated to any tone, possibilities which are realized as 'floating tones' and toneless vowels, respectively. A corollary is that a sound change deleting a tone-bearing unit may leave behind the tone previously associated with it, allowing it to link up with some other phoneme.

Autosegmental representations are constrained by the inviolable principle that association lines may not cross. This imposes (correctly) a locality constraint to the effect that a tone cannot be assimilated across another tone.[18] Second, unassociated tones are assumed to link to free tone-bearing units one to one and left to right. The rightward direction of tone

---

[18] As long as assimilation is treated by multiple linking of a tone to several tone-bearing units and unrestricted melody copying is disallowed.

association lies behind the typological generalization that perseverative assimilation ('rightward spread' of tone) is more common than anticipatory assimilation.[19]

One of the most far-reaching principles of the theory, and perhaps the most problematic, is the *obligatory contour principle* (OCP), which prohibits sequences of identical tones on a tier.[20] The OCP accounts for such characteristic processes as 'tone absorption' (Goldsmith 1984).

Autosegmental representations were soon generalized to 'segmental' phenomena. The result of this was a fully autosegmentalized conception of phonological representations, in which feature bundles are organized into quasi-independent tiers and linked to timing units.[21] The geometries of phonological representations currently being proposed are extremely rich (Clements 1985; Sagey 1986).

Most of the tonal processes mentioned above turn out to have 'segmental' counterparts which can be explained in the same way. Recall that one of the crucial properties of tiered phonology is that it permits many–one association in both directions. Two feature bundles may be linked to a single slot. This representation accounts for the possibility of a sequence of articulations with the status of a single segment (e.g. affricates, or phonologically short diphthongs).[22] Conversely, one feature bundle may be linked to two slots. This is the standard representation of long vowels and consonants. Lengthening and shortening can then be seen to result from the addition and elimination of skeletal slots on the timing tier. If a new slot is added, it will be linked with a feature bundle in the melody in accordance with the principles of autosegmental phonology. If a slot is eliminated, the feature bundle linked to it will be 'set afloat' and deleted by convention unless it is associated with some other slot. The insertion and elimination of skeletal slots is characteristically determined by syllable structure. The common process of open syllable lengthening and closed syllable shortening is thus the implementation of a constraint requiring the rhyme to have two slots.[23]

*Compensatory lengthening*, in the simplest case, results from the deletion

[19] Maddieson (1978); see e.g. McCawley (1978) for Japanese and Kiparsky (1982c) for Vedic.
[20] Leben (1973, 1978), Pulleyblank (1986; apparent exceptions accounted for by lexical linking of tones), Goldsmith (1979; no universal OCP); Odden (1986; the OCP is not inviolable and not a formal constraint on phonological representations).
[21] These timing units have been represented as CV slots (Clements & Keyser 1983) or as unspecified X slots bracketed into syllables, hierarchically (Levin 1985) or not (Hyman 1985).
[22] See e.g. Clements & Keyser (1983), Keyser & Kiparsky (1984).
[23] These processes are studied (from a syllabic point of view) in Reis (1974), Leys (1975), Árnason (1980), Anderson (1984). Extrametricality explains why open syllable lengthening can apply to *closed* syllables if they are word-final (Kiparsky 1984). Interaction with the resyllabification rules (attraction of consonants to stressed syllables) unifies closed syllable shortening with 'trisyllabic shortening' and related shortenings in English, as in *seren+ity*, *con+ic*, *Span+ish* (Stampe 1972/1980; Myers 1986).

of the features associated with a slot and the spread of features from a neighboring segment into the vacated slot.[24]

*Geminate consonants* were a puzzle for earlier phonological theory in that they behave unlike clusters of distinct consonants in a number of ways. These special properties have turned out to be largely derivable from the principles of autosegmental phonology, specifically the OCP (extended to the nontonal domain) and the ban on crossing association lines. See Steriade (1982) and Steriade & Schein (1984) for an account of the 'integrity' of geminates (resistance to anaptyxis), Hayes (1986b) for 'inalterability' (resistance to processes that would modify one half of a geminate), and Prince (1984) on their equivalence to single consonants in morpheme structure rules. The theory in fact predicts, correctly, that integrity and unalterability should hold specifically for morpheme-internal geminates and for geminates originating by assimilation across morpheme boundaries.[25] For morphological aspects of the OCP see especially McCarthy (1986).

*Coalescence and split.* Another possibility inherent in tiered phonology is that a sequence of feature bundles on different tiers may coalesce into a single feature bundle, or that conversely a feature bundle may be linearized into a sequence of separate feature bundles. Coalescence is a common source of complex segments, particularly secondary articulation such as glottalization (Sapir 1938; Greenberg 1970),[26] aspiration (Wetzels & Hermans 1985), palatalization (Bhat 1978), and, for vowels, nasalization (Ferguson, Hyman & Ohala 1975; Ruhlen 1978), breathy voice, etc. In addition, monophthongization processes such as $ai \rightarrow e$ and $au \rightarrow o$ are extremely common. The converse process is the linearization of feature specifications, as in diphthongization[27] and in such consonantal processes as prenasalization ($m \rightarrow {}^{m}b$).

*Epenthesis and anaptyxis.* At the level of phonetic realization, these processes result from shifts in the relative timing of articulations on different tiers, yielding an intrusive articulation with no skeletal slot of its own in the lexical phonology (Clements 1986). Like all sound changes, such timing shifts appear to originate postlexically, as changes in the phonetic realization of

---

[24] See de Chene & Anderson (1979), Ingria (1980), Steriade (1982: ch. 2), Clements (1982), Miranda (1984), Hock (1986 – who reviews some of the older and recent work), and the studies collected in Wetzels & Sezer (1986).

[25] The prediction is regrettably compromised by the possibility (and apparent necessity) of treating some assimilations as melody copying processes (Steriade 1986); see fn. 18 in this chapter.

[26] See also Blust (1980) for discussion of other sources of glottalization.

[27] Andersen (1972) suggests that features are linearized in the order 'unmarked, marked'; the assumed markedness relations are, however, not well-supported and are at variance with those proposed in other works (Chomsky & Halle 1968; Kean 1981).

lexical representations. This intrusive articulation may be *phonologized* under certain conditions, acquiring a skeletal slot of its own. For example, some Finnish dialects develop a svarabhakti vowel in certain liquid clusters (Skousen 1975). Operating postlexically, this yields schwa, which is not a phoneme of Finnish, and does not count for lexical rules such as word stress, e.g. *kýlmässä→ kýləmässä* 'cold' (inessive sg.). Phonologized into a rule of lexical phonology, it must (by structure-preservation, Kiparsky 1985) yield a phoneme of the language (normally a copy of the preceding vowel) and may feed lexical rules (hence *kýlymässä*, lexically four syllables as shown by the secondary stress on the third syllable). A similar interpretation can be given for consonant epenthesis, e.g. *warmth→ warmpth* (phonetic) and *thimle→ thimble* (phonologized, in fact lexicalized).[28]

## Weakening processes: lenition, assimilation

Weakening processes result from loss of feature specifications associated with a segment, with or without concomitant spread of marked feature specifications from a neighboring segment. They apply typically to segments in prosodically weak positions (unstressed syllables, syllable codas; Szemerényi 1973; Hock 1976).

Assimilation tends to spread marked feature specifications to segments (Schachter 1969: 344ff). For example, vowels tend to get nasalized by nasal consonants rather than denasalized by oral consonants. This asymmetry can be derived as a theorem within autosegmental phonology if we assume that marked values are specified and unmarked values unspecified (Poser 1982; Harris 1984; Mascaró 1984; Kiparsky 1985; Hayes 1986a).[29] In total assimilation of consonants, the less sonorous consonant tends to win, e.g. Sanskrit *dharma, sūtra→* Pāli *dhamma, sutta* (Hankamer & Aissen 1974); given that the sonority hierarchy can be derived from the markedness hierarchy (Farmer 1979) this may be a special case of the general principle.[30]

A second basic generalization is that assimilation takes place first between

---

[28] That the former type results from phonetic (though language-particular) realization rules is argued in Liberman & Pierrehumbert (1984). Wetzels (1985) proposes to distinguish them in terms of the linking configuration on the CV tier. This seems plausible for the intrusive consonants, but it is not clear how it could be generalized to vowel epenthesis. He also suggests that the former type occurs with liquid clusters and the latter type with other clusters. Presumably, the phonologization of the intrusive transitional stop articulation is governed by (language-particular as well as universal) constraints on syllable structure. For example, /warmpth/ is not syllabifiable in English (Kiparsky 1981), and stop+liquid is a possible onset in English but stop+nasal is not. Wetzels' discussion does not indicate that a hierarchical theory of syllable structure is in any way incompatible with the autosegmental decomposition of phonological representations into tiers.

[29] See also Gvozdanović (1982, 1985) on the idea that hierarchically dominant features are more likely to be preserved under weakening processes.

[30] For the role of the sonority hierachy see Zwicky (1972), Hooper (1976a: chs 10, 11), Selkirk (1982), Steriade (1982). Foley (1977) proposes several other 'strength' scales; for discussion see Drachman (1980), Smith (1981 – with Foley's reply in Goyvaerts 1981), Harlow (1982), Harris (1985: ch. 2).

segments which are already most similar in their feature composition (Hutcheson 1973; Lee 1975, 1976). This is reflected in the common prohibition on sequences of minimally distinct consonants (Trnka 1936; Trubetzkoy 1939: 220–4; Greenberg 1978b; McCalla 1980). A principled derivation of this generalization is still lacking, although feature tiers in conjunction with the OCP (McCarthy 1986) suggest a promising approach.

*Tonal assimilation*. Low tone assimilates to high tone more often than the reverse (Hyman & Schuh 1974; Maddieson 1978). This follows directly from the marked status of high tone (Maddieson 1978; D. Pulleyblank 1986), given the principle that assimilation is spread of marked feature specifications. Since for similar reasons in a three-tone system mid tone is unmarked relative to low and high we would also predict that mid tone should assimilate both to high tone and to low tone more often than the reverse.

*Tonogenesis*. The laryngeal articulation of consonants can affect neighboring vowels in a way which is then phonologized as tone.[31] This process can give rise to tonal systems, and increase the number of tones in languages which are already tonal.[32] The best-documented type, found throughout Southeast Asia and scattered elsewhere, is the development of low tone after voiced obstruents.[33] The phonetic mechanisms behind this lowering tendency are disputed. The following causes have been proposed: decrease in transglottal pressure accompanying voiced obstruents (Kohler 1985), decrease in vocal cord tension accompanying voicing, due either to intrinsic slackening of the vocal cords (Halle & Stevens 1971) or to lowering of the larynx (Hombert, Ohala & Ewan 1979).[34] For a recent review see Rischel (1986).[35]

---

[31] Voicing and continuancy also have a lengthening effect on a preceding vowel (Peterson & Lehiste 1960; Chen 1970) which has been phonologized in some dialects of English (Aitken's law, Harris 1985: ch. 2).

[32] Major pioneering studies are Maspéro (1912), Haudricourt (1954, Vietnamese), Karlgren (1915, 1926, Chinese), Brown (1965, Thai). For more recent findings, on both Asian and African languages, see Hyman (1973, 1978), Lea (1973), Matisoff (1973), Hagège & Haudricourt (1978), Hombert, Ohala & Ewan (1979), Henderson (1982), Laughren (1984), Rischel (1985, 1986).

[33] Including voiced aspirates, but not, apparently, implosives (Hombert *et al.*, 1979: 47–8). In some Thai and Chinese dialects it is voiceless obstruents which have caused low tone on the following vowel, while voicing on the contrary has had a *raising* effect. It may be that the rising vs. falling pitch contour arising from the voicing distinction may be reinterpreted either as high vs. low or as low vs. high, perhaps depending in some way on the structure of the phonological system. See Maddieson (1978: 353), Rischel (1985, 1986) for reference and discussion.

[34] Other consonantal effects on tone include lowering before [h] and raising before glottal stops.

[35] Rischel concludes: 'Obviously, sound change has both an articulatory, a perceptual, and a high-level organizational aspect. Therefore, one cannot hope to arrive at a unified explanation of any mechanism of tonal change without taking into consideration the psychological role played by already existing or incipient tonal distinctions (e.g. such that have to do with syllable quantity or types of syllable termination), and the degrees of freedom inherent in the tonal development. Thus, the conditions for tonogenesis must be considered anew in all detail *for each particular language*, and with reference to *all chronological stages* that seem relevant to the explanation.' (1986: 80)

## Strengthening processes: vowel and consonant shifts

It would not be surprising if phonological systems tended to be organized in such a way as to permit maximum use of the available perceptual space, and if vowel and consonant shifts were motivated by that end. For various proposals to this effect see Vendryes (1902), Trubetzkoy (1939), Jakobson (1941), Martinet (1955: 62, 151), Zinder (1979 – structural as well as perceptual relevance of redundant features), Liljencrants & Lindblom (1972), Janson & Schulman (1983), Lindblom (1986a, b – typology of vowel systems derivable from maximization of contrast, see Bromberger & Halle 1986 for discussion), Stevens, Keyser & Kawasaki (1986 – enhancement of contrasts by means of redundant features).

Vowel shifts have recently received considerable attention. Labov *et al.* (1972) suggest that they fall into a few limited types: tense (or 'peripheral') vowels tend to be raised, lax (nonperipheral) vowels tend to fall, and back vowels are fronted. Stockwell (1978: 338) attributes these shifts to the interplay of strengthening and weakening processes. He analyzes peripheral vowels as phonologically centering diphthongs; vowel shifts are taken as results of the 'conflict between glide maximization (the *perceptual* ideal) and glide minimization (the *productive* ideal). Perception wants maximum dis-similation ([æə]→ [iɑ], [ii]→ [ai]), while production wants the minimum articulatory movement. See also Wolfe (1972), Donegan (1978), Schane (1984), Morin (1984). What remains puzzling on all accounts is the persistence of these shifts (or of the kinds of vowel systems that give rise to them) in certain languages such as English and the other Germanic languages (Wallace 1975), and their total absence in others, such as Japanese. It has been speculated that this persistence is ultimately traceable to certain properties of the prosodic system.[36]

It is not clear that analogs exist in the tonal domain. A striking trait of many tone systems, however, are polarity switches, such as the interchange of high and low tone (Maddieson 1978: 352). Whether these are elementary processes or derive from the interaction of independent tone shifts remains to be discovered. Evidence for the latter is Pulleyblank's (1986) explanation of a polarity switch in Margi through the interaction of tone spread and default tone assignment (rather than by simple interchange of tonal values).

## Naturalness paradoxes and how to live with them

As should be clear even from our cursory survey, identification of 'natural processes' is a tricky matter. For many ostensibly natural processes it is

---

[36] Van Coetsem, Hendricks & McCormick (1981) argue this for consonant shifts as well.

possible to produce the exact contrary cases, for which, moreover, it is often possible to devise equally plausible explanations. As we have seen, voiced stops often induce low tone on the following vowel, but sometimes high tone (fn. 33). Assimilation is natural, but so is dissimilation. Nasalized vowels are sometimes lowered, sometimes raised.[37] Another striking example is the loss of final vowels in words of the form CV̄CV. In such cases, the distinction between the new monosyllables and original CV̄C monosyllables is sometimes rephonologized in terms of a contrast between long and overlong syllables. Which will be the overlong ones? Will it be the original monosyllables, since other things being equal, a monosyllabic word is longer than the stressed syllable of a disyllabic word? Or will it be the new monosyllables, since they would become overlong by compensatory lengthening when the second syllable is lost? The answer is: both! Ternes (1981) shows that some German dialects undergoing apocope have developed overlength on the original monosyllables, others, in exactly the reverse development, on the shortened disyllables.

This fact of linguistic life should not cause surprise or despair[38] once we recognize that in language, as in other biological and social systems, there is no simple relation between mechanism and function: process can serve many functions, and a given function can be served by many processes. In consequence, functional requirements only constrain the historical development of such systems, but do not uniquely determine it. The characteristic 'opportunism' of biological evolution[39] is typical of language change as well.

### 14.2.3. The nature of phonological variation

The discovery by Labov and his collaborators of stable patterns of variation in speech, governed by features of the linguistic context as well as by style and social class, raises two interconnected issues of fundamental importance for grammatical theory, which any account of sound change must come to grips with: (a) how is the patterning of variation to be characterized, and (b) what are its causes? (See Fonagy 1956, 1967, for earlier discussion of this issue.) Statistical models of variation (Cedergren & Sankoff 1974; Rousseau & Sankoff 1978) posit for each variable rule an input probability $p_0$ which represents the rule's basic 'strength,' and probabilities $p_1, \ldots p_n$ associated with particular features of the environment ('variable constraints'), in such a way that the probability of applying the rule in a given specific environ-

---

[37] Schourup (1973) and Ruhlen (1978) propose that this depends on whether nasalization is distinctive or not; Chen (1973) suggests that the basic tendency is lowering and the raising is due to tensing which accompanies nasalization.

[38] As in Lass (1980, 1981).

[39] See Gould (1980) for some pretty examples.

ment is obtained as a function of the probabilities associated with the features present in that environment. Cedergren & Sankoff formulate the following linguistic interpretation of these statistical models:

> . . . the statistically patterned variation . . . reflects an underlying probabilistic component in the competence of each speaker. The probability of rule application [is] a well-defined function of the features present in the environment of the variable.

These models can be interpreted as embodying certain hypotheses about the character of variation:

1. *The rule hypothesis:* variation arises from contextually determined probabilities of grammatical rules.
2. *The independence hypothesis:* each contextual factor affects the probability of rule application independently of the others.
3. *The competence hypothesis:* linguistic competence has a probabilistic component.

On each point, different interpretations are of course possible and have in fact been proposed many times. The rule hypothesis was challenged by a number of variationists who argued that the observed frequency patterns are artifacts of collating different sets of speakers and/or the same speaker in different circumstances, and contended that variation patterns are really governed by *implicational scales* (Bickerton 1971; Bailey 1973). For example, a rule deleting final stops might apply with varying degrees of generality, but is always constrained by implicational constraints such as:

(i) Deletion before vowels implies deletion before consonants.
(ii) Deletion of voiced stops implies deletion of voiceless stops.
(iii) Deletion in formal style implies deletion in casual style.

The argument is that the statistical spread of variation shrinks as we reduce the size of the sample and the stylistic range of the sample. At the limit (single speaker, single style) we would therefore have an invariant pattern. But even if there were such a limit, we could probably never identify it because there are too many variables involved, and because some of them, such as style and class, have a subjective component which cannot in principle be measured independently to a sufficient degree of precision.

The independence hypothesis was challenged by Kay (1978) and Kay & McDaniel (1979) on the basis of the fact that the relative weight of variable constraints can vary for different groups of speakers. For example, groups of Black teenagers studied by Labov (1972b) differed in that for some groups, variation in the application of final *-t*, *-d* deletion depended more on the phonological environment, and for others, it depended more on the presence

of a grammatical boundary. It turned out, however, that the relative importance of the grammatical boundary correlates exactly with the speaker's age,
the reason being, as Labov himself showed, that speakers analyze the derivational morphology of past tense clusters more deeply as they grow older. So it
would be wrong to attribute the difference between the two groups of
speakers to a reversal of the variable constraints. Instead, the deletion
pattern is dependent on the speaker's grammatical system.[40]

The competence hypothesis is logically related to the independence
hypothesis in the following way: if the contribution of each feature of the
environment to the probability of applying a rule could vary independently,
then the variable constraints associated with those environments would have
to be learned by speakers, which would mean that they are part of their
linguistic competence. This would have the corollary for historical linguistics
that sound change could involve redistribution or reweighting of variable
constraints. The alternative, or *functionalist* hypothesis is that the relative
frequency of variants across different environments is not learned, and not
part of grammatical competence, but results from processing constraints that
come into play in language use.[41] On the functionalist view, the progress of
linguistic change could not consist of environment-specific changes in the
frequency of application of rules, but only in an overall increase (or decrease)
in the frequency of application of a rule (i.e. in $p_0$), with all environments $p_1$,
$\ldots p_n$ moving in lockstep. Empirical support for the functionalist view
(proposed speculatively in Kiparsky 1971) has been found for syntactic
change by Kroch (1986). Short of historical work such as Kroch's, it could be
tested empirically by means of crossdialectal comparison of variable rules.
Since the variationist position entails that in principle any of the factors
controlling the relative frequency with which optional rules are applied in
different environments is subject to independent variation and therefore to
change, it should be possible to find dialects differing minimally with respect
to the pattern of variation in some rule. The functionalist account, on the
other hand, entails that the contribution of each variable constraint is fixed.
Variationists can establish their case by demonstrating dialectal diversity in
the conditioning of optional rules, and supporters of the processing explanation can establish theirs by demonstrating its crossdialectal and crosslinguistic
uniformity.

Such comparisons must however be based on the grammars of the dialects

---

[40] Even so, Sankoff & Labov (1979) concede to Kay & McDaniel (1979) that the assumption of the
independence of constraints is empirically wrong, taking the position that the apparatus of variable
rules is not a theoretical model but a heuristic device (p. 206), and denying that the independence of
constraints has been assumed in theory or in practice, in variation studies. The conjecture we make in
the text, instead, is that the independence of variable constraints is actually one of the virtues of the
model.

[41] Curiously, Fasold (1978: 87) refers to this as the 'weakest' position on variation, whereas it in fact is the
strongest, since it holds that variation patterns are predictable.

and not just the frequencies of linguistic alternants. The reason is that seemingly dialect-specific variation patterns are not necessarily the result of a rule having dialect-specific variable constraints. They might also be the result of the interaction of different rules with dialect-independent variable constraints. Consider in this regard one of the few phonological variation studies to have addressed this problem, Guy's (1980) investigation of *-t, -d* deletion in New York and Philadelphia. Guy (p. 51) finds that the process 'is omnipresent in a range of English speakers, and very stable and uniform with regard to its major constraints.' In particular, all speakers show the grammatical effect which retards deletion of *-t, -d* in suffixes (e.g. *walked, rained*) as opposed to stems (e.g. *start, hold*) and all speakers show the phonological effect which favors deletion next to consonants, e.g. *test me* vs. *test us, test me* vs. *get me*. However, Guy found that (among white speakers) a following pause *impedes* deletion in Philadelphia but *promotes* it in New York, as shown in the following figures giving the frequencies of deletion:

(2) | *Environment* | __ #C | __ #V | __ ## |
|---|---|---|---|
| New Yorkers | 1.0 | 0.56 | 0.83 |
| Philadelphians | 1.0 | 0.38 | 0.12 |

This is *prima facie* evidence for a dialect difference, but the nature of the difference is not at all self-evident. Quite possibly the data reflect the *interaction* of different individually well-behaved variable rules. To show how such interaction can yield apparently arbitrary variation patterns, we will construct a small artificial example. Assume that the *-t, -d* deletion rule applies specifically to *unreleased* stops such as typically occur in syllable-final position in English. Imagine now two hypothetical dialects of English. In dialect A, word-final stops are obligatorily unreleased ($t^-$). In dialect B, this is true only in connected speech; before a pause, stops are optionally (say half the time) released ($t^+$).

(3) | *Environment* | __C | __V | __ ## |
|---|---|---|---|
| Dialect A | $t^-$ | $t^-$ | $t^-$ |
| Dialect B | $t^-$ | $t^-$ | $t^-/t^+$ |

As a result, dialect A will show the universal pattern of consonant deletion rules (Poplack 1980 etc.): it will apply most often before C, next most often before pause, and least often before V. But in dialect B, the optional release before pause deprives deletion of half its input, so that the very same deletion rule now yields a partially reversed pattern of variation:

(4) | *Environment* | __C | __V | __ ## |
|---|---|---|---|
| Dialect A | most frequent | least frequent | intermediate |
| Dialect B | most frequent | intermediate | least frequent |

Our fictitious dialects A and B illustrate how what appears to be a reversal of variable constraints could in reality be due to the interference of a distinct phonological process. They are not intended as serious analyses of New York and Philadelphia speech, although they resemble the respective patterns discovered by Guy in those dialects. On the contrary, the actual phonological analysis of New York and Philadelphia speech will have to relate the *-t*, *-d* deletion rule not only to stop release, but also to the glottalization and 'flapping' to which these consonants are notoriously subject in many dialects of English, including the ones in question. As is well-known, these processes interact in a way which makes it quite misleading to investigate any one of them in isolation. Much of the variability in these and other processes of English low-level phonology, moreover, can be traced to variation in syllabification (Kahn 1976). The much discussed 'variable constraints' on such rules as '*-t*, *-d* deletion' may therefore be artifacts.

The alternative view suggested here should not be construed as an attempt to escape empirical responsibility by shielding the functionalist theory of variation from potential refutation by statistical data. On the contrary, it leads to important testable predictions which do not follow from the standard variationist view. First, if some of the variability of *-t*, *-d* deletion is mediated by phonetic processes such as release and glottalization, then the deletion pattern should be more uniform across dialects for consonants such as *-s*, *-z*, which are not subject to those processes, and which therefore appear with more uniform allophones. And if the variability is ultimately a matter of alternative syllabification, then deletion of final consonants should be sensitive to variable constraints determining resyllabification across word boundary (Singh & Ford 1984). This would predict that the lower the initial consonant of the next word is on the sonority hierarchy, the more it should trigger deletion of a preceding consonant. This prediction is in fact confirmed for final *-t*, *-d* deletion, as Singh and Ford point out, by Guy's finding that liquids and glides were uniformly ordered between consonants and vowels as triggers of deletion. Finally, on the suggested functionalist interpretation significant covariation is predicted between different syllable-sensitive rules, whether related or not.

The fundamental problem is that although variationists in principle associate probabilities with *rules*, they in practice usually end up associating them with *alternants* without worrying much by what rule system the alternants are derived. In this way variationist research has tended to put out of court the interesting empirical question to what extent the grammatical system is in fact implicated in the pattern of variation.

In conclusion, it is necessary to problematize the variation data, and to put its analysis on a more systematic phonetic and phonological footing. This is undoubtedly not easy to do but it is essential if the problem of the relationship between structure, variation, and change is to be resolved.

## 14.2.4. Sound change and linguistic structure

If the considerations of the preceding sections are put together with the assumptions of lexical phonology, the following picture of sound change emerges: natural phonological processes, originating in production, perception, and acquisition, result in inherent, functionally controlled variability of speech. 'Sound change' takes place when the results of these processes are internalized by language learners as part of their grammatical competence.[42] Internalization as lexical representations or lexical rules is subject to structure-preservation and other relevant constraints on the lexical component, and may involve selective grammaticalization and lexicalization of variants preferred at the optional stage. In consequence, conditions on sound change reflect functional factors.[43] Internalization as postlexical rules is not subject to the principles governing the lexical component, and cannot result in morphological conditioning, lexical diffusion etc. In this way we derive the desired result that only 'phonemic' changes can be morphologized and undergo lexical diffusion.

In the following sections we consider some factors that appear to be relevant to the incorporation of change in linguistic structure.

### The role of acquisition in sound change

Since the neogrammarians (Osthoff & Brugmann 1878; Paul 1880/1920) it has been speculated that, in addition to gradual articulatory drift, the discontinuous transmission of language is a factor in sound change, and that this mechanism is specifically responsible for certain so-called 'minor sound changes.' These changes, notably dissimilation (Grammont 1895; Posner 1961) and metathesis (Grammont 1933; Ultan 1978), differ from ordinary sound change in being (1) abrupt rather than gradual, (2) often sporadic,[44]

---

[42] Hellberg (1978, 1980) has made a good case for the proposition that learners internalize phonological 'processes' as 'rules' *before* these become either opaque or unnatural, contrary to what some interpretations of natural phonology (but not all, cf. Dressler 1985) would imply. See also Anderson (1981) for relevant discussion.

[43] Hence the possibility of sound changes conditioned by certain morphological factors, stylistic level ('learned' vs. colloquial), sex (male vs. female dialects), class (caste dialects). It also follows that morphophonemic conditioning of sound change should be impossible. Thus, Lachmann's law must be an analogical change rather than a sound change (Kuryłowicz 1968; Watkins 1970, King 1973; Strunk 1976; Perini 1978; Drachman 1978).

[44] Hoenigswald (1964) shows, however, that many allegedly sporadic changes of this type are actually regular changes once their contextual restrictions are correctly defined. Hock (1985) argues that metathesis is regular if it is structurally motivated, e.g. by syllable structure constraints of the language.

and (3) structure-preserving, in the sense that they do not result in new segment types but simply redistribute existing ones (Hoenigswald 1978b). It has been proposed that dissimilation arises by a mechanism akin to hypercorrection; as Vendryes (1902) succinctly put it, 'it is the fear of assimilation that produces dissimilation.' Along these lines, Ohala (1986) hypothesizes that dissimilation arises when listeners misinterpret what they hear as being the result of assimilation, and then in careful speech actualize the supposed source. For example, the dissimilation of Slavic [čæ] to [ča] would have happened when speakers assumed that [čæ] was 'really' an assimilated version of /ča/, and proceeded to undo this putative assimilation process. The abovementioned properties of abruptness, sporadicity, and structure preservation are immediately explained by this hypothesis. Also explained is the fact that dissimilation typically involves the same features as assimilation, viz. features defining places of articulation (aspiration, glottalization, palatality, rounding) rather than features defining manner of articulation.

Andersen (1973, 1978) assigns a much more pervasive role to acquisition in sound change. He conjectures that sound change in general can originate in much the same way that analogical change is usually pictured as taking place, namely by 'abduction': learners get stuck with their own misperceptions or miscategorizations, and, by a sort of hypercorrection, devise *adaptive rules* that map their own 'wrong' underlying forms into something that approximates the ambient norm. Loss of those adaptive rules would then constitute sound change. Empirical study of child phonology gives little support for this theory.[45] Moreover, a general problem with locating sound change in language acquisition is that the class of typical or potential sound changes does not match the class of typical or potential child language processes (Drachman 1978; Vihman 1980).[46]

## Structural constraints on sound change

A corollary of postulating nonphonetic levels of phonological representation is that for each sound change we must ask not only what the innovation is but what its consequences are for the linguistic system. Claims about the latter depend entirely on the *linguistic* theory that is being assumed, not on any aspect of the theory of change. For example, in phonemic terms the Great Vowel Shift of English caused a major restructuring of the English vowel

[45] Relatively little is known about children's phonological perception, but there is some evidence that they are quite acute at discriminating phonetic nuances (Read 1971) and that they freely reanalyze their grammar en route to the adult system (Kiparsky & Menn 1977). Accounts of analogical change by imperfect learning (Kiparsky 1968) or other 'abductive' mechanisms are more plausible, to the extent that these changes eliminate analyses which are in some way hard to learn (opaque, etc.).

[46] See also Weinreich, Herzog & Labov (1968) and Bybee & Slobin (1982) on the general issue; also relevant is Janson (1981, 1982) on the perceptual motivation of sound change, and Labov (1974) on what might be termed subminimal contrasts. See further, Parker (1981), Lahiri & Blumstein (1983).

inventory; from the viewpoint of the phonological theory worked out in Chomsky & Halle (1968) it hardly changed it at all. However, in so far as change may depend on structure, historical considerations may constrain and provide evidence bearing on the linguistic theory.

For this reason, Jakobson's classification of types of phonological restructuring processes is more than an idle taxonomy. Its importance derives from the point we already noted (p. 372) that sound changes are determined by overriding structural principles, universal as well as language-specific. If change is structure-dependent then we had better know what the structure is in order to understand the change.

Examples of studies which explain sound change on the basis of typological parameters are Reis (1974), for quantity, and Murray & Vennemann (1983), for syllabification. Symmetry considerations have long been considered a motivation of change (Martinet 1955; Moulton 1960, 1961; Ronneberger-Sibold 1985); given phonological features, they usually translate into simplicity considerations, so the need for symmetry as an autonomous factor is unclear. For exemplification and discussion of the relationship between sound change and morphosyntactic structure see Korhonen (1969, 1982), Gussman (1976), Nyman (1977), Cooley (1978), Harris (1978), Keyser & O'Neil (1980a, b), Ronneberger-Sibold (1980), Hewson (1982), Moulton (1983).

These considerations are also crucial for comparative linguistics. In an influential paper, Jakobson (1958) re-emphasized the uniformitarian tenet that reconstructed languages must be compatible with the universal principles that govern phonological systems. For example, since aspirated consonants presuppose the existence of /h/, an /h/ is predicted for Proto-Indo-European, which is confirmed by laryngeal theory. In the same way, recent proposals that the 'voiced' stops were glottalic (Hopper 1973; Gamkrelidze & Ivanov 1984) would imply the existence of a glottal stop. In Proto-Semitic, the comparative method leads to an overcrowded inventory of front fricatives; typological considerations alone would point to reconstructing one of them as a voiceless lateral, which is confirmed by a wealth of independent evidence (Steiner 1977).

## Functional causes

Gilliéron's amusing examples of homonyms arising from sound change and being sorted out by 'therapeutic' lexical replacement are well-known. It is not surprising that speakers should begin to avoid a homonym that causes repeated misunderstanding or embarrassment and resort to paraphrases, which eventually may replace the original word (Gilliéron 1918; Dworkin 1975). More problematic are two popular extensions of this idea. One is that homonymy may be avoided not just therapeutically by repairing its damages by lexical replacement, but 'prophylactically' (pre-emptively) by blocking the sound change itself from applying to that word. To my knowledge, the apparent cases of this phenomenon all involve *phonemic* changes, and thus effectively reduce to the previous case of selection among lexical alternants. For example, in Finnish the sound change $t \rightarrow s/$ ___ $i$ has not applied in the past tenses of certain verbs where it would have produced homonymy (e.g. *kut+i* 'spawned,' from *kute-* does not become *kusi* which means 'pissed,' from *kus(e)-*). However, it is a lexical neutralization rule and so there is the possibility of a lexical choice between the alternant forms, resolved in favor of the unambiguous variant with $s$.[47]

An even more radical extension of functionalism is the idea that the threat of homonymy may actually prevent or cause entire sound changes. A demonstration of this effect would be of considerable significance because no existing model of sound change shows how genuine teleology of this kind could be implemented. Two claims in point (Martinet 1955) are: (1) that the likelihood of mergers is inversely proportional to the amount of homonymy that would result (to what Martinet calls the *functional load* of the merged phonemic distinction); and (2) that the threat of merger from one sound change will tend to be averted by another sound change ('push chains'). Considering the importance of the issue, the scarcity of systematic studies of the problem is amazing. The first claim has been investigated, with negative results, by King (1967). As for the second, since mergers are obviously common events, the problem is how to support a functional interpretation of chain shifts, specifically, how to tell whether a sequence of sound changes $A \rightarrow B$, $B \rightarrow C$ (where $A \nrightarrow C$) is a push chain. By definition, it is a push chain if the former change *caused* the latter, in the relevant sense. The alternatives to be excluded are: (1) that there is no causal connection, but simply a random sequence of changes; and (2) that the causality is the other way round (and related to symmetry of the phonological system rather than to homonymy), in which case we have a 'drag chain'. One way of establishing causality would be to show statistically in a large corpus of changes that shifts tend to come in chains. King did such a study (1969a) and got negative results; proponents of teleology have criticized its design, without however proposing a better one. (Chain shifts which can be subsumed under one process, such as raising of tense vowels, of course do not support a teleological interpretation.) In individual cases, a causal connection would be indicated if contextual restrictions on $A \rightarrow B$, the more arbitrary and specific the better, are replicated in $B \rightarrow C$, so that the latter only applies where the distinction between A and C 'needs' maintaining. Assuming causality is established,

---

[47] Moreover, the rule applies in a largely idiosyncratic fashion in past tense forms. See Paunonen (1973), Kiparsky (1973), Campbell (1974) for details.

push chains can be distinguished from drag chains by careful attention to the chronology of the changes (as in Eliasson 1986).[48] See Campbell & Ringen (1981), Drachman (1981) for discussion of the general issues at stake, and Vincent (1978) for a statement of the case against teleology.

## 14.3. Analogical change in phonology

In this section we will be concerned only with phonological aspects of analogical change, and with boundary questions relating to sound change and analogical change. For morphological analogy, see Anderson (Chapter 13 in this volume) and Anttila (1977).

## 14.3.1. Phonetic and phonological analogy

The neogrammarians drew a sharp conceptual boundary between analogy and sound change, but as we already saw in section 14.1, that boundary can be hard to find in practice. Anti-neogrammarians have attempted to 'deconstruct' the distinction theoretically as well, by showing that the process of sound change itself involves an analogical mechanism. Schuchardt (1885: 7f, 22f): argued that sound change originates in specific environments and generalizes by *phonetic analogy*:

> Inspection of any group of related dialects will show that the
> conditioning factors of the sound change vary in diverse ways from
> place to place; this can be seen as the spatial projection, as it were, of
> time differences.                                    (Schuchardt 1885: 61f)

Exactly how does this spatial projection of time differences come about? The traditional idea is that sound changes are attenuated in the course of their geographic spread. For example, the Old High German consonant shift is assumed to have started in full force in the south and to have petered out as it spread northward before coming to a complete halt. Becker (1967) and Bach & King (1970) questioned this assumption on the grounds that one would expect a borrowing dialect to generalize a rule rather than restrict it, and suggested that the direction of spread might have been the opposite. Since this fails to explain why sound changes are more limited on their *whole* periphery, Robinson & van Coetsem (1973) propose instead that the reason rules are most general where they originated is that they had the most time to become simplified there. Noting that lexical diffusion of innovations is also most advanced at the point of origin, Barrack (1976) adds the suggestion that the successive waves of generalization themselves could spread in wave-like

---

[48] On relative chronology in general and in relation to synchronic rule order in particular, see Chafe (1968), Kiparsky (1968), Voyles (1969), Chen (1976), Anderson (1978), Markey (1978), Janson (1979).

fashion. See Adams (1977) and Ralph (1981) for further discussion of the geographical spread of sound change.

Independent evidence that phonetic/phonological analogy must be recognized as a mechanism of change is that it can also generalize regularities which do not arise directly as sound changes at all. For example, the voiceless aspirated palatal /ch/ of Sanskrit happened to originate for the most part as a geminate [cch]; in the relatively few cases where it was originally ungeminated it was later geminated by analogy with the bulk of the geminated ones (Wackernagel 1896: 156). Such purely phonological analogical processes fit poorly into the neogrammarian scheme of things, there being no morphological process which can provide the basis for a proportion of the usual sort. From the viewpoint of the theory that analogical change is grammar simplification, on the other hand, such cases are to be expected. Thus, the analogical gemination of /ch/ in Sanskrit is a generalization of (i.e. the elimination of exceptions to) the phonotactic rule 'aspirated palatals are geminated.'[49]

## 14.3.2. Non-surface analogy

The neogrammarian notion of analogy as an intrinsically morphological process is only one of the reasons which has led historical linguists to overlook analogy in the purely phonological domain. Another reason is that analogy was classically defined on surface forms, and phonological analogy may involve crucial reference to abstract rules and representations, in which case it is simply beyond the reach of traditional conceptions of analogical change.

Kuryłowicz (1948, 1964, 1977) recognized this problem and attempted to remedy it, within the limitations of structural theory, by enriching and constraining the proportional schema in certain ways. He suggested that both the terms of the proportions and the relation between them have to meet certain structural conditions. In particular, the terms have to be related as *forme de fondation* and *forme fondée*, and their representation may crucially abstract away from the actual pronunciation in some respects. In the following analogical proportion, proposed to account for the rise of lengthened grade (*vṛddhi*) in the Sanskrit ablaut system (Kuryłowicz 1956), which critically depends on the phonological equivalence of syllabic and nonsyllabic resonants (*ṛ=r*) and of long vowels and geminate vowels (*ā=aa*):

(5) ṛ : ar = a : X (where X = aa = ā)

Two other enrichments of the basic proportional schema are Leed's (1970) proposals that proportions can operate on distinctive feature representations

---

[49] On phonetic analogy see also Vennemann (1972b).

and that a single analogical change can be the result of several analogical proportions operating simultaneously.[50]

The structuralist approach thus amounts to an attempt to retrofit analogical proportions with certain rule-like properties. The relation between *forme de fondation* and *forme fondée* (Kuryłowicz 1977) is similar to the relation between input and output of a rule, and proportions with 'virtual' terms which abstract away from certain overtly present surface features, such as (5), are comparable to rules which apply to representations at nonfinal stages in derivations. Thus, (5) can be thought of as representing a straightforward generalization of the ablaut rule if we take into account the fact that ablaut applies at a point in the synchronic derivation which precedes the application of vowel contraction and syllabification. Indeed Kuryłowicz (1964) has explicitly justified the abstract nature of proportions by the principle that *redundant* features or elements can be disregarded in setting up proportions. A grammar-based account of analogical change captures those properties *inherently*. In our terms, for example, Kuryłowicz's idea that redundant features can be ignored in proportions translates into the claim that rules can generalize even when followed in the derivation by other rules which add those redundant features or elements. Similarly, Leed's simultaneously applicable multiple proportions that operate on feature matrices are close to the rule systems of a generative phonology. What the proportional mechanism cannot mimic with such annotations is the *sequentially ordered* character of rule application, a major weakness in the domain of morphophonology.

An example of a change traditionally considered a sound change which has turned out to be a case of phonological analogy (rule loss) is the 'second fronting' in the Mercian dialect of Old English ([dag+as]→[dægas], [fat+u]→[fæətu]). The problem is how to unify the changes of [a] to [æ] and to [æə]. Dresher (1980) argues that Mercian had a rule of *a*-restoration which retracts [æ] to [a] before a back vowel in the following syllable, and a rule of back mutation which diphthongizes front vowels before a front consonant followed by a back vowel:

(6) *a*-restoration: æ→ a/ ___ $C_0$[+back]
(7) Back mutation: ∅→ ə/[V,−back] ___ [−back][V,+back]

The sound change according to Dresher is actually the *loss* of *a*-restoration, causing a word like /fæt+u/ to undergo back mutation:

(8)

| | Older stage | Innovating stage |
|---|---|---|
| | /fæt+u/ | /fæt+u/ |
| *a*-restoration: | /fat+u/ | ― |
| back mutation: | ― | /fæə t+u/ |

---

[50] On the relation between analogy and sound change see further Malkiel (1968, 1971, 1976), Bazell (1974), King (1980).

### 14.3.3. Analogical change and the phonemic level

We concluded in section 14.1 from the English example discussed by Bloomfield that the principle of separation of levels is inconsistent with the facts of linguistic change. In this section we will look more closely at the relation between analogical change and the phonemic level of representation and consider how the problem may be resolved in the theory of lexical phonology.

Not all structuralists agree with Kuryłowicz that abstract morphophonemic representations must be recognized as part of linguistic structure, let alone that they can play a role in language change. According to a common view (Trnka 1968: 342), 'morphological analogy cannot affect the inventory and the organization of phonemic features':

> ... the transference of a sound into the position of any other by way of analogy is conclusive evidence of their phonemic status. Thus Old English *æ* must be regarded as a phoneme different from *a*, because the latter appears in closed syllables (cf. 2nd pers. sg. imper. *far* 'go') and in open ones when followed by a front vowel (cf. gen. sg. *paðes* 'path' masc. gen. sg. *glades glad* past part. *faren* etc.) by analogy on other forms in which the interchange between *æ* and *a* is based on phonological laws. (Trnka 1968: 349)

Similar claims have been defended in Darden (1971), Flier (1982), and Manaster-Ramer (1984); cf. Hogg (1979), for related discussion.

However, clear cases of morphological analogy giving rise to new phonemes are known. Jakobson (1931) cites the rise of palatal /k'/ in Russian by analogy with the alternations between palatal and nonpalatal consonants in the conjugation, e.g. *rv+u : rv'+ot=tk+u : tk'+ot*, replacing original *\*tčot*. In Swiss German dialects, analogical extension of umlaut has given rise to new phonemes (Moulton 1967).[51] In Western Bosnian dialects of Serbo-Croatian, a new phoneme /δ/ has arisen analogically in past participles (Ivić 1973).

These facts cause difficulty for any theory which recognizes an autonomous phonemic level and maintains a strict separation of levels. Ebeling (1960) and Zinder (1979) attempt to cope with the paradox by supposing that the allophones somehow became phonemicized *before* their analogical introduction into the contrasting environment:

> ... /k'/ became a phoneme not because the word /tk'ot/ appeared: on the contrary, the word /tk'ot/ became possible because /k'/ entered into a phonemic opposition with /k/ ... each sound in the word is a

---

[51] These cases are analyzed as rule reordering in Kiparsky (1968) and Niepokuj (1985); Moses (1982) argues for lexicalization.

representative of some phoneme. If this is true, the function of sense discrimination can shift from one element to another. From the point of view of the word's entire shape, it had always been necessary that the word *peki* ['bake!'] should have ended in the vowel /i/, and that the preceding consonant as well should have been palatalized, even though it did not represent the phoneme /k'/ opposed to non-palatalized /k/. Under certain circumstances . . . it could happen that palatalization could have become connected with meaning. (Zinder: 243, quoted from Liberman 1981).

This is a major departure from classical phonemics, since it requires sounds which are in complementary distribution to be independent phonemes in their own right. The move is analogous to that of the post-Bloomfieldian autonomous phonologists (see p. 367 above), only Ebeling and Zinder want to move the phonemic level even further 'south'. However, they do not actually state any new principles for determining phonemic representations; the conclusion is based only the *post hoc* inference from analogical change.

Synchronic paradoxes of similar type led Halle (1959) to propose that the structuralists' phonemic level should be dropped. In classical generative phonology (Chomsky & Halle 1968), underlying phonological represen-tations are mapped by phonological rules into systematic phonetic represen-tations, which are related to articulation by principles which are (with certain provisos), universal. From this point of view, the failure of phonological analogy to respect the phoneme inventory is a welcome fact. On the other hand, the existence of generalizations about distinctive as opposed to redundant phonological features (section 14.1.5) becomes problematic again.

Recently, this picture has again been questioned. The theory of lexical phonology posits a level of lexical representation between underlying representations and phonetics.[52] Lexical representations are derived by phonological rules operating in the lexicon, which are subject to marking conditions which prohibit certain features from being marked in the lexi-con.[53] On this theory, the analogical changes in question could be interpreted as resulting from simplifications in the marking conditions. Thus, prior to the change, Russian had a marking condition prohibiting the feature combina-tion [−back, +high], blocking the palatalization rule from applying to velars. The analogical change, then, was the loss of this restriction from the lexical phonology of Russian. The prediction is that the change should have coincided with the lexicalization of palatals in underived words in the

---

[52] Mohanan (1986), (Kiparsky (1982a, b, 1985), Kaisse & Shaw (1985), Rubach (1984).

[53] The level of lexical representations is, however, not the same as the level of classical phonemics and plays a very different role in the theory. For example, the mapping of lexical representation into phonetics permits neutralization, which is by definition precluded in allophonic rules.

language. More generally, this entails that only features which play a distinctive role in the language could be generalized by phonological analogy.

Further implications of lexical phonology for phonological change will be examined in the next section.

## 14.4. On the nature of lexical diffusion: a conjecture and a case study

Proponents of lexical diffusion do not question that sound change of the neogrammarian type exists as well.[54] The question arises how the two types of change can be differentiated. Labov (1981) argues in detail that we must recognize both types of sound change, with the characteristics listed in (9):

| (9) | *'Neogrammarian'* change | *Lexical* *diffusion* |
|---|---|---|
| Discrete | no | yes |
| Phonetic conditioning | fine | rough |
| Lexical exceptions | no | yes |
| Grammatical conditioning | no | yes |
| Social affect | yes | no |
| Predictable | yes | no |
| Learnable | yes | no |
| Categorized | no | yes |
| Dictionary entries | 1 | 2 |

The properties in (9) differentiate two types of phonological rules. Do those rule types *result* from the two kinds of sound change, or is the existence of two rule types itself the reason why there are two kinds of sound change? We shall here argue for the latter position. The typology presented in (9) closely resembles the distinction between lexical and postlexical rules (Kiparsky 1982a, b; Kaisse & Shaw 1985; Mohanan 1986) and we propose to identify the two.

An alternative is that the distinction between neogrammarian sound change and lexical diffusion is intrinsically connected to the particular phonological feature involved (Labov 1981). Labov suggests that lexical diffusion is found most often in changes in phonological features that define 'subsystems' in that their phonetic realization involves several phonetic features, while phonological features with a more 'concrete' phonetic manifestation will tend to change in neogrammarian fashion:

> . . . where lexical diffusion does occur, it is to be found most often in changes across subsystems – particularly lengthenings and shortenings

---

[54] 'The neogrammarian conception of language change will probably continue to be part of the truth' (Wang 1979: 369).

in vowels, and changes of place of articulation in consonants. Diphthongization and monophthongization appear to be intermediate cases.

We find regular sound change in a wide range of vowel shifts that represent movements within the subsystem of short vowels, or the subsystem of up-gliding diphthongs, or in-gliding diphthongs: raising, lowering, fronting, backing, rounding, unrounding, nasalization.

In consonants, Labov suggests that change in manner of articulation is typically regular.

Such a relationship between the modality of change and the substantive character of the feature involved would be a purely empirical one; there is no theoretical reason to expect it. But in any case, it runs counter to a number of reasonably well-documented cases of lexical diffusion involving raising, voicing, and other features with intrinsic phonetic interpretation (Kiparsky 1980: 412; Phillips 1984: 321).

The position to be defended here is that lexical diffusion is a property of lexical rules. That is, we take the differences in (9) not as *results* of the two types of sound change but as *preconditions* for them. This relationship, we propose, is a principled one because the theory of lexical phonology already specifies as one of the essential distinctions between lexical and postlexical rules that only the former may have lexical exceptions. It follows that lexical diffusion must be a redistribution of phonemes among lexical items and cannot create any new phonological contrasts. This prediction is borne out by the attested examples of lexical diffusion, which invariably involve *neutralization* processes, i.e. processes whose output can be lexicalized – an observation which suggests that lexical diffusion is the 'selective progressive lexicalization of the output of neutralizing variable rules (Kiparsky 1980: 412). In addition, this hypothesis fully reconciles lexical diffusion with Bloomfield's 'stray sounds' argument against the possibility of lexically sporadic sound change (see p. 366).

Our hypothesis further predicts that the very same feature, indeed the same rule, should be subject to lexical diffusion in one language or dialect and not in another depending on whether the feature is lexically distinctive or not. We will now show that this is borne out in a well-known English example, the tensing of short /æ/.

The tensing of /æ/ applies in all dialects of American English, but it takes several quite different forms. In the MidAtlantic states it is a lexical rule; the Philadelphia version is stated in (10) (Ferguson 1975; Labov 1981, 1986):

(10) Philadelphia tensing pattern:
   ǽ→ Á before (normally tautosyllabic) $f, s, \theta, m, n, (d)$

This rule causes stressed [æ] to become tense (we will write the tensed form as *A*), regularly before certain tautosyllabic consonants (see (11a), in three words before *d* (11b) and in scattered words in open syllables (11c):

(11) a. grAph, pAss, pAth, hAm, mAn
    b. bAd, mAd, glAd (vs. sæd, dæd, læd . . .)
    c. p[æ/A]l, pl[æ/A]net, person[æ/A]lity

In a given word, Philadelphia speakers either apply or do not apply tensing uniformly. This feature-specifying rule is to be sharply distinguished from the *degree* of tensing and raising with which the tense vowel is pronounced, which varies in a gradient manner depending on style and social class. As shown by the contrast in (11b) between tense *bAd*, *mAd*, *glAd* and lax *sæd*, *dæd*, *læd*, etc., the rule has been subject to lexical diffusion. Labov argues that it is an ongoing change in the dialect, which is currently being extended to words like those in (11c).

A similar tensing process operates in most dialects of American English, such as at least the Midwest and New England, but in those other dialects it operates *categorically* with no lexical conditioning whatsoever. So we may ask why Philadelphia and more generally the MidAtlantic area including New York City and Washington implement the tensing in so radically different a way from the rest of the country.

To begin with, let us establish that tensing in Philadelphia is a rule of lexical phonology, in fact a rule ordered at level 1. The data which shows this was obtained partly from Labov (1981) and partly from native Philadelphians interviewed by Lori Levin and myself.[55] The relevant facts and their explanation in the framework of lexical phonology are as follows.

1. A syllable that is closed at level 1 retains its tense vowel even when its coda later becomes the onset of a following 'word boundary' suffix or word:

(12) a. mAnn#ing, tAnn#ing, hAmm#ing, clAmm#y, glAss#y,
      mAdden#ing, scAnn#er, mAdd#est[56]
    b. plAn it, pAss us

This is because tensing operates at level 1 and word boundary suffixes are not added until level 2, while the combinations in (12b) are not formed until the syntax.

2. Because of the inherent cyclicity of lexical derivations we predict that the tenseness of basic words will be retained in words derived from them at level 1 regardless of resyllabification in later cycles. We found this to be the prevalent pattern in the words:

---

[55] Labov (1986) reports additional data which is in agreement with our findings.
[56] The # boundary is written before these affixes merely to show their level 2 status. The same goes for the + boundaries in (13). In lexical phonology boundaries are eliminated from phonological representations.

(13) clAss+ify, gAs+ify, gAs+eous, photogrAph+ic

A number of speakers were found with lax [æ] in these words; and [æ] was even preferred in *massive*. There are several possible explanations for this fact. One is that these speakers treat the words as underived, or as root-based rather than word-based derivatives. Since roots are not cyclic domains, tensing would in that case first become applicable only *after* the suffix is added, at which point the final consonant will already be resyllabified as an onset.[57] The [æ] may also be a residue of the earlier system where, as I shall argue below, tensing operated at a later stage in derivation. In fact, this pronunciation seems to be characteristic of older speakers in my data, although I do not have enough material for a firm conclusion.

Lax [æ] is correctly predicted for words like *humæn+ity*, *titæn+ic* (since [æ] is unstressed on the first cycle and the syllable is open on the second cycle), and *sæn+ity*, *Spæn+ish* (since [æ] is long on the first cycle and the syllable is open on the second cycle).

3. Syllables which become closed only after level 1 do not undergo tensing. For example, the process which deletes an unstressed vowel before an unstressed syllable beginning with a sonorant cannot apply until level 2 at the earliest because it must 'wait' until the word stress is assigned. If it applied cyclically at level 1 we would get *\*op'ratic* instead of *operatic*, from *op'ra*. This deletion produces a closed syllable but, as predicted, it does not feed tensing.[58]

(14) fæm'ly, cæth'lic, anæph'ra

4. Tensing does not apply to the past tenses of strong verbs (15a), though it does apply to their present tenses (15b) and of course to weak verbs (15c):

(15) a. ræn, begæn, swæm
   b. stAnd, understAnd
   c. scAnned, hAmmed

So tensing is ordered before the ablaut rule:

(16) i→ æ in the past tense of strong verbs

whose output must clearly be æ, not A, because of *sæt, spæt, drænk, sæng*,

---

[57] Morphological indeterminacy should accordingly lead to phonological variability. It is not unlikely that speakers should differ in whether they derive a word like *massive* from *mass*. On that hypothesis one would predict educated speakers to have A more often in these derivatives than uneducated speakers, but I do not know whether that is so.

[58] Hence tensing provides a diagnostic for underlying representations. Words like *camera* regularly have lax æ, suggesting that they are lexically represented as trisyllabic in spite of the fact that they are practically always pronounced as disyllables and have no stress-shifted derivations either, so that the elided middle syllable is actually never heard. It is not necessary to attribute the trisyllabic underlying form to the orthography (though that is certainly a possibility). The unusual cluster *-mr-* might be a sufficient clue to the deleted vowel.

*ræng*, *etc.* Rule (16) has to apply at level 1 for other reasons;[59] this entails that tensing must also be at level 1. in (15).[60]

5. Tensing never applies to non-lexical categories, such as auxiliaries or the indefinite article:

(17) hæd, æm, cæn, æn

Hence the well-known contrast *I cæn* vs. *tin cAn*. Since word stress is also assigned by lexical rules, the items in (17) get no word stress (as witness the fact that they are liable to vowel reduction unless they receive a postlexical stress in their sentence context) and consequently they do not meet the structural description of tensing.

Given what has been said so far, it follows that we could account for why æ-tensing undergoes lexical diffusion in the MidAtlantic states if we could show how it became a lexical rule in the first place. To this end let us look first at the simpler types of dialect.

(18) *Midwest*:
  a. Backing (lexical)
     [+low] → [+back] in env. __ r
  b. Tensing/raising (postlexical)
     /æ/ → {[æ] . . . . . . . . . . . [ih]} (continuum of tensing/raising)

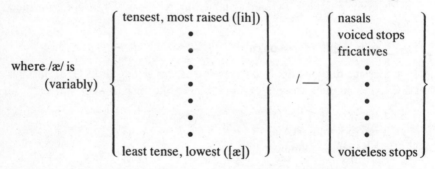

where /æ/ is
(variably)

In the Midwest (see (18)) there are two phonemes /æ/ and /a/ in *lather* and *father*. The opposition between them is neutralized in favor of *a* before tautosyllabic *r* by the lexical backing rule (18a). The vowel /æ/ is subject to a variable postlexical tensing rule of which an approximate formulation is given in (18b). This rule is totally uninfected by any lexical idiosyncrasy.

In New England the situation is a bit more complicated because lexical backing applies more generally there, not just before *r* but in roughly the

---

[59] Because it belongs to level 1 it does not apply to verbs derived from nouns at level 2, e.g. *inked* rather than *\*ank* (Kiparsky 1982a).

[60] Note that tensing does not *have* to be ordered before (16). It *could* be ordered also after (16), still at level 1. There are indications that this possibility is also realized, in that some speakers have lax [æ̆].

same contexts as the British English broad *a* rule, before fricatives and nasal clusters, in a lexically specified set of words as those listed under (19b).

(19) a. car, Harvard
    b. half, laugh, bath, pass, ask, aunt, dance, example
    c. father, balm

The vowel is realized as the well-known [a] of *Park your car in Harvard yard*. I will assume this to be characterized by the feature [+ATR], though I will continue to call the rule 'backing' for convenience. There are many æ's to which this backing rule does not apply, either because its context is not met or because they are lexically specified as [−ATR] so that the strict cycle condition will block the lexical rule from applying to them. All these æ's are then subject to tensing *postlexically* by the same rule as in the Midwest. So in this dialect we again have two phonemes but with a rather different distribution because of the more general backing rule.

(20) *New England*:
    a. Backing (lexical)
        [+low, −back] → [+ATR] / ___ r, $C_f$ (in certain words)
        (where $C_f$=f, θ, s, N+C)
    b. Tensing/raising (postlexical)
        /æ/ → {[æ] . . . . . . . . . . . [ih]} (continuum of tensing/raising)

The Mid-Atlantic states, like New England, had a special broad *a* rule before fricatives and nasal clusters, but broad *a* coincided not with the vowel of *car* and *father* – but with the tense æ that was also the output of the postlexical tensing rule. The result was that these dialects acquired a *lexical* tensing rule. Now this lexical tensing rule overlapped with the old postlexical tensing rule, and eventually merged with it; the result is precisely the system that prevails in Philadelphia, shown in (21):

    a. Backing (lexical)
        [+low] → [+back] / ___r
    b. Tensing (lexical)
        [+low, −back] → [+ tense] / ___ $C_f$, in a set of words whose core is
        the old broad [*a*] class
    c. Raising (postlexical)
        /A/ → {[æ] . . . . . . . . . . . [ih]} (continuum of tensing/raising)

As we have seen, having acquired lexical status, tensing then spreads to new lexical items, that is, it undergoes lexical diffusion. So we see that the lexical status of æ-tensing in the MidAtlantic states is ultimately due to the fact that here and only here it continues in part the lexical backing rule of British English.

There is perhaps some contact between my claim that lexical diffusion is a property of lexical rules, and Labov's claim that lexical diffusion is a property of features defining 'abstract subsystems.' However, Labov identifies the abstract subsystems not by the phonological system of the language but by the phonetic nature of the distinctive features. In his view, features like tenseness and length are subject to lexical diffusion because they do not define any single physical dimension but rather 'a set of features that may include length, height, fronting, the directions and contours of glides, and the temporal distribution of the overall energy' (p. 299), while features like front/back and high/low will *not* manifest lexical diffusion because their physical realization is more direct. On this view it is, of course, mysterious that *a*-tensing, which after all involves the same feature in all dialects, is subject to lexical diffusion in some dialects and not others. By linking lexical diffusion to the *function* of the feature in the abstract phonological system as we have done – specifically with the lexical vs. postlexical status of the rule that specifies it – we predict exactly the observed dialect differences.

I draw the conclusion that the existence of two types of sound change, lexical diffusion and 'neogrammarian' sound change, is a consequence of the existence of two types of phonological rules, lexical rules and postlexical rules.

## 14.5. **Concluding remark**

There is no dearth of either data on theoretical alternatives in historical phonology. As usual, the hard part is to connect them in a way which will give us a more precise understanding of 'what really happened,' while narrowing down the theoretical options. When does sound change spread word by word? How is sound change constrained by the phonological system? By the vocal tract? What is the right interpretation of the variable rule technology? These and other basic questions of historical linguistics are at the moment being answered in radically different ways, some of which we have attempted to sort out here. Progress in our understanding of sound change is likely to come from an integration of theories of phonology, phonetics, acquisition, and language processing (perception, production, variation). It is this interplay of mutually constraining factors which gives historical linguistics its focal role in the study of language.

## REFERENCES

Adams, D. Q. 1977. Inter dialect rule borrowing: some cases from Greek. *General Linguistics* 17: 141–54.

Andersen, H. 1972. Diphthongization. *Language* 48: 11–50.

Andersen, H. 1973. Abductive and deductive change. *Language* 49: 567–93.

Andersen, H. 1978. Perceptual and conceptual factors in abductive innovations. In J. Fisiak (ed.) *Trends in linguistics: studies and monographs*. Vol. 4: *Recent developments in historical phonology*. The Hague: Mouton.

Anderson, S. R. 1978. Historical change and rule ordering in phonology. In J. Fisiak (ed.) *Trends in linguistics: studies and monographs*. Vol. 4: *Recent developments in historical phonology*. The Hague: Mouton.

Anderson, S. R. 1981. Why phonology isn't 'natural'. *Linguistic Inquiry* 12: 493–540.

Anderson, S. R. 1984. A metrical reinterpretation of some traditional claims about quantity and stress. In M. Aronoff & R. T. Oehrle (eds.) *Language sound structure*. Cambridge, MA: MIT Press.

Anttila, R. 1972. *An introduction to historical and comparative linguistics*. New York: Macmillan.

Anttila, R. 1977. *Analogy*. The Hague: Mouton.

Árnason, K. 1980. *Quantity in historical phonology*. Cambridge: Cambridge University Press.

Bach, E. & King, R. D. 1970. Umlaut in modern German. *Glossa* 4: 3–21.

Bailey, C.-J. N. 1973. *Variation and linguistic theory*. Washington: Georgetown University Press.

Baldi, P. & Werth, R. N. (eds.) 1978. *Readings in historical phonology*. University Park: Pennsylvania State University Press.

Barrack, C. 1976. Lexical diffusion and the High German consonant shift. *Lingua* 40: 151–75.

Bauer, R. S. 1979. Alveolarization in Cantonese: a case of lexical diffusion. *Journal of Chinese Linguistics* 7: 132–41.

Bauer, R. S. 1983. Cantonese sound change across subgroups of the Hong Kong speech community. *Journal of Chinese Linguistics* 11: 301–54.

Bazell, C. E. 1974. Marginal'nye zvukovje zakony. *Voprosy Jazykoznanija*, pp. 81–6.

Becker, D. A. 1967. Generative phonology and dialect study: an investigation of three modern dialects. Doctoral dissertation, University of Texas.

Bhat, D. N. S. 1972. *Sound change*. Poona: Bhasha Prakashan.

Bhat, D. N. S. 1978. A general study of palatalization. In Greenberg (1978b).

Bickerton, D. 1971. Inherent variability and variable rules. *Foundations of Language* 7: 457–92.

Bloomfield, L. 1933. *Language*. New York: Holt.

Bluhme, H. 1980. Uber die Ursachen des Lautwandels. In H. Lüdtke (ed.) *Kommunikationstheoretische Grundlagen des Sprachwandels*. Berlin: deGruyter.

Blust, R. 1980. More on the origin of glottalic consonants. *Lingua* 52: 125–56.

Bromberger, S. & Halle, M. 1986. On the relationship between phonology and phonetics. In J. S. Perkell & D. H. Klatt (eds.) *Invariance and variability in speech processes*. Hillsdale: Erlbaum.

Brown, M. 1965. *From ancient Thai to modern dialects*. Bangkok: Social Science Foundation Press of Thailand.

Bybee, J. L. & Slobin, D. I. 1982. Why small children cannot change language on their own: suggestions from the English past tense. In A. Ahlqvist (ed.) *Papers from the 5th International Conference on Historical Linguistics*. Amsterdam: Benjamins.

Campbell, L. 1974. On conditions on sound change. In J. M. Anderson & C. Jones (eds.) *Historical linguistics I–II*. Amsterdam: North-Holland.

Campbell, L. & Ringen, J. 1981. Teleology and the explanation of sound change. In W. Dressler (ed.) *Phonologica 1980*. Innsbruck: Institut für Sprachwissenschaft der Universität Innsbruck.

Cedergren, H. & Sankoff, D. 1974. Variable rules: performance as a statistical reflection of competence. *Language* 50: 335–55.

Cerrón-Palomino, R. 1974. Morphologically conditioned changes in Wanka-Quechua. *Studies in the Linguistic Sciences* 4, 2: 40–75.

Chafe, W. 1968. The ordering of phonological rules. *International Journal of Applied Linguistics* 34: 115–36.

Chan, M. 1982. Lexical diffusion and two Chinese cases reanalyzed. University of Washington, Linguistics Dept. ms.

Chen, M. Y. 1970. Vowel length variation as a function of the voicing of the consonant environment. *Phonetica* 22: 129–59.

Chen, M. Y. 1972. The time dimension: contribution toward a theory of sound change. *Foundations of Language* 8: 458–98.

Chen, M. Y. 1973. On the formal expression of natural rules in phonology. *Journal of Linguistics* 9: 223–49.

Chen, M. Y. & Hsieh, H.-I. 1973. The time variable in phonological change. *Journal of Linguistics* 7: 1–13.

Chen, M. Y. & Wang, W. S.-Y. 1975. Sound change: activation and implementation. *Language* 51: 255–81.

Chen, M. Y. 1976. Relative chronology: three methods of reconstruction. *Journal of Linguistics* 2: 209–58.

Chene, B. de & Anderson, S. R. 1979. Compensatory lengthening. *Language* 55: 505–35.

Cheng, C.-C. & Wang, W. S. Y. 1977. Tone change in Chao-zhou Chinese: a study in lexical diffusion. In W. Wang (ed.) *The lexicon in phonological change*. The Hague: Mouton.

Chomsky, N. & Halle, M. 1968. *The sound pattern of English*. New York: Harper & Row.

Christy, C. 1983. *Uniformitarianism in linguistics*. Amsterdam: Benjamins.

Clements, G. N. 1982. Compensatory lengthening: an independent mechanism of phonological change. Distributed by Indiana University Linguistics Club.

Clements, G. N. 1985. The geometry of phonological features. *Phonology Yearbook* 2: 223–50.

Clements, G. N. 1986. Syllabification and epenthesis in Barra Gaelic. ms.

Clements, G. N. & Ford, K. 1979. Kikuyu tone shift and its synchronic consequences. *Linguistic Inquiry* 10: 179–210.

Clements, G. N. & Keyser, S. J. 1983. *CV phonology in a generative theory of the syllable*. Cambridge, MA: MIT Press.

Coetsem, F. van, Hendricks, R. & McCormick, S. 1981. Accent typology and sound change. *Lingua* 59: 295–315.

Cooley, M. 1978. Phonological constraints and sound change. *Glossa* 12: 125–36.

Crothers, J. 1978. Typology and universals of vowel systems. In Greenberg (1978b).

Darden, B. 1971. Diachronic evidence for phonemics. *CLS* 7: 323–31.

Donegan, P. 1978. On the natural phonology of vowels. *Working Papers in Linguistics* 23. Ohio State University.

Donegan, P. 1985. How learnable is phonology? In W. U. Dressler & L. Tonelli (eds.) *Natural phonology from Eisenstadt*. Padova: CLESP.

Donegan, P. & Stampe, D. 1979. The study of natural phonology. In D. Dinnsen (ed.) *Current approaches to phonological theory*. Bloomington: Indiana University Press.

Drachman, G. 1978. Child language and language change: a conjecture and some refutations. In J. Fisiak (ed.) *Trends in linguistics: studies and monographs*. Vol. 4: *Recent developments in historical phonology*. The Hague: Mouton.

Drachman, G. 1980. Phonological asymmetry and phonological analogy: or, will the real Lachmann's Law please stand up. In M. Mayrhofer, M. Peters & O. E. Pfeiffer (eds.) *Lautgeschichte und Etymologie*. Wiesbaden: Dr. Ludwig Reichert Verlag.

Drachman, G. 1981. Teleological explanation in phonology. In W. Dressler, O. E. Pfeiffer & J. Rennison (eds.) *Phonologica 1980*. Innsbruck: Innsbrucker Beiträge zur Sprachwissenschaft.

Dresher, B. E. 1980. The Mercian second fronting: a case of rule loss in Old English. *Linguistic Inquiry* 11: 47–73.

Dressler, W. 1984. Explaining natural phonology. *Phonology Yearbook* 1: 29–51.

Dressler, W. 1985. *Morphonology: the dynamics of derivation*. Ann Arbor: Karoma.

Dworkin, S. N. 1975. Therapeutic reactions to excessive phonetic erosion. *Romance Philology* 28: 462–72.

Ebeling, C. L. 1960. *Linguistic units*. The Hague: Mouton.

Egerod, S. 1982. How not to split tones – the Chaozhou case. *Fangyan* 4: 169–73.

Eliasson, S. 1986. Is sound change teleological? The case of the central Scandinavian vowel shift. University of Uppsala. ms.

Farmer, A. 1979. Phonological markedness and the sonority hierarchy. In K. Safir (ed.) *Papers on syllable structure, metrical structure, and harmony processes*. Department of Linguistics, MIT.

Fasold, R. 1978. Language variation and linguistic competence. In D. Sankoff (ed.) *Linguistic variation: models and methods*. New York: Academic Press.

Ferguson, C. 1975. 'Short A' in Philadelphia English. In M. E. Smith (ed.) *Studies in linguistics: in honor of George L. Trager*. The Hague: Mouton.

Ferguson, C. A. 1978. Phonological processes. In Greenberg (1978b).

Ferguson, C. A., Hyman, L. & Ohala, J. 1975. *Nasálfest: papers from a symposium on nasals and nasalization*. Stanford: Stanford University.

Fidelholtz, J. L. 1975. Word frequency and vowel reduction in English. *CLS* 11: 200–13.

Flier, M. 1982. Morphophonemic change as evidence of phonemic change: the status of the sharped velars in Russian. *International Journal of Slavic Linguistics and Poetics* 25/26: 137–48.

Foley, J. 1977. *Foundations of theoretical phonology*. Cambridge: Cambridge University Press.

Fónagy, I. 1956. Über den Verlauf des Lautwandels. *Acta Linguistica Hungarica* 6: 173–278.

Fónagy, I. 1967. Variation und Lautwandel. In J. Hamm (ed.) *Phonologie der Gegenwart*. Graz: H. Böhlaus Nachfolger.

Gamkrelidze, T. V. & Ivanov, V. V. 1984. *Indoevropeiskii jazyk i indoevropeicy*. Tbilisi: Izdatelstvo Tbilisskogo Universiteta. An English translation *Indo-European and the Indo-Europeans* is forthcoming, to be published by Mouton.

Gerritsen, M. & Jansen, F. 1979. Een 50-jarige theorie over klankverandering getoetst aan 18 *ui*-woorden in 100 jaar. In M. Gerritsen (ed.) *Taalverandering in Nederlandse Dialekten*. Muiderberg: Dick Coutinho.

Gilliéron, J. 1918. *Généalogie des mots qui désignent l'abeille*. Paris: Champion.

Gilliéron, J. 1921. *Pathologie et thérapeutique verbales*. Paris: Champion.

Goldsmith, J. 1979. *Autosegmental phonology*. New York: Garland. (Doctoral dissertation, MIT, 1976.)

Goldsmith, J. 1984. Meeussen's rule. In M. Aronoff & R. T. Oehrle (eds.) *Language sound structure*. Cambridge, MA: MIT Press.

Gould, S. J. 1980. *The panda's thumb*. New York: Norton.

Goyvaerts, D. (ed.) 1981. *Phonology in the 1980's*. Ghent: Story-Scientia.

Grammont, M. 1895. *La dissimilation consonantique*. Dijon: Darantière.

Grammont, M. 1933. 2nd edn. 1939. *Traité de phonétique*. Paris: Delagrave.

Greenberg, J. H. 1966. Synchronic and diachronic universals in phonology. *Language* 42: 508–17.

Greenberg, J. H. 1969. Some methods of dynamic comparison in linguistics. In J. Puhvel (ed.) *Substance and structure of language*. Berkeley: University of California Press.

Greenberg, J. H. 1970. Some generalizations concerning glottalic consonants, especially implosives. *Working Papers on Language Universals* 2: 1–38.

Greenberg, J. H. 1978a. Some generalizations concerning initial and final consonant clusters. In Greenberg (1978b).

Greenberg, J. H. (ed.) 1978b. *Universals of human language*. Stanford, California: Stanford University Press.

Gussmann, Edmund 1976. Recoverable derivations and phonological change. *Lingua* 40: 281–303.

Guy, G. 1980. Variation in the group and in the individual: the case of final stop deletion. In W. Labov (ed.) *Locating language in time and space*. New York: Academic Press.

Gvozdanović, J. 1982. On establishing restrictions imposed on sound change. In A. Ahlqvist (ed.) *Papers from the 5th International Conference on Historical Linguistics*. Amsterdam: Benjamins.

Gvozdanović, J. 1985. *Language system and its change*. Berlin: Mouton/deGruyter.

Habick, T. 1980. Sound change in Farmer City. Doctoral dissertation, University of Illinois.

Hagège, C. & Haudricourt, A. 1978. *La phonologie panchronique*. Paris: PUF.

Halle, M. 1959. *The sound pattern of Russian*. The Hague: Mouton.

Halle, M. 1984. Remarks on the scientific revolution in linguistics 1926–1929. Presented at the First Roman Jakobson Colloquium.
Halle, M. & Stevens, K. 1971. A note on laryngeal features. *Quarterly Progress Report, Massachusetts Institute of Technology Research Laboratory of Electronics* 101: 198–213.
Hankamer, J. & Aissen, J. 1974. The sonority hierarchy. *CLS Parasession* 10: 131–45.
Harlow, R. B. 1982. Phonological changes in Polynesian. In A. Ahlqvist (ed.) *Papers from the 5th International Conference on Historical Linguistics*. Amsterdam: Benjamins.
Harris, James W. 1984. Autosegmental phonology, lexical phonology, and Spanish nasals. In M. Aronoff & R. T. Oehrle (eds.) *Language sound structure*. Cambridge, MA: MIT Press.
Harris, John 1985. *Phonological variation and change*. Cambridge: Cambridge University Press.
Harris, M. B. 1978. The inter-relationship between phonological and grammatical change. In J. Fisiak (ed.) *Trends in linguistics: studies and monographs*. Vol. 4: *Recent developments in historical phonology*. The Hague: Mouton.
Hashimoto, M. 1981. Review of W. Wang (ed.) *The lexicon in phonological change*. *Language* 57: 183–91.
Haudricourt, A. 1954. De l'origine des tons en Vietnamien. *Journal Asiatique* 242: 69–82.
Hayes, B. 1981. A metrical theory of stress rules. Doctoral dissertation, MIT.
Hayes, B. 1986a. Assimilation as spreading in Toba Batak. *Linguistic Inquiry* 17: 467–99.
Hayes, B. 1986b. Inalterability in CV phonology. *Language* 62: 321–52.
Heath, J. 1981. A case of intensive lexical diffusion. *Language* 57: 335–67.
Hellberg, S. 1978. Unnatural phonology. *Journal of Linguistics* 14: 157–78.
Hellberg, S. 1980. Apparent naturalness in phonology. *Nordic Journal of Linguistics* 3: 1–24.
Henderson, E. J. A. 1982. Tonogenesis: some recent speculations on the development of tone. *Transactions of the Philological Society* pp. 1–24.
Hewson, J. 1982. Shifting systems: evidence for systemic change in French historical phonology. In A. Ahlqvist (ed.) *Amsterdam Studies in the Theory and History of Linguistic Science. Papers from the 5th International Conference on Historical Linguistics*. Amsterdam: Benjamins.
Hock, H. H. 1976. Final weakening and related phenomena. *Mid-America Linguistics Conference Papers* 10: 219–59.
Hock, H. H. 1985. Regular metathesis. *Linguistics* 23: 529–46.
Hock, H. H. 1986. Compensatory lengthening: in defense of the concept 'mora'. *Folia Linguistica* 20: 139–60.
Hockett, C. F. 1965. Sound change. *Language* 41: 185–204.
Hoenigswald, H. 1960. *Language change and linguistic reconstruction*. Chicago: University of Chicago Press.
Hoenigswald, H. 1964. Graduality, sporadicity, and the minor sound change processes. *Phonetica* 11: 202–15.
Hoenigswald, H. 1973. *Studies in formal historical linguistics*. Dordrecht: Reidel.
Hoenigswald, H. 1978a. The *annus mirabilis* 1976 and posterity. *Transactions of the Philological Society*, pp. 17–35.
Hoenigswald, H. 1978b. Secondary split, typology, and universals. In J. Fisiak (ed.) *Trends in linguistics: studies and monographs*. Vol. 4: *Recent developments in historical phonology*. The Hague: Mouton.
Hogg, R. 1979. Analogy and phonology. *Journal of Linguistics* 15: 55–85.
Hombert, J.-M., Ohala, J. J. & Ewan, W. G. 1979. Phonetic explanations for the development of tone. *Language* 55: 37–58.
Hooper, J. B. 1976a. *An introduction to natural generative phonology*. New York: Academic Press.
Hooper, J. B. 1976b. Word frequency in lexical diffusion and the source of morphophonological change. In W. Christie, Jr. (ed.) *Current progress in historical linguistics*. Amsterdam: North-Holland.
Hopper, P. 1973. Glottalized and murmured occlusives in Indo-European. *Glossa* 7: 141–66.
Hulst, H. van der & Smith, N. 1982. *The structure of phonological representations, 1–2*. Dordrecht: Foris.
Hutcheson, J. 1973. Remarks on the nature of complete consonant assimilation. *CLS* 9: 215–22.
Hyman, L. (ed.) 1973. *Occasional Papers in Linguistics*. Vol. 1: *Consonant types and tone*. Los Angeles: University of Southern California.

Hyman, L. 1978. Historical tonology. In V. Fromkin (ed.) *Tone: a linguistic survey*. New York: Academic Press.

Hyman, L. 1985. *A theory of syllable weight*. Dordrecht: Foris.

Hyman, L. & Schuh, R. 1974. Universals of tone rules: evidence from West Africa. *Linguistic Inquiry* 5: 81–115.

Ingria, R. 1980. Compensatory lengthening as a metrical phenomenon. *Linguistic Inquiry* 11: 465–96.

Ivić, P. 1973. Sound laws and the distinctive power of phonological patterns. *Language Sciences* 24: 1–6.

Jakobson, R. 1929. Remarques sur l'évolution phonologique du russe comparée a celle des autres langues slaves. *Travaux du Cercle Linguistique de Prague*, vol. 2. Reprinted in *Selected writings*, vol. 1.

Jakobson, R. 1931. Prinzipien der historischen Phonologie. *Travaux du Cercle Linguistique de Prague* 4: 249–67. Reprinted in *Selected writings*, vol. 1.

Jakobson, R. 1941. *Kindersprache, Aphasie, und allgemeine Lautgesetze*. Uppsala: Språ kvetenskapliga Sällskapets Förhandlingar.

Jakobson, R. 1958. Typological studies and their contribution to historical linguistics. In E. Sivertsen (ed.) *Proceedings of the Eighth International Congress of Linguists*. Oslo: University Press.

Janson, T. 1977. Reversed lexical diffusion and lexical split: loss of -*d* in Stockholm. In W. Wang (ed.) *The lexicon in phonological change*. The Hague: Mouton.

Janson, T. 1979. *Mechanisms of language change in Latin*. Stockholm: Almqvist & Wiksell.

Janson, T. 1981. Identical sounds and variable perception. In W. U. Dressler, O. E. Pfeiffer & J. R. Rennison (eds.) *Phonologica 1980*. Vienna: Institut für Sprachwissenschaft der Universität Wien.

Janson, T. 1982. Sound change and perceptual compensation. In J. P. Maher, A. K. Bomhard & E. F. Koerner (eds.) *Papers from the 3rd International Conference on Historical Linguistics*. Amsterdam: Benjamins.

Janson, T. & Schulman, R. 1983. Non-distinctive features and their use. *Journal of Linguistics* 19: 321–36.

Jespersen, O. 1886/1933. Zur Lautgesetzfrage. In *Linguistica: selected papers in English, French and German*. Copenhagen and London. (Originally published in 1886. Reprinted in Wilbur (1977)).

Johnson, S. 1982. Morphological influences on sound change. In A. Ahlqvist (ed.) *Amsterdam Studies in the Theory and History of Linguistic Science. Papers from the 5th International Conference on Historical Linguistics*. Amsterdam: Benjamins.

Joos, M. 1952. The medieval sibilants. *Language* 28: 222–31.

Kahn, D. 1976. Syllable-based generalizations in English phonology. Doctoral dissertation, MIT. Published 1980. New York: Garland Press.

Kaisse, E. & Shaw, P. A. 1985. On the theory of lexical phonology. *Phonology Yearbook* 2: 1–30.

Karlgren, B. 1915. *Études sur la phonologie chinoise*. Leiden and Stockholm: Archives d'études orientales.

Karlgren, B. 1926. *Philology and ancient China*. Oslo: Instituttet for sammenlignende kulturforskning.

Kay, P. 1978. Variable rules, community grammar, and linguistic change. In D. Sankoff (ed.) *Linguistic variation: models and methods*. New York: Academic Press.

Kay, P. & McDaniel, C. K. 1979. On the logic of variable rules. *Language in Society* 8: 151–87.

Kean, M. L. 1981. On a theory of markedness: some general considerations and a case in point. *GLOW 1979*.

Keyser, S. J. & Kiparsky, P. 1984. Syllable structure in Finnish phonology. In M. Aronoff & R. T. Oehrle (eds.) *Language sound structure*. Cambridge, MA: MIT Press.

Keyser, S. J. & O'Neil, W. 1980a. The evolution of the Old English plural rule. *Journal of Linguistic Research* 1: 17–35.

Keyser, S. J. & O'Neil, W. 1980b. Exceptions to high vowel deletion in the Vespasian Psalter and their explanations. In M. Davenport, E. Hansen & H. F. Nielsen (eds.) *Current topics in historical linguistics: Proceedings of the Second International Conference on English Historical Linguistics*. Odense: Odense University Studies in English.

King, R. 1967. Functional load and sound change. *Language* 43: 831–52.

King, R. 1969a. Push chains and drag chains. *Glossa* 3: 3–21.

King, R. 1969b. *Historical linguistics and generative grammar.* Englewood Cliffs: Prentice-Hall.

King, R. 1973. Rule insertion. *Language* 49: 551–73.

King, R. 1980. The history of final devoicing in Yiddish. In M. I. Herzog, B. Kirschenblatt-Gimblett, D. Miron & R. Wise (eds.) *The field of Yiddish: studies in language, folklore, and literature. Fourth collection.* Philadelphia: Institute for the Study of Human Issues.

Kiparsky, P. 1968. Linguistic universals and linguistic change. In E. Bach & R. Harms (eds.) *Universals in linguistic theory.* New York: Holt.

Kiparsky, P. 1971. Historical linguistics. In W. Dingwall (ed.) *A survey of linguistic science.* College Park, Maryland: University of Maryland.

Kiparsky, P. 1973. Phonological representations. In O. Fujimura (ed.) *Three dimensions of linguistic theory.* Tokyo: TEC.

Kiparsky, P. 1980. Concluding statement. In E. Traugott, R. Labrum & S. Shepherd (eds.) *Papers from the 4th International Conference on Historical Linguistics.* Amsterdam: Benjamins.

Kiparsky, P. 1981. Remarks on the metrical structure of the syllable. In W. U. Dressler, O. E. Pfeiffer & J. R. Rennison (eds.) *Phonologica 1980.* Vienna: Institut für Sprachwissenschaft der Universität Wien.

Kiparsky, P. 1982a. Lexical morphology and phonology. In I. S. Yang (ed.) *Linguistics in the morning calm.* Seoul: Hanshin.

Kiparsky, P. 1982b. From cyclic phonology to lexical phonology. In H. van der Hulst & N. Smith (eds.) *The structure of phonological representations 1.* Dordrecht: Foris.

Kiparsky, P. 1982c. The Vedic and Pāṇinian accent systems. In P. Kiparsky *Some theoretical problems in Pāṇini's grammar.* Poona: Bhandarkar Oriental Research Institute.

Kiparsky, P. 1984. On the lexical phonology of Iceland. In C. C. Elert, I. Johansson & E. Strangert (eds.) *Nordic prosody* III. Umeå: University of Umeå.

Kiparsky, P. 1985. Some consequences of lexical phonology. *Phonology Yearbook* 2: 85–138.

Kiparsky, P. & Menn, L. 1977. On the acquisition of phonology. In L. Macnamara (ed.) *Language learning and thought.* New York: Academic Press.

Koch, W. A. 1970. *Zur Theorie des Lautwandels.* Hildesheim: Olms.

Kohler, K. 1985. $F_0$ in the perception of lenis and fortis plosives. *Journal of the Acoustical Society of America* 78: 21–32.

Korhonen, M. 1969. Die Entwicklung der morphologischen Methode im Lappischen. *Finnisch-Ugrische Forschungen* 37: 203–62.

Korhonen, M. 1982. Reductive phonetic developments as the trigger to typological change: two examples from the Finno-Ugrian languages. In A. Ahlqvist (ed.) *Amsterdam Studies in the Theory and History of Linguistic Science. Papers from the 5th International Conference on Historical Linguistics.* Amsterdam: Benjamins.

Krishnamurti, B. 1978. Areal and lexical diffusion of sound change. *Language* 54: 1–20.

Kroch, A. 1978. Toward a theory of social dialect variation. *Language in Society* 7. Reprinted in H. Allen & M. Linn (eds.) *Dialects and language variation.* New York: Academic Press.

Kroch, A. 1986. Function and grammar in the history of English periphrastic *do.* In R. Fasold & D. Schiffrin (eds.) *Language variation and change.* Orlando: Harcourt.

Kuryłowicz, J. 1948. La nature des procés dits 'analogiques'. *Acta Linguistica* 5: 15–37.

Kuryłowicz, J. 1956. *L'apophonie en indo-européen.* Warsaw: Polska Akademia Nauk.

Kuryłowicz, J. 1964. *The inflectional categories of Indo-European.* Heidelberg: Winter.

Kuryłowicz, J. 1968. A remark on Lachmann's Law. *Harvard Studies in Classical Philology* 72: 295–99.

Kuryłowicz, J. 1977. Problèmes morphologiques généraux. In *Prace Językoznawce.* Vol. 90: *Problèmes de linguistique indo-européenne.* Warsaw: Wydawnictwo Polskiej Akademii Nauk.

Labov, W. 1965. On the mechanism of linguistic change. *Georgetown University Monographs on Languages and Linguistics* 18: 91–114.

Labov, W. 1972a. The internal evolution of linguistic rules. In R. Stockwell & R. K. S. Macaulay (eds.) *Linguistic change and generative theory.* Bloomington: Indiana University Press.

Labov, W. 1972b. *Sociolinguistic patterns*. Philadelphia: University of Pennsylvania Press.
Labov, W. 1974. On the use of the present to explain the past. In L. Heilmann (ed.) *Proceedings of the Eleventh International Congress of Linguistics*. Bologna: Mulino.
Labov, W. 1981. Resolving the neogrammarian controversy. *Language* 57: 267–308.
Labov, W. 1986. The exact description of the speech community: short A in Philadelphia. ms.
Labov, W. & Sankoff, D. 1979. On the uses of variable rules. *Language in Society* 8: 189–222.
Labov, W., Yaeger, M. & Steiner, R. 1972. *A quantitative study of sound change in progress*. Philadelphia: U.S. Regional Survey.
Lahiri, A. & Blumstein, S. 1983. Acoustic invariance in speech: contributions towards an explanation of natural rules in phonology. Brown University. ms.
Lass, R. 1980. *On explaining language change*. Cambridge: Cambridge University Press.
Lass, R. 1981. Explaining language change: the future of an illusion. In W. Dressler, O. E. Pfeiffer & J. Rennison (eds.) *Phonologica 1980*. Innsbruck: Innsbrucker Beiträge zur Sprachwissenschaft.
Laughren, M. 1984. Tone in Zulu nouns. In G. N. Clements & J. Goldsmith (eds.) *Autosegmental studies in Bantu tone*. Dordrecht: Foris.
Lea, W. A. 1973. Segmental and suprasegmental influences on fundamental frequency contours. In L. Hyman (ed.) *Consonant types and tone*. Los Angeles: University of Southern California.
Leben, W. 1973. *Suprasegmental phonology*. Doctoral dissertation, MIT. Published (1979) New York: Garland.
Leben, W. 1978. The representation of tone. In V. Fromkin (ed.) *Tone: a linguistic survey*. New York: Academic Press.
Lee, G. 1975. Natural phonological descriptions. I. *Working Papers in Linguistics, University of Hawaii* 7: 85–125.
Lee, G. 1976. Natural phonological descriptions, II. *Working Papers in Linguistics, University of Hawaii* 8: 25–61.
Leed, R. L. 1970. Distinctive features and analogy. *Lingua* 26: 1–24.
Leskien, A. 1876. *Die Deklination im Slavisch-Litauischen und Germanischen*. Leipzig.
Leslau, W. 1969. Frequency as a determinant of linguistic change in the Ethiopian languages. *Word* 25: 180–9.
Levin, J. 1985. A metrical theory of syllabicity. Doctoral dissertation, MIT.
Leys, O. 1975. Die Dehnung von Vokalen im Niederländischen und im Deutschen. *Leuvense Bijdragen* 64: 421–49.
Liberman, A. 1981. Review of Zinder 1979. *Language* 57: 725–7.
Liberman, M. & Pierrehumbert, J. 1984. Intonational invariance under changes in pitch range and length. In M. Aronoff & R. T. Oehrle (eds.) *Language sound structure*. Cambridge, MA: MIT Press.
Lightfoot, D. 1979. *Principles of diachronic syntax*. Cambridge: Cambridge University Press.
Liljencrants, J. & Lindblom, B. 1972. Numerical simulation of vowel quality systems: the role of perceptual contrast. *Language* 48: 839–62.
Lindblom, B. 1986a. On the origin and purpose of discreteness and invariance in sound patterns. In J. S. Perkell & D. H. Klatt (eds.) *Invariance and variability in speech processes*. Hillsdale: Erlbaum.
Lindblom, B. 1986b. Phonetic universals in vowel systems. In J. Ohala (ed.) *Experimental phonology*. New York: Academic Press.
Maddieson, I. 1978. Universals of tone. In J. H. Greenberg (ed.) *Universals of human language*. Stanford: Stanford University Press.
Malkiel, Y. 1967. 'Each word has a history of its own.' *Glossa* 1: 137–49.
Malkiel, Y. 1968. The inflectional paradigm as an occasional determinant of sound change. In W. P. Lehmann & Y. Malkiel (eds.) *Directions for historical linguistics*. Austin: University of Texas Press.
Malkiel, Y. 1971. Derivational transparency as an occasional co-determinant of sound change: a new causal ingredient in the distribution of ç and -z- in ancient Hispano-Romance. *Romance Philology* 25: 1–52.
Malkiel, Y. 1976. Multi-conditioned sound change and the impact of morphology on phonology. *Language* 52: 757–78.

Manaster-Ramer, A. 1984. How abstruse is phonology? Distributed by Indiana University Linguistics Club.

Mańczak, W. 1968. Le développement phonétique irrégulier dû a la fréquence en russe. *Lingua* 21: 287–93.

Mańczak, W. 1969. *Le développement phonétique irrégulier des langues romanes et la fréquence.* Kraków: Nakładen Uniwersytetu Jagellońskiego.

Mańczak, W. 1978. Irregular sound change due to frequency in German. In J. Fisiak (ed.) *Trends in Linguistics: Studies and Monographs.* Vol. 4: *Recent developments in historical phonology.* The Hague: Mouton.

Mańczak, W. 1980. Frequenz und Sprachwandel. In H. Lüdtke (ed.) *Kommunikationstheoretische Grundlagen des Sprachwandels.* Berlin: deGruyter.

Markey, T. L. 1978. *On dating phonological change.* Ann Arbor: Karoma.

Martinet, A. 1955. *Economie des changements linguistiques.* Bern: Francke.

Mascaró, J. 1984. Continuant spreading in Basque, Catalan, and Spanish. In M. Aronoff & R. T. Oehrle (eds.) *Language sound structure.* Cambridge, MA: MIT Press.

Maspéro, A. 1912. Etudes sur la phonétique historique de la langue annamite: les initiales. *Bulletin de L'école Française d'Extrême Orient* 12: 114–16.

Matisoff, J. 1973. Tonogenesis in Southeast Asia. In L. Hyman (ed.) *Consonant types and tone.* Los Angeles: University of Southern California.

McCalla, K. I. 1980. Phonological and morphological forces in syntagmatic change. *Lingua* 51: 1–16.

McCarthy, J. 1986. OCP effects: gemination and antigemination. *Linguistic Inquiry* 17: 207–63.

McCawley, J. 1978. Notes on the history of accent in Japanese. In J. Fisiak (ed.) *Trends in Linguistics: Studies and Monographs.* Vol. 4: *Recent developments in historical phonology.* The Hague: Mouton.

Miranda, R. 1974. Sound change and other phonological change. *Minnesota Working Papers in Linguistics and Philosophy of Language*, vol. 2.

Miranda, R. 1984. Temporal compensation and phonetic change: the case of compensatory lengthening in Hindi. *Papers from the Minnesota Regional Conference on Language and Linguistics.*

Mohanan, K. P. 1986. *The theory of lexical phonology.* Dordrecht: Reidel.

Morin, Y.-C. 1984. La loi de position ou de l'explication en phonologie historique. *Revue québecoise de linguistique* 15: 199–232.

Moses, J. 1982. The Swiss German case of vowel lowering and umlaut: rule reordering or restructuring. *CLS* 18: 367–76.

Moulton, W. G. 1960. The short vowel systems of Northern Switzerland. *Word* 16: 155–82.

Moulton, W. G. 1961. Zur Geschichte des deutschen Vokalsystems. *Beiträge zur Geschichte der deutschen Sprache und Literatur* 83: 1–35.

Moulton, W. G. 1967. Types of phonemic change. In *To honor Roman Jakobson.* The Hague: Mouton.

Moulton, W. G. 1983. Dimensions, explanations, and universals in phonology. In F. B. Agard, G. Kelley, A. Makkai, V. Becker Makkai (eds.) *Essays in honor of Charles F. Hockett.* Leiden: E. J. Brill.

Murray, R. W. & Vennemann, T. 1983. Sound change and syllable structure in Germanic phonology. *Language* 59: 514–28.

Myers, S. 1986. The long and the short of it: a metrical theory of English vowel quantity. *CLS* 21, part 1: 275–88.

Niepokuj, M. 1985. A rule's progress: reordering in Swiss German. *BLS* 11: 287–93.

Nyman, M. 1977. Where does Latin *sum* come from? *Language* 53: 39–60.

Nyman, M. 1978. Lexicalization out of casual speech: the Greek–Latin synizesis. In *Four linguistic studies in classical languages.* Helsinki: Department of General Linguistics, Univěrsity of Helsinki.

Odden, D. 1986. On the role of the obligatory contour principle in phonological theory. *Language* 62: 353–83.

Ohala, J. 1974. Phonetic explanation in phonology. *CLS Parasession*, pp. 251–74.

Ohala, J. 1983. The direction of sound change. In A. Cohen & M. P. R. van den Broecke (eds.) *Abstracts of the 10th International Congress of Phonetic Sciences.* Dordrecht: Foris.

Ohala, J. 1986. Phonological evidence for top-down processing in speech perception. In J. S. Perkell & D. H. Klatt (eds.) *Invariance and variability in speech processes*. Hillsdale: Erlbaum.

Osthoff, H. & Brugmann, K. 1878. *Morphologische Untersuchungen*. Leipzig.

Parker, F. 1981. A functional perceptual account of final devoicing. *Journal of Phonetics* 9: 129–37.

Passy, P. 1890. *Étude sur les changements phonétiques*. Paris: Firmin-Didot.

Paul, H. 1880. (5th edn, 1920). *Prinzipien der Sprachgeschichte*. Halle: Niemeyer.

Paunonen, H. 1973. On free variation. *Suomalais-ugrilaisen seuran aikakauskirja* 72: 285–300.

Perini, M. A. 1978. The latest note on Lachmann's law. *Linguistic Inquiry* 9: 114–16.

Peterson, G. E. & Lehiste, I. 1960. Duration of syllable nuclei in English. *Journal of the Acoustical Society of America* 32: 693–703.

Phillips, B. 1984. Word frequency and the actuation of sound change. *Language* 60: 320–42.

Poplack, S. 1980. Deletion and disambiguation in Puerto Rican Spanish. *Language* 56: 371–85.

Posner, R. 1961. *Consonantal dissimilation in the Romance languages*. Oxford: Oxford University Press.

Poser, W. 1982. Phonological representations and action-at-a-distance. In H. van der Hulst & N. Smith (eds.) *The structure of phonological representations, II*. Dordrecht: Foris.

Postal, P. 1968. *Aspects of phonological theory*. New York: Harper & Row.

Prince, A. S. 1984. Phonology with tiers. In M. Aronoff & R. T. Oehrle (eds.) *Language sound structure*. Cambridge, MA: MIT Press.

Pulleyblank, D. 1986. *Tone in lexical phonology*. Dordrecht: Reidel.

Pulleyblank, E. G. 1982. Review of W. Wang (ed.) *The lexicon in phonological change. Journal of Chinese Linguistics* 10: 392–416.

Ralph, B. 1975. *Phonological differentiation*. Gothenburg: Acta Universitatis Gothoburgiensis.

Ralph, B. 1977. Rule extension in historical phonology. *Studia Linguistica* 21: 164–91.

Ralph, B. 1981. Rule naturalness and rule diffusion. In W. U. Dressler, O. E. Pfeiffer & J. R. Rennison (eds.) *Phonologica 1980*. Vienna: Institut für Sprachwissenschaft der Universität Wien.

Read, C. 1971. Pre-school children's knowledge of English phonology. *Harvard Educational Review* 41: 1–34.

Reighard, J. 1980. The transition problem: lexical diffusion vs. variable rules. In E. Traugott, R. Labrum & S. Shepherd (eds.) *Papers from the 4th International Conference on Historical Linguistics*. Amsterdam: Benjamins.

Reis, M. 1974. *Lauttheorie und Lautgeschichte*. Munich: Fink.

Rischel, J. 1985. *Thai phonetics and phonology* (Annual Report 19). Copenhagen: Institute of Phonetics, University of Copenhagen.

Rischel, J. 1986. *The tone split in Thai* (Annual Report 20). Institute of Phonetics, University of Copenhagen.

Robinson, O. W. 1976. A 'scattered' rule in Swiss German. *Language* 52: 148–62.

Robinson, O. W. 1977. Rule reordering and lexical diffusion. In W. Wang (ed.) *The lexicon in phonological change*. The Hague: Mouton.

Robinson, O. W. & van Coetsem, F. 1973. Review of R. King, *Historical linguistics and generative grammar. Lingua* 31: 331–69.

Ronneberger-Sibold, E. 1980. *Sprachverwendung – Sprachsystem: Ökonomie und Wandel*. Tübingen: Niemeyer.

Ronneberger-Sibold, E. 1985. The history of New High German *qu/zw* (*quer/Zwerchfell*) and natural generative phonology. In W. U. Dressler & L. Tonelli (eds.) *Natural phonology from Eisenstadt*. Padova: CLESP.

Rousseau, P. & Sankoff, D. 1978. Advances in variable rule methodology. In D. Sankoff (ed.) *Linguistic variation: models and methods*. New York: Academic Press.

Rubach, J. 1978. Phonostylistics and sound change. In J. Fisiak (ed.) *Trends in linguistics: studies and monographs*. Vol. 4: *Recent developments in historical phonology*. The Hague: Mouton.

Rubach, J. 1984. *Cyclic and lexical phonology*. Dordrecht: Foris.

Ruhlen, M. 1978. Nasal vowels. In J. H. Greenberg (ed.) *Universals of human language*. Stanford: Stanford University Press.

Sagey, E. C. 1986. The structure of the melody. Doctoral dissertation, MIT.
Sankoff, D. & Labov, W. 1979. On the uses of variable rules. *Language in Society* 8: 189–222.
Sapir, E. 1938. Glottalized continuants in Navaho, Nootka, and Kwakiutl. *Language* 14: 248–74.
Schachter, P. 1969. Natural assimilation rules in Akan. *International Journal of Applied Linguistics* 35: 342–55.
Schane, S. A. 1984. Two English vowel movements: a particle analysis. In M. Aronoff & R. T. Oehrle (eds.) *Language sound structure*. Cambridge, MA: MIT Press.
Scherer, W. 1868. *Zur Geschichte der deutschen Sprache*. Berlin: Duncker.
Schourup, L. 1973. A cross-linguistic study of vowel nasalization. *Ohio State University Working Papers in Linguistics* 15: 190–221.
Schuchardt, H. 1885. *Über die Lautgesetze. Gegen die Junggrammmatiker*. Berlin.
Schuchardt, H. 1928. *Hugo Schuchardt-Brevier 2*. Halle.
Selkirk, E. 1982. The syllable. In van der Hulst & Smith (1982, vol. 2).
Sherman, D. 1975. Noun–verb stress alternation: an example of the lexical diffusion of sound change in English. *Linguistics* 149: 43–71.
Sieberer, A. 1964. *Lautwandel und seine Triebkräfte*. Vienna: Notring.
Sievers, E. 1901. *Grundzüge der Phonetik*. Leipzig: Breitkopf & Härtel.
Sihler, A. 1977. Morphologically conditioned sound change and OE participles in *-en*. *General Linguistics* 17: 76–97.
Singh, R. & Ford, A. 1984. A closer look at some so-called variable processes. In R. Fasold (ed.) *NWAVE XI*. Washington, DC.
Skousen, R. 1975. *Substantive evidence in phonology*. The Hague: Mouton.
Smith, N. S. H. 1981. Foley's scales of relative phonological strength. In Goyvaerts (1981).
Stampe, D. 1972/1980. *A dissertation on natural phonology*. New York: Garland. (Originally, doctoral dissertation, Ohio State University, 1972.)
Stampe, D. 1985. On the two levels of phonological representations. In W. U. Dressler & L. Tonelli (eds.) *Natural phonology from Eisenstadt*. Padova: CLESP.
Steiner, R. C. 1977. *The case for fricative-laterals in proto-Semitic*. New Haven: American Oriental Society.
Steriade, D. 1982. Greek prosodies and the nature of syllabification. Doctoral dissertation, MIT.
Steriade, D. 1986. Yokuts and the vowel plane. *Linguistic Inquiry* 17: 129–46.
Steriade, D. & Schein, B. 1964. Geminates and structure-dependent rules. *WCCFL* 3: 263–91.
Stevens, K., Keyser, S. J. & Kawasaki, H. 1986. Toward a phonetic and phonological theory of redundant features. In J. S. Perkell & D. H. Klatt (eds.) *Invariance and variability in speech processes*. Hillsdale: Erlbaum.
Stockwell, R. 1978. Perseverance in the English vowel shift. In J. Fisiak (ed.) *Trends in linguistics: studies and monographs*. Vol. 4: *Recent developments in historical phonology*. The Hague: Mouton.
Straka, G. 1964. L'évolution phonétique du latin au français sous l'effet de l'énergie et de la faiblesse articulatoire. *Travaux de linguistique et de littérature*, pp. 17–98.
Strunk, K. 1976. *Lachmann's Regel für das Lateinische*. Göttingen.
Szemerényi, O. 1973. Marked–unmarked and a problem of Latin diachrony. *Transactions of the Philological Society*, pp. 55–74.
Ternes, E. 1981. Über Herkunft und Verbreitung der Überlänge in deutschen dialekten. In W. U. Dressler, O. E. Pfeiffer & J. R. Rennison (eds.) *Phonologica 1980*. Vienna: Institut für Sprachwissenschaft der Universität Wien.
Timberlake, A. 1978. Uniform and alternating environments in phonological change. *Folia Slavica* 2: 312–28.
Trnka, B. 1936. General laws of phonemic combinations. *Travaux du cercle linguistique de Prague* 6: 57–62.
Trnka, B. 1968. On analogy. *Zeitschrift für Phonetik, Sprachwissenschaft und Kommunikationsforschung* 21: 345–51.
Trubetzkoy, N. S. 1939. (3rd edn. 1962). *Grundzüge der Phonologie*. Göttingen: Vandenhoeck & Ruprecht.
Ultan, R. 1978. A typological view of metathesis. In J. H. Greenberg (ed.) *Universals of human language*. Stanford: Stanford University Press.

Vendryes, J. 1902. Réflexions sur les lois phonétiques. In *Mélanges linguistiques offerts à Antoine Meillet*. Paris. English translation in Keiler (ed.) 1972.

Vennemann, T. 1972. Phonetic and conceptual analogy. In Vennemann & Wilbur (1972).

Vennemann, T. & Wilbur, T. H. 1972. *Schuchardt, the neogrammarians, and the transformational theory of change*. Wiesbaden: Athenaion.

Verner, K. 1877. Eine Ausname der ersten Lautverschiebung. *Zeitschrift für vergleichende Sprachforschung* 23: 97–130. English translation in Baldi & Werth (1978).

Vihman, M. M. 1980. Sound change and child language. In E. Traugott, R. Labrum & S. Shepherd (eds.) *Papers from the 4th International Conference on Historical Linguistics*. Amsterdam: Benjamins.

Vincent, N. 1978. Is sound change teleological? In J. Fisiak (ed.) *Recent developments in historical phonology*. The Hague: Mouton.

Voyles, J. 1969. Simplicity, ordered rules, and the First Sound Shift. *Language* 43: 636–60.

Wackernagel, J. 1986. *Altindische Grammatik, I*. Göttingen: Vandenhoeck & Ruprecht.

Wallace, S. 1975. Structure, change, and typology: the case of Germanic. *Orbis* 24: 391–403.

Wang, W. S.-Y. 1979. Language change – a lexical perspective. *Annual Review of Anthropology* 8: 353–71.

Wang, W. S.-Y. 1982. Variation and selection in language change. *Bulletin of the Institute of History and Philology, Academia Sinica* 53: 495–519.

Wang, W. S.-Y. & Cheng, C.-C. 1977. Implementation of phonological change: the Shuangfeng Chinese case. In W. Wang (ed.) *The lexicon in phonological change*. The Hague: Mouton.

Wanner, D. & Craven, T. D. 1980. Early intervocalic voicing in Tuscan. In E. Traugott, R. Labrum & Shepherd S. (eds.) *Papers from the 4th International Conference on Historical Linguistics*. Amsterdam: Benjamins.

Wartburg, W. von 1943. *Einführung in die Problematik und Methodik der Sprachwissenschaft*. Halle. Quoted from the English translation (1969) *Problems and methods in linguistics*, New York: Barnes & Noble.

Watkins, C. 1970. A further remark on Lachmann's law. *Harvard Journal of Classical Philology* 74: 55–65.

Weinreich, U., Herzog, M. & Labov, W. 1968. Empirical foundations for a theory of language change. In L. P. Lehmann & Y. Malkiel (eds.) *Directions for historical linguistics*. Austin: University of Texas Press.

Wells, J. C. 1982. *Accents of English I–III*. Cambridge: Cambridge University Press.

Wetzels, W. L. 1985. The historical phonology of intrusive stops. A non-linear description. *Canadian Journal of Linguistics* 30: 285–333.

Wetzels, W. L. & Hermans, B. 1985. Aspirated geminates in Pāli. In H. Bennis & F. Beukema (eds.) *Linguistics in the Netherlands, 1985*. Dordrecht: Foris.

Wetzels, W. L. & Sezer, E. F. (eds.) 1986. *Studies in compensatory lengthening*. Dordrecht: Foris.

Wilbur, T. H. 1977. *The Lautgesetz-controversy*. Amsterdam: Benjamins.

Winteler, J. 1876. *Die Kerenzer Mundart des Kantons Glarus*. Leipzig-Heidelberg.

Wolfe, P. 1972. *Linguistic change and the great vowel shift in English*. Berkeley/Los Angeles: University of California Press.

Zinder, L. R. 1979. *Obščaja fonetika*. Moscow: Vysšaja Škola.

Zwicky, A. 1972. Linguistic change and generative theory. In R. Stockwell & R. Macaulay (eds.) *Note on a phonological hierarchy in English*. Bloomington: Indiana University Press.

# 15 Mathematical properties of grammars*

*Amy S. Weinberg*

## 15.0. Introduction

How do we learn and process our native language? In the majority of
current linguistic theories, systems of rules and representations are judged
by their ability to answer these questions. That is, they are evaluated on the
extent to which they shed light on how language learners acquire their
mother tongue in a short amount of time and under realistic environmental
conditions, and how native speakers are able to understand sentences in
basically the time it takes them to hear them. As far as the latter feat is
concerned, since the linguist's grammar represents the stored representation of linguistic knowledge it would be quite peculiar if this knowledge
did not play a part in explaining our ability to understand the sentences
spoken in it. Put bluntly, a theory that characterizes what we know about
our language in such a way that this knowledge could never be efficiently
put to use would not seem to be a very promising psychological candidate.[1]

We would certainly prefer a grammatical theory that could provide part
of the explanation for *all* of our linguistic abilities, including the speed with
which we understand linguistic input. Thus, a psychologically plausible
theory of grammar must play a central role in the theory of language
processing. While many have concluded on the basis of mathematical results
that a model based on a transformational theory of grammar is too slow to
serve as the basis for a fast language comprehension system, we will see
below that there is reason to think that such conclusions are incorrect.

Mathematical characterization of the kinds of formal operations allowed

* I would like to thank Robert C. Berwick, Norbert Hornstein, and Fritz Newmeyer for very helpful
comments. All errors are my own.
[1] Despite the remarks in Kroch & Joshi (1985: 2), this has always been Chomsky's position. Indeed, he
has often stressed the potential relevance of the theory of language use for the construction of an
adequate theory of linguistic knowledge: 'If we accept – as I do – . . . [the] contention that the rules of
grammar enter into the processing mechanisms, then evidence regarding production, recall, and
language use in general can be expected (in principle) to have bearing on the investigation of rules of
grammar, on what is sometimes called "grammatical competence." ' (Chomsky 1980: 200–1)

by particular theories of grammar has made it possible to determine roughly how hard it will be for a system that has the power to encode these formal operations to perform various tasks. The formal power of transformational grammar was investigated in the early 1970s by Peters & Ritchie (1973). Since then it has been the general wisdom that a system with transformational power is unsuited for the task of fast language comprehension because it makes that process inordinately slow (for a recent statement of this position see Kroch & Joshi 1985: 1–2).

This interpretation of what mathematical modeling tells us about transformational grammar has influenced the course of linguistic research. A consensus has emerged that we must jettison the transformational component of our grammars in order to make these theories acceptable components of both processing and acquisition models, and therefore many now attempt to capture linguistic generalizations without recourse to transformational rules.

This chapter evaluates these negative conclusions about transformational grammars in three stages. First, it will explain the relevance of the problem of modeling fast language comprehension to the critical assessment of linguistic theories. Second, it will explain why mathematical characterization of transformational grammars suggested that modeling fast comprehension would be a problem. This will involve explaining the basic mathematical concepts that tell us how hard it is to use a certain grammatical system to perform a given task. Third, it will show that many of the mathematical results were inappropriately applied by those studying natural language comprehension. In particular, it will show that while the general mathematical characterization of transformational grammar legitimately abstracts away from many factors in purely formal analysis, such factors become crucial when mathematically modeling actual natural language. The general moral will be that while mathematical models can shed great light on problems relevant to cognitive science, they must be applied with care. More positively, we will see that once the results are analyzed more carefully, transformational grammar re-emerges as a plausible candidate to explain both the ease of language learning and language understanding.

## 15.1. Language understanding – an informal view

Before turning to formal results we will review some general and uncontroversial assumptions about what is involved in language understanding. We assume that a language comprehension model (processing device) must explain our ability to understand a sentence in more or less the time that it takes us to hear or read it. Part of language understanding involves constructing a syntactic representation of an utterance. Moreover, it is assumed that this representation is constructed by matching input to a set of stored grammatical rules.[2]

Language comprehension, then, is in part a process of matching the input (the sound stream) with the syntactic rules that provide its appropriate analysis. To understand a sentence, we have to read the input tokens (words) and retrieve the grammatical rules that appropriately analyze it. The time involved in this computation is dependent at least in part on the number of words in the sentence. Likewise, the size of the grammar (how many rules it contains) is also crucial, because matching the appropriate rule to the input forces its retrieval from a stored list of rules. The time needed to find the appropriate rule depends also on the nature of the particular devices that we actually use to process input. For example, if we are fortunate enough to have a machine that does not have to plod through a list of rules from beginning to end, but rather has intelligent strategies for assessing where a particular rule is in a list, the process of finding that rule will be faster. The exact representation of the rules in the list (e.g. whether each symbol of each rule must be specified or whether they can be collapsed in some compact way) also affects parse time. Since the grammars of various linguistic theories differ in their number of rules, different theories would seem to have different sized grammars and thus make different predictions about parse time. Less obviously, grammatical characterizations of the same phenomena differ with respect to the length of input as well. Consider, for example, (1), which is the output of an analysis of (2) in current transformational approaches:

(1) Who$_i$ does John like [e$_i$]
(2) Who does John like?

The assumption that questions are analyzed by movement and that a moved category leaves an empty copy of itself in the position from which it was moved (and assigned its semantic role) entails that the output derivation is one token longer than its associated input string. It is worth asking then, whether analyses employing copying, deletion, or other operations sanctioned by TG add inordinate length to the output structure and thus predict an inordinately long processing time.[3]

To investigate this matter, we could use a strictly empirical method,

---

[2] We will suppose the correctness of the latter assumption, as do critics of TG. However, current work in transformational grammar suggests that better explanations of how language is learned are possible if we replace language-particular rules with universal modular constraints (see Chomsky 1981 for a theory of this type). Some recent work (Berwick & Weinberg 1985; Barton 1986) also suggests that better explanations of our language processing abilities will come from this sort of modification, though such ideas need to be worked out in more detail before their mathematical implications can be assessed.

[3] While the particular case discussed in (1) and (2) is not problematic, cases that are problematic for TG will be discussed below.

constructing some representative derivations where transformational operations are applied to input strings and seeing how long it actually takes people to process these cases. This method is tedious, and moreover risky, because an apparent compatibility between grammatical theory and processing data might simply result from our failure to have considered some relevant hard cases. What we really want is a method that can predict what the costs of allowing a grammar to use certain types of formal operations will be. We want to know what the hard cases for this system are going to be before we go to the trouble of constructing a complete comprehension system incorporating the grammatical theory. The promise of mathematical characterization is that it seems to offer a general way of predicting how hard a processing task is going to be for a given system, which in turn involves deciding which class of formal languages most closely characterizes natural language. Since classes of grammars can be characterized as 'machines' that actually analyze input strings and associate them with their appropriate output representations, we can use mathematical techniques to analyze how difficult it will be for particular automata to partake in the task of processing.

## 15.2. Formal language and grammar classes

Strings of symbols can be described by a variety of different formalisms. For example, sentence (3) could be described simply as the linear pattern (4):

(3) John likes linguistics
(4) noun verb noun

We can construct grammars that describe only the linear (non-hierarchical) aspects of a particular pattern. These grammars, called *regular grammars*, allow only rules with a single nonterminal symbol on the left-hand portion of the rule and at most one nonterminal symbol (noun, verb, etc.) and one terminal on the right-hand side. If the nonterminal symbol is the leftmost symbol on the right-hand side, the grammar is a *left-linear* grammar and if it is the rightmost, the grammar is a *right-linear* grammar. A right-linear grammar has rules of the form (5) and generates sentence (3) using the rules in (6):

(5) $A \rightarrow a B$
    $B \rightarrow b$
(6) $S \rightarrow John\ V_1$
    $V_1 \rightarrow likes\ N_1$
    $N_1 \rightarrow linguistics$

It can be proven that regular grammars can generate all and only a mathematically well-understood class of languages: *finite-state* (regular) languages. The limitation of regular grammars is that they do not express the hierarchical patterning of natural language. Most importantly, there is no direct way to express the notion of a *phrase* using this type of notation.[4] To express the notion of a phrase it is necessary to expand the type of permissible rewrite rules. We retain the restriction that only a single nonterminal can appear as the left-hand side of a rule, but allow a string with any number of terminals and nonterminals in any order to appear on right-hand expansion. Such a rule is called *context-free* (CF) because it allows categories to be expanded regardless of the context.[5] Sentence (3) could be generated by context-free grammar (7):

(7) S  → NP VP
    NP → N
    VP → V NP
    V  → likes
    N  → John, linguistics

The rules in (6) and (7) both generate (3), but they analyze it differently. The context-free grammar groups the words of (3) into phrases, but the regular grammar does not. Formalisms that can generate all the same strings are called *weakly equivalent*, and those that generate all the same strings and give them the same structural analyses are called *strongly equivalent*. Two grammars that are weakly equivalent are said to *recognize* the same strings. Recognition thus requires a simple yes/no answer to the question, 'Can the rules in the grammar generate this sentence?' The set of strings recognized using a given grammar is its *language*. If two grammars give the same structural analysis to a string, then they *parse* it in the same way. Parsing, unlike recognition, is not just a yes/no matter, since it must be explicitly specified which rules match a string's pattern so as to provide the string's parse according to a particular grammar. We can also use these concepts in describing the relationship between grammars and their associated automata. Thus, *regular grammars* are weakly and strongly equivalent to a class of mathematical devices called *finite-state automata*, because for every regular grammar we can construct a finite-state automaton that both recognizes all and only the strings recognized by that grammar and gives these strings the same structural descriptions that the grammar would assign. Context-free grammars are also strongly equivalent to a well-known class of automata called *push down storage automata* (pdsa).[6]

It turns out that regular grammars and context-free grammars are neither weakly nor strongly equivalent. They obviously give different analyses to the same strings, as can be seen by comparing the grammars in (6) and (7). In

---

[4] See Kimball (1973) and Berwick (forthcoming) for details.
[5] By 'context' we mean the linguistic symbols that appear within the same phrase or in phrases next to the category to be expanded.
[6] This result was proven in Chomsky (1962).

addition, though, there are some languages that a CF grammar can recognize that a regular grammar cannot. The class of languages generated by regular grammars is properly included in the class generated by context-free grammars.

Crucially, sentence comprehension is dependent upon parsing difficulty rather than mere recognition, since the appropriate structural analysis must be matched to a given input string.

Given these basic notions, one can ask several questions about the appropriateness of a particular formal system as a characterization of a natural language. Taking into account questions of weak generative capacity (the class of strings that the grammar can recognize), one can ask whether the grammar can generate all the construction types that are actually found in the language. Chomsky (1956, 1957) argued that certain constructions found in natural languages are not in the class of finite-state languages and so cannot be generated by regular grammars or recognized by finite-state automata, and concluded that these systems are thus excluded as possible candidate grammars for natural languages.[7]

As far as their strong generative capacity is concerned, regular grammars fail to capture many pervasive generalizations about natural languages, or do so only clumsily (see Chomsky 1957). Likewise, CF grammars do not unfailingly assign the appropriate structural analyses to the strings that they generate. For example, Bresnan *et al.* (1982) show that although a CF grammar can generate a certain construction type (the 'crossed serial dependencies' in Dutch), the structural analysis that it provides does not support appropriate semantic interpretation.

We can extend our repertoire of rule-writing possibilities still further, characterizing classes of languages with greater weak generative power. *Context-sensitive* rules may contain more than one symbol on their left-hand sides; their right-hand sides are restricted only to the extent that they must contain at least as many symbols as the left-hand side contains. The term 'context-sensitive' is applied because they allow certain constituents to be rewritten only if certain context restrictions are satisfied. A typical example of a context-sensitive phenomenon is subject–verb agreement, in which a verb has plural marking only if the subject NP is plural. A context-sensitive rule like (8) captures this generalization in a more direct and less cumbersome fashion than would be possible with context-free rules or regular grammars:

(8) NP+plural V → NP+plural V+plural[8]

---

[7] Though Langendoen (1975) and Church (1980) disagree, and claim that while the kinds of sentences that Chomsky discusses are in principle part of linguistic competence, given memory system limitations only a subset of them are understandable – a subset that can be generated by regular grammars and recognized by finite-state automata. However, regular grammars look like much less promising candidates once their strong generative capacity is taken into consideration (see below).

[8] We take NP+plural to be a complex lexical item.

The most powerful family of grammars are those using unrestricted rewrite rules. The only 'restriction' on such rules is that their left-hand sides must be non-empty. These grammars allow a great discrepancy between the surface and the underlying string, since they permit potentially unbounded deletions, where the length of the underlying representation need not be a function of the surface representation at all.

## 15.3. **The complexity of formal language classes**

We turn now to the question of how much time is needed to give an analysis to a string. For example, generating a sentence according to a right-linear grammar involves reading the input, deciding what categories the input consists of and figuring out what symbol appears to the right or left of a given token. Recognizing a sentence using a context-free grammar means doing all of this and structuring the input into the appropriate phrases. This means that the context-free grammar has to do more work to analyze the same number of tokens. We would suspect that since more work is associated with the analysis of a unit of input by a context-free grammar in some cases, more time would be needed to recognize a string using this grammar than would be needed to recognize the same string using a regular grammar or to recognize a string that cannot be recognized by a finite-state grammar at all. In fact, this informal suspicion can be confirmed. It has been proven that the amount of time needed to recognize a string using a regular grammar is proportional to n where n equals the number of words in a sentence (its length). However, so far as CF grammars are concerned, we can guarantee only that they can recognize a string in a time proportional to the cube of the length of the input $(n^3)$. Both of these results place a bound only on the time that is required in the worst case to recognize a given string. They do not say whether we will find cases in natural language that will force the grammar to use its worst case time. Furthermore, it is important to emphasize that these are results about recognition time and not about parsing time. Since we are interested in the time it takes us to parse human languages, we can see that we must exercise some care in applying recognition results in our analysis of the complexity of human language comprehension.

If unbounded deletions are available to unrestricted rewriting systems, we cannot guarantee that there will be any general time bound on the recognition of strings. If we allow unrestricted deletions, then the parser's output representation can contain arbitrarily many more tokens than its corresponding surface string. Since each of the tokens of the underlying representation will have to be written down during the analysis of this string, we cannot put a time bound on how long it will take in the worst case to give an analysis. In addition, it might take an arbitrary amount of time using these types of grammars to process sentences not in the language simply in order to reject them.

Do we need to use the full power of unrestricted rewrite grammars to construct an adequate analysis of natural language? This issue was discussed by Peters & Ritchie (1973) and by Peters (1973), who showed that analyses from early transformational frameworks made use of this power. For example, in a sentence like (9), the surface subject serves as the subject of both the matrix and the embedded clause:

(9) The wind's howl threatened to scare the baby

Early theories of TG expressed 'dual subjecthood' by having the surface subject appear in both clauses. Thus, the underlying representation of (9) was (10):

(10) [The wind's howl] threatened [the wind's howl] to scare the baby

A rule called equi-NP deletion applied to delete the coreferential embedded subject in infinitival and gerundive sentences. This rule was stated as in (11):

$$ (11) \qquad X - (NP) - Y\,[\,\left\{ \begin{array}{l} FOR \\ POSS \end{array} \right\}\,] - NP - Z - ] - W - (NP) - P \rightarrow $$

| | SD | 1 | 2 | 3 | 4 | | 5 | 6 | | 7 | 8 | 9 |
|---|---|---|---|---|---|---|---|---|---|---|---|---|
| | SC | 1 | 2 | 3 | 4 | | 0 | 6 | | 7 | 8 | 9 |

Since coreferentiality between the overt and the understood subjects is represented by having two fully specified NPs, the underlying string has more terminal symbols than its associated surface string. Assuming that each terminal element takes one unit of time to process, it follows that interpreting this sentence (associating the surface string with its underlying representation) is going to take more time than would be taken by simply reading the surface string. This problem is quite serious, given that nothing prevents subjects being embedded inside subjects, and thus the generation of sentences like (12):

(12) Their sitting down's promising to steady the canoe threatens to spoil the joke[9]

The subject of the clause *to steady the canoe* is *their sitting down*, so the equi analysis gives (13) as the underlying structure for this part of the clause:

(13) [$_{NP}$ Their sitting down's] promising [$_{NP}$ their sitting down] to steady the canoe . . .

[9] This sentence is taken from Peters (1973). It is certainly not natural and many people find it unacceptable. Therefore it may be possible to argue that the time cost of computing these sentences is irrelevant, since they violate some independent principle. For the purposes of this paper, though, we will ignore this possibility.

Since the subject of the most embedded clause is interpreted as (13), the full underlying representation for this sentence is (14):

(14) [Their sitting down's] promising [their sitting down] to steady the
     canoe threatens [their sitting down's promising to steady the canoe] to
     spoil the joke[10]

Since this process may be iterated indefinitely, the marking of coreference with an actual lexical copy of the surface antecedent gives the grammar the power to produce derivations where the underlying representation has taken arbitrarily longer to interpret than the time it takes to write down the surface string.

Lapointe (1977) suggested that the weak generative capacity of transformational grammar could be reduced and the length of the underlying string limited to a time proportional to $2^n$ of the length of the surface string, given that current versions of the theory mark coreferentiality between positions in a string by an empty category (a PRO or trace) co-indexed with a lexical antecedent, rather than having the coreferential NP literally copied. (This conclusion depends upon the assumption that empty categories cannot be 'layered', i.e. embedded inside another to indicate which subpart of a complex antecedent is coreferential with them.) If we assume such antecedent–empty category relationships, we can guarantee that there will be only a fixed number of empty categories per sentence and the length of the input/output string will in fact be proportional to some factor of the length of the input. Thus, as proven by Berwick & Weinberg (1984), a government–binding grammar (which incorporates this sort of empty category analysis) strongly and weakly generates at most context-sensitive languages.

## 15.4. The relevance of claims about weak generative capacity

Many would argue that restriction of weak generative power to the context-sensitive class is not much of a restriction at all, because the worst case recognition, which takes time proportional to $2^n$ times the length of the input string, cannot guarantee that this exponent will be small (say 'the cube' as in the context-free case or '0' as in the regular grammar case). Thus, if we focus just on the role that the length of the output string plays in determining how hard it is to recognize a string, it seems that, all other things being equal, the more restrictive the grammar, the better. However, recall that language comprehension involves parsing rather than simply recognition. Also, as mentioned above, length is not the only factor that influences the complexity of recognition or parsing. The size of the grammar also plays a role. In ignoring this factor we have done no more than follow standard mathematical

---

[10] That is, it is the fact that their sitting down promises to steady the canoe that threatens to spoil the joke.

complexity analyses. Thus we discussed the relative merits of grammars, given the conclusion that a context-free grammar can recognize a sentence in a time equal to the cube of its length. But in fact a more accurate assessment of recognition tells us that a context-free grammar can recognize a sentence in time $Kn^3$, that is in a time *proportional* to the cube of its length where (K) is the constant of proportionality that reflects the contribution of the size of the grammar and other related details. The standard complexity analyses abstract away from the role of grammar size by considering the cases where the fact of sentence length is sure to predominate. These are cases of *asymptotic* length, where the input length becomes unboundedly long and approaches the limit. Therefore, a point is ultimately reached where factors contributed by length simply swamp out the complexity contributed by the grammar, no matter how great its size. Consequently, in asymptotic length cases, the grammar size factor does not prevent an accurate measure of the total complexity of the sentence.

One adopts asymptotic complexity measures to preserve the generality of one's results. Recall that the 'grammar size' factor is actually shorthand for a host of idiosyncratic factors that can vary from device to device. Thus, an analysis that depends on their particular setting will be correspondingly less general, applying only to the class of machines that set these details in the same way. By concentrating on inputs of a length great enough to allow us to drop these factors, we make our analyses applicable to the full class of possible machines. Unfortunately, mathematical generality may have cognitive cost. Asymptotic results must be applied to cognitive issues with a great deal of care. As cognitive scientists, we are interested in analyzing how difficult it will be to comprehend sentences that human beings are likely to hear. Thus knowing that a given theory of grammar is very efficient at comprehending sentences of asymptotic length is irrelevant to our enterprise. And we must furthermore remember that these complexity results are worst-case results. Thus the fact that a grammar can only recognize a sentence of asymptotic length in time $x^n$ does not mean that it cannot recognize sentences that human beings actually hear much faster (i.e. move much faster to end of sentence). This would be true if 'worst case' is never represented in natural language samples or if it is represented so rarely that parsing these strings fast does not confer any real biological advantage (see Berwick & Weinberg 1984:96 for discussion). It could turn out that it is the ability to parse the very short sentences used in daily conversation that is crucial to the design of the human parsing mechanism. In fact, we will see below that the grammar size factor is probably the crucial factor in determining the complexity of cognitively relevant inputs.

One could still argue, though, that since theories with weaker weak generative capacity than context-sensitive and transformational grammar cannot in principle exceed a time proportional to $n^3$, considerations of restrictiveness should still invite us to limit our attention to grammars with a weaker generative power. That is, we should focus our attention on cases that even in the limit are associated with fairly fast recognition times and then try to use extra constraints to restrict their associated times still further. The idea behind this is that these theories have a faster worst-case recognition time and we cannot be sure that some of the cases that the device must recognize will not include the worst case for sentences of sub-asymptotic complexity. In this situation, a less powerful system will be faster than its slower cousin for the sub-asymptotic cases, and so, the argument goes, we should pick the theory with the 'best' efficiency rating overall. Such an argument was made in Pullum (1981). Pullum criticizes Berwick & Weinberg (1981), who claimed that when these complexity results are applied to cognitively relevant cases as suggested above, transformational grammar becomes an extremely plausible parsing grammar. Pullum (1981) remarks that:

> the claims about recognition of [context-free languages] do not stop at saying that by good fortune there happens to be a fast recognition algorithm for each member of the class of CFLs. The claim is that there is a single universal algorithm that works for the class and has a low deterministic polynomial time complexity. That is what cannot be said of the context-sensitive languages. (Pullum 1981: 4).

Pullum's argument fails for two reasons. First, as we mentioned, we are not interested in recognition complexity, but in the complexity of a string's parse. The recognition results guarantee that there will always be some context-free grammar that can recognize a string in polynomial time, but not that any context-free grammar will be able to do so. As long as we are simply talking about recognition, this is not a problem because, as mentioned above, recognition is not done relative to a particular grammar. Any grammar that recognizes a string will report the same 'yes' or 'no' answer back and we do not record any of the details about the analysis that the grammar performed while making this decision. By contrast, providing a parse for a string means retaining the structural analysis provided by the grammar. When we take parsing into account, it is not true that all finite-state grammars will be faster than formalisms with greater generative capacity. It is even possible to show that there are certain finite-state languages that can be parsed by some context-free grammars but not by some regular grammars in linear time (see Berwick forthcoming). That is, it takes longer than linear time to assign the grammar's particular set of structural analyses to a given language. This does not affect the recognition results, because these results claim only that there will be some other regular grammar yielding a different structural analysis that can recognize this and every other finite-state language in linear time. This interchangeability of grammars of course does not extend to the parsing case and therefore, even if we stick to systems of the weakest generative power, we cannot bar the possibility that the particular grammar from this class that best describes or expresses generalizations about the language in question will not be among the set of grammars that can parse the language efficiently.

Secondly, even if we restrict our attention to recognition, Pullum illicitly idealizes away from the contribution of the size of the grammar. As we mentioned above, once we deal with sub-asymptotic cases, this factor may be crucial and we have to open-mindedly approach the issue of whether grammar size or sentence length is likely to predominate in determining the complexity of parsing the class of sentences we are likely to hear. Once we allow these factors into our calculations, restricting our attention to grammars of low asymptotic complexity is not restrictive at all. In fact, it may mean that we fail to consider grammars that are actually faster for inputs whose length is in the range of sentences that we are most likely to hear. For example, consider a grammar that could parse a sentence in a time proportional to the actual length of a sentence using a grammar that contained 1000 rules. In the limit, such a grammar would be faster than a grammar that had five rules and could parse in time $n^2$. However, for sentences of even 100 words or less, the second alternative would be faster. Until we know which factor, grammar size or sentence length or both, is likely to predominate in our calculations of complexity, we don't know what to restrict. If length predominates, we may want to look at theories with weak generative power, but if grammar size predominates, then at least for a wide range of cases a rise in weak generative capacity may be compensated for if there is a corresponding shrinkage in the size of the grammar. With this in mind, consider the results of Meyer & Fischer (1971), who show that as one moves to more and more powerful formalisms one can use more and more compact representations to describe phenomena. If information can be analyzed more compactly, then it would seem that for all the cases where grammar size predominates, a system with greater weak generative power would be more 'restrictive' because of the corresponding reduction in the size of the associated grammar.[11]

It is difficult to be more specific without a particular algorithm to discuss. Assuming, though, that most sentences that a comprehension device will have to process will be 20 words or less and that a grammar that is powerful

[11] For discussion of the problems for computation caused by the grammar size of systems with weak generative capacity like generalized phrase structure grammar (GPSG), see Barton (1986) and Ristad (1986).

427

enough to describe all the constructions in a natural language will consist of a few hundred rules, one would suspect that grammar size would predominate in our calculation.[12]

Once the grammar size factor is taken into account, we get a very different assessment of what types of grammars are computationally complex. Generative grammarians have been motivated by considerations of learnability to try to express linguistic generalizations as compactly as possible. The preceding arguments suggest that compact grammars may also be crucial in ensuring that linguistic knowledge can also be used to guarantee fast language comprehension.

Thus we have concluded on a markedly different note from that with which we began. The perceived incompatibility of TG and fast language comprehension stemmed both from a too narrow focus on the weak generative capacity of this formalism and on a too pessimistic assumption about the weak generative power of a transformational grammar. The fascination with weak generative capacity stemmed in turn from the failure to see that the asymptotic complexity of a grammatical system was not likely to be cognitively relevant. Once factors (like grammar size) that are likely to be crucial in evaluating parsing complexity for the cases that human beings are likely to be able to comprehend (the sub-asymptotic cases) are taken into consideration, we see that TG has exactly the right kind of features (small grammar size) to guarantee fast language comprehension as well as fast language learning.

*REFERENCES*

Barton, E. 1986. On the complexity of ID/LP parsing. *AI Memo no. 812*. MIT Artificial Intelligence Laboratory.
Berwick, R. Forthcoming. *Computational linguistics*. Cambridge, MA: MIT Press.
Berwick, R. & Weinberg, A. 1981. Parsing efficiency, computational complexity, and the evaluation of grammatical theories. *Linguistic Inquiry* 13: 1–61.
Berwick, R. & Weinberg, A. 1984. *The grammatical basis of linguistic performance*. Cambridge, MA: MIT Press.
Berwick, R. & Weinberg, A. 1985. Deterministic parsing: a modern view. *NELS* 15: 15–33.
Bresnan, J., Kaplan, R. M., Peters, S. & Zaenen, A. 1982. Cross serial dependencies in Dutch. *Linguistic Inquiry* 13: 613–35.
Chomsky, N. 1956. Three models for the description of language. *IRE Transactions on Information Theory*, pp. 113–24.
Chomsky, N. 1957. *Syntactic structures*. The Hague: Mouton.
Chomsky, N. 1962. Context free grammars and pushdown storage. *MIT Research Lab of Electronics Quarterly Progress Report*.
Chomsky, N. 1980. *Rules and representations*. New York: Columbia University Press.
Chomsky, N. 1981. *Lectures on government and binding*. Dordrecht: Foris.

[12] As an example of the predominance of grammar size, Berwick & Weinberg (1984: 96–7) showed that this factor contributes approximately 2/3 of the complexity of recognizing an input of 10 tokens using the Earley algorithm (the fastest current general parsing method for context-free grammars) and a grammar of 500 rules.

Church, K. 1980. On memory limitations in natural language parsing. Indiana University Linguistics Club. ms.

Gazdar, G., Klein, E., Pullum, G. & Sag, I. 1985. *Generalized phrase structure grammar*. Oxford: Blackwell.

Kimball, J. 1973. *The formal theory of grammar*. Englewood Cliffs: Prentice-Hall.

Kroch, A. & Joshi, A. 1985. The linguistic relevance of tree adjoining grammar. University of Pennsylvania. ms.

Langendoen, T. 1975. Finite state parsing of phrase structure languages and the status of readjustment rules. *Linguistic Inquiry* 7: 4.

Lapointe, S. 1977. Recursiveness and deletion. *Linguistic Analysis* 3: 227–65.

Meyer & Fischer 1971. Economy of description by automata, grammars, and formal systems. *Proceedings of the ACM symposium on switching and automata theory* 12: 185–94.

Peters, S. 1973. On restricting deletion transformations. In M. Gross, M. Halle & M. Schutzenberger (eds.) *The formal analysis of language*. The Hague: Mouton.

Peters, S. & Ritchie, R. 1973. On the generative power of transformational grammars. *Information Sciences* 6: 49–83.

Pullum, G. K. 1981. Context-freeness and the computer processing of human languages. *Proceedings of ACL* 21: 1–6.

Ristad, E. 1986. GPSG – recognition is NP – hard. *AI Memo no. 837*. MIT Artificial Intelligence Laboratory.

# 16 Linguistics and the philosophy of language*

*Alice ter Meulen*

For centuries, empirical questions of grammatical analysis have been closely intertwined with philosophical reflections on language. Modern linguistics has been, on the one hand, fully emancipated as an independent empirical discipline from the 'mother of the sciences,' but, on the other hand, import-ant and mutually beneficial influences continue to shape current linguistic theory and philosophy of language. The purpose of this essay is to record some of these current trends and lively topics of common research, restric-ted to the Western academic environment.[1]

The first section traces some twentieth-century roots from which con-temporary linguistic theory and philosophy of language have developed. Various theories of meaning that presently have adherents both among linguists and philosophers are discussed in the second section. Current topics in the semantics of natural language, as a new interdisciplinary field of research where linguists and philosophers fruitfully cooperate, are presented in the third section, which also sketches some of the most recent developments.

## 16.1. The historical background

### 16.1.1. The linguistic turn in philosophy

A well-recognized shift in philosophical method, known as the linguistic turn in philosophy, took place at the onset of the twentieth century with the rise of the British school of analytic philosophy primarily at Oxford and Cambridge.[2] Its central tenet was that any philosophical problem should be clarified by analyzing the language in which it is couched. G. E. Moore, its

---

* I wish to thank Johan van Benthem and Fritz Newmeyer for their useful comments.

[1] Due to their apparent lack of active interaction with empirical linguistic research and theory of grammar, the recent developments in French philosophy of language and 'grammatology' associated with Jacques Derrida, Michel Foucault, Helene Cixous, Luce Irigaray, and Julia Kristeva are outside our scope as well as 'Jurgen Habermas' 'Theorie der kommunikativen Kompetenz' of the German Kritische Schule.

[2] See Rorty (1967) for an excellent source of classical texts, and for general reference Passmore (1957).

founding father, initiated the method of *conceptual analysis* (CA), in which the analysis of a concept consists in relating it to other concepts, in such a way that a sentence expressing identity of the concepts constitutes an analytic assertion, which is necessarily true in virtue of the meaning of its words. For instance, the concept *brother* is thus analyzed as *male sibling*. This analytical method later found extensive linguistic usage as lexical decomposition in interpretive (Katz & Fodor 1963) and in generative semantics (McCawley 1968; Lakoff 1971) and is still applied in various forms in other linguistic theories concerned with lexical or conceptual meaning (Fodor 1977; Dowty 1979). Both among philosophers (Kripke 1972; Putnam 1975) and linguists (Katz 1972; Jackendoff 1983) skepticism has developed whether this method could ever provide necessary and sufficient conditions for word meaning.

In early analytic philosophy under the influence of Wittgenstein and Austin, conceptual analysis was converted later into a more explicitly linguistic method which clarified the meaning of an expression by a description of how to use it. This form of semantic theory became known as *ordinary language philosophy*, whose method is often referred to with the slogan 'meaning is use,' and which is commonly (but incorrectly, as we will see below) thought to be in direct opposition with truth-conditional or referential theories of meaning. It places strong emphasis on the context dependence of meaning and semantic interpretation, and attempts to analyze how one and the same expression may mean different things in different contexts of use. Linguists have adopted aspects of this philosophical analysis in pragmatic theories of meaning, which are concerned with other than descriptive and declarative uses of language (see 16.2.3).

Closely correlated to the linguistic turn in philosophy was the development of modern logic by Frege, Russell, Wittgenstein and subsequent generations of logicians. Although most logicians in the first half of this century, with the notable exceptions of Frege, Strawson and Quine, showed a rather derogatory attitude towards natural language for its inherent ambiguities and vagueness, or for containing its own metalanguage and being hence prone to the truth-functional paradoxes (Tarski), the methods and results of logic currently find important linguistic applications, and furthermore, linguistic insights significantly influence new developments in logic. For modern logic, reasoning in natural language has always been a major source of semantic puzzles and inspiration for formal inferential systems, which analyze some abstract aspects of our linguistic or cognitive abilities.

The two linguistic puzzles which preoccupied Frege (see Geach & Black 1952) still constitute major foundational problems of linguistic and philosophical semantics: (1) informative identity statements with coreferential NPs and (2) opaque contexts, where existential generalization and substitution of equivalents fail. Frege illustrates the first problem as the question why, for instance, the sentence *Hesperus is the Evening Star* is informative whereas *Hesperus is Hesperus* is not, or is only trivially informative. Both sentences contain NPs that refer to the same planet, but the informativeness of the first one is attributed to the difference in Fregean sense (*Sinn*) of the two NPs. The second problem is illustrated by the difference between the sentences *Peter believes that Hesperus is the Evening Star* and *Peter believes that Hesperus is Hesperus*. The first sentence may or may not be true, but the second one must be true, although the NPs in the embedded sentences are all coreferential and should therefore be substitutable for each other, while preserving truth value. Hence sentences embedded under what are generally called 'attitude verbs' refer not simply to their truth value, as they would when they occur by themselves, but to their Fregean sense. Furthermore, NPs in sentences embedded in opaque contexts are systematically ambiguous between a *de re reading*, i.e. the NP is interpreted by what actually has the property denoted by the noun, or a *de dicto reading*, when the NP is interpreted depending on the beliefs the subject holds. Linguistic paraphrases make clear that only in de re readings can the NP be preposed while binding a pronoun embedded under the main verb, i.e. *Of Hesperus John believes that it is the Evening Star*, or *Of the Evening Star John believes that it is Hesperus*. A proper account of belief should represent these two beliefs as different, but both as true if, as in our stellar system, the Evening Star actually is Hesperus. Much of the subsequent research in the semantics of natural language can be understood as a search for an adequate and mathematically satisfactory explication of this Fregean notion of sense, an adequate account of opaque contexts, and a context-sensitive analysis of the abstract concept of informative use of language.

## 16.1.2. Philosophical and logical foundations of linguistics

Generative linguistic theory, which was initially developed by Chomsky (1957, 1977), incorporated insights and further developed the theory of formal grammars and abstract automata, which itself resulted from the important work on computability in recursion-theory by the mathematical logicians Turing, Church, Gödel, Kleene and Post. A starting assumption of the generative paradigm is that natural languages can be usefully viewed as sets of structured strings, suited to mathematical analysis and formal representation. Together with this logical foundation of the theory of grammar, but conceptually independent of it, Chomsky reintroduced a rationalist theory of mind and linguistic competence in strong opposition to the then pervasive empiricist, narrowly inductivist and often behaviorist methodologies in linguistic research. This gave rise to the famous controversy about the innateness hypothesis in the 60s and 70s, which saw philosophers of language such as Putnam and Quine disputing the need for a rationalist foundation for linguistic theory, and Chomsky disclaiming in turn the possibility of adequate empiricist explanations of language learning and linguistic universals.[3]

The development of transformational generative grammar, with its claim of the autonomy of syntax from semantics, can be understood as an attempt to separate the issues of form methodologically from those of meaning. It assumes a decidedly syntactic perspective on any linguistic notion or process, not unlike the heuristically fruitful separation in the foundations of mathematics of the syntactically oriented proof-theory and abstract recursion-theory from the model-theoretic and semantic interpretation of formal systems. Philosophers of language have traditionally been concerned primarily with semantic concepts, such as meaning and the relation between language, mind and the external world, paying little, if any, attention to the rich syntactic variation of linguistic phenomena in ordinary languages. However, explicit recognition of the need for a formally precise account of the syntax of natural language has always been common amongst those logicians (Ajduciewicz 1935; Lambek 1958) and philosophers (Bar-Hillel 1953a, b, 1964; Geach 1972) working in *categorial grammar*, a context-free syntax which generates surface structures and reflects the function/argument structure of their semantic interpretation. A variety of such grammars are nowadays finding acceptance among linguists, notably *generalized phrase structure grammar* (GPSG) and *Montague grammar*.

Presently there is general agreement that any suggested boundary between syntax and semantics is heavily theory-dependent. Although we may have a crude, pretheoretical intuition about the proper division of labor between syntax and semantics, only detailed comparisons of rival syntactic and semantic accounts of the same empirical phenomena provide interesting arguments for locating their linguistic explanation in one or the other component, or possibly even maintaining a parallel account in both syntax and semantics (see, for example, Chapter 9 in this volume, by Enç for a comparison of syntactic and semantic accounts of quantifier scope).

## 16.2. Theories of meaning

Although there is a general consensus among philosophers of language and linguists that a theory of meaning must minimally provide an account of the relation between linguistic structure and the external world, opinions

---

[3] The innateness debate is well-documented in Chomsky (1966, 1980, 1986). See also Hook (1969), Searle (1971) and Block (1981).

diverge widely on what methods it should employ and on the question whether it should incorporate or even be identified with a theory of language understanding to provide an explanation of linguistic behavior. We review here some current theories that have advocates among both philosophers and linguists, grouped under three general headings primarily according to their methods.

### 16.2.1. Psychological representationalism

Part of what competent speakers of a language have acquired is knowledge of what the expressions of the language mean or how they may use the language to express their thoughts or mental states. They know, for instance, what sort of thing they call *table*, and that *It is raining* is true when it is raining, but also what it takes to correctly use the sentence *I believe that it is raining*. Any theory of meaning will have to characterize the meaning of such sentences about external as well as internal, or mental, states, but this leaves entirely open which tools are appropriate to represent meaning. Psychological representationalism requires a level of mental representations to mediate between the language and the world, whose precise nature and primitives are to be determined by cognitive psychology, of which linguistics is considered to be a branch. The mental representations are represented in some internal code, as innate language of thought (J. A. Fodor 1975). The relation of a natural language expression to its internal representation is a mapping by projection rules (Katz & Fodor 1963) or correspondence rules which decompose the meaning of any expression into the primitives of the internal code, reminiscent at the lexical level of the method of conceptual analysis. The language of thought is assumed to have its own syntactic structure, described by 'conceptual wellformedness rules' (Jackendoff 1983), and is intended to serve as sole interface to other psychological input from perceptual sources or memory. Although rules of inference should apply at this level of internal representation, the language of thought is not considered to be one of the formal languages developed in logic, which are often rejected for having been designed for mathematical purposes with little consideration for the grammar of natural languages. Chomsky, Hornstein, and Jackendoff emphasize repeatedly that logical languages are unsuitable tools for linguistic analysis, but often their criticism seems to be directed towards first-order predicate logical languages only, although recent semantic research is rarely so restricted in formal method.

Subjects which are in the same mental state are to be related to formally equivalent representations, and in this sense the internal code represents mental states, constituting a representational theory of mind. J. A. Fodor (1983) advocates a strongly syntactic conception of the internal code, drawing on an attractive analogy to the 'internal' machine language, which interprets a programming language, causing its computational behavior. Internal representations of natural languages similarly function in the causation of linguistic and other behavior. Since 'computational processes are, by definition, *syntactic*' (Fodor 1983: 40, his italics), semantic categories are assumed to be of no use in the internal representations.[4] Identifying mental states with such internal representations offers a possible explanation why opaque contexts are psychologically more informative than transparent ones, since the former report essentially how subjects represent the world to themselves, which is directly reflected in the internal representation (see J. A. Fodor 1981: 234–40).

Psychological representationalists meet with strong skepticism and opposition from philosophers and linguists outside the transformational generative paradigm.[5] A recurrent point of their criticism is that either a complete language of thought as part of the species-specific innate endowment is nothing but an empirically unsupported theoretical hypothesis, or it is subject to a vicious infinite regress. Certainly there is plenty of psycholinguistic evidence showing that development of conceptual structure partly determines first language acquisition, but nothing in these studies forces us to assume that the *entire* conceptual apparatus of an adult competent speaker is innate to the infant. It seems more plausible from an empirical point of view that it is only through acquaintance with an external world that children gradually develop their conceptual schemes, which enable them to assign meaning to expressions. Yet a psychological representationalist cannot admit that conceptual structure is in any sense acquired, since the very argument for its innateness would lead then to an infinite regress. J. A. Fodor (1975), for instance, argues that linguistic development is possible only due to the completely innate cognitive structure, since in order for children to formulate hypotheses about the language, the relevant conceptual dimensions must already be available to them. Suppose the language of thought were not completely innate, but at least partly acquired. If so, then a second language of thought would be needed to contain the relevant conceptual dimensions to interpret the first. This argument shows that an infinite number of distinct internal languages would be needed, which the opponents to psychological representationalism take to show that the very idea of a language of thought is fundamentally misguided (though appealed to by its proponents as showing the necessity of its innateness).[6] An

---

[4] See Stich (1983) for more discussion concerning the connection between a purely syntactic theory of mental representations and methodological solipsism.

[5] See Lewis (1972a) for a strong criticism of Katz's semantics as nothing but translation into the uninterpreted language 'Markerese'.

[6] The idea that anything one learns, one already tacitly 'knows' is found in Plato's dialogue *Meno*, where Socrates by maieutic method elicits a geometric proof from a slave (Plato *Meno*: 80d). Blackburn (1984) points out this historical connection between psychological realism and Platonist epistemology.

intermediate position is advocated by Jackendoff, who argues that a language of thought is not sufficient to represent meaning and that cognitive structure partly independent of language helps to shape the development of the language of thought.

The identification of meaning with mental state has been called into question by Putnam's well-known Twin Earth argument. In succinct form, his point is that we cannot maintain two theses at the same time: (1) that intension (meaning) determines extension (range of application), and (2) that meanings are mental states, i.e. that meanings are 'in the head.' Imagine two situations $s_1$ and $s_2$, in which someone is holding a glass filled with a transparent liquid and says *This is water*. Now at $s_1$ the liquid is $H_2O$, but at $s_2$ the liquid is XYZ. Furthermore, $s_1$ actually happened, but $s_2$ is a hypothetical situation, which resembles our actual world in all respects except for the fact that everyone typically calls XYZ *water*. Now the speakers at $s_1$ and $s_2$ are in the same mental state when uttering *This is water* and referring to the contents of the glass in their hand. But they refer to different extensions with their *water*, and hence cannot assign the same meaning to that word. If we construe mental states in such ways that their representations carry no existential presupposition concerning anyone or anything but the subject who is in that state, the two speakers are in type-identical mental states. On the other hand, if mental states are represented as non-identical when the object of the state, $H_2O$ in the one case, XYZ in the other, differs, the two speakers are not in the same mental state, for they are thinking about different liquids. The arguments are bound to remain inconclusive, as long as clear formal criteria for equivalence of mental representations are lacking. This obviously requires an independently specified syntax of the medium of mental representations, and the burden of proof is with those who claim that equivalence of representations is a purely syntactic notion, to show how it is determined while avoiding any appeal to semantic conditions in explaining how equivalent representations hook up to the external world.

### 16.2.2. Semantic realism

Semantic realism analyzes meaning as a direct relation between linguistic expressions and parts of the external world, which is commonly represented by abstract models, set-theoretic, operational or otherwise formalized, of the sort originally developed for formal languages. This mode of representation of meaning is tailored to a theory of inference, entailment, and semantic equivalence. The meaning of opaque contexts, attitude verbs and mental states is also analyzed in terms of this relation, so no special internal medium is needed for their representation. Different primitives of interpretations are assumed by various realistic theories of meaning, but the best-known theory of interpretation to have found linguistic application is Montague grammar, which is based on models with primitive possible worlds and individuals. The meaning of an expression in such models, its intension, is a function from possible worlds to its set-theoretic extensions at such worlds. The intension and the extension of an expression can be viewed as a set-theoretic analysis of the Fregean notions of sense and reference (*Sinn* and *Bedeutung*). Semantic realism offers no account of language learning nor of conceptual development, leaving such issues to cognitive psychology, of which it considers itself independent. The way in which the intension or extension of an expression is determined, either generally or for an individual speaker, is not part of the descriptive goals of a realist semantics, although some of its proponents have emphasized that stereotypes, experts, and various social processes constitute a 'division of labor' influencing the actual way in which a linguistic expression is hooked up into the world.[7] Realism as an ontological stance, which admits of gradation, is committed to viewing the different possible worlds as alternative realities, a position which is taken to all its consequences in Lewis (1972b).

Perhaps not surprisingly, the major challenge to a realist semantics is to account adequately for the interpretation of sentences embedded under attitude verbs. In possible world semantics the intension of the sentence *It is raining* is a 'proposition,' set-theoretically explicated as a function from worlds to worlds in which it is actually raining, or equivalently, the set of possible worlds at which it is raining. An epistemic attitude, like belief, is analyzed as a relation between its subject and the intension of the embedded sentence reporting his or her belief. Suppose now that a model is specified in which at all worlds in which Hesperus is the Evening Star, and only there, the Evening Star is the Morning Star. Then in that model the two sentences *Peter believes that Hesperus is the Evening Star* and *Peter believes that Hesperus is the Morning Star* are interpreted equivalently, since the intension of the embedded sentences is one and the same function.[8] Similarly, a proposition like *Peter believes that the Evening Star is the Morning Star* is entailed by the belief report, i.e. interpreted by the same set or a subset of the worlds. Hence, any necessarily coreferring expression may be substituted in the embedded sentence preserving the truth value of the entire belief-reporting sentence, since substitution of intensionally equivalent or weaker expressions is a general logical rule. This has the undesirable consequence, called *the problem of logical omniscience*

---

[7] 'Traditional semantic theory leaves out only two contributions to the determination of extension – the contribution of society and the contribution of the real world!' (Putnam 1975: 275).

[8] Assuming (as in the example) that functions are set-theoretically represented as sets of ordered pairs, functions are identical if and only if they are represented by the same set. If functions are not reduced to set-theoretical notions, the argument does not keep its force.

in possible world semantics, that the set-theoretic interpretation of any epistemic attitude, or any other sentence-embedding verb, is closed under logical consequence. Although from a purely logical point of view, logical omniscience simply reflects the nature of valid inferences, which are to be distinguished sharply from any psychologistic interpretation of logical laws, pressure from more linguistically motivated criticism of possible worlds semantics challenges the framework to provide a sound function for a linguistic theory of semantic competence, including a more natural account of inferential processes which could provide a finer-grained notion of equivalence of meaning (see especially Partee 1973, 1982). The debate whether semantics of natural language should be a branch of mathematics or psychology has thus ended with the requirement that it provide realistic representations of semantic competence, and with a general acceptance of the reality that competent people may not know all consequences of their beliefs. (For more discussion, see 16.3.2 below.)

In order to develop such a realistic semantic theory, recent research in natural language semantics is directed towards a more procedural and dynamic conception of interpretation and evaluation. This development was preceded by attempts to represent contextual parameters within a possible worlds semantics, separating the context-dependent interpretation for indexical expressions from the context-independent meaning of other descriptive expressions. Two well-known accounts of indexicals and context dependence are briefly discussed here, as they have been very influential in recent linguistic research.

If possible worlds are taken as partial states of affairs or partial specificatons of the way the world is or can be, they must still be distinguished from possible contexts of use, which determine the reference of indexical expressions like *I*, *you*, *here*, *now* etc., and demonstratives like *this*, *that*, *over there*. An account of various forms of context-dependent meaning was originally thought to belong properly to pragmatics, which appealed to speakers, hearers, utterances (rather than sentences or propositions) and contexts of use.[9] The semantic characteristic of indexicals and demonstratives is their constant reference in intensional and extensional contexts. For instance, in *John believes that I am a fool*, an intensional context, the indexical *I* has the same reference as in the extensional context *I am a fool*, if uttered by me. Even in counterfactual contexts indexicals and demonstratives maintain their extensional reference e.g. *I could have been in Paris now* still refers to the utterer of the sentence. After unsuccessful attempts to pack contextual parameters into an extended index or point of reference

---

[9] See Morris (1938) for early thoughts on the division of labor between syntax, semantics and pragmatics. Other terms for indexicals are 'token-reflexives' (Reichenbach), 'egocentric particulars' (Russell) or 'token indexical elements' (Katz).

including possible worlds,[10] Kaplan (1979a, b) presented a semantic 'double-indexing' theory of demonstratives which separated the context-dependent part of meaning, the *character*, of an expression from its *content* or intension. The character of *I* is a function that assigns to each context the content or intension of the expression, the role of the speaker. A competent speaker of English, Kaplan claimed, knows the constant character, rather than the variable content, of such expressions, which determines their referents.

In Stalnaker (1979) the idea that every utterance is interpreted in a context constitutes the core of his semantic theory, which analyses the meaning of an expression as the way in which its utterance affects the common ground and the shared presuppositions of the speakers. The context is adjusted to accommodate the information expressed by an assertion, and the content of the assertion is added to the common ground of the conversational participants.[11] Recent developments in semantics of natural language have been strongly influenced by this more dynamic approach to interpretation and meaning, which is essentially context-dependent and blends pragmatic factors with a standard possible worlds model theory (see section 16.3).

### 16.2.3. Pragmatics and language use

Pragmatics, though less so than syntax and semantics, is characterized by a set of central research issues forming a coherent scientific program of linguistic inquiry. Traditionally it covers those theories of meaning and interpretation which appeal to speakers/hearers, their knowledge of the world, contexts of use, and to linguistic acts or performances and their effects. Many of its current questions are rooted in early British ordinary language philosophy, and the influence of Austin and Grice on analytic philosophy. Austin's philosophical papers (Austin 1962) emphasized the importance of nondescriptive and non-truth-functional uses of language, maintaining that an expression may be used to obtain a multitude of desired goals or effects, due to its context-dependent *illocutionary force* (the act performed by uttering an expression, e.g. making a promise, asking a question) and *perlocutionary force* (the effect obtained, e.g. getting a window closed, convincing someone). Such uses of language, it was claimed, could not be analyzed adequately by truth-conditional theories of meaning, nor by possible worlds semantics, although they constitute an important part of our rule-governed

---

[10] See Montague (1970), Lewis (1972a). Perry (1977, 1979) points out the inherent difficulties of demonstratives and indexicals for a Fregean theory of meaning. The first use of double-indexing in an intensional semantics for temporal indexicals is Kamp (1971).

[11] Similar in spirit is Lewis (1979).

linguistic behavior. The claim of incompatibility of such analyses of meaning with logical semantics was fueled especially by the academic separation, enforced by his followers, of Wittgenstein's philosophy of language into an 'early Wittgenstein,' based on the *Tractatus* (1922) and a 'later Wittgenstein,' (1953), which advocated linguistic practices and conventions as central to a theory of meaning.[12] Later pragmatic theories of meaning have been presented rather as complementary to semantic theories, and currently the distinction is blurred still further in logical theories of context-dependent meaning and interpretation (see 16.3.3). The goal of a theory of speech acts and performative verbs, developed originally by Austin's student, Searle (1969) is to describe necessary and sufficient conditions for various types of linguistic acts. Generative grammarians attempted at first to capture such information directly in the syntactic structure, a project that has now been abandoned (see Sadock 1974 as well as his chapter in Volume II of this series). Nevertheless, despite the failure of a syntactic treatment of speech acts, with our present hindsight we might understand such an attempt as a recognition of the need for a semantic theory of interpretation of utterances rather than of sentences isolated from their contexts of use – a theory which captures, besides truth conditions, the conditions in which an utterance is informative or successfully used to obtain certain effects.

Grice (1957, 1968) stressed the conceptual relation between natural meaning in the external world where, for example, smoke means fire, and non-natural, linguistic meaning of utterances. He developed an analysis of utterance meaning based on irreducible intentional idiom: a speaker *s* means something by uttering *u* is analyzed as: *s* intends *u* to produce an effect (belief or action). Understanding an utterance is partly recognizing the speakers intentions. For Grice, utterance meaning is primary and sentence meaning derivative, but his pragmatic theory contributes little towards a compositional semantics along Fregean lines. Grice's influence in linguistics is primarily due to his account in Grice (1975) of conversational maxims, that is, social conventions of communication, which concern additional, secondary aspects of utterance meaning and so called *implicatures* or invited inferences which are not entailed by the sentence uttered. One example is the *maxim of quantity*: make your contribution to a conversation as informative as required for the current purposes of exchange. Suppose someone asks the question *Who did you kiss last night?* and you answer *Jim and Jack*. The questioner may legitimately infer that you did not kiss anyone else, although you did not say so. Gricean maxims are essential to any linguistic theory which purports to explain how inferences are made from

---

[12] Kenny (1973) rightly emphasizes the continuity in Wittgenstein's thought.

what is said in interaction with the speakers' presuppositions[13] and their knowledge of the world.

## 16.3. **Semantics of natural language**

The present section surveys some of the major current issues in the interdisciplinary field of semantics of natural language, which includes a number of disparate semantic frameworks, of which we mention here only Montague grammar (Montague 1974), situation semantics (Barwise & Perry 1983), discourse representation theory (Kamp 1981), file change semantics (Heim 1982) and game theoretic semantics (Hintikka 1973; Saarinen 1978). Its main methodological principle, the *compositionality principle*, often attributed to Frege, says that the meaning of an expression is a function of the meaning of its parts and the way they are put together. The nature of the principle is open to much debate and it is sometimes misunderstood as an empirical claim about natural language. Its importance and force lie in its nature as a formal constraint on the interaction of syntax and semantics and (possibly) pragmatics. Consequently, compositionality may come in degrees, depending on the extent and way in which a particular theory espouses the principle. In most rigorous mathematical form, adopted in Montague grammar, it requires that the syntax, structured as term-algebra with syntactic operations on trees, can be homomorphically embedded into the semantic term-algebra with semantic operations on intensions.[14] The syntax may be a categorial or a phrase structure grammar, as long as every syntactic rule has a corresponding semantic effect (identity-functions are allowed if no semantic change is required). This so-called 'rule-by-rule hypothesis' (Bach 1976) is the particular way Montague grammar implements compositionality, allowing distinct semantic rules to use the same semantic operation, which is taken to be at least in practice equivalent to strong compositionality. The semantic component specifies the meaning and interpretation of the syntactically generated expressions, which include conditions of truth or falsity, traditionally conceived of as the only purely semantic part of meaning. But if the theory of meaning and interpretation is

---

[13] Presuppositions, i.e. conditions which must be fulfilled for an expression to be interpretable, have a long history in philosophy of language and linguistic semantics and pragmatics. Much current discussion centers on the projection problem of presuppositions, i.e. how the presuppositions of an expression are or are not preserved within larger expressions. See Karttunen (1973), Kempson (1975), Wilson (1975), Gazdar (1979), Oh & Dinneen (1979), Soames (1979) and Heim (1981).

[14] See Janssen (1983) for an algebraic analysis of compositionality. Partee (1984) contains a comprehensive survey of linguistic arguments for or against compositionality as a working hypothesis or methodological constraint on grammar. Cooper (1983), which includes ideas originally developed in Cooper's dissertation of 1975, presents the first attempt at weakening Montegovian compositionality in a principled and restricted way for scope ambiguities.

441

more broadly concerned with context-dependent meaning and interpretation, it will also include pragmatic conditions of informativeness, conditions of correct or incorrect use of expressions, and incorporate a representation of the conversational common ground. An important question, open to much debate, is whether strong compositionality can be maintained overall or only locally, i.e. within stable contexts, for such comprehensive theories of interpretation.[15]

Although within this general research program, semantic theories may differ in their specification of the way operations and functions actually execute algorithms computing meaning, these kinds of difference do not matter to semantic theory. Semantic description is independent of the actual computational processes or performing operations in a structure, set-theoretic, algebraic, operational, or otherwise so long as they can be characterized up to isomorphism at an appropriate level of mathematical abstraction.

### 16.3.1. Logical form and semantic representation

In analytic philosophy, the received method of conceptual or linguistic analysis often employs some or another logical language with a clear intended interpretation, matching the analysandum with a formula or semi-formal expression. Reformists, like Russell, intended such a language to 'regiment' the misleading forms of natural language expressions, for example, by analyzing nonreferring definite descriptions as containing hidden existential quantification. Rather than reformation of natural language, the common goal of semantics of natural language is now to represent aspects of the meaning of a linguistic expression in a form suitable for a 'broad' theory of inference, which includes pragmatic factors and accounts for invited inferences. The compositionality principle imposes a stringent recursive format of the translation algorithm to a formal language, whose syntax and interpretation should be specified independently of the syntax of the natural language. Current research (especially Kamp 1981; Heim 1982; Barwise & Perry 1983) provides new formal means of semantic representation for such a broad theory of meaning, interpretation, and inference. The distinctive feature of these developments is the shift from static notions of interpretations and satisfaction of truth conditions, adopted from logic, towards dynamic semantic operations and the central use of partial functions in constructing representations of given and new information and an analysis

---

[15] Barwise & Perry (1983) reject strong compositionality for their notion of meaning (cf. Kaplan's level of *character*), but seem to maintain it for the evaluation (cf. extensional denotation). Kamp's DRS-theory (Kamp 1981) is not strongly compositional, but a rather cumbersome indexed reformulation of it is compositional as Zeevat (1984) showed. See also Chierchia & Rooth (1984) on this point.

of the meaning of an expression in terms of its ability to modify a given representation.

A fundamental open question is whether a theory of meaning and interpretation must include an intermediate level of representation of informational dependencies between the natural language syntax and the model-theoretic interpretation. In Montague grammar, direct interpretation, i.e. mapping linguistic expressions immediately into mode-theoretic objects, is thought to be a mere notational variant of the more commonly used indirect interpretation via an intermediate stage of translation to a formal language of typed intensional logic. Situation semantics (Barwise & Perry 1983) advocates direct interpretation rather than indirect interpretation, rejecting the idea that the meaning of a linguistic expression can be represented in its logical form in any way that does justice to context-dependent interpretation. Kamp (1981) and Heim (1982) do use an intermediate representational level, which is to a certain extent comparable with the level of logical form in syntactic theories.

## 16.3.2. Intensional contexts and attitudes

In the important, and by now traditional controversy on attitude-reports and scope ambiguities in the philosophy of language,[16] Montague grammar provided the first compositional semantics of opaque contexts, relating the syntactic structure of belief- or attitude-reports to their interpretation in an intensional logic with a possible world semantics which accounted in a general way for quantifier-scope ambiguities. Linguists have criticized this approach, though, for requiring syntactic disambiguation of semantic phenomena, and have therefore developed alternatives relocating the explanation to the semantics (see Enç & Ladusaw in this volume.)

The recent development of dynamic semantics has shed a quite different light on puzzles of scope ambiguities. De re beliefs can be analyzed by unifying previously assigned 'existing' referents in the representation with the relevant NP interpretation, whereas new referents are to be introduced in 'belief-domains' for de dicto interpretations of an NP (for fuller discussion, see Kamp 1984). Compared to the traditional 'static' analysis of scope ambiguities as linear dependencies between quantifiers in formulas, dynamic interpretations discriminate innovatively the way in which meaning is assigned to an expression from the product of that process, its meaning. This may prove to be the right foundation for a unified account of the ambiguities which arise due to the meaning of the expressions and those which depend on the common ground of speakers, their shared information

---

[16] The most important sources here are Quine (1953, 1960, 1966, 1969), Kaplan (1969) and Hintikka (1973).

and on their beliefs about the world. It does not imply, however, as Barwise & Perry (1983) suggest, that the possible worlds must be abandoned. Within the possible worlds paradigm, Stalnaker (1984: 71) argues that 'Semantic complexity lies in the means of determining a proposition and not in the proposition itself,' and Cresswell & von Stechow (1982) and Cresswell (1985) present a compositional theory of structured meanings which are intended to serve as semantic objects of attitudes.[17] The viability of these new theories will have to be tested in future research, but the current methodological trend towards refinement in structuring the representation of meaning distinctively sets out the cooperative program for syntax, semantics, pragmatics, and philosophy and logic.

[17] See also Soames (1985) for a critical discussion of the 'semantic innocence' of situation semantics regarding attitudes, suggesting that Russellian propositions, which have internal structure related to the syntactic structure of the attitude-report, will provide a better solution.

*REFERENCES*

Ajduciewicz, K. 1935. Die syntaktische Konnexität. *Studia Philosophica* 1: 1–27. English translation in S. McCall (ed.) 1967. *Polish logic*. Oxford: Oxford University Press.

Austin, J. L. 1962. *How to do things with words*. Oxford: Oxford University Press.

Bach, E. 1976. An extension of classical transformational grammar. In *Problems of linguistic metatheory. Proceedings of the 1976 Conference*, Michigan State University.

Bar-Hillel, Y. 1953a. Logical syntax and semantics. *Language* 29: 47–58.

Bar-Hillel, Y. 1953b. A quasi-arithmetical notation of syntactic description. *Language* 29: 47–58.

Bar-Hillel, Y. 1964. *Language and information: selected essays on their theory and application*. Reading: Addison-Wesley.

Barwise, J. & Perry, J. 1983. *Situations and attitudes*. Cambridge, MA: MIT Press.

Blackburn, S. 1984. *Spreading the word. Groundings in the philosophy of language*. Oxford: Clarendon Press.

Block, N. (ed.) 1981. *Readings in the philosophy of psychology*. Vol. 2 of the *Language and thought* series. Cambridge, MA: Harvard University Press.

Chierchia, G. & Rooth, M. 1984. Configurational notions in discourse representation theory. In C. Jones & P. Sells (eds.) *NELS* 14: 49–63.

Chomsky, N. 1957. *Syntactic structures*. The Hague: Mouton.

Chomsky, N. 1966. *Cartesian linguistics*. New York: Harper & Row.

Chomsky, N. 1977 (1955). *The logical structure of linguistic theory*. New York: Plenum.

Chomsky, N. 1980. *Rules and representations*. Oxford: Blackwell.

Chomsky, N. 1981. *Lectures on government and binding*. Dordrecht: Foris.

Chomsky, N. 1986. *Knowledge of language: its nature, origin and use*. Series Convergence. New York: Praeger.

Cole, P. (ed.) 1979. *Syntax and semantics*. Vol. 9: *Speech acts*. New York: Academic Press.

Cooper, R. 1983. *Quantification and syntactic theory*. Dordrecht: Reidel.

Cresswell, M. 1985. *Structured meanings. The semantics of propositional attitudes*. Cambridge, MA: MIT Press.

Cresswell, M. & von Stechow, A. 1982. De re belief generalized. *Linguistics and Philosophy* 5, 4: 503–35.

Davidson, D. & Harman, G. (eds.) 1972. *Semantics of natural language*. Dordrecht: Reidel.

Davidson, D. & Harman, G. (eds.) 1975. *The logic of grammar*. Encino: Dickinson.

Dowty, D. 1979. *Word meaning and Montague grammar*. Dordrecht: Reidel.

Fodor, J. A. 1975. *The language of thought*. New York: Thomas Y. Crowell. Paperback edn (1979). Cambridge, MA: Harvard University Press.

Fodor, J. A. 1981. *Representations. Philosophical essays on the foundations of cognitive science.* Cambridge, MA: MIT Press.

Fodor, J. A. 1983. *The modularity of mind. An essay on faculty psychology.* Cambridge, MA: MIT Press.

Fodor, J. D. 1977. *Semantics: theories of meaning in generative grammar.* Sussex: Harvester.

French, P., Uehling, Th. & Wettstein, H. (eds.) 1979. *Contemporary perspectives in the philosophy of language.* Minneapolis: University of Minnesota Press.

Gazdar, G. 1979. *Pragmatics – implicature, presupposition and logical form.* New York: Academic Press.

Geach, P. 1972. A program for syntax. In Davidson & Harman (1972).

Geach, P. & Black, M. 1952. *Translations from the philosophical writings of Gottlob Frege.* Oxford: Blackwell.

Grice, H. P. 1957. Meaning. *Philosophical Review* 66: 377–88. Reprinted in Steinberg & Jacobovits (1971).

Grice, H. P. 1968. Utterer's meaning, sentence-meaning and word-meaning. *Foundations of Language* 4: 225–42. Reprinted in Searle (1971).

Grice, H. P. 1975. Logic and conversation. In Davidson & Harman (1975).

Grice, H. P. 1979. Further notes on logic and conversation. In Cole (1979).

Heim, I. 1981. On the projection problem for presuppositions. *WCCFL 2 Proceedings.* Stanford: Stanford University Dept. of Linguistics.

Heim, I. 1982. The semantics of definite and indefinite noun-phrases. Doctoral dissertation, University of Massachusetts/Amherst.

Hintikka, J. 1973. *Logic, language-games and information. Kantian themes in the philosophy of logic.* Oxford: Clarendon Press.

Hook, S. 1969. *Language and philosophy.* New York: New York University Press.

Hornstein, N. 1984. *Logic as grammar. An approach to meaning in natural language.* Cambridge, MA: MIT Press/Bradford Books.

Jackendoff, R. 1983. *Semantics and cognition.* Cambridge, MA: MIT Press.

Janssen, Th. 1983. Foundations and applications of Montague grammar. Doctoral dissertation, The Mathematical Centre, Amsterdam.

Kamp, H. 1971. Formal properties of 'now'. *Theoria* 37: 227–73.

Kamp, H. 1981. A theory of truth and semantic representation. In J. Groenendijk, M. Stokhof & Th. Janssen (eds.) *Formal methods in the study of language.* Mathematical Centre Tract 135. Amsterdam: Mathematical Centre. Reprinted (1983) as *Truth, interpretation and information.* GRASS 2, Dordrecht: Foris.

Kamp, H. 1984. A DRS-theory of belief. University of Texas/Austin. ms.

Kaplan, D. 1969. Quantifying in. *Synthese* 19: 178–214.

Kaplan, D. 1979a. Dthat. In P. Cole (1979). Reprinted in P. French *et al.* (1979).

Kaplan, D. 1979b. On the logic of demonstratives. In P. French *et al.* (1979).

Karttunen, L. 1973. Presuppositions of compound sentences. *Linguistic Inquiry* 4: 169–93.

Katz, J. 1972. *Semantic theory.* New York: Harper & Row.

Katz, J. & Fodor, J. A. 1963. The structure of a semantic theory. *Language* 39, 2: 170–210.

Katz, J. & Postal, P. 1964. *An integrated theory of linguistic descriptions.* Cambridge, MA: MIT Press.

Kempson, R. 1975. *Presuppositions and the delimitation of semantics.* Cambridge: Cambridge University Press.

Kenny, A. 1973. *Wittgenstein.* London: Alan Lane/Penguin.

Kripke, S. 1972. Naming and necessity. In Davidson & Harman (1972). Reprinted (1980) as monograph with same title. Cambridge, MA: Harvard University Press.

Lakoff, G. 1971. On generative semantics. In Steinberg & Jakobovits (1971).

Lambek, J. 1958. The mathematics of sentence structure. *American Mathematical Monthly* 65: 154–69.

Landman, F. & Veltman, F. 1984. *Varieties of formal semantics.* GRASS 3, Dordrecht: Foris.

Lewis, D. 1972a. General semantics. In Davidson & Harman (1972). Reprinted (1983) in *Philosophical Papers 1.* Oxford: Oxford University Press.

Lewis, D. 1972b. *Counterfactuals.* Cambridge, MA: Harvard University Press.

Lewis, D. 1979. Score-keeping in a language game. In R. Bäuerle, U. Egli & A. von Stechow (eds.) *Semantics from different points of view.* Berlin: Springer.

McCawley, J. D. 1968. Lexical insertion in a transformational grammar without deep structure. In B. Darden, C. Bailey & A. Davison (eds.) *CLS* 4.

Montague, R. 1970. Pragmatics and intensional logic. *Synthese* 22: 68–94. Reprinted in Montague (1974).

Montague, R. 1974. *Formal philosophy*. Ed. R. Thomason. New Haven: Yale University Press.

Morris, C. 1938. Foundations of the theory of signs. In *International encyclopedia of unified science* 1. Chicago: University of Chicago Press.

Oh, C. K. & Dinneen, D. A. (eds.) 1979. *Syntax and semantics*. Vol. 11: *Presupposition*. New York: Academic Press.

Partee, B. 1973. The semantics of belief-sentences. In J. Hintikka, J. Moravcsik & P. Suppes (eds.) *Approaches to natural language*. Dordrecht: Reidel.

Partee, B. 1982. Belief sentences and the limits of semantics. In S. Peters & E. Saarinen (eds.) *Processes, beliefs and questions*. Dordrecht: Reidel.

Partee, B. 1984. Compositionality. In Landman & Veltman (1984).

Passmore, J. 1957. *A hundred years of philosophy*. Harmondsworth: Penguin.

Perry, J. 1977. Frege on demonstratives. *Philosophical Review* 86: 474–97.

Perry, J. 1979. The problem of the essential indexical. *Nous* 13: 3–21.

Putnam, H. 1975. *Mind, language and reality. Philosophical papers, vol. 2*. Cambridge: Cambridge University Press.

Quine, W. V. O. 1953. *From a logical point of view*. Cambridge, MA: Harvard University Press.

Quine, W. V. O. 1960. *Word and object*. Cambridge, MA: MIT Press.

Quine, W. V. O. 1966. *The ways of paradox and other essays*. New York: Random House.

Quine, W. V. O. 1969. *Ontological relativity and other essays*. New York: Columbia.

Rorty, R. (ed.) 1967. *The linguistic turn. Recent essays in philosophical method*. Chicago: University of Chicago Press.

Saarinen, E. (ed.) 1978. *Game theoretical semantics*. Dordrecht: Reidel.

Sadock, J. 1974. *Toward a linguistic theory of speech-acts*. New York: Academic Press.

Searle, J. 1969. *Speech acts. An essay in the philosophy of language*. Cambridge: Cambridge University Press.

Searle, J. (ed.) 1971. *Philosophy of language*. Oxford: Oxford University Press.

Soames, S. 1979. A projection problem for speaker presuppositions. *Linguistic Inquiry* 10, 4: 623–66.

Soames, S. 1985. Lost innocence. *Linguistics and Philosophy* 8, 1: 59–71.

Stalnaker, R. 1979. Assertion. In P. Cole (1979).

Stalnaker, R. 1984. *Inquiry*. Cambridge, MA: MIT Press.

Steinberg, D. & Jakobovits, L. (eds.) 1971. *Semantics: an interdisciplinary reader in philosophy, linguistics and psychology*. Cambridge: Cambridge University Press.

Stich, S. 1983. *From folk psychology to cognitive science: the case against belief*. Cambridge, MA: MIT Press.

Wilson, D. 1975. *Presuppositions and non-truth-conditional semantics*. London and New York: Academic Press.

Wittgenstein, L. 1922. *Tractatus logico-philosophicus*. London: Routledge & Kegan Paul.

Wittgenstein, L. 1953. *Philosophical investigations*. Oxford: Blackwell.

Zeevat, H. 1984. A compositional approach to discourse representations. University of Amsterdam. ms.

# 17 Linguistic typology

*Bernard Comrie*

## 17.0. Introduction: what is linguistic typology?

The overall aim of linguistic typology is to classify languages in terms of their structural properties, in other words to answer, in general but revealing terms, the question: what is language X like? In linguistics, there are other ways of classifying languages, and it is important to appreciate the difference between these other possible classificatory principles and the principles of linguistic typology.

Perhaps the best-known way of classifying languages is in terms of their genetic relatedness, as when English and German are classified as members of the Germanic branch of the Indo-European family; Russian and Polish are classified as members of the Slavic branch of the Indo-European family; and Arabic and Hebrew are classified as members of the Semitic branch of the Afroasiatic family. Essentially, claiming that two languages are related means claiming that, at some time in the past, they shared a common ancestor language. Thus English and German are claimed to have had a common ancestor, Proto-Germanic, in the past, while all of English, German, Russian, and Polish had a common ancestor, Proto-Indo-European, in the even more distant past. The evidence for claiming that two languages are genetically related is, of course, the existence of shared similarities, but there is no supposition that the features that happen to be shared by descendants of a common ancestor are of particular structural signficance in a descriptive account of any of the languages in question. For instance, some of the evidence for the genetic relatedness of Indo-European languages comes from shared basic vocabulary, such as words for kinship terms, numerals, and common everyday objects, but such vocabulary items are of no particular importance in characterizing the overall structure of any individual Indo-European language or of the putative ancestor language, Proto-Indo-European.

Another way in which one might classify languages is in terms of areally shared properties. It has long been known that if languages are in close contact, then they will probably start developing features in common. The simplest example of this is loanwords: the intense contact between English and French in England during the Middle Ages has resulted in the infusion of a vast number of French lexical items into the English language, including even such basic lexical items as *very*. In some cases, the similarities that come to be shared as a result of contact are more spectacular, affecting more basic aspects of the structure of the languages involved. The most famous example of such mutual influence is the Balkan sprachbund: the term 'sprachbund,' incidentally, is used for a group of geographically contiguous languages which share features in common that have arisen through mutual contact. The core of the Balkan sprachbund consists of Modern Greek, Albanian, Bulgarian (with the closely related Macedonian), and Rumanian. All four languages are in fact Indo-European, but from different branches – Greek is a member of the Hellenic branch; Albanian is a branch of its own; Bulgarian is a member of the Slavic branch, while Rumanian is a member of the Romance subbranch of the Italic branch – and they share a number of features with one another that are not shared with languages more closely related genetically. That is, Modern Greek shares some features with the other Balkan languages that it does not share with Ancient Greek; Bulgarian has some such features that are not shared by other Slavic languages; Rumanian has some such features that are not shared by the other Romance languages or Latin.

Among the characteristic features of the Balkan sprachbund are: (a) merging of the expression of the genitive (possessive) and dative (indirect object, recipient) relations, as in Bulgarian *na žena* 'of/to (a) woman'; (b) development of a postponed definite article (except in Modern Greek), as in Rumanian *om-ul* 'man-the'; and most spectacularly of all from the viewpoint of closely related languages, (c) large-scale loss of the infinitive and its replacement by finite subordinate clauses, as in Modern Greek *θel-o na maθ-o* 'I want to learn,' literally 'want-I that learn-I.'

But although the features shared by areally related languages can go quite deep into the grammatical structure of the individual languages, the set of shared features does not in any way constitute a coherent whole: for instance, there is no intrinsic relation between loss of the infinitive and development of a postposed definite article, as can be seen from the Scandinavian languages, which have a postposed article (e.g. Swedish *mann-en* 'man-the') but no infinitive loss. Moreover, it is not necessary that any of the individual features be particularly significant structurally: thus, loss of the overt distinction between the expression of genitive and dative relations is hardly a major revolution in the grammatical structure of a language. The study of shared areal features is, incidentally, often referred to as 'areal typology,' but given the rather different aims of areal typology and what is understood by the more general term 'linguistic typology,' I will not deal in any more detail with areal typology in this contribution.

Linguistic typology is thus the classification of languages in terms of those structural properties that are not shared by virtue of common genetic origin or areal contact. In particular, in carrying out linguistic typology it will quite often be appropriate to group languages together typologically even though those languages are spoken in areas geographically remote from one another and even though, as far as we are aware, the languages are not genetically related: for instance, Turkish and Quechua share many syntactic properties in common (e.g. head-final constituent order and widespread use of special dependent verb forms in dependent clauses), but are geographically remote from one another (Turkey and South America respectively), and are, as far as can be established, not genetically related. In individual cases, it may be difficult to establish whether similarities between two languages are purely typological or the result of common genetic origin or intense contact – this is one of the problems faced, for instance, by the Ural-Altaic hypothesis, since the most obvious features shared by, say, Turkish and Finnish are typologically quite common across the languages of the world, many of them being shared, for instance, with Quechua. But in principle the difference is clear, and provided one selects one's language sample from languages that are genetically and areally diverse, it should be possible to guard against biases introduced into linguistic typology by the consideration of genetically or areally related languages.

The enterprise of linguistic typology has two important presuppositions. First, it is assumed that languages can be compared with one another in terms of their structures. This implies that there are some universal properties of language, namely the basis of the structural comparison. For this reason, the study of linguistic typology has in general gone hand in hand with the study of language universals. Indeed, certain statements about language are regarded by some investigators as statements about language universals, by others as statements about linguistic typology, and by yet others as demonstrating the absence of any clear division between the two enterprises. A good example would be an implicational universal, for instance: if a language has voiceless nasals, then it also has voiced nasals. This statement is a universal in the sense that it restricts the class of possible languages: there can be no language that has voiceless nasals but lacks voiced nasals. But equally, it can be viewed as establishing a tripartite typology of languages: those with only voiced nasals (e.g. English), those with both voiced and voiceless nasals (e.g. Burmese), and those with no nasals (e.g. some Salishan languages, spoken on the northwest coast of North America).

Secondly, linguistic typology presupposes that there are differences among languages, since clearly if there were no differences then all individual instantiations of the human linguistic potential would belong to a single type, which would have a single member. While the observation that there are differences among languages may seem trivial, it is important always to bear this observation in mind in practice. Certainly, some linguistic approaches have suffered and do suffer from almost exclusive concentration on a single language (such as Latin in the Middle Ages, English until quite recently in generative grammar). The overall aim of the combined enterprise of language universals and linguistic typology is the study of the range of possible variation across languages and of the constraints on that variation. The more specific approaches to linguistic typology examined below should be considered against the background of this remark.

In principle, any structural property of a language could be chosen as the basis of a linguistic typology. For instance, one could in principle typologize languages depending on whether or not they have a voice opposition in the consonant system. English, Russian, and Japanese would then be assigned to the language type having this opposition, while Quechua, Hawaiian, and Dyirbal (an Aboriginal language of Australia) would be assigned to the language type lacking this opposition. While this is in principle a well-formed typology, linguists would probably readily agree that it is not a very useful typology, for the simple reason that it does not tell us anything significant about linguistic structure. From the fact that a language has or lacks a voice opposition in its consonants, one cannot predict any other properties of the language and indeed, on many other typological parameters English and Japanese, or Hawaiian and Dyirbal, are radically different from one another.

Thus in practice, in carrying out linguistic typology the aim is to find significant typological parameters, where by significant we mean 'characterizing a large area of the structure of the language.' Some attempts at linguistic typologies, in particular earlier attempts from the nineteenth century, tried to provide a single typological characterization of the whole language. Such holistic typologies assume that there is some single typological feature that is so salient that it can be used to typologize the whole structure of the language – the remaining features of each individual language presumably being relatively insignificant to the overall enterprise. Nowadays, few linguists would attempt to establish holistic typologies of this kind. For instance, two languages might have clear typological similarities in their phonology, but be radically different in their syntactic typology. Tone languages, for example, represent a well-defined type in terms of one aspect of phonology, but different tone languages may be radically different from one another on other parameters: thus, tone languages of West Africa have segmental phoneme inventories very different from tone languages of Southeast Asia.

In what follows, I have not attempted to give a detailed historical overview of work on language typology; a survey of this kind is already available in Greenberg (1974). Rather, the individual sections below examine typological parameters that have been advanced as possible bases for linguistic typologies assessing their merits and defects.

## 17.1. **Morphological typology**

The first systematically developed theory of linguistic typology was in relation to morphological typology, i.e. to the ways in which individual morphemes are combined into words in different languages. As will become clearer in the course of the exposition throughout this contribution, progress in language typology is heavily interdependent with overall progress in linguistic theory. From the early nineteenth century until quite recently, linguists' understanding of morphology was much firmer than their understanding of syntax, and in part the earlier development of morphological typology can be viewed as a reflection of this.

Morphological typology groups languages into three or four types: isolating, agglutinative, fusional (also called flectional), sometimes with the addition of a fourth type, polysynthetic (also sometimes called incorporating). In an ideal isolating language, each word would consist of just one morpheme. Some languages come closer to this ideal, for instance Vietnamese:

(1) Tuy    nghèo, nhu'ng anh thích giúp bạn
      though poor  yet     he  like  help friend
      'Though poor, he likes to help friends'

Each of the words in this sentence consists of a single morpheme, and is invariable: thus *anh* does not change to show case (cf. the difference between English *he* and *him*), and *thích* does not change to show person and number or tense (cf. English *like, likes, liked*).

In an agglutinative language, words do change to show different morphological categories, but the morpheme indicating each morphological category is readily segmentable from adjacent morphemes, i.e. one ends up with a linear sequence of morphemes corresponding to a linear order of grammatical categories. Turkish is often cited as a language close to the ideal agglutinative type. The Turkish for 'to my hands' is *el-ler-im-e*, in which *el* is 'hand' and the suffixes are, in order, 'plural,' '1st person,' 'dative.' A fusional language likewise expresses several grammatical categories in a single word, but segmentation is impossible or difficult. The older Indo-European languages, such as Latin, are good examples of fusional languages: in Latin *can-um* 'of the dogs,' for instance, the genitive plural inflection *-um* cannot be segmented into one phoneme sequence expressing 'genitive' and another one expressing 'plural,' as can be seen by comparing the genitive singular *can-is* and the nominative plural *can-ēs*.

A polysynthetic language is one in which so many categories can be expressed in a single word that a whole sentence regularly consists of just a single word. Eskimo is an example of a language (or more accurately, group of languages) with widespread polysynthesis; example (2) is from Siberian Yupik:

(2) Angya-ghlla-ng-yug-tuq
  boat-big-get-want-3sg.
  'He wants to get a big boat'

However, polysynthetic does not really represent a different type in terms of the parameters used in defining the other three types: it is simply agglutination taken to the extreme.

A better way of looking at these types, following ideas of Sapir (1921), is to consider the interaction of two parameters: the index of synthesis, which counts the number of morphemes per word; and the index of fusion, which counts the extent to which the morphemes in a word are fused together (as opposed to being segmentable); clearly, the index of fusion is only relevant if the index of synthesis is greater than 1. An ideal isolating language thus has a low index of synthesis, while a polysynthetic language has a high index of synthesis. Languages usually classified as agglutinative or fusional occupy an intermediate position; they are distinguished according to their index of fusion (low for agglutinative, high for fusional languages). Polysynthetic languages usually have a low index of fusion (with so many grammatical categories packed into a single word, it would presumably impose too great a load on the memory to have to remember a distinct single sequence for every possible combination), though there might well be individual instances of fusion of adjacent morphemes (as is in fact the case in Eskimo).

In defining morphological types above, I referred to ideal types, In fact, probably no language corresponds exactly to one of the types as defined above. Thus, Vietnamese has a large number of compound words incorporating two or more morphemes, e.g. *vê-sinh* 'hygiene' (lit. 'guard life'). In Turkish, it is often impossible to segment person from number in verb forms (e.g. *git-ti-m* 'I went,' *git-ti-z* 'we went,' where *git* is 'go' and *-ti* is the past tense morpheme). In Latin, the stem *can-* is segmentable from the infectional suffix. Although English is to a large extent isolating, it does have some agglutination (e.g. *cat*, *cat-s*; *love*, *love-s*, *love-d*, *lov-ing*), and even some fusion (e.g. *tooth*, *teeth*; *be*, *am*, *is*, *are*, *was*, *were*). This is an important observation that will recur below: in typologizing languages we often find that the individual linguistic types are not discrete, all-or-nothing categorizations, but rather represent polar values; individual languages then belong to a given type to a greater or less extent.

Morphological typology occupies an important place in the historical development of linguistic typology – many of the principles were first worked out in relation to morphological typology – and morphological typology is the kind of typology that most often finds its way into general introductions to linguistics. However, it is now generally acknowledged that morphological typology is an extremely limited view of typology: in particular, from the fact that a language is of a particular morphological type, one can predict very little about other aspects of its structure. Thus, in the sense defined in section 17.0, morphological typology does not isolate a really significant aspect of language structure. The typological parameters discussed below are all attempts to isolate more significant parameters.

## 17.2. Word order typology

One set of parameters that has gained widespread attention in recent years as a possible basis for linguistic typology is word order, or more accurately, constituent order (i.e. the order of constituents within constructions; a constituent may, of course, consist of more than one word, as when the subject *the man* is defined as a constituent of the sentence *The man ran away*). The starting point for this area of investigation, as for so much of current work on language universals and linguistic typology, is Greenberg (1966). In this article, Greenberg examined a number of logically independent word order parameters, including in particular: (a) the order of the verb relative to the subject and object; (b) the order of attributive adjectives relative to their head noun; (c) the order of genitives relative to their head noun; (d) the order of adpositions relative to their dependent noun, i.e. whether a language has prepositions or postpositions. Although these four parameters are in principle logically independent, Greenberg noted that there are strong correlations among individual parameter values. For instance, if a language is verb-initial (i.e. the verb precedes both subject and object), it invariably has prepositions. (More recent work suggests that this should perhaps be modified to *almost* invariably has prepositions.) In fact, Greenberg noted that of the logically possible number of combinations of different word order parameters, only a limited subset is attested among the languages of the world, and even fewer are attested with frequency. If we leave out of consideration the subject, then the two most common combinations are: (i) object before verb, adjective before noun, genitive before noun, postpositional, and (ii) object after verb, adjective after noun, genitive after noun, prepositional.

Some later researchers (though, it should be emphasized, not Greenberg himself) attempted to generalize Greenberg's results, by positing two major ideal language types in terms of word order. Here, I will follow essentially the proposal of Vennemann (1972). Vennemann argues that the various parameter values listed under (i) above are all instances of a single ordering principle: operator before operand; while those listed under (ii) above are all instances of the converse: operand before operator. Thus the two language types are operator–operand and operand–operator. They can be illustrated by Japanese and Welsh respectively:

(3) Taroo ga    Ziroo o       but-ta
    Taroo SUBJ Jiroo DIR OBJ hit-PAST
    'Taroo hit Jiroo'

(4) Lladd-odd    y   dyn y   ci
    kill-PAST 3 sg. the man the dog
    'The man killed the dog'

Sentences (3) and (4) illustrate the order of constituents, in particular verb and object, in the clause. For adjectives, compare Japanese *akai hon* 'red book' and Welsh *llyfr goch*, lit. 'book red'; for genitives, Japanese *kodomo no hon* 'the child's book,' lit. 'child GEN book,' and Welsh *llyfr y bachgen*, lit. 'book the child.' Japanese has postpositions, e.g. *uti ni*, lit. 'house in,' whereas Welsh has prepositions, e.g. *yn y ty* 'in the house.'

This approach to word order typology has more recently been incorporated into generative grammar, in particular into $\overline{X}$-grammar (Jackendoff 1977). Within $\overline{X}$-grammar, the basic schema specifying the structure of different kinds of phrases (e.g. noun phrase, verb phrase, prepositional phrase) is the same, so that languages like Japanese have a basic phrase-structure rule specifying that the head is preceded by its adjuncts, while Welsh has the mirror-image rule, specifying that the head is followed by its adjuncts. Vennemann's terms 'operator' and 'operand' can simply be replaced by 'adjunct' and 'head,' and languages are either head-final or head-initial.

While word order typology is clearly a more significant basis for linguistic typology than was morphological typology, it is not without serious problems. In addition to problems that arise in establishing a basic word for many languages, the establishment of two main types, head-final and head-initial, involves a considerable idealization of the data. Many languages are exceptional on one or more parameters from the overall type. Thus English and Persian are both overall head-initial, but English has prenominal adjectives and Persian is verb-final. A large number of languages with overall verb-final word order nonetheless have the adjective following the noun (e.g. Basque) – indeed in Greenberg's study almost as many languages are of this type as of the consistent head-final type.

Although one can establish ideal types as a standard against which to measure individual languages, one would hope that the ideal types established are indeed typologically significant, rather than just arbitrarily chosen measuring standards. Within generative grammar, it has proven necessary to set up other principles which can override the strict head-final/head-initial distinction. Chinese, for instance, is claimed to be a head-final language (with preposed adjectives and genitives) where case assignment takes place to the right (so that the fact that objects follow their verb is handled by case assignment) (Koopman 1984: 122–6). Whether the interaction of conflicting principles can be sufficiently constrained to avoid vacuity remains a topic for future research. The work of Hawkins (1983) suggest that if universals of word order are to have any empirical validity, they may be so specific that they are of restricted typological relevance.

## 17.3. Functional approaches

For many years the idea has been around in linguistics that there is some interplay between word order and case marking, in particular in that languages with rich case-marking systems (like Latin, Turkish, Japanese – the postpositions of Japanese function in the same way as the bound case markers of the other languages) tend to have freer word order, while languages with poorly developed case marking (like English) have more fixed word order, often relying on the word order to provide information on the grammatical relations. Thus, English *The man loves the woman* and *The woman loves the man* have radically different meanings, whereas Latin *Vir amat mulier-em* and *Mulier-em amat vir* have the same cognitive meaning: in Latin the fact that 'man' is subject is shown by the nominative case of *vir*, while the fact that 'woman' is object is shown by the accusative case of *mulier*. To say 'The woman loves the man' in Latin, it would be necessary to change the cases, e.g. *Mulier vir-um amat*.

More recently, it has become clear that another way in which languages can be typologized is in terms of the interrelations that hold among grammatical (syntactic) relations, semantic (thematic) relations (roles), and functional sentence perspective (pragmatic relations/roles, topic–comment structure). Grammatical relations are, for instance, subject and direct object. Semantic roles are such notions as agent and patient. Pragmatic roles include topic (what the sentence is about) and focus (the most essential new information conveyed by the sentence). In role-and-reference grammar, for instance, a distinction is made between two major (ideal) types of language: role-

455

dominated and reference-dominated languages (Foley & Van Valin 1984). In a role-dominated language, for a given constellation of semantic roles there is in general only one possible syntactic encoding, in particular a given semantic role cannot be encoded by means of different grammatical relations. Thus in Tepera, a non-Austronesian language of Irian Jaya (West New Guinea), while sentence (5) is possible, there are no corresponding passives in which some noun phrase other than the agent would appear as subject:

(5) Di detero miré   ne opo te da jéy  te i-ke-nere
    that person female the pig OBJ this child OBJ give AORIST-
    3 sg. SUBJ, 3 sg. OBJ
    'That woman gave a pig to this child'

In English, a reference-dominated language, by contrast, it is possible for either the patient or the recipient to appear as subject, as in (6) and (7):

(6) The pig was given to this child by that woman
(7) This child was given the pig by that woman

Shifts in the syntactic encoding of semantic roles in reference-dominated languages often serve to indicate differences in functional sentence perspective: in (6), the topic is most likely to be *the pig*, while in (7) it is most likely to be *the child*.

The distinction between role-dominated and reference-dominated languages is, like so many other typological parameters, a continuum rather than a discrete categorization. Thus, English is more reference-dominated than Tepera, but less so than Tagalog (a member of the Philippine branch of the Austronesian family), where a far greater range of semantic roles can appear as subject. In (8), the subject encodes the semantic role of instrument; the closest English equivalent would be something like, 'The knife was used to cut some bread':

(8) I-p-in-utol ng     lalaki ng     tinapay ang kutsilyo
    cut AGENT man PATIENT bread SUBJ knife
    'The man cut bread with the knife'

In the morphology of the verb *putol* 'cut' in (8), the combination of prefix *i-* and infix *-in-* indicates both past tense and that the subject corresponds to the instrument.

In a recent study, Hawkins (1986) has drawn together these various strands – word order, case marking, grammatical relations, semantic roles, functional sentence perspective – in order to provide a more general basis for a language typology. His work involves primarily the comparison of English and German, although it is readily extendable to other languages. Although English and German are quite closely related genetically, they differ on a number of important structural points. German has a richer case-marking system and freer word order. English has a number of syntactic processes that change the grammatical relations of noun phrases (for instance allowing all of agent, patient, and recipient to appear as subject, as was shown above); although German has some syntactic processes of this kind, they are much more heavily restricted: the German passive, for instance, allows the patient to appear as subject, but not the recipient:

(9) Der      Mann gab dem      Lehrer den      Apfel
     the-NOM man    gave the-DAT teacher the-ACC apple
     'The man gave the apple to the teacher'

(10) Der Apfel wurde      dem Lehrer (vo-m   Mann) gegeben
             became PAST                by-the-man   give PAST PARTICIPLE
      'The apple was given to the teacher (by the man)'

(11) *Der Lehrer wurde den Apfel (vom Mann) gegeben
      'The teacher was given the apple (by the man)'

The integrated consideration of these various logically independent parameters enables a very general characterization to be given of a number of significant differences between English and German. The lack of case marking means that English must rely crucially on word order, i.e. English cannot simply change word order in order to encode differences in functional sentence perspective; the existence of grammatical relation changing rules, however, means that, by changing the syntactic encoding of a given semantic role, the linear order of that semantic role can effectively be changed by altering its grammatical relation. The richer case-marking system of German enables noun phrases to be moved more freely, thus providing a more direct means of encoding differences in functional sentence perspective, so that grammatical relation changing rules are not needed for this function. Incidentally, the differences between English and Russian in this respect are even greater than those between English and German; for the English–Russian comparison, reference may be made to Comrie (1981: 68–78).

The preceding discussion has introduced an important additional strand into our overall consideration of linguistic typology. This discussion has become functional, in the sense that structural properties of language are considered in relation to their communicative functions: word order and case marking are alternative means of indicating the grammatical relations of the noun phrases in a clause, and given this functional identity we might expect to find some give-and-take between them, e.g. if case marking is used to encode grammatical relations, then word order is not required for this purpose, and can be requisitioned to some other purpose, such as marking functional sentence perspective.

A number of current investigations into linguistic typology adopt a functional perspective. Space limitations preclude detailed consideration of individual projects, but at least bibliographical references can be given. The Sector for Theory of Grammar and Typological Study of Languages (Leningrad Branch, Institute of Linguistics of the Academy of Sciences of the USSR) has published the results of a number of projects in which some topic, often defined semantically, is selected (e.g. causatives, passives, resultatives), and then a typological survey is given of the different ways in which the phenomenon so defined is encoded syntactically and morphologically in a range of languages. Their most recent study is of resultative constructions (i.e. expressing a state as the result of a preceding event), and an English edition of this monograph is in preparation (Nedjalkov forthcoming). The universals and typology project of the University of Cologne, UNITYP, has adopted an aggressively functional perspective; the detailed application of their approach to 'apprehension' (ways in which objects are identified linguistically, for instance by use of determiners, semantic classification, etc.) can be seen in Seiler & Lehmann/Seiler & Stachowiak 1982). In my own most recent typological work, I have adopted a functional approach to coreference by studying the ways in which different languages rely on radically different devices, both grammatical and extralinguistic, in order to keep track of the referents of noun phrases in a text (Comrie forthcoming).

## 17.4. Generative syntax

One of the most interesting recent developments in linguistic typology has been the entry of generative syntax into the field. Until the late 1970s, generative syntax was largely English-dominated, and studies of the syntax of other languages from a generative perspective (usually by scholars outside the mainstream generative school) were often little more than adaptations of the canonical English examples into the other language. A radical shift began, however, in the late 1970s, first with the inclusion of a wider range of European languages (such as Italian and Dutch), and more recently with the inclusion of a number of languages from other parts of the world (e.g. Chinese, Japanese, and the Australian Aboriginal language Walbiri). A useful compendium of the results of the first stage of this broader interest on the part of generative syntax is provided by Chomsky (1981).

During the earlier period of the history of generative syntax, the prime emphasis was on language universals, in the sense of properties that are common to all languages, with correspondingly little emphasis on differences among languages. In the more recent generative syntactic work, however, it has become clear that many properties of language can be parameterized. This means that, for certain phenomena, language as a whole has open to it a limited number of possibilities, or parameters, and each individual language selects one of these parameter values. Crosslinguistic variation is constrained by the fact that only a limited number of parameter values are permitted, but some degree of variation is permitted by the fact that different languages can choose different parameter values. This notion of parameter is, of course, nothing other than a reformulation of linguistic typology: each individual parameter choice defines a linguistic type, and our earlier discussion could easily be reformulated in these terms (e.g. one parameter might have the two values operator–operand and operand–operator).

Just as in typology more generally, the generative approach to parameters strives to find parameters that are structurally significant in the sense that they bring together a number of logically distinct individual language differences. A good example of this is the pro-drop parameter, discussed, for instance, by Chomsky (1981: 240–8, 253–75). Perhaps the most obvious reflex of a positive choice on this parameter is that unstressed pronouns can be dropped, as in Italian *credo* vs. English *I believe* – Italian is a pro-drop language, while English is not. However, a number of other properties are claimed to correlate with this. Pro-drop languages typically have a rich system of verb agreement, so that Italian distinguishes *cred-o* 'I believe,' *cred-i* 'you believe,' *cred-e* 'he/she believes,' *cred-iamo* 'we believe,' *cred-ete* 'you-all believe,' *cred-ono* 'they believe,' whereas English has the verb form *believe* for all of these except the 3rd person singular *believe-s*. Pro-drop languages allow free inversion of subject and verb in simple sentences, so that in Italian alongside *Giovanni ha mangiato* 'Giovanni has eaten' one can also say in the same cognitive meaning *Ha mangiato Giovanni*; in English such free inversion is impossible – inversion is either controlled by a limited set of sentence-initial constituents (as in *Away ran the bear*), or has a semantic effect in question-formation (e.g. *Has he eaten?*). Apparently even less closely related to the basic possibility of dropping pronouns, pro-drop languages like Italian allow movement of subjects of subordinate clauses with an overt complementizer, whereas languages like English do not:

(12) Chi cred-i    che parti-r-à?
     who think-2sg. that leave-FUTURE-3sg.
     'Who do you think (*that) will leave?'

In English, the translation of (12) is grammatical only if the complementizer *that* is omitted.

In citing the example of the pro-drop parameter, I do not want to give the impression that this typological parameter is trouble-free, or even that it is the strongest example from generative typological research (it is one of the easiest to present). The precise relation between dropping unstressed pronouns and verb agreement remains unclear: languages such as Chinese and Japanese allow dropping of unstressed pronouns although they lack verb agreement. But perhaps their phenomenon is different from that in languages with verb agreement, such as Italian; see, for instance, the discussion of the zero topic parameter in Huang (1984). However, one still finds languages like German and Brazilian Portuguese, where German has a richer agreement system than Brazilian Portuguese, but Brazilian Portuguese is pro-drop while German is not: German verbs make a four- or five-way distinction according to person and number of the subject, while Brazilian Portuguese verbs have a three- or four-way distinction. Moreover, although generative syntax has considerably broadened its horizons in terms of the range of languages investigated, this range is still extremely limited relative to most other work in linguistic typology – and once the possibility of parametric variation is recognized, there is no excuse for not examining a wider range of languages, given that this may uncover otherwise undreamed of instances of parametric variation.

Nonetheless, I believe that the convergence of interests between practitioners of linguistic typology and generative syntax has the potential to create important new advances in both fields. By this I do not want to advocate mindless eclecticism – a good approach does not arise through mixing several poor approaches. In this contribution I have tried to show the extent to which good work in linguistic typology is dependent on developments in general linguistic theory, and I believe firmly that genuine interaction and mutual respect between linguistic typology and grammatical theory will lead to significant advances in our overall understanding of language, which is surely the goal of all linguists.

*REFERENCES*

Chomsky, N. 1981. *Lectures on government and binding: the Pisa lectures.* Studies in Generative Grammar, 9. Dordrecht: Foris.
Comrie, B. 1981. *Language universals and linguistic typology.* Oxford: Blackwell; Chicago: University of Chicago Press.
Comrie, B. Forthcoming. Coreference and conjunction reduction in grammar and discourse. In J. A. Hawkins (ed.) *Explaining language universals.* Oxford: Blackwell.
Foley, W. A. & Van Valin, R. D. Jr. 1984. *Functional syntax and universal grammar.* Cambridge Studies in Linguistics, 38. Cambridge: Cambridge University Press.
Greenberg, J. H. 1966. Some universals of grammar with particular reference to the order of meaningful elements. In J. H. Greenberg (ed.) *Universals of language.* 2nd edn. Cambridge, MA: MIT Press.
Greenberg, J. H. 1974. *Language typology: a historical and analytic overview.* Janua Linguarum, Series Minor, 184. The Hague: Mouton.
Hawkins, J. A. 1983. *Word order universals.* Quantitative Analyses of Linguistic Structure. New York: Academic Press.

Hawkins, J. A. 1986. *A comparitive typology of English and German.* London: Croom Helm; Austin: University of Texas Press.

Huang, J. 1984. On the distribution and reference of empty pronouns. *Linguistic Inquiry* 15: 531–74.

Jackendoff, R. 1977. *X̄-syntax: a study of phrase structure.* Linguistic Inquiry Monograph 2. Cambridge, MA: MIT Press.

Koopman, H. 1984. *The syntax of verbs: from verb movement rules in the Kru languages to universal grammar.* Dordrecht: Foris.

Nedjalkov, V. P. (ed.) Forthcoming. *The typology of resultative constructions: resultative, stative, passive, perfect.* Typological Studies in Language. Amsterdam: Benjamins. Russian original (1983) *Tipologija rezul'tativnyx konstrukcij: rezul'tativ, stativ, passiv, perfekt.* Leningrad: Izd-vo 'Nauka'.

Sapir, E. 1921. *Language: an introduction to the study of speech.* New York: Harcourt, Brace & World.

Seiler, H. & Lehmann C./Seiler, H. & Stachowiak, F. J. (eds.) 1982. *Apprehension: das sprachliche Erfassen von Gegenständen.* 2 vols. Language Universals Series, 1/I–II. Tübingen: Gunter Narr Verlag.

Vennemann, T. 1972. Analogy in generative grammar, the origin of word order. In L. Heilmann (ed.) *Proceedings of the Eleventh International Congress of Linguists,* vol. 2. Bologna: Il Mulino.

# Appendix. History of linguistics
*R. H. Robins*

## A.0. Introduction

Linguistics, the systematic study of human language and human languages, looks back to more than two thousand years of unbroken interest and continuity of scholarship. It can trace its origins in many cultures and in at least four major civilizations, in which folk linguistics, arising from our fascination with and respect for our gift of tongues, developed independently into a culturally recognized specialist field of study such as we would today recognize as linguistics.

This diversity of origins presents us at once with a problem of presentation, of combining the various traditions into a coherent narrative and survey. In this chapter we shall organize our account around the course of linguistic scholarship in Europe and America from classical Greece up to the present day, when current conditions of scholarly work allow us to speak of 'world linguistics.' This may be done without any disparagement or neglect of work from outside Europe, from which in several cases European linguistics benefited enormously. The main factor behind this plan is simply the fact that over the past 2500 years there has been a continuous tradition of thinking and writing about language in Europe, in which each generation made itself aware of what had been done (or left undone) by its predecessors and sought to build on or to rectify what it found. This tradition passed through the Greco-Roman world, the Middle Ages, Europe of the Renaissance and Reformation, the scientific developments of the seventeenth, eighteenth, and nineteenth centuries, and into our contemporary world. At different periods, as the result of cultural contacts of one sort or another, European linguists became aware of what had been done and what was being done in other parts of the globe, and enriched their own understanding by studying and exploiting the insights, theoretical and practical, of scholars in other civilizations. We shall take notice of these extra-European contributions at the points of their first or their maximal impact on Europe as they passed into the stream flowing into general linguistics as it is now taught and researched all over the world.

462

## A.1. **The Greek world**

Linguistic studies as a recognized branch of learning arose from two main sources: our natural curiosity about ourselves, our powers, and our place in the world, and the satisfaction of perceived needs such as today would fall under the purview of applied linguistics. In ancient Greece both such drives were operative, but the response to curiosity was the first in time, so far as we can tell, and linguistic speculation began sporadically and fragmentarily among the pre-Socratic philosophers and rhetoricians as the Greeks manifested their 'gift of wondering at things that other people take for granted' (Bloomfield 1935: 4). Two rather general, and at first imprecisely formulated, questions were discussed: (1) how far was language 'natural,' i.e. imposed by the nature of the world, and how far 'conventional,' i.e. tacitly agreed by particular speech communities for communicative convenience; and (2) analogy vs. anomaly: how far was language inherently structured and rule-governed ('analogical'), and how far irregular, variable, and unpredictable ('anomalous'). This debate continued through Greek and Roman times and fleetingly into the Middle Ages.

Plato (427–348 BC) devoted one of his Socratic dialogs to linguistic questions (the *Cratylus*), and he made statements about syntax and semantics in some others. This at least makes it probable that Socrates discussed linguistic topics with his audiences, something confirmed by the fact that his contemporary writer of comedies, Aristophanes, pokes fun publicly at Socrates for arguing about such abstruse things as animate sex and grammatical gender (*Clouds* 658–99). Plato's interest in language within philosophy was taken over by Aristotle, who treated linguistic questions also within rhetoric and literary criticism. From their works we see emerging a phonology of Attic (Athenian) Greek, based on the phonetic values of the Greek alphabet, and a first analysis of the major sentence structure (*logos*) into NP–VP (*onoma* and *rhēma*). Arising from this first dichotomy came the beginnings of a word class (parts of speech) system for the Greek language.

Plato and Aristotle wrote about language, but the philosophers who first gave recognition to linguistics as a separate branch of philosophy were the Stoics, who, like some linguists today, saw language as the key to understanding how the human mind works. A considerable number of specifically linguistic treatises were written in the years following 300 BC by members of the Stoic school, and it is clear that a general theory of language, and with it theories of phonology, syntax, and semantics, were worked out. Unfortunately, none of these writings survives except in fragments, and we have to rely on later, often inferior, summaries and comments by linguists of other schools for a reconstruction of Stoic linguistics, which must have contained a great deal of interesting material particularly in the field today designated as the philosophy of language (see further Mates 1953; Long 1971).

At the same time as Stoic linguistic philosophy was being developed, political conditions were occasioning a different motivation for linguistic scholarship. The Alexandrian or Macedonian conquest of Asia Minor and Egypt in the name of Greece and of Greek civilization brought for the first time large areas inhabited by non-Greek-speakers under the rule of people who publicly and officially used the Greek language and justified their rule by spreading Greek culture and Greek standards over their subjects. This was the Hellenistic Age, which lasted in essentials through Roman rule, it being Roman policy to leave the Greek world under Greek administration, and through into the Byzantine era of the fifth to the fifteenth centuries.

Schools were established for the teaching of Greek literature to non-Greeks, and this work had to be supported by the more elementary teaching of Greek as a second language. Pergamum and Alexandria were two notable centres of this work. Additionally, scholars felt the need to preserve the literary standards of Greek grammar and Greek style as exemplified by the great authors of the classical age in times when a different variety of Greek, the *koinē*, seen in the Greek *New Testament*, was spreading all over the Greek world, much of it written and spoken as a second language. This was the context for Alexandrian scholarship in literary criticism, in Homeric textual studies, in glossaries of words difficult to interpret (the beginnings of lexicography), and of the didactic grammars of Greek, the most famous of which is attributed to Dionysius Thrax of about 100 BC. There is some controversy whether the text that we have is the work of Dionysius or of a later writer, but it seems clear that the text does set out the orthographic phonology and the morphology of Greek as it was taught at the end of the pre-Christian era.

The attitude of the Alexandrian grammarians was openly didactic and literary. In a passage that is certainly genuine, Dionysius defined grammar as the empirical study of the usage of poets and prose writers and declared that its finest objective is the critical appreciation of literature (text in Robins 1979: 31). This was a very different view of linguistic studies from that of the earlier philosophers and of the contemporary Stoics, and it appears that controversy continued between those who wanted to keep linguistics as a philosophical discipline based on what were held to be truly scientific principles and those who were unashamed empiricists, looking to the external observation of the products of writers as their method and their justification. Dionysius's definition by its use of the word *empeiria* 'observational knowledge' caused offence to some, who wanted the subject to be raised to a higher level of esteem by laying emphasis on *technē* 'science,' and by making reference, as did the Stoics, to the logical and psychological principles underlying language (Robins 1974). Stoic linguistics continued, until Stoic schools along with other pagan schools were closed by Justinian in 529 in the interests of Christian learning; but it is clear that in Greco-Roman antiquity the view of grammar and of linguistics in general set out by the Alexandrians became the standard view, and Dionysius's definition was not seriously challenged before the rise of speculative (philosophical) grammar in the scholastic age.

The controversy is of considerable importance historically. It may be seen as the first manifestation of the recurrent debate between two attitudes to linguistics, broadly labelled *empiricist* and *rationalist*, though such a crude dichotomy conceals many variations. We notice this division of scientific attitudes in different forms at several periods in European linguistic studies. Essentially the question turns on whether the linguist should treat his subject matter like any other empirical scientific observer must treat his, through systematic external observation and classification of the data, or whether in a different but equally valid interpretation of science, he should take advantage of his privileged position as a speaker–listener as well as an observer of language in order to relate the working and the structure of language to the working and the structure of the human mind, making use of data necessarily accessible to him alone (judgements, feelings, thought processes) and only indirectly available from others, mostly through the observation of their use of language.

The Alexandrians were strict empiricists. Their data were equally accessible to all in the texts of the classical authors. The Stoics were more mentalistically and rationalistically inclined. For them, linguistics was a part of philosophy, or, as we would say today, part of cognitive psychology. But Alexandrian views prevailed and Alexandrian purposes satisfied the continuing needs of the Hellenized eastern provinces of the Roman Empire and in the education of upper-class Romans in the Greek language and in the appreciation of Greek literature.

Moreover, the presentation of Greek phonology and morphology as set out in Dionysius's grammar as we have it became standard. The Stoics had played a major part in identifying the relevant grammatical categories in Greek (for example nominal case), their semantic analysis of the Greek verb was highly sensitive, and they successfuly developed the original syntactic division of the sentence by Plato and Aristotle to a more delicate system of four, and then of five, distinct word classes. But there, as far as we can see, they stopped. The Alexandrians' eight word classes (noun, verb, participle, article, pronoun, preposition, adverb, and conjunction) as they finally emerged, and the categories ascribed to them (case, tense, number, gender, etc.) became the model for other Greek grammars and for the detailed description of the syntax of Greek around 200 AD by Apollonius

Dyscolus. Dionysius's morphology and Apollonius's syntax became the foundation of Greek language teaching and gave rise to a large body of commentaries (*scholia*), summaries, and other didactic aids throughout the Eastern Empire and the Byzantine period, ultimately providing the material and some of the personnel for the revival of Greek studies in the West in the later Middle Ages and the beginning of the Renaissance.

## A.2. The Roman world

The Romans were not in the main original abstract thinkers. In the famous lines of Vergil justifying the Augustan peace and Roman imperial power, Rome was bidden to keep order, maintain stability, and leave others (the Greeks) to develop under benign Roman protection their superior artistic, literary, and scientific talents (*Aeneid* 6.847–53). By the time Rome became generally in contact with and under the influence of the Greek world, Greek linguistic science was well-developed and, encouraged by some Greek grammarians, Roman scholars on the whole conceived their objective to be the presentation of Latin phonology and Latin grammar through the same sets of phonological and grammatical categories and word classes as had been successfully applied to Greek. The typological similarities between the two languages greatly assisted this, and the presence in the Latin lexicon of a large number of Indo-European inheritances shared with Greek along with an increasing volume of recent Greek loanwords encouraged the quite erroneous but widely held view that Latin was itself directly descended from Greek with some barbarian admixture.

Those places where Greek and Latin were not obviously isomorphous were singled out for comment and discussion. Two notable instances were the Latin six-case system as against the five Greek cases, and the absence in Latin of an equivalent for the Greek definite article (the definite article in the Romance languages emerged later out of semantically weakened demonstrative pronouns). Five of the Latin six cases were matched one-to-one with the Greek cases, on semantic grounds, and the sixth, now called the ablative, whose syntactic and semantic functions were divided between the genitive and dative cases in Greek, was at first named the 'Latin case' and the 'sixth case,' thus emphasizing its peculiar position. The absence of a definite article class was duly noted; in fact, the number of word classes was maintained at eight through the separate recognition of the interjection as a class in it own right, the Greeks having treated this set of words, not unreasonably, as a subclass of adverbs.

Only one Latin scholar, who appeared relatively early in the history of linguistics in Rome, showed real originality – the long-lived and prolific polymath Marcus Terentius Varro (116–27 BC). Varro did not write a grammar of Latin, and in his time there were no grammars of Latin yet written. He was well-versed in Greek literature and Greek linguistics, and he was aware of the grammar of Dionysius and of its famous definition of grammar, as well as of current Stoic work. Among his many writings Varro produced a long and rather rambling disquisition on the Latin language, in which he investigated so far as he could its earlier history, it current usage, and its grammatical structure. Only part of this work (*De lingua Latina*) is now extant, but what we have gives a clear picture of Varro's method.

Varro took the categories of Greek and tried them out on Latin; this was how he first noticed the extra Latin case. His analysis of the semantics and the formal structure of the Latin verbal system was based on Stoic rather than on Alexandrian principles, and it shows insights quite beyond the presentations given in the later standard grammars of Latin. He studied the inflectional and derivational formations of Latin in an attempt to show how language can and does increase its lexical and grammatical resources to meet changed circumstances and a developing civilization. In this he showed a unique insight into Latin morphology, even though his historical perspective was severely constrained and warped by lack of knowledge of more than one or two centuries. Rather than simply following the Greek word class system, as did the other grammarians, with the substitution of interjection for article, Varro interestingly divided the Latin lexicon into inflecting ('productive') and non-inflecting ('sterile') words, further classifying inflecting words into four classes by reference to case and tense: nouns being plus case and minus tense, verbs plus tense and minus case, participles plus case and plus tense, and adverbs minus case and tense; and to these morphologically distinguished classes he assigned distinct syntactic functions.

In his more general reflections on language, Varro dealt extensively with the analogy–anomaly controversy, deploying the arguments on either side, quoting Greek authors on Greek and applying their statements to Latin. Ultimately he reached the only tenable position, that language is inherently regular and rule-governed, that it is the linguist's task to discover and formalize the rules, but that exceptions (anomalies), whether semantic (plural nouns for single entities, neuter nouns for male or female animates, and so on) or grammatical (irregular verbs, derivational gaps, etc.), must be accepted and recorded, and that it is no part of the linguist's work, as some had thought, to try to improve the structure of the language in defiance of established usage.

From early in the Christian era grammars of Latin appeared in considerable numbers. They varied in length but in broad outline they presented Latin in the same way, as far as possible in the framework provided by existing Greek grammars. All were literary in their educational setting and didactic in their orientation. The two best-known may be taken as typical representatives: Donatus (fourth century) wrote a short manual summarizing partly in catechistic form the essentials of Latin orthography, phonology, and morphology: Priscian (c. 500) was much more prolix, and his *Institutiones grammaticae* contain books and run to 1125 pages in their modern printed form (Keil 1855/1859).

Priscian, writing in Constantinople, the capital of the eastern half of the Empire and later of the surviving Byzantine Empire, may be seen to form the link between classical antiquity and the Middle Ages in Europe as far as linguistics is concerned. In his extensive account of Latin grammar he draws entirely on the Greek models for his method and theory; Apollonius is in places almost translated word-for-word into Latin and provided with Latin examples. He, together with another Greek grammarian, is hailed in several places as 'artis grammaticae maximus auctor.' Priscian's text is liberally illustrated with quotations from classical Latin and from Greek authors as well, where they instantiate the same point. He was almost certainly working and writing as a teacher of Latin in a predominantly Greek-speaking city (later the knowledge and use of Latin in the Byzantine Empire declined sharply).

## A.3. **Medieval Europe**

If retrospectively Priscian's *Institutiones* represent a summary of the achievement of the Greco-Roman tradition in descriptive linguistics, his work, with the work of Donatus, looks forward to the linguistic studies of the Middle Ages. These two authors provided the principal resources for the teaching of Latin, the universal language of education and of international usage, and the language of the Church in medieval western Europe, and for the teaching of grammar as a basic component of education itself. Latin grammar, quite apart from the acquisition of Latin as the medium of education, was itself a central discipline, the first member of the 'seven liberal arts' (along with dialectic, rhetoric, music, arithmetic, geometry, and astronomy), on which secondary and tertiary education was organized. Furthermore, as we shall see, it was Priscian and Priscian's Latin grammar that provided the material for the very differently oriented scholastic grammars of the later Middle Ages.

Donatus and Priscian were essential texts for medieval education. Donatus, being short, concise, and arranged for rote learning, was at first the most widely known, and it gave rise to the word *Donat* to refer to any elementary Latin grammar book. Priscian was more a complete reference book of Latin grammar; its standing can be illustrated by the fact that despite its length several hundred copies of his *Institutiones*, individually made of course, were in existence in medieval Europe.

European education and European linguistic scholarship in the Middle Ages were Latin-based. Latin had been and remained the lingua franca of the former Western Roman Empire, and it was the official language of the Church. The only significant work on vernacular languages lay in the independent study of Irish at the hands of the Irish schools, and the isolated and for long ignored piece of phonological analysis and orthographic reform undertaken by the twelfth-century Icelandic scholar known only by his nineteenth-century title as the 'First grammarian' (O'Cuív 1965, 1973; Haugen 1972). Apart from these, linguistics and evangelistic activity have been close allies throughout the Christian era, as we see today in the work of K. L. Pike and his colleagues in the Summer Institute of Linguistics; early examples of this are to be seen in the devising of an alphabetic writing for the Goths by Bishop Ulfilas (fourth century), who translated parts of the New Testament into Gothic, and the creation of the first form of the Cyrillic alphabet for converted Slavic speakers in the ninth century by St Cyril.

In the first centuries after the breakdown of the Western Roman Empire the Church was the single strongest supporter for education and for the continuity of linguistics and of other forms of scholarship. A reassertion of civic responsibility for educational standards, in alliance with clerical institutions, was made by Charlemagne (742–814), who invited the British grammarian Alcuin to be both his own tutor and the man in charge of the teaching of grammar in his domains. Charlemagne's action in this field marked the first part of what is known today as the Carolingian Renaissance. In this the authority of Priscian was increasingly recognized and became the scholarly basis of the teaching of grammar, and this had far-reaching consequences. Unlike Donatus, Priscian's *Institutiones* had not been intended and could not be used as a school textbook. It had to be epitomized and explained by commentaries. At first these were written with purely didactic ends in view, but gradually as time wore on the commentators conceived their objective as more profound. By the eleventh century there was, within the Church of course, a revival of European philosophy at the hands of such men as Anselm and Abelard; the writings of Aristotle, which in the 'Dark Ages' had been almost lost to western Europe except for Latin translations of parts by Boethius and others, were becoming available again, and the study of Greek, which had also sunk to a very low level, was reviving. All this was greatly helped by European contacts with Greek scholarship in the East as a consequence of the Crusades, and in Spain where Aristotelian philosophy and the thoughts of its Arab interpreters, such as Averroes, became known to Europeans through certain centres of co-existence and collaboration between Christian and Islamic scholars in Toledo and elsewhere.

This development ultimately transformed scholarly attitudes to Latin grammar into a philosophical rather than a literary and didactic discipline. The movement was at its height in the thirteenth and fourteenth centuries, with particularly strong representation in the University of Paris. The vehicle of this transformation, to which Grabmann gave the title 'Die Logisierung der Grammatik' (1926: 114), was the succession of commentaries on Priscian, which were more and more directed not to making his work easier for schoolboys and schoolmasters but to finding an explanation for its having been written in the way it was written and to finding a philosophical justification for Latin grammar as Priscian had described it. A twelfth-century commentary by Petrus Helias marks a notable step in this process (Hunt 1980).

The philosophic reinterpretation of grammar took its final form in numerous treatises setting out and justifying Priscian's work within Catholic philosophy in the form established by St Thomas Aquinas (1224–1274). This philosophy, generally known as Thomism, was in essence a synthesis of Aristotelian logic and metaphysics and the Christian faith as taught by the fathers of the Church. Thomas saw no repugnance between Aristotelianism and Christianity. A recent census of these grammars (Bursill-Hall 1981) has identified numerous manuscripts extant in various European libraries. They were collectively known as speculative grammars (*grammaticae speculativae*), and despite their number the theory that they expounded was remarkably uniform. Two are readily available in edited texts today, those by Siger de Courtrai (Sigerus de Cortraco 1977) and Thomas of Erfurt (1972). None of the grammars is easy to read; though fairly short, they are written in a specialized form of medieval Latin, with an extensive set of technical terms designating the theoretical concepts involved. The actual description of Latin was left more or less as Priscian had left it, but these grammars aimed at explaining just why his grammar had taken the form that it had. A twelfth-century writer, William of Conches (Peter Helias's teacher), was quite explicit on this; in terms remarkably like the writings of some generative grammarians today (Roos 1952: 93) he said that Priscian and the older commentators were quite adequate at the descriptive level in setting out the grammar of Latin, but they did not try to explain and justify their description, saying why, for example, Priscian made use of his eight word classes and the various grammatical categories associated with them. Such a level of explanatory adequacy, relating a descriptive framework to a theory of language, was the prime objective of the speculative grammarians.

Grammar was now firmly under the control of the philosophers. The long predominance of Dionysius's literary and empirical grammar was for the time being eclipsed over a large part of Europe. Grammar was now redefined as relating language to the human mind (Siger's definition, 1977:

1, ran: 'Grammatica est semocinalis scientia, sermonem et passiones eius in communi ad exprimendum principaliter mentis conceptus per sermonem coniugatum considerans'). Gone from these grammars was the array of literary quotations to exemplify rules; in their place are purely formulaic examples, without contextual reality, simply providing lexical fillings to syntactic positions: *Socrates hits Plato* and *Socrates runs well* are two such examples.

The theory of language within which the speculative grammarians operated embraced three interrelated levels: external reality, or the ways in which the world existed, its real properties (*modi essendi*); the capabilities of the mind to apprehend and understand these (*modi intelligendi*); and the means whereby mankind could communicate this understanding (*modi significandi*). These last were the province of the grammarian, and for this reason these grammarians were often referred to as *Modistae*.

Priscian's word classes were distinguished by their specific *modi significandi*. As an illustration, the two most important classes, noun and verb, presented reality, as understood, through two basic *modi* or aspects, things as continuing existents (*modus entis*) and time-bound transient phenomena (*modus esse*) in which existents participated (*dolor* 'pain' or 'grief,' for example, designates a permanent part of sentients' experience in the world; *dolere* 'to be in pain,' 'to grieve,' and its various inflections, refer to time-bound, transient states of one or other sentients). Each of Priscian's grammatical categories further specifies apprehended reality under some aspect: number (one or more), tense (temporal relation), case (relations between entities and between entity and states or processes), and so on.

It is virtually impossible to summarize modistic speculative grammatical theory, as it rests on a highly integrated set of metaphysical, logical, and grammatical concepts within an overarching Catholic philosophy, ultimately serving, as did all medieval science, the world view of the Christian faith (*Scientia ancilla fidei*). It had a number of important achievements and consequences in the history of linguistics. Despite its sticking closely at the descriptive level to Priscian, whose work is constantly mentioned, some advances in grammatical understanding were made: the actual role of Greek and Latin prepositions, which had not been grasped either by Apollonius or by Priscian, was clearly explained (Thomas of Erfurt 1972: 262). More importantly, for the first time in the mainstream tradition of European linguistics, a general abstract theory of syntax was formulated, founded on the union (*compositio*) of the *modus entis* of the noun and the *modus esse* of the verb and making provision for embedding and for recursion (Robins 1980). This theory was intended for application to all languages, and in its abstractness and generality it went far beyond the work of Apollonius and

471

Priscian, who had provided not so much a syntactic theory as a wealth of individual construction types in Greek and Latin, illustrated, classified, and compared.

The major legacy of medieval speculative grammar, however, is the theory of universal grammar or linguistic universals. Antiquity had largely ignored languages other than Latin and Greek, except for purely practical purposes, and these two languages were structurally very similar. Medieval Europe was aware of its own vernaculars, and since the official recognition of Christianity and the expansion of Islam, Europe had to take Hebrew and Arabic seriously. Despite the typological differences involved, the speculative grammarians had no doubts. The world was one, the capacities and operations of the human mind, genetically inherited or, as they would say, created by God, were the same in all men, and therefore in essentials language was one and the same everywhere; surface differences, inconvenient though they might be, were no more than accidents (in the words of Roger Bacon, himself an Arabist and Hebraist, given in Wallerand 1913: (43), 'Grammatica una et eadem est secundum substantiam in omnibus linguis, licet accidentaliter varietur'). Universal grammar has remained a continuous inspiration and a problem ever since.

Speculative grammarians downgraded mere grammar teaching as theoretically uninformed and uninteresting. But, of course, this did not disappear. Epitomies of Priscian were in continued use along with Donatus, and a number of new manuals of grammar were written. One, in hexameter verse for easier memorization, became a standard textbook for several generations, Alexander de Villedieu's *Doctrinale* (c. 1200) which, in fact, showed certain theoretical advances over Priscian in syntax, as in the concept of government or rection, which the speculative grammarians were able to take up and to take further.

The speculative grammarians had also rejected the literary grammar which, the Stoics apart, had dominated Europe for a thousand years. But the study of Latin classical literature, though under suspicion as pagan, and the study of grammar in this context did not cease. Such studies went on at some universities, notably at Orleans, and its practitioners were determined to maintain their position. This was the factual basis of the medieval allegory *The Battle of the Seven Arts* (Waddell 1926: ch. 6), a tale of the classical authors (*auctores*) going forth from Orleans against Paris, stronghold of the *artes* dominated by Aristotle. In the fighting the *auctores* are driven back, but as they withdraw they vow that their time will come and one day their studies will be restored to full favour. And this is just what did happen in linguistic work in the Renaissance.

## A.4. **The Renaissance: linguistics in Modern Europe**

The Renaissance certainly took its name from the rediscovery and renewed study of classical Greece and Rome, the rebirth of ancient European civilization, first in Italy and then over the whole of Europe. From the fifteenth century the corpus of classical literature, more or less as we have it today, became known and was soon available in print, and the classics, *Literae humaniores* (secular as against medieval Church-governed literature), established themselves as the basis of a full education for the upper and rising classes of Europe. This led to a change in the study of Latin grammar, to which Greek grammar had now been added; the Latin that was respected and therefore taught was now the once-living native language of Vergil and Cicero, not the medieval second language, and still less the specialized philosophical Latin of the scholastics, which was despised for its neologisms and grammatical forms unknown to antiquity. Serious attention was now given, as it had not been given before, to the recovery and use of the proper pronunciation of classical Greek and Latin as it had existed in the golden age. Erasmus, one of the stars of the Renaissance, wrote a celebrated dialog on the correct pronunciation of the two classical languages. And a definition of grammar in 1473 returned it to the literary setting of Dionysius (Padley 1976: 31): 'ars scriptorum et poetarum lectionibus observata'.

This was not, however, anything like the whole story of linguistic studies in Renaissance Europe. In fact, a number of separate but interrelated factors were operative in the fifteenth, sixteenth, and seventeenth centuries. Three major movements in European thought were to transform first Europe and then the entire world as it came under European influence or control. The Renaissance, the rebirth of classical learning and the recovery of humanist as against clerical values, was one. A second, within the Church itself, was the successful challenge in northern Europe to the supremacy of Rome and the Papacy by the various Protestant sects in the Reformation. A third, allied both to humanism and to Protestantism, was the rise of the natural sciences and of the viewpoint of empirical science, wherein knowledge is to be derived from observation and experiment and not from authority, whether secular or divine. It was this last movement, whose force is by no means spent today, that assured the creation from the seventeenth century on of the 'modern world' as we have come to accept it over the last few centuries. The seventeenth century in particular, the 'century of genius' as it has been called, was a century of ferment in scientific, political, philosophical, and religious thinking, and, no doubt partly in consequence of this, it was a century that saw the Civil War in England and the devastating Thirty Years War in central Europe.

Besides these major developments, other events directly impinged on linguistic studies. 1453 marked the final extinction of the Byzantine Empire, the direct descendant of the old Roman Empire. The troubles of Byzantium had already assisted the renewal of Greek studies in Europe by encouraging several notable Greek scholars to migrate westward and to take up teaching posts in Italy and elsewhere. Not long after 1453, in 1492 the discovery of the New World inaugurated the expansion of Europe to the west, to the east, and to the south, exposing European linguists to the challenge of an unprecedented number of newly discovered languages, phonologically and grammatically unlike any languages they had known before.

In Europe itself, Latin as a *lingua franca* lived on for several centuries, but it faced the increasing rivalry in this role of the vernacular languages of the larger European speech communities, English, French, Italian, Spanish, and German. The rise of nation states and of a commercial and secular middle class, and especially in Protestant countries the regular use of vernacular languages in Church services and in translations of the Bible, all led to a much enhanced status and importance for the modern languages of Europe.

By 1500 printing was well-established and printed books were in full production and regular use. This, of course, enormously speeded up the diffusion of knowledge, including knowledge of languages old and new, facilitated the spread of education and literacy, and set teaching and learning of all sorts in the context in which they have been familiar up to the present time, when the primacy of printed words in certain areas and to a certain extent is in some danger from the electronic wizardry of information technology. Printing had, of course, additional specific effects on linguistic studies themselves.

All these factors make the history of linguistics far more complex than it has been so far, and render it no longer feasible, even if it ever has been, to follow this history in linear progression. What can and must be done is to identify and interpret the various contemporaneous and interconnected developments in the study of language that took place during these centuries.

Linguistics in Europe could no longer be largely equated with the linguistic study of Latin and Greek. These languages continued to be studied in their classical forms as major fields of learning, but the linguistic horizons of Europe were vastly extended, ultimately over the entire globe. Early in the Christian era Europeans had had to make themselves acquainted with Hebrew, the language of the Old Testament, and Arabic came into prominence from the seventh century. With these languages, Europeans faced not just typologically unfamiliar grammar and phonetics but also the products of indigenous linguistic traditions and schools, in some respects unlike what had been their experience hitherto.

Arabic linguistic scholarship, which exerted an important influence on Hebraic linguistics, was the joint product of the Islamic religion and of Arabic secular power. Non-Arabic-speakers in the Arabic dominions needed the language in various walks of life, much as non-Latins had needed Latin in the Roman Empire, and the Islamic faith, now greatly extended, required, as it still does, the use of classical Arabic in its public observances. In the eighth century, Sibawayh, author of *Al-kitab* (*The Book*), the first known full grammar of the language, established the morphological description of it substantially as it has remained ever since, leading to the lexical identification of the consonantal, usually 'triliteral,' roots of verbs, shown to underlie a vast array of inflected and derived formations (*k - t - b*, 'write,' from which *kitab* is formed, is the best-known example). This alone confronted Europeans for the first time with a morphological concept of a far higher level of abstraction than their own tradition, wholly 'word and paradigm,' had hitherto envisaged. It is noteworthy that Reuchlin, author of *De rudimentis Hebraicis* (1506), unlike the universalist Roger Bacon, expressly warned his readers of the fundamental grammatical differences between Hebrew and Latin.

Once colonial, missionary, and commercial expansion was under way, Europe was deluged with new languages. Native America, Africa, the Indian subcontinent, Southeast Asia, and the Far East showed the Europeans languages of unbelievable morphological complexity, as with so many American-Indian languages, and languages with virtually no morphology, such as classical Chinese and some Southeast Asian languages. In all these areas linguistic scholarship marched in step with Christian evangelism, as it has continued to do. The *Propaganda Fide* department of the Roman Church was as prominent in the sixteenth and seventeenth centuries in high-grade linguistic work as the Protestant Summer Institute of Linguistics is today.

Chinese made a notable impact. Three of its salient characteristics, lexical tone, isolating structure, and ideographic or logographic writing, though wholly familiar today, made an extraordinary impression on seventeenth-century Europe. This was intensified by the absence before the beginning of the eighteenth century of any sound grammar of Chinese written in a European language. In China itself lexicographical and phonological studies had been undertaken since early in the Christian era, in order to maintain an understanding of the Confucian and other classical texts as the language itself gradually changed.

At first Europeans felt, as some have continued to do ever since, that

'Chinese has no grammar,' because it has little or no morphology, at least in its classical form. This and the ubiquity of a single ideographic writing system over a vast range of different languages (the so-called 'Chinese dialects') inspired Europeans with the idea that China had pioneered the way towards a genuine universal language, directly representing thoughts in writing, without the intermediate hindrance of separate grammars of different languages. Wilkins's 'real character' was the best-known example of this type of widespread European research (Wilkins 1668). A separate encouragement came from the apparently language-neutral, universal, communicative value of mathematics; Leibniz looked forward to the day when much theological and philosophical controversy would be settled by the invitation to 'sit down and calculate.'

Medieval linguists, being mainly concerned with the teaching and study of a second language, did little more than repeat Priscian's phonetic observations on Latin, and the *Modistae* generally thought that phonetics was not their province as grammarians. Vernacular language studies changed this attitude, and from the sixteenth century grammars of living languages included considerable numbers of pages on pronunciation under one head or another. Petrus Ramus, famous as a sixteenth-century educational reformer, wrote a grammar of French that bears witness to this practice.

The spread of literacy, the social trends already noticed, and the invention of printing gave rise to the large-scale production of dictionaries and grammars of European languages. From their original function as limited glossaries of 'difficult words' dictionaries grew in size and scope to their present-day comprehension of books ideally registering every word in use in a language. An idea of the amount of grammar writing that went on may be formed from the listing of no fewer than 112 separate grammars of English up to the year 1800 (Alston 1965, 1973).

Most of these were practical didactic grammars based on the usage of the educated classes of society and serving their needs and the needs of others wishing to improve their social standing and of foreigners learning a language. In so far as they had an explicit theoretical basis this was strongly observational and scientifically oriented. It is interesting to see several English linguists among the early members of the Royal Society, founded in 1660 for the encouragement of scientific research and discovery. But the tradition of universalistic philosophical grammar continued, seeking in rather different ways to explain language by reference to logic and human thinking. An Italian philosopher, Campanella, in the seventeenth century distinguished the two contrasting approaches to grammar as *grammatica philosophica* and *grammatica civilis* (practical grammar). Scaliger and Sanctius are notable representatives of *grammatica philosophica*, as is the later

Port-Royal *Grammaire générale et raisonnée* (Lancelot & Arnauld 1660). Here a significant illustration of the different methods of the two types of grammar may be seen: in relation to the same grammatical rule, on the use of relative pronouns after certain types of noun phrase, Vaugelas, author of *Remarques sur la langue françoise*, justifies it by reference to the usage of authors and the practice of upper-class and court speakers (1670: 277–9); the Port-Royal grammar insists on going further by providing an explanation of the logical and semantic factors involved in the speakers' minds (1660: 75–83). That such grammarians were more sympathetic to rationalist philosophy is not surprising.

A joint product of European vernacular studies, the revival of classical Latin and Greek, and the expansion of European linguistic horizons was the beginning of serious typological and historical linguistic studies, as compared with the sporadic, isolated, and usually underinformed observations on these aspects of linguistics that had been made in earlier days. In the fourteenth century Dante had contrasted the Latin-derived Romance languages with Latin itself, and modern Europe could not fail to notice the grammatical and structural differences between most current languages and the earlier, obviously lexically related, classical and other ancient languages (Gothic, for example). Typological comparisons were prominent in the linguistic articles in the seventeenth-century French *Encyclopédie*, and this subject was further developed by the Schlegel brothers in Germany and later by Wilhelm von Humboldt, who was responsible for popularizing the tripartite typology of isolating, agglutinative, and inflectional languages. Such studies continued through the nineteenth century but were greatly overshadowed by the strictly historical comparison of languages, for reasons that will be seen. Typology has, of course, been taken up with renewed interest and insights in the resurgence of descriptive linguistics in the present century.

There was official encouragement, especially in Russia, for the collection of vocabularies and texts from diverse languages, which ultimately provided the material for comparative-historical research. Such research made progress during the eighteenth century; in 1770 Sajnovics published his proof that Hungarian and Lappish were part of the same language family. But the major impulse in this branch of linguistics, making it the dominant theme in the next century, arose from the discovery of Sanskrit, its linguistic literature and its historical connection with the classical, and most of the modern, languages of Europe. The language had been known to earlier Europeans as the classical language of India, and certain likenesses with Greek and Latin had been reported, but the full awareness and appreciation of the whole tradition of the language came in the last quarter of the eighteenth century.

## A.5. Sanskrit and nineteenth-century historical linguistics

The original purpose of the study of the Sanskrit language in India had been the preservation and the proper understanding of the Vedic Sanskrit sacred literature, some of which is dated as early as the twelfth century BC. From this essentially practical, 'applied linguistics,' requirement there developed an extraordinarily vigorous and successful tradition of phonetic, phonological, morphological, syntactic, lexical, and semantic studies. The most famous products of this tradition are Pāṇini's Sanskrit grammar (Aṣṭād-hyāyī, perhaps c. 500 BC), the basis of all subsequent description and teaching of the language, and the phonetic treatises (c. 500–150 BC), which enable us to know more about the pronunciation of Sanskrit than of any other ancient language. Allen's observation on the writers of these treatises may be taken as applying to the Indian tradition as a whole (1953: 6): '[They] were phoneticians rather than priests . . . and must surely have transcended their original terms of reference.' Chinese phonological analysis was greatly stimulated after contact through Buddhist missionary scholars in the first centuries of the Christian era with Sanskritic phonetic work, but it was in Europe that the effect was the most far-reaching, and without it the course of contemporary linguistics might have been very different.

In India, the linguistic study of Sanskrit had been continuously maintained, and when European scholars began to understand it they realized for the first time that they faced a line of scholarship not just different from, but in some important respects manifestly superior to, their own or to any other known to them. In phonetics the Indians, by concentrating on the processes of articulation rather than on acoustic impressions, had advanced their knowledge remarkably, and it was only through their work that Europe was able fully to understand the physiological basis of phonetic voicing. Equally, the morphological analysis of Sanskrit in the work of Pāṇini and his many commentators so impressed Europeans with its accuracy, detail, and economy that for a time they transferred their admiration to the language itself, in Sir William Jones's famous words (Robins 1979: 134): 'more perfect than the Greek, more copious than the Latin, and more exquisitely refined than either.'

In addition to this, the simultaneous realization of the historical connections of Sanskrit with the languages of Europe came at a time when the Romantic movement and nationalistic sentiments were at their height, especially in German-speaking areas. Linguistics became effectively concentrated, usually in conjunction with Sanskrit studies, on research into the history and composition of what was later to be known as the Indo-European family of languages.

The Indo-European family and concomitantly other similarly based genetic families were the progressive creation of nineteenth-century scholarship, mainly in the German universities. This work went hand-in-hand with the steady refinement of the actual methodology of comparison and of the understanding of the nature of language change. At first, attention was directed to the obvious similarities in the inflected forms of the languages (hence the enduring term *comparative grammar, vergleichende Grammatik*). Later, the more sophisticated relationship of systematic correspondences of forms between related languages replaced mere similarity, and whole lexica were brought into the comparison, making etymology now a strictly scientific discipline.

As historical linguistics established itself as a science in the learned world of the nineteenth century it faced the question of what sort of science it was. In the first half of the century biological notions, in part derived from comparative anatomy, gave rise to expressions like the 'growth,' 'life,' 'decay,' and 'death' of languages, which were not just metaphors. In the mid-century, Schleicher, once a dominant figure in linguistics, fully aligned the subject with the biological sciences, and interpreted the typology of isolating, agglutinative, and inflectional structures as a progression of growth and maturity, followed by a long period of decline as inflectional forms were replaced by more isolating phrases in the later history of the Indo-European languages. In one of his latest books he claimed support for his biological view, which he had been expressing for some time, from Darwin's theory of evolution and natural selection (Schleicher 1863).

Such a position could scarcely be maintained, and historical linguistics achieved something of a paradigm in the Kuhnian sense (1970) in the final years of the century at the hands of a loosely knit group of scholars known as the *Junggrammatiker* or neogrammarians (the title *Juggrammatiker* was first given them as a quasi-political nickname, but it has since become part of established linguistic terminology). The essence of the neogrammarian principle was an insistence on strict methodology: no etymology could be accepted as evidence of a historical relationship unless the words concerned followed regular patterns of correspondences or, if not, unless the apparent deviance could be satisfactorily explained. This basic rule was known as *Die Ausnahmslosigkeit der Lautgesetze* (the 'regularity hypothesis,' Hockett 1965: 186). Method rather than theory building was the important thing, and the scientific model for historical linguistics was not biology but the exact physical sciences, together with psychology and sociology to help explain certain historical changes. In this respect nineteenth-century historical linguistics allied itself with the observational-empirical side as against the universalist philosophical grammar side (cf. Pott 1833–6: xii).

By the end of the century the theory and methodology of comparative-historical linguistics had been well understood, and the Indo-European family had been established in substantially its present-day membership, with the exception of Hittite, whose script was deciphered in 1915, and which is now known certainly to be genetically related to the rest of the family. Other genetic families were likewise firmly established (such as Finno-Ugrian and Altaic), and comparative-historical methods have been progressively applied with success to languages in all parts of the world, for example to the Bantu languages, now included in a wider Niger-Congo family (Greenberg 1963: ch. 2), and to the languages of native America, where Sapir and Bloomfield, well trained in Indo-European studies, achieved notable results. Historical linguistics continues to be an important and essential component of general linguistics, and the present century has seen the neogrammarian position, while essentially intact, modified in various ways in the course of changes in general linguistic theory. But the most prominent movement in linguistics in the twentieth century has been the revival and then the extraordinary growth of synchronic, descriptive studies and in the theoretical investigation of language from several different viewpoints.

## A.6. **Descriptive and theoretical linguistics in the twentieth century**

This resurgence of synchronic linguistics is usually ascribed to de Saussure and his great influence in Paris and Geneva in the first decade of the century. Whether he actually created the ideas with which he is credited, or whether he rather articulated and propagated general trends that were developing in any case in the scholarly world, cannot be finally decided; but it is certain that all contemporary linguists are heavily indebted to him.

Besides his successful insistence that general linguistics comprises the distinct and equally essential synchronic (descriptive) dimension and the diachronic (historical) dimension, de Saussure is best known for establishing the structural treatment of language in the synchronic dimension (later it was seen that this should be extended to historical linguistics as well). In brief, languages should be viewed not as aggregates of entities, but as structured wholes in which at each level, lexical, grammatical, and phonological, elements function through their relationships with other elements at that level and must be defined in such terms.

The phoneme theory was the first direct consequence of Saussurean thought. The term and the concept had emerged in the nineteenth century, but the Prague School, at the height of its influence during the interwar years, exploited structural ideas to develop a fully fledged phonological theory based on the phoneme, as set out in Trubetzkoy's *Grundzüge der Phonologie* (1939). A most important part of the Prague phoneme concept was the distinctive feature, perhaps the single linguistic notion that has irreversibly affected almost the whole of linguistics in this century. Reinterpreted by Jakobson on acoustic lines it won a place in American structuralist phonology in alliance with acoustic and experimental phonetics, subsequently to become almost the 'official' version of the phoneme in generative linguistics, and later again modified back towards articulatory phonetics by Chomsky and Halle in 1968. Before that, again through the original impulse of Jakobson, the distinctive feature concept had been applied revealingly to morphological analysis and to semantics, and in the formal syntactic specification of words in current generative grammar it now dominates syntax (cf. Robins 1977 and further references).

In the interwar period, and for a decade thereafter, phonology was the pace-maker in theoretical linguistics, a place taken by syntax since 1957. Phonology was largely under the control of one or other version of the phoneme theory. One conspicuous rebel in these years was J. R. Firth, of London, whose prosodic theory, then a little-understood development, has now found partial acceptance under different headings among such current versions as autosegmental phonology and metrical phonology; and Firth's view of phonology as the link between (prior) grammar and phonetics, in vigorous opposition to the independent 'biunique' status of American phonemics of the 1950s, is now wholly shared by the Chomskyans.

Linguistics as a widely recognized and eagerly studied subject came into its own with the worldwide expansion of university education after the second world war, and nowhere more than in North America. Up to 1957 under the powerful influence of Bloomfield and the generation inspired by his teaching, a rigorously empiricist, observational, and formal version of descriptive linguistics, subsequently designated, often reproachfully, as 'taxonomist,' commanded the field. Inspired by the methodological requirements of American-Indian languages, presenting a special challenge to American linguists, and by Bloomfield's conviction that physicalism was the only true scientific method, these linguists insisted that only publicly observable phenomena in speech or writing could be accepted as valid data, and that every abstraction made from them must be justified by publicly stated and publicly replicable procedures; in Bloomfield's words (1939: 13): 'Science shall deal only with events that are accessible in their time and place to any and all observers – or only with events that are placed in coordinates of time and space.' Those areas of language study unamenable to such rigorous discipline were simply abandoned or relegated to the periphery: psycholinguistics, philosophy of language, and much of semantics (again in Bloomfield's words (1935: 140): 'The statement of meaning is . . . the weak point in language-study, and will remain so until human knowledge advances very far beyond its present state.')

This was empiricist linguistics in its extreme form. The material was an observed corpus of externally recorded data, regarded as a fair sample, whether of literary texts (in the manner of Dionysius Thrax), of the results of a field trip to Indian territory, or of fifty hours of recorded English conversations, on which Fries based his *Structure of English* (1952), explicitly refusing to make use of his own private knowledge and command of his native English in the interests, as he saw them, of scientific linguistics. Harris's *Methods in structural linguistics* (1951) is a good illustration of the work and attitude of this school.

The structuralists' work gave to linguistics an unprecedented rigor and precision, as well as a variety of excellent descriptions of many languages, familiar or newly discovered. Chomsky has paid justified tribute to them (1964: 75–6), but, like the medieval speculative grammarians in their criticism of Priscian, he claims, no less in the interests of science, that linguistics can and should transcend this descriptive adequacy by an explanatory adequacy and a deeper understanding of what it is to be a speaker–hearer. In this most modern form of the ancient and enduring rationalist–empiricist debate he sees language as a key to the mind and linguistics as a branch of cognitive psychology; universal grammar is part of our biological endowment, by which alone can be explained the effortless acquisition of our first language in childhood. This 'generativist' aspect of Chomsky's work and that of his numerous and often divergent disciples is of far more permanent significance than the exploitation of transformations in syntactic description that figured so prominently in their earlier studies but which has now been much reduced in its role and status.

It is clear that the major shift in the theory and practice of linguistics inaugurated by Chomsky in 1957, and the various versions and developments that have arisen from it and within it, have become the dominant themes among many of the world's linguists. But Chomskyans and persisting structuralists are not the only contenders on the linguistic stage. The stratificationalists are psychologically and mentalistically inclined; but the tagmemicists, very active in the mission field under Pike's inspiration and leadership, are methodologically orientated and concentrate on the external observation of little-known languages. Halliday's systemic grammar, deriving from one aspect of Firth's linguistic theory, his contextual semantics, is sociolinguistically rather than psycholinguistically directed.

What the future holds can only be surmised and awaited, but the present generation of linguists can rejoice at the public interest and public support that the subject now enjoys, since, across the wide spectrum of the discipline and through its major theoretical controversies, some of the finest minds of the age, Trubetzkoy, Jakobson, Sapir, Bloomfield, and Chomsky, have devoted to it the full measure of their intellectual vigor and conviction.

## BIBLIOGRAPHY

Only a few references have been given in the text of this article, where the source material may be unfamiliar or where direct quotation has been made. In recent years there has been much writing on the history of linguistics, and for further study and very full bibliographies one may refer to the following: Arens(1969), Bursill-Hall (1971), Mohrmann *et al.* (1961, 1963), Padley (1976, 1985), Robins (1979), Rosier (1983), Sebeok (1966, 1975) and the articles and reviews in the specialist periodical *Historiographia linguistica* (*HL*; 1974–   ).


Allen, W. S. 1953. *Phonetics in ancient India*. London: Oxford University Press.

Alston, R. C. 1965. *Bibliography of the English language from the invention of printing to the year 1800*. Vol. 1: *English grammars written in English*. Leeds: Arnold.

Alston, R. C. 1973. *Supplement* to Alston (1965). Leeds: University Press.

Arens, H. 1969. *Sprachwissenschaft: der Gang ihrer Entwicklung von der Antike bis zur Gegenwart*. Munich: Karl Alber.

Bloomfield, L. 1935. *Language*. London: Allen & Unwin.

Bloomfield, L. 1939. Linguistic aspects of science. *International encyclopedia of unified science*. Vol. 1, part 4. Chicago: Chicago University Press.

Bursill-Hall, G. L. 1971. *Speculative grammars of the Middle Ages*. The Hague: Mouton.

Bursill-Hall, G. L. 1981. *A census of medieval Latin grammatical manuscripts*. Stuttgart: Frommann-Holzboog.

Chomsky, N. 1964. *Current issues in linguistic theory*. The Hague: Mouton.

Chomsky, N. & Halle, M. 1968. *The sound pattern of English*. New York: Harper & Row.

Fries, C. C. 1952. *The structure of English*. New York: Harcourt Brace.

Grabmann, M. 1926. *Mittelalterliches Geistesleben I*. Munich: Hüber.

Greenberg, J. H. 1963. The languages of Africa. *International Journal of Applied Linguistics* 29: 1.

Harris, Z. S. 1951. *Methods in structural linguistics*. Chicago: Chicago University Press.

Haugen, E. (ed.) 1972. *First grammatical treatise*. London: Longman.

Hockett, C. F. 1965. Sound change. *Language* 41: 185–204.

Hunt, R. W. 1980. *Collected papers on the history of grammar in the Middle Ages*. Amsterdam: Benjamins.

Keil, H. 1855/1859. *Grammatici Latini*. Vols. 2 and 3. Leipzig: Teubner.

Kuhn, T. S. 1970. *The structure of scientific revolutions*. Chicago: Chicago University Press.

Lancelot, C. & Arnauld, A. 1660. *Grammaire générale et raisonnée*. Paris: Pierre le petit.

Long, A. A. (ed.) 1971. *Problems in Stoicism*. London: Athlone Press.

Mates, B. 1953. *Stoic logic*. University of California Publications in Philosophy, no. 26. Berkeley: University of California Press.

Mohrmann, C., Norman, F., Sommerfelt, A. (eds.) 1963. *Trends in modern linguistics*. Utrecht: Spectrum.

Mohrmann, C., Sommerfelt, A., Whatmough, J. (eds.) 1961. *Trends in European and American linguistics 1930–1960*. Utrecht: Spectrum.

Ó Cuív, B. 1965. Linguistic terminology in the mediaeval Irish bardic tracts. *Transactions of The Philological Society*, pp. 141–64.

Ó Cuív, B. 1973. The linguistic training of the medieval Irish poet. *Celtica* 10: 114–40.

Padley, G. A. 1976. *Grammatical theory in western Europe 1500–1700: the Latin tradition*. Cambridge: Cambridge University Press.

Padley, G. A. 1985. *Grammatical theory in western Europe 1500–1700: trends in vernacular grammar I*. Cambridge: Cambridge University Press.

Pott, A. F. 1833–6. *Etymologische Forschungen auf dem Gebiet der indogermanischen Sprachen*. Lemgo: Meyer.

Reuchlin, J. 1506. *De rudimentis Hebraicis*. Pforzheim: Anshelm.

Robins, R. H. 1974. Theory-orientation versus data-orientation: a recurrent theme in linguistics. *HL* 1: 11–26.

Robins, R. H. 1977. Distinctive feature theory. In D. Armstrong & C. H. van Schoonveld (eds.) *Roman Jakobson: echoes of his scholarship*. Lisse: P. de Ridder.

Robins, R. H. 1979. *A short history of linguistics*. London: Longman.

Robins, R. H. 1980. Functional syntax in medieval Europe. *HL* 7: 231–40.

Roos, H. 1952. Die modi significandi des Martinus de Dacia. *Beiträge zur Geschichte der Philosophie und Theologie des Mittelalters* 37: 2.

Rosier, I. 1983. *La grammaire spéculative des modistes*. Lille: Presses Universitaires.

Sajnovics, P. 1770. *Demonstratio idioma Ungarorum et Lapponum idem esse*. Copenhagen: Royal Asylum.

Schleicher, A. 1863. *Die darwinsche Theorie und die Sprachwissenschaft*. Weimar: Böhlau.

Sebeok, T. A. (ed.) 1966. *Portraits of linguists: a biographical source book for the history of western linguistics 1746–1963*. Bloomington and London. Indiana University Press.

Sebeok, T. A. 1975. *The historiography of linguistics*. Current Trends in Linguistics, no. 13.

Sigerus de Cortraco. 1977. *Summa modorum significandi; sophismata*. Ed. J. Pinborg. Amsterdam: Benjamins.

Thomas of Erfurt. 1972. *Grammatica speculativa*. Ed. G. L. Bursill-Hall. London: Longman.

Trubetzkoy, N. S. 1939. Grundzüge der Phonologie. *Travaux du Cercle Linguistique de Prague* 7.

Vaugelas, C. 1670. *Remarques sur la language françoise*. Paris: Jolly. First published in 1647.

Waddell, H. 1926. *The wandering scholars*. 7th edn. 1949. London: Constable.

Wallerand, G. (ed.) 1913. *Les oeuvres de Siger de Courtrai*. Les philosophes belges, no. 8. Louvain: Les Institut supérieur de philosophie de L'Université.

Wilkins, J. 1668. *Essay towards a real character and a philosophical language*. London: Gellibrand.

# Index of names

# Index of subjects

494

# Index of subjects

Syntax – *cont.*
theory; Lexical functional grammar,
etc.) 1–2, 8–12, 18–56, 60–86, 303–21:
diachronic 6–7, 303–21; interface with
phonology 6, 255–78; interface with
semantics 239–53; morphologization
of 336–54
Synthesis, index of 452

Target undershoot 230
*That*-trace effects 251–2
Thematic roles 48, 65–6, 75–6, 85–6, 92–4,
149, 239–40, 242–3, 253, 455–6
*There*-insertion 2, 268
Theta-criterion *See* Theta-theory
Theta-roles *See* Thematic roles
Theta-theory (*See also* Thematic roles) 20,
51, 242
Thomism 470
Tone 200, 202, 204, 208, 259, 264, 288,
290–1, 378–9, 382: sandhi 264
Tonogenesis 298–9, 382
Topic–comment structure 455
Traces 8, 36, 37, 242, 269–70, 424
Transformational grammar (*See also*
Standard theory; Syntax, etc.):
mathematical properties of 416–28
Transformational rules *See* Move-alpha;
Passive construction; Raising construction,
etc.

Truth conditions *See* Semantics, truth-
conditional
Truth-functional paradoxes 432
Twin Earth argument 436
Type assignment 240–1
Typology 447–60, 475–7: areal 449;
functional approaches to 455–8; word-
order 68–9, 453–5

Unbounded dependencies *See Wh*-
movement
Unification categorial grammar 12
Uniformitarian principle 363–4
Universal grammar (UG) 304–5, 313–14,
317–18

Variable binding 247–52
Variables, bound 249–51
Voice onset time (VOT) 223–5, 227–8

Weak crossover 249–51
*Wh*-constructions 2, 8–9, 22–43, 248–51
*Wh*-island constraint 23–4, 40–1
Word formation rules *See* Morphology

X-bar theory 21–2, 39, 42, 176, 454

# Contents of Volumes II, III, and IV